Lermontov self-portrait, 1837-38.

William Edward Brown

A History of
Russian Literature
of the
Romantic Period

Volume Four

Ardis, Ann Arbor

Ardis Publishers
2901 Heatherway
Ann Arbor, Michigan 48104

Library of Congress Cataloging in Publication Data

Brown, William Edward, 1904—
A history of Russian literature of the romantic period.

1. Russian literature—19th century—History and
criticism.   2. Romanticism—Soviet Union.   I. Title.
PG3015.5.R6B76 1985   891.7′09′145   85-18556
ISBN 0-88233-938-9 (set: alk. paper)

Contents

LIST OF ILLUSTRATIONS

A History of
Russian Literature
of the
Romantic Period

I

Fyodor Tyutchev (Before 1841)

Fyodor Tyutchev's association with the Wisdom-lovers was of short duration and much less significant for his poetical development than was the case with other members of the group. S. E. Raich was his private tutor, and through him Tyutchev became acquainted with the literary friends who were later to constitute the "Raich circle." During Tyutchev's attendance at Moscow University, from which he was graduated in 1821, he had close associations with the Raich group, with the Society of Lovers of Russian Literature, with Professor Merzlyakov, etc. In 1822, however, before the official formation of the Society of Lovers of Wisdom, Tyutchev had entered government service in the Department of Foreign Affairs, and been sent to the Russian Embassy in Bavaria. With a few brief intermissions he remained abroad, in Germany and north Italy, for the next twenty-three years. After his return to Moscow and St. Petersburg in 1843 he resumed government service, which had been interrupted in 1841, now in the Bureau of Censorship, with which he remained until his death.

A diplomat and civil servant for most of his life, Tyutchev always regarded his verse-writing as a sideline, distinctly secondary. In fact, he was incredibly casual about the products of his pen, never making any effort to see them published, and even evincing the most complete indifference toward them when they were seen into print by others. When his son-in-law Ivan Aksakov, for instance, got together the second collected edition of his poetry in 1868, and asked the poet to read over the text with a view to making final corrections, he returned the manuscript unread. He often wrote his verse on scraps of paper during meetings which bored him (he had a very low boredom tolerance!) and then mislaid them or casually gave them away. In a letter to his friend I. S. Gagarin of July 7, 1836 he remarks, with no particular indication of feeling, on the loss of most of his verse written during his residence abroad: "What I have sent you constitutes a tiny portion of the pile accumulated by time, which has perished by the will of fate, or rather, of some sort of predestination. On my return from Greece [at the end of 1833], when I had undertaken somehow or other in the dusk to sort out my papers, I destroyed the greater part of my poetical efforts, and noticed this only considerably later."[1]

Were Tyutchev a third-rate or even a second-rate poet, one might attribute such perverse carelessness to a well-merited diffidence in the value of what he had composed. He was, however, a supremely intelligent person with excellent literary taste and judgment, and the only Russian poet of the nineteenth century who can stand beside Pushkin and Lermontov at the very summit of the poets' Helicon. But he was, in this as in most other aspects of his life, sharply divided against himself. He might very truly, with Faust, have said: "Two souls, alas, dwell in my breast."

The year 1841 marks a distinct break in Tyutchev's verse; for several years he apparently composed nothing, returning to writing only about 1845. His later verse accordingly falls outside of the scope of this study, and will not be considered. To this period belongs most of his Panslavic verse, which is of little artistic value, but also some of his best love poetry, especially the cycle dedicated to his mistress E. A. Denisova. Certain qualities in this later verse link it with the rise after about 1848 of the realistic psychological novel, and make it more reasonable to discuss it in that connection.

Although Tyutchev began writing verse when he was ten or eleven years old, it was only at the ripe age of fifteen that his first piece was published. After his departure for Germany he occasionally sent poems to his friend Raich for publication in the latter's rather obscure almanacs. In 1836, at the urging of his friend Gagarin, Tyutchev sent a batch of verse to Pushkin's newly launched periodical *The Contemporary:* 24 of these pieces were published in this year, under the title "Poems Sent from Germany." The poet's name, evidently at his request, was never given, but only indicated as "Mr. F. T."[2] After Pushkin's death *The Contemporary* continued to publish "Poems Sent from Germany" to the eventual total of 39. The poems made no stir at all at the time of their appearance. It was not until 1850 that the poet Nekrasov, at that time editor of *The Contemporary,* published in his journal a long and very laudatory essay on the "Poems Sent from Germany," whose author he even then did not know except as "Mr. F." From 1850 begins the public recognition of Tyutchev as a poet; in 1854 *The Contemporary* published as a separate brochure a collection of 92 of Tyutchev's poems, accompanied by an essay by their editor, Ivan S. Turgenev.[3] The second, and last, collection published in Tyutchev's lifetime has been mentioned: its editors were the poet's son and son-in-law (1868).

Collected, as it was, almost in spite of its author, and never with his full cooperation, the "Complete Verse of F. I. Tyutchev" inevitably contains a great deal of dross, which does the poet no credit and would doubtless have been eliminated with a more conventional author. The editor of the latest Soviet collection, K.V. Pigarev, who is also the author of a capital book on Tyutchev's poetry,[4] has interestingly divided the work into two volumes, of which the first collection contains the "pure gold" (some 80 poems belonging to the period with which we are concerned), the second the baser metal—juvenilia (1816-24), translations, occasional verse, epigrams, etc., and the bulk of the Panslavic propaganda pieces. Each volume is arranged as far as possible in chronological order, although exactitude in this matter is usually impossible to attain. For the purposes of this study the only portion of the second volume which need be of concern is the translations, which often reveal a good deal about the views and interests of the one who has selected them for translation.

The period of Tyutchev's creative life with which we are concerned— mainly the 1820s and 1830s—he spent almost entirely outside of Russia, mostly in Germany. As a result he was pretty much cut off from significant contact with the other Russian writers of his time, and far more closely associated with the literary elite of Germany. His two wives were both Bavarian noblewomen. He was personally acquainted with Schelling, who wrote enthusiastically about the Russian's acumen; he visited Goethe in Weimar, and he was a friend of Heinrich Heine, some of whose verse, like that of Goethe, he translated. Not surprisingly, there is more German romanticism than Russian in his poetry. Pushkin in a quite different connection noted in 1836 that "Poetry has remained foreign to French influence; it is becoming more and more friendly to German poetry, and proudly maintains its independence from the tastes and demands of the public."[5] In this prevailingly German orientation Tyutchev is close to the Wisdom Lovers, as he is for example also in his rhetorical and sometimes didactic tone, in his reversion to eighteenth-century poetical models (Derzhavin et al.) and in his slightly archaistic and uncommon language. But Tyutchev, for all his early association with Vladimir Odoevsky and other members of the Society of Wisdom Lovers, was always independent, and he by no means shared the group's hostility to French influence. He was well versed in French literature, spoke the language almost to the exclusion of Russian during his twenty-two years abroad, wrote most of his letters in French, and even composed verse in it. English literature he knew less intimately, but he was enthusiastic about Byron, and Shakespeare was a favorite author.

Tyutchev has not fared well with English translators: there are a good many scattered versions of extremely varied quality, some quite good, but the great majority so bad that a literal prose translation, where needed, seems preferable.

The loss of what was probably the bulk of Tyutchev's original verse of the period of his foreign residence makes it appear that he was mostly occupied during those two decades with translations. Even of these, however, we now possess only a portion: it is known, for example, that he translated a large part, perhaps all, of *Faust: Part I,* but destroyed most of his version—intentionally this time. His translations do not have the quality of Zhukovsky's, of sounding as though they were genuinely original works, but they are accurate and sensitive, and his choice of subject is often very revealing of his own poetical attitudes.

One of the earliest, done at some date between 1820 and 1822, when Tyutchev would have been still in his teens, is a rather free version of Lamartine's elegy *L'Isolement*.[6] Here Zhukovsky's example seems to have been operative: the form of the original, quatrains of Alexandrine lines rhyming alternately aBaB, is not kept, and the Russian version takes the form of an unbroken sequence of 48 lines of "free iambics," with lines of from six to four beats irregularly placed with no pattern. The sense of the poem, moreover, is treated as freely as the form: certain passages of the original are ignored and in one place at least the translator has added material of his own. Some of these changes reveal characteristics of Tyutchev's thought which will reappear later in his original verse. Thus, when Lamartine meditates over the possibility of finding in a world after death the "vague object of his desires," he writes:

> Là, je m'enivrerais à la source où j'aspire,
> Là, je retrouverais et l'espoir et l'amour,
> Et ce bien idéal que toute âme désire,
> Et qui n'a pas de nom au terrestre séjour!

The corresponding passage in Tyutchev's translation reads:

> That world, where there are no orphans, where faith has fulfilment; where the sun of Truth is in a heaven incorruptible? There, perhaps, will be made clear the saving [*spasitel'nyî*] object of secret hopes, toward which the soul still strives even here, and only there, in its native land [*otchizne*] will embrace.

"The ideal good that every soul desires, and which has no name in the earthly abode" has been transformed into "the saving object of secret hopes"; but the striking adjective "saving" certainly has here no religious connotation. Rather it points to the pantheist's longing for a complete revelation of the identity of man's soul with the World-Spirit. Lamartine continues with a quatrain which the translator omits altogether:

> Que ne puis-je, porté sur le char de l'Aurore,
> Vague objet de mes voeux, m'élancer jusqu'à toi!
> Sur la terre d'exil pourquoi reste-je encore?
> Il n'est rien de commun entre la terre et moi.

Perhaps for the intensely life-loving Tyutchev the sense of the last two lines was repugnant; in any case he replaces the whole passage with something altogether different: "How brightly flame the throngs of the stars above me, the living thoughts of divinity! What a night has thickened over the earth, and how dead is the earth, in the sight of the heavens!" The very characteristic phrase, "living thoughts of divinity," with which the stars are described, is all Tyutchev, and belongs to German romanticism, not French.

Of Tyutchev's other translations, only three from the earlier period are from French originals: the messenger's speech in Racine's *Phèdre* (Act V, sc. 6) describing the death of Hippolyte; Don Carlos's soliloquy at the tomb of Charlemagne, from Victor Hugo's *Hernani* (Act IV, sc. 2); and the Béranger piece *The Old Vagabond* [*Le vieux vagabond*]. None of these tells very much about the translator. There are two interesting but isolated bits from Shakespeare (*A Midsummer Night's Dream,* Act V, sc. 1: Theseus's speech on "The lunatic, the lover and the poet,"and Puck's song, Act V, sc. 2: "Now the hungry lion roars"). Among the very early pieces (it was published in 1819 when Tyutchev was sixteen) is a version of Horace's epistle to Maecenas (*Carmina* III, 29). Like the Lamartine translation, and like several of the original poems of the same period, this is composed in "free iambics," without regard for the verse form of the original—a practice which Tyutchev abandoned with his first translation from the German, "Hector and Andromache," a version of Schiller's *The Departure of Hector* [*Hektors Abschied*].

A major, and quite successful, translation is that of Schiller's great hymn *To Joy* [*An die Freude*],[7] which was published in the almanac *Northern Lyre* for 1827, with the notation: "Munich. February, 1825."The strophic form, rhyme-scheme and wording of the German are here scrupulously reproduced, and Tyutchev's version is still the standard Russian rendering of the ode. It is to this, it may be remembered, that Dmitry Karamazov refers in his conversation with Alyosha ("Confessions of a Passionate Heart"). Evidently Tyutchev considered this piece of more significance than he usually attached to his verse, for he wrote an original poem in the form of an epistle, "To Friends," to accompany the translation. It begins:[8]

> What the divine [poet] sang, O friends, in the flaming transport of freedom and in the full feeling of Being, when at the banquet of Nature the singer, her beloved son, bound the nations into a single circle, and with soul enraptured, life-creating light in his eyes, from the foaming cup of Genius he drank to the health of men.
>
> And is it for me to sing this joyous hymn, far from those close to my heart, in a melancholy unshared—is it for me to sing of Joy on toneless lyre?

After this effort Tyutchev translated no more Schiller until, about 1850, "The Victory Feast"[*Das Siegesfest*]. For the next twenty years most of his translations are from Goethe, and from his friend Heinrich Heine. There are a few isolated exceptions that may be noted: from a work of the Austrian poet Joseph Christian von Zedlitz (1790-1862) called *Totenkränze,* the section on the death of Byron; and from Manzoni's ode on the death of Napoleon, "The Fifth of May"[*Il cinque maggio*] (Napoleon died on May 5, 1821), strophes 7-16. Tyutchev's admiration for Byron and his poetry is reflected in a version of "Lines Written in an Album, at Malta," where, however, for his own purposes he has completely changed the sense.

A comparison of Byron's original and Tyutchev's paraphrase is instructive:

> As o'er the cold sepulchral stone
> Some name arrests the passer-by;
> Thus, when thou view'st this page alone,
> May mine attract thy pensive eye!
>
> And when by thee that name is read,
> Perchance in some succeeding year,
> Reflect on me as on the dead,
> And think my heart is buried here.

Tyutchev: "In an Album to *Friends*":[9]

> As the wayfarer's attention lingers on the cold sepulchral stones,
> So shall the inscription of a well-known hand attract my friends!...
>   Many, many years hence it will remind them of a former friend:
> "He exists no longer in our circle; but his heart is buried here!"

Byron's verses were addressed to a woman whom he had met in Malta, but Tyutchev has rephrased the piece so that it is his "friends" who will be reminded of him when in years to come they read his album entry.

The bulk of the translations done in the years 1822-41 are from Goethe and Heine. Aside from five passages from *Faust: Part I,* the Goethe versions are from *Wilhelm Meisters Lehrjahre* (the Harper's two songs); one poem from the *West-östliche Divan* ("Hegire"), the ballad "Der Sänger," and "Der König in Thule." The Heine translations, which are particularly good, are of the lyrics: "Ein Fichtenbaum steht einsam," "Das Herz ist mir bedrückt, und sehnlich," "Fragen," "Der Schiffbrüchige," and "In welche soll' ich mich verlieben." In addition to these renderings of Heine poems, there is one curious and significant oddity—a translation into Russian blank verse of one chapter (no. 31) of the third book of Heine's prose *Pictures of Travel* [*Reisebilder,*] which describes the German poet's ruminations when in his travels he visits the battlefield of Marengo. It was at Marengo, it will be recalled, that Napoleon in June, 1800, won a brilliant victory over the Austrians, after which he was able to establish an ostensibly republican government in northern Italy.

On the surface it may seem that Tyutchev's translations form a very motley grab-bag without any internal coherence. Closer examination, however, reveals a pattern emerging from a group of them, and this pattern is significant for the poet's outlook on the world, both in his period of foreign residence and during his later official career. Schiller's ecstatic vision of the millions of mankind embracing in universal brotherhood; Zedlitz's admiring but slightly disapproving rhapsody on the tempestuous Byron; and Manzoni's majestic picture of the Titan who had died on St.

Helena: "He experienced everything! good fortune, victory, captivity, all of fate's favor and all its cruelty! Twice was he hurled in the dust, and twice on a throne!"[10]—all this answers Tyuchev's own romantic temperament, his impatience of restraints on his individuality, and his abstract love of freedom. The culminating pinnacle of this is the version from Heine's *Reisebilder*. We are inclined to forget the degree to which Napoleon represented for his own age and later the spirit of freedom. We see him as he was after 18 Brumaire, and are astonished that a Russian, of all Europeans, should idealize the man who brought such suffering on his country in 1812. It would be well for us to remember the picture that Tolstoi draws of the situation in 1806, when Pierre Bezukhov at Anna Schérer's soirée is still, seven years after 18 Brumaire, the admiring defender of Napoleon. Tyutchev was in Munich, and he was a friend of Heinrich Heine. The German poet's feelings may not have been exactly his, and if there was any influence from one to the other it would be hard to decide in which direction it went. Nevertheless what Heine has to say on the subject will by and large have been true for Tyutchev at this time also. In the beginning of Chapter 29 of the Italian book of his "Travel Pictures," Heine writes:[11]

> I ask you, dear reader, not to consider me unconditionally a Bonapartist; my allegiance is not to the acts, but only to the genius of the man. I love him unconditionally only up to the 18th of Brumaire—then he betrayed freedom.

He reflects on the battlefield he is about to visit:

> Here General Bonaparte took such a mighty draft from the cup of fame that in his intoxication he became consul, emperor, world conqueror, and only sobered up on St. Helena. We did not fare much better; we were drunk along with him, we had all the dreams along with him, woke up in the same way, and [now] in the misery of sobriety we are making all kinds of sensible reflections.

In Chapter 30 comes a startling passage, which, while departing from the immediate subject of Napoleon, is certainly of capital importance for Tyutchev's later development as a Panslavist. Heine's travelling companion is a German from Livonia, which was a part of the Russian Empire. As they are about to visit the battlefield, this companion remarks: "Who now thinks about Marengo!... Now all eyes are fixed on the Balkans, where my countryman Diebitsch is straightening out the Turks' turbans, and we shall capture Constantinople yet this year. Are you a good Russian?" When Heine takes the time to think over this strange question, he has to admit, Yes, he is a good Russian! The champion of liberty which Napoleon had been is now, of all people, the Russian Tsar!

And in fact, with the strange turnabout of slogans and representatives in the great struggle, things have turned out so that the most ardent friend of revolution sees in Russia's victory alone the world's salvation, and must regard Emperor Nicholas as the standard-bearer of freedom!... We took the banner back again from Downing Street and planted it in St. Petersburg, and chose for its bearer Emperor Nicholas, the knight of Europe, who protected Greek widows and orphans against Asiatic barbarians, and won his spurs in so good a fight.[12]

Chapter 31[13] in Tyutchev's verse paraphrase alters somewhat the order of thought of the original, but is otherwise remarkably literal. It begins with the Livonian travel-companion's observation: "It will be a beautiful day." The "I" of the poem (Heine or Tyutchev or their respective personae!) echoes the remark, giving it a more extended meaning: "It will be a beautiful day! The sun of freedom will shed a livelier and warmer glow than the aristocracy of the night's stars!" He looks forward to a new generation, sired in freedom:

And in those free-born souls will boldly blaze a purer fire of ideas and feelings— incomprehensible for us natural slaves.
    Ah, and equally incomprehensible for them will be the night in which their fathers languished cheerlessly all their lives through, and carried on a battle desperate, cruel, against vile owls and subterranean specters, the monstrous spawn of Erebus!... Ill-fortuned warriors, all the powers of our spirit, all the blood of our hearts we spent in battle—and the final day of victory will illumine us, pallid, decrepit before our time!... The fresh immortality of the youthful sun will not bring life to hearts exhausted, will not fire once more cheeks grown dim. We shall hide ourselves before it, like the pale moon!

The scene has become allegorical, as the physical sun rising over the battlefield becomes the symbol for the new, free generation, the physical moon, pale and wan in the sky, for the old generation of freedom-fighters. At the end of the passage Heine declares that he has no concern whether future generations shall put the laurels of the poet on his grave,—"But the sword, my friends, lay on my tomb! I was a warrior! I was a fighter for freedom, and I served her with faith and truth all my life long in her holy battle!"

For one looking at the world of 1829 from the Russian intellectual's ordinary point of view, it is nothing less than grotesque to see in the tyrant Nikolai I the "knight of Europe," the great white hope of all friends of revolution. Doubtless Heine was seeing the situation from a very distorted angle, and doubtless events of a few years later would bring him a bitter disillusionment, but in the war against the Turkish Empire, which was certainly many degrees more rotten and reactionary even than the Russian, his sympathies could only be with the Russian side. In the same year of 1829 Tyutchev translated and presented to the Tsar a curious poem written by King Ludwig I of Bavaria, entitled: "Nicolaus: das ist, der Volksbesieger."

The first line of Tyutchev's Russian carries out the Bavarian King's rather academic pun (the Tsar's name comes from two Greek roots meaning "victory" and "people"): "O Nikolai, *conqueror of peoples,* you have justified your name!"[14] The first strophe of the ode ends: "Exult, O Christians! Our God, the God of mercy and of war, has wrested the bloody sceptre from impious hands." The final strophe sounds almost like Heine's travel companion:

> Your soul does not thirst for worldly glory, your eyes are not fixed on the earthly. But, O Tsar, He by whom empires are maintained has pronounced their sentence upon your foes ... He Himself turns his countenance away from them, blood has long since washed away their evil sovereignty, above their head the angel of death is hovering; Stambul is passing away—*Constantinople* is resurrected anew.

Of course alarmed British diplomacy saw to it that Istanbul was *not* taken by the victorious Russian armies, and this first real opportunity of recreating under Russia's protection the fallen Byzantine Empire was lost. It seemed a quarter of a century later that the opportunity was presented again. 1853 was the four-hundredth anniversary of the fall of Constantinople to Mehmet I—and the Slavophiles were not the only Russians who saw in the Crimean War the foreordained instrument for reversing that disaster. The disillusionment this time was extreme, and when Nikolai I, that "knight of Europe," breathed his last in 1855 when the war was already lost, Tyutchev wrote him a bitter epitaph:[15] "Not God you served, and not Russia. You served only your own vanity, and all your deeds, both good and bad,—everything in you was a lie, everything an empty phantom. You were not a Tsar, but an actor." But this was in 1856; in 1829 even such otherwise clear-sighted men as Fyodor Tyutchev and Heinrich Heine could still see in Nikolai I the champion of the oppressed, the divinely ordained instrument for driving the Turks out of Europe.

Tyutchev's translations and political verse have little or no artistic value; they are important only as clues to his ways of thinking—and these, in turn, are important only because Tyutchev is one of the great poets of his age and land. It is time now to turn to the real poetry, what Pigarev calls the "pure gold" of Tyutchev's heritage.

Tyutchev was a romantic, and in his attitude toward poetry very close to the Wisdom-lovers, with whom he was early and for a short time associated. He was much closer to the German romantics, however, than were any of the others. German romanticism, however, is a very large and formless entity, self-contradictory in many respects. German scholars very frequently classify Schiller and Goethe as classicists, distinct from the romantic movement. This they were not: even in their most classical period, when the two great poets were turning for their inspiration not to the middle ages and folk poetry, as some of the other romantics did, but to

Greece and Rome, they were still very different from the classicists of the eighteenth century. The classicism of Goethe and Schiller is a special variety of German romanticism, peculiar to them and to Hölderlin, but shared by no others. It was alien to the Jena romantics: Schiller, who had been idolized at first by the Schlegels, coldly repudiated them and was subsequently regarded by their school as an apostate. The truth of the matter is that the Jena group represented only one aspect of a very complicated phenomenon, just as did the Heidelberg group after them; the Weimar classicists were still another fraction of the same movement. Tyutchev, as his translations show, was drawn to Goethe and Schiller, and it is certain that from them, and particularly from Goethe, he learned most of what he had to learn about poetry. This is not to say that he imitated: but in the utilization of lyric verse for conveying profound philosophical thought, which the Wisdom-lovers attempted but without genius, Tyutchev is very close to Goethe. He is close also to Pushkin, and in the later period of his life, which falls outside of our present purview, he is even closer than in the 1820s and 1830s. His poems are mostly short; his metrical forms are simple; his style is solemn and elevated, "difficult." The poems are dense with meaning. The thought is strikingly original; if it at times shows similarity to the philosophical systems of Fichte or Schelling, one must never imagine that the poet is simply turning philosophers' prose into verse. He appropriates what harmonizes with his own thought, but erects no system.

Tyutchev, from the moment when Nekrasov first discovered the "Poems Sent from Germany," has been hailed as a poet of nature. A great many of his verses are miniature landscapes which depict various moods of nature. An example of the kind is "Morning in the Mountains," composed apparently on a visit to Salzburg:[16]

> The azure of the sky smiles, washed by the storm in the night,
> and the valley winds dewily between the mountains in a bright band.
> Only the slope of the highest mountains is covered to their
> middle with mists, like the airy ruins of palaces reared by magic.

Probably composed at the same time (the two are side by side in Tyutchev's autograph) is "Snowy Mountains":[17]

> Already the noontide hour is blazing with perpendicular rays—and the mountain with its black forests has begun to smoke.
> Below, like a steel mirror, the waters of the lake are blue, and from the rocks, glittering in the sultry heat, the brooks are hurrying to their native deep [*rodnuiu glub*].
> And while our earthly world, as though half-asleep, pervaded by a fragrant voluptuousness, rests in the noonday haze,
> Aloft, like native deities, above the gasping earth the icy heights are playing with the fiery azure of the sky.

These are true landscapes, objective representations of reality; they are not symbols of anything. But one is immediately struck by certain peculiar features. "The azure of the sky *smiles* [*smeetsia*]"; the "earthly world . . . is half-asleep" and "rests"; the snow-covered mountains "are playing," etc. Twice in the second poem the adjective *rodnoi* is used, which I have arbitrarily translated "native"; the word properly means "belonging to one's own family," and in the first instance of its use here means that the brooks streaming down the mountain sides are *akin* to the depth of the valley to which gravity brings them; in the second instance, the snowy mountain-tops are likened to "kindred gods" of the earth. Nature, for Tyutchev, is always *alive;* and since the best way of indicating aliveness is by using human terms, nature is always anthropomorphized, shown in human likeness. One of his most famous poems, unfortunately mutilated by the censor, begins with a passionate assertion of the poet's belief:[18] "Nature is not what you suppose: not blind, not a soulless face—she has a soul, she has freedom, she has love, she has a language." Tyutchev's attitude twoard nature is pantheistic—nature and man are kindred, and both are parts of a World Spirit that can be called God, though the concept is remote from religious orthodoxy. In this connection it may be noted that the Panslavist verses, which should be regarded as propaganda rather than poetry, emphasize the Orthodox Christian church along with autocracy as cornerstones of Russian uniqueness and superiority. Here, as in many other places, Tyutchev is a dual being, at odds with himself. As a poet, he sees the world in one way; as a politician, in quite another.

Plato defines the soul, the principle of life, in terms of motion: that which moves of itself is alive. Tyutchev's pictures of nature are always in motion, not static: the brooks "are hurrying," the "icy heights . . . are playing"; the mountain "has begun to smoke [*zadymilasia*]." The aspects of nature that the poet most frequently portrays are what may be called the cosmic aspects—the alternation of day and night, of the seasons, the coming and passing of storms, and the like. The milder, more intimate sides of nature do not interest him. He would have understood and sympathized with Tennyson's "Flower in the crannied wall" for its implication of the oneness of all nature, but he would never have used a flower as illustration. Typical of his nature poetry is the 1828 "Spring Thunderstorm":[19]

> I love a thunderstorm in the beginning of May, when the first spring thunder, as though it were sporting and playing, peals in the blue sky.
> The young peals reverberate,—and look, the rain has splashed, the dust is flying, the raindrop pearls are hanging, and the sun is gilding the threads.
> The brisk torrent is running down the mountain, in the woods the birds' hubbub is not stilled, and the woods' hubbub and the noise in the mountains—everything gaily echoes the thunder.

You would say: flighty Hebe, while feeding Zeus's eagle, laughing, has poured out on the earth the thunder-foaming goblet from heaven.

One of the most vivid examples of the anthropomorphizing of nature is Tyutchev's verse in "Summer Evening" (1828):[20]

Already earth has rolled off from her head the incandescent ball of the sun, and the sea wave has swallowed up the powerful conflagration of evening.

Already the bright stars have risen and lifted with their watery heads the vault of heaven that weighs down upon us.

The river of the atmosphere flows more fully between sky and earth, the breast breathes more easily and freely, liberated from the sultry heat.

And a pleasant shiver like a water-jet [struia] has run along the veins of Nature, as though the waters of a spring had touched her fevered feet.

Sometimes the small vignettes of nature are more mood-pictures than visual presentations; such is the lyric, written in 1830 during the poet's journey from Munich to Moscow:[21]

Here, where the vault of heaven gazes so sluggishly at the emaciated earth,—here, sunk in an iron sleep, exhausted Nature reposes . . .

Only here and there pale birches, a small bush, grey moss, like feverish dreams trouble the dead repose.

When nature is given human attributes, these need not be merely physical, such as the shiver when overheated feet feel the coolness of spring-water; they can be emotional as well, as "Autumn Evening" (1830) attests:[22]

There is in the brightness of autumn evenings a touching and mysterious charm: the ominous brilliance and colorfulness of the trees, the languid, light rustle of the purple leaves, the quiet, hazy azure above the sadly orphaned earth, and, as though it were the premonition of coming storms, the fitful, cold wind at intervals, loss, exhaustion—and upon everything that gentle smile of fading, which in a being with reason we call the godlike diffidence of suffering.

The sea plays an impressive part in Tyutchev's poetry; it is not, for him, a threatening and chaotic element, but the embodiment of Nature's restless creative force. With him waves always "sing"—unless, as in the poem "Sea Horse" (1830) they are otherwise animated:[23]

O fiery horse, O horse of the sea, with pale green mane, now quiet, affectionately tame, now wildly playful! You were reared by the turbulent whirlwind on God's wide plain; it taught you to prance, to gambol, to gallop at will.

I love you, when headlong in your proud strength, thick mane dishevelled and all steaming and in a lather, directing your stormy course toward the shore, you dash with a gay whinny, plant your hooves on the sounding shore and scatter in spray!

Tyutchev is unlikely to have known the wonderful chorus "in praise of Colonus" in Sophocles's *Oedipus at Colonus,* in which the same metaphor occurs, but the similarity is striking.

Mention has been made earlier of the poet's most explicit declaration of the living quality of nature ("Nature is not what you suppose—"). Docked of two strophes by the censor, evidently because they contained something at odds with orthodoxy, the poem is a fragment without the necessary inner connections; it ends, however, with an indignant comment on those blind beings who do not see that Nature is alive:[24]

> They do not see and do not hear, they live in this world as though in the dark; for them evidently suns do not breathe and there is no life in the sea's waves.
>
> Sunlight has not descended into their souls, spring has not bloomed in their breast, in their presence the woods have not talked, and the night in its stars has been dumb!

Like the sea, the starry sky is for Tyutchev a fertile source of images. The night is an ambiguous entity for him: at times it is the welcome, reposeful moment of escape from the noise and tumult of the day; but at other times it is a menacing being that unveils the latent chaos in things. In its more benign aspect it is the time of dreams. These surround the earth like an ocean, but only in the night may the soul set sail on this tempting path:

> An ocean embraces the earthly ball, earthly life is embraced round about by dreams; comes the night—and with resounding waves the element beats on its shore.
>
> This is its voice: it compels us and beseeches... The magic boat has already come to life in the harbor; the flood-tide is rising and speedily carries us away into the infinity of dark waves.
>
> The vault of heaven, burning with the stars' glory, gazes mysteriously out of the depths—and we sail, on all sides surrounded by the glowing abyss.[25]

The poetical fancy that night sets free a restless horde of human thoughts and dreams is the theme of another wonderful Tyutchev lyric:[26]

> How sweetly drowses the dark-green garden, embraced by the voluptuousness of the blue night; through the apple tree, whitened with blossoms, how sweetly shines the golden moon!...
>
> Mysteriously, as on the first day of creation[a reminiscence, perhaps, of Goethe's "Herrlich, wie am ersten Tag"—the song of the archangels in *Faust I,* "Prologue in Heaven"?] burns the throng of stars in the fathomless sky; the exclamations of a distant music are audible, the nearby brook speaks more audibly....
>
> A curtain has been let down upon the world of the day; movement has grown faint, labor fallen asleep. Above the slumbering city, as in the forest treetops, has awoken the wondrous, nightly hum [*gul*]....
>
> Where does it come from, this incomprehensible hum?... Is it the disembodied world of mortal thoughts, set free by sleep, audible but invisible, now swarming in the chaos of night?...

Night is the time when man comes closest to achieving the complete identification with the external world which is the pantheist's and mystic's goal. Such identification comes rarely, and only in "a flash" [*problesk*], which is the title of an early poem of Tyutchev.[27] Beginning with a description of the ethereal sounds of an Aeolian harp in the night, he turns to the state of a listener who hears these sounds as though wafted from heaven:

Oh, how then from the earthly circle we fly in soul to the immortal! The past, like the phantom of a friend, we long to press to our breast ... But, ah, not for us was it intended; we soon grow weary in heaven,—and it is not given to paltry dust to breathe the fire divine.

Hardly have we with a momentary effort broken for an instant our charmed slumber, and standing up, sweep the firmament with confused and tremulous glance,—

When with head weighed down, blinded by one single ray, we fall once more, not to repose, but into exhausting dreams.

Rare as is this moment of complete communion, it is so much the more ecstatic. Tyutchev catches it in two marvelous strophes that were one of Lev Tolstoi's favorite poems:[28]

The grey shadows have been kneaded, color has faded, sound fallen asleep—life, motion resolved into a wavering dusk, a distant hum [*gul*] ... The moth's invisible flight is audible in the night air ... hour of inexpressible longing! ... All in me, and I in all! ...

Still dusk, slumberous dusk, pour into the depths of my soul, still, languid, fragrant, flood and quiet everything. Overflow the cup of feeling with the dark of self-forgetfulness! ... Give me to taste annihilation, mingle me with the drowsing world!

There is an almost Oriental feeling in the cry "Give me to taste annihilation" [*Dai vkusit' unichtozhen'ia*]. Nirvana, the blissful renunciation of personality, is not a normal aspiration of this intensely individualistic poet.

Night, as we have noted, may be the time when the human soul most closely approaches this mystic union with the All; but it is also the time when a terror is uncovered which the day has masked. In Schelling's philosophy the history of the universe and of the human soul is an almost Manichaean tale of eternal struggle between light and dark, between the forces of chaos and of order, between a dark, unconscious principle in both nature and man and a conscious striving toward ever higher stages of consciousness. Tyutchev appropriated this poetical idea, without, of course, embodying it in any rigorous system. The theme appears in the striking lyric that begins "About what are you wailing, wind of the night?"[29] The poet says to the night wind: "In a language intelligible to the heart you tell over and over about an incomprehensible torment." In the second strophe he exclaims:

> Oh, do not sing these terrible songs about ancient, about kindred [*rodimyi*] chaos! How greedily the soul's nightly world takes in the loved tale! It is torn from the mortal breast, it thirsts to be merged with the infinite! . . . Oh, do not wake the sleeping storms—beneath them chaos is stirring!

The chaos which the night wind threatens to disturb is inner—and it may be the primeval, irrational passion of love which for Tyutchev belongs to the world of chaos. Note that the adjective he uses is *rodimyi*—a word which implies that the chaos of which the wind sings, which is external, is "of the same family" [*rod*] as that within the human soul.

The image of chaos as an abyss of horror cloaked by kindly Day is developed in the poem "Day and Night":[30]

> Over the mysterious world of spirits, over this nameless abyss a gold-tissued cloak is thrown by the gods' high will. The day—the day, animation of the earth-born, the healing of the sick soul, friend of men and gods!
> But the day grows dim—night has drawn near; she has come—and from the world of fate she tears and casts away the blessed fabric of the cloak . . . and the abyss is laid bare before us, with its terrors and its dark, and there is no barrier between it and us—that is why we are terrified of the night!

When he was in Italy, Tyutchev was intrigued by the Italian habit of pessimistically finding "bad air," *(mal' aria),* a harbinger of death, in all sorts of apparently innocent and benign phenomena. In a poem titled "Mal' Aria"[31] he declares: "I love [the idea of] this mysterious Evil, invisibly infused in everything." It suggests the thought that perhaps indeed Death "when he summons the sons of Earth from life, covers his form as with a light veil so as to keep secret from them his terrible coming!" It is a notion analogous to that of the cloak of day that hides the abyss of chaos.

Schelling's philosophy, which is essentially optimistic, has no place for the concept of a "Final Cataclysm"[32] that would bring the ordered world back into primal Chaos. Tyutchev, however, sees the struggle of man and nature to bring cosmos—an ordered, civilized world—into being out of chaos as hopeless and ultimately futile. In "The Final Cataclysm" he reverts to a Biblical figure and envisions a kind of reversal of Genesis: "When Nature's last hour shall strike, the cohesion of earth's parts will be destroyed, the waters will once more cover everything visible, and God's face will be reflected in them!" Of about the same date (1829) as "The Final Cataclysm" is the powerfully disturbing poem "Sleeplessness":[33]

> The monotonous striking of the clock, wearisome tale of the night! A tongue equally foreign to all, and yet as intelligible to each as conscience!
> Who of us has heard without a pang, amid the universal silence, the dull groans of time, a prophetic-valedictory voice?
> It seems to us: irresistible Fate has overtaken the orphaned world—and we, in battle, have been abandoned to ourselves by all of nature;

> And our life stands before us, as a phantom, on the earth's extreme verge, and along with our age and friends, it grows pale in the twilit distance;
> And a new, youthful tribe meanwhile has come to bloom in the sun, and carried us, O friends, and our time into oblivion!
> Only now and then, performing a sorrowful rite at the midnight hour, the metal's sepulchral voice, from time to time laments us!

The poignant thought that in the eternal struggle between chaos and cosmos a whole generation has been abandoned by nature to fight hopelessly by itself makes this one of Tyutchev's most tragic poems.

Fyodor Tyutchev was one of the most contradictory thinkers of his age. Almost everything that can be asserted about his views can as readily be denied on the basis of evidence apparently equally valid. His highly poetical vision of an animate nature was based on no solid philosophical system, such as he might have derived from Schelling or other German idealists, but was intuitive. Evidently at times he doubted the validity of this intuition. A particularly telling evidence of skepticism in regard to Schelling's *Naturphilosophie* is embodied in a poem titled "Lunacy."[34] Personified "Lunacy" is represented as dwelling in a parched, waterless desert, where it "watches with glassy eyes for something in the clouds." Then, with evident ironical reference to a curious feature of Schelling's doctrine, he shows Lunacy with ear to the ground, listening intently "to something, with secret satisfaction on its brow." "It supposes that it hears the seething of streams, that it hears the flow of subterranean waters, and their cradle song, and their noisy issuance from the earth!" Schelling used to cite as evidence of sympathetic communion between man and external nature the phenomenon of men who professed to be able to detect the location of underground springs—what we know colloquially as "water-dowsers." But in the poem it is Lunacy itself which deludes itself with the expectation of finding some sympathetic sign in the sky or life-giving water in the midst of a burning desert. In another, almost epigrammatic, piece the crucial question: Is nature alive or not?—remains unanswered. The poem is entitled simply: "Problème":[35]

> A stone lay in the valley, having rolled down from the mountain. How did it fall? No one now knows—Did it break away from the summit *of its own accord,* or *was it hurled down by another's will?* Century has been borne after century: no one has yet answered the question.

Incidentally one may wonder whether the French title of the poem conceals an esoteric play on words. The Greek *problema* is derived from the verb "to throw," and means literally "something thrown forward,"—which might well apply to the problematical stone.

Another natural symbol poses an answer to the question as pessimistic as that of "Lunacy." In a short piece first published in 1836[36] the poet addresses a willow-tree that bends over a stream:

> Why do you bend your head over the waters, O willow? Or with trembling leaves like thirsty mouths catch at the running stream?
>
> Though your every leaf should grow weary, should quiver over the stream . . . yet the stream runs on and splashes, and glistens as it basks in the sun, and laughs at you . . .

Just as the willow will never succeed in catching the eternally flowing stream, so the human soul will be ever mocked by delusive nature.

Symbols as explicit as this are not common with Tyutchev, although they occur often enough to have led the "symbolist school" (Bryusov, Bely, Balmont et al.) of the end of the nineteenth century to proclaim the poet as one of their forerunners. Another very explicit symbol is that of the "Fountain."[37] In this, the typically romantic despair at the limitations of human knowledge is voiced—the despair that leads the aged Faust to thoughts of suicide. The fountain rises buoyantly toward the sky—but it comes inevitably to an invisible limit, after which it falls impotently back to the ground. Structurally this poem follows a pattern quite frequent with Tyutchev: in two strophes are presented first the natural analogy, then the application, almost in the fashion of a fable. Here the second strophe ends: "Fountain of mortal thought . . . How greedily you break away toward the sky! . . . But an invisible and fateful hand, bending your stubborn beam, makes it glitter in fragments from the height."

The gulf between human consciousness and the life of nature is the theme of the poem "Assuagement" (*Uspokoenie:* 1830).[38] The figure used is strikingly reminiscent of the third of the "three deaths" in Lev Tolstoi's story of that name—the death of the young tree cut down to become the marker of an old man's grave. The feeling of story and poem is the same: the indifference of nature to death. In the Tolstoi story the fall of the tree leaves more sunlight and growing space for the rest of the forest:

> The storm had passed—still smoking, the lofty oak was lying, smitten by the thunderbolt, and the grey smoke drifted from its branches over the green, made brighter by the storm. But for some time already the birds' song had been resounding louder and fuller in the groves, and the rainbow with the end of its arch had come to rest on the green treetops.

Doubtless the rainbow is used here with a hint of its Biblical meaning as a sign of reconciliation between heaven and earth.

When he is not entertaining corrosive doubts of the possibility of communion between man and nature, Tyutchev abandons himself to an ecstatic acceptance of life in all its fullness that is reminiscent of Goethe. It is usually the coming of spring that seems to evoke this mood. Poems of this sort breathe a healthy sensuality, yet notably this does not, as with most romantics, lead directly (cf. Tennyson's "young man") to "thoughts of love." Love belongs in another realm; as we shall see, it is mostly associated in the poet's mind with storms, and it is an emanation of Chaos. Spring belongs to the bright side of existence:[39]

> No, my partiality for you, mother-Earth, I am powerless to conceal! Incorporeal spirits of voluptuousness, I, your faithful son, do not crave. What, in comparison with you, is the delight of Paradise,—O season of love, season of spring, blooming blessedness of May, ruddy light, golden dreams?
>
> Every day, in profound inactivity, to drink in the warm springtime air, in the pure and lofty sky at times to follow after the clouds; to wander without business and without aim and accidentally, on the wing, to happen on the fresh scent of lilac or on a bright dream.

Similar is the lyric that begins: "The earth's aspect is still mournful, but the air already breathes of spring."[40] Spring has not yet begun, but nature in her sleep has already begun to smile; just so has the soul been sleeping, but now "the blocks of snow are shining and melting, the azure is radiant, blood is racing."

In Schelling's philosophy the natural harmony and oneness of all animate creation with the World-Spirit is broken by man's development of individuality, of a "particular life" severed from the life of the All. This breach in the world unity is in fact the origin of evil. For Tyutchev, a supreme individualist, this concept had intellectual but not emotional appeal. It is mostly found in his later verses with Slavophile orientation, where he stresses the principle of individualism as a "Western," "un-Christian" element, alien to the Slavic mentality. In one notable poem of the late 1830s, however, the concept appears in combination with the motif of spring ("Spring," 1838):[41]

> However heavily weighs the hand of fate, however wearying the deceit of men, however wrinkles furrow the brow and however full of wounds the heart; to whatever stern trials you have been subjected,—what will resist the breath and first meeting with spring!
>
> Spring...she knows nothing of you, of grief and evil; her look is radiant with immortality, and there is not a wrinkle on her brow. Obedient to her own laws alone, she flies down to you at the appointed hour, bright, blissfully indifferent, as befits divinities.
>
> She scatters blossoms over the earth, as fresh as the primal spring; if there has been another [spring] before her, she knows nothing of it; over the sky wander many clouds, but they are her clouds; she finds not even a trace of the being of faded springs.
>
> Not of what has been are the roses fragrant, and the nightingale sings in the night; not over what has been does Aurora shed scented tears,—and the terror of the inevitable end is not wafted from tree or leaf; their life, like a shoreless ocean, is all spread out in the present.
>
> Plaything and victim of particular life! Come, turn back the deception of feelings and plunge, cheerful, your own master, into this life-giving ocean! Come, wash in its ethereal stream your martyred breast—and become part, if but for a moment, of divinely universal life.

Here may be noted the characterization of vividly personified Spring as a being indifferent to man, and particularly, indifferent to that peculiarly human quality, a sense of duration, of time, of history. Spring comes as though it were for the first time—the "primal spring"; the roses' fragrance and the nightingale's song have nothing in them of the past—and concomitantly, they know nothing of what is to come, as man in his "particular life" does—of the "inevitable end." In the *Duino Elegies* Rainer Maria Rilke speaks of the animal's eyes that are turned inward, so that it does not see its ending; Tyutchev's "Spring" feels no sense of time, of either past or future. The poet exhorts himself to find healing from his wounds in the blissful non-consciousness of non-human nature. To be sure, it can be "but for a moment," as he has already noted sadly in "Flash," more than a decade earlier.

One of the best-known of Tyutchev's poems of any period is "Silentium!" (1830).[42] The general sense of the piece is clear enough, and is pregnantly conveyed in the line from the second strophe: *Mysl' izrechennaia est' lozh'*—"a thought once spoken is a lie." But is the injunction "to be still" based on despair of ever finding comprehension from one's fellowmen? Or is it, as Bukhshtab seems to feel,[43] conceived as a path to a mystic's higher knowledge? Silence, immersion in "the dark night of the soul" is a recognized part of the physical discipline necessary as a preliminary to mystical illumination. Indeed, "mystery" and "mysticism" themselves are etymologically derived from the Greek verb meaning "to keep one's mouth shut." There are other Tyutchev poems, e.g., "Vision" [*Videnie*], which lend some color to the Bukhshtab interpretation; but on the whole the explicit questions at the beginning of the second strophe seem to imply the easier meaning: "How can the heart express itself? How can another comprehend you? Will he understand what you live by?" In any case, the adjuration, surely directed to the poet himself, is toward a secret, inner life: "Know how to live only in yourself—there is a whole world in your soul of mysteriously captivating thoughts; noise from outside will drown them out, the rays of daylight drive them away,—hearken to their singing—and be silent!"

Divided against himself in so many ways as Tyutchev was, it is not surprising to find disunity in his religious conceptions. In a sense, of course, his Schellingian *Naturphilosophie* is a kind of religion—but it is intuitive, a poetical way of looking at the world, not a reasoned or faith-based attitude. In his Slavophile verse he naturally makes much of the superiority of Russian Orthodoxy to individualistic Western Catholicism. Yet he was, as even a very sympathetic biographer (Ivan Aksakov) notes, almost wholly irreligious in his ordinary life. Probably the abrupt little snarl addressed to an unknown woman[44] reveals well enough his actual feelings toward revealed religion:

> There is no feeling in your eyes, there is no truth in your speech, and there is no soul in you.
> Be manful, heart, to the end: and there is no Creator in creation! And there is no sense in prayer![45]

Two of his poems of the mid-1830s reveal his ironical attitude toward the Lutheranism of the Germany where he spent so many years. The earlier of these begins: *"Ia liuteran liubliu bogosluzhen'e."* It is a mistake to translate the verb *liubliu* here literally as "I love," which would give the idea that he prefers the bare, unadorned Lutheran service to the colorful and sumptuous service of the Orthodox church. The verb here, as in the first line of "Mal' aria," means rather "I like the idea of—," with an underlying tone of amusement. After describing the simple service and the bare walls of the Lutheran church, he draws the moral: "Setting out on a journey, religion stands for the last time before you; she has not yet crossed the threshold, but her house is empty and bare. She has not yet crossed the threshold, the door has not yet been shut behind her . . . but the hour has come, has struck . . . Pray to God! you are praying now for the last time." The second of the "Lutheran" poems vividly presents the scene of a Protestant funeral:[46]

> And the coffin has already been lowered into the grave, and all have crowded around . . . they jostle each other, breathe with difficulty; the breath of decay oppresses the breast.
> And over the open grave, at the pillow, where the coffin rests, the learned pastor, impressive, pronounces the graveside sermon . . .
> He proclaims the frailty of man, original sin, the blood of Christ . . . and the intelligent, seemly sermon affects the crowd in different ways.
> And the sky is so incorruptibly pure, so infinite above the earth. . . . and the birds soar with loud song in the blue abyss of the air . . .

In the number and turbulence of his amorous attachments Tyutchev ranks high among poets. In sheer numbers probably Pushkin has the advantage, but for chronological spread few but Goethe can compete. Tyutchev, like Goethe, had his last affair at the age of seventy; his first marriage was at the age of twenty-three, and this is unlikely to have been the beginning of his experiences. He was a very passionate man, and various incidents in his life make it clear that where love was concerned few other considerations had any weight. After the death of his first wife he applied to the Russian Foreign Office for permission to marry another Bavarian lady and have a leave of absence for the purpose. Permission to marry was granted, but no leave—so Tyutchev, who was at the time in charge of the Russian mission in Turin, simply locked the embassy doors, made his way to Switzerland and married Ernestine Dornberg. Not surprisingly, after this the Foreign Office found his services dispensable, and he remained without employment from 1831 to 1844. In 1850 he became infatuated with Elena Alexandrovna Denisova, one of the instructresses in the school where his daughters were students. This affair lasted for fourteen years, until Denisova's death, and resulted in three children. The affair was carried on in complete defiance of scandalized public opinion, even of the disapproval of the Court.

A poet's love life is of concern to a critic only in so far as it affects his poetry. Tyutchev wrote some of his most magnificent verse in direct connection with his various loves. The summit of his poetry is probably to be found in the Denisova cycle, but this belongs to his later period and is outside the scope of this study. We shall consider only the love poems that fall within the period 1830-36. The identity of the addressees is unimportant, and in any case is often in doubt.

Tyutchev's intuitive view of the world, reinforced no doubt by Schelling's philosophy, is essentially dualistic—a pattern of light and dark, of chaos and cosmos, of bright repose and of stormy passion. Love, as we have noted, falls on the dark side of this dichotomy. It is an elemental force refractory to human reason, and the very embodiment of chaos. In Tyutchev's verse it is usually associated with storm—a non-human incarnation of chaos which in itself attracted the poet (cf. the poem "Spring Storm"). The earlier pieces, however, are serene, and reflect the poet's own feelings, where the best of the later ones depict rather his partner's emotions. From 1830 comes this lyric:[47]

That day, I remember, was for me the morning of the day of life: she stood in silence before me, her breast heaved like a wave, her cheeks grew scarlet as the dawn, reddening and burning ever hotter! And suddenly, like the young sun, the golden avowal of love was wrested from her breast... and I beheld a new world!

Another poem, dated 1834, paints a delicate and idyllic picture of another less serious attraction:[48]

I remember a golden time, I remember a region dear to my heart. The day was turning toward evening; there were two of us; below, in the shadow, the Danube was noisy.

And on the hill, there where showing white the ruin of a castle looked afar, you stood, a young fay, leaning against the mossy granite,

Touching with your youthful foot the fragments of the age-old pile; and the sun lingered, saying farewell to the hill, and the castle, and you.

And the quiet breeze in passing played with your dress, and from the wild apple-trees blew down blossom after blossom on your young shoulders.

Unconcerned, you gazed into the distance... the border of the sky was dimming mistily in the light; the day was dying out; more loudly sang the river in its darkened banks.

And you with careless gaiety were seeing off the happy day; and sweetly over us flew the shadow of swift-flowing life.

The description of the dawn of passion in this piece from about 1836 has been compared with a novelist's technique; indeed, in the mastery with which Tyutchev handles psychology in the small compass of a lyric there is a great resemblance to Dostoevsky. Note here the pervasive atmosphere of sultriness, climaxing in the final line:[49]

> In the close stillness of the air, like the premonition of a storm, the roses' fragrance is hotter, the locust's voice louder.
> Hark! behind the white, smoky cloud the thunder is dully rolling; the sky is girt round about with flying lightning.
> A certain gross superfluity of life suffuses the sultry air, it tingles and burns in the veins like a potion from the gods!
> Maiden, maiden, what makes the muslin heave over your young breast? Why does the moist brilliance of your eyes grow turbid, melancholy?
> Why does the flame of your virginal cheeks grow pale and fade away? What so oppresses your breast and makes your lips hot?...
> Through your silken eyelashes two tears have oozed... or are they the raindrops of the coming storm...?

Of about the same date as the piece just cited, and doubtless belonging to the same emotional context, is this:[50]

> The east grew white. The boat glided, the sail sounded gaily,—like a sky inverted the sea trembled beneath us...
> The east grew red. She said a prayer, pushing the veil away from her forehead,— the prayer breathed on her lips, the sky exulted in her eyes.
> The east flamed. She bent, her gleaming neck drooped,—and over the childish cheeks streamed drops of fire...

As a final example of Tyutchev's earlier love poetry may be cited these two strophes:[51]

> I love your eyes, my darling, with their fiery-wondrous play, when you suddenly raise them, and, as with the lightning of heaven, take in a whole circle with a glance...
> But there are enchantments stronger: your eyes, cast down, at the moment of a passionate kiss, and between the lowered lashes, the somber, muted fire of desire.

Tyutchev's political verse is uniformly bad, or at least indifferent. It is a cerebral artifact, untouched by the heart. Most of it belongs to his Slavophile years and is hence outside the scope of the present study. Its chief theme is that which he treated (in French prose) in the treatise *La Russie et la Révolution* (1849): there are two forces confronting one another in Europe, revolution (an emanation of chaos!) and Russia, the guardian of order. This was doubtless the reasoned attitude of the diplomat Tyutchev, but there is evidence that the revolutionary aspect of chaos was not without attractions for Tyutchev the man of feeling. One of the evidences of this is the poem "Cicero":[52]

The Roman orator said, amid civic storm and turmoil: "I got up late—and on the road was overtaken by the night of Rome!" Yes!... but, in saying good-bye to Roman glory, from the height of the Capitoline you saw in all its greatness the setting of its bloody star!...

Fortunate is he who has visited the world at its fateful moments! The blessed [gods] have invited him as a companion to their feast. He is the spectator of their lofty spectacles, he has been admitted to their council—and, alive, he has, like a dweller in heaven, drunk immortality from their cup!

Whatever his intellectual attitude may have been, the fateful moments of his world held emotional attraction. One of these was the July Revolution in France (1831); a later one was 1848, "the year of revolutions." Russia's wars with Turkey also aroused his intense interest, especially the war of 1853-56, which he saw as Russia's great opportunity of liberating her Slavic brothers from Ottoman oppression. This theme appears only sporadically in the poems before 1840: we have noted it in the semi-official translation of the poem by Ludwig of Bavaria to Tsar Nikolai I. It is hinted at in this symbolic lyric of 1830, "The Alps":[53]

Through the azure twilight of the night peer the snowy Alps; as pale as death, their eyes strike with an icy terror. Bewitched by some kind of authority, they drowse, misty and terrible, until the ascension of the Dawn, like fallen kings!...

But the East will only begin to grow red, and there is an end to the deadly charms—first in the sky will the oldest brother's crown grow bright. And from the great brother's head the stream runs to the lesser [brothers], and all the family, reborn, glitters in crowns of gold!...

It hardly needs to be pointed out that light comes from the east, and that the light strikes first the elder brother—which can hardly be other than Russia—and thence is spread to the lesser members of the family. The poem, however, although evidently symbolic, can be read as a purely descriptive piece of landscape-painting, and perhaps better appreciated so.

Although there is some basis for the belief that in his post-1840 period Tyutchev was moving in the direction of realism, and thus coming closer to Pushkin's mature style, certainly in the earlier period the two greatest poets of their time were at opposite poles stylistically. Pushkin began in the Karamzinist camp, and was influenced in his development chiefly by the major poets of the 1810s, Zhukovsky and Batyushkov. Tyutchev, who was only four years younger than Pushkin, began to write verse under the tutelage of the rather conservative Raich. His earliest extant poems, e.g., "On the New Year of 1816" and "Urania," accordingly belong in the tradition of Derzhavin, who was Raich's model. To this tradition Tyutchev remained faithful in several important ways—in his preference for a rather archaic language, in his didacticism, and in a prevailingly rhetorical tone. The genres which he cultivated, however, are not those of Derzhavin; neither are they those of the Karamzinists. They are a development of his own. Some of his earliest pieces approach Derzhavin's type of ode, but nothing of this sort appears in his mature verse; and the epistles and elegies of the Karamzinists are equally missing.

Perhaps the most notable feature of the Derzhavin style to be found in Tyutchev's verse of all periods is archaism of both language and style. Any one of his lyrics will be marked by the use of words not in the ordinary Russian vocabulary of his time—Slavonicisms and obsolete, bookish "poetical diction." Not only the vocabulary shows this trend, but even such stylistic characteristics as the fondness for compound adjectives, which give a heightened solemnity to the verse, the trick of placing a noun in a middle position, with a modifier both before and after it, and the like. His frequently awkward, even unparsable, periods are another archaic feature, a relic of the "poetic disorder" which eighteenth-century poets imagined contributed to the elevation of their verse.

Where Derzhavin and the other poets of the eighteenth century tend toward large, expansive forms, such as the ode, Tyutchev prefers the small form. His favorite is a poem of two strophes, each often of only four lines— an almost epigrammatic brevity. Very rarely do Tyutchev's mature poems exceed five strophes, and this concision extends to the individual strophes as well: the individual sentences are tightly constructed, with no unnecessary verbiage.

Very typical of Tyutchev's poetical practice is the abrupt, unexplained beginning, sometimes giving the effect of breaking into the middle of a conversation. "Yes," "No," "And" often function as the first words of a poem, and very often "he" or "she," with no previous introduction or identification, appears in the first lines. The effect of discourse interrupted in Tyutchev's verse is suggested by his frequent use of the second person pronoun, with a verb either in the indicative or imperative mode, as though he were directly addressing another person or persons. This is of course a part of his rhetorical and didactical tendency: thus, he begins a poem with the abrupt ejaculation: "Nature is not what you [plur.] suppose." Several of his nature lyrics, which open with descriptions of the natural scene, begin with the imperative *smotri,* "look!" "Silentium" begins with a line of three imperatives: "Be silent, hide yourself and keep secret..."

Quite in Derzhavin's manner is Tyutchev's argumentative style, in which he provides logical connectives of a fairly prosy sort to hold his thought together, e.g., "Yes! But—," "But nevertheless," "But if," "Meanwhile," etc. Again, one may note the abundance in Tyutchev of rhetorical questions and exclamations. This, however, is no more a trait of Derzhavin than it is of Zhukovsky, for whom it is a very characteristic stylistic feature. Rhetorical question and exclamation belong to the high style, and their prevalence in Tyutchev means no more than that he strives to get away from the flatness of the Karamzinian middle style. In his political verse, with which we are not concerned, the rhetorical element dominates.

Tyutchev's verse never attracted the general public of Russian readers. He remained caviar to the general, the object of great admiration on the part of a few critics, themselves writers—Turgenev, Nekrasov, Lev Tolstoi—but little known or appreciated by the wider literate public. It was not until the end of the century that a new generation of poets arose in Russia, happily dissatisfied with the dreary "civic verse" of the poetical wasteland of the 1870s and 1880s, and rediscovered Tyutchev. The Symbolists posthumously adopted Tyutchev as one of their own. Valery Bryusov, in his article "F. I. Tyutchev,"[54] wrote: "Tyutchev has methods of composing and apprehending verse which are his own entirely, and which in his time, the beginning of the nineteenth century, stood out in complete isolation." Tolstoi ranked Tyutchev as a poet ahead even of Pushkin; few today would go this far, but many would give him second place in his century, ahead of the very uneven Lermontov. Ranking writers, however, is a futile task at best: it suffices to say of Fyodor Tyutchev that he belongs among the greatest poets of his nation, and indeed of any nation.

II

Other Major Poets of the 1830s-1840s

Alexander Ivanovich Polezhaev (1804-1838)

Many of Russia's literary figures have suffered misfortune of one kind or another at the hands of a tyrannical government, from the noose that ended Ryleev's life to the relatively mild form of exile meted out to Pushkin, but few have endured more protracted torments than Alexander Polezhaev, forced at the age of twenty-two into military service under the harshest conditions, and dead twelve years later of tuberculosis directly resulting from incarceration in a noisome military prison.

Alexander Polezhaev[1] was the bastard son of a vicious landowner, Leonty Struisky, and a serf-girl of his household. Liberated the year after her son's birth, the girl was forcibly married to a merchant named Ivan Polezhaev, who officially recognized the child as his and thus legitimated him. It may be noted that Yury Struisky, Leonty's brother, fathered the poet "Triluny" in similar fashion, but eventually married his mistress and so gave his son his own name ("Triluny's" real name was Dimitry Yurevich Struisky). Polezhaev lost his foster-father in 1808 and his mother in 1810, after which he was brought up on his father's estate by his mother's relatives until 1816, when Struisky sent him to Moscow for an education. Leonty Struisky in the same year brutally killed one of his serfs and in consequence was exiled to Siberia, where he died in 1823. Alexander, after finishing preparatory school, entered Moscow University, where he proved to be a brilliant student. In 1824 he journeyed to St. Petersburg for a visit to his uncle Alexander N. Struisky, a visit which he recorded in his bawdy and irreligious narrative poem *Sashka,* written in the first half of 1826. His first published poems appeared in late 1825 and early 1826, and he was graduated in 1826 from the University with high honors. At the moment, however, when a promising literary career seemed in sight for him, a denunciation was made to Emperor Nikolai, who was in Moscow for his coronation, against the "free-thinking" students of Moscow University, and a manuscript copy of Polezhaev's *Sashka* was submitted to confirm the denunciation. At the end of June, accordingly, Polezhaev was abruptly summoned to appear before the Emperor, compelled to read his poem to his imperial audience, and forthwith sentenced to military service in an infantry regiment with non-commissioned rank.

The lamentable tale of Polezhaev's subsequent life may be quickly told. In 1827 he attempted to escape from his regiment, with the hazy idea of going directly to St. Petersburg to plead with the Emperor for release. He returned voluntarily, but was sentenced to be reduced in rank to a common soldier without the privilege of ever attaining officer rank. Soon after this an investigation in Moscow uncovered a "subversive" group in which Polezhaev had allegedly read some agitational verses by Ryleev. Polezhaev was accordingly imprisoned for a month or more. The next year he insulted a sergeant and spent six months in military prison. In 1829 his regiment was ordered to the Caucasus, where he saw active service against the insurgent mountaineers of Daghestan. In the years 1830-33 he took part in a number of engagements, some of which are chronicled in his narrative poems *Erpelí* and *Chir-Yurt*. For "exceptional bravery and presence of mind" private Polezhaev was promoted to non-commissioned rank. When the regiment to which he had been attached was withdrawn from the Caucasus, Polezhaev was transferred to another, which was stationed in the Ryazan province. Here he made the acquaintance of Alexander Herzen, Ogaryov and the poet Satin, and in the home of the friendly Colonel Bibikov met the latter's daughter Ekaterina, with whom he fell hopelessly in love. The regiment was moved to Kaluga province in June 1834, however, and the Zaraisk idyll was terminated. In 1836-37 Polezhaev was on detached duty in Moscow, but for some infraction of discipline was subjected in 1837 to severe corporal punishment, as a result of which he was sent to a military hospital. In January 1838 a personal decree of Nikolai I promoted Polezhaev to the lowest commissioned rank. Nine days after receiving his promotion Lieutenant Polezhaev died of tuberculosis, brought on by the unspeakable conditions of a military prison augmented by heavy drinking.

It is impossible not to sympathize with a person whose entire life was an ordeal of almost unrelieved bleakness. At the same time it is impossible not to agree with Belinsky:[2] "Polezhaev was not the victim of fate and had no right to blame anyone but himself for his ruin." Unquestionably the punishment initially meted out to him for the indiscretions of the poem *Sashka* was severe out of all proportion to the offence; but unquestionably Polezhaev's flight in 1827 was the worst kind of folly, and the punishment which it entailed was one which the victim certainly brought on himself. Doubtless the prospect of twenty-five years of hardship, danger and intolerable boredom, with no hope of mitigation even by good conduct, induced in Polezhaev a desperation which resulted in the several breaches of discipline for which he was punished later. Had he been able, however, to discipline his own conduct more successfully, he might have avoided much of the suffering which he had to endure. A more submissive and rational Polezhaev, however, would have been an entirely different person.

Ordinarily a poet's external biography is, if not an irrelevant matter, at least of secondary importance in the consideration of his work. With Polezhaev it is totally impossible to dissociate life from work. He is one of the least objective of poets, and the "lyric hero" of his verse is almost identical with the poet himself. There is, however, a good deal of exaggeration and posturing in his verse, a good deal of self-dramatization. As Belinsky pointed out, Polezhaev never had a chance to mature: even his last verse has the defects of immaturity.

His earliest efforts belong to the year 1825 and were published in the *European Herald* while the author was still a student in Moscow University. They are, as might be expected, conventional: light verse (e.g., "Inconstancy"), elegies ("Remembrances," "Night"), the usual romantic effusion on "genius," etc. There are also translations: "Morni and the Shade of Kormak," from Ossian, and an excellent version of Byron's long ballad, "Oscar of Alva." There is a rather pointless bit of satire ("A New Misfortune") mocking the clergy and their families when a proposed decree of Alexander I would have forbidden them to wear secular clothes. But among this undistinguished stuff one poem stands out. It is tentatively dated 1826, probably before Polezhaev's fateful audience with the Emperor and his condemnation to military service. "Burial"[3] was first published in 1836, in Polezhaev's first volume of verse:

> I saw death's cruel festival—the sombre rite of burial: a young girl had tasted the peace of eternity in the gloom of nothingness. No long line of equipages, no black crepe and no censers in a crowd of courtiers and pages crowded behind her to the grave. Ah, no! A simple plank coffin was carried by a file of her girl-friends, and without elaborate service, the parish-priest walked ahead. The family circle and on the day of sorrow the griefstricken bridegroom, among young girls of the same age, accompanied the coffin with tears. And now the physician of souls has chanted the last prayer, and there is more violent wailing and weeping... and death has finished his capture! The loud nail resounds lingeringly, the grave of death has been closed, and the girl committed, as a new guest, to the unfeeling ground.... I saw it all; in dumb silence I stood at the fateful place and in the depth of my soul I said: 'Farewell, farewell, young bride!' Involuntarily some sort of trembling possessed me with wondrous power, and from the mysterious tomb I did not want to depart for a long time. There came to my mind at that time innocent dreams, and the sweet burden of sorrow I brought to the memory of beauty. I knew her—she, in play, gave me a flower not long before,—and suddenly, playing, drooping, had faded away like the flower she had given.

Vivid realistic traits stand out in the poem and make it harrowing—the grief-stricken family, the lone priest heading the procession, the dreadful sound of the coffin cover being nailed shut; and the simile of the flower at the end, which could have been utterly banal and meaningless, is given vitality by its personal application.

The whole of Alexander Polezhaev's life after 1826 was fatally affected by the poem *Sashka*.[4] The impulse to write the poem was given by the publication in the middle of February 1825, of the first chapter of Pushkin's *Eugene Onegin*. Polezhaev, whose ambivalent social status disposed him to hostility toward the aristocracy and high society, determined to create an "anti-Onegin" whose adventures take place in the lowest of low society. For a poet such as Polezhaev it was the most natural thing in the world to make himself the hero of his poem; this is, of course, not quite literally true—*Sashka* is not written in the first person, although in first-person comments the narrator refers to the hero as a friend—but the third stanza of the poem gives the hero's surname as Polezhaev, and Sashka is of course the diminutive of Alexander. Perhaps all the incidents and thoughts attributed to Sashka may not have belonged to the author, but the visit to his uncle, where the reference to *Onegin* is particularly obvious, definitely does. The language of the poem is deliberately vulgar, often so obscene that the prudish Soviet press has never reprinted the poem in full, The two "chapters" are divided into stanzas of twelve lines each (the "Onegin stanza" has fourteen) rhyming aBaBcDcDeFeF.

What probably infuriated Nikolai I about the piece was not so much the obscenity as the mockingly irreligious tone of it, and the almost equally offensive contempt which it shows for accepted social and political values.

Sashka begins with a short address "To My Readers," who must be envisioned as fellow-students for the most part, since there could never have been any thought of publication:

> Not for fame, but for amusement I write! Approval or criticism I do not ask for! Let whoever will, laugh, and I am glad; but the debauched, unfriendly—let them wail. And whoever wants to take anything else here for evil, whoever spreads [tales] and denounces,—he can ————.[5]

The first chapter, pointedly copying the *Onegin* situation, presents the hero's thoughts as he rides from Moscow to the capital to visit his uncle. Uncle is portrayed as a terribly sharp-tempered person, but quick to forget his tantrums—probably a true picture of Alexander Struisky. In the third strophe the author introduces the hero whose thoughts he has been giving:

> Students of all lands and regions! He is your comrade and my friend; his surname is Polezhaev, and furthermore... well, friends, not all at once! I'm a talkative fellow even without you,—provided I don't put you to sleep, just listen patiently: I'd be glad to talk all my life![6]

Sashka's birth and early childhood are described:

> Sashka's first teacher was one of the household lackeys. Let's pass over the fact that this famous mentor was also a Solomon in French, and that the child prattled splendidly: *Jean f[outut], un v[is], un c[on]*; let's pass over the fact that at six years old he played "The Young Lady" on the balalaika, and that he was the coachmen's equal in obscenity, shooting craps and pitch.

At ten Sashka was suddenly hurried off to Moscow to a French boardingschool, and thence to the University; here the author digresses on the difference between "the student" in Göttingen or Oxford and in Russia:

> Among you [i.e., Germans or English] a boy doesn't get the idea of puffing himself up and hissing: "I'm a student!" You judge: though he be a prince's brat, there isn't a drop of sense in him! With you a student is a respected man, not a scrimy snot-face[!], not an educated half-wit and not a fool with dough! With you talents are esteemed, and not bows at three versts distance; with you there is reward for merits, and not for salutations in hallways!
>
> No rector governs your spirit—natural intelligence shows you the way, and it supplies you with honor and rank, and not "no way, nohow!" But you [i.e., Russia], land notorious only for goatlike beards, land that burdens minds with chains, my stupid fatherland! When will the time come for you to open your eyes to your savagery, when will you throw off from yourself the burden of your contemptible hangmen?[7]

It was probably this outburst against sacrosanct Russian traditions, as much as anything else in *Sashka,* that convinced Nikolai that here was a "dangerous thinker," plotting to overthrow the government—for who could Russia's "contemptible hangmen" be, if not the Tsar and his minions, who had in fact actually hanged Ryleev and four others of the Decembrists just a few months before?

The scene shifts to a presumably typical student orgy in a Moscow tavern, with floods of liquor and willing girls. "Seneca was a fine philosopher," the poet opines, "and the sage Plato still more intelligent; but for two or three centuries now they have not been, so help me, a model. Both in them and in the modern charlatans there's only a baggage of absurdities and our whole society rests on deceptions, whether spiritual or secular."[8] This strophe ends with four lines of dots: apparently the poet's hedonism took him into areas of such frank sensuality that the Soviet censor had to leave them to the reader's imagination.

More characterization of Sashka follows: he has some knowledge of French and German and mathematics, and can even write verses in his native Russian—but, the poet hastens to say, "I have no intention of holding forth on learned men or on the sciences."

> Amen! Not a word about the sciences . . . the features of this character: freedom in thought and conduct, acknowledgment of no man as his judge; neither cowardly submissiveness nor hypocritical piety, but a thirst for obstinate liberty and passions unrestrained! To judge decisively and boldly with his own mind on all matters and to smoulder with deep-rooted hostility toward the shaggy rascals in horse-collars [i.e., the clergy].
>
> He couldn't for the life of him tolerate them, and into his system of thought neither saints' relics nor angels nor devils nor either books [i.e., the Old and New Testaments] entered at all, neither this way nor that; and however much the learned Plato along with Socrates might teach him to believe in Jesus[!], he believes none of this: "All this is stories," he says; he measures God with his own yardstick, and gives not a penny for the church.

> The reason I am expatiating on such divine matters is that I flatter myself that I am showing Sashka as though he were naked, in all his parts; that all may know him as they ought, from his good side and his bad, and I swear, so help me, he himself will infallibly say that this is the way he is. Of course, such a godless scapegrace isn't to the taste of many people; but even if he doesn't believe in Jesus, he really is a fine fellow![9]

The "fine fellow," however, is a vulgarian on principle: "Not theaters and masquerades and the finest flower of Moscow's ladies, not dudes, not costumes are the objects of his seething thoughts. No, my Sashka's principles are not such. He was not *bon-ton* from birth, and he didn't direct his swift and eagle flight in this direction at all."

The first chapter of *Sashka* ends with the adjournment of the drinking party to a brothel,—a scene rather abbreviated in the printed text—followed by a skirmish with the police, the capture of Sasha, his rescue by a husky student friend, and a final riotous celebration of victory over the forces of law and order.

The second, and last, chapter of Polezhaev's poem brings the rowdy hero to St. Petersburg, where he meets with the expected reception from his uncle—a furious dressing-down which rapidly diminishes in intensity until finally all is affection and pampering. Sashka is outfitted with stylish new clothes, given plenty of pocket-money, and turned loose to live the fashionable life in St. Petersburg. The fashionable life, however, is not for him, whose tastes run to cruder amusements. He dutifully accepts the tickets to concerts and plays, but usually leaves after a little and goes somewhere to do some drinking. His conduct with his uncle, however, is the height of respectability:[10]

> With what ardor of rapture he would praise uncle's dreams, demonstrate the providence of God, go deep into the beauties of nature; with what fire he expressed admiration for the intelligence of Napoleon, and how he would go into raptures over the deeds of Moreau and Ney and Davout; he abused all Russians without exception, and in the Hermitage he didn't remove either his mouth or his eyes from the pictures. Oh, the rascal! Oh, the scamp, the son of a bitch!
>
> And he indulged, and played the hypocrite, and flattered shamelessly, and lied! And honest uncle believed everything, and kept giving the scamp money ... often-times, he would have just come from Millionaia [a disreputable street in the capital], and uncle [would say]: "Where have you been, friend?" And he (as bold as you please.) [would reply]: "I've been walking along the boulevard, sir, and then I watched the launching of a steamer, and then I inspected the Winter Palace. And what calm weather it is!"—Oh, you————rascal!

Inevitably Sashka's St. Petersburg holiday has to come to an end, and abruptly he is shipped back to Moscow, where he suddenly makes his appearance in the midst of a Muscovite street carnival, is rapturously greeted by the narrator, and sets off on a new series of escapades, with which the poet ends his tale. In an epilogue Polezhaev writes:[11]

Friends, here are a few events from my Sashka's life ... Perhaps a hail of abuse and scolding will fall like rain on him, and on me, as the coryphaeus of his debauchery and excesses, and some seminarist or other, blazing with malice, will make his sudden appearance ... But I despise them so much that I'm unwilling even to listen, and what more I shall learn about Sashka—so help me, I shan't keep any of it quiet.

Possibly Polezhaev actually did intend to add other chapters to his tale; if so, his intentions were forever frustrated by the Emperor's stern punishment, and the carefree life of his student years came to an abrupt end.

Sashka is obviously not a work of art, nor was designed to be. It has the merits of liveliness, humor and youthful bravado. The depiction of Moscow low-life is probably accurate, but there is no attempt to render the descriptions realistic by generalization. The characterization of Sashka is the only one in the poem, all the other persons being incidental; since Sashka is transparently a double of the author, the characterization is quite detailed, with the chief emphasis on what were decidedly Polezhaev's leading traits, a love of freedom intolerant of any kind of subordination, and an extravagant intensity of passion.

Of about the same period as *Sashka,* that is, the first part of 1826, is an insignificant pseudo-Oriental poem, *The Goat-Imam.*[12] An avaricious Muslim clergyman tries to swindle a neighbor out of a windfall treasure by masquerading as the devil in a goatskin and horns. The swindle backfires: the goatskin adheres to the imam's body and he is discovered by the villagers, who punish him properly and deprive him of the spiritual office he has abused. The Oriental color is obviously only a disguise for an attack on the covetousness of the Orthodox priesthood.

Polezhaev's first published collection of verse appeared in 1832, titled simply *Poems of A. Polezhaev.* In the same year the two long narratives *Erpeli* and *Chir-Yurt* came out in separate volumes. The collection *The Hookah (Kal'ian)* appeared in 1833 and was reprinted in 1836 and 1838. In additition to these collections of lyrics, translations and narrative poems deemed printable by the censors, a certain number of other verses exist which Polezhaev wrote as epistles to friends, and evidently with no thought of publication in complete form. Of the latter group the most interesting is an epistle written in 1828 to Alexander Petrovich Lozovsky,[13] who had become the poet's close friend and literary executor. Portions of this epistle were published in the journal *Galatea.* It relates chiefly to the period of Polezhaev's incarceration in a military prison after his second arrest.

In the first section of the epistle the poet addresses Lozovsky directly, whom he had only recently met, but who had from the first manifested a friendly sympathy toward the unfortunate conscript quite in contrast to the indifference of the fair-weather friends of which he complains in section V of this epistle. Of himself at this juncture he says: "Beneath the yoke of misfortune the whole world is suspect to me; the features of perished truth are only dreams in my eyes ... it [i.e., the truth] to my truculent mind is both hateful and laughable!" Lozovsky's affection, which in his despair he still finds scarcely credible, has nevertheless been his only comfort:

> But granting that I, a plaything of my passions, shall be a puppet for men; granting that the cruel poison of their perfidy will magnify the hell in my breast ... even you are no better than they.... I myself do not know for what reason, to what end I have come to love you.... Your look is not a reproach to the unfortunate. Your voice, the sound of your words are dear to me as the sweet brook. So the nightingale in the stillness of night sings for the sorrowful soul, so spoke Uriel to Abbadon in the darkness of Gehenna [Uriel, one of the "good angels" in Klopstock's *Messias* remained a friend to the fallen angel Abbadon, and eventually redeemed him].

In the second section of the epistle Polezhaev gives a vivid and horrifying picture of the military prison in which he was confined:

> And on the enormous court, as it were in a pit or hole, a hole long since hollowed out, or a guard-house, it's all the same ... And in the depths of this hole, still another hole in the wall, called the prison; in it perpetual dampness and darkness, and a gleam of the sun's rays shines feebly in it through the windows; the cracked brick vault is just on the point of falling and crashing on the floor ... In the prison for the five or six victims there is a row of small plank beds by the stove. And ten bold heads, decided enemies of the Tsar, sit on the little plank-beds, and the irons on them rattle.... and every evening as they lie down to sleep, and in the morning, in their prayers to the Lord Christ they in unison consign the Russian Tsar to————and all want to serve him because he's a hard master at making men run the gauntlet for trifles....
>
> Here.... lies the poet, made recruit.... here for three hundred sixty-five days in a circle of villainous people he drinks in the stinking air of life and curses the autocracy. Here he, in the flower of his youth, disfigured, like a skeleton, with a half-shorn beard, languishes in cruel anguish ... He is no longer alive in mind—soul and mind are killed in him; but like a roving automaton or an unfeeling soldier begotten by a bayonet for a bayonet, he breathes with the life of a fool; twice a day he eats and drinks and renders his duty to nature.

Section III of the epistle consists of the prisoner's roseate recollections of happier days, now lost forever. Section IV begins with a stern and reproachful address (enciphered, of course!) to his persecutor, Tsar Nikolai; then returns to the realities of the filthy cell where he is confined,— he who in time past has been the singer of the Bacchic delights of student banquets. The section ends as it began, with an enciphered allusion to Nikolai, which credits him with the destruction of the poet's dreams: "The second Nero, Iscariot, Brazilian python, and Nimrod honored him [i.e., the poet] with his enmity, and strangled him with a kiss!" Section V, as mentioned above, is a satirical reproach addressed to the egotistical society "friends" who once flocked around the man they now shun.

The Sixth is the most interesting, from an intellectual point of view, of the epistle's divisions, since it consists entirely of an argument on the existence of God and on free will:

> The system of the stars, the cricket's jump, the movements of the sea and of the fiddle-bow—everything is the free will of the creative hand...Or is belief in God nonsense? To say that He does not exist is ridiculous; to say that He exists is difficult. If He exists, if He is mind, far above our proud thoughts, just, eternal and good, living in Himself and by Himself, the alpha and omega of existence...then He is not the judge of us: is it possible for Him to judge what He Himself has taken thought to create? In condemning His own creation, He would be disproving Himself!....To repeat the traditions of antiquity, that we are free in our actions, is to run counter to intelligence and so fall into another darkness...If His providence could see the evil of my freedom—He must from myriads of ages have called forth my atom for chains...One of two things: either He desired that I should suffer though innocent, or else a blind, implacable destiny has pulled me into the gulf of misfortune?....If He saw, then He desired it; if He desired it, then He ordered it, everything is through Him and from Him; the conclusion for this is—if I am free, He is a tyrant; if I am a puppet, He is a blockhead.

This whole syllogism, which derives from Baron d'Holbach's *Système de la nature,* is a model of concision and intellectual vigor. It is also a very rare instance for nineteenth-century Russia of an unqualified agnosticism.

Section VII is a rather pathetic address to the "uncle" (Alexander Struisky) whom Polezhaev had treated in *Sashka* with such amused condescension, and to whom he now turns for forgiveness: "In ruining my rebellious life, I implore you, in tears of repentance!....I would call you by the sacred name of father!...I call...And I beg for the forgiveness of love upon my submissive head for my sins!...Forgive! Forgive!...my fault has been avenged with a terrible vengeance!" In the final short section the poet foresees the uselessness of all his hopes and appeals, and envisions his own end in prison and a grave unmarked by either stone or cross.

The "Epistle to Alexander Petrovich Lozovsky" is typical of Polezhaev's best verse—intensely, grippingly personal, passionate and emotional. It runs the gamut from the most touching expressions of love and friendship, for Lozovsky and Struisky, to contempt and hatred for the Tsar, disdain and loathing for his fellow prisoners, through a dry, tight philosophical discourse, to an almost hysterical despair. An extraordinary document!

The "Epistle to Lozovsky" is written in the four-foot iambic meter traditional for its genre. It is a meter that Polézhaev often uses for other purposes as well, as do all the romantics. Almost unique and specifically his own, however, is the two-foot anapaestic line in which many of his most characteristic lyrics are composed. When Belinsky spoke of the strength of Polezhaev's verse, he may have had this peculiarly intense, fast-moving meter in mind. The anapaest is a foot not often employed by Russian poets, who favor rather the amphibrach. Much of the effect of stern stoicism of the famous "Song of the Captive Iroquois"[14] (between 1826 and 1828) derives from its anapaestic meter, of which the first strophe will serve as an example:

Ia umru! na pozor palacham
Bezzashchitnoe telo otdam!
   Ravnodushno oni
   Dlia zabavy detei
   Otdirat' ot kostei
   Budut zhily moi!
   Obrugaiut, ub'iut
   I moi trup razorvut!

["I shall die! To the shame of my executioners / I shall give my defenseless body / Indifferently, they / Will flay from my bones / For their childrens' pleasure / My veins and sinews! / They will curse and kill me / And tear my corpse asunder!"]

This, incidentally, is one of the few of Polezhaev's poems which can be regarded as, at least outwardly, impersonal and objective, although of course even here the captive brave who defies death and the worst torments that his enemies can inflict on him with the words: "But I shall endure! I shall say nothing. I shall not wrinkle my brow!" is Polezhaev himself in one of his moods.

Another of his moods is that of melodramatic despair, such as pervades "The Evening Twilight"[15] (between 1826 and 1828). This is composed entirely in the short two-beat anapaestic meter with couplet rhyme which he uses so often. His lyric hero views the sunset and senses the falling of the beneficent dew which heals and revives the wilted foliage in the parched fields. Why, he asks, does not a like balsam revive his own being? But no:

Anguish crushes the young singer, as the gravestone crushes the corpse in the earth . . . I have withered, I have withered, forever, forever! And happiness I have known, never, never! And I lived—but I lived to my own ruin. . . . With my stormy life I killed my hopes . . . I did not flower—and I faded in the morning of my gloomy days; what I loved [freedom, doubtless] I have found in that the ruin of my life.

The effectiveness of the piece, its almost hectic movement, is lost in any translation that does not reproduce the regular anapaestic rhythm with its lines that end so insistently on strongly accented syllables.

"Chains,"[16] written during the same period as "Evening Twilight," is much less effective in its use of the four-foot iambic verse, but it has some powerful lines: "Without the feeling of life, without desires, like a loathsome shadow, I drag the chain of my sufferings and die night and day!" The lyric hero contemplates regicide as vengeance for his sufferings—"but the chain of enslavement clanks on the fettered legs and the steel of vengeance dies away in cold and trembling hands! As a frightened, soulless slave, then I curse my lot and once more look indifferently upon the new Tsar's chains." "The Living Dead,"[17] another lyric of the years 1826-28, uses the figure of the restless ghost for the poet himself, and hints at suicide as the way of ending his half-life:

The plaything of passions, I stand living at the doors of the tomb, and soon, soon, vengeance and malice will fall asleep forever in my breast! The idols of happiness and freedom do not exist for me, and, a useless member of existence, I shall not defile nature with myself! For me the world is a desert, the grave a palace! I shall descend into it without regret, and let God judge the suicide for his moment of desperation!

Perhaps Polezhaev may actually have attempted suicide—it would hardly be surprising—but, if the poem "Providence,"[18] of the same years, reflects a real experience, he was deterred at the last moment somewhat as Faust was:

I was perishing... my evil genius was triumphing.... Yet a moment more, and... it is finished!... but suddenly an unexpected ray of hope, like a purple light, gleamed from the clouds. Some hidden, by me long-forgotten, God pulled me back from the open darkness!... He infused once more into the breast of the atheist and sham-sophist the fire of love! He gilded once more the days of sorrowful anguish, and illumined me with the dawn-light of forgiveness [*proshchal'noi*]! Burn, be radiant, holy light! And burn to the end, without growing pale!

It seems likely that "Providence" represents a later stage of Polezhaev's spiritual biography than the epistle "To Alexander Petrovich Lozovsky," the atheistic arguments of which he is probably referring to in calling himself a "sham-sophist." Unfortunately there is no possibility of dating the poems more precisely. In any case it is time wasted to look for consistency of outlook in a poet so passionately volatile as Polezhaev.

Early in 1829 the Moscow Infantry Regiment to which Polezhaev had been assigned was ordered to the Caucasus. Whatever the hardships this move entailed, including separation from friends and literary associates in Moscow, the active campaign life and the stimulation of a new and exotic scene evidently did much to brighten Polezhaev's outlook on life. The lyrics of the period 1829 to 1832, although by no means free of self-pity and despair, are markedly more restrained than those of 1826-28.

The poem "Tarki"[19] (May 1831), the first—censorable—portion of which was published in Polezhaev's *Poems* in 1832, records the poet's unflattering first impressions of the Daghestani center Tarku, residence of Russia's ally, the elderly Shamkhal. It may be recalled that Alexander Bestuzhev-Marlinsky's novel *Ammalat-Bek* is laid in this part of present-day Azerbaijan, and in fact only a few years before Polezhaev's visit. The two men saw service in the eastern Caucasus during almost the same years, and died within months of each other, Bestuzhev in battle, Polezhaev in a military hospital. The poem "Tarki," written in the short, two-foot lines (here iambic) so typical of our poet begins: "I have been in the mountains— what a joy! I have been in Tarki—what an abomination!" Throughout the poem the author exerts himself to the utmost to "debunk" the popular, romanticized picture of the exotic Muslim East. He goes on to show Tarki as it really is, in a few short, sharp strokes:

> I shall say, and not in jest: the Shamkhal's *aul* is not a little similar to a Russian cattle-shed. Big and long, smeared with clay, dirty inside, unclean outside; some three mosques, brooks and puddles, a cemetery, a ditch and fishing-place, a *dukhán* [i.e., tavern], five shops, and finally, to top it all, the very advantageous and two-storied palace at the top [of the village], where the prince Shamkhal sits and judges everyone on the spot.

The customary attraction of the romantic Caucasus—its gorgeous women—has to be mentioned, but they fare little better than the Shamkhal's capital:

> And how charming are the girls in Tarki—more beautiful than Eve! Always in trousers of red material, and they don't take a bath once in a year. Five hundred rubles—and not half a word [of objection]! The loving mother is ready then and there to sell you her daughter—to go to bed with her, and do as you please...though it may be forever!

Then the poem turns from the general to the particular, and relates with humor the narrator's own experience with one of Tarki's available beauties— "a real treasure, fifty years old." The assignation takes place while the husband is presumably absent, but he returns unexpectedly and is mollified only when he receives "my purse and silver," after which he allows proceedings to go on as planned!

"Tarki" is close in tone and outlook to the long narrative poem *Erpelí* (1832), written at about the same period. As we shall see, in this realistic piece the outlook is that of the common Russian soldier, with whom Polezhaev identifies himself, almost obliterating the figure of the suffering and despairing poet. But the more romantic persona recurs in the lyrics of the period. Thus, in "The Song of the Perishing Sailor"[20] (1832), using the rather hackneyed image for his fate which the title explains, he pictures the raging elements that threaten to engulf his frail boat, but views the inevitable with defiant equanimity:

> The secret son of nature, the constant friend of freedom, from youthful years upon the sea of misfortunes, I have been directing my swift flight, and have left the peaceful shore behind! (sect. v)
> The white sail of migration, the bold, carefree anchor, the dull ray from behind the clouds, the gleam from afar in the darkness of night—took the place of friends for me! (sect. viii)
> What is there for me in obscure life? What is there in a fatherland that is everywhere? What terror has the wave for me? Let it come with eternal darkness, and let the living corpse perish! (sect. ix)
> Ever blacker is the starless vault, ever more terribly howl the deeps; the wind whistles, the thunder roars, the sea groans—the way is far... Sinking, sinking, my little boat. (sect. x)

Despair of a much quieter sort pervades "Night on the Kuban"[21] (1832), an elegy in almost traditional meter (four-foot iambic lines) and structure. The poem begins by establishing the scene: a warm summer night, a distant mountain range, the setting sun, and "on the wings of the light zephyr descends the friend of nature, sleep." The toilworn peasant sleeps, happy in the security of his home and the love of his wife; the sybarite sleeps, oblivious of the voice of conscience. Then the poet returns to the scene—the new moon hanging over the roaring river (Kuban) and the "New Hellespont," i.e., the straits of Kerch, known to antiquity as the "Cimmerian Bosporus." Here once the Cossack frontier guards used to keep constant watch against nocturnal Tatar raids; but now all is peaceful, and "the neighborhood of battles is shrouded in dark and sorrowful silence, and the battle-land is stricken as it were with a graveyard peace." Then the poet turns to himself. Why does sleep not come to him? "Why do I summon it in vain? Or is it in reality so terrible to lose freedom and repose!... Are they really never to return, the idols of my youth, and are the violent gusts of passion never to be tamed?" Abruptly another theme enters the meditation—the friendship of the one person who has ever showed gentle pity for the sufferer—Alexander Lozovsky, of course, though he is not named: "I shall be he, he shall be I, into one of us both shall be merged, and then let enmity and malice, and death and the grave-digger's spade clatter above our head!" But the elegy ends plaintively, with the poet still alone:

> And I on a solitary rock, I, the destroyer of the general quiet, sit in profound obliviousness, like a spirit from the region underground. And the days and the years will go forward in their accustomed course, but to me they will not bring back with them repose and freedom!

If Polezhaev's wretched life can be said to have had any bright spot, it would have been the years 1833 and 1834. He had been transferred to the Tarutin Chasseur Regiment, stationed in Ryazan province, and in June 1834 he made the acquaintance of the Bibikov family and fell in love with Ekaterina Bibikova. His situation in the army had been improved at least to the extent that he had been given non-commissioned rank. The black despair of his earlier lyrics gives way to other moods, of which the poem "Repentance"[22] (1833) is typical. It begins with confession: "I have sinned against reason; for a moment I fell out of love with it...I have sinned against the conditions of the soul and of youthful glory, which the dream of idle talk is now hissing with calumny." Then the poet asks himself: "Where is the harmonious lyre, where the young bard's crown? Surely vice has not thrown them at the feet of a contemptible idol?" The poem ends positively:[23]

> Oh, no!...It is finished!...The rebellious fire has grown cold on the sombre brow...As a son of earth, I have paid tribute to the earth in my inevitable turn: I have come to know dishonor, shame under the mask of savage ignorance,—but before the face of the Caucasian mountains I tear my unclean garments! Like in pride to the

mountains, visible in the abysses and in the azure, I shall soar, like the incense from the flowers of the wilderness to the skies, and give back my strings the roar and the wail of the tempest that is past.

The change in Polezhaev's outlook on life in this period is reflected in "A Fragment from an Epistle to A[lexander] P[etrovich] L[ozovsky]" (1833), which begins abruptly: "And they *are* no more, no more! The years of spiritual storms and rebellions have sped past, and I am far from the confines of war, brigandage and freedom."

Early in 1833 Polezhaev had the opportunity of making a brief visit to Moscow, a record of which is the poem "Ivan the Great"[24] (1833). The sight of the grand old Kremlin bell-tower inspires the poet to an almost eighteenth-century solemnity and grandiloquence:

Once more she is before me, Moscow once more! The wavering vapor of the mist grows thin, and radiant are the head and cross of Ivan the Great! There he is—the gigantic Briareus, who battles valiantly with thunder, but is the friend of people and of Tsars with his hundred bells! His tocsin and his quiet ringing are always pleasant to the patriot...And he, your husband, Josephine, iron of will and hand, gazed on the age-old giant with involuntary melancholy! Moscow beneath the yoke of the foe, and night, and riot, and the Kremlin aflame—often perturbed the new Sarmatian in the sorrowful silence...Kingdoms arose; the fire of battle went out under the sky of Africa, and resoundingly, resoundingly with the clapping of hands, merged Ivan's noisy voice! [*zvuchno, zvuchno s pleskom dlanei / Slilsia Ivana shumnyi glas!*]

The solemn and exalted style quite suddenly gives way to a mocking, familiar tone as the poet imagines himself at the top of the tower, looking down and seeing "proud Moscow, to whom good report has always given the name of marvel—only a heap of sand and stones." "Without perfidious and empty words I can add that the people, whom the mother-capital cherishes more than others, are visible from there without spectacles, believe me, as a line-up of ordinary capons..." At the end of the poem, however, mockery is once more displaced by affection for the old monument, as the poet recalls:

The half-savage peasant not without reason said with tears: "Great is the Lord in Heaven, and great in Moscow is Ivan the Great!" So, praise to you, praise; live, flourish, Ivan of the Kremlin, and comforting Moscow's ears, resound with all your bells!

There are a number of fine poems of Polezhaev composed during and immediately after the brief idyll of July 1834, when he was with the Bibikovs on their estate of Ilinskoe. One pathetic short piece, addressed to Ekaterina and known only from the copy which was given to her, was composed as an inscription for the water-color portrait which Ekaterina painted of Polezhaev, and which is reproduced as frontispiece in the *Poet's*

Library edition of his verse: "Fate killed me in childhood! I have not known life *for thirty years* [Polezhaev was born in 1804, and the poem was written in 1834], but your brush suddenly commanded: 'Rise from the darkness, live, poet!' And the cold tomb blossomed, and once again I saw the light... "[25] But of course his resurrection was only momentary, and perhaps the return to his living tomb was so much the more crushing for the short experience of life and love that had been accorded him. The highest point which Polezhaev's poetry ever reached is the long elegy "Black Eyes," written in July 1834.[26] The first 12 strophes (out of 27) were published by the *Moscow Observer* in 1838, after the poet's death. Belinsky realized the meaning of the poem, and termed it the poet's "terrible funeral song to himself."[27]

The poem's first strophe sets the theme:

> Oh, I am sad!... All my life is a storm! I am tired of earthly habitation! Why do you burn before me, like the rays of Paradise before Satan, you magical black eyes?

Before the appearance of the black eyes, the poet had been resigned to his hapless lot: "Alas! Sorrowful, indifferent, I had long since grown accustomed to my evil fate; violent, pitiless to myself, I despised it in desperate battle, and was proudly obedient to misfortune!... " The thought of the possibility of a change in his condition frightened him:

> And, sunk in criminal doubts of the purpose of existence, cursing fate, I trembled for fear that truth, like the bright sunshine, suddenly illuminating me, might draw me out of my embittered darkness.
>
> Terrible to me was the great passage from daring thoughts to the light of providence; I avoided the innocent creature who might, out of pity, give my soul a lofty flight.
>
> And suddenly it, like a precious angel... Oh no! Like a punishing and malicious spirit, brighter than day, appeared before me, with the smile of roses blazing in the springtime on the turf of an aromatic valley.
>
> It [i.e., the "innocent creature"] appeared—everything disappeared for me: I forgot in tormenting adversity my love and hatred for nature, my mad ardor for lost freedom, and everything I had lived and breathed for hitherto...

The abstract "innocent creature," with its neuter gender, changes in the tenth strophe to the feminine "she":

> And the Paradise-maiden, the Beauty-maiden with an inexpressible look poured into my heart innocent love with a secret reproach, and the soul in her sang in heavenly chorus:
>
> "Love me—and on eyes and lips kiss me, orphan poet, as the butterfly kisses the lily in the morning! Love me as a beloved sister, and I shall once more direct your deadened reason toward heaven and toward good!"

There follows an extraordinary section in which the poet recounts his battle against the softening influence which he fears: "In vain I summoned to my aid my proud genius, my evil fate." He finds himself at last "in chains before a shamefaced girl. In chains!... Creator!.... A weak child is playing with me at her unaccountable will, punishing me with a carefree smile, and I, like a slave, drag myself voluntarily after her, consecrating my whole life to suffering!" Yet despite his abhorrence of the thought of dependence on "a weak child," he torments himself with remembrance of strolls and communion with her, "when among ruins and graves we wandered with sombre dreams, and eternal sleep over the peaceful crosses, and death and life floated before us, and I sought the repose of the dead"—a typical romantic setting for a love affair! He recalls Ekaterina's tears over the blighted romance of *La Nouvelle Héloise,* and her white arms and shoulders as she modestly bathed. The poem ends:

> The deadly poison of irresistible love has torn and slowly destroyed me; once more the world, as formerly, has grown cold... Perhaps... No! My hour has already struck, the terrible hour that nothing can avert.
>   Wherefore insanely anger heaven? She exists no longer!... She blooms even now... But where? For whose pride does she bloom? Whose incense burns for the goddess?... Tell me,—O black eyes!

Some of Polezhaev's later verse, between 1834 and 1837, is very good, and deserves mention, as for example the "Garland on the Grave of Pushkin,"[28] published in mutilated form first in 1842 in the posthumous collection entitled *Hours of Recuperation,* but in full only in 1916; and the touching retelling of the "Eighth Chapter of John"—the story of the woman taken in adultery. There is also the curious dramatic poem translated from *La Mort de Pompei* of Ernest Legouvé (1807-1903), called "The Last Day of Pompei" (1837). The title of the poem in Russian is of course taken directly from the famous painting of Karl Bryullov, itself inspired by Bulwer-Lytton's well-known novel (1834).

A considerable amount of Polezhaev's verse belongs in the category of narrative—Russian *poèmy.* Aside from *Sashka* and the *Imam-Goat,* which have already been considered, there are the inconsequential *Creditors, The Eccentric* and *A Day in Moscow,* all published in the 1832 collection of poems. They are unoriginal, mildly satirical pieces showing nothing whatever of their author's individual personality. The first genuinely interesting and original narrative poem of Polezhaev after *Sashka* was composed in 1830, after the poet had seen action in the Caucasus. It bears the name of the Daghestani village near which the action of the poem takes place, *Erpelí.*[29] A couple of years later *Chir-Yurt,* the record of the bloody battle at the village of this name (October 19, 1831) was written. A third, much shorter piece, *The Cemetery of Germanchug* (between 1832 and 1833), belongs to this series.

The Caucasian poems are unique in Polezhaev's work. They are realistic, almost ostentatiously unromantic in tone, as though the author were deliberately trying to dispose of the highly colored picture of the Caucasus as the land of exotic beauty of both nature and humanity, the land of freedom, the land of exciting adventure. We have seen in "Tarki" the same debunking preoccupation. Polezhaev in these poems, or at least in the first two, identifies himself with the common Russian soldier, and depicts the Caucasus and its people from the soldier's point of view. *Erpeli* bears in fact the parenthetical dedication: "To the warriors of the Caucasus." The second chapter of *Erpeli* begins with a contrast between the romanticized picture of the mountains and the soldier's reality:

> He who loves wild pictures in their primal nakedness, forests, hills, valleys in the naked beauty of nature; who is captivated by the spirit of liberty, which has gone out of fashion in Europe some years ago—I beg him, if convenient, to leave the university and in marching equipment follow me. I'll show him in the world the original of such things, which in his study he has probably not seen on his maps; and marching along the front, on the expedition he will see them at the sides like so many turnips and garlics in beds in his garden.

Evidently, with all his urge to play down the attractions of mountain scenery, the poet remains alive to the beauty around him:

> And I shall point out to him with a smile the steppes extending 500 versts on which only rarely and by mistake the feather-grass grows with the thistle, and spreading out into the ruddy day, this flower glows in a long streak, like a purple ocean, in its prickly beauty.
>
> I shall show him the Titan, grey and old as a demon, in an enormous region of mist, always at war against the skies. From his stony flanks, icy with a million waves, streams clatter both summer and winter, with violent speed. In vain the noonday heat blazes, contending with his triple crown; angry and sullen, he breathes only snow-storms and ice. Around, from sea to sea, the ridges of granite and snow, contending like Elbrus with nature, have been standing from time immemorial; and their unapproachable heights shine out of the clouds. Thither only the bold dream can fly with the king of birds.[30]

The description continues, growing more ironical, until finally the narrator imagines himself clapping his guest on the shoulder and telling him that it is no wonder that, fresh from the capitals, he should be amazed at what he sees: "I too thought just like you, was ready all my life on earth to look for marvels and beauty in nature,—wise and extremely wise, as the learned chorus reiterates." "And so what? I pray you, proceed to the Caucasus!.... With what kind of face, do you think, you recognized the order to service? Weren't you as entranced as before at the mere mention of the Caucasus?" He lists some of the romantic attractions: "to look over the Circassian girls, to be entranced day and night by the mountains!... by Elbrus, by the swift horses that Pushkin described, etc." The poet acknowledges that this was his outlook when he first arrived, but—

> Here are these marvelous pictures: cascades, mountains and precipices... with stony soul, murdered by my bitter lot, I gaze on them against my will, and believe me, I see in it all—ugliness, and nothing more! Maybe, my friend... in quarreling frivolously with fate, you too will find the coat too tight, or just as like me as two drops of water; then you will judge more intelligently, having always inclined toward dreams—and you will stop marvelling at the rubbishy wonders of the Caucasus.[31]

The "action" of *Erpelí* is confined to the movement of the author's Moscow Infantry Regiment from its station near Tarki to another in the mountains farther to the south and west—a movement seen from the soldier's point of view, who has only the vaguest notion of the military situation as a whole and the objective he is heading for or the reasons for his going. The officers are also seen from below as it were—Yermolov, Velyaminov (in *Chir-Yurt*) etc. It is the same with the mountain tribes, whom other poets of the age often idealize and depict with lively admiration: after all, their fierce resistance to Russian encroachment is only the reflection of their native love of liberty! Polezhaev, like the common soldier at his side, sees them only as "the enemy." He shows a real revulsion from the inevitable horrors of war, but oversimplifies the motives of the Avar and Chechen resistance by pinning the responsibility for it almost entirely on a single mad fanatic:[32]

> And so, the heroes of the Caucasus in shaggy fur-hats and cloaks, reluctantly abandoning their raids in the mountains, thieving and brigandage, and exchanging their own violent laziness for domestic labor, were raising maize and barley with wondrous success, when suddenly one stormy day, to their unexpected misfortune and woe, from the sea or from beyond the sea—rumor is silent on this—there appeared among them an arrogant guest, some sort of mad genius, the prophet and priest Kazi-Mullah. As a man sent down from God for the instruction of the Muslims, carrying an open Koran, he cried at first sternly against the host of vices and sins of his esteemed countrymen.

This generalized attack on vice is followed shortly by a more specific one; the prophet proclaims:

> The determinations of destiny are preparing a new lot for us: Russia shall disappear, an end to fighting—you shall recover your freedom! God lives, and I am His prophet! His mouth speaks in me; in my right hand are life and death and destiny itself! Like the unexpected and abundant rain we shall war against the enemy, chase them with powerful hand from the pastures and meadows of Anapa, from the lush hills of Daghestan, and the hated tyrant of the free mountains, defenceless, we shall push back behind the Don!

Deluded by this religious rhetoric, the ignorant tribesmen, according to Polezhaev, were goaded into general revolt.

In the fifth chapter of *Erpelí* the poet includes a vivid little dialogue, set in the regimental cook-tent, as several soldiers discuss high matters of politics and strategy. Polezhaev's humor is friendly and his characterization sharp. The insurgent mountaineers are like a bewildering show of "Chinese shadows":

They have hidden themselves... What for? Where from, and also why?
     I shall not put forward my conclusions, I shall not explain anything for you, for the reason that I know very little. What little I know, I shan't say, but rather show you a place where the veil of every kind of secret is always bright and transparent as an emerald or glass. Here is this precious place: it's in the kitchen by the kettles. There is all worldly wisdom; there, from heads cheerful, kind, carefree and always loquacious, every day one can easily learn about such matters in the wide world as one does not often dare discuss even in the study. There they'll show you everything in detail, and at its conclusion, say with an oath by God, that this is what they have heard from Kozma Savelich Skotov himself. "If that's so, then there's not a word to be said," they'll shout, with open mouth,—"Kozma Savelich doesn't lie." And who is he?—you will ask by chance; why, the General's man... Surely that must have occurred to you? Such is the custom of the Russian military. Please be so good as to follow me to the kettles... A little closer... so... sit down. Here's a spoon for you; cross yourself... The soup is healthy and meaty... Hark! The talk is about the Tavlintsy [one of the Daghestani tribes]:
First Cook. Yes, yes, they're natural-born thieves! If it weren't for our boys, then look out—they'd bust your noggin like vicious beasts; but just show up a detachment, and they're all peaceful friends.
Second Cook. Everyone in red, and ever so much silver on his trousers and jacket.
First Cook. Why shouldn't he have the goods, when he's butchered us in broad daylight?
A Musketeer (lighting his pipe). First off he coaxed us with words into believing he really wasn't going to revolt, and later he signed an oath.
Ten Voices. Never mind, he doesn't put it over on the Moscow lads!
First Cook. I, says he, haven't any intention of going to war with the Russian Tsar, and so that he may trust me, I'm ready to give the oath of allegiance, and silver, and much gold. But there are in our mountains two brothers, whom the whole Caucasus are scared of. They're making the war against you.
Second Cook (from behind a kettle). We won't quiet down such brazen fellows.
First Cook. But I, the Mirza Shamkhalov [i.e., Suleiman Mirza, son of the Shamkhal of Tarki], says he, am your everlasting tributary and servant!
Musketeer. He'll forget his anger... Aha!... and how many versts more is it to the place?
First Cook. Why! With a good mount we'd get there in about four hours.
Second Cook. And kill them all off tomorrow! Yes, if it should happen to me to get anything into my hands, how quick I'd chuck the tiresome misery in the kitchen, and I'd always be cheerful, drunk.
First Cook. Hey, you, get up—there's the drum![33]

The drum is of course the signal to march, so the kitchen dialogue is abruptly broken off.

The sixth chapter of the poem brings the author and his reader to the regiment's objective:

> And here we've arrived at last before famous Erpelí! In the five parts of my notes [i.e., the five preceding chapters of the poem] having set forth the whole expedition in brief, I ought here, like Walter Scott or Byron, to provide a record from lively, striking pictures for you, my dear sir, or for you, esteemed lady (for whom instead of powders an affectionate mama has had the thoughtfulness to offer a copy of my verses. An effective prescription, I don't dispute).

But unfortunately the poet has never learned to sketch; he can only offer a few amateurish scenes, such as this:

> On a level expanse of muddy ground stands in enormous majesty the *aul* of the Tavlintsy, Erpelí. Fragments of rocks and flinty mountains are its age-old foundation; alleys of shady poplars are the beauty of the shapely mass. Everywhere the roving glance encounters native houses [*saklí*] and fences, wattle and earthen walls; every house is a blockhouse with embankment and moat. Over the river that has broken through, running from the mountains' height, by the wondrous hand of art, bridges have been constructed; whirlpools, cascades, a mill, levees—everything breathes of the stark nakedness of a savage and simple nature. In the *aul* noise and the trampling of horses, the silence of wives and the laughter of children; on the roofs, in the windows, at the gates, a seething populace, richly adorned, dressed like the Persian *kizilbashi* [Turkish "red heads," that is, warriors who wore red bands on their turbans]. There is a chieftain's yataghan [scimitar]; there rifle, sabres, pistols glisten, gleam with silver in their warlike parade. Here are the strange fittings of the horses: bows, bridles, stirrups; the ornaments of embellished beards, pieces of cloth, linen that scarcely covers the shoulders of grey-haired, dirty old women, and the barking of dogs at the Russian scent, and shouting and whistling and scenes of meeting, and the chatter of the waves and the noise of the wind—there's the *aul* copied for you![34]

Polezhaev has an observant eye, and his description is realistic and vivid, though here and there, as in the ironic references to the village's "enormous majesty" or "the wondrous hand of art" that builds its bridges, one may detect his usual concern for debunking the romantic attractions of the scene.

The expedition to Erpelí is enough, apparently, to overawe the mountaineers, and no military demonstration beyond it is necessary to insure submission. The description ends with a reunion of the separated Russian regiments and general celebration. The poet rejoices that his task is finished. At the end of Chapter VII he remarks significantly: "I don't know whether the strict censorship will condemn me or not; but no matter—I'm not a poet, but only a caricature of one."

The end of Chapter VIII of *Erpelí* constitutes a reversion, from the impersonal, objective approach of the first chapters, to the self-concerned subjectivism of Polezhaev's lyrics. Though he foresees an early death, the poet hopes for immortality for his verses:

> A self-loving worshipper of the Muses, I see death not far off; but still the pen in my hand sketches its capricious plan. In going to my fathers in others' wake, to remain in some men's memory! Perhaps tomorrow or even now, before I have experienced a

Circassian bullet, they'll put me into a flour-sack and commit me to the desert ground . . . In a remote, god-forsaken country I waste away, separated from those dear to my heart . . . as pleases the malevolent tyrant, my hostile destiny!

No one will regret the corpse that lies in its bast shroud; his slippers and jacket will go to some survivor who will forget their former owner; there will be no memorial services for the dead, funeral cakes and the rest: "This is my lot! I have foreseen it very clearly with no far-reaching prophecies . . . And what will be the poet's memorial? . . . It cannot be. . . . His sins? . . . They're the quit-rent of the other world . . . Verses, my friends, verses!" In the last lines of the chapter he writes, as it were, his own epitaph: "In the flower of his years he lived without life, he died without death in the wide world! . . . There's good people's memory of the poet!"[35]

The second of the Caucasian narratives, *Chir-Yurt* (May 1832)[36] is in general more serious and more conventional in tone. Its climax is not, as with *Erpelí*, a battle expected but happily averted—the unfortunate village which gives its name to the poem was stormed with great carnage and reduced to ruins. From the first the author of the poem is present, not in his capacity as a common soldier, as in *Erpelí*, but as Polezhaev, the suffering poet: "Forgotten, sombre and low-spirited, I live alone in the midst of people, wearied by my own torment, which is inseparable from me." But, rather unexpectedly, the unwilling soldier now evinces a desire to serve not only his country, but the Tsar:

Yes, destroyed for life, I long with my last blood for my fatherland to wash off my stain! Oh, if only some time it might disappear with the trace of reproach! . . . The noise of war resounds in the mountains; the perjured Daghestani, the Lesghian, the Chechen, the Zakubanets [i.e., man from beyond the Kuban River] will meet with me in battle! I shall not betray Tsar and duty, I shall fly everywhere with honor, I shall pave a way for myself toward my lost star . . . [37]

There are again in *Chir-Yurt* descriptions of the mountain villages, sketches of the mountaineers deluded by the fanatical Kazi-Mullah, and an admiring picture of General Velyaminov. The first part of the poem ends with the frustrated Russian attempt to ford the swift Sulak River for an attack on Chir-Yurt, the village on the high ground of its right bank. The second part begins with a passage in solemn "high" style, denouncing war and the bloody fate of the unhappy village:[38]

Accursed be that ill-starred man who first felt the torments of importunate envy: he first murdered his brother! Accursed be that unfortunate who first drew the sword of war against those unhappy lands where lived a peace-loving people! . . . [eight lines cut out by the censor]. Sad genius of fallen kingdoms, witness of great truth: law and the sword!—there is virtue! The sword alone is the soul of perfidy; as long as they are both in union, so long is man free; if there is no law, wickedness awakes and the sword carves out its rights. . . .

Here is the root of anarchic life, here is the scourge beloved of Satan! The cause of brigandage and war, the Caucasus's sepulchral torch! And you experienced this lot, Chir-Yurt, courageous, unsubmissive! You fought terribly, fell terribly with your stubborn pride. Oh, how fearfully was spread the vengeance of the destroying sword! How loudly, terribly resounded your fall in the mists of the mountains!... The hour has struck: Chir-Yurt is no more! In the walls of Chir-Yurt is the son of victory—fire, storm and destruction.

This general meditation breaks off, and there follows a description of the second, and successful, attempt to ford the river at a different location, and the resulting panic of the Chechens. Abruptly the poet changes his solemn, tragic tone—a jarring dissonance characteristic of Polezhaev:[39]

Forgive me, dear friends, if after grandeur of narration there is always inappropriately born in me jest and mischief! So help me, I don't know why it is, I'm fond of wilfulness, and I admit to you, I'm not a drone for learned tedium and good sense... I'm afraid as death of various rules which, for the rest, of necessity I have prudently not abandoned in the moral life and in misfortune; but the rules of heavy intellect, but the rules of reading and writing I cannot abide, I hate, and, most amusing of all, I have never seen and do not see any great loss from this. I count up the loss with the profit, and here's what I conclude: when I write, then I think; when I think, then I write.

This capricious episode seems designed only to relieve the tension of a tale that quite evidently harrows the teller and presumably his audience. At the end of the account of the battle of Chir-Yurt the solemn tone resumes:[40]

Oh, who, with violent hand, lover of war and destruction, O battlefield, has watered you with a bloody dew? Who over crags and hills, to the joy of demons and of hell, has scattered the warrior mass for a banquet of jackals and eagles? From what land, from what country are the fallen heroes of war? All is quiet, dead above the waves; there is mist and peace upon the banks; Chir-Yurt with bowed head stands dejected upon the cliffs. Around her, upon the field of battle, a streak of smoke shows black, and the greedy scythe of death is gathering its sorrowful tribute.

Then in a final outburst of horror and revulsion the poet cries:

Come hither, O misanthrope, come hither in your malicious reveries to listen to the wails, to see the grave of those whom you hate, but who are your like! Look, O confidant of Satan, self-sacrificing murderer, at these corpses, these faces, the prey of furious war! Do you not see on them the stamp of the finger of an invisible hand that has put the groan of curses in the mouth of suffering and anguish? Gaze, in the darkness of the dreadful night, in its sorrowful silence, at the sunken eyes in a half-purple shroud.... Half an hour ago they were animated by a dream of mad fury; but the bullet of death whistled, and there was darkness on the stern eyes. Look here, at this hand—it shared to the end the bitterness and torture of the warrior killed by a shell; the disfigured fingers cramped in cruel pain, stony—open, cold as Siberian ice... Here is the tremor of the dying: an old man with bloody skull... His numbing tongue still emits a long-drawn babble... The spirit of life is wafted and awakened in the brain of the cloven head... he grows black... a shudder... he stretches out—and Allah's worshipper is no more.

The final paragraph of the poem asks the poet's hopeless question:

> When shall the martial lyre, the thunderous note of sorrowful strings, forget battles and the lightning-bolt and sing of the comfort of peace? Or shall the pensive singer, deceived by secret thought, ever sorrowful and gloomy, find his end in battle?

To the years just after Polezhaev's service in the Caucasus belong two works of a very different sort from *Erpeli* and *Chir-Yurt.* "The Dream of Brutus"[41] (1833) is a four-page account, seemingly inspired by Lucan, of the "liberator" Marcus Brutus on the eve of the battle of Philippi (43 B.C.) and of the vision portending his death. Brutus is of course, as always in the nineteenth century, seen as the supreme patriot, and his victim Caesar as the archetypical tyrant. The poem ends with a brief summation of the meaning, for the poet, of the battle itself: "The day of the fateful battle has come. The standards of martial honor clatter—the triumvirate is unconquered, and the son of valor, the warrior of vengeance fell, a free man, for fallen Rome!"

The second of these Roman poems is longer and more elaborately constructed, but on the whole rather less successful. As Belinsky notes:[42] "His poem *Coriolanus* is marked by a rhetorical character; there are many sonorous lines in it, but very few that are poetical." *Coriolanus* (1834)[43] is divided into four "chapters," each in several sections. The story is of course one well known from Shakespeare's play of the same name, itself derived from Plutarch's life of the hero. Apparently Polezhaev utilized both Livy and Plutarch, but not Shakespeare, which is a pity, because Shakespeare's drama portrays a real, three-dimensional person; Polezhaev's hero is a shadowy lay-figure. The story's entire meaning is perverted by the depiction of Coriolanus as a wronged and innocent sufferer, the victim of an unreasonable and fickle mob. Shakespeare's—and Plutarch's—hero is not only a valiant and patriotic Roman, but an arrogant patrician, contemptuous of the plebs and rebellious against their magistrates, the tribunes. He imagines that his military services to Rome justify him in flouting the law, and when the populace which he despises exiles him, his patriotism is turned to an embittered desire for vengeance and he leads the Volscian enemy against his own city. By suppressing all reference to Coriolanus's arrogance Polezhaev perhaps hoped to show him as a martyr, but succeeded only in robbing him of all personality and presenting the Roman people as an irresponsible and ungrateful canaille. The crucial character of Coriolanus's mother Volumnia, moreover, fails entirely to come through effectively, since she is seen only momentarily, weeping when her son leaves for exile, before her appearance in the last chapter to beg him to spare his fatherland,—and even in this climactic scene her appeal is too short—fifteen lines—though eloquent, to make plausible Coriolanus's abrupt about-face and declaration: "O my mother, you are victorious! Your son has perished, but Rome is saved!"

Polezhaev should perhaps not be held at fault for a defect in his poem which is general to his age, and which perhaps only Pushkin realized and made a serious attempt to overcome. This is his completely unhistorical approach to history. As any reader of Livy must have been aware, the episode of Coriolanus, whatever historical basis it may ever have had, belongs to the fifth century before Christ; and a mere glance at the map must have revealed that Antium, the Volscian capital, lies only some thirty miles to the south of Rome. Yet Polezhaev treats the hard-pressed little Italian city-state of Rome, whose perspective was of necessity limited to about a fifty-mile radius about it, as an opulent metropolis, subduer of kings and arbiter of Italy! It was perhaps hard in the 1830s to think of Rome of any age without the power and the glory that belonged to it by the middle of the second century—but even with only Livy and Plutarch as sources Polezhaev could have avoided some of his grotesque anachronisms. As Belinsky astutely remarks:[44] "he understood neither the Roman people nor the historical significance of his chosen hero."

Before we leave Polezhaev, one of his later translations deserves a word. This is the 1833 version of what he calls a "cantata," *The Trojan Women,* from *Les Troyennes* by Casimir Delavigne.[45] The scene is of course that familiar from Euripides's *Trojan Women*—the aftermath of the capture of Troy, as the wives, sisters and mothers of the fallen heroes of Troy mourn their country and their own fate as slaves of the victorious Greeks. Delavigne, and following him his Russian translator, do not individualize the women, except as "first, second," etc. Their lamentations take the form of contrasted pictures of the pastoral joys of Priam, Polyxena, of Hector et al. and their terrible wartime fates. Polezhaev's version is in this short fragment beautifully classical, a superb rendering both of the original French and of the spirit, which is astonishingly close to the Euripidean model in its restraint and simplicity. A Trojan woman sings just before the final chorus:

> You desire to listen to a slave woman's song, O unfeeling people?[i.e., the Greeks]. Give us back mothers, give us back fathers, children and brothers and husbands! Wrest Ilion from the pitiful desert into which you have succeeded in converting her! But if your dominion has not power to return the majesty of the burned Pergamum, if you cannot give life to the sons and warriors of Priam,—then listen to a wail; but the hymn of fateful servitude will not fill the foreign land!...*Chorus.* Farewell to you, native fields of Troy, the quenched kin of kings, perished heroes, beauty of our sacred fatherland! And Ida, with its lush hills, and the bright sun with our native skies, farewell forever!...

Polezhaev is one of the most uneven of poets. At his best his verse is marked, as Belinsky said, by a powerful energy and compression. But it seldom remains at this level for long, and side by side with the best passages are others which, as Belinsky complains,[46] are "bad to the point of meaninglessness." There is no doubt that the reason for this unevenness is not want of ability, but lack of patience. He seems to have dashed off his verses in a fit of inspiration, but never sat down with cold self-criticism and worked them over. Acknowledging all the good qualities of his verse, Belinsky still writes:[47] "But with this there is a lack of polish, of exactitude in words and expressions. The reason for this is as much the fact that he had a careless attitude toward poetry and never gave the finishing touches to his verses... as that, stopping with a single immediate feeling, he did not develop it and heighten it, by learning and meditation, to *taste.*" The last point is particularly well taken: Polezhaev's deficiencies are perhaps chiefly attributable to a lack of taste. He seems, however, to have been moving in the right direction in his later verse, and perhaps if he had lived long enough to mature, there would have been fewer regrettable lapses. Belinsky also notes his tendency to a monotonous reiteration of a single theme. He was too subjective ever to succeed in picturing another character than his own—hence the inferiority of his Roman pieces. But even in depicting his own feelings, he stopped, in Belinsky's words, "with a single one, forever uncontrolled and forever locked in itself, forever turning around on itself without moving forward, always monotonous, and always expressing itself in the same old formulas."[48] Yet, with all the imperfections that must be noted in Polezhaev, he cannot be denied an important place in Russian literature of the 1830s. He had something new and fresh to say, and in many respects he seems almost like a premonition of Lermontov. Belinsky ends his critique with some verses of Pushkin's ("A Portrait") referring to the subject as "a lawless comet, in the ordered circle of the stars," and adds: "A comet is a monstrous phenomenon, if you will, but its terrible beauty is more interesting for everyone than the momentary flash of a falling star, which penetrates by chance and disappears without trace on the horizon of the night sky."

Viktor Grigoryevich Teplyakov 1804-1842

Both the life and the poetry of Viktor Teplyakov mark him as the romantic par excellence. His was the typically short life of his generation of poets, but one quite untypically restless and adventurous. He was born into a nobleman's family from Tver and received a good education, first at home and then in the preparatory school for the nobility attached to Moscow University. In 1820 he entered the service as a hussar, but poor health and the military routine combined to make this service distasteful, and he was able to obtain release in 1825. Although not connected with the Decembrist conspiracy, he refused at first to take the oath of allegiance to Nikolai I, and as a result both he and his brother, who was also implicated, were arrested. He spent from April to June of 1826 in the prison of the

Petropavlovsk fortress. Pardoned at last by the Emperor, he began a career in the civil service which was mostly carried on in the southern regions of the Empire under the Governor-General M. S. Vorontsov. In March 1829 he was ordered to Varna in Bulgaria for archaeological research. Russia was at the time at war with Turkey, and the military front was in southern Bulgaria. Teplyakov witnessed some action and was for a time confined to a camp at Sozopol, where a cholera epidemic was raging. He was able during this mission, however, to acquire a valuable collection of antiquities which now form part of the collections of the Odessa Museum. At the same time he was writing his best verse, the seven *Thracian Elegies*. A collection of his verse was published in two parts in the years 1832 and 1836. His prose account of his activities, *Letters from Bulgaria,* was published in 1834.

Subsequent travels in 1834-35 took him to Constantinople, Asia Minor and Greece. After about a year of residence in St. Petersburg (1835-36) he returned once more to the East—Greece, Egypt, Syria, Palestine and Constantinople. Finally he turned his attention to western Europe, visited Paris, Germany, Switzerland and Italy. His final sortie was again to Paris in 1842, where he died suddenly of an apoplectic stroke.

Teplyakov's literary interests date from his period of military service, when he and his friend P. P. Kaverin shared enthusiasm for Byron and Pushkin. Like most of the young poets of the early 1820s, Teplyakov was for a time drawn to civic, libertarian themes. One of his earliest poems is a fragment from what would have been a long narrative poem entitled "Bonifaci" (1823),[49] built upon the life of the Provençal poet of Marseilles, who tried to rouse his fellow-citizens against Charles of Anjou, and was eventually put to death by the usurper. A few semi-autobiographical lyrics ("The Prisoner" and "The Exile") seem to have been composed during or immediately after his incarceration; but the first really important body of poetry which Teplyakov wrote is the cycle of *Thracian Elegies*. Most of the poet's contacts during the early 1830s are with the literary circles of Odessa, but through his brother he was in touch at long distance with the editors of *Northern Flowers* and *The Literary Gazette*. Pushkin continued to be Teplyakov's literary model and the object of his greatest admiration, but his verse already gives evidence of a certain movement away from Pushkin in the direction of a more intensified individualism. He did not actually meet Pushkin until the period of his residence (1835-36) in St. Petersburg. A native tendency to pessimism seems to have been heightened by Pushkin's tragic death. Most of Teplyakov's verse after 1837 is marked by gloom and cynicism. Characteristic are the pieces inspired by the theme of "the demon," which quite independently of Lermontov show a similar hopelessness.

When *The Thracian Elegies* appeared (1836), Pushkin wrote an enthusiastic review for his *Contemporary*. Although most of the review concerns the elegies, it ends with the words: "If Mr. Teplyakov had written nothing else but the elegy 'Solitude' and the stanzas 'Love and Hate,' he would even then take an honored place among our poets."[50] He then quotes entire the elegy "Solitude." To these high points of Teplyakov's verse must also be added the strangely powerful "House of Wonders" (1831) and "Two Angels" (1833). Before considering *The Thracian Elegies* in detail, we may have a look at this material.

"The House of Wonders"[51] had its genesis in an actual experience of the poet which he related in a letter to his brother. He had taken up residence in a house in Odessa which was reputed to be haunted and visited at night by strange apparitions (the house existed down to the end of the century). The letter describes it in hyperbolic fashion:

> This whole summer I have been spending in a strange, absurd structure, known in [Odessa] under the intriguing designation of *House of Wonders*. Imagine a spacious stone structure not belonging exactly to any single architectural order, or rather including in itself all the kinds of architecture from the time of the building of Solomon's temple down to our age... The inner arrangement of rooms is still more unusual: parallelograms, squares, triangles, halls and cubby-holes.... They say that the original owner and builder of the house, a being resembling Byron's Manfred, took up quarters, from the time of the Russian conquest of these regions, among some enormous ruins, the beginning of which, according to the belief of certain antiquarians, belongs to the time of one (I don't remember precisely which) of the Tauro-Scythian kings.[52]

The letter goes on to say that on the first night of the poet's residence one of his servants insisted on sleeping with his head thrust through the door of his master's bedroom, while the other, "who, as you well know, talks, both asleep and awake, both in strange and in familiar houses, with the powers of darkness, in a short while began to snore, began to moan, and embarked on an endless conversation with the house-spirits." The poet himself, his imagination stirred by the strange stories of the "House of Wonders," lay awake all night concocting the phantasmagoria which he later wrote down and which constitutes the poem.

The poem begins with conventional observations on nightfall, the silence broken by the sound of the midnight bell, etc. Suddenly the poet hears footsteps, and a shrouded figure approaches his bed. It seems to be the wraith of a soldier friend of his youth, his breast pierced by a Turkish sword. The poet addresses him with reminiscences of their idealistic youth together and queries about subsequent disillusionment:

> Do you recall our golden conversations, when, beside the bivouac fires, we woke in each other our own true dreams? And, leafing through the mysterious volume of life, found quite empty the whole vulgar romance for us both... Say, did your earthly ideal take flesh? Is beauty in truth incorruptible?... and sadly the newcomer shook his head, and flew off like smoke, and drew me after him by an inexplicable force.

The ghost leads the poet through halls and passages, down mysterious stairs into subterranean vaults, where "nothingness merged with splendor, with earthly bliss, the voiceless past with the mute future in the mysterious cell." Here are figures symbolizing love of money, of fame, etc., and a vast table at which sit scientists and scholars with the tools of their disciplines before them—"but in a black line everywhere upon it was inscribed 'Nothingness.'" At the beginning of the second part the dreamer queries: "Trust in life, hope, love, love of all nature—shall your blessed fire not again flare up in my breast?" He witnesses another series of figures, symbolizing this time the arts—sculpture, painting, music—culminating in a dance of beautiful maidens. One of these stands out from the rest: he recognizes her, and in rapture rushes to clasp her in his arms, but suddenly the lights go out and he finds himself clasping a skeleton, upon whose skull he sees written "your ideal." After a blank of seven lines, evidently representing something too cynical for the censor to pass, the final lines sum up the meaning of the whole: "Since that time I have seen in the arts, in youthful beauty, in the treasures of knowledge and in earthly glory NOTHINGNESS."

The romantic spirit that soars too high above the vulgar earthly existence is almost certain sooner or later to suffer a painful fall. The ideal turns out to be unrealizable, and there is a cynical revulsion that willfully rejects even the commonplace goods which life holds for the ordinary man. This rather childish reaction seems to be but a pose, but it is not so with Teplyakov, as it is not so with Lermontov. They suffer genuinely from a shattering disillusionment. This is one of the particular marks of Russian romanticism of the 1830s, found in varying manifestations in Teplyakov, Lermontov, Polezhaev and Gogol. Pushkin felt a touch of it, and in his poem "The Demon" (1823) he gave the phenomenon an enduring symbol:[53]

> In those days when all the impressions of existence were new to me—girls' glances, and the rustle of forests, and the nightingale's singing at night,—when exalted feelings, freedom, glory and love and the inspired arts so powerfully agitated my blood,—some malevolent genius then began secretly to visit me, shadowing with sudden boredom the hours of hopes and enjoyments. Sorrowful were our meetings: his smile, strange look, his venomous discourse poured a cold poison into my soul. With calumny inexhaustible he tempted providence; he called the beautiful a dream; he was contemptuous of inspiration; he believed in neither love nor freedom; he looked upon life with mockery, and nothing in all nature was he willing to bless.

Pushkin's was a healthy nature, able to repel the demon's assaults without permanent damage, but others were not so fortunate. Teplyakov's brother, writing the poet's biography, quotes from his last letter, written from Paris just before his sudden death: "What is there for me now to do with myself? I've seen everything, whatsoever there is interesting in this sublunary world, and it has all bored me to an inexpressible degree."[54] The vision in "The House of Wonders" which puts the label of "Nothingness" on all human life is matched by other workings of the same theme in the poems "Love and Hate" and "Two Angels."

"Love and Hate" (1832),[55] which bears as epigraph a half-line from Dante wrenched out of context and turned into a question—"Conosceste i dubbiosi desiri?" ("Have you come to know dubious desires?") begins with a question directed to the poet:

> When around you, amid giddy tempests, glimmers the frosty glitter of vulgar merriment, when magnate and rich man, and the worthless motley swarm of worldly butterflies flashes tiresomely past,—do you remember that there, like the lot cast for you, gloomy or joyful, your slave or your master, like a snake or a dove, your evil spirit or your good, everywhere in the crowd an invisible spectator keeps vigil?

The questioner does not reveal himself until the fourth strophe: he is the "invisible spectator." As a friend he will show the poet all the beauties of existence as the idealist envisions them:

> He will transport you to gardens above the clouds, to where hearts do not waste away from love; where above the sea of being gleam the nests of angels in the blossoms of heavenly roses, in the rubies of the stars . . . But, if you are seduced by worldly vanity, do not understand me and lay your breast open to lofty passion. . . . suffer! I am your foe. . . .

As long as the ideal remains that, and the poet makes no effort to actualize it, the mysterious spectator is a friend; but if he lets himself be drawn into contact with the real world, the friend becomes an enemy, and will poison all existence: "Your intellect, your beauty I, like a malicious demon, shall turn to ice with the poison of my mockery."

The definitive appearance of this theme in Teplyakov is in the poem "Two Angels" (1833).[56] The first angel is described in Part I—beautiful, childlike, compassionate, comforter of mankind in sorrow. The two epigraphs which accompany the poem give the clue to its interpretation. The first is from Milton's *Paradise Lost* (Book V, 309-311): ". . . what glorious shape / Comes this way moving; seems another morn / Ris'n on mid-noon . . . " After the description of the bright angel the poet queries: "When the blind man divine [i.e., Milton] sang of man's perfect state, the innocence and bliss of the two first-created hearts,—was it not this angel who showed the sun of Paradise to the eyes of his soul, and chasing away the darkness of the fall, revealed Eden to it?" Then, in a personal postscript, he remarks: "Upon the bosom of mother nature he [i.e., the angel] once crowned with roses my young years; he animated with his blessing the babe's golden playing, and breathed the holy harmony of worlds into the heart of the youth!" The second part of the poem describes the other angel:

> His beauty is like the stormy night; his eyes gleam with the serpent's sting, his mouth with the red of blood. A crown, fashioned of sharp lightning, burns around his proud brow, and his cheeks, white as snow, are covered with the shadow of unfathomable thoughts. He looks with mockery on holy good in the claws of black evil; earthly greatness in his eyes is the worm of the grave, the dust of nothingness.

He poisons with his mockery every earthly aspiration; but yet at times even the mocker feels a sorrowful longing for "lost Paradise, and then his heart has pity for something, and a stream of involuntary tears rolls down." In harmony with the second epigraph, which is from Byron's *Cain* ("... sorrow seems / half of his immortality") the symmetrical second query is put to the reader:

> When upon the pinions of black thoughts, far from the regions of earth, measuring the spaces of the abyss, soared the Giant's dark intellect, counted the steps of eternity over the graves of extinguished worlds,—was it not this angel who with the rays of storm, with his own discourse with Cain, impregnated the poet then?

The "Giant" is of course Byron, thus paired with Milton; and the poet's autobiographical note completes the parallelism:

> Since that time when you, O terrible angel, visited my darksome mind—some sort of wild, strange voice has begun to speak in my soul.... Since the time when tears died out in my breast, I have looked on everything with mockery, and I trample upon the roses of life in the garden of earthly existence.

Pushkin in his review article on Teplyakov's poetry singled out, along with "Love and Hate," the elegy "Solitude"[57] as a work that by itself would assure the poet an honored place in his country's literature. The poem begins with a conventional bit of atmosphere: the poet is alone before a dying hearth-fire as the autumn winds howl and the rain beats at his window. He thinks how pleasant such a situation would be for husband and wife, surrounded by family and friends, and compares his own solitude with their enviable lot. But, he exclaims, if for him there is destined no such blissful fate,—

> Oh, kindle in my soul the ardor of holy prayers! Let the ray of ardent faith shine in its wilderness, let healing unction be poured into my breast—let not the dreams of yesterday torment the heart today!
> Let my soul, drunk with hope not of earth, be united with the world-soul, let this dark vale disappear before me, let the autumn winds in their fury not rap at my window.
> Oh, let my spirit be borne above the storm, thither, where the Creator's glance kindles their throngs! In the world above the sun let my greedy ears hearken, enraptured, to the organs of the angels...

Perhaps, he concludes wistfully, "when I have recovered from earthly sorrow, I shall not then pine for a dear one in the present world!" "Solitude" stands out in isolation among Teplyakov's poetry, both for its mystical craving for union with the "world-soul" and its almost religious fervor, and for the perfectly human and evidently autobiographical wistfulness of this perennial wanderer for the prosaic joys of a home and family life. Here, it would seem, speaks the dark angel's sorrowful side.

The seven *Thracian Elegies,*[58] composed during Teplyakov's sojourn in Bulgaria in 1829-30 and first published in full in 1836, were regarded by the poet himself as his principal work, and as a permanent contribution to the elegiac genre. His appraisal was perfectly correct: the elegies are superb poetry and they bring a great deal that is new to a moribund form. The poems were evidently composed *pari passu* with the letters which form the basis of the prose account of Teplyakov's experiences in Bulgaria: in the commentary with which the poet accompanied the elegies there are numerous citations from the *Letters from Bulgaria,* explaining allusions, describing places, etc. The cycle of elegies moves chronologically from "The Sailing" (no. 1), "Tomis" (no. 2), "The Shores of Moesia" (no. 3), "The Ruins of Gebedzhin" (no. 4), "The Fountains of Gebedzhin" (no. 5), "Eski-Arnautlar" (no. 6) to "The Return" (no. 7). There is great variety in the group; the first, as Pushkin noted, obviously inspired by Byron's *Childe Harold,* describes the poet's feelings on leaving his native land; the second, paralleling the episode in Pushkin's *Gypsies* in which the old gypsy tells the story of a poet of old banished to the Moldavian steppe, and even more closely Bobrov's utilization of the same theme, makes the story of Ovid a parallel to the poet's own misfortunes; the third meditates on the stirring ancient history of the shores of the Dobrudja; the fourth and fifth are set in the region of some impressive basaltic columns in the neighborhood of Varna, which the poet takes for ancient ruins; elegy six describes a battle in which the Russian forces are victorious over the Turks; and the final elegy of the cycle intertwines an account of the poet's return by land with reminiscences of the plague-stricken camp where he was for a time quarantined. In most respects the last two of the group are of far less interest to a modern reader than the earlier five.

Teplyakov sailed from Odessa in March 1829 on the Venetian brig *La Perseveranza,* bound for Varna. In a letter of March 1829 to his brother, he relates his feelings on his departure, which the first elegy elaborates. The poem has two epigraphs: the second—two lines from the first canto of Byron's *Childe Harold*—is self-explanatory: "Adieu, adieu! my native shore / Fades o'er the waters blue." The first is a quotation from the mystic Pierre-Simon Ballanche (1776-1847), apparently from his *Essais de palingénésie sociale,* which Teplyakov clearly applies to his own writing— an extreme statement of the romantic theory of inspiration: "Ma bouche se refuse à tout language qui n'est pas le vêtement même de la pensée... et d'ailleurs... ma lyre est comme une puissance surnaturelle qui ne rend que des sons inspirés." The Ballanche quotation evidently is intended to apply not to the first elegy alone, but to the whole group.

The first elegy begins with the preparations for sailing:

> The cable whistles; from the billowing depths
> The anchor comes up, the wind begins to blow;
> The sailor on the rigging of the creaking masts

> Has spread the last sail—
> And lo, on the blue waves
> The free ship has already flapped
> Its white wings!

The voyager is at first exultant, and addresses the receding shore in Byron's words:

> We are sailing! . . . the day grows pale; my native shores are fleeing;
> A golden glow pours over the blue path.
> Farewell, land! Farewell, Russia.
> Farewell, O native land, farewell![59]

Then suddenly he realizes that his joy is mingled with regret; he upbraids himself: whom has he left behind that cares for him? It is the past that he regrets, and lost youth. In his letter to his brother he remarks: "It seemed to me, as Washington Irving said, that at that moment I had closed the first volume of my life with all that it contained." In the confusion of his feelings he turns to his lyre—"Come, dear companion of my cherished thoughts! In every sound of the friendly strings / Let my soul fly, O native land, to thee!" He then inserts in the midst of the irregular long lines of the elegy proper a three-strophe "song," with the couplet refrain at the end of each strophe: "Bluer, bluer, foreign distances! Gray waves, do not slumber." The substance of the song is a self-addressed exhortation to forget the disappointments of the past and look forward to the exciting future: "I shall behold the land of gods, / I shall uncover eloquent dust." Then the elegy resumes with a description of the sunset, the gathering clouds, the tall dark waves, and the scene on the deck:

> And lo, already in imperceptive slumber
> Upon the silent deck the mariners' eyes are closed . . .
> All sleeps,—only at the tiller the sailor on watch
> Hums a quiet song about his far-off native land,
>   Or, having ended his watch,
> Noisily wakes a comrade to relieve him.

As he watches the play of the waves, they become for the poet a symbol of disillusionment:

> Only the wanderer-wave, surging up in the mute distance,
> Like a wraith in a shroud, with bended knees,
>   Stands above the sleeping abyss;
>   It moans above the waste of waters—
> And scatters in foamy dew.
>   So does some proud hope raise
>   The breast of lively youth;
>   So does the soul, surfeited with dream,
>   Smash in the wasteland its holy ideal!

> But enough! What is our ideal?
> Love, friendship, the charmer fame?
> Their vial is Circe's cup.
> In it is hidden bitter poison![60]

Having reassured himself that all the "ideals" which were so precious to his youth are only an illusion, the voyager turns resolutely once more to bid the swift ship speed on its way. His last words are: "Farewell, distant Russia! Farewell, O native land, farewell!"

There is less of the innovative in the first elegy than in those that follow; but some elements may be noted nevertheless. The very scene is an innovation—the deck of a ship is not the usual vantage-point from which the elegist watches the sunset and the heaving waves. Then there is the relative realism of the description—the hoisting of the anchor, the setting of the canvas, the sailor at the tiller humming a song or rousing a comrade to take over the watch. Finally, although there are moments of typically elegiac nostalgia and regret, there is a pervasive mood of defiance and of anticipatory relish for what the future may bring which may be Byronic, but is certainly far indeed from the usually passive atmosphere of the romantic elegy.

Elegy II bears the explanatory title "Tomis" and a quotation from Ovid's elegy V of the Third Book of *Tristia*—the poet's own epitaph composed for his exile's grave in distant Tomis: "I who lie here, the playmate of tender loves, am Naso the poet, whose own genius was my ruin. Let it not be a burden to you who pass by, whoever you may be, who have loved, to say: 'Let Naso's bones rest gently.'" The theme of Ovid's banishment by Augustus to one of the remotest and most desolate spots in the Roman Empire, and of his unavailing efforts to obtain pardon and repatriation from Augustus's successor Tiberius is one that other Russian poets before Teplyakov had treated. Most recently Pushkin in *The Gypsies* had made it a legend of the steppes where his poem was laid; at the very end of the eighteenth century Semyon Bobrov, in his "ballad" called "The Tomb of Ovid," had utilized the theme in a fashion so similar to Teplyakov's treatment that one wonders if Bobrov's version was known to the later poet.[61] The reason for Ovid's banishment has never been determined—the exile himself never discloses it, and aside from the mysterious remark that it resulted from "a writing and a mistake," never alludes to it. Modern scholars have conjectured that the *Ars amandi* is probably the writing, but are at a loss as to the "mistake." For the romantic poet, Ovid becomes the symbol of genius persecuted by arbitrary power, and can be readily identified with any other poet thus afflicted. When Pushkin began *The Gypsies* he was enduring his "southern exile" at the orders of Alexander I; and although the circumstances are not clear, it is probable that Bobrov's long residence in the south was not entirely voluntary. Teplyakov puts in the mouth of Ovid's shade an explicit comparison of the fate of his younger fellow-poet with his own.

In *Letters from Bulgaria*[62] Teplyakov the archaeologist and antiquary gives a detailed and scholarly argument for identifying ancient Tomis with the then Turkish town Küstenci, modern Rumanian Constantsa, instead of with other sites north and south of it. His identification is undoubtedly correct, and although no one has ever discovered the actual tomb of Ovid, the Russian poet is no doubt justified in writing: "I venture to think that in any case Ovid's tomb existed not in my imagination alone; but it could be concealed (even at no great distance from me) in the vicinity of Küstenci, which presented itself to my eyes on March 24, at the time of my voyage to Varna."

The second elegy is symmetrically constructed; between two portions in the irregular combination of long and short lines which is characteristic of the whole group is inserted the address of Ovid's specter. Written in six strophes each of sixteen lines, alternating six-foot and five-foot iambic lines and masculine and feminine rhymes; this metrical device is obviously intended to set apart the "antique" from the "modern" portions of the poem, and in the "antique" portion to imitate the effect of the elegiac distich in which Ovid's own *Tristia* and *Epistulae ex Ponto* are composed. The framing portion of the elegy (lines 1-48 and 145-197) pictures the poet's ship in a storm (prosaically related in *Letters from Bulgaria*) and contrasts the terror and despair of the mariners with the voyager's delight in the tempest. In the first section the "stranger" (the poet himself) addresses the helmsman with the exclamation: "Isn't this a storm, my helmsman! How the sea swirls and splashes!" The steersman replies reassuringly that conditions have not yet made it necessary to fire a cannon as a signal for help. Then the "stranger" espies a sandy promontory and recognizes it as an indication of ancient Tomis: "Is it you I see, dismal region of exile? Is it you, land of immortal suffering? O steppe, rich with Naso's tomb!" Then, as he meditates on Ovid's fate, he imagines that he sees an apparition crowned with light and holding a lyre above the tumbling waves:

> Mournful is the tinkling of its strings:
> in it the heart hears exile;
> in it sounds the moan for its native land,
> the wail of a soul without hope. It sings:
>> "Do not say that over my urn
>> You mourn, O solitary wanderer;
>> The ray of fame does not burn above your head,
>> But we are equal in our cruel fate!"

Using actual quotations from Ovid's elegies, the wraith describes the exiled poet's sufferings, which have become a legend to subsequent ages. He remembers his last farewell as he left his Roman home:

Oh, how I greeted on the Tiber's banks
The Roman dawn for the last time!
How speedily, O dust of the Capitoline, you hid
the world's capital from my eyes!
And you disappeared behind it, my home, my earthly Paradise,
Dwelling of my fathers' gods!
Exile! Where is a roof for you?—all the world is before you,—
Only to you farewell, O native hearth!
But no! Even the whole world has been taken from me:
Exile awaited the poet there
Where the air is a snowy vapor, mist is the day's clothing,
There, where is earth's end or its beginning!
Where only the noise of battle or the howl of constant storms
The wilderness echo repeats afar,
The ferocious Sarmatian goes out to brigandage,
Or the rapacious Getan spreads murder!

The third strophe of Ovid's lament is almost a resume of Book III, elegy X of the *Tristia,* with its vivid description of the difficulties of poetic composition in the unfamiliar wintry land, where barbarian horsemen ride on the ice of the frozen Danube "with the fire of war, with the threat of devastation" to the townsmen. The fourth and fifth strophes continue the account of the exile's homesickness:

Shall I see you once again, shadow of my native roof?
Shall I behold you, my fathers' gods?
And that magical region, where the sun every day
Gilds the green palaces of springtime?
And you, O eternal city! Shall I see at your feet
The world spread out before the seven hills,
The gleam of sumptuous porticoes and golden temples,
And the foam of streams beneath bronze lions?

At the end of the fifth strophe the Roman exile turns to his Russian counterpart with the words: "You yourself are walking a thorny path, / Smitten by the curse of blind fate!" "Like me, you are orphaned and alone among all, / And know yourself the cold of a life without comfort," he continues in the final strophe, then turns back to his own fate: whatever his enemies may have intended, Ovid's fame is eternal. But what does this matter to the dead? "In vain does rumor's trumpet summon / Worshippers from all sides to the unanswering dust,—What is there for the cold ashes in those resounding eulogies, / Behind which life dies every hour!"[63]

The apparition disappears and the scene returns to the present and the furious storm. Once more the "stranger" accosts the steersman: "Isn't this a storm, my helmsman? Already the sea is whipping against the mast, and in the face of the monstrous wave, as a mute slave before a tyrant, your ship bows and trembles!" This time the steersman admits the gravity of the situation and orders the signal gun to be fired—but there is no answering signal. The stranger exclaims: "My helmsman, how pale your face is!" The mariner turns to his questioner with: "You wouldn't dare in this moment, O stranger, to smile at the storm?" But to himself the stranger thinks: "With all my heart I would wish every moment to become one with it; I could wish to merge with the strife of the elements." But then he pauses—after all, stronger than the noise of battling sea and sky "the words of the perished poet now resound in my soul!"

The third "Thracian Elegy," "The Shores of Moesia,"[64] carries as epigraph a quotation from Schiller's "Die Vier Weltalter," describing the blissful life of the shepherd in the golden age of Saturn. As the poet's ship coasts along between the Danube mouth and Varna, he meditates on the eventful past of the region—the invasion of Darius at the end of the sixth century B.C. and of Trajan in the second century A.D., then the waves of barbarians crossing the great river into the Roman Empire. Why did they leave their homes to carry devastation into the civilized world? "Ask why the clouds of hungry locusts speed their flying shroud along the wind to the gardens, the rich corn-lands and the meadows." "The remnants of these wild tribes transformed the world and were transformed with it!" But surely their lives were happier on their native steppes—and the poet launches into a description of the idyllic existence of the nomad, living close to nature and wandering at will over the steppe, "Until, above a silvery streamlet, a luxuriant meadow, under the shadow of willows, with its fresh beauty, with its fragrant sward would tempt them,—then over the new pastures would spread the nomads' noisy herds and a new sun would illumine their movable cities." The poet laments that he was not born in that happy time. His meditations are interrupted by the sight of a bold headland looming up over the sea, and he recognizes it as a one-time Venetian fortress. This sight leads to another meditation on the great past of St. Mark's city: "And where now is thy scepter? Where are the days of triumph and resounding fame? The heel of Nothingness has been raised upon you, O magnificent Rome of the Ocean!" The final section of the elegy brings the poet and his ship to the point where he hears the sunset gun from Varna, now in Russian hands: "O joy! Tomorrow we shall see the country of the worshippers of the Prophet, beneath a sky eternally blue we shall drink in your air, O land of the sumptuous East!" With imaginings of marble fountains, roses and springtime beauty, the poem ends.

The fourth elegy, which Pushkin singled out for particular praise, and which, along with the second, marks the high point of the cycle, is called "The Ruins of Gebedzhin."[65] Its epigraph is a portion of the tenth chapter of the prophet Jeremiah, describing the desolation of a forsaken city. The poem requires a certain amount of explanation. Teplyakov discovered, in the course of his archaeological explorations, a site some ten miles from Varna, toward Providiya, which was covered with what seemed to be countless columns of such a regular appearance that they could be imagined to be man-made. He did not discover the origin of these, and Vatsuro's commentary on the elegy gives no hint, but a friend of mine who has visited the site assures me that they are basalt and of volcanic origin. Teplyakov probably knew this, but preferred for his own poetic purposes to think of them as the ruins of an unimaginably ancient city. His prose description from *Letters from Bulgaria,* which he cites in his own commentary, deserves full quotation both for the light it throws on the poem and as an example of Teplyakov's poetic prose style, which resembles Lermontov's:[66]

> An extensive level area spreads out before you as you emerge from the depths of the forest that surrounds it on all sides. On this level area, cut in several places by tall bushes, extend masses of these gigantic columns, or to put it better, are strewn over a space of more than three versts. I say strewn, because in their position there is evident neither order nor ordinary architectural consistency. Whole thousands of these wonderful columns strike you with the strangest forms. In some places they rise as perfectly regular cylinders; in others they present the appearance of a tower, of a broken pyramid, of a truncated cone; some become thicker toward the bottom and seem girdled by broad cornices. There are elevations upon which several such columns are set so close together that they make one think involuntarily of the remains of an ancient portico ... The complete absence of capitals, of regular cornices and various other architectural ornamentation destroys, for me at least, any possibility of judging as to an order of architecture, by which it might be possible to guess at the beginning of these gigantic ruins ... In speaking of their artificial origin, I must meanwhile admit that all this is far from satisfactory to explain a *human* purpose for these numberless columns, so symmetrical, so unusual, almost uniform everywhere, but strewn over an area that exceeds every measure of human structures. Is it possible that these majestic masses are nothing else but masses of simple *basalt* fragments? Is it possible that this striking regularity of forms and proportions is only a caprice of nature, deceiving man with so perfect an imitation of art, in a country that is peopled with the monuments of antiquity and hosts of famous historical memories? In this latter case scholarly investigators of nature apply, of course, to such phenomena their curious hypothesis of the existence of *mute witnesses* of these unknown, enormous revolutions, before which all the alterations of our sphere caused by man, by hurricanes, by volcanic eruptions, by marine inundations and similar convulsions of the organic world disappear.

In the poem the wanderer confronts the bewildering spectacle of the Gebedzhin "ruins," and queries: "Are not the fragments of an ancient world before me? Are not phantoms from before the flood passing before my eyes?" He compares the scene to a grainfield flattened by hail, to a grove of trees laid low by a storm, and to a battlefield strewn with corpses:

> Here is a harvest crumpled by Saturn's heel,
> Here are the branches of oaks laid low by time,
> Here is a soldiery slain by Annihilation's hand,
> Sleeping in the dust beneath the winding-sheet of the ages!

Remembering the tales told by Herodotus about the wisdom of the ancient Scythians Anacharsis and Avaris, he wonders if here is a memorial of those times:

> Bands of the granite dead!
> Are you not sentinels of those pillars
> On which the marvels of the ages,
> Of the arts and knowledge of the primeval world
> Were engraved by the hand of the sons of the Scythians?

Perhaps the builders of the ruins belonged to the fabled race of giants, of the time—

> When a stripling's head
> Reached to the tops of our towers,
> And the hunter summoned to combat
> The mammoth, mighty and terrible!

He imagines a great city, with sumptuous palaces, hanging gardens and heaven-piercing towers where now all is desolation:

> And the foam of streams from above, amid palm trees,
> Gushed from the maw of bronze behemoths!
> And here upon the blood of sacrifice
> Perhaps, garlanded with peaceful flowers,
> The colossi of jasper gods
> Gazed cheerily with diamond eyes.

Here was surely a place where human wisdom reached a high point—but now "everywhere death, everywhere dust in the stranger's sorrowful eyes!"

But if all living traces of man have disappeared, nature is lavish, garlanding the fallen pillars with flowers and covering the gaunt corpses with fresh ivy. In the dusk the traveller hears the song of the nightingale and watches as a family of lizards scuttles away at his approach and rustles in the rocks. He turns to address the "ruins" directly: why does he feel drawn to them? "Age-old hieroglyphs, Mausoleum of a bygone world! Between you and my soul, say, what kind of sympathy is there?" The ruins are "Fate's lesson to the vanity of descendants." Better than the laurel, a symbol of a glory that vanishes with time, would be a crown of leaves from these fallen pillars, testimony of the vanity of human efforts.

Returning to the earthly scene, the poet describes the nightfall, the moon casting its light through the trees on the fallen giants, the stars glittering above. As he contemplates the scene, he thinks of Byron's words:

> There is the moral of all human tales; 'Tis but the same rehearsal of the past: First freedom, and then glory,—when that falls, Wealth, vice, corruption,—barbarism at last. (*Childe Harold* IV, 108)

So far in the elegy there has been little intrusion of the elegist's own personality; now, however, he abruptly and with little apparent relevance to the rest of the theme, pictures his disillusionment—a typically Byronic theme:

> But I, a humble friend of nature,—my bloom, grown by hope, so early faded—is it because I refused to crawl toward happiness behind the thoughtless crowd by the paths of pygmy intrigues? Because heaven's gift, the fire of the heart, I desired to preserve in my breast and in carefree simplicity of soul, blocked no one's path with the endless net of self-assertiveness?

Again he reiterates his youthful feeling for Nature—an almost Wordsworthian attitude—but contrasts it with his Byronic disillusionment with men:

> Oh! I remember when, once, all nature was insufficient for my divine love—What a sympathy in my feelings, what a fire burned in my blood! ... But I learned to know human hearts, I came to know the sting of calumny, I endured the persecutions of injustice, I wept for the betrayals of friendship, the flowers of trampled hope.

There is something more than a little repellent in the exaggeration of the poet's woes which follows, and the wild accumulation of figures of speech makes the passage a little ridiculous:

> In his eyes is no magnet of love, grief is hidden in caustic mockery, and a brow furrowed by the thunderbolts of thought, like a stormy sea; and the ardor of former raptures has become metal thrown from the crucible!

In the final section of his meditation the poet asks himself if, despite his melancholy experiences with men, it is in vain that his spirit has been capivated by "invisible beauty." He hastens to answer "No, no!" and comparing his soul to a captive eagle carrying its broken chains into a world above the storm, he dreams of a universal reconciliation at "the Creator's throne," when the "fallen angel" Abbadona (from Klopstock's *Messias*) will return to his celestial brother Abdiel, and "From the sun's chalice will slake with him the thirst of immortal love."

The elegy ends with more description; as the morning breaks, strange, unearthly sounds are heard. The Cossack orderly is stirring, the poet's horse paws the ground and strikes sparks from the rocks: "Let us take to the saddle and ride; the way is far; where we are riding to,—Fate knows! Farewell, O swarm of my visions! Sacred dust of a world gone by; And thou, mysterious genius of the ruins, accept my farewell bow!"

The Fifth "Thracian Elegy,"[67] with the subtitle "The Fountains of Gebedzhin," is preceded by an epigraph from the so-called "Golden Verses" attributed to Pythagoras. The relevance of the epigraph becomes apparent later in the reference to "the Proteus of Croton" and his teachings. As the poem begins the traveller is climbing, apparently toward Gebedzhin, under a pitilessly burning sun and is tormented by thirst. He reaches the shelter of the forest, and discovers to his delight two cool springs in the shade. Here he rests on the green sward and meditates. Was it not such an idyllic spot to which the Roman poet Tibullus invited his beloved Delia? He too, having abandoned the illusory objects of his youthful dreams, longs for such repose. Human conduct is contradictory: "Hungry Harlequin is solicitous for the rights of his street-corner friends; he becomes a Croesus—and whets a vengeful ax against men" (probably a reference to the French Revolution). "The Brahmin fell upon the pariah, but he was deprived of Brahma's favors—and he became a brother to the persecuted and fell in love with humanity!" Procrustes' bed is universal—if you are too long, the ax will shorten you, if too short, the noose will stretch you: "In the wild chaos of this darkness, what is to be sought for, what is to be striven for, where is one to flee, what's the purpose of being born?" Is the eternal and vain struggle for happiness "the heritage of Adam's fall?" "Alas! By whatever path we go toward happiness—earthly sorrow stands before the rainbow palace, barring to the heart all entrances, like the sentinel of Paradise Lost, the archangel with the flaming sword!"

In his meditation the thinker longs to be free of material trammels and able to grasp the harmony of the whole, as did Pythagoras when he heard the singing of the spheres:

> Sated with the fruits of bitter heritage, having comprehended this world with the eyes of the soul, what's to do? *To be or not to be?* Oh, if I might grasp the whole chain of existences with the soul's wings! Might throw off earthly vanities, trample upon worthless desires... Perhaps contemplation of the universal soul might reveal to me the angels' dreams, and the primal archetype of beauty, and the radiance of the Eternal thought in it! Was it not thus that once the Proteus of Croton lived? He heard with his soul the harmony of the Universe and the choir of the heavenly spheres, intoxicated in the holy stillness of the passions!

More modestly the poet thinks of a solitary rustic existence in the lap of nature, where everything would inspire to poetic creation:

> Poetry of solitude, in your inspiration the grace of Eden would be poured out for the heart! When shall an upland spring once more in a still and patterned valley whisper of it to me? When amid the dull delirium shall I listen to the rustling of the woods, the trembling of the rain among the leaves, as I bend over the bough of a grey stump? When shall the river's streams at times, breaking against the steep banks, with a surge of earthly joys represent to me their vanity? When shall I comprehend the connection with myself of everything that ripens in the world, that lives or grows or is stony [i.e., of the entire animal, vegetable and mineral world]—and when shall I, moved by the common motion, pour out together with all creation my own heart's gamut [*klavir*] in a united hymn?

The hymn to "Mother Nature" is continued in a rhapsody that is distinctly suggestive of Wordsworth:

> But without thee its tinkling is a coupling of inharmonious sounds. O thou whose beneficent gaze pours life-giving radiance into the depths of the seas and into the bowels of the mountains! Thou, for whom the morning rises through golden mist upon the dewy meadow, noonday shines over the river, evening wanders in the silent grove

and brings to the sea-shore the fantastic flower of the soul's dreams! Thou of whom in the thick branches silvered by the pearly moon the sleepless nightingale sings as he admires the garden lake,—Thou, whose magical string is in the moan of the shy dove and in the shriek of the mother eagle, and audible in the sounds of the air!

Once more the elegist turns to his own woes: nature has been grudging to him alone. He has never known "her whose tenderness might have reconciled her lover with hope"—his ideal mate, whom he calls "Psyche." With the bliss imagined with her, "other eternity I would not have needed." A brief description of the coming of evening to the heat-weary world ends the poem: "Round about is poured a scarcely perceptible melody, the quiet voice of the evening sacrifice [the angelus?], and it is as though an ethereal swarm of pure souls were being borne away from us toward a homeland above the stars."

The Sixth "Thracian Elegy"[68] doubtless had an immediacy when it was published that it can never have again. It stands out from the entire cycle as the only one which is purely descriptive and contains none of the author's personal notes, beyond his occasional claims that the bard's function is to sing the glory of warriors so that their descendants may admire them—which is the tenor of the four lines quoted as epigraph from Zhukovsky's "The Bard in the Camp of the Russian Warriors." In his commentary on the elegy Teplyakov remarks:[69]

> Certain details of the engagement of May 5 at Eski Arnautlar, with which the campaign of 1829 opened, have been set forth by the author in his *Letters from Bulgaria* (pp. 180-192). Finding himself quite unexpectedly on the field of this memorable battle, he mentally drew a sketch of the present elegy during the very heat of the battle. Subsequently he tried to embellish it with the color only of those impressions which his soul had taken in the bloody action itself of the drama that had been played before him.

The description of the battle is vivid and factual; it is enhanced by many perfectly realistic details such as the ordinary atmospheric battle picture of romantic poets omits. Thus at the first alarm of the Turkish attack—

> The summoning drum thunders, like a storm howls the trumpeting horn. The bright bayonets sparkle, horses neigh, scenting the enemy, over them a winged forest of spears. Blinking, the Cossacks are on the move, and the cannon in threatening ranks are dragged heavily among the regiments; in the smoke of burning slow-matches the sparks die out with a crackling flash, and through the mists yellower, redder, the floods of the morning's rays line up the slope of the sky.

The Turks are repelled and the battle is over by evening. The beauty of the setting sun contrasts with the gruesome sight of the battlefield:

> And now firing is no longer heard, the shadow of night descends on the valley and the dying sun is splendid as on the first day of creation. And like so many viands after a

feast, the purple flow of spilled wines, here a cup thrown down and there a lyre, here a garland from a girl reveller's head—so the corpses of the valiant strewed with their throng the patterned vale. Here a red fez, there a black shako in the dust, with the severed head. There a face blued from torment, with bloody foam on the lips; there a curse in clenched teeth, in the eyes lightning turned to stone. There a fallen horse, in the transport of torment, has torn up the lush grass with his hoof; on a cannon the bloody print of convulsive hands.

The elegy ends with the theme suggested by the Zhukovsky epigraph: the pride and admiration of the descendants of the heroes of the battle whom the poet has celebrated.

The Seventh "Thracian Elegy"[70] with the subtitle "The Return," has as epigraph a quotation from Béranger's *Couplet aux jeunes gens,* the substance of which is a call to honor those who have undergone danger and toil for the sake of others. Teplyakov evidently intends it to apply to the sufferers from the plague (cholera?) which the poem describes.

The elegy lacks the internal unity of the others; one must mentally reconstruct the poet's movements, piecing them together from references in *Letters from Bulgaria.* He remained in the Varna area until after the battle described in Elegy VI (May 5); on May 12 he sailed south to Sozopol, on the south coast of the Gulf of Burgas, where there must have been a Russian outpost; the camp was stricken by a fearful epidemic which spread into the town of Sozopol and the poet was quarantined there until July. When the main force of the Russian army crossed the Balkan Mountains on its way to besiege Adrianople, it occupied the coast of the Gulf of Burgas, including the town of Ankhialo, north of the gulf. Teplyakov was allowed to leave Sozopol, which he did, as he tells in his *Letters,* on a Greek caique which he engaged, and which was overloaded by Greeks anxious to escape from the plague-stricken area of Sozopol. He got pleasant quarters in Ankhialo, including a bed with satin pillows (!) and a beautiful black-eyed daughter of the house, and apparently remained there for a time before finally leaving by land. He was back in Odessa in 1830.

The elegy begins with reminiscences of the earlier poems of the cycle: "And where, and where, are the thunderbolts of war? Where the sweetness of the nomad life? The phantoms of giants upon the age-old dust and the chain of lively memories?" A vision of the oceans of blood spilled over the ages in the regions which he is leaving appalls him. But he is now returning in the autumn to the cold and rainy north; the memories of his experiences will remain with him, and he will not forget their charm: "Today—the town [Sozopol?], tomorrow the waves, the seething camp, the silent crag, and horse, and pilgrim staff, and boat." He recalls the first approach of Russian warships across the bay toward Mesemvria and the salvo of guns which in the *Letters* he says sounded to him like the trump of resurrection, heralding as they did his deliverance from quarantined Sozopol:

> At the hour of noonday once I was sitting by the bright sea and carrying the mirror of my soul to the azure world. Above it the Balkan Mountains are blue in the distance, a hundred-gunned warship is white, gliding like a swan among the rocks. Already it is near—and suddenly it disappears in smoke over the blue waves, as though covered by clouds; a bright fire tears them apart—and muffled thunders from the ship burst toward the smitten shores: thus distant Russia sends her native greeting to her sons!

Then the elegist turns to his escape on the Greek caique; all goes well at first, the sky is blue and the sea bright and the boat slips through the waves like a dolphin; but the wind freshens and the overloaded boat has heavy going. But here at last is the harbor, "before us is the conquered town! There a bed with a satin pillow under a white canopy awaits me; a maiden with a voluptuous smile offers me her country's wine. In my soul the glances of the black-eyed girl pour deeply their liquid fire—but it is already time for the wanderer to be on his way! Long since my steed, my captive Arab, has been gnawing his bit, and dancing in his eagerness on the stones of the courtyard!"

The next section of the poem describes the swift ride of the poet on his "captive Arab," accompanied by his Cossack orderly. The travellers are overtaken by evening at a site with ruins:

> The valley is covered with a sapphire dusk; the eternal vault burns with stars; the silent moon silvers a chaos of ruins before me. I wander over the dead heaps of them; how melancholy and how comforting to seek the traces of bygone wonders, to tread the cold dust of heroes! There the swarm of centuries turns into one moment, space into a point; from the dark gulfs of the past comes a mysterious word. There the sons of colossal kingdoms, with their proud fame and fall—All and Nothing—are laid bare to stern meditations.

After a night spent on the ground the travellers push on and reach the Russian army camp, where there also appears to be an epidemic raging. An unidentified soldier questions the traveller about his experience with the plague:

> Were you beneath its sickle?... Did your brain become frost or fire, bewitched by the Black Reaper? Listen! At night, among the tents, yesterday she wandered like a thief, and as in a field a row of sheaves, she counted them with a sickle of lightning.... And suddenly—think of it! it was not in sleep—something, gliding over my heart, hissed like a snake in my ears. I look: she has pressed with her burning lips to my lips and greedily clasped me with a mocking smile to her icy breast!

In the very moment of telling his tale the unfortunate falls dead; on his face are the tell-tale marks of the plague.

The description of the plague in the town—presumably Sozopol—concludes the elegy, with intimations, mutilated by the censor, that the poet found a lover in the devastated city and lost her to the plague.

The final section of the poem presents again the poet's persona as the lonely wanderer, persecuted by fate:

> The journey is ended; the noise of battle no longer disturbs my sound sleep; bayonets do not glisten around battle-flags; the slow-match does not spark over the cannon; the redoubt does not spout like a volcano, and its fire does not pierce the darkness of night with a whistling hail, and the Euxine's waves do not burn with the bright glare of grenades.
>
> What now—will my life now speed by in a silent backwater, as an unloaded boat rocking in the sea without flood-tide? No, friends, no! I am not yet committing my pilgrim staff to the Penates; I sit on the bank—and with my soul summon a favoring wind!

In Pushkin's review of Teplyakov's poetry, the *Thracian Elegies* occupy the largest space, and of these the First, Second and Fourth are quoted in large part and commented on extensively. The First, despite its obvious derivation from *Childe Harold,* pleases Pushkin. "Here is harmony, lyric movement, truth of feeling!" The Second comes in for more censure than the rest: "the poet greets the unseen tomb of Ovid with verses that are too careless"—"'the silence of the tomb,' 'loud as the distant sound of a chariot,' 'a groan that sounds like the wail of a soul,' 'words more holy than the murmur of the waves'—all this is inexact, false, or simply means nothing." He takes the poet to task for making Ovid "rush joyously into deadly battle" when the latter plainly says in the *Tristia* that from childhood he has abhorred war. "The Ruins of Gebedzhin" Pushkin considers the best of the cycle: "In it is disclosed an unusual artistry in description, clarity in expression and power in ideas." After quoting a long passage, he exclaims: "That is beautiful! The energy of the last verses is amazing!" He summarizes his criticism of the *Elegies* before turning to the rest of Teplyakov's work:

> The remaining elegies (among which the sixth is very remarkable) contain the flaws and beauties which we have already noted: a power of expression which often passes into inflation, a clarity of description sometimes darkened by inexactitude. In general the principal qualities of *The Thracian Elegies* are: radiance and energy; the chief flaws: bombast and monotony.[71]

Certainly no exception can be taken to Pushkin's appraisal. There is a striking originality often apparent in Teplyakov's verse, but it is often marred by what Pushkin terms "inexactitude"—by a muddiness of imagery. It is in his use of figures of speech particularly that Teplyakov errs: where Pushkin himself is parsimonious in metaphors, similes, apostrophes, et al., the younger poet scatters them with an all too liberal hand, with results, as we have seen, that are often confusing and sometimes absurd. He has too a young poet's tendency to make use of the ready-made phrases of poetic diction without giving them the transforming touch of his own originality. And finally, he is often only high-flown and bombastic when he means to be impressive—but so, to be candid, is even such a genuinely great poet as Lermontov at times. And a great deal of *The Thracian Elegies* is pure poetic gold, as Pushkin saw and pointed out.

In terms of their relation to the elegiac genre, what can be said of the poems? They bear evident traces of the tradition of their kind: conventional descriptions of "moody" landscapes, such as tempestuous seas, moonlit forests and the like; the almost obligatory figure of a lyric hero obsessed by his own melancholy fate; vague references to a lost and golden youth, and the like. This is the weakest part of the poems. What constitutes their originality and uniqueness is precisely where Teplyakov transcends the hackneyed conventions of the genre and infuses the elegy with an intellectual content unfamiliar to it. The poet's persona is, one might say, another Childe Harold—a deeply pessimistic, fate-driven wanderer, victim of unspecified injustice, who finds pleasure in meditating on the ironies of human fate. But the substance of his meditations is something new for the elegy: far more of the cycle is devoted to the mournful spectacle of the inevitable decay of civilizations and the nullity of human achievement than to the poet's own sorrow. In the second elegy the fate of Ovid, drawn so as to suggest a parallel with his own, drives home the lesson that genius is always misunderstood and persecuted. There is nothing new in this, of course—one may think of Batyushkov's "Dying Tasso." But the last words of Ovid's phantom give the theme an entirely unexpected and original twist: the fame of a great genius will last as long as civilization does—but what is that to the dead? "The paths of glory lead but to the grave"—and even civilization itself is mortal. It is in this latter theme that one may see the greatest originality of Teplyakov's elegies. In "The Ruins of Gebedzhin" particularly the picture of a desolate tract strewn with ruins completely devoid of identifying trace, so that the very name and age of their builders is lost in oblivion, powerfully emphasizes the "Nothingness" that is the poet's final word for civilization. "Nothingness" for the creation of a single genius (Ovid), "Nothingness" for the entire fabric of a people's cultural history.

The same theme, I would suggest, lies behind the sixth and rather unsatisfactory seventh elegies. It is not made explicit, but the picture in the sixth of military glory, of the triumphant course of "the Russian eagle," perhaps to convert "the dust of Stamboul into Byzantium" once more is painfully paired with the grim picture of the plague, with the inexplicable force that annihilates that glory at the moment of triumph. The symmetry of the composition is blurred by the tasteless personal intrusion at the end of the seventh; it would have been far more effective if the poet had left himself out, or shown himself only as an impersonal mourner in reverie over the plague-stricken camp.

Finally, in the third and the fifth elegies appears a theme which I have called an almost Wordsworthian attitude toward nature, which is new in the elegy. If all civilization is sooner or later obliterated, "Mother-Nature" is eternal; the picture of the nomad Scyths as true "children of nature," whose idyllic life the poet wishes he might have shared; and the memories of a childhood when the poet had actually enjoyed for a brief moment an almost pantheistic feeling of oneness with Nature—these pictures contrast sharply with the unrelieved pessimism of much of the rest of the cycle. There is even a suggestion, muted no doubt out of regard for the censor, that union with Nature is equivalent to union with God.

If in *The Thracian Elegies* Teplyakov did not succeed in creating a perfectly flawless work of art, which would be rather much to expect of a twenty-five-year-old poet, he did most certainly create one of the most original and interesting bodies of elegiac poetry to be found in Russian literature.

Alexei Vasilyevich Koltsov (1809-1842)

The *Poet's Library* edition[72] of Koltsov's verse contains only some 180 pages, and of these about thirty include valueless juvenilia, poems of questionable authenticity, and the like. Even the 150 pages of relatively mature work include some material which might more profitably be forgotten. A judicious winnowing of Koltsov's verses would yield probably only a few score of songs that deserve serious consideration—but these are among the most beautiful of their kind in the language.

Koltsov's significance in the history of Russian literature is thus of a very special and limited kind. He is unsurpassed in one narrow genre. His friend and "discoverer" Vissarion Belinsky understandably exaggerated Koltsov's importance, and others of the so-called "democratic" critics of the later nineteenth century followed Belinsky's lead. Ogaryov even ridiculously paired Koltsov with Lermontov. Soviet critics, for whom Belinsky's dicta usually have the authority of holy writ, have unanimously promoted the poet to a major status.

An explanation of this peculiar situation is not far to seek. At the time when Belinsky first encountered Koltsov (about 1831), one of the critic's primary preoccupations was the vexing problem of "nationality," i.e., Russianness. The triad of values enunciated first by S. S. Uvarov and subsequently elevated to what has become known as "official nationalism," consisted of: orthodoxy, autocracy, and nationality [*narodnost'*], but the third of these in this formulation was construed to mean, or at least to include as an essential part, the institution of serfdom, which was anathema to all right-thinking intellectuals. At the same time the Slavophile ideology, which was just crystallizing, emphasized certain qualities as inherently Russian and preeminently embodied in the common people, such as respect for authority, resignation and passivity. To Belinsky and other westernizers, the Slavophile view of the Russian peasant was totally mistaken and only a more sophisticated version of the crass official doctrine. Therefore when in 1831 the young cattle-dealer Alexei Koltsov made his first visit to Moscow on business and was introduced to Belinsky, the latter immediately saw in the self-made poet of Voronezh a living refutation of the interpretations of "nationality" which he abominated. Koltsov's peasant songs and other poems showed the Russian people as active, buoyant, cheerful, but resentful of tyranny, critical of the arbitrary authority of both the landowner and the Tsar. This, for Belinsky, was obviously the true and complete picture.

Alexei Koltsov was not a peasant, but a *meshchanin;* his father was a wealthy cattle-dealer of Voronezh. The business into which he had been born, however, and which his tyrannical father never let him escape, inevitably brought young Alexei into the closest contact with peasant life; and being naturally intelligent and observant, he absorbed the peasant outlook on life. When through contact with the philosopher and poet Nikolai Stankevich and later with Belinsky the young man was weaned away from the artificial and stilted mode of writing which he had first learned, and had begun to ignore the polite conventions of versification and put his own experiences directly into verse, he created something genuinely new and, as Belinsky and his fellows felt, genuinely Russian.

Koltsov had first encountered poetry when, at the age of sixteen, he happened on a volume of verse by I. I. Dmitriev—a rather unlikely initiator into the art. It is significant that, according to his own account, Koltsov's rapture at the exciting discovery was expressed by his learning the poems by heart and *singing* them to tunes of his own devising. Poetry for Koltsov from the beginning meant song.

Vasily Koltsov despised everything that was not financially profitable, and his son was not even permitted to go to a secondary school, but forced to help in the cattle business, often by driving herds of cattle over the steppes from one place to another. When Alexei, with the help of a friendly Voronezh bookseller and a professor in the local seminary began to try his hand at writing verse, his father was contemptuous. It was only in the 1830s, when Alexei's contacts with the literary world through Belinsky, Stankevich, and eventually Pushkin, whom he met in 1836, seemed to his miserly father likely to open doors to him which could be made to yield material gain, that Vasily grudgingly accepted his son's peculiar proclivities. When, however, Alexei attempted in 1840 to break away from the uncongenial world of a small-town bourgeoisie and devoted himself fully to the immense task of self-education and creativity, which he so passionately enjoyed, his father refused him all aid, and he was obliged to abandon the project. In 1842 tuberculosis, probably exasperated by the despair of ever freeing himself from his hopeless situation, brought him to an untimely end. It should be added that parental tyranny had twice thwarted Alexei's plans for marriage. He fell in love with one of his father's peasant girls and proposed to marry her, but during his absence on a business trip in 1828 his father sold Dunyasha to another village, where she died soon after. Later, when he was attracted to Varvara Grigoryevna Lebedeva, daughter of another bourgeois family of Voronezh, his family succeeded in breaking off the relationship.

Most of Koltsov's verse before 1831 is written in the forms and style of late romanticism—elegies, epistles, album verses and the like. Sometimes, these are quite revealing of his own ambiguous position, e.g., "Last Verses" (January 1830): "Let the world rail with cruel mockery at my meagre labor; I shall say with a noble smile: I am a *meshchanin,* not a poet."[73] One short, untitled piece (Jan.-Apr. 1829) probably reflects his grief over the loss of Dunyasha:[74]

> Nothing, nothing in the world gladdens me since I parted with my beloved forever; since that time, if I glance at young maidens at play, I sigh, and bitter tears pour from my eyes. Circling about me, they sport like the swallows in spring, they laugh at my tears with the smile of love. Young beauties, I too was happy here, and I too joked at gay feasts, like you. But early a stern fate said: part from her. Since that time I no longer meet anywhere with gladness.

A number of the early pieces have a biographical interest, e.g., "Epistle to V. G. O." (i.e., Varvara Grigoryevna Lebedeva, née Ogarkova), or "On the Departure of D. A. Kashkin for Odessa" (Kashkin was the bookseller who befriended the young man). Of some interest is also the 1829 poem: "Reply to a Question about my Life":[75]

> All my life is like the blue sea, in dispute with the stormy winds—it rages, foams, seethes, splashes with waves and roars. The winds depart—and it becomes as level as a cloth. At other times, in days of bad weather, everything in the world weighs on the soul; at times happiness smiles, life begins to speak responsively; at times grief from all sides hangs like a cloud over me and like a black wave for the while the soul is cold; now for a moment fair weather comes again and the soul drinks gladness, breathing joy! Everything then is once more beautiful for it, warm, quiet, lively, bright as the magical glass of the waters, and it is as though sorrow did not exist . . .

The best, however, of the poems written before 1831 is one that gives a preview as it were of the realism and naturalness of Koltsov's later songs. This is entitled "Nochleg chumakov" (1828),[76] which could be approximately translated as "A teamsters' night encampment." The *chumaki* were Ukrainian peasants who with teams of oxen hauled grain south over the steppes to the Crimea or the region of the Don, and returned with loads of salt and dried fish. Koltsov, himself a drover, evidently encountered such people on some of his passages across the steppes:

> Close to the high road the roving encampment of the sons of the free Ukraine is settled for the night. In the steppe it is dark and gloomy: in the sky there are neither glittering stars nor moon; nothing disturbs the quiet of the night. Only at times a passerby plays, and the bells of a post-carriage ringing on the spirited troika interrupt the silence for a moment. Among the wagons burns a fire; a kettle hangs on a trivet; a teamster,

undressed, bearded, sits with his legs folded under him and boils buckwheat porridge with suet. Not far from the camp the tired oxen are pasturing; they are watched over by no one. Carefree in the circle in front of the fire the Ukrainian teamsters, [some] grey-haired, [some] young lads with moustaches, lie stretched out on the grass and gaze glumly into the distance. What have the teamsters to drive away drowsiness? How long since have they lost desire to sing their songs of olden times? With what do they now entertain themselves? It used to be that often during the dark night I would spend time with them and, I remember, I used to listen to their songs with a sort of involuntary gladness... But hark, in the darkness to the playing of the pipe, and hark! they have begun to sing quietly to the pipe about the life of their grandfathers, sons of the free Ukraine... And how dear to the heart are those songs, how expressive, somber, long-drawn-out, resonant and full of the traditions of their native land!

By 1830 Koltsov had begun to outgrow the conventional themes and style of his earlier efforts and to make use of the rich traditions and colorful life of the Russian peasant, which poets before him had rarely known and even more rarely exploited. Often he uses a very short line, with only two beats, and unrhymed—a line that approximates that found in genuine popular songs. In using this almost popular meter, however, he is prone to divide the poem into symmetrical strophes, which is not normal in folk songs. A good example of this transitional type of song is the 1830 piece with the title "The Ring." The song is put in the mouth of a peasant girl, who is trying to find out if her lover is faithful by the traditional means of holding his ring in a candle flame to see if it will melt. The closeness of Koltsov's song to genuine popular tradition can be seen in this case from a portion of a folk song on the same theme:[77]

> How would I, a young girl, have known, found out
> My dear one's unkindness,
> The un-love of my heart's beloved,
> Had I not sat late of an evening,
> Had I not kindled a candle of the fiery wax
> Had I not waited for my beloved,
> Not burned the red gold,
> Not melted the gold of the ring?

> Kak by ia znalá, mladá, védala
> nepriiátstvo drúga mílogo,
> neliubóv' drúga serdéchnogo,
> ne sidéla by pózdno vécherom,
> Ia ne zhglá by svechí vósku iárogo,
> ne zhdalá by drúga mílogo,
> ne topíla by krásnogo zólota,
> ne lilá by ia zólota pérstnia.

The meter of the folk song is a three-foot line, unrhymed, and without prosodic definition as iambic, trochaic, or the like, although the dactylic clausula is commonest. Koltsov's poem maintains a two-foot line, and the dactylic clausula appears in less than half the lines:[78]

I light a candle of the fiery wax, I [try to] unsolder the ring of my beloved.

Burn, burn, fateful fire, unsolder, burn the pure gold. Without him for me you are of no use, without him on [my] hand [there is] a stone on my heart.

Whatever I look at, I sigh, I become sad, and my eyes begin to run with the bitter sorrow of tears.

Will he return? Or will he bring me, comfortless, to life with a little message? There is no hope in my soul... So you melt down in a golden tear, memento of my dear one!

Unharmed, black is the ring in the fire, and it rings on the table: eternal memory.

As an example of the meter the first and fourth strophes will serve; note the inner rhyme in the fourth strophe—a common feature of Koltsov's verse:

I
Ia zatépliu svechú
vóska iárova
raspaiáiu kol'tsó
drúga mílogo.

IV
Chto zaglianú—to vzdokhnú,
Zatoskúiusia,
i zal'iútsia glazá
gór'kim górem slëz.

Of about the same date as "The Ring" is a much longer poem, "Village Feast,"[79] with a lively and realistic description of a peasant banquet. The piece begins without prelude: "The plank doors have been opened; on horses, in sleighs the guests have ridden in; the host and his wife have bowed low to them, led them from the porch into the bright living-room [gorenku]. Before the Holy Savior [i.e., an icon] the guests say prayers." Then follows the description of the food: "At the oaken tables, all set, on pine-wood benches the invited [guests] have taken seats. On the tables are many roast chickens, geese, pies, dishes full of ham." Later, when their hunger is satisfied, there is talk: "The guests drink and eat, and begin chattering [gutoriat—a provincial word]: about the grain, about the haymaking, about olden times; what kind of grain harvest will the Lord God send us? How will the hay on the steppe get green?" The feasting lasts until midnight and cockcrow; the poem ends simply: "The talk and the noise have grown still in the dark living-room; from the door the bend [in the road] is visible in the snow."

Apparently written on the same day (September 21, 1830) as "Village Feast" is a haunting "Old Man's Song"[80] in four strophes:

I saddle a horse, a swift horse, I dash, I fly lighter than a falcon.
Across fields, beyond seas, into a distant land—I shall pursue, call back my youth!

> I shall tidy up and appear the lad I once was, and I shall exchange looks again with
> the pretty girls.
> But alas, there are no roads to the unrecallable! Never will the sun come up in the
> west!

Throughout his short life Koltsov was obsessed by what Dostoevsky was to call "the cursed questions" that man has never answered. Philosophical lucubrations do not as a rule result in superior poetry, and Koltsov was not only not a philosopher, but not even a formally educated layman. Among his published verse (mostly in the posthumous volume put out by Belinsky in 1846: his first volume of 1835, published at the expense of Stankevich and his group, contained only eighteen pieces in total) are a considerable number of what he titled *dumy,* meaning here something like "meditations." There are fourteen pieces specifically so titled, besides a number of others with the same kind of content, but not thus qualified. Among the latter is the 1830 poem "What do I signify?" or "What is the meaning of my life?"[81]

> What do I, a petty crumb, signify? I live, I labor assiduously, I waste time in desire for happiness, and, eternally discontented, I weep! What am I seeking? Toward what am I striving? In what sort of country, what am I good for? There are people: they are mortally anxious to unriddle these questions. But what do I care for them? Let them ponder everything as seriously as they like. I'm a stripling [*nedorosl'*], I'm not a wise man; and for me it's more necessary to know a little; on a rather rough road I walk with short steps like a blind man; if I meet with something laughable, I laugh; if I encounter something beautiful, I'm captivated by it; with the unfortunate I will weep with all my soul, and I don't try to know what I signify.

A number of the *dumy* take a religious form, as for example "The Great Word," dedicated to Zhukovsky (1836), or this of the same date, entitled "Prayer":[82]

> Savior, Savior! Pure is my faith as the flame of prayer! But, O God, even for faith the tomb is dark! What will replace my hearing? My quenched eyes? The profound feeling of my heart grown cold? What will be the life of the spirit without this heart? Upon the cross, upon the tomb, upon heaven, upon earth, upon the point of beginning and the goal of creation the Almighty Creator has thrown a veil, has set a seal—a seal for the ages that the worlds will not destroy and tear away, fire will not burn nor water wash away!...
> Forgive me, O Savior! the tear of my sinful evening prayer: in the darkness it shines with love for Thee!

On one occasion (December 7, 1840) Koltsov in a *duma* ("The Poet")[83] attempted to deal with the questions that at one time or another have perennially vexed poets: what *is* poetry? What is the poet's place in the scheme of things?

> In the soul of man thoughts appear as in the misty distance do the stars of the sky... The world is God's mystery; nature entire is in the soul of man. Penetrated by feeling, warmed by love, from her [i.e., Nature] proceed all forces in images... the sovereign-artist creates a picture, a great drama, a history of a kingdom. In them the spirit of eternal life, conscious of itself, manifests itself in endless forms. And it lives for centuries, reflecting our mind, triumphing eternally over soulless death. Wondrous creations of omnipotent thought! All the world before you disappears with me!...

One of the most interesting and significant of Koltsov's "meditations," though not so called, is one written only a few months before his death (Dec., 1841) and oddly titled "From Horace."[84] Koltsov did not know Latin, and the poem has only the most tenuous connection with Horace; he probably knew enough about the Latin poet to realize his Epicurean "this-worldliness," so antithetical to Christian teachings. Belinsky hailed this poem as the poet's "escape from the fogs of mysticism." Whether it represents a definitive turning-point in Koltsov's outlook on life is a question to which no answer can be given. The only piece of personal verse written between "From Horace" and Koltsov's death on October 29, 1842 is: "On the New Year, 1842,"[85] which in its pathetic final strophe evidently reflects a premonition of death, but gives no indication of its meaning other than as the frustration of unfulfilled hopes:

> What is concealed in it [i.e., the darkness of the new year] for me? Surely not new sufferings? Surely I shall not go untimely from the world, without having accomplished even my sincere desire?

"From Horace," which Belinsky had to bowdlerize a bit in order to get it through the censor's office, reads in its original version:

> Isn't it time for us to stop dreaming about heaven, disparaging earthly life, wishing that it be, or be not?
> It's easy, of course, to build airy worlds, to assert and to dispute; how important we are in these!
> But does feeling at times speak from the soul in us [and say] that we must not set value on earthly life?
> The tomb is the end of everything; beyond the distance is thick murk; neither answers nor echoes to our fateful wail!
> But here are earthly gifts, the fragrance of flowers, golden days and nights, the riotous noise of woods;
> And the heart's living life, and the holy fire of feeling, and a young girl gleaming in beauty!

Koltsov's philosophical, or abstract, poems are only a very secondary part of his output, and some of them do indeed deserve the epithet "frightful" which Dmitrij Čiževskij applies indiscriminately to them all.[86] Some are, however, if not great poetry, at least very interesting personal documents.

The genuinely valuable portion of Koltsov's verse is to be found in the pieces which he often calls "Russian songs," or sometimes just "songs," and sometimes leaves without any genre definition. They are composed in colloquial Russian, with numerous echoes of the language of genuine anonymous songs. To convey in another language the linguistic differences between peasant speech and standard literary usage is a hopeless task. Koltsov has often been called (e.g., by Stender-Petersen)[87] "the Russian Burns," but the analogy is misleading. Robert Burns wrote the best of his verse in a dialect which is not English at all, but is as distinct from English as Ukrainian is from Russian. Burns was moreover no semi-literate peasant, although he reflects the outlook and interests of the Scots peasant just as Koltsov does his Russian counterpart. The chief aspect of the two men's verse where the analogy is applicable is in singability. In Burns's poetry the song occupies a very prominent place, although not so dominant a one as in Koltsov's. L. Plotkin in the *Poet's Library* Koltsov[88] states that "for 92 works of Koltsov 300 composers have created 700 romances and songs." It would be interesting to see how this might compare with Burns, but I know of no such statistics.

If the actual linguistic divergencies from standard Russian of Koltsov's peasant songs can not adequately be represented in another language, there is one area where such representation is not impossible— the stylistic. Among the peculiarities of the Russian popular song is the use of compounds in which two nouns are linked together by a hyphen to form a single word, e.g., *ogon'-molniia*, "fire-lightning"; *kovyl'-trava*, "feather-grass," or *kruchina-duma*, "sorrow-thought." Some such combinations are extremely common, e.g., *mat'-zemlia*, "mother-earth," or *dusha-devitsa*, "soul-maiden," i.e., "the girl of one's dreams." Sometimes the combination consists of adjective and related noun, e.g., *zima-zimskaia*, "wintry-winter," or of verb and adverb, e.g., *gorit-goria*, "burns-burningly." Another earmark of the language of popular song is the procedure of breaking up a phrase consisting of preposition, adjective and modified noun, e.g., *iz sinego moria*, "from the deep-blue sea," into two, with the preposition repeated before the adjective, i.e., *iz moria iz sinego*, "from the sea, from the deep-blue [one]." Again, Russian popular song, like English ballads or Homeric epic, abounds in "constant epithets," that is, modifying words or phrases habitually used with certain substantives; such would be "*stormy* winds," "*swift* steed," "*bright* eyes," "*white* breast," "*dark* cloud," "*bitter* tear," and many more. Even in a translation such peculiarities can be felt, as can sometimes even such very common peasant usages as the diminutive of a noun or adjective instead of the word itself, e.g., *solnyshko*, lit. "dear little sun" instead of the colorless, unemotional *solntse*. Such diminutives, however, are usually very hard to convey in English, which is poorly provided with suffixes of that kind and in which such emotional coloration generally sounds rather silly.

Something more needs to be said about Koltsov's versification. It was noted above that a line of two beats, unrhymed, in strophes usually of four lines, is perhaps his most characteristic unit. The three-beat line, more common in folk-song, is rare with Koltsov. However, rather unfortunately it seems, in his later verse he shows a tendency toward a more regular alternation of syllables and toward rhyme, usually only in the even lines of a quatrain. In some cases this results in lines which can be scanned in regular prosodic units, e.g., the first strophe of an 1840 "Russian Song":[89]

> Mnogo ést' u meniá
> teremóv i sadóv
> i razdól'nykh poleí,
> l dremúchikh lesóv

> [I have many towers and gardens and
> broad fields and thick woods]

Here the lines form a pattern of regular anapaestic dimeter, with rhyme-scheme XAXA.

In a series of poems from the middle 1830s Koltsov employs certain syllable combinations almost with the effect of a new kind of compound prosodic foot, like the Greek dochmius. The long, un-strophic poem "The Mower" (1836)[90] begins:

> Ne voz'mú ia v tólk
> ne pridúmaiu . . .
> otchegó zhe ták—
> ne voz'mú ia v tólk?
> Okh, v neschástnyi dén',
> v bestalánnyi chas,
> bez soróchki iá
> rodilsiá na svét.

> [I don't get it, I don't understand . . .
> why is it so—I don't get it!
> Oh, on an unhappy day, in a luckless hour
> without a shirt I was born into the world.]

Here the syllables form a quite regular pattern of an anapaest followed by an iamb (xx́ x́); this regularity, however, does not extend throughout the poem.

The short line and lack of rhyme, whole or partial, is, along with the vocabulary and style of popular song, characteristic of only one portion of Koltsov's verse—the songs, scenes from peasant life, and some of the "meditations." When he has occasion to write formal verse, even in his later period, he reverts to the regular syllabo-tonic system, with rhyme; such, for instance, is the 1838 "World of Music,"[91] written in Moscow when he attended a musical soirée at the home of V. P. Botkin: the piece is written in perfectly regular trochaic tetrameter, with alternating masculine and feminine lines, and rhyme in the even lines. It is as though the peasant lad had put on formal dress for the occasion!

Koltsov's songs are very much alike in their themes and situations. They are put in the mouth now of a lover, now of his lass, now of an old man recalling his youth, now of a bold young lad whose life has unexplainedly turned sour, e.g., "Second Song of Dare-Devil Curly-Hair" [*Likhach Kudriavich*]. One of the best, known in many musical versions by various composers, was thought, perhaps rightly, by Belinsky, to reflect Koltsov's personal grief at the death of his Dunyasha:[92]

> Do not rustle, rye, with your ripe ear! Do not sing, mower, of the broad steppe! I have no reason now to gather grain, I have no reason now to become rich! The young man intended, intended his gain not for his own soul—but for his soul-maiden. It was sweet to me to look into her eyes, into eyes full of loving thoughts! And those bright eyes have gone out, the lovely maiden sleeps the sleep of the grave! Heavier than a mountain, darker than midnight lies the black thought on my heart!

The passing of youth, such a common theme of romantic elegy, takes on a concreteness and immediacy with Koltsov unknown to more conventional poets:[93]

> Like a migrant nightingale youth has flown by; like a wave in stormy gladness, it has roared by.
> There was a golden time, and it has been cut short; young strength has been used up, along with the body.
> From sorrow-thought the blood in the heart has grown cold; what I loved as my soul,—that too has betrayed me.
> Like a blade of grass the wind sways the young man; winter chills his face, and sun burns it.
> Untimely, unseasonably I have spent myself utterly; even my blue caftan sags to the ground from my shoulders!
> Without love, without luck I wander over the world: should I part with misfortune—I meet up with sorrow!
> On a steep mountain grew a green oak; at the mountain's foot now it lies, it rests.
> ("A Bitter Lot," 1837)

Misfortune seems to be the general lot of the peasant; the unfortunate of "Village Calamity" (1838) loses his beloved to a wealthier suitor, then his house accidentally catches fire, and he ends with the sad quatrain: "Since that time I and sorrow-need have been wandering by strange corners. I work for a piece of daily bread, I am bathed in bloody sweat."[94] A luckless lad is jilted by his betrothed ("The Betrayal of the Betrothed," 1838):[95]

> The summer sun is in the sky, but it does not warm me, a young man;
> My heart has stopped from the cold, from the betrayal of my betrothed.

Heavy grief-longing has fallen on my poor woeful head [dim.]; mortal torment torments my soul, my soul wants out of my body.

I went to people for help,—the people laughed and turned away; [I went] to the grave, to father, mother,—they do not rise up at my voice.

The light grew dull in my eyes, I fell on the grass unconscious...

In the solitary night a terrible storm raised me up on the grave...

In the night, in the storm, I saddled my horse; I set out on a journey without a road—to drag my woe around, to take comfort in life, to come to terms with my evil lot.

One of the woes that was probably commonest for a peasant woman was to be forcibly married to an old man she did not love. In this song of 1838 it is the parents who force the unwelcome marriage, but it could equally well have been a tyrannical landowner. The girl's song constitutes a Russian version of that common medieval genre, the *Chanson de la mal mariée,* with the difference that the satirical and defiant element of the French type is wanting:[96]

Oh, why did they marry me by force to an unloved, an old husband? I suppose it's a cheerful thing now for my mother to wipe away my bitter tears;

I suppose it's a cheerful thing for father to look on my wretched life-existence; No doubt the heart in them will break asunder when I come alone to the great day;

Gifts from my dear one I shall bring with me; on my face grief, in my soul—longing.

It's too late, parents, to accuse fate, to conjure, to cast lots, to promise gladness! Let ships sail from beyond the sea, let gold be piled on the ground; the grass won't grow after autumn, the flowers won't bloom in winter in the snow!

Another girl who has suffered the same fate ("A Russian Song," Nov. 15, 1839)[97] remarks bitterly: "My parents say: 'It's live-together—love together; but choose by the heart, and bitterness will come.' It's a fine thing, when they've grown old together, to reason, to give advice, and bring youth to their own level without consideration."

There is an abundance of calamity of all sorts in Koltsov's peasant poems, yet one of the most striking features is the sturdy determination which the sufferers evince to face their misfortunes courageously and overcome them. Thus the jilted lover in the poem quoted above mounts his horse and rides off "to take comfort in life, to come to terms with an evil lot." The hero of a Russian song of 1838 ("On the field the wind is blowing... ")[98] is comforted in his lot by the knowledge of a girl's love: "A bold young lad will whistle like a nightingale! Without a path, without light he will find his own lot. What's a road to him! [What are] thunder-clouds! When there come into his heart—blue eyes!" Another lyric hero ("Last Struggle," 1838)[99] finds his strength in religion:

Over me the tempest howled, the thunder rumbled in the sky; fate frightened the weak understanding, the cold penetrated to the soul.

But I did not fall from suffering, I proudly sustained the blow. I preserved my desires in my soul, strength in my body, fire in my heart!

What is downfall! What is saving! Let be what will be—it's all the same! To holy providence I have long since committed myself!

In this faith there is no doubt, of this my heart is full! Without end is the striving in it!... In it is repose and quiet...

Do not threaten me with misfortune, do not, fate, challenge me to battles; I am ready to do battle with you, but you will not come to terms with me!

In my soul there is strength, in my heart there is blood; *beneath the cross* is my grave; *on the cross* is my love!

"The Path" (1839)[100] begins hesitantly: the hero of the poem sees his path before him, but has no inclination to take it. He knows that he should face the unknown confidently and cheerfully, but the will is lacking:

But for the path I have no strong will in my soul, to look on people in a foreign land;

To stand by myself at times in the face of misfortune; to go back not a step beneath a storm;

And with grief at a feast to be of cheerful countenance; to talk to destruction and sing songs like a nightingale!

If cheerfulness and pluck are characteristic of Koltsov's peasant heroes in their attitude toward adversity, endurance and pride in strength mark their toilsome daily lives. To the upper-class intellectual, for whom physical labor was a terrifying and repellent unknown, such an attitude must have seemed mysterious. He was appalled by the dehumanizing, degrading aspects of agricultural labor, and probably few could have imagined themselves in the position of Tolstoi's Levin, glorying in his own strength and endurance as he mows alongside his peasants. But Koltsov saw the peasants as they were, not as they looked to a white-handed intellectual, and portrayed them accordingly. "Plowman's Song" (1831)[101] is typical; the plowman addresses his horse:

Now then! Pull, Gray, over plowland, over tithe-land; let's whiten the iron [of the plow] against the damp earth.

The pretty little dawn-maiden has begun to burn in the sky, from the big forest the dear sun [dim.] is rising.

It's cheerful on the plowland. Now then! Pull, Gray! You and I together, servant and master.

Cheerfully I ready harrow and plow, I prepare the wagon, I pour out the grain.

Cheerfully I look at the threshing-floor, at the ricks, I flail and I winnow... Now then! Pull, Gray!

Gray and I will get our plowing done early, we'll get ready the holy cradle for the dear grain [dim.].

Damp mother-earth will water it, will feed it, the little blades will come up on the field—Now then! Pull, Gray!

The little blades will come up on the field—and the ears will grow, will get ripe, will dress themselves in golden cloth.

> Our sickle will shine here, the scythe will ring here; sweet will be the rest on the heavy sheaves!
>
> Now then! Pull, Gray! I'll feed you all you want, I'll give you water to drink, water from a spring.
>
> With a silent prayer I plow, I sow. Grant me a good harvest, God, bread [or grain]—my wealth!

The "sower" in the poem of that name exhibits the peasant attitude toward the natural world that surrounds him—almost an animistic attitude, like the plowman's, who prepares a "cradle" for his seed-grain, and sees "mother earth" suckling and feeding the infant plants. He goes out into the steppe to mow the hay, and addresses it familiarly:[102]

> The free-spaced steppe is distant all around, it lies broadly, it is spread with feather-grass!...Oh you, my steppe, free steppe, you have stretched yourself out, you have moved yourself away from the Black Sea! I have come to visit you not alone; I and my keen scythe have come together. I've long since wanted to walk over the steppe grass up and down with her [i.e., the scythe]...Exert yourself, shoulder! Swing, arm! You, puff in my face, wind from the south! Freshen, make waves of the wide-stretching steppe! Begin to hum, scythe, like a swarm of bees! Flash, scythe, scatter sparks around! Rustle, grass that's cut from beneath...

Perhaps the fullest picture of peasant life in Koltsov's verse is given in the 1835 "Harvest."[103] The poem begins descriptively: the dawn comes up like a red flame; the clouds gather and thicken and grow ominous; a short thunderstorm ensues, then the sun comes out:

> At the fields, at the orchards, the green ones, the village folk do not look their fill. The village folk have waited with trembling and prayer for God's grace; their cherished, peaceful thoughts have awoken together with the spring. The first thought: to pour the corn from the corn-bin into sacks, to put away the carts; and their second thought [dim.] was: to ride out from the village on wheels at the right time. The third thought they thought—they said a prayer to the Lord God.
>
> With the morning light they all rode out into the field and set out to walk one after the other, to spread out the corn in full armfuls; and we can begin to turn the ground with plows [*plugami*], and till again with the curved plow [*sokhoi*], to comb it over with the teeth of the harrow.
>
> The people in families have come out to reap, to mow at the root of the tall rye. In frequent stooks the sheaves are laid; all night long creaks the music of the wagons. On threshing-floors everywhere the stacks sit widely, like princes, with heads bowed. The sun sees the reaping finished; it has gone more coldly toward the autumn; but warm is the candle of the villager before the icon of the Mother of God.

Most of Koltsov's occasional poems are inferior and better forgotten. One, however, stands out as an exception, and can serve as a fitting close to this sketch. Written in 1837, "The Forest"[104] is, as the poet makes explicit, "Dedicated to the Memory of A. S. Pushkin." The forest is the murdered poet, envisioned as the folk-hero bogatyr Bova:

Why, thick-set forest [*dremuchii les:* lit., "sleeping forest," a folklore phrase meaning "thick, impenetrable, primeval forest"], have you grown pensive, become overcast with dark sorrow?

Why, enchanted Bova-strongman, do you stand with uncovered head in battle, [Why] have you bowed down, and do not fight with the passing storm-cloud?

Your thick-leaved green helmet the stormy blast has torn away—and strewn it in the dust.

Your cloak has fallen to your feet and been scattered—you stand, you are bowed, and you do not fight.

What has become of the lofty speech, the proud strength, the kingly valor?

Did you not once have the nightingale's liquid song in the silent night?

Did you not have once, in the daytime, a luxuriance—your friend and foe refreshed themselves in it.

Did you not have once, late in the evening, terrible converse with the storm?

It will fling wide the black cloud, envelop you with wind-cold. And you say to it with roaring voice: "Turn back! Stop where you are!"

Where now is your green might? You have turned all black, you are covered with darkness...

You have grown wild, fallen silent...only in bad weather you wail a complaint against untimeliness.

Yes, dark forest, bogatyr Bova! All your life long you labored in battles.

The strong did not overpower you, but the black autumn cut you down.

In the time of sleep, it seems, enemy forces rushed on the defenceless one.

They took the head from the bogatyr's shoulders—not with a great mountain, but with a straw.

Alexei Koltsov is an unique phenomenon in Russian literature. There had been other peasant poets, before him and contemporaries—genuine peasants, such as Fyodor N. Slepushkin (1783-1848), Mikhail D. Sukhanov (1801-1842) and Yegor I. Alipanov (1802-1860). Some of these had succeeded in acquiring a good deal more polite education than did the young drover from Voronezh, and all of them had succeeded in shedding their peasant outlook on life. Their verses are conventional, bookish, even when they deal with peasant life. Once having freed themselves from the soil, they made themselves as bourgeois as possible, and wrote third-rate stuff of no possible interest.

Not so Koltsov; perhaps it was fortunate for literature that he did have a tyrannical miser for a father and was prevented from getting the education he so craved. Had he succeeded in his purpose, he too might have become another faceless versifier. It was certainly fortunate, both for literature and for him, that he fell into the hands of Vissarion Belinsky, who was astute enough to see in the young man's not very distinguished early verse a genuine poetical promise and was able by wise guidance to bring this promise to fulfillment.

Russia never produced another Koltsov during the nineteenth century. His influence, however, may be seen in such Nekrasov poems as "Who Lives Happy in Russia?" and "Red-Nosed Frost." The twentieth century soil than any of the other poets of his period, except perhaps Klyuev. But there is a strain of hooliganism in Yesenin that betrays a want of self-assurance. Koltsov, for all the diffidence he felt before his friends of the intelligentsia, was never unsure of himself. His was a strong, life-affirming character, and his verse reveals the tough, resilient, essentially optimistic nature of the peasantry among whom he spent his short and hapless life and with whom he identified himself.

III

Minor Poets of the 1830s-1840s

As has been stressed many times in this study, the romantic era in Russia was an era preeminently of verse. Not until well toward the end of the 1830s did prose begin to take a position of comparable importance. In both capitals literary periodicals abounded, of various shades of aesthetic and crypto-political opinion, and in their pages scores of versifiers exhibited their skills. Some of these, as must be expected, are best left in a merciful oblivion; but a surprising number of them reveal themselves, even to a critical modern eye, as writers, if not of genius, at least of impressive competence and with something original and interesting to say. Sometimes what they have to say seems only to reinforce what the major poets of the era were saying; but in some cases they represent directions which a critic of a later age, with unerring hindsight, can say that Russian poetry might have taken, but for such and such a circumstance. And sometimes, when one of these minor figures has evidently nothing original to contribute, he is yet in his very eclecticism worth noting as a kind of index of the shifting literary tastes of his time. No extensive treatment need be accorded these luminaries of the third magnitude, but their names at least deserve mention, and the place they fill in the story of Russian romantic verse indicated. The eighteenth-century sentimentalist poet I.I. Dmitriev described himself, with becoming modesty, as "a common soldier on Pindus." Some of the dozen-odd group whom we shall briefly review would have vehemently disputed a private's status, but the verdict of time is inexorable.

Pyotr Alexandrovich Pletnyov (1792-1865)[1]

Taking our company of "private soldiers on Pindus" in order of seniority, we begin with a man whose name has been encountered more than once in discussions of Pushkin, Delvig, Baratynsky et al. Pletnyov was a commoner, the son of a priest, whose life work was performed in the classroom and in editorial offices. He taught at numerous institutions, finally in St. Petersburg University; and as a literary figure his importance is greatest as a critic and as editor of the *Contemporary* after Pushkin's death until the periodical was taken over by Nekrasov (1837-1846). In spite of Pushkin's frank appraisal of his verse as "pallid as a corpse," he dedicated *Eugene Onegin* to him, and remained a warm friend for some twenty years. Pletnyov, as his epistle "To A. S. Pushkin" (1822) shows, realized his inadequacies as a poet, and after the 1820s abandoned verse altogether.

Pletnyov's earliest verse shows the evident influence of Zhukovsky and Batyushkov, and although other influences make their appearance later, it was the "gloomy elegy" that he cultivated with greatest assiduity and success throughout his poetical career. Under the influence of some radical friends in the Society of Lovers of Russian Literature, perhaps chiefly of Ryleev, he wrote some mild "civic" verse, of which the most notable example is the ode "A Citizen's Duty," dedicated to the liberal Admiral N. S. Mordvinov. He was never, it seems, very close to the Decembrist group of radicals, but found the association of Gnedich and Fyodor Glinka and similar moderates more congenial. After 1826 Pletnyov's verse shows more similarities with the light, "anthology" type, of which his friend Anton Delvig was a master, than with any other.

The genres which Pletnyov cultivated were chiefly those of the Batyushkov-Zhukovsky school—the elegy first and foremost (e.g., "The Tomb of Derzhavin," 1819; "To My Homeland," 1820), the friendly epistle (e.g., "To Delvig," 1820; "To. N. I. Gnedich," 1822; "To Vyazemsky," 1822; "To A. S. Pushkin," 1822; "To Zhukovsky," 1824 et al.); and short, scarcely classifiable pieces of a reflective nature, such as the stanzas" "Fate" (1823), the miniature epistle "To the Manuscript of Baratynsky's Poems" (1821) and the "album verses" "To a Gay Beauty" (1825). A fair example of Pletnyov's style is the sonnet, in the style of Anton Delvig, to his one-time pupil Alexandra Nikolaevna Semyonova (1824).[2]

> Repose of soul, enjoyments, expectations,
> the joyful habits of youthful years,
> all the joys with which our world is beautiful
> at the whispering of playful daydream,
> fate takes from us without compassion,
> and time wafts their light trace away
> as the cold wind carries away the last flower
> when the time of fading has come.
>   One thing the soul solicitously preserves
> like the secret gift of first love:
> from early years to sorrowful old age
> her first friend is with her. His smile, his look,
> movements, glance—everything speaks with her,
> everything flies to her, like the sound of distant music.

The pose of the gloomy elegist could be readily exchanged for that of the indolent Epicurean luxuriating in rustic solitude—the persona, that is, of Zhukovsky for that of Batyushkov. The "Stanzas to D[elvig]" (1826)[3] show us the other side of the coin:

Delvig! how good it is in our indolence to live in the country; beneath the ancestral shade to drink the linden-mead of our forefathers. To rest unconcerned on a sultry midday in the overgrown garden; to go out under the quiet evening before a long, sweet sleep; to wait in bed in the morning in case the Muse might come to us; to forget to call by their names all the days of the week; and with no jealous love, without ceremony and without fuss, as in the happy age of Saturn, to live year after year!

In 1822 the Arzamas group was offended by some lines in Pletnyov's poem "B[atyushk]ov from Rome" which they interpreted as derogatory to their friend, and they exhibited considerable coldness toward Pletnyov in consequence. In a letter to his uncle Vasily Lvovich, Alexander Pushkin wrote: "Prose is more appropriate for Pletnyov than verse. He has no feeling, no liveliness—his style is as pallid as a corpse."[4] Indiscreetly the recipient of the letter showed this damning criticism to Pletnyov. The result was the epistle "To A. S. Pushkin," written in the autumn of 1822.[5] Pletnyov begins:

I am not angry at your biting rebuke: upon it is the seal of your frankness; and perhaps the severe lesson will rouse my weakened wings. Your proud anger, I shall say without needless words, is more comforting than the common people's praise. I recognize a judge of my verses, and not a flatterer with a cold smile.

Away with pretence: in my career I have not accomplished anything worthy of a poet. But my thought in moments of meditation has more than once warmed with the divine fire.

The epistle is dignified and free from reproach; it evidently touched Pushkin, for in a letter to his brother Lev he wrote:[6] "Pletnyov's epistle is perhaps his first piece to be torn out of him by a fullness of feeling. It sparkles with real beauties. He knew how to take advantage of his favorable position as regards me; his tone is bold and noble."

Nikolai Mikhailovich Konshin (1793-1859)[7]

Konshin's first career was in the army, in which he worked his way up to a captaincy. He was stationed for a considerable period in Finland, where he became acquainted with Baratynsky. Both Finland and Baratynsky exerted marked influence on his writing, which dates from 1820. After resigning his commission in 1824, he took up a civilian career, in the course of which he became from 1829 to 1837 part of the commission that governed the Lycée of Tsarskoe Selo. Later posts as director of educational institutions in Tver and Yaroslavl followed.

Konshin's literary direction was first set by Zhukovsky and the elegiac school; Baratynsky remained his chief model, although he became associated with Delvig and even with Pushkin. In the 1840s and 1850s he turned more and more to prose, with which he was by no means successful, and to the study of history. During this period he came into conflict with Belinsky and the leaders of the "natural school," to which he harbored a strong hostility. His later verse exhibits a strain of black pessimism rather similar to that of Baratynsky. Individual features in Konshin's style are a tendency in his earlier pieces to intermingle the traditional elegiac clichés with a deliberately prosaic vocabulary; and after 1825, a fondness for allegorical or even mystical themes.

The early elegies and epistles are undistinguished: they repeat the usual complaints over passing youth, the celebration of Bacchus and Venus, the exhortation to put aside sloth and take up the dusty lyre, and the like. In a short epistle of 1820 "To Boratynsky" (of four epistles addressed to Eugene Abramovich in the *Poets of the 1820s-1830s* collection, three use this spelling of his name—but the owner of the name was himself no more consistent!). Konshin begins conventionally:[8]

> Let us forget, my friend, the noisy camp, and the troublesome trooping of the colors; to us is given blissful rest on the bosom of mother nature. Upon the fresh verdure of the fields let us go and teach love to the beauties, and hide ourselves from days of bad weather beneath the cottager's peaceful roof.

But evidently the inroads of old age are already apparent to the twenty-seven-year-old poet, for he continues ruefully:

> But something still is not cheering; ah, something is not what it was! Already rapture in the breast is silent and the heart has grown cold to everything; it is as though joy has been taken away, as though there were no longer any pleasure! The life of the imagination has disappeared, the capacity to feel is not the same!

If the "capacity to feel" suffered momentary atrophy, it seems to have rapidly recovered. In the epistle "To Our Set" [*K nashim*],[9] which pretends to be an invitation to tea, he calls on his boon companions "Eugene" (Baratynsky) and Delvig, and two other army friends, to come help him "dedicate an evening to the gods who give bliss." "Friends," he concludes, "there's no censorship for banquets to friendship and equality!" The poem was obviously composed during one of the periods when Konshin's regiment was stationed in St. Petersburg, where Baratynsky and Delvig shared an apartment together. But such a time of non-military leisure was always subject to sudden interruption. In a poem entitled "March" [*Pokhod*] of 1822[10] he artfully introduces into the trite elegiac language a startling prosaism: "The summoning drum is sounding. Phoebus's service is at an end; the bard casts a sorrowful glance to heaven—and hides his lyre in his trunk." The rhyme *baraban* ("drum") and *chemodan* ("trunk") stresses the "bard's" irony toward his own predicament. Similar is the ending of an 1823 epistle "To Boratynsky":[11]

So, friend, now I see myself, and I no longer have need of advice—there is no science of happiness in the world, and happiness can't be given us. Fortunate is he who in a cozy nook is not poor in what life needs, and has been able in a moment's ecstasy to forget himself with love; he who has never entrusted himself to the world, who feasts alone on life's feast, to whom the world has not presented the look of a Flemish cheese under the microscope [i.e., maggotty]!

The same kind of slightly mocking attitude toward the very poses of the elegiac poet may be seen in "Finlandia" (1823),[12] addressed to an unidentified girlfriend of Konshin's. He laments in perfectly conventional fashion that "he has already forgotten the dear form of the sweetheart of his springtime years—he has put in his gloomy breast the memories of old days; in the wildernesses of the northern distance he treads the antediluvian dust; godlessly have the gods cheated him of health and years; he knows no union with people; he has abandoned lyre and pen." Then in a mischievous change of tone he remarks: "His fussy Muse wipes the dust off his desk [*biuro*]." As for the impressive scenery of Finland, whose eternity so inspired Baratynsky, it has quite the opposite effect on his friend. He ends his "Finlandia" with the words: "Fleeing behind the door of my hut the *imperishable* masses, I philosophize, yawning, on the dear *fragility of things!*" The italics are Konshin's.

As a final example of Konshin's verse may be cited the short poem "The West" (1826),[13] printed in 1827 in the *Neva Almanac* under the title "The Door." The poem has in its original form an epigraph, attributed to "King David"—"When Thou shalt give Thine holy one to see incorruption" (Psalm XV [XVI], 11):

There is in the dark West a rock like a wall,
a secret door keeps guard over the rock.
That door is set in, sunken in, that door has put out roots,
it is merged with the eternal granite.
You cannot scratch under the rock—there's no digging beneath:
there the spade's clatter is dumb;
you cannot scratch over the rock—into the distant height of heaven
the inaccessible ridge is lost.
Why does the rock lie in wait—what does the granite bar—
what does the secret door keep in guard?...
But in the dark *West* lies that rock
and is silent behind the secret door!

The poem sounds startlingly like something of Bryusov's or Bely's; certainly here at least Konshin is a symbolist before "symbolism."

Alexei Damianovich Illichevsky (1798-1837)[14]

Illichevsky, one year older than Alexander Pushkin, was his classmate in the Lycée of Tsarskoe Selo and was there regarded as a worthy poetical rival of Pushkin. He wrote extensively during his years in the Lycée and published in all the numerous collections of verse put out by the institution. Upon graduation in 1817 Illichevsky took a governmental post in Siberia, where his father was at the time governor of Tomsk. After resigning from the service in 1823 Illichevsky made a pilgrimage to Paris, then reentered the civil service in 1825 and continued in it, now in St. Petersburg, to the end of his life. The only collection of his verse, *Essays in the Anthology Genre,* was published in 1827. After this year he wrote and published very little; his style by that time was obsolete and uncongenial to the contemporary literary world.

Illichevsky's style was formed while he was a student at the Lycée and never changed, except to undergo some polishing. In his student years "light verse," such as M. N. Muravyov and N. A. Lvov had represented in the last years of the eighteenth century, and as I. I. Dmitriev chiefly represented in the first decade of the nineteenth, was in great vogue. Muravyov's pupil and editor, Konstantin Batyushkov, in his own early verse and in his famous essay "On the Influence of Light Verse on Language" (1816), had popularized the genre at just the time when Pushkin and Illichevsky were undergraduates. Pushkin and Batyushkov himself fortunately soon matured beyond the "light" style; Illichevsky never did. Ten years after he left the Lycée his literary ideal was still that of the pre-romantic *Anthologie française* of 1816. The notion of "anthology verse" was derived from the *Greek Anthology,* a huge and miscellaneous collection of epigrams, composed over the course of many centuries, of which the unifying characteristic is an elegant and lapidary brevity. V. E. Vatsuro's note on Illichevsky in the *Poet's Library* volume *Poets of the 1820s and 1830s*[15] succinctly defines Illichevsky's concept of "anthology verse": "He conceives of 'anthology' in the spirit of eighteenth-century poetical practice, as a collection of small poems of a gallant and erotic, epigrammatic or moralistic character, distinguished by elegance of style and poetical technique and aphoristic point." Of the vast *Palatine Anthology* it was chiefly Books V (amatory epigrams) and IX (rhetorical and epideictic epigrams) that afforded models for French and Russian poets.

Illichevsky's "anthology verses" are among the best of their kind, but needless to say, that kind is very limited and the monotony and triviality of subject matter outweighs for a modern reader the elegant polish of the style. Perfectly in the spirit of the Greek rhetorical epigram is this short 1827 piece entitled "Actaeon and Menelaus":[16] "By the vengeful nymph Actaeon was punished with horns because he saw with daring eyes what he should not have seen. Venus's son [i.e., Cupid] adorned the brow of Helen's husband [i.e., Menelaus] with them because he shared with others a sight which he should have viewed alone." A similar play on classical mythology is the four-line epigram "To N. N., with an Apple:"[17] "I have been chosen judge, like Paris; you, like Cypris, are victorious. I have made no worse a decision than did Paris; will you give me a reward like his?" Turning a pathetic classical legend on its head, Illichevsky writes:[18]

> When Orpheus, tradition reports, penetrated the depths of Hades, to punish the singer for his boldness they ordered him to take back his wife; then the poor husband touched his strings and deafened Tartarus with his lyre: Pluto was touched by his playing, and freed him from his wife.

Sometimes Illichevsky's verses fit the "moralistic" category mentioned by Vatsuro; "The Hour-Glass," if a little more concise, could well have been written by Palladas:[19]

> As it pours down ceaselessly in the glass, how convincingly this sand teaches us that so also does life depart, growing shorter, and with each day the mortal hour comes closer to us. Oh, weak man! What are your days? A moment! On this short course you are slipping at every step; without noticing it, you have been running to the tomb since the day of your birth; created of dust, you are crumbling into dust.

In 1828 Illichevsky published in the almanac *Northern Flowers* translations of three of Adam Mickiewicz's *Crimean Sonnets* (1826). These are among the very few of Illichevsky's verses to stray outside the limits of "anthology verse." They are serious, romantic poems, filled with the Polish exile's longing for his homeland. Illichevsky translates them in the same rhyme-scheme as the originals, without of course keeping the uniform feminine line-endings of the Polish. "The Steppes of Akkerman" (Mickiewicz's "First Crimean Sonnet") is a good example:[20]

> Sailing on the spacious circle of a waterless ocean,
> in a cart, as in a boat, I rock among the flowers
> on the waves of rustling grasses, on the shorelessness of meadows,
> I pass by purple islands of tall weeds.
> Dusk has already fallen, ahead there is neither path nor kurgan;
> I seek in the heavens for the stars that guide mariners:
> yonder gleams a cloud—it is the Dniester between its banks;
> yonder has blazed out a flare—it is the lighthouse of Akkerman.
>   How quiet! Let us pause! I hear afar off
> how, scarce visible even to a hawk, the cranes are winding,
> how the light moth is fluttering on the grass,
> how the snake with slippery breast touches the earth:
> a stranger to boundaries, my greedy ear is borne to Poland [*Litva*]...
> But let us move on—no one will answer my call.

Alexander Ardalionovich Shishkov (1799-1832)[21]

The talented nephew of Admiral A. S. Shishkov, founder of the *Beseda,* shared none of his uncle's literary or political views. Orphaned at an early age, Alexander Ardalionovich was brought up by his uncle, probably through his influence became interested in poetry, but turned not to the "old archaists," but to the Arzamas group. Pushkin addressed a friendly epistle to him in 1816 as to one of his own group, a writer of "light verse," follower of Tibullus and Parny. None of Shishkov's verse of this date has survived. In 1815, at the age of sixteen, the young man had already enlisted in the army. In 1818 he was transferred, through his uncle's help, to a post in the Caucasus under General A. P. Yermolov. Difficulties with the commander led to a transfer to the Ukraine, to the Odessa Infantry Regiment. During this period he became associated with the southern branch of the Decembrist conspiracy, and with Pushkin, then in his "southern exile." After the coup of December 14, 1825, Shishkov was taken to St. Petersburg on suspicion of complicity with the conspirators, but apparently owing to his uncle's efforts was almost immediately released. He was, however, arrested again in 1827 as a result of some incautious language in one of his poems. Transferred to the fortress of Dunaburg, where Küchelbecker was confined at the time, the unfortunate Shishkov was once more (1829) brought to trial, this time for an infraction of army discipline, and discharged from the service, with orders to settle in Tver and never enter either St. Petersburg or Moscow. Being almost destitute, since he owned no property, he was obliged to try to make a living by his pen. In 1831 he published a four-volume collection of translations of the German romantic theater; he also contributed to several publications in Moscow and St. Petersburg translations of the verse and prose of the German romantics, as well as original poetry. In 1832 Shishkov met a tragic end in a scuffle with another man on a dark stairway, in the course of which he was fatally stabbed.

Three collections of Shishkov's verse were published during his lifetime: *The Eastern Lute* (1824); *Experiments of 1828 by Alexander Shishkov II,* and the first part of *Works and Translations by Captain A. A. Shishkov,* which was not issued in full until after the poet's death (in 1834, by the efforts of his friends Sergei T. Aksakov, N. I. Nadezhdin and M. P. Pogodin).

Three principal influences are observable in Shishkov's poetry—the eastern or Caucasus inspiration, seen in the epistle "To N. T. A[ksakov]" (1821) and "Osman" (1824); the civic or libertarian trend, inspired by Pushkin and the Decembrist poets, exemplified by the "Roman masquerades" "To Metellius" (1824), "To Emilius" (1832), the epistle "To Rotchev" (1827) et al.; and the interest in German romanticism which characterizes the latest period of his life, e.g., "El'fa" (1829), the ballad "Agrippina" (1831) and the paraphrase of the "Prologue in the Theater" of Goethe's *Faust: Part I* (1831). Of Shishkov's earliest work, which must have been in the Batyushkov tradition, judging from Pushkin's epistle, nothing has survived.

It is characteristic of the average verse of the 1820s and 1830s, even of some of the superior and more original creations of the period, that certain sharply defined styles can be distinguished, each marked by the prominence of what the Soviet critic V. A. Gofman, writing about Ryleev, termed "signal words." Such are, in civic verse, the terms "chains," "slavery," "tyrant," "law," "dagger," etc. For the "mournful elegy" "tears," "urn," "moon," and the like automatically evoke the mood—they are the words and concepts which Küchelbecker makes fun of in his essay "On the Direction of Our Poetry—". Similar "signal words" for the "eastern style" are almost anything from Turkish, Persian, Arabic or eastern languages. Note from Shishkov's work the epistle of 1821, addressed to his friend Nikolai Timofeevich Aksakov (ca. 1797-1882), brother of the author of *The Family Chronicle*. The mention in the first part of the epistle of exotic southern flora conveys the tone; then in the second part there is a heaping up of foreign words, familiar indeed to literate Russians, but obviously the "signals" of an eastern culture:[22]

> I have seen the Kur [river in Georgia], it rolls its waters beneath the shade of vines; I have been in the country, the homeland of roses, abounding in the charms of nature. Pure and bright is the firmament there; there the sumptuous anemone is red, the chinar [the Oriental plane-tree] is proud in its beauty, and the traveller in the time of noon-day heat is lured by peach and lemon tree to rest and forgetfulness.
>
> I saw charming maidens there: their running was the light running of the *dzheiran* [an Asiatic antelope]; like the vapor of the springtime mist the gauze was drawn over their breasts from the face to their slender waist. They were more splendid than the roses of Gilan [northern province of Iran], more delectable than the sweet *sherbet* [a Persian drink], etc.

The vogue for "Caucasus" atmosphere in the early nineteenth century was strong in Russia, and one need only think of the immense popularity of Bestuzhev-Marlinsky's novels *Ammalat-bek* and *Mullah-Nur*. Lermontov's *Mtsyri* and *The Demon* belong to the same tradition.

Shishkov's relations with the Decembrists were, as we have noted, close enough to get him into trouble after the suppression of the revolt. His epistle "To Rotchev" (1827) got into the hands of Benckendorff, the ruthless head of the notorious "Third Section" (i.e., the secret police) and led to Shishkov's arrest in 1827. The epistle begins with a definition of the civic poet in the exalted terms typical of the Decembrists:[23]

> Great, O friend, is the poet's vocation; for him is made ready the crown of immortality when the singer dedicates his lively inspiration to his fatherland; when his golden strings tell of the glory of his ancestors; when hearts seethe through them, and the youthful warrior threatens battle, and the mother blesses her child for strife.

The poet adjures his friend to sing so as to inspire the people: "But do not lull the ears of your fellow-citizens with your splendid lyre: even as it is they are slaves of passions, slaves of magnates, slaves of tsars. There is not in them the exalted spirit of the Slav or the virtues of fearless heroes." The exhortation concludes with the demand: "They crawl to the steps of the throne, to them has been given contemptible flattery. To summon slaves out of slumber Tyrtaeus's trumpet is needed, and not the pipes of Anacreon."

"To Rotchev" was of course not published in Shishkov's lifetime; the satires "To Metellius" and "To Emilius" were. This was made possible by their use of a device often employed to evade censorship—the so-called "Roman masquerade." The French Revolution had first popularized this device; the picture of the Roman Republic as the citadel of civic virtue, which the *Parallel Lives* of Plutarch had done much to disseminate, was often utilized to inspire the creators of a new "republic." Russian followers of the tradition evoked a vaguely Roman atmosphere by the use of genuine Roman republican names—e.g., Licinius, Aemilius and the like—republican institutions, e.g., Senate, lictors, etc., and allusions to the Capitoline Hill, the Tiber et al. They almost never attempted to recreate a specific historical situation. Sometimes, indeed, a satire got past the censor by the impudent device of pretending to be a genuine work, "translated" from the Latin. Often the "situation" presented as of ancient Rome was close enough to that of current Russia to need no commentary. Such was that of Shishkov's "To Metellius" of 1824, behind which can be readily seen the realities of the dominance of the infamous Arakcheev. The Roman persona, addressing his appeal to Metellius, cries out:[24]

> Oh! Shall the thunder of heaven, that avenger of justice, speedily be launched upon the head of powerful wickedness, and your power, O arrogant dictator, disappear, and in Rome freedom and repose come to flower? Metellius! Shall I live to see so happy a moment? Or shall I end my sorrowful life amid *Roman slaves?* No, no! The day will come. Free from chains, like the Arabian horse at the sounds of battle nearby, the Roman shall spring up, and with sword in bloody hand, wipe out his disgrace and the shame of his fathers!

Aside from the title there is virtually no Roman disguise at all in "To Emilius." The satire is directed against a *scheiss-freundlich* and ignorant landowner, whose features are so sharply painted that it would seem that they might have been recognizable to a contemporary: to what does he owe his position, the poet queries; has he distinguished himself in war, or the administration of justice, or defence of the weak and helpless?[25]

> No—his late mother left him three hundred muzhiks, poor and tormented; portraits of his great-grandfather and grandfather in copper frames, a stupid head with a contemptible soul, a landlord's arrogance—and not a single book. Reared in the backwoods, not knowing what learning is, he often used to sit in idleness with folded hands, or else with a pack of greyhounds and hunting dogs would trample in the fields on the crops of the muzhiks.

The writer would protest this kind of conduct and draw an eloquent picture of the virtues of the ideal landowner: "But vain was all my toil, and there is poor success where the stern truth engenders only laughter. I hear their whisper: 'What a peevish eccentric!'—and they leave me once more for the cornfields with their dogs."

Shishkov's interest in German romantic poetry and drama, which is so markedly antithetical to the civic themes which he had so successfully treated in the 1820s, seems paradoxical. Perhaps in his desperate struggle to scrape together a living he turned to what seemed the safest literary field available. He translated works of Zacharias Werner, Schiller and Theodor Körner. Ludwig Tieck, however, occupied him chiefly: he translated the *Märchen* "Der blonde Eckbert" and "Der Runenberg," the play *Fortunatus,* and other pieces, and on the basis of Tieck's *Märchen* "Die Elfen" he constructed his semi-dramatic fairytale "Elfa."[26] Ossianic influence, perhaps mediated by the German romantics, is evident in the "Bard on the Field of Battle," where, however, the fate of Shishkov's Decembrist friends is the unacknowledged sub-text.

One of the most interesting of Shishkov's German-inspired poems is a very free and reinterpreted paraphrase of the "Prologue in the Theater" of Goethe's *Faust.* Shishkov renders only a portion of the whole, reducing considerably the part of the *Komik* (Goethe's "Lustige Person") and making the Poet the mouthpiece of an entirely romantic and un-Goethean concept of poetry. In his final speech Goethe's *Dichter* looks back nostalgically at his season of inspiration, when feeling in him was fresh and uninhibited; his last words are: "Gib meine Jugend mir zurück." Shishkov is faithful to this principal theme, but gives his Poet a more decidedly romantic physiognomy than Goethe's possesses:[27]

> Give me back the golden years, when I myself lived in the future; when, care-free son of nature, I fell in love with the sweetness of songs. When they poured in a seething stream from my youthful breast, when the world and men were hidden in a mist before me, when with gay hand I plucked fragrant flowers and was satisfied with myself, and was rich amid poverty—rich in the attraction toward lofty truth, and in wondrous dreams! Give back to me, give back my tormenting happiness, and the power of feeling and the fire of love, all the former ardor of my blood and the former flame of passion—give me back Paradise, give me back Hell, give me back my youth!

There is in Shishkov's sympathetic picture of the Poet none of Goethe's half-amused irony.

Vasily Ivanovich Tumansky (1800-1860)[28]

Vasily Tumansky was the son of a Ukrainian landowner from the Chernigov district. After a primary education at home, partly under a

German tutor, he attended the Kharkov Gymnasium, and later the Petropavlovsk school in St. Petersburg. In 1819 he travelled to Paris, where he attended lectures at the Collège de France; he was particularly attracted by Victor Cousin, who at that time was propagandizing the German idealist philosphers. Tumansky met Wilhelm Küchelbecker while in Paris, and was infected with the civic enthusiasm which marks Küchelbecker's early verse. Upon returning to Russia, Tumansky in 1821 began to take an active part in the literary life of St. Petersburg. He had already in 1818 been elected to membership in the Society of Lovers of Literature, Learning and the Arts, but in 1821 had found it rather too conservative for his taste, and gravitated toward the Society of Lovers of Russian Literature. While in the capital he became an intimate of the circle of Ryleev and Alexander Bestuzhev. In 1823 Tumansky migrated to Odessa as a clerk and translator in the College of Foreign Affairs. During his service there he met Alexander Pushkin and became his ardent admirer. The two dispatched a joint letter to Küchelbecker, as has been mentioned earlier, protesting the latter's defection to the archaism of Katenin and Griboedov. Tumansky continued in the civil service until 1846, almost entirely in the Ukraine, the Crimea and Moldavia. After retirement in 1846 he settled on his Ukrainian estate, but in his last years took some part in the preliminary studies conducted in preparation for the liberation of the serfs. He died in 1860. No collection of his verse was made until 1881; a much more complete one appeared in 1912.

Tumansky throughout his literary career remained a faithful follower of the traditions of Karamzin and Zhukovsky. His orientation toward German romanticism is particularly significant. For a short period in his early life he was brought through Küchelbecker into the orbit of Decembrist thought and wrote some notable verse under this influence, but this episode was not long-lasting. Most of his production is that of a typical elegist.

Lidia Ginzburg in her foreword to the *Poet's Library* edition of *Poets of the 1820s and 1830s* quotes from a letter of Tumansky to his cousin Sophia Grigoryevna Tumanskaya, with whom he was in love:[29] "We realized by our own experience that the happiness of virtuous souls is in sincerity, that a proven [friend] is necessary for our happiness. We have realized that the first condition of every union is perfect confidence on both sides, perfect dependence on one another, and therefore we maintain those beautiful rules of friendship in our relations. I am convinced that our letters, as the frank jottings of two enlightened persons, will include an entire chronicle of our feelings, our passions, and griefs and joys...." Here is obviously German sentimentalism in its quintessential form. Much the same spirit is apparent in Tumansky's verse epistle to this same cousin, accompanying his gift of Zhukovsky's works.[30]

In 1823 a rift occurred in the Society of Lovers of Literature, Learning and the Arts between the more conservative older wing, whose spokesman was Prince N. A. Tsertelev, and the young radicals. In connection with this dispute Tumansky wrote his programmatic epistle "To Prince N. A. Tsertelev."[31] The definition of a poet with which the epistle begins deserves quoting:

> My friend! That man is not yet a poet who, devoted to the Muses from his youthful years and grown old under their law, with wonted tenderness caresses the young world with his lyre's monotonous sound. That man is not yet a poet who, having forgotten with his weak soul the lofty principles of art, in the throng of friends, with shepherd's pipe or trumpet, takes a broad path through the noisy promenades of journals. No! The immortal laurel does not gleam upon the brow of the slaves of public opinion, accustomed to proclaim the truth without conviction, who spare injustice and vice upon the earth. The laws of Genius are freedom! It knows no other bonds, inexhaustible in its lofty fancies as Nature; like the angel of being from the heights above the stars, having penetrated the mysteries of creation, it beholds there the rebellious throng of suffering merged with the beautiful throng of quietness. It hears the voice of the fates, the predestination of the ages and, able to transfer its flame to our souls, it sets upon its living songs the seal of lofty mind. Now, the interlocutor of days gone by, it uncovers the ancient dust of peoples and kings—the daring preacher of peoples and kings; now it sings of the bright world of the future, and spirits from on high from the cloudless region, still involuntarily sighing from the sweet sounds of the lyres that sing in heaven, fly down in choirs to the voice of the earthly singer.

After his picture of the true poet, Tumansky gives his example—and it is precisely that Byron whom the conservatives rejected.

There is, however, little Byronism in Tumansky's own verse. Most notable, perhaps, of this brief phase of his poetry are two sonnets, written in Odessa in 1825 and entitled simply "Greece."[32] They are among the best verse that the Greek revolution inspired among Russian poets. It may be recalled that Tumansky and Küchelbecker had the fleeting dream of going themselves to help the Greek insurgents. The first sonnet gives a dark picture of Greece enslaved:

> Has not thy moan, a widow's piteous moan, long been a just reproach to thy sons? O Greece, it seems that God has doomed thee to the sword of the punishing right hand! More barren than rocks, darker than prison walls, it seemed, thou hadst perished forever, and the Greek vegetated upon a glorious dust like the limp moss on the marble of a tomb.
>
> Beholding thee, we exclaimed: "No! The tribe of great men has been completely annihilated there! There is a land of slaves: for them the weight of shackles is no burden; the legacy of inherited rights for them is not sacred." But thou didst keep for us a wondrous answer, and didst prepare a time of terror.

The second sonnet pictures an aroused Greece:

> Hearken! Whose call has shaken the vaults of these caverns, the profound peace of these age-old oaks? Hearts tremble, recognizing the well-known voice, as do sensitive

waters before the storm. It has risen, it has risen, the great spirit of freedom! Raising the cross, girding on the steel, like the angel of battle, it calls you, oppressed peoples, to the redemption of your glorious rights!

And lo, all around the sound of battle has coursed; like an army camp, Hellas has raised a clamor; the warriors of the holy cause have joined ranks, more terrible than strongholds, more unshakable than rocks,—like God's thunder, their sword has trampled the foe, and their glory has thundered across the world!

Tumansky's usual themes are the private ones of love, communion with nature, regret for passing youth, the exaltation of poetic creation, and similar sentimental and romantic commonplaces. A good example of this side of his inspiration is the ode-like poem "Lament" (1825).[33] It is composed in strophes, each of six lines, the first two and the fourth being Alexandrines, the third, fifth and sixth iambic tetrameter; the rhyme scheme is AAbCCb. The piece begins with the image of a ship becalmed in harbor: such is the poet's spirit, languishing in "dumb idleness," unable to escape its lethargy. The ship suddenly breaks away and is off, but no such fortune is the poet's: "No, in very idleness my noble mind with the pride of past days, with the surplus of new thoughts, has often been thrown into turmoil like the sea, like the sea amid rocks, and beaten there, and avid of glory, avid of deeds, has striven to pour itself forth in songs." In the ecstasy of returning inspiration he compares himself to "God's sacrifice, seized by the greedy flame":

My former lofty path opened up before me, my breast was rocked by an influx of buoyant feelings, my heartstrings began to tremble! Ah! Give me the lyre, fate's immortal gift; let me pour out my prescient fire into its resounding thunders!

I, like an eagle, shall direct my flight from the heights! At my name the persecuted shall have rest and the insolent persecutor shall tremble! To smite wickedness I shall penetrate into hell itself and sate my spiritual hunger and be glory's subjugator!

I was not doomed by my destiny, like a piteous slave of earth, from my cradle days to the unfeeling cares of the world; the treasure of lofty thoughts was given me by heaven, and with eternal fire, like a volcano, my soul was warmed.

The poet looks back on his youth and acknowledges that love and the lusts of the flesh lured him like Sirens from his poet's path: "But by my heart I swear—even in that slavish voluptuousness I was not lulled by earthly vanity, by the idol of earthly happiness! My spirit was put to sleep, but still I was a singer, and the crown destined for me was not trampled by the world in its flower!" Thus, sitting on a rock by the side of the sea, the poet says, he communed with himself and trembled with longing to break away from his spiritual sloth—but in vain: "With the evening sweetness, with the evening moon everything sank into a divine repose, and my soul inclined to its former voluptuousness. Only now and again there whispered in it an obscure voice, like the sound of the light, slow surges dying away on the shore."

Tumansky's fondness for the German romantics allies him to a certain

degree, spiritually at least, with the Wisdom Lovers. His two brief poems—
the Greeks would have called them epigrams—on the death of Venevitinov
(1827) show his sympathy, as they show also the created image of the young
poet which sprang up so soon after his death. The first is the better:[34]

> He shone for a moment, like the charming sunshine of May; he sang for a
> moment, like the May-time nightingale; and heeding neither love nor glory, he soared
> into the land of his dream. Do not weep for him, cherished friend of the poet! Outside
> of life, he has not disappeared from the world: he will be a ray of the light divine, he will
> be a sound of heaven's harmony.

Something of the same mystical intuition of beauty that Venevitinov and
his friends the Wisdom Lovers sought is in Tumansky's poem "The
Ideal":[35]

> When wandering without participation
> Amidst worldly festivity,
> we await from heaven the secret of happiness,
> await a revelation of divinity,
> at times, in a bright moment,
> like a shadow there passes before us
> an inexplicable apparition—
> Beauty, which lives for but an hour,
> glances past and then is hidden from the eyes...

In the 1830s Tumansky ventured into a novel area of verse—the
descriptive poem, in which the physical features of a landscape suggest
moods and thoughts to the contemplative poet. Such is his lengthy and
rhapsodic "Strand-Weg" (1833),[36] inspired by the road along the Baltic Sea
shore from Memel to Königsberg—a road, as he notes, through a region
almost deserted by man, between the desolation of the sea and the
monotonous waste of sand. The sight of a wrecked boat on the seashore
brings him to exclaim at the end of the piece: "Know, O wanderer! that I
too here recalled in just the same way the regions of my spring-time, the
mouldered garb of my love, and the shattered hopes of my youth, shattered
like this poor boat!" His "House on the Bosporus" (1836)[37] is a vivid and
picturesque evocation of the life of a Muslim gentleman, as seen by an
envious northerner. Mention should also be made of two matching poems,
"Thoughts of the South" (1830) and "Thoughts of the North" (1830-31) in
which the poet describes with relish the contrasting attractions of a
southern landscape enlivened by the obligatory black-eyed and sultry
beauties and wintry merry-making in his native land.[38]

Baron Yegor Fyodorovich Rozen (1800-1860)[39]

Here and there in the correspondence and occasional writings of
Vyazemsky, Delvig and Pushkin may be found references to the German-

born Livonian nobleman Baron Georg Rosen, who learned Russian first in his nineteenth year and thereafter ambitiously threw himself into a hectic literary activity in his adopted language. A combination of colossal self-esteem and indefatigable industry enabled him to turn out not only an impressive amount of lyric verse but also numerous historical tragedies in verse, prose tales, histories, critical articles, and even a treatise *On Rhyme.* Although in his autobiographical reminiscences Baron Rozen records with great satisfaction the flattering opinions of Pushkin on his verse, it is evident that there must have been a good deal of irony, undetected by the recipient, in these praises. It seems that Rozen's Russian was never that of a native; he was particularly insensitive to the nuances of usage among the various language levels of Russian, and was capable of jumbling together in one piece high-flown and obsolete Slavonic poetical diction and expressions from the vulgate of the prosiest sort.

Rozen's principal contribution to literature is probably to be found in the translations which he made of Pushkin and other Russian romantic poets into German. He served in many ways as an intermediary between the German romantics and their Russian counterparts, and his critical writings often contain insights of considerable value.

Of his original Russian verse some belongs with the elegiac effusions of the Zhukovsky-Batyushkov school (e.g., "Regret for Youth," 1826), some are attempts to utilize Russian folklore for quasi-popular narratives (e.g., the prolix and highly unsuccessful "Domovoi," 1833), and some represent German fashions imported into Russian (e.g., "The Vestal," 1829, an "antique ballad" of the kind popularized in Germany by Schiller and Goethe). "Tasso's Vision" (1828), a dialogue between the mad poet of *Jerusalem Delivered* and his friend Manso, utilizes the theme of the misunderstood and persecuted genius that Batyushkov had popularized, and which was to furnish a dramatic subject for Kukolnik.

In the poem "The Shepherd's Horn in Petersburg" (1831) Rozen pretends most improbably that he hears in the morning the pastoral horn (Russian substitute for the classical pipes) in the midst of the bustling capital. This leads to meditations on the simple life of the village, reminiscences of childhood, and the analogy of the simple-hearted poet pursuing in solitude his craft in the midst of the populous city. "Shepherd's horn, shepherd's horn! Speak: Do these vain souls heed you—each an enemy to himself? No! Corrupted by debauchery, the children of voluptuousness and vanity, they are still sleeping, in a wealthy mode of life, the sleep of the heart's emptiness!"[40]

Naturally Rozen composed love poetry, most of which is as conventional as the rest of his verse. "To the Unknown Beloved" (1831), however, has some good lines. After several strophes recounting the exaggerated and rapturous encomiums of others on the unknown beauty, the poet turns to his own feelings:

But I see you only while walking, at the window sometimes, of evenings; you are wordless, like a creation of my dreams, and clothed in a mantle of mourning.

Thus for me the sight of you shines mysterious and dear as the gentle ray of the moon; you are for me the luminary of evening, the goddess of dreams and angel of quietness![41]

Vasily Nikiforovich Grigoryev (1803-1876)[42]

Grigoryev, the son of a poor official of St. Petersburg, had no institutional education beyond that which he acquired in a very poor preparatory school in the capital. He continued on his own, however, and acquired enough knowledge of German and French to be able to make translations in the 1820s from Ossian, Klopstock, Salis, Lamartine et al. Grigoryev entered the civil service after finishing his Gymnasium course and remained in it for the rest of his life, ending in a rather high post in the treasury department. After about 1835 he gave up writing verse almost entirely; he had apparently never regarded himself as a genuine poet or his writing as anything more than an avocation.

During the 1820s Grigoryev came under the influence of Fyodor Glinka and Ryleev, and composed a certain amount of verse of a libertarian inspiration, using the device so characteristic of Glinka for concealing his real meaning from the censor, the Biblical disguise. Thus "The Fall of Babylon," (1822) ostensibly the utterance of an exultant Hebrew at the downfall of the hated tyrant city, gives an opportunity for some vigorous but wholly abstract denunciations of tyranny in general:[43] "Monster, rejected by nature, curses and oblivion are your lot! Your corpse lies solitary, unburied, only the rapacious raven has clothed it with his wing! Where are thoughts of pride and greatness? Like the dry leaf torn off by the winds even the trace of your thunderous glory has disappeared... Tremble, tyrant, your avenger does not sleep!" The same Biblical masquerade is used in "The Feelings of the Captive Hebrew" (1823), subtitled "Imitation of the 136th Psalm," and in "Lamentation: an Israelite Song" of 1827; the latter undoubtedly refers to the fate of the Decembrists. It ends with the pathetic words, applicable to the exiles in Siberia:[44] "To the eagle is given a nest, a lair to the lion, shelter to slaves... to Jacob a tomb!"

Some of Grigoryev's verse of the 1820s is inspired by the national history of his own land. Such is "The Banks of the Volkhov" (1823), with its vision of the great days of free Novgorod, and such is the "Song of Bayan" entitled "The Attack of Mamay" (1825), glorifying the great victory of Dmitry Donskoi over the Tatars in 1378. The most ambitious piece of this kind is "Prince Andrei Kurbsky"[45] (1829), perhaps inspired by Ryleev's *duma* "Kurbsky." The historical Prince Kurbsky had been a loyal and successful general of Tsar Ivan IV, particularly distinguished at the capture of Kazan. Alienated by Ivan's ruthless suppression of the boyar class and warned in time of his own impending fate at the hands of "the terrible" Tsar, Kurbsky abruptly changed allegiance in the course of the Livonian War and defected to the Polish King Stefan Batory. At this time he wrote his famous letters to Tsar Ivan, justifying his conduct and denouncing the Tsar's mad tyranny. Grigoryev's poem is largely a paraphrase of Kurbsky's epistles, drawn from Karamzin's *History of the Russian State,* in which they are cited, but making more than Karamzin does of the tragedy of the Prince, who in order to save himself and oppose Ivan's tyranny, finds himself in the position of shedding the blood of his fellow-citizens. The poem is a quite impressive piece of "Decembrist" pseudo-historical pamphleteering.

Grigoryev was in the Caucasus region from April 1828 to December 1830, studying economic conditions. During his stay there he encountered Griboedov both alive and dead (like Pushkin, he met the funeral cortege returning with the poet's body from Teheran), and the exiled Decembrists Alexander Bestuzhev and V. S. Tolstoi. Like most other Russian poets who visited the Caucasus, Grigoryev was inspired to some descriptive verse, e.g., "Evening in the Caucasus," "Beshtau" (the five-peaked mountain near Piatigorsk that gives its name to that town) and "Georgian Woman." "Winter Night on the Steppe"[46] (1826) is short enough to quote *in toto* as a satisfactory example of Grigoryev's verse:

> The cold blast whirls with snow; and the steppe, like a victim of the bad weather, holds up with its meagre sides the vault of heaven, glittering with bright stars. The frost crackles invisibly, and the incandescent half-moon stands on a fiery pillar, throwing light over the exhausted world, and the steppe, it seems to me, is shelterless. Thither, O dreams, to the starry heights! Abandon the field of your life! Upon it, like the steppe, the blizzard of misfortune whirls away the traces of cheerfulness; and, as though in spite, the light of hope illuminates a shelterless path; like the stars, joys glitter above the wayfarer—he strives toward them, and upon his soul the cold of the earthly lies like a heavy chain!

Mention should be made also of Grigoryev's tribute to the Greek War of Independence, the poem "The Greek Woman [*Grechanka*]" (1824), which can stand beside Tumansky's "Greece" as one of the best pieces of Russian verse which that conflict inspired.

Lukyan Andreevich Yakubovich (1805-1839)[47]

Genuine Bohemians are rare in Russian nineteenth-century literature, but there seem to be more of them in the 1830s than earlier. Yakubovich and his poet friends Polezhaev and Sokolovsky are notable examples.

Yakubovich was the son of a small landholder who had a dilettantish interest in literature. The young man received a good education in the preparatory school for nobles attached to the University of Moscow, from which he was graduated in 1826. Having evidently neither interest nor aptitude for the government service, he tried to break into the literary world. He published his poems first in various Moscow periodicals, and then migrated to St. Petersburg, where apparently through an uncle who was a school friend of Pushkin Yakubovich was introduced to his idol. He even was suggested to Pushkin as a collaborator in publication of *The Contemporary,* but Pushkin's death put an end to the project, which would probably in any case not have materialized. Although Pushkin had earlier accepted three of Yakubovich's poems for publication, their calibre is so inferior that there could have been no permanent rapport between the poets. Yakubovich was devastated by Pushkin's death.

He had become acquainted, probably while still in school, with Alexander Polezhaev, and through him with Sokolovsky and other politically radical young poets. Yakubovsky himself gives no evidence in his verse of any deeply held political convictions, however. Polezhaev was soon punished for his notorious poem *Sashka* by being sent as a private soldier to the Caucasus; Yakubovich continued attempting to earn a living by writing for the St. Petersburg journals and giving lessons as a private tutor. He lived, according to friends, in an attic, unheated and almost unfurnished; owned nothing but an overcoat and a dress coat and a few books, and was often too poor to eat properly. The inevitable result of this kind of life was poor health; he returned in 1839 to his father's estate near Kaluga, where he died shortly.

Yakubovich's sole interest in life was literature; for it he sacrificed everything, finally even his life. It is a melancholy fact that despite this single-hearted devotion he had almost no talent. It is said that the apparent demand for his verse was quite unrelated to its literary merits—he wrote almost nothing but extremely short pieces, which were very useful as space-fillers! His orientation was toward extreme romanticism, but he had nothing original to contribute. He was known to almost everyone in the literary world, a very familiar figure, but he was treated generally with contemptuous irony.

Two brief specimens of his verse will suffice to characterize it. He was fond of obvious symbolism, of which "The Waterfall"[48] is a good example:

> Yonder, where eternally over the ledges the waterfall thunders and glitters and where the dark-blue granites stand like dead corpses,—grown torpid, the neighborhood drowses. Only the wild animal, having happened on the rock, heeds the falling of the highland waters, gazing into their heaving crystal.
>
> Like the waterfall, the poet, mighty in thought, seethes and rushes; the crowd does not echo his sound, the mob has no sympathy for feeling. Only the enlightened friend of nature, among his own forests, in the deep wilderness, fully values the sacred labor, the soul's divine fire.

One of his best poems is a fifteen-line "philosophical lyric" entitled "To a Wise Man":[49]

The booty of corruption and the worm, what do you still dream of, wise man, when in the silence of night, not closing your eyes, you read the book of knowledge?

What have you read in it? What have you learned? Always the same truth from the ages, the world revealed to us no other: man lived, loved, suffered, and man is no more!...

There is one law for the living: swaddling-clothes are replaced by winding-sheets! And King Solomon spoke the truth: "All is vanity of vanities and dream!" So what do wise men dream about?

Dmitry Yurevich Struisky *(Triluny)* (1806-1856)[50]

If Yakubovich is a rather pathetic example of the determined poet whose whole-hearted devotion to his art was coupled with no talent, Struisky is the enthusiastic dilettante whose evidently considerable gifts were dispersed in a dozen different directions without real success in any.

Dmitry Struisky was the illegitimate son of Yury Struisky, a landowner of the Penza district, and a serf girl. He was thus the first cousin of the poet A. I. Polezhaev, bastard son of Leonty Struisky. Unlike Polezhaev, Dmitry, at the age of twelve, was legitimated by his father and as a nobleman's son given a good education, including three years at the University of Moscow. He left the University to enter the civil service in 1824, saved up enough money from his small salary to resign in 1834 and take an extensive two-year tour of western Europe. He had begun publishing verse as early as 1827, and continued sporadically thereafter, but also wrote short stories, critical articles on music and painting, and even some amateurish music—songs and a one-act opera, produced in 1840-41 with a libretto by N. A. Polevoi, called *Parasha the Siberian Girl.* In 1829 Struisky had begun to use the pseudonym "Triluny" in signing his verse, a name derived from his father's coat-of-arms, which featured "three moons." According to contemporary accounts he was always eccentric and erratic, extremely absent-minded and unconventional in conduct, giving an impression of mild insanity. At the end of the 1840s he became genuinely insane, and was sent by his brother to an asylum in Paris where he died, probably in 1856.

Triluny's verse, like his music, is amateurish. He never acquired the fundamental knowledge in either sphere which would have enabled him to find the appropriate form for his often grandiose ideas. It is typical of his careless attitude that his first published piece of verse, a historical poem of 1827 entitled "Hannibal at the Ruins of Carthage," presented the great Carthaginian general mourning over the ruins of his native city, which was destroyed in 146 B.C. Hannibal died in 183! In 1840 was published a volume entitled *The Poems of Triluny. Almanac for 1830,* a hodge-podge of verse and prose, including fragments of what was apparently conceived as a lengthy poem, called "Pictures." Some of the fragments are vigorous satires, but no unifying principle can be detected, and the name presumably refers merely to the poet's own kaleidoscopic view of the world.

Byron, whom Triluny knew in his original language, was his particular idol, and he translated portions of *The Giaour* and of *Childe Harold.* He also published a poem called *The Siege of Missolonghi,* which he called "an imitation of Byron's poem *The Siege of Corinth."* It seems that the melancholy, anti-social Byronic attitude, which with so many of his contemporaries was no more than a fashionable pose, corresponded with Triluny's real alienation and disharmony which later manifested itself in insanity.

Some of Triluny's best verse is in the tradition, though not the form, of classical satire. In one of the fragments of "Pictures" a Poet engages in a colloquy with a Buffoon. The Buffoon is, of course, the voice of the philistine, of common sense, while the Poet speaks for high ideals. In the course of his tirade the latter utters the usual romantic denunciation of the city, with considerable vigor:[51]

> Unbearable to me is this fashionable chaos, where everything tends to the breaking of intelligence and natural simplicity; where there is everlasting noise, where everything is a-boil, where often night burns as bright as day from street-lights and smoky lampions, and where the smartly dressed bevy of goddesses shamelessly beckons to all from the windows, with a love as bitter as wormwood. Here everything's for sale, and even love, the holiest of feelings, numbered among the inspired arts, is to be bought from shameful witches! I hate cities, they are the training-grounds of vice. Here without reproaches, without shame, brother impudently flays his brother, fathers shun their children, friends their friends. Trailing after this noisy crowd, I look with contempt on everything, and alone and orphaned I wander with disenchanted soul! Gazing at this furious Sodom, I think with a bitter smile: by what cruel mistake have I been thrown into this madhouse?... Let them find fault with my malicious tongue, let me win enemies, but I cannot endure your Mitrofanushkas, shameful caste, like an ulcer!

The short 1837 poem "The Suicide" is a powerful piece, with its combination of pity and horror:[52]

> *He* forestalled death with death; the earth has given her prey a refuge, but not in the family of kindred graves is *his* grave black. I saw the pale corpse in a corner, the hand with the dagger had grown stiff, and the blood had spread itself on the floor like a purple veil. The suicide's bloody aspect, like God's wrath, was terrible to me,—as a warrior without glory is despicable in his native land. They did not sing a mass for the disgraced corpse, but timidly carried it away at midnight, and reproachfully a sorrowful cross stands over earth's stepson.

Much more conventional, and despite its exaggerated and lurid, effect-seeking language, much less moving is Triluny's contribution to the romantic collection of "Demon" poems:[53]

In darkness in which there is no dawn, like a lawless comet he wanders, darker than the darkness. He is the genuine phantom of the poet! Intellects subject to him have raised idols in his honor, and he has temples in the world, crowds of priests, slaves and lyres, and the incense of disgusting flattery. But he has not forgotten, inconsolable, the wonderful radiance of heaven, and he curses the world of hell, and the moment when its brightness disappeared! And he, like a worm, gnaws the universe, summons the Eternal to combat, and guffaws with furious laughter when, raising his right hand with the thunder, he brings it down on the sinful kingdom, dries up the spring of truth in it and suddenly with pitiless tread wipes it out from the face of the earth! O foe irreconcilable of good, you are dreadful, elusive! Everywhere your form is visible to us, you are named chance, destiny, and under the cover of a subtle mask you convert the holy truths of the ages into empty tales. Amid the secret graves your delusive torch shines in the gloom; hastening toward it, the godless sage draws after him a crowd of unfortunates by the fatal star ... But even your woe is dreadful! There is no rainbow in your night, it is like the sea in icy armor, or a grave without the rays of the sun! With soul condemned, hopeless, you are eternally given over to the torment of a shoreless eternity. Demon, weep! He who was an effulgent Cherub, has become a tormentor and executioner! For your ungrateful soul there is comfort nowhere, in nothing; you hate God's world! You would fain destroy it! But there is a limit to your thunder—you sow death in your own graves, but life will burst forth from the tomb; and you, gloomy miscreant, gaze on God's eternal world: and for you there is no *hope*!

Pushkin's "demon" is easy to identify—he is "the spirit that ever denies." It is hard to be quite sure what Triluny's fiend means to him—perhaps he was not quite sure himself. When the eternal "denier" of the first part of the poem seems metamorphosed at the end into one of Milton's fallen angels, and the poet wastes his words in denouncing abstract evil, the piece loses interest.

As a final example of Triluny's verse, written, or at least published, in 1845, may be quoted "Literary Note,"[54] which is supposed, probably correctly, to refer to Pushkin's death. The government strictly forbade any glorification of Pushkin in print, or lamentation over his slaying, especially immediately after the event:

With your sudden death songs in the North fell into long silence! The Russian wilderness drowses without echo ... Neither woman's charm nor the tales of forefathers nor the cup of friendship nor hero's exploit will call forth your prescient lyre! Far from the wondrously beautiful capital that you celebrated, you have fallen to rest alone in a wilderness tomb; and your grave-mound has been grown over with country grass, without a funeral feast of your friends. The people's bard has been snatched away! Russian strings have been broken!

Alexander Gavrilovich Rotchev (1806-1873)[55]

Like Struisky-Triluny, Rotchev also has a connection, though not a familial one, with the unfortunate soldier-poet Alexander Polezhaev. During Rotchev's student years in the University of Moscow he became an intimate of Polezhaev, and in 1826 was accused of having collaborated with him in writing some anti-government verse. In his case he was fortunate enough to escape with nothing worse than police surveillance.

Rotchev's published verses date from 1826; they appeared in various almanacs, in Raich's *Atheneum,* in *The Moscow Telegraph* and elsewhere. In 1829 he became embroiled in a literary feud that raged between Raich and Polevoi, in which he took sides with the latter and so parted company with the *Atheneum.* Rotchev wrote some rather voluptuous erotic verse ("Song of the Bacchante," "Solomon," etc.) and imitations of Byron. He appropriated a literary gambit much in favor for evading censorship, i.e., the imitation of Biblical or eastern prophetic material devoted to denunciations of injustice, threats of divine retribution, and the like. In this genre he composed a cycle of "Imitations of the Koran" (1827) and of poetical versions from the Apocalypse (1831). Rotchev also turned his hand to drama writing: he translated Schiller's *The Bride from Messina* [*Die Braut von Messina*], *The Maiden of Orleans* [*Die Jungfrau von Orleans*] and *Wilhelm Tell,* Shakespeare's *Macbeth* and Victor Hugo's *Hernani* and *Cromwell.* Reviewers of these efforts accused him of unheard-of unfaithfulness to the originals. After the beginning of the 1830s Rotchev almost ceased to write verse; he took service in 1835 with the Russian-American Company, did a good deal of travelling, and was for a time commandant for the Company in a Russian fort in California. In his last decade and a half he did mostly editorial and journalistic work; in 1869-71 he covered the Franco-Prussian War as correspondent.

As may be seen, Rotchev was a poet for only a short while, and at no time a very serious one. His "Imitations of the Koran"[56] are an interesting parallel with Pushkin's cycle of the same name, which preceded Rotchev's by less than a year. While Pushkin's "Imitations" are a serious attempt to reproduce the entire atmosphere of the patriarchal Arabic way of life, Rotchev's are no more than an "oriental masquerade" designed to allow the poet in prophet's guise to preach justice and denounce social evils. The first of the cycle is a typical example: it utilizes material from the One Hundredth Sutra of the Koran, and from some others:

> I swear by the steed's waving mane and by the shower of sparks from his hooves that the righteous voice of God will soon thunder over the world!
> I swear by the evening sunset and by the golden gleam of morning: with His hand He has raised the seven heavens one upon another!
> Is it not He who with bright fires has kindled this boundless firmament? And He it is also who with their light wings preserves the flight of the soaring birds.
> And when the heavens flash terribly with fiery stream above the illumined earth, is it not God's beauty that shines?
> Without faith in God the joy of existence darts past, darts past; will He send fire without smoke, and smoke will He send without fire?

More apocalyptic is No. 7, with no obvious Koranic original:

Mighty, O Creator, is thy hand! Thou didst raise the mountains with a mighty word, and over the earth the clouds lay like a veil, like an eternal smoke. Earth and heaven hear a voice: "Now my power has created all things, and my love, my wrath and might constrain you to honor me! The trumpet shall thunder the first time: life shall be quenched in the breast of nature; a second time—and my day shall begin to shine, the peoples shall rise up from their graves! On that day, fateful to unbelievers, hearts shall be filled with confusion and like terrified locusts, all shall be carried to the throne of God!"

Vladimir Grigoryevich Benediktov (1807-1873)[57]

If in 1836 any literate Russian had seen Vladimir Benediktov classified among the "minor poets," he probably would have been both amazed and outraged. Benediktov's first book of poems, which was published in 1835, was a sensational success, and a chorus of hyperbolic praise, led by such respected masters as Zhukovsky, greeted the young poet. Shevyryov ranked Benediktov above Pushkin[58] and proclaimed him as the greatly longed-for "poet of thought." This acclaim continued for some seven years, but there were a few dissenting voices. Panaev recalled Pushkin's cool reaction: when asked what he thought of the new poet he praised a single striking image in his verse, but would say nothing more about it.[59] Turgenev remembered how as a young man he had idolized Benediktov, and read Belinsky's and Polevoi's negative comments with indignation, but soon found himself unconsciously agreeing with them. Belinsky's 1835 review of the poems pointed out their serious deficiencies of language, imagery—even of common sense. In a second article in 1842, reviewing the second, two-volume edition of Benediktov's verse, Belinsky gave the *coup de grace* to the poet's ridiculously inflated reputation. During the 1840s Benediktov's popularity declined as fast as it had earlier risen; he attempted a comeback in the 1850s with some "civic verse," but without much success. By his death he was nearly forgotten.

Summing up his conclusions in his second (1842) article, Belinsky wrote:

Mr. Benediktov's poetry is not the poetry of nature, nor of history nor of the people—it is the poetry of the middle classes of the bureaucratic population of St. Petersburg. It reflected them fully, with their loves and compliments, their balls and politeness, their feelings and conceptions—in a word, with all their peculiarities, and it reflected them open-heartedly, without any irony, without any arrière-pensée.[60]

Benediktov was in fact the literary mouthpiece of the bureaucratic class to which he belonged and the values of which he faithfully reflected. His father was a *chinovnik*, stationed in the Petrozavodsk area near the capital. The boy had a good secondary-school education in the Olonets Gymnasium then in St. Petersburg, after which he saw military service in one of the Guards Regiments, was decorated for bravery in the 1831 Polish War and in 1832 resigned his commission to enter the civil service. He served for the next thirty years in the Ministry of Finance. He had all the qualities of a good civil servant, and rose by 1860 to the post of director and member of the governing board of the State Loan Bank. His final decade was spent in retirement.

Benediktov, along with Kukolnik, is a representative of the late-romantic style which Ivan Turgenev devastatingly dubbed "the style of fake grandeur." He appropriated all the paraphernalia of romantic elegy—the night and its stars, the stormy sea, the abyss, the waterfall, the music of the spheres etc., and applied it to subjects of the utmost commonplaceness and triviality. These subjects he invested with a hectic exuberance of language. Benediktov is never content with one word where half a dozen will serve as well—and these words, as Belinsky was among the first to point out, are often coinages of his own, unknown to the Russian language before him (the Polonsky edition of Benediktov's *Works* [1902] is provided with a glossary of his neologisms [Vol. II, pp. i-iii]. It is evident that he made every effort to transcend the vulgar commonplaceness of his subjects by enhancing the "elevation" of his style.

A good example of the nature of Benediktov's themes and of his treatment of them is the poem "Curls."[61] One may imagine as background a prosaic enough scene: a ballroom (one of the poet's favorite locales) where, in the heat of a waltz, the hair-do of a pretty blonde has fallen down and covered her face and shoulders. Note the piling up of images for the "curls"—"lustre and aroma, rings, little jets, little snakes—a silken cascade!" The curls are personified and addressed as sentient beings; they are "sung to sleep" by the music, and dropping off in slumber, have fallen from their proper position. In the eyes of the avid young men at the ball they become a gold mine, a royal crown, etc. Then, in the final metaphor, they become shining waves receding into the distance—the owner of the curls carries them away from St. Petersburg!

> Curls of enchantress-maiden, curls—lustre and aroma, curls—rings, little jets, little snakes—a silken cascade! Twist, pour, pile up together, luxuriantly, like sparks, like pearls! You have no need of diamonds! Your elusive winding gleams more beautifully without embellishments, without a pearly diadem. Let the rose only—the flower of love—the rose—emblem of tenderness—beautify with the charm of Eden your soft jets! I recall: in the sphere of a ballroom night, you, lulled to sleep, fell from the head over bright eyes; hundreds of eyes surrounded you, and in the light of the flickering candles wondrously the shadows from you trembled on breast and shoulders; a tender hand threw you carelessly behind a little ear; the heart of the youth flamed and leaped high. With greedy glance we captured the scattering of these locks, lips did not find words, but the question burned in eyes: Who shall be the full possessor of this gold mine? Who will scoop these waves with greedy hand? Who of us, friends and sufferers, shall devour their amber, twine their silk on his fingers, sear with a kiss, tangle voluptuously, rumple with love, and in the darkness on the pillow, scatter wholeheartedly? Curls, golden curls, luxuriant, thick curls, a maiden's royal crown!

The young men were entranced by you, to you their prayers were expressed by the knocking of ardent hearts; but, devoured by the night, and accessible to it alone, you were entrusted as an earthly, priceless treasure to none; you appeared, romped,—and, as the crystal of the waters of the sea, your waves rolled away into the unknown distance.

A once very famous poem, which Belinsky quotes in full in his first (1835) review, is "The Waltz."[62] Again, a banal scene: a crowded ballroom and a lively waltz, from which one after another all the couples drop out, leaving a single pair whirling alone, as though bewitched by the music. Here one may note first of all the smart unexpectedness of the combinations of words—a typical Benediktov trait: "everything glitters.... epaulets, necklaces, rings and bracelets, curls, *phrases* and eyes ... "; "hearts oppressed by passions *and corsets.*" Then the forced and pretentious metaphors that describe the scene as one after another the glittering couples leave the waltz—"dust from a diamond ring carried away by a whirlwind," etc. And finally the key metaphor upon which the major part of the poem is constructed: the ring of dancers becomes the solar system performing the revolutions that Copernicus described! The final image is almost as startling—the girl in white and her black-garbed partner become angel and demon!

> Everything glitters: flowers, hanging-lamps, diamond and turquoise, candelabras, stars, epaulets, necklaces, rings and bracelets, curls, phrases, and eyes. Everything is in motion: the air, the people, blondes, locks and breasts, and little feet that deserve a crown, with their mysterious promise, and hearts oppressed by passions and corsets.
>
> The circle, from the exhausted storm of the waltz gradually thinning, has already lost much of its glitter. Amid the heat, pair after pair stops circling and falls out. It is the dust [*prakh*] from a diamond ring, carried away by a whirlwind, the dust [*pyl'*] from a pearl diadem, the scattering [*osyp'*] from a royal crown; it is sparks from falling stars, which at times in flying circles, cutting across the heavens, scatter upon the regions of earth, as it were, the dispersed [*osypnye*—a coined word] radiances, with iridescent colors, from a fiery wheel. Now only one pair [*para*] is left, only *she* and *he*. She is wearing white gauze like vapor [*para*—Benediktov loves puns!]; he is all in black, blacker than storm-clouds. The genius of darkness and the spirit of Eden, they are soaring, it seems, in the clouds. And Copernicus's system has its triumph in their eyes. Evidently the world goes around, everything revolves, circles, everything in the bounds of nature is an eternal waltz! The fiddle-bows scatter thunder in livelier fashion; faster in the new brightness of triumph the couple sketches lightning with its circlings, and the two flying beings have twined their wings more tightly together. In vain the black-winged one wants to hold back his flight; drawn on by an incomprehensible force, as over the abyss of the ocean, he flies in layers of mist, all embraced by fire. In the sphere of rainbow light, through chaos and fire and smoke rushes the dark planet with his bright companion. In vain the white cherub seeks for strength or exorcism to break the ring of embraces; her breast is weary, her speech breaks off, her fruitless exertions die away; over the fire of bare shoulders wave blonde wings, the river of tresses cascades, in the breast there is no room for breath; her inflamed hand is firmly grasped by a hellish hand, while with the other the angel burningly, in the horror of the fall, holds fast to the demon of the whirl by his iron shoulders.

Metaphor is Benediktov's chief stock in trade. Very often a whole poem will be built around one, as e.g., his farewell to his hussar's sabre, where the weapon, a feminine noun [*sablia*] in Russian, becomes his beloved.[63] A very well-known example of the sort, which in its time aroused fervid admiration, is "The Crag" [*Utës*],[64] which is the opening poem of the 1835 collection. After the first line the reader realizes that "the crag" stands for the Byronic poet,—perhaps for Benediktov's complacent self-image. But the metaphor swallows up the real crag, and almost everything that is said about the rock as a rock is lifeless and abstract. The effect is heightened by the use of the masculine pronoun to refer to the subject of the poem: "crag" is masculine, so the use is natural, but the attribution to the rock of such epithets as "sombre" and "stern," the reference to its "heels," "brow," "cloak," "head," etc., cancels its "rockness" and leaves it only a thinly disguised romantic poet:

> On all sides surrounded by the plain of the sea, the crag rises proudly,—sombre, stern, unmoved [*nezyblem*] it stands, in its might contesting with the surges of the waves and the pressure of ages. The waves only lick the mighty one's heels, from time there are only furrows along its brow; grey moss crawls on the broad slopes,—the grey summit is a throne for eagles.
>
> The giant is all wrapped in gloom as in a cloak; he has bent, as though in meditation, his shaggy head. Fearlessly with all his stature he has bowed over the sea, and terribly he has risen over the sea's abyss; you wait for him to fall—do not wait for his falling! Sloping he has taken his stand so as to gaze from above on the feeble waves with the mockery of contempt and to frighten with his valor the gaze of a mortal!
>
> He is cold, but nature's heat is forged in him; in the days of the wonder-working of the forces that build, he, the first-born son of fire, was powerfully forced up from the heart of the earth by the force of fire!—he rushed up and cooled in the solidity of granite. The ray of sunshine is not animating to him; to sensual delights his age-old breast is forever closed, and he is savage and morose—that is why he is mighty!
>
> On the other hand, he brightens with furious gladness when the winds rush on their abandoned path, when the sea lashes against him with its breakers, and leaps greedily upon the giant's breast—see, the lightning's flame has flashed over him, the thunderbolt borne its blow on his head—what of it?—the fiery serpent has broken its sting, and the crag laughs, all unscathed.

Benediktov's uninhibited use of metaphor can at times be effective, but it can also be quite ridiculous, especially when, as often, the metaphor is "realized," that is, carried out logically. Thus, a pretty girl can reasonably be called "a magnet for all eyes," but the metaphor degenerates into what the Italians call a *concetto* when it is said that "her charms are a magnet that attracts *iron hearts.*" The metaphor of love as a flame and the lover's heart as burning with passion is ancient and hackneyed; here is what Benediktov does with it:[65]

> Take as a gift the poet's heart! Here it is! Fire is blazing in it. You are silent... Surely you do not want to reject this precious gift? Oh, how slyly you smiled! I understand the language of your eyes: you gave me an excellent hint about my former

> love. You are saying: "God be with you! Before another maiden you burned your whole heart, O careless poet, and now you mean before me to ignite the spark in your heart's ashes." No, you are mistaken, I say; it is not with my former heart that I burn! It has long ago been reduced to ashes, but from the ashes a new one has been born—it is a phoenix that I give to you.

Belinsky quotes a Benediktov metaphor for love: "a drop of honey on the sharp sting of beauty," and another for love's passing: "the streams of time have grown the moss of forgetfulness on the ruins of love." In the poem "Black Eyes"[66] we find that "in them [i.e., black eyes] is the tomb of impassivity and the cradle of bliss." Perhaps the most famous (or infamous) such "Benediktovism" is the phrase with which he describes the male partner of a pair of lovers: "the son of thunder, the eagle-man!" But it would be hard to surpass for sheer absurdity the metaphor of "The Abyss."[67] The abyss, it appears, is a woman's heart: "There shine golden sparks, but there is darkness lying hidden in the depths. There are hidden precious pearls, and monsters sleep on the bottom.... Fear with the outburst of stormy forces to disturb the mystery of the deep, where quietly drowses a crocodile!" Shevyryov's comparison of a young girl's heart to the neat and pretty contents of her boudoir is not much better, but Shevyryov's is an exceptional lapse, Benediktov's is habitual.[68] Whether Benediktov had any knowledge of seventeenth-century "metaphysical poetry," or such Baroque masters as Góngora or Marino, it is certain that his efforts to astonish his readers with startling and bizarre metaphors, verbal cleverness and novelty, etc., belong exactly in their tradition. Like them, for example, he often uses scientific concepts as a basis for his comparisons (e.g.,in the Copernican metaphor, in "The Waltz" quoted above). Another astronomical phenomenon is the basis for the whole sonnet "The Comet":[69]

> Behold the heavens! There is the harmony of the ages; how entrancing is the silence of the constellations, how full of harmony is the whole family of worlds, and how calculated [*raschetistyi*—one of B.'s coinages] is their circular dance!
> But, laying out its own peculiar path among them, a bright comet is not true to the systems, and seemingly threatens the other worlds, screening half the sky with its dazzling tail.
> The astronomer is tranquil: this guest in the sky, he perceives, is proceeding on a commensurate path; but fearful is the new radiance for the superstitious mob.
> Even so a radiant thought, a lofty dream, frightens earth's rabble in their cavern's darkness, but is tranquilly accepted by the bright intellect.

Occasionally Benediktov drops his Baroque manner and composes verse that is not remarkably different from that of other romantic poets of his time. "The Poet's Sorrow" (1830s)[70] is a perhaps sincere self-portrait of Benediktov in the pose of the idealist vainly looking for sympathy from unfeeling fellow-beings:

No—when you have unriddled the singer's lot, you will not call him happy. At times even the very glitter of a crown is grievous to one inspired. Have you seen how at a sorrowful moment under the cruel burden of misfortune, wearied by a hermit's melancholy, he seeks the sympathy of men? The movements of his heart he would fain share with [other] hearts, and his lofty sorrow comes out in sonorous waves, and men listen to the singer, their cries of approbation resound, but their hearts do not apprehend the meaning of the sad song. He sings to them of his losses, and with the flame of his heart's torments he, possessed by their mightiness, animates every sound— and he asks for their tears, for burning tears: but those tears he does not wring from them, and behold—the crowd offers him its frozen rapture.

As a final exhibit, with what seems to be Benediktov's poetical program embedded in another romantic picture of the misunderstood and unappreciated poet, may be cited the fourth "Extract from the Book of Love".[71]

Write, Poet! Compose your symphonies of the heart for your beloved! Pour into resounding melodies the unhappy ardor of your suffering love! In order to express the despairing torments, in order that all your fire may permeate your words—discover unheard-of sounds, invent an unknown language!

And he sings: she doesn't listen to him; he sheds tears; she doesn't see them. But when rumor, cancelling all mysteries, carries the burning song into the world and perhaps another beauty feels it darkly without understanding it: she [i.e., the poet's beloved] will accept it without feeling it; she will pass by, will measure without reflection all the depths of the poet's heavy thoughts; her lively, swift-flying mind will apprehend the language of the heart's sadness—and full of the proud sense of power before her worshipper, she will at times point to his stormy verse, where burns all his soul, and say with a smile: "How nice this is!" then lightly flit away to her amusements. But you proceed, unfailing dreamer, to squander once again your fruitless dreams! Or again, inspired workman, to forge a crown for the haughty beauty, artisan for the glory of the beautiful!

Nestor Vasilyevich Kukolnik (1809-1868)[72]

The outstanding example of the "fake majesty" school of writing, as Turgenev so appropriately named it, was the son of a Slovakian scientist and teacher who had settled early in the nineteenth century in Russia and become thoroughly naturalized. Nestor Kukolnik was educated in the same Ukrainian school (Nezhin) where Gogol was at the same time a pupil. Upon graduation in 1829, he taught for two years in Vilno, then migrated to St. Petersburg to make his career in literature. His first published work, which appeared in 1833, was the "fantasy," as he called his verse tragedy, *Torquato Tasso*. Resounding success came with his second verse drama, which was first played on January 15, 1834: *The Hand of the Almighty Saved the Fatherland*. The sentiments of this inflated and static version of the events of 1613 were so in keeping with the principles of the "official nationalism" of Nikolai I that the young dramatist became from that point almost the Emperor's "pocket poet," as Catherine II used to call Vasily Petrov. It became indeed tantamount to treason even to pass unfavorable criticism on a Kukolnik drama, as Polevoi discovered when his journal the *Moscow Telegraph* was abruptly suppressed for a hostile review of *The Hand of the Almighty Saved the Fatherland.*

Kukolnik's contemporary fame rested largely on his dramas—a long series of pieces, reaching into the 1860s. Except for one experiment in tragedy of plot and character (*Roxolana*, 1834), he learned to keep strictly within the bounds of two types which had proved successful. The archetype of the first group was *Torquato Tasso*, the romantics' favorite misunderstood poet, the genius hounded by fate and the innocent victim of calumny and intrigue. On this general model were composed the "fantasias" *Meister Mind, Giacopo Sannazaro, Giulio Mosti*, the diptych *Domenichino, Johann Anton Leisewitz, The Improvisator* and the unfinished *Pietro Aretino*. The heroes of all these pieces are either Italian or German poets or artists, and the "plot" is regularly founded on the motive of the jealousy and hatred of a less successful rival of the hero. Characters are always black or white, and the "positive" hero's posthumous fame and recognition are assured at the end, as a kind of compensation for his miseries in this life. Later Kukolnik branched out a bit, and wrote one play of this series on an eighteenth-century Russian poet, *Yermil Ivanovich Kostrov*, and one on an English actor, *David Garrick.*

The other, and even more successful group of Kukolnik dramas begins with *The Hand of the Almighty . . .*, followed by *Prince Mikhail Vasilyevich Skopin-Shuisky, Lieutenant-General Patkul, Ivan Ryabov, Fisherman of Archangel, The Statue of Christoff in Riga*, or *There Will Be War, Prince Daniel Dimitrievich Kholmsky* and *Boyar Fyodor Vasilyevich Basenok*. In these quasi-historical dramas the subjects are all drawn from Russian history and the episodes are uniformly such as to give an opportunity for glorifying the Tsar and the Almighty. Again, characters are one-dimensional and either black or white. If white, they are in the highest degree passive: thus Minin relies, like his colleague Pozharsky, on "the hand of the Almighty" to save the fatherland, in defiance of the facts of history; and Patkul not only takes no active steps to escape from the Saxon officers sent to arrest him, but even deliberately lets himself be taken, serene in his confidence in Tsar Peter and the Almighty. The negative characters, on the other hand, are very active and contrive all sorts of devious plots, which usually come to nothing without even any very active effort on the part of the hero or heroes. From a dramatic standpoint the plays are tiresome, and their only interest apparently lay in the high-flown patriotic sentiments which all the positive characters poured forth in interminable monologues. The language of all the dramas is the most outrageous fustian, which like the similar language of Benediktov's lyrics, appealed to the "bureaucratic population of St. Petersburg," in Belinsky's words.

Besides dramas, Kukolnik wrote stories and even novels in the 1840s and 1850s, when it appeared that prose was soon to take over the hegemony of the literary world. He published, usually in *The Reading Library,* some lyric verse, mostly love poetry addressed to a mysterious lady who, he liked to hint, was of extremely high birth—in this way putting himself in the position of his hero Tasso, in love with the sister of the Duke of Ferrara, and of David Rizzio, the hero of Kukolnik's unfinished narrative poem, who loved Mary Stuart, Queen of France and later of Scotland.

As a fair example of Kukolnik's dramatic style, which dominated the Russian stage for a decade, a portion of one of Tasso's soliloquies will serve; the dying poet has come to Rome, where the Pope has prepared a great celebration at which he will be given "the laurel crown of Virgil" (actually, of Petrarch). But the fate that has persecuted Tasso from the first thwarts the Pope's good intentions—death overtakes him before he receives the crown. Addressing a crowd of "the Roman people" from the doctor's house on the Capitoline where he is domiciled, on the eve of the day set for the celebration, he declaims:[73]

> And all this for a poor singer! For the poor singer of Jerusalem!—When I look around, methinks I have lived some sort of great epic. I have lived an enormous tragedy.... The day will come! The denouement is preparing, and in the morning I shall sleep the sleep of evening... The time is coming, and I shall not be, and all my dreams and inspirations will pour together into memory alone! In my Italy art will fall asleep, poetry will fall out of love with Torquato's land, and pass from here to the West and the North!...

Mention of "the North" then leads the dying poet to a clairvoyant vision of the great flowering of poetry in an unnamed, but obvious, "northern land."

To a taste less sympathetic than that of the Russian *chinovnik* to grandiloquence, Kukolnik's short lyrics, interspersed through his plays and other works, offer more interest. "Rizzio's Romance," which Mikhail Glinka set to music, is one of the best:[74]

> Who she is and where she is— / Is known to the skies alone,
> But my soul is allured / By the wondrous unknown.
> I believe, I know: the day will come, / My heart is in glad confusion,
> It will find its mysterious maiden, / And the dream will come true.
> The wind knows who she is, / The clouds have seen her,
> When above her from afar / They run with their light shadow.
> The nightingales sing of her, / The bright stars glitter
> With the glances of her eyes, / But they will not tell her name.

This extract ("December 7") from "Notes of a Man in Love" (1837)[75] will give an idea of Kukolnik's "personal" lyric:

Oh, my God! How I love her!...

Neither the cries of enemies, nor the riotous noise of the feast draws my winged thoughts away from my idol! I always sing of *her!*

But the verse of my sufferings is dull, unintelligible, it has become accustomed to the enigmatic darkness; but the assemblage of feelings is a peculiar language, and it will be comprehensible to but a few.

In my love there is no revelation to people! What though I fall beneath the weight of my secret, what though in life I shall see no inspiration, yet I will not surrender *love* to the judgment of men! I shall not make the sorrowful admission either to her, or to you, enemies of sacred passions! From your suffering to mine there are no passages or earthly stairs. Away, sincerity! Sooner would I be a light bird, if it were really necessary to be candid! Still sooner, to a ruined tomb am I decided to reveal my unfortunate love; but never shall I send to my beloved Eleonora [not the lady's real name, of course, but the name of Parny's mistress] either passionate words or looks, but I shall whisper gloomily to myself: "Oh, my God, how I love her!"...

Nikolai Mikhailovich Satin (1814-1873)[76]

When Alexander Herzen and his friend Nikolai Ogaryov, later leaders of Russian liberalism, were students in Moscow University (1830-1834) they formed a small circle of like-minded students around them, one of whom was the young nobleman Nikolai Satin. Another was the Siberian-born Vladimir Ignatyevich Sokolovsky (1808-1839).[77] The Herzen circle was not conspiratorial, but was decidedly anti-governmental and hostile to the entire trend of Russian life under Nikolai I, its materialism and philistinism. Immediately after their graduation from the University, Herzen, Satin and Sokolovsky were arrested and interrogated by the police of the Third Section on the charge of having sung scurrilous and anti-governmental songs. The most offensive of these songs was one composed by Sokolovsky, with reference to the confused "interregnum" of 1825, when the country for a time was in doubt whether the heir of the deceased Alexander I was to be his brother Constantine or his younger brother Nikolai:[78]

The Russian Emperor [Alexander I] commended his spirit to God, and the embalmer stuffed his belly. The state is in mourning, all the people are in mourning— and there rides to us to be our Tsar the monster Kostyshka [Constantine]. But to the Universal Tsar, the God of highest powers, the Blessed Tsar [Alexander] submitted a document. Reading the manifesto [Alexander's secret will, naming Nikolai as his successor] the Creator took pity and gave us Nikolai—a son of a bitch! A scoundrel!

Nikolai quite understandably preferred not to have a regular public trial, which would air the "scurrilous songs," so after the offenders had been held some while in custody, they were unofficially sentenced by imperial decree: Sokolovsky, as the most guilty, was to serve a three-year prison sentence in Schlusselberg, after which he would be sent as a civil servant to the remote region of Vyatka; Satin was relegated to Simbirsk, Herzen to Perm, and Ogaryov to Penza.

For Sokolovsky, a frail and consumptive youth, this "mild" arrangement was a death sentence. He served only a little over half his term in the damp and unhealthy prison before friends obtained his release, Vyatka was little better, and in 1838 he obtained permission to go to the Caucasus for his health. He died in Pyatigorsk in 1839, leaving a body of curious verse, mostly unpublished, and a published and indifferent novel. Sokolovsky's verse is almost entirely inspired by the Old Testament and belongs stylistically in the line of the archaizing verse of Küchelbecker et al. The long poem *The Creation of the World* is a poetical version of the first chapters of Genesis; the dramatic poem *Khever'* is a retelling of the book of Esther, with all the names of the characters changed to evade the ecclesiastical censor, and the poem *The Destruction of Babylon,* composed in Sokolovsky's last year, is a turgid series of alternating proclamations from the Almighty of the impending destruction of the city of sin, and of meditations on the theme by an earthly prophet. Sokolovsky's verse is pretentious and intolerably verbose, and his choice of Biblical subjects seems to have been determined not only by the possibilities they offer of verbal denunciations of iniquity, but more simply because of the obligatory elevation of language which they require and which coincided with the poet's personal taste.

A much truer poet than Sokolovsky is the second one of the singers of scurrilous songs, Nikolai Satin. Like Sokolovsky, Satin was sickly and plagued all his life by physical weakness. He escaped the prison experience of his friend, however, and lived to the comparatively advanced age of fifty-nine. His forced residence in Simbirsk lasted until 1837, when he too was permitted to recuperate in the Caucasus. Full pardon of his crimes was later obtained, and he even travelled abroad, visiting Herzen and Ogaryov in London. In his earlier years, during the 1830s, Satin made a considerable contribution to Russian verse, but after the middle 1840s he became silent. His verse is reminiscent in some degree of that of Venevitinov. He is particularly preoccupied with the theme of the poet's nature and mission, and the contrasting world views of the idealist and materialist.

Typical of Satin's poetry is "The Dying Artist" (1833),[79] which is the monologue of a young sculptor whom Satin imagines on his deathbed, mourning that he has been unable to complete his masterpiece, a "statue of religion":

And I dreamed: the moment of delight will come at last after all my labors, Inspiration will descend from heaven upon my soul, and my chisel will be obedient to me... It would happen that I, impatient to create, would summon all art to my aid, but vain was my self-loving labor, and in my creations I was conscious of a defect perceptible to me alone,—I could not transfer all my soul to them, upon them lay the

> seal of the earthly—but I desired to create the heavenly! Oh, a heavy thing it is with soul overfilled, to live among the children of cold earth! Not to have the power with mighty hand to show forth all the soul's feelings in one's creations!

Inspiration comes at last to the despairing sculptor:

> Once I, exhausted by my labors, laid my head upon my couch, and suddenly given wings by light slumber, I visited the supra-astral world of visions: there phantoms with airy beauty swirled in the form of a rainbow shroud, like a light swarm there were borne above me the free sons of fantasy.

Among these entrancing, but familiar creations of fancy suddenly appeared the heavenly one herself—Religion, here evidently a philosophical concept, a mystical communion with the Deity, in no way related to the ordinary meaning of the term. Awaking from his dream the sculptor in rapture succeeded in reproducing in stone the features of his heavenly model. But, alas, the vision faded before he could finish the statue—and now he faces death, which will forever destroy the possibility of completing his work. But at the last he sees himself transfigured: he will be transported to a sphere where there will no longer be any limitations to possibility, and another with love will take up his unfinished work and carry it to completion.

To all appearances Satin was an ecstatic dreamer with the most exalted notions of the function of the poet as a prophet commissioned by heaven to lead mankind out of the stagnation of its material life to a world of the spirit. He would seem to have been a sort of Lensky, totally disoriented in the real world, at home only in some misty sphere above the stars. Yet his verses give evidence that he had enough contact with reality to understand the nature of the "other life" that he personally shunned. The dialogue "The Poet"[80] (1835) presents a down-to-earth "friend" in conversation with a poet who is doubtless, like the "youth" of "The Poet's Repentance" an idealized self-portrait. The "friend" finds the "poet" in rapt meditation, from which he comes to with a start when a hand is laid on his shoulder. The friend asks: "Where have you been roving?" The poet replies:

> In a far-off region. And it seemed to me that I had abandoned the world below and the genius of the storm had snatched me away into fields of azure. Ether flowed at my feet, and the heavenly vault above my head glowed with sapphire blue; crowds of worlds around me burned with the flame of fire; flowing together into bright clusters, then scattering into the immensity. And the genius of the storm, my companion, abandoned the terrible face of the earth, clothed himself with the rays of the rainbow, and covered me with gilded pinions, pressed my lips and breathed rapture into my breast. Straightaway I understood the miraculous, and in sweet perturbation I fell before him: it was inspiration! And the genius infused my heart with joy, fledged me with winged dream—and launched me among the stars! I flew in infinity, I breathed proud freedom. I was enraptured by the heavens; my verse resounded like God's

thunder and poured out over the worlds like sunshine in the blue expanse... I lived, I felt!

To this ecstatic dithyramb the poet's friend opposes the realities of life:

> Dreamer! While you are soaring, friend, in the haze of the blue expanse, our age, long abandoned by dream, has been forging with iron hand greatness to the earth. Believe me, my friend, our cold age does not value the free dream. A despot, prosaist, it wants Apollo to throw away his lyre. It wants the favorite of Phoebus to come down from the heaven above and forgetting that a fire burns in his breast, to write about people's domestic life and the manners of society... Who is able to stand against the age? The time is past for writing verse: the demand of the age is prose, prose!

When the poet protests that it is not his fault that the Creator has endowed him with a sensitive soul and a natural propensity for poetry the friend replies:

> But, friend, you feel deeply, yet the human race has long since shut the window on feeling. Believe me, my friend, your free verse will not touch the cold mind of men; and the sounds of your golden lyre, that melody of wondrous harmonies, will die away like a sound in the empty distance, like a call in the midst of the desert steppe.

The poet has the last word: he instances Homer, Tasso and Camões as poets whose genius their own age failed to recognize, but whom subsequent ages have declared divine. "A terrible posterity will come, will pay tribute of reverence, and clothe his [i.e., the poet's] creations in the garb of bright incorruptibility." It is perhaps worth noting that in the second half of the 1830s Russian literature was in fact turning definitively to prose. Not to mention Pushkin, Lermontov and Gogol, even the secondary writers of the time, such as Veltman and K.P. Masalsky, were abandoning verse, and there was a notable decline in the quantity of verse published in the more popular journals of the day. Benediktov, in fact, seems to have been one of the few versifiers who continued to enjoy popularity during the period. We have seen how coolly a genuinely significant volume of verse, such as Baratynsky's *Twilights,* was received.

Satin, as we have noted, had been in his student years an intimate of the Herzen-Ogaryov circle, and even after leaving the University, continued to maintain a close friendship with these liberals, whose lives were to be devoted to combatting autocracy and serfdom. Satin, however, was not a fighter, and his mouthpiece the "Poet" in the piece of that name, speaks for him in claiming an innate and ineradicable penchant for poetry. Evidently, however, his temperamental incompatibility with political activism weighed on his conscience. In 1835 he composed a "fantasy" which he at first entitled "Resignation," after the Schiller poem which furnishes its theme, but later, and more suitably, called "The Poet's Repentance."[81] In letters to his friend Ketcher, who had rather adversely criticized the poem,

Satin makes clear that he and his lyric hero, the "youth," are not identical, and that he himself doubtless could not be capable of the heroic self-abnegation which he attributes to the former:

> On what basis have you undertaken to censure me for self-praise? On what basis have you concluded that my "youth" is I? Must the hero of a work necessarily be the author himself? Believe me, I know well my own shortcomings, my own weaknesses, and by no means rate myself . . . as high as I would like to rate my "youth." This "youth," if you like, is I, but an ideal I, cleansed of all shortcomings, invested with new merits, and consequently this "I" is a perfectly new, independent person, in no way to be confused with the real me. And why accuse me of self-praise, when in the whole piece I don't say a word about myself? Byron's Conrad (in his *Corsair*) is Byron himself, but Byron isn't Conrad! All the heroes of Byron's poems are Byrons, but Don Juan isn't Childe Harold, isn't Conrad, and so on. Byron clearly tells his reader not to confuse the *real him with the ideal him,* and even strophes in which he speaks of himself personally, he detaches as it were from the rest of the poem.

The fantasy is headed by a brief epigraph: "Faith without works is dead" (Epistle of James II, 26). The "youth" who is Satin's lyric hero, his idealized self, has withdrawn from the ungrateful and unfeeling crowd and is enjoying an idyllic existence in a beautiful rustic retreat, in company with his beloved, and happy in his god-given gift of poetry. His monologue begins with an account of his disillusionment with "the crowd": "I was then," he remarks, "filled with the conviction that the spirit of love binds all men, that he preserves in them the sparks of renewal, and builds them mausoleums of greatness." But now he has come to realize the hopeless gulf that lies between him and his fellow-men:

> Now farewell, family of my kindred brothers, farewell forever, farewell, you and I have no community of feelings, aspirations and conceptions; we were created with souls of different kinds! . . . I exhausted all the means of temptation, I kept repeating to them that deep in them is the wondrous imprint of predestination, and how worthless and pitiable is their life! But for them the summoning voice was incomprehensible, it was sweet for them to live under the burden of fate; in them there is no love and consciousness of their powers, and their name is—worthless slaves!

Having renounced the hopeless task of trying to reveal the ideal world to his materialist brothers, the youth has retreated to his "three friends," whom he celebrates lyrically: "the black-eyed maiden," who is his beloved; nature, which is for him "earnest of immortality, the source of eternal harmony," and the gift of poetry. He remembers "the gloomy poet, the poet of misty England," and his fate to be misunderstood by his own people; he breaks off with the exclamation: "But peace with your brethren, peace with you! Poet, your hopes have been fulfilled, and you yourself have been merged with your soul in the soul of the universal fabric! . . . " More than even Lord Byron, however, it is the great German romantic who has inspired Satin's youth:

> Schiller, limitless Schiller, long ago you told me of a blessed fatherland, of a
> kindred region! You proclaimed that for the poet with inspiration on his brow there is
> no familial greeting here, that he is a stranger on earth, that before him the deceptive
> glitter of the earthly realm has disappeared and that in heaven Zeus awaits him with
> open arms! I am a poet—wherefore sufferings? There is a fatherland, there is a father!
> There in rays of radiance the promised crown awaits me!

As the youth's monologue ends he hears the sounds of a harp and the voice
of his beloved singing. Her "romance" begins with the significant words:
"World of egoism, world of suffering, abandon, poet, without regret!" The
youth has already complained of the "egoism" of his unappreciative fellow-
mortals. At the end of her song he confirms his decision to live with his
"three friends" and be happy.

The second part of "The Poet's Repentance" introduces the "maiden"
and the "youth" in what Satin calls a "duodrama." At first the maiden's
caresses confirm the youth in his pleasure in having said farewell to his
fellow-men. In exaltation he feels that he is inspired to create great poetry:

> Hearken to me now, to the prophet of renewal: my word will proclaim blessed
> tidings, flow with speed together to the meeting-place [veche] of inspiration, while in
> me burns the fire of omniscience...Hearken!...(he suddenly stops, looks around
> him, and says quietly after a slight pause) Woe is me, vain are all summons, I have been
> withdrawn by fate far from men, who will hearken here to the word of prophecy? In
> whom will it here bring to life the extinguished fire of the passions?

It is in vain for the prophet to utter his words to rocks and trees—they
must be addressed to men. The maiden vainly reminds him of her love: he
replies: "Strong is my love for you, but there is another love: you, a weak
maiden, do not understand it! Yes, too broad are the arms of my soul: I
must embrace all mankind in them!" The maiden sings another "romance,"
the gist of which is a call for the most callous kind of selfishness and
disregard of others. Her lover is horrified and realizes at last that he and his
"black-eyed maiden" have little in common: "No, no, you and I pray to
different gods: yours demands a sacrifice, mine commands to sacrifice!"
Hoping to divert the youth from his dangerous train of thought, the maiden
leaves, saying that she will bring the youth's favorite poet, who may change
his mind. Alone, he meditates on the inconsistency of his conduct: he has
seen in the "sacred mirror of truth" as though written out, his own
condemnation: "Take leave of the creature that you love, and be once more
where are glory and shame! Did you dare to cast the stone of accusation,
and reproach men for their fall? You are an egoist, in the embraces of self-
indulgence, you are the pitiful slave of furious passions!" When the maiden
returns, he has decided that he must leave her and his other two "friends,"
nature and poetry, but still hesitates, knowing that his beloved's whole life
is wrapped up in him. She brings him a volume of Schiller's poems and bids
him read; he opens the book at random and reads:

Gieb mir das Weib, so teuer deinem Herzen,
Gieb deine Laure mir!
Jenseits der Gräber wuchern deine Schmerzen!
Ich riss sie blutend aus dem wunden Herzen,
Und weinte laut, und gab sie ihr![82]

The lines are from the poem "Resignation," and in their original context mean something rather different from the meaning that they assume in Satin's fantasy. Schiller's lyric hero, near the end of his life, imagines himself before the throne of eternity, never having enjoyed happiness in the world. The "divine child," called truth, demands first his youth, and then his beloved wife, with the promise: "I shall repay you in another life." The sacrifice is made with tears, and then begins the mockery of "the world": "For hopes ... you have given up *certain* goods? For six thousand years death has held his peace: has a corpse ever risen from the tomb to give you tidings of the recompenser?" The hero pays no attention to the mockery, but declares to his judge that he has sacrificed all, and would now claim his reward. A "genius" gives him the answer: "Two flowers.... bloom for the wise discoverer: they are named *hope* and *enjoyment*. He who has plucked *one* of the flowers may not desire the other sister. Let him enjoy, who cannot have faith. The teaching is as eternal as the world. He who can have faith must forbear ... You have *hoped,* your reward has been received; your *faith* was the happiness meted out to you!" In Satin's use of the passage, the "resigning" of earthly love, communion with nature and selfish poetical creation is not involved with any faith in a posthumous recompense, but is done with the intention of bringing enlightenment to fellow-men who are wandering in darkness. Heartened by the support of his favorite poet, the youth says farewell to his beloved, and professes himself ready, like his revered Dante, to follow his Virgil through hell and purgatory to Paradise: "I shall accomplish my predestination, I shall renounce everything: mate, glory, honor; I shall offer myself as a holocaust! Oh! the cross is heavy, but it must be borne!"

Evidently the idealistic self-abnegation of the youth in "The Poet's Repentance" represented only one side of Satin's nature. Accounts of the poet's later life picture him as a morose hypochondriac, a gambler and compulsive drinker. From the evidence of an 1841 piece, "Fragment from an Overheard Conversation,"[83] it would appear that Satin—if the "young man" of the "Fragment" is in any way a self-portrait—had elements of that typical nineteenth-century Russian phenomenon which takes its usual name from the title of one of Ivan Turgenev's stories, "the superfluous man." The "Fragment from an Overheard Conversation" is headed by an epigraph of eight lines from a monologue by Faust in *Faust: Part I,* of which the first two lines sum up the Young Man's situation:

Ich bin zu alt, um nur zu spielen, zu jung, um ohne Wunsch zu sein.

The "overheard conversation" takes place between a middle-aged doctor and his friend, the "young man." The latter has not slept well and is suffering, as the doctor soon discovers, from *khandra,* an ailment typical of the romantic, but with no very adequate modern English equivalent: the nineteenth-century British idiom called it "spleen," John Gay "the dumps"; a modern psychologist might speak of "chronic depression." The doctor tries to diagnose its characteristics:

> Tell me, what's your *khandra* for? It's an anachronism in this age! When all around you life is seething in contemporary man, when everything is straining, everything is rushing to embrace nature and the sciences, when both mind and spirit and hands—everything is animated with the genius of labor, you, like stagnant water, have gone stale with melancholy and boredom! Believe me, friend, life is good; in it mind and body and soul will easily find their proper place, only provided there's a little will-power. But if in life we blunder along an uneven path, as though in darkness,—it's not life that's to blame, but we!

The young man answers rather impatiently to this sensible diagnosis:

> Whether I'm to blame or life is to blame, or someone else,—it's all the same to me! I know only one thing for certain: that I'm alive, and I'm suffering, that each day that rises over me I meet with secret trepidation and pass with tears; that there are desires in my soul, that there is thirst for belief, there is love—and along with them the bitter realization that with every day I shall once more desire, be sad, strain toward something, feel doubts of myself and of life, and never....
> *Doctor.* Stop! Define your desires, give your life a purpose, your dreams a name, and what is impossible—renounce! To chase after a shadow, believe me, is in vain!
> *Young Man.* Yes, *renounce*!...Always the same old story, long since familiar to me!...What has bloomed so magnificently, so beautifully in the soul, what has been the breath of your life, what you have striven, suffered for—tear it all away! It's nothing but dreams! Sacrifice them to life, and then measure your desires according to your powers, as with a yardstick!—No, no! Leave me sufferings, in them is bliss—
> *Doctor.* Perhaps; but how reconcile life with them?
> *Young Man.* Oh, better to part with life! Without them what can life give me? *I am too old to be entertained, and too young not to desire!*

With this quotation from the *Faust* epigraph the "Overheard Conversation" ends. One thinks involuntarily of the confrontation between Alexander Aduev and his uncle in Goncharov's novel *An Ordinary Story.*

Pyotr Petrovich Yershov (1815-1869)

The case of P. P. Yershov is almost unique in Russian literature. Although his verse fills a modest volume in the *Poet's Library* series,[84] he is decidedly a *homo unius libri.* None of his later works approached with contemporaries the success of his *Konek-Gorbunok* ("Little Hunchback Horse"), and are hardly accorded even mention by modern critics.

Moreover, his "one book" was composed when the poet was eighteen and still a student at St. Petersburg University. The poem had four editions in Yershov's lifetime, and has been republished many times since; it is known and loved throughout Russia.

Yershov was born in Siberia, in a village near Tobolsk, and after graduation from the University returned to his native land, where he spent the rest of his life in the capacity of a dedicated but not overly successful teacher and educational administrator. His isolation from the literary circles of St. Petersburg and Moscow undoubtedly contributed to the paucity of his literary output, but without question the want of success of his later works was fully deserved. They are imitative and unoriginal.

"The Little Hunchback Horse," on the other hand, is original and reveals the best side of Yershov—his genius as a storyteller. The poem was undoubtedly inspired by Pushkin's *skazka,* "The Tale of Tsar Saltan," which had been published in 1832. Like the Pushkin *skazka,* it is a free reworking of several folklore motifs, and is composed in a swift-moving trochaic tetrameter with paired rhymes. The 2510 lines of the poem are divided into three parts, devoted to three major episodes in the story of Ivan the Fool and his magical "little hunchback horse."

Part One of the poem relates the background circumstances: how a peasant father and his three sons were plagued by a nightly visitor who devastated their field of wheat; how the two elder sons, who were both intelligent, i.e., practical fellows, failed to catch the marauder, while Ivan, "who was altogether a fool," i.e., a dreamer and impractical, succeeded in apprehending the culprit, a beautiful mare, which submitted to him and told him that in three days she would give birth to two such beautiful horses as had never been seen,—and a third, "a little horse, only three *vershki* in height [i.e., about six inches!], with two humps on his back and ears an *arshin* [28 inches] long." Ivan is bidden to sell the two beautiful stallions, but keep for himself the "little hunchback horse." The two elder brothers try to steal the two golden-maned stallions, but Ivan catches them with the aid of his little horse; the golden-maned pair are sold at length to the King, and Ivan becomes his groom.

Part Two continues with Ivan's story; earlier on Ivan and his miraculous little horse had found a feather which lights up the whole neighborhood like a fire. The little horse warned his master: "Here lies the feather of a Fire-Bird. But for your own happiness, do not take it. Much, much disquiet it will bring with it." Ivan disregarded the warning and put the feather inside his cap. When he becomes a groom in the King's stables, the *spal'nik* ("gentleman of the King's bedchamber") sees him as a rival and denounces him to the King as having in his possession a treasure that should be the King's, a Fire-Bird's feather. The King, seeing this treasure, demands on pain of death that Ivan get him the bird itself! The little horse reminds his master that this misfortune is the result of his own disobedience, but gives him advice which enables him to catch a Fire-Bird and bring it to the King in a gilded cage. The *spal'nik* continues his machinations, this time inciting the King to demand that Ivan bring him "the beautiful Tsar-Maiden," the daughter of the Moon and sister of the Sun. Again with the little horse's aid the exploit is accomplished. But all is not yet well. The King would marry the Tsar-Maiden, but she demands that first her ring be brought, which is on the bottom of the "pagan ocean," and naturally it is to Ivan that this feat is entrusted.

Part Two ends with the storyteller's words: "On the next day our Ivan, taking three onions in his pocket, and dressing himself quite warmly, seated himself on his little horse and rode off on his distant journey.—Give me, brothers, a chance to catch my breath!" Part Three relates the success of Ivan's third mission. On the banks of the Ocean he finds a stranded monster—*"Chudo-iudo ryba-kit"* ("Wonder-Monster Whale-Fish"), which has been banished from the ocean and lies off-shore, inert, impotent and despairing; on his back a village with woods and pastures has grown up. The little horse rouses the monster, tells of their mission, and enlists the Whale's aid on condition of their obtaining from the Moon or Sun the reason for its banishment. Ivan and the horse ride on to the place where earth meets sky, leave earth and continue their way to the dwelling-place of the Moon, who rather oddly is the Tsar-Maiden's mother, even though the word *mesiats* is masculine! Ivan addresses the Moon, who entertains him hospitably, as Mesiats Mesiatsovich ("Moon Moonovich") and receives the information that the Whale-Monster's banishment is due to his having swallowed three dozen ships, crews and all, without divine permission. If he will give them their freedom, he will be pardoned. The little horse hurries to the peasant village on the monster's back and gets that evacuated before the Whale returns to the Ocean. Then the Whale-Monster fulfills his part in the bargain, dives to the bottom of the sea and after a bit of doing obtains the aid of a school of herring, the ruff (*ërsh*) and some sturgeon, which bring the casket with the Tsar-Maiden's ring to the surface. Ivan and the little horse ride off with the treasure to the King's palace.

At this point the Tsar-Maiden balks: she will not marry an old man such as the King; he must first regain his youth, which can be done by submitting to being boiled! Prudently the King demands that Ivan first submit to the ordeal. The little horse gives his master an antidote to hot water, and he jumps into the boiling cauldron and comes out younger and handsomer than ever. The King is delighted and tries the same experiment, but of course is scalded to death. The Tsar-Maiden then announces that she will marry Ivan, and the people joyfully acclaim him King. Presumably he, the Tsar-Maiden and "the little hunchback horse" live happily ever after.

Many of the incidents in this fairy tale originate in a *skazka*, "The Fire-Bird and Princess Vasilissa," which is No. 103 in the collection of A. N.

Afanasiev.[85] Thus, the miraculous helper of "the young strelets" in the first version is "a bogatyr steed," of "the fine young fellow" in the second version, a *zherebёnochik*, "a tiny little stallion." Neither of these horses appears to have the two humps or the long ears of Ivan's steed, which are probably Yershov's addition. The "young strelets," like Ivan, finds a Fire-Bird's feather, is warned by the "bogatyr horse": "Don't take the golden feather; take it—and you'll know sorrow!" but takes it anyhow, with the predicted result. The place of the Tsar-Maiden is taken by Princess Vasilissa, and it is her wedding garments which must be fetched from under a large stone in the middle of "the blue sea." There is no "Wonder-Monster Whale-Fish" in the folk tale, which is probably a Yershov invention; its place is taken in the first version by a giant crab, in the second by a pike. The final episode in both versions is the same: "The King saw that he [the young strelets] had become such a handsome fellow, and wanted to try it himself; like a fool he got into the water and was boiled to death in a moment." This motif is unquestionably a genuine part of Russian folklore, in spite of its startling similarity to the classical Greek legend of Medea's disposal of Jason's usurping uncle Pelias.

Yershov's delightful poem owes much of its charm to the roguish humor with which the story is told, the straight-faced mingling of the fantastic and the commonplace, as in the scene in which the Tsar-Maiden's mother "Moon Moonovich" entertains Ivan, just as in a peasant's *izba*; and to the extraordinary speed of the narration, which never has a chance to become tiresome. Marxist critics regularly stress the Russianness of the tale and the evidence, e.g., the unflattering picture of the King, of the poet's "democratic" turn of mind. No doubt these are in fact qualities of the work, but neither the most distinctive nor contributing the most to the poem's long-lasting popularity. Needless to say, the language is strongly popular, and often even dialectal. The poet frequently employs typical folklore turns of phrase, such as: "Whether they ride near or far, whether high or low and whether they saw anyone, I know nothing [of this]. Speedily the tale is told—the business is carried out with difficulty" (lines 1729-34).

Yershov's other works, besides a number of quite banal romantic lyrics, consist of a long ballad, "The Siberian Cossack," on the *Lenore* theme of the ghostly bridegroom; a dramatic fragment, "Foma the Smith," a libretto for a "fantastic opera" called *The Terrible Sword*, and a narrative poem, *Suzgé*, "A Siberian Tradition," which deals with Yermak's conquest of Siberia, and the heroism of Suzgé, wife of Khan Kuchum. Of these only the last named has any literary interest.

IV

Mikhail Lermontov: Lyric Verse

Mikhail Lermontov occupies a peculiar position in Russian literature. His life was cut short at the early age of twenty-six, and his published work at that date consisted of one volume of lyrical verse, four narrative poems, and the novel *A Hero of Our Time.* Yet even when he was killed in 1841 he was already recognized as Pushkin's worthy successor, the second greatest poet of his age—and this verdict has seldom been put in question. Clearly he was an extraordinary genius. He was one of the least objective of writers: almost every work of his is intensely personal. Yet so little is really known of his inner biography, of the actual evolution of his world outlook, of his artistic creed, that the Soviet critic Boris Eikhenbaum[1] could say of him: "Lermontov, really, is an enciphered enigma" [*zashifrovan*].

The external facts of his biography are well enough known to require no considerable treatment. Born in 1814, he was the child of an unhappy marriage; his mother died when he was ten years old, and at the insistence of his maternal grandmother, she assumed responsibility for his upbringing, in view of his father's impecunious condition. Yury Lermontov died when his son was seventeen: there had been little contact between the two, but there was evidently a great deal of natural affection. Mikhail was educated in the Pension, or preparatory school for noblemen's sons, attached to Moscow University, had a short and unsatisfactory experience with the University itself, then migrated to St. Petersburg, where he enrolled in a training school for army officers. Upon completion of this uncongenial course he was commissioned, and served until 1837 as an officer in a Guards Regiment in the capital. His incendiary poem written on the occasion of Pushkin's death, "The Death of a Poet," brought government retaliation upon him. He was briefly exiled to the Caucasus, but his grandmother's efforts secured his recall. Several acts of folly—a notorious duel with the son of the French ambassador, in which neither party was injured was one—brought upon him another exile to the Caucasus. While waiting in Pyatigorsk for his grandmother and Zhukovsky to intervene for him again, he got into a silly quarrel with another officer, was challenged to a duel, and killed on June 15, 1841. Lermontov was never married, but his lyrics record a number of amorous infatuations, most serious of which seems to have been that for Natalya Fyodorovna Ivanova (1813-1875), daughter of the minor dramatist Fyodor F. Ivanov.

This affair began when the poet was sixteen, and seems to have been terminated by Natalya's decision to marry not Lermontov, but a friend of his. The semi-autobiographical tragedy *A Strange One*[2] records Lermontov's version of the episode. A second serious attachment was to Varvara Alexandrovna Lopukhina, sister of a university friend; numerous poems are addressed or dedicated to her, and she appears to have been the original of the Vera and perhaps also of the Princess Mary of *A Hero of Our Time*. Her marriage (the result of parental pressure) to N. F. Bakhmetev Lermontov regarded as a betrayal. All of Lermontov's letters to Varvara Lopukhina before her marriage were destroyed by order of her husband. Several friends played an important part in Lermontov's life: Svyatoslav Afanasyevich Raevsky (1808-1876), the novelist Vladimir Fyodorovich Odoevsky (1803-1869), the latter's cousin the young Decembrist poet Alexander Ivanovich Odoevsky (1802-1829), whom Lermontov met in the Caucasus, the Slavophile theorist Yury Samarin (1809-1876), the poetess Yevdokia Petrovna Rostopchina (1811-1858) et al. Among the poet's letters many are addressed to various women, some cousins and other relatives, among them Alexandra Mikhailovna Vereshchagina. In this connection it may be observed that nearly all the 51 letters of Lermontov which have so far been discovered are of a routine, factual nature, or else conventionally gallant epistles, often in French, to members of the opposite sex, carefully calculated to reveal nothing of the poet's serious thoughts and feelings. Nowhere in his letters does he, like Pushkin, reveal himself intimately to his correspondent. Neither his political views nor his literary theories are ever aired in the letters. This may be only an accident due to the very small number of letters extant, almost none of which is addressed to the poet's literary associates, but whatever the cause, it is one of the major reasons why Lermontov still remains "an enciphered enigma." It must also be remembered that, again unlike Pushkin, Lermontov was never involved in journalism and wrote no critical articles, either for publication or for his own eyes alone. Virtually everything that can be said about Lermontov's literary or philosophical positions has to be gleaned from his literary works; and since such material is seldom unequivocal, estimates of the writer's position have varied all the way from Dmitry Merezhkovsky's mystical interpretation to the earlier Soviet attempts to make him little more than a version of Mayakovsky, the poet of *agitki*. It hardly needs to be said that such extremes are ridiculous; but evidently with a poet such as Lermontov any critical opinion must, in the nature of things, be highly personal. The subject simply does not lend itself to an objective treatment.

Although Lermontov has fared better in the matter of English translations than most Russian romantics, comparably far less of his work is accessible in English than is the case with Pushkin. Some of his lyrics are available in prose translations in Obolensky's *Penguin Book of Russian*

Verse, and an extract from *The Demon.* Eugene Kayden, in *The Demon and Other Poems,* gives satisfactory verse translations of *The Demon, Mtsyri (The Novice)* and two other long narratives, together with less satisfactory versions of 65 lyrics, from 1829 to 1841. In Guy Daniels's *A Lermontov Reader* there is a small selection (19) of lyrics, in generally good verse translation, three complete narrative poems, together with portions of *The Novice,* the prose play *A Strange One,* and the unfinished prose novel *Princess Ligovskaya.* C. M. Bowra's *First* and *Second Books of Russian Verse* contain translations by various hands of twenty-three lyrics. There are several translations of *A Hero of Our Time,* of which Vladimir Nabokov's is the best. The tale *Shtoss,* Lermontov's last prose work, is available in a translation by David Lowe,[3] and the unfinished youthful novel *Vadim* has been translated by Helena Goscilo.[4] Quantitatively this is not a great deal; Lermontov's lyric verse comes to some 365 pieces, exclusive of translations and disputed poems; his narrative poems number 27, several of them only fragmentary and incomplete; to this it must be added that *The Demon* is known in no less than eight separate versions, partial or complete. There are seven plays, *Masquerade* in two quite different versions; of these we have Roger Phillips's translation of *Masquerade* (*RLT,* no. 7) and Daniels's translation of *A Strange One.* The bulk of the untranslated narrative verse, however, belongs to the early years, when Lermontov was from fourteen to eighteen years old; the five best narrative poems have been translated entire, but *Sashka,* a first-rate, although possibly incomplete, narrative, is unavailable.

There is a puzzling feature about Lermontov's attitude toward his own work. He began writing verses when he was fourteen, and from then until he left officer's training school at twenty he wrote nearly two-thirds of all the lyrics that he was ever to write. Yet almost none of this mass of material was ever published in his lifetime—and indeed, it is very evident that had he lived, it never would have been published. It is, to be sure, immature verse and in no way comparable with what he composed after 1834—but it is quite comparable with almost anything that was being written *and published* by most of the poets of the 1830s, even much older than he. Only two explanations of this peculiar circumstance are possible: either Lermontov wrote only as a private diversion, never intending the results to be seen outside of a very small circle of intimates; or else he was extraordinarily self-critical. All the evidence indicates that the second is the true explanation. There are plenty of references in the unpublished early verses to the young poet's thirst for fame, which would hardly have come to him from the minuscule circle in which they were seen. Moreover, the theme of the poet as prophet, so common among the romantics, appears in his verse as in that of Küchelbecker, Pushkin and many others. A prophet has to have an audience, as Satin's "repentant poet" was to realize. When Lermontov's notebooks were examined after his death and most of the unpublished material put out in the posthumous edition of 1842, Belinsky defended the action against hostile critics by remarking:[5] "Poets such as Lermontov are stricter toward themselves than their strictest and most exacting critics." He goes on to say that Lermontov had no reason when his 1840 collection of poems was published to expect an early death, and hence would reasonably have viewed what he had written before about 1837 as so inferior to what he believed he would write subsequently that it might best be forgotten. This is in all probability the correct appraisal of the situation.

Since the 1842 edition of Lermontov's complete works, it has been traditional to present him, either in an edition or in a critical study such as this, as first a lyric poet, with a division around 1834 between "early" and "late" verse; second as the composer of long narrative poems; third, as dramatist; and fourth, as prose novelist. Although the division presents some difficulties, it is roughly chronological as regards the sequence of the poet's literary interests, and is less confusing than the alternative would be, of taking the entire *oeuvre* chronologically, especially as precise dates of composition are in many cases impossible to determine. Some cross references from one category to another will of course be necessary from time to time.

Lermontov's Early Lyric Verse (1828-34)

The concerns of any poet are two: his own inner world of thought and feeling; and the world about him, which includes both other beings like himself and his relations with them, and the world of external nature. Any beginning poet, however, is likely to start, if he has had any exposure to them, with the realm of books and with imitations of other poets' work. Lermontov is no exception. Although we know very little about his early reading, evidences from the works that he translated indicate that besides Russian poets, especially Pushkin, his favorites were German, especially Schiller and Goethe, and above all English, preeminently Shakespeare (he translated the scene of the three witches from Schiller's version of *Macbeth* at the age of fifteen) and Byron. He outgrew direct imitation of Byron by the time he was twenty, but the indirect influence of that arch-romantic remained with him all his life.

Lermontov's earliest extant work belongs to 1828, when he was fourteen. He was a boy of extraordinary sensitivity and a brilliant mind, and he had done a great deal of reading. This is evident in the four pieces from 1828, which are good imitations of current themes of elegy ("Autumn," "The Pipe") and "light" or "anthology verse" ("Cupid's Mistake"). In "The Pipe"[6] he assumes the persona of an aging and classical singer: "There once my lost love nurtured my heart and agitated my blood!... All has now disappeared; but you are left me, comfort of the suffering, salvation in quietness, O beloved memory, sacred to the soul!" "The Pipe" has many verbal echoes of Batyushkov. Even in this period of overt imitation, however, some of the traits of the mature poet come through, e.g., the quite surprising insight into the nature of "inspiration," which "The Poet" shows. One may note also the ability to pack a great deal into a single line, e.g., the last of "Cupid's Mistake": "Those who are the most submissive, on them falls the blame!"[7]

Elegies or epistles to friends, in the early romantic mode, constitute the first genuinely personal verse of Lermontov. "A Dedication. N. N."[8] is a good example. On the autograph of the poem Lermontov wrote, at some later time, "On the occasion of a quarrel with Saburov." Saburov was a school friend, apparently of a rather flighty disposition. "Here, friend, are the fruits of my careless Muse," the fifteen-year-old poet begins: "I am bringing you as a gift a fine shading of my feelings, even though you have despised the ties of sacred friendship, even though you have rejected the ardor of my soul. I know you: you are fickle, reckless, and a false friend has already enticed you into his toils. But remember, the path to happiness is difficult from that land where vice is king...." The piece ends with more dark hints and dire threats. Naive and childish though it is, it gives evidence of some psychological acumen on the poet's part; and thematically, at least, it is original.

Lermontov was a moody, introspective youth, evidently touchy and hypersensitive, and to judge from his own verse professions, doomed by his nature to loneliness. The commonest theme in his early verse is people's lack of understanding and his resulting sense of isolation. Sometimes this theme is dramatized in Byronic fashion by the projection of the lyric persona as an outcast, or especially, as the mythical figure of that quintessential outcast, the "demon." The earliest appearance of this figure is in a short piece from 1829 entitled "My Demon,"[9] evidently inspired, though quite differently treated, by Pushkin's poem of the same title, published in 1824. To the year 1829 belongs also the earliest of Lermontov's sketches for the narrative poem *The Demon,* which he completed only in the year of his death, 1841. The 1829 piece has some characteristic Byronic traits:

> His element is the totality of evil. As he is borne amid the misty clouds, he loves the fateful storms and the foaming of rivers and the noise of forests. Amid the yellow, scattered leaves stands his invisible throne. Upon it, among the muted winds, he sits gloomy and sombre. He implants distrustfulness, he has contempt for pure love, he rejects all prayers, he looks indifferently on blood, and he stifles the sound of lofty feelings with the voice of the passions, and the Muse of gentle inspirations shuns his unearthly eyes.

It may be noted that Pushkin's is a Mephistophelean demon, "The spirit that ever denies," the deflater of all lofty feelings with the dry voice of cynical reason. Lermontov's is a rebellious figure, whose favorite haunt is the storm: he hates repose and harmony, and it is with "the voice of the passions," not of reason, that he drowns out "the sound of lofty feelings." We shall often encounter such a figure in Lermontov's verse; perhaps the most famous embodiment is in "The Sail": "And he, rebellious, seeks the storm, as though in storm were repose!"[10]

In Lermontov's lyrical verse, after the very earliest, traditional genre distinctions are entirely meaningless.[11] Content, rather than form, must determine classification. It is possible on the basis of content to distinguish roughly three groups of pieces here, although very often, and increasingly as the poet matures, one such group encroaches on another and merges with it. These subject groupings are: poems of a philosophical, religious or existential introspection; poems of a social or political, usually critical, cast; and poems dealing with intimate personal relationships, chiefly love. Outside these categories are the relatively few pieces among the early verse which are fully objective in character, in which the poet assumes a persona remote from his own time or place, e.g., "Pan" (1829) or "Georgian Song" (1829).

"My Demon" belongs, of course, to the first, which is also the largest, of the three groupings. Another rather notable one, from the same year (1829) is "Monologue."[12] Here the general reflection on human life merges with a particular criticism of the lot of "the children of the north." The theme is given in the first line: "Believe: insignificance is a good in the world we're in," and the final two sum up the conclusion: "And bitter for us is the cup of chilly life; and *nothing* delights the soul." To the same year, when Lermontov was fifteen, belongs the first of the three poems entitled simply "Prayer."[13] This is a plea to the Almighty to forgive the young petitioner his attachment to earthly life, the "wild agitations" of his soul, and the "sinful songs" which often impede his prayer. Significantly, the last supplication is: "From the terrible thirst of singing [i.e., verse writing] let me be freed, O Creator," How sincere this plea was cannot, naturally, be said; fortunately, in any case, the Almighty ignored it.[14]

There are in Lermontov's work three rather long meditations, headed simply "Night," and all written in 1830. "Night" is of course a common romantic theme (e.g., Novalis), going back to Edward Young's *Night Thoughts*. Lermontov's "Nights" are, however, visions of terror rather than the sombre but comforting Youngian dreams. "Night I"[15] is connected with Byron's "Darkness" ("A Dream," 1819) which Lermontov, according to a note made to himself,[16] intended to translate in prose for his cousin Alexandra M. Vereshchagina. Byron's poem is a vision of intolerable darkness in a world without sun or moon: Lermontov dreams that he has died, and his soul is condemned by an angel to remain for his sins with the decaying body in the tomb until the Second Coming. Just before the tortured soul cries out in blasphemy, the dreamer wakes. The poem is ostentatiously horrifying, e.g., "With despair I sat and watched as the insects swarmed and avidly devoured their food; the worm now crept out of my eye-sockets, now hid itself again in the disfigured skull, and its every movement tore me with convulsive sickness." The climax comes in the final words: "Then I hurled wild curses at my father and mother, at all men—and the thought flashed through my mind (a creation of hell): what if time shall accomplish its course and be sunk irrecoverably in eternity, and there is nothing to give me peace, and they do not come hither to forgive me?... And I was minded to pronounce blasphemies against Heaven, but my voice died—and I awoke."

The second "Night"[17] is shorter but no less harrowing. The dreamer sees the heavens overshadowed by a huge skeletal apparition which announces itself as Death. It mocks the dreamer's terror, reminding him how often he has called upon Death in the past. But in his grasp he holds two persons dear to the poet, and gives him the choice: one of them must die, but he may save the other. Startlingly, the despairing answer is:

> [Take] both, both!... I believe: there is no reunion, there is no parting!... They have lived sufficiently for their punishment to continue eternally. Oh! Take me too, an earthly worm—and break the earth to pieces, the nest of vice, of madness and of sorrow!... All, all it takes from us by deceit and gives us nothing, save birth!... A curse on this gift!—without it we should never know thee, and so also [we should never know] poor futile life, in which there is no hope, and danger everywhere. Let my dear ones perish, let them perish!... Only for one thing will I still weep: why are they not children!...

"Night III"[18] is not a philosophical piece, but an unfinished elegy, introducing an enigmatic hero simply as "he." "And who is *he?* Who is he, this destroyer of sleep? With what is this rebellious breast filled? Oh, if you could but guess in his eyes what he is minded to conceal! Oh, if but a single poor friend might be able to soften the malady of his soul." It is evident that "he" is the poet himself.

Of the themes which the youthful Lermontov treats in his philosophical verses that of the meaning (or meaninglessness) of life, and of the place of man in the scheme of things is certainly the commonest. A black pessimism is his habitual attitude, as in the first and second "Night." Sometimes there is a hint of hope that the bleak human fate will in some remote future be brightened. Thus, in "Fragment" (1830)[19] the poet in the second strophe states his own situation: "A flame not of earth has been preserved in me since my days of babyhood. But fate has decreed that it perish, as it has lived, in silence. I firmly expected its fruits, loving to converse with myself. The sound of my heart's words will grow still: alone, alone I shall remain." In the third strophe the "fruits" of this "flame not of earth" (i.e., the gift of poetry) are specified as "secret meditations" for which the poet has neglected "the path of love and the path of fame." But omnipotent death poisons everything; the lyric hero cries: "Gaze on my brow, look into my eyes, into their pallid hue; my face could not tell you that I am fifteen years old!" But the last three strophes of "Fragment" (which are translated in Kayden's collection under the title "This World of Loneliness"[20]) envisage a happier future humanity, who "will not curse," and whose "days will flow as innocent as those of children." "But we shall behold this Paradise of earth, chained above the abyss of darkness," and our punishment "for whole ages of wickedness" will be an eternity of envy and regret.

The poet's criticism of life in one exceptional poem[21] is balanced by a confident assertion that the innate desire for good in human souls must have been implanted by the Creator and is a clear indication that in some future they will have fulfillment:

> If the Creator had condemned us to live in the submission of ignorance, He would not have put unrealizable desires into our souls. He would not have allowed us to strive toward that which was not to be accomplished. He would not have allowed us to seek perfection in ourselves and in the world, if we were not to know perfect blessedness forever.
>
> But [as it is] there is in us a holy feeling, hope, the god of future days,—it is in the soul, where everything earthly lives, in despite of passions; it is an earnest that in heaven or in another wilderness there is such a place where love will appear before us, like a tender angel, and where the soul will be unable to know again the rebellious longing for it.

As the writer of the entry in the *Lermontov Encyclopedia* remarks:[22] "This [poem] explains in many ways the depth and force of Lermontov's doubt and negation—as the parameters within which youthful hopes, faith and ideals were born, and with the elimination of which these were tragically lost." Any such happy place, where true love may exist, is of course either "in heaven" or in "some other wilderness" like that of earth; here any hope of such a thing is vain. Such is the burden of "The Cup of Life" (1831).[23]

The romantic's yearning to transcend the trammelling weaknesses of human existence is beautifully and succinctly expressed in "Sky and Stars,"[24] where as usually with Lermontov, "stars" serve as symbols of the unattainable ideal:

> The evening sky is clear, the distant stars are bright, bright as a child's happiness: oh! wherefore may I not think: stars, you are bright as my happiness!
>
> "Why are you unhappy?" people will say to me. This is why I am unhappy, good people, because the stars and the sky are stars and sky! and I am a man!...
>
> Men nurture envy of each other; but I, on the contrary, envy only the beautiful stars, would fain take their place.

Although Lermontov's attitude toward life is a negative one in most of the early poems, there are exceptions, when it appears that life may be worth living in spite of everything. "My Home"[25] declares that: "There is a sense of justice in the heart of man, the sacred seed of eternity," and the wide and beautiful world which is "my home" is built for this sense, even though I am condemned to suffer in it. As in the poem beginning "If the Creator had condemned us to live . . . " examined above, "My Home" views the sense of justice innate in the human being as implanted by the Creator; but there is nothing about the corollary that this innate desire must have satisfaction in a future life. Instead, the conclusion is that a Stoic acceptance of this life of injustice is man's only choice: "And the Almighty has built my beautiful home for this sense [of justice], and I am condemned to suffer long in it, and in it only shall I be at rest." In the last lines of a poem "To a Friend" (1829)[26] the poet declares: "I too in days gone by have soared in soul toward the lofty, in rapture of living thoughts; but to me the sufferings of earth are dearer: I have become used to them, and do not leave them." Perhaps the most striking formulation of the poet's attachment to the world of the here and now is the poem "Earth and Heaven" (1830-31):[27]

> How should we not love earth more than heaven? Heavenly happiness is obscure to us; though earthly happiness may be a hundred times less, yet we know what it is.
>
> To recollect hopes and torments that have been, a secret inclination seethes in us; the unreliability of earthly hopes disquiets us, and the beauty of sorrow delights us.
>
> The dark distance of the future is terrible to the soul in the present; we would desire bliss in heaven, but we regret to part with the earth.
>
> That which is in our control is pleasanter to us, though we seek at times for something other; but at the hour of parting we see more clearly how it has become akin to the soul.

Lermontov's attitude toward religion, like so much in his world view, is somewhat ambiguous. "Earth and Heaven" expresses an unquestioning faith in the reality of a future of posthumous bliss, even though we earthly creatures prefer to postpone its enjoyment. It is evident also from other poems, e.g., "The Angel,"[28] the three "Prayers" (1829, 1837, 1839), etc., that he was a believing Christian, but it is equally evident from much else in his verse that his beliefs could hardly be regarded as either Orthodox or orthodox. The official church is no less guilty than the state of bigotry, hypocrisy and inhumanity.

One of the most striking of Lermontov's psychological traits, as we see from his life as well as from his verse, was a turbulent and restless spirit, for which repose was tantamount to stagnation and inner death. His famous and much-anthologized poem "The Sail"[29] is the classical expression of this aspect of his personality: the sail—"rebellious, seeks the storm, as though in storm were repose." Another poem from the same year (1832) voices the same longing for action and combat, this time without the symbolic disguise:[30]

> I want to live! I want sorrow in despite of love and happiness; they have coddled my mind and too much smoothed my brow. It's time, it's time to the jeers of

the world to drive away the fog of quietness; what is the poet's life without suffering? And what is the ocean without storm? *He* [i.e., the poet] desires to live at the price of torment, at the price of exhausting cares. He buys the sounds of heaven [i.e., his verses], he does not win fame for nothing.

Many of Lermontov's early poems refer to his longing for fame—a puzzling attitude in view of his evident reluctance to commit his verse to print. Fame, he admits, in the poem of that name (1830-31) is not eternal, but he still ardently desires it:[31]

> To what end do I seek for fame? It is evident there is no bliss in fame, but yet my soul desires to reach perfection in everything. Penetrating the murk of the future, she [i.e., my soul] suffers, powerless, and in the present encounters everything otherwise than as she would wish it. I would not fear judgment if I were confident that the world through the ages would not with calumnies offend [my] inspired labor; that [men] would come to believe and heed the tale of [my] bitter torment, and not dare to equate the living sounds of heaven with the earthly. But I shall not attain in anything that which so disquiets me; everything is brief on the earthly globe, and fame cannot live forever. What though posterity illumine with praise the poet's sorrowful dust—where is fame in brief eulogies? Man's falsity is well known. Another with his lofty song will cause to be forgotten the singer who has ceased to live, who loved so all alone.

The great majority of Lermontov's early poems are short in scope and are constructed around only one or two themes. A striking exception is the 32-stanza poem named simply for the day (presumably) when it was composed, or at least begun—"June 11, 1831."[32] The poem defies a classical genre classification: it is in octains, rhyming ABABCCDD; all the rhymes are masculine, as with a number of the 1830 poems. It has been suggested[33] that Byron's "Epistle to Augusta" served Lermontov as a model for this poem, both metrically and thematically. Byron's poem is in octave stanzas of the usual sort, which normally in English have exclusively masculine rhymes. It is less than half as long as Lermontov's piece (16 strophes), is addressed to a definite person (the poet's sister) and although it is psychologically revealing of Byron's personality, it is thematically far less varied and inclusive than the Russian poem. Byron gave his piece a genre title—"Epistle"—and the content is fully appropriate to that eighteenth-century variety. Lermontov made no attempt to classify his work, but probably "meditation" would come closest to defining the character of the piece. In it the poet touches one after another on most of the themes which appear individually in the rest of his work. Although obviously devoid of external unity, the picture of the lyric hero which emerges contributes an inner cohesion. It is a remarkable document.

It begins with the poet's profession that from childhood's days he has loved "all the enchantments of the world, but not the world." In the world he has known real life only for moments; but these moments have peopled his dreams. In a short hour he has lived lifetimes; the figures of his dreams are altogether unlike the beings of earth: "everything in them was hell or heaven." The third strophe voices the age-old complaint of the poet that cold common words are powerless to convey "the desire for blessedness"; yet he would gladly sacrifice life itself to be able to impart even a shadow of what he has experienced to another. The theme of glory returns in the fourth strophe:

> Notoriety, fame, what are they?—but they have dominion over me; and they bid me sacrifice everything to them. And I drag out tormenting days without a goal, slandered, solitary; but I trust them! An unknown prophet has promised me immortality, and, living, I have surrendered to death everything that was a gift of earth.

The fifth strophe begins: "But for the heavenly there is no tomb." The poet's dreams may be revered by the world when he is dead. And his beloved too shall know immortality. "Men are just toward the dead," and "the son will bless what the father cursed." But man's life is no longer lasting than a flower's: "Only the soul alone must outlive its cradle." And so too the soul's creations. Then comes a rather conventional description of the poet meditating on a river bank and watching the flowing waves. "Then I was happy... Oh, if I might forget the unforgettable! A woman's look!" But "the sorrowful phantom of former days is always alive." In the ninth stanza the thought of the beloved who has not returned his love leads the poet to a Byronic self-characterization:

> No one on earth holds me dear, and I am a burden to myself as to others; melancholy strays across my brow. I am cold and proud; and to the crowd I even seem malicious; but may the crowd penetrate boldly into my heart? Wherefore should it know what is locked therein? Whether there is fire there or darkness, it is all the same to it.

The poet resorts to a simile to clarify the mystery of his being—the cloud in which is concealed the swift-striking lightning bolt—"and who shall explain its source, and who shall look into the depths of the clouds?"

Suddenly, with stanza 11, a new theme is introduced—disquiet about a future life: "When I shall end my life, where will my soul be condemned to wander, in what region shall I meet with the objects of my love?" But no one has returned that love: "And with anguish I see that to love as I do is a vice, and I see that to love more feebly I have not been able." Most people do not trust love, and in this they are happy: "but for me to love is a necessity; and I have loved with all the intensity of my soul's powers." Even disillusionment has been unable to break the habit of love; just as a birch-tree that has taken root in a crevice of a ruined wall, and is buffeted by storm and parched by heat, but still clings firmly to its foothold: "So only in a broken heart can passion have limitless dominion." The proud soul does not tire beneath the burden of being, nor grow cold." Such a soul "breathing vengeance against the unconquerable" is capable of doing much evil, though it could make thousands happy. "With such a soul you are either a god or an evildoer."

Stanza 16 is purely descriptive—the picture of the free and boundless steppe which the hero has always so loved. The picture is carried into the next strophe in a powerful figure:

> And the thought of infinity, like a giant, suddenly strikes the mind of man, when the shoreless ocean of the steppes is blue before his eyes; every sound of the universal harmony, every hour of suffering or of gladness becomes intelligible for us, and we are able to render ourselves account of our own fate.

The scene changes from the steppe to sunset in the high mountains. Contemplating the scene, "the heart is full, full of years gone by." The dreams of the poet are almost as beautiful as the reality. In stanza 20 it is again a natural scene that evokes an observation on the human condition. The sight of the changeless snow-clad mountain-peaks, unscathed by the lightning that plays around them, calls forth the aphorism: "He who is close to heaven is not harmed by the earthly."

Once more the steppe landscape recurs in stanza 21: it is mournful, an endless, unobstructed expanse where the silvery feather-grass waves in the wind, and the human gaze is met only by two or three forlorn birch trees. Again the mood of nature is interpreted in human terms: "just so tiresome is life, where there is no struggle." "I must have action," the poet cries, "I would immortalize every day like the shade of a great hero; I cannot understand what it means to rest." Here once again is the theme of "The Sail."

The same train of thought continues in the succeeding stanzas: something in the poet's soul is always seething and ripening—but life is so short—will it be possible to accomplish anything? "The thirst for life is stronger in me than fate-inflicted sufferings." But the time comes when "the swift mind grows icy." This is a "half-world, betwixt gladness and sorrow," when "life is hateful, but death is terrible." The root of your torment, however, is in yourself: "heaven cannot be blamed for everything." "I am used to this condition," the poet continues in stanza 25, "but to express it clearly the tongue of neither angel nor demon has been able." Angel and devil know no such perturbations: "only in man could the blessed meet with the accursed. All his torments come from this"—a sentiment clearly echoing the doctrines of Friedrich Schelling.

No man has ever attained all that he desired; and if one whom heaven has destined to be fortunate looks back over his past, he must confess that he might have been more fortunate if destiny had not poisoned his hopes. "But the wave has no power to return to the shore." Pursued by the fateful storm, seething and foaming, the wave always remembers the quiet gulf of its birth. It may find such another gulf, but—"he who has roamed the seas will not fall asleep in the shade of the cliffs of the shore."

In stanza 28 the poet suddenly abandons the nature imagery which he has used through so much of the rest of the poem, and addresses himself:

> I foreknew my lot, and upon me is the early seal of grief; how I am tormented, only the Creator knows, but the indifferent world must not know. I shall not die forgotten. My death will be terrible: foreign regions will wonder at it, and in my native land all will curse even the memory of me.

What lies behind this strange prophecy is hard to say. Lermontov seems to have been dreaming here of some heroic, revolutionary action; but if all in his native land are to curse even his memory, it is clear that this action cannot be such a self-sacrificing exploit for the good of his people as the Decembrist poets sometimes envision. The tone of the stanza suggests rather the warped and sinister figure of Vadim, in the unfinished novel of that name, and in the melodramatic vision of his end, the object of universal malediction, there is a suggestion also of "The Demon."

Abruptly stanza 29 contradicts the last line of the preceding: "All. No, not all: there is one creature capable of loving—though not me." This creature (*sozdan'e*—intentionally neuter, to conceal the sex) pays no heed to public opinion, and will remember the prophecy and shed an idle tear. There follows a description of the poet's "bloody tomb, a tomb without prayer and without cross," in the untenanted wilderness. Here some young stranger will sometimes pause in sympathy, and say: "Why did the world not understand the great one? How is it that he found himself no friends, and that love's greeting brought no hope to him again? He was deserving of it." The stranger will meditate thus, and look afar "and see the clouds with the azure of the waves, and a white sail, and a scudding boat." The emphasis on "the white sail and the scudding boat" is significant, recalling immediately the theme of the poem "The Sail," though that poem was actually written only in the following year (1832).

The final (32nd) stanza returns to the poet's imagined fate:

> And [he will see] my grave-mound! my beloved dreams are like this. There is a sweetness in everything not realized,—there are beauties in such scenes; only to transfer them to paper is difficult: the thought is powerful when it is not constricted by the measure of words, when it is as free as the play of children, as the sound of the harp in the silence of night.

The theme of an early death is one of the most pervasive of Lermontov's themes. Most commonly, even in his extreme youth, he views death as a welcome escape from the stupid and indifferent world. The poem "Death" [*Oborvana tsep' zhizni molodoi,* 1831-32][34] is typical. It is time, the young poet writes, to "go home, to where there is no future, nor past, nor eternity, nor years; where there are neither expectations nor passions, nor bitter tears, nor fame, nor honors; where memory sleeps a deep sleep, and the heart in its confined sepulchral home does not feel the gnawing of the worm." He asks himself whether he will be lured toward life again by "the clamor of soulless satisfactions, or the tortures of fruitless thoughts, or the self-loving crowd that is stupid from its wisdom, or by the perfidious love of maidens." "Shall I long to live again so as to suffer in soul once more, and love as much? Almighty God, Thou knowest: I could no longer endure; what though all hell should seize me, what though I should be tormented—I am glad, I am glad, though it should be twice as much as in former days, so it be only far, far from people." In its almost hysterical loathing of humanity this has something pathological. Fortunately this mood is not always with him; one might be inclined to label it a Byronic pose, were it not that the pieces which Lermontov wrote at this date were never published in his lifetime nor meant to be. Could the poet have posed before himself?

The influence of Byron is everywhere apparent in these early verses as it is even more strikingly in the narrative poems of the period. "No, I am not Byron, I'm another," he declares in one well-known piece.[35] Like the English poet, he feels himself a stranger and an outcast—but his is "a Russian soul." He equates his thoughts, rather grandiosely, with the ocean's mysteries, and at the end of the poem asks: "Who shall tell my thoughts to the crowd? I—or God—or no one!"

Lermontov's contemptuous and hostile attitude toward "the crowd" or "the mob" is Byronic and characteristic of many romantics, but is in the sharpest possible contrast to the humanitarian ideology of the Decembrist poets. Yet there are a few, and rather important, pieces among Lermontov's early verse that may be classified as political or social in theme. The earliest such is "The Turk's Complaint" (1829):[36] "the Turk" who so bitterly describes the land where "at times minds are as cold and hard as rock," where "early the quiet flame of good goes out" in men, where "man groans from slavery and chains," and then exclaims: "Friend! That land is my fatherland!" is of course the fifteen-year-old poet himself. But there is nothing in the conventional mention of "slavery and chains" to indicate that Lermontov was animated, now or later, by the dream of combatting serfdom. As a matter of fact, he may have had an abstract sympathy for the oppressed peasant class, but he knew them not at all, as Pushkin did. Lermontov's despised "crowd" is the class to which he himself belongs, and the tyranny which rouses him to a prophetic vision in the famous "Prophecy" (1830)[37] is the military and bureaucratic regime under which he himself chafes, not the slavery of Russia's peasantry. His feelings of indignation at the insensitive "citizen" who is not even aware of his servitude is expressed forcefully in "The Bard's Song" (1830).[38] Using as his persona a medieval bard returning to his homeland, now enslaved to the Tatars, he writes:

Who could sing a single song? Having tuned the trembling strings with a despairing movement of my hands, it would happen that I wrung out a sound: but it died away so soon! And if it was heard by the son of chains, the groaning of perishing freedom did not touch his ears.

Of a sudden someone asked me: Why do I so often shed tears where man lives so free? Of whom do I strum my string, of whom do I sing? This speech pierced me through and through. The last swarm of hopes fell dead. I hurled my *guzla* to the ground and in silence shattered it with my foot.

The theme of the poem's last line obviously reflects Thomas Moore's "The Minstrel Boy": "The harp he loved ne'er spoke again, for he tore its chords asunder." Nikolai Yazykov's 1823 poem "Song of a Bard in the Time of the Tatar Dominion in Russia" served Lermontov also as a model, as O. V. Miller notes in the *Lermontov Encyclopedia* (p. 409). For both poets the "Tatar Yoke" is associated with the contemporary scene.

Similar in inspiration is the fragment that begins "Three nights I passed without sleep" (1831),[39] which was intended by the poet to form part of a narrative based on the struggle of Mstislav the Black against the Tatars.[40] The date assumed for the action of the poem would be 1238 when the defense of the city of Vladimir took place. Lermontov's note apropos of the projected poem begins: "Mstislav prays for three nights on the Kurgan, that the beloved name of Russia may not perish." In the course of Mstislav's monologue he says: "What though I may not accomplish my intent, yet it is great, and that is enough: my hour has come—the hour of glory or of shame: I shall be immortal, or forever forgotten." The monologue takes on a romantic coloration when the prince speaks of his relations with "Nature":

I questioned Nature, and she took me into her arms; in the cold forest at the terrible moment of the snow-storm I drank sweetness from her bewitching lips. But for my desires the world was empty—they saw no object in it for themselves. I often bent my gaze upon the stars, and upon the moon, the night skies' ornament, but felt I was not born for them...But having lost fatherland and freedom, I suddenly found myself, in myself alone I found salvation for the whole people, and I plunged with my entire mind into one sole thought, perhaps vain and unprofitable for my native land, but, pure and beautiful as hope, strong as freedom and as holy.

Doubtless the thoughts attributed to the thirteenth-century Mstislav are those of the poet himself, but it should be noted that the thirst for fame and immortality plays a far greater part in his motivation than does any concern for his people's salvation. The purpose for which he comes may be "vain and unprofitable" for his native land; but for himself it may prove the source of posthumous glory.

Another historical figure whom Lermontov apparently thought of at one time as a mouthpiece for thoughts of his own was the Livonian nobleman Johann Reinhold Patkul (1660-1720), whose letters, written from prison before his execution by Charles XII, were published in Moscow in 1806. Patkul is the real hero of Lazhechnikov's novel *The Last Novik,* published in 1831, and the romanticized picture of his career which the novelist gives is doubtless the inspiration for Lermontov's fragment "From Patkul" (1831).[41] Patkul is the imagined speaker:

> Vain is the enormous malice of my enemies. God will be our judge, and the traditions of the people. Though separated by Destiny, let us both battle for happiness and the glory of our fatherland. What though I perish... close to the darkness of the tomb, insensible of fear, unknowing chains, my spirit shall soar ever higher and higher and be blown like smoke over the iron roof!

The fragment is apparently thought of as part of a letter addressed to one of Patkul's fellow-fighters against Sweden—perhaps his mistress Rosa, perhaps even Peter the Great.

The most impressive of Lermontov's earlier political verses is entitled: "July 30, 1830 (Paris)."[42] It is addressed to the Bourbon king Charles X, dethroned and exiled by the "July Revolution." The poem, of four eight-line stanzas, is in foor-foot iambic lines, with exclusively masculine rhymes—a device probably learned from Zhukovsky, which contributes a particularly energetic effect:

> You might have been a better king; you did not choose[to be],—you thought you could subdue the people under the yoke, but you did not know the French: There is an earthly judgment even for kings. It proclaimed your end: from your trembling head you dropped the crown in flight.
> And terrible battle flared up, and the banner of freedom goes like a spirit before the proud throng. And one sound filled[all] ears: and blood spurted in Paris. Oh! With what, O tyrant, will you pay for this righteous blood, for the blood of the people, for the blood of citizens!
> When the last trump shall rend the blue vault with its sound; when the graves shall open, and their dust resume its former aspect; when the scales shall appear, and the Judge shall raise them... will not your hair stand on end? Will not your hand begin to tremble?
> Fool! What will you be on *that* day, when even now there is shame upon you? An object of hell's mockery, shade, phantom, deceived by Destiny! Smitten with an immortal wound, you will turn an imploring gaze, and the bloody ranks will shout: "He is guilty! He is guilty!"

There is no doubt of Lermontov's dislike and contempt for royalty, but the abstract notion of "freedom" which in this poem and elsewhere he opposes to it has nothing to do with liberation of the people from slavery; it connotes only the gentleman's dispensation from the vexations of autocratic rule. The notion that an autocratic regime, whether of Charles X or of Nikolai I, could have anything good about it, either actually or potentially, makes him very impatient. Particularly odious in his eyes are the sycophantic "crowd" of the nobility who surround the autocrat. In this connection the poem "To***" (1830-31),[43] which begins: "Oh, enough of excusing vice!" is of particular interest. There is no direct evidence anywhere for the identity of the addressee behind the asterisks, but a conjecture going back to 1909 and Maxim Gorky very plausibly suggests Pushkin. In 1830 Pushkin published an epistle under the title "To a Grandee" [*K Vel'mozhe*],[44] which Gorky's conjecture would make the motivation for Lermontov's poem. The "Grandee" in question was Prince Nikolai Borisovich Yusupov (1751-1831), one of the last magnates of the court of Catherine II. The Prince had invited Pushkin to visit him at his estate near Moscow, and the epistle is a poetical acceptance of the invitation. The visit, of course, never took place, since Yusupov died in the summer of the next year at the age of eighty, of cholera. Pushkin was very fond of the old man, and from the evidence of the epistle used to take particular delight in drawing out of him stories of his youthful relations with poets and beautiful women. He relates a typical anecdote in a letter (10/23 January 1831) to Peter Vyazemsky:[45]

> Yesterday I saw Prince Yusupov and discharged your commission. I asked him about Fonvizin, and here's what I got. He knew Fonvizin very well—he lived in the same house with him for a short time. *C'était un autre Beaumarchais pour la conversation* ... He knows how to squander his *bon mots,* and not even remember them. And meanwhile he told me the following: the tragic poet Maikov, meeting Fonvizin, asked him, stammering as usual: "Have you seen my *Agriopa?*" "I have." "What do you say to this tragedy?" "I say: *Agriópa—sranaia zhópa* ('Agriopa is a shit ass')." Witty and unexpected, isn't it? Put it in your biography [of Fonvizin] and I'll thank you.

The characterization of Prince Yusupov which Pushkin gives in the poem is clear evidence of the reasons for Pushkin's fondness: e.g., "You have come to understand the good of life: a happy man, you live for life. From childhood you have intelligently diversified your long, bright life, sought for what was possible, dissipated in moderation; diversions and honors came to you in turn." Yusupov is envisioned as listening in Paris to Diderot's fascinating conversation: "He would sit on his shaky tripod [like the Pythia!], throw off his wig, shut his eyes in rapture, and preach. And you would listen modestly, over the slow cup, to atheist or deist, like a curious Scythian to an Athenian sophist." Pushkin recalls the old man's hospitality and entertaining stories:

> In stepping across your threshold I would be suddenly transported to the days of Catherine. Bookcases, statues, and paintings, and orderly gardens bear witness to me that you revere the Muses in quiet, that they are your breath of life in noble idleness. I listen to you: your free conversation is full of youth. You have a lively feeling for the influence of beauty. Rapturously you appraise the brilliance of Alyabeva and the charm of Goncharova [two contemporary beauties, the second of whom was Pushkin's fiancée and later wife]. Nonchalantly surrounding yourself with Correggio, Canova, you, without participating in the agitations of society, sometimes gaze mockingly out of the window at them, and see in everything the turning of a circle.

Evidently this picture of a placid, self-indulgent, Epicurean existence struck Lermontov as intolerable—he certainly never understood Pushkin, whom he heroized as the author of the ode "Liberty" and whose famous "Stanzas" (1826) addressed to Nikolai I on his accession he considered, as did others, to be a bit of odious sycophancy. The poem "To ***" is important enough to quote entire:

> Oh, enough of excusing vice! Shall the purple be a shield for evildoers? Let fools deify them, let another lyre sound for them; but you, O singer, hold off: the crown of gold is not your crown.
> For exile from your native land be praised everywhere, as for Freedom; Nature early endowed you with lofty thought and soul: you saw evil and you did not bow your proud brow before evil.
> You sang of liberty, when the tyrant thundered and punishments threatened; fearing only the eternal judgment, and alien to fear on earth, you sang—and in this land there is one who has understood your song.

Lermontov at seventeen doubtless did understand the youthful Pushkin of the ode "Liberty"; but for the mature man and his all-embracing, life-affirming wholeness the passionate young fanatic had no understanding. The Pushkin whom he celebrates in "The Death of the Poet" (1837) is largely a Pushkin of his own creation.

Lermontov's entire poetic work is, to borrow Dostoevsky's phrase, "the confession of an ardent soul." As might be expected, the lyrics that directly mirror his own emotional life, particularly his relations with women, are the most numerous in his oeuvre. A strict separation, in any case, between what may be called "philosophical meditations" and love lyrics is often impossible to make with him: the varieties interpenetrate. Thus it is in the five-stanza meditation that begins: "I saw the shadow of happiness" (1831).[46] In the short compass of this piece he touches on many themes: "Happiness is false, and not worth the tears it costs"; "Is the object of my love an angel of Paradise, but created by God as an instrument of punishment?" "No, she is not to blame for the 'spot of boredom' in my mind, which threatens to engulf me entire"; "My beloved is everything to me, but I love my native land where I was born and will be buried"; "My dead father, where are you? Is there a heaven? The question is un-answerable, and for this reason I seek consolation for my being in a woman's heart." Such a poem is a fascinating study of Lermontov's psychological make-up, but entirely wanting in logical structure or unity. In another lyric of the same year ("The Day Will Come—and By the World Condemned—")[47] Lermontov envisions his fate as execution, apparently, despised and hated by the mob, but if his beloved feels grief at the news of his death, he will be content; if she joins the universal rejoicing at it, his ghost will make her life intolerable.

The theme of the poet's loneliness and the world's incomprehension forms the background of the love lyric "We were brought together

accidentally by fate" (1832),[48] which has the heading: "To *"—probably
Varvara Lopukhina. In the third and fourth strophes he writes:

> Be, O be my heaven, be the comrade of my terrible storms; then let them thunder
> among us—I was born not to live without them. I was born that the entire world
> should be witness of my triumph or my downfall; but with you, my guiding light, what
> is the praise or the bitter mockery of men!

Quite remarkable for the insight it affords into Lermontov's feeling
for his father, whom he scarcely knew, is the 1831 poem, written shortly
after the death of Yury Lermontov: "A terrible fate of son and father—."[49]
The young poet realizes that his grandmother has done her best to keep
them apart: "But in vain were their wishes: we did not find enmity one in
the other, though both became the victims of suffering! It is not for me to
judge whether you are guilty or not—you have been condemned by the
world. But what is the world? A crowd of people, now malicious, now well-
intentioned, a collection of undeserved praises and calumnies just as
ridiculous." The poem ends with a pathetic hope that the father has at least
kept love for his son in the other world: "Surely now you do not completely
cease to love me? Oh, if so, then I do not put heaven the equal of this earth
where I am dragging out my life; what though I do not know happiness
here—at least I love!"

Eighteenth-century love poetry is notoriously abstract: the beloved is
seldom given concrete features and the relations between poet and mistress
are seldom portrayed specifically. Parny was one of the first poets to break
away from this convention. Lermontov's love poetry, while undoubtedly
reflecting a perfectly genuine passion, or passions, and psychologically
revealing as far as the poet is concerned, is usually conventional and
abstract in the depiction of his beloved. As he matures, however,
Lermontov overcomes this abstractness, and with Ivanova and Lopukhina
particularly he succeeds in creating a credible portrait—not of their
external features, which remain wholly conventional, but of their per-
sonalities. He subjects Natalya Ivanova to a searching analysis ("I am not
worthy, perhaps...," 1831):[50]

> You are not sly as a serpent, only your soul often surrenders itself to new
> impressions. It is attracted by the moment; many are dear to it, but none yet fully; but
> this cannot serve me as a consolation.

The poem that begins melodramatically: "The Most High has pronounced
His sentence,"[51] in which the poet acknowledges the end of his relations
with Natalya Fyodorovna, is full of his contradictory feeling for her: "You
have abused the rights you acquired over me, and after first flattering me
with love, you have betrayed me—God be with you! I would not resolve to
curse! Everything in you is sacred for me, the bewitching eyes and that

breast where the young heart beats. I remember, I once plucked through devotion a flower that kept the poison of suffering—from your innocent lips at the hour of parting, an unforced kiss; I knew it was not love—and I bore it; but I could not then guess that a moment of gaiety was dearer to you than all my hopes and torments and tears! Be happy in my unhappiness, and having heard that I am suffering, do not you be wearied with empty repentance." The elegiac tone of this poem is mingled in a quite unusual way with bitter oratorical invective, as in the final lines: "What have I deserved, that the fresh brightness of your eyes should be darkened with tears? Better that you should school yourself for laughter, for life is laughing at us!"

Varvara Lopukhina is portrayed quite otherwise than the rather shallow, flighty Ivanova. Of Lopukhina Lermontov writes (1832):[52]

> She does not entice lively youths with proud beauty, she does not lead behind her a throng of mute sighers. Her figure is not the figure of a goddess, her breast does not rise up like a wave, and in her no one, falling to the ground, acknowledges his divinity. Yet all her movements, smiles, speeches and features are so full of life, of inspiration, so full of a wonderful simplicity! But her voice penetrates the soul like a memory of better days, and the heart loves and suffers, almost ashamed of its own love.

Something of Lermontov's psychological acuity may be seen in an 1831 piece, "To Princess L. G----a,"[53] which may perhaps have been addressed to Elizaveta Gorchakova, cousin of Natalya Ivanova:

> When you listen coldly to tales of others' sorrow, and shake your young head unbelievingly; when brilliant apparel delights you madly, or when your soul is agitated by childish vexation; when I see, see clearly that for you at seventeen everything is attractive, beautiful, everything—even people, life and society [svet],—then, tormented by memory, I say to my soul: Happy is he who can give himself to earthly desires in the flower of his days! But do not be envious; you [i.e., my soul] will not be content with this, as she is; you will not forget your hopes, but you were not born for others. Yes! A great thought has been kept in you until now, like a seed: it was born with you into the world—it is not destined to perish!

Not unnaturally Lermontov's love-related verse often contains a great deal of self-analysis. Note the poem "Repentance" (1830-31):[54]

> To what purpose is rebellious murmuring, reproach to overmastering Fate? She was kind to you, you created your own suffering. Senseless one, you possessed a pure soul, an open one, uninfected by the general evil, and you lost this treasure.
>
> The fire of first love you resolved to bring to birth in her, and you could not love any longer once you had attained this sorrowful goal. You despised everything; you stand among people like an oak in a desert land, and the quiet weeping of innocent love could not shake your soul.
>
> God does not twice grant us joy, cheering us with mutual passion; without consolation, weary, your life will pass like your youth. You will meet *her* kiss on the lips of a beautiful deceiver, and hourly before you will be the features of the first object [of your love].

Oh, implore her forgiveness, fall, fall at her feet; otherwise you will prepare your own hell, in rejecting reconciliation. Though you will still love, there is no return to former feelings. You will not have the power forever to replace the first loss.

The little poem "Evening"[55] echoes the self-reproach of "Repentance":

When the crimson day is setting behind the earth's blue edge; when the mist rises, and shadow hides everything afar—then in the quietness I think of eternity and love, and someone's voice whispers to me: You will not be happy again. And I gaze at the heavens with submissive soul; they have wrought miracles, but not for you and me, nor for the worthless fool to whom your look will be dearer to the end than all heaven's rewards.

One of the best of Lermontov's early poems is the indignant reproach to Natalya Ivanova, headed simply "To *" (1832).[56] There is so much in this passionate *cri de coeur* of both self-analysis and of belated understanding of Natalya's character that it is worth citing entire:

I shall not abase myself before you; neither your greeting nor your reproach has dominion over my soul. Know: we are strangers from this time forth. You have forgotten: I shall not give up freedom for delusion. Even as it is, I have sacrificed years for your smile and your eyes; even as it is, I have seen in you for too long the hope of my young days, and grown to hate the whole world so as to love you the more strongly. How can I know—perhaps those moments that ran by at your feet I was taking away from inspiration! And what did you give to take their place? Perhaps, overcome by heavenly thought and the power of the spirit I might have given the world a wondrous gift, and [the world] in recompense given me immortality? Wherefore did you so tenderly promise to make up for its crown; wherefore were you not at the beginning what you became in the end? I am proud! . . . Farewell! love another, dream of finding love in another; I will not make myself the slave of anyone on earth. In foreign mountains beneath the sky of the south I shall perhaps sequester myself; but we know each other too well to be able to forget each other. From henceforth I shall begin to enjoy myself, and I shall swear to my passion for all; with all I shall laugh, but I care not to weep with any. I shall begin to deceive godlessly, so as not to love as I have loved; or is it possible to respect a woman, when an angel has betrayed me? I was prepared for death and torment, and ready to challenge the whole world to combat, so as—fool that I was!—to press your young hand one more time! Ignorant of your perfidious betrayal, I gave you my soul; did you know the worth of such a soul? You knew—but I did not know you!

Even in the midst of this tempestuous outcry of wounded love and self-esteem may be heard the characteristic note of supreme confidence in a poetical immortality—this in a boy of eighteen who had published scarcely anything! Mingled with this certainty of his genius is the equal certainty of a short life (cf. the 1832 poem "No, I'm not Byron"), and the consciousness of the gulf between himself and the crowd. In "No, I'm not Byron" he calls himself a "chosen one [*izbrannik*], still unknown"; in an earlier poem (1831) he uses the same word, but in a significantly different context:

I was not created by Almighty God for angels and Paradise; but for what purpose I live in suffering—*He* knows more about this.

Like my demon, I am a chosen one of evil; like the demon, with a proud soul, I am a careless wanderer among men, a stranger to earth and heaven.

Read, compare in remembrance my fate with his, and believe with soul unpitying that he and I are one in this world.[57]

Lermontov's Later Lyric Verse (1835-1841)

The year 1833 marks a hiatus in Lermontov's lyrical production. Apparently his "Muse" deserted him altogether during the ordeal of the Cavalry Cadets' School: we have only one poem from 1833 as contrasted with the 51 of 1832. The following years are no better—there are two lyrics from 1833-34 and four from 1836. Three of the four from 1836 are translations of poems by Byron—"The Dying Gladiator,"[58] "Hebrew Melody" (Byron's "My Soul is Dark"),[59] and "Lines, Written in an Album at Malta"—a two-strophe piece which Ivan Kozlov had also translated.[60]

With 1837 begins the period of Lermontov's fully mature verse, heralded by the magnificently denunciatory "Death of a Poet."[61] Metrically this is unique. It begins in the octosyllabic iambic verse so often used by both Pushkin and Lermontov for narrative; then, after a contemptuous reference to Pushkin's French assassin d'Anthès, the meter changes, through five lines comparing Pushkin's death to that of his Lensky in *Eugene Onegin*. These transitional lines, as it were, modulate the four-foot beginning to a solemn six-foot passage: iambic tetrameter, iambic pentameter, iambic tetrameter, iambic pentameter, iambic hexameter (Alexandrine). After five Alexandrine lines lamenting Pushkin's fatal involvement with the society that he had learned to despise, the meter shifts again, and there are twelve lines of varying lengths and unpredictable rhymes reminiscent of the "free iambics" of certain late classical odes.

The final sixteen lines, which continue the "free iambic" form, with lines ranging from three-beat to six-beat, were an afterthought, according to the testimony of Lermontov's friend S. A. Raevsky. It was written a few days after the rest of the poem, as an indignant protest against the attempt of court circles to discredit Pushkin and defend d'Anthès. These despicable toadies, whom he calls "hangmen of Freedom, Genius and Glory," are of course beyond the reach of any human law; but—"There is the Terrible Judgment: it waits / it is not accessible to the clink of gold." At the Last Judgment not all the black blood of the calumniators will wash away "the Poet's righteous blood!" The metrical freedom which Lermontov has chosen for this final passage allows him to make several magnificently effective contrasts. Thus, the denunciation begins: *A vy, nadmennye potomki* ("But you, arrogant descendants"), a four-foot line with feminine ending, which is followed by a thunderous Alexandrine: *Izvestnoi podlost'iu proslavlennykh otsov* ("of fathers renowned for notorious baseness"). In the center of the passage an Alexandrine pronounces solemnly: "But there is the judgment of God, [you] confidants of vice!" Immediately follows a line that cracks like a whip: *Est' groznyi sud: on zhdët!* ("There is the Terrible Judgment: it waits!")

The predictable consequence of Lermontov's bold denunciation of Russia's governmental caste, and by implication of the Emperor himself (who certainly condoned the killing of Pushkin, whether or not he connived in it) was the arrest of the outspoken critic and his brief incarceration (February 1837); following his trial he was demoted and sent to serve in the Caucasus as a private in the Nizhni-Novgorod Dragoon Regiment. During the enforced idleness of his prison stay Lermontov wrote, according to the information of his cousin Akim Pavlovich Shan-Girei, four poems: "The Prisoner,"[62] "My Neighbor,"[63] "When Fields of Rye Wave Golden"[64] and "Supplication."[65] These four lyrics, together with "Death of the Poet" mark the rather abrupt change of Lermontov's poetical style from romantic posing to a mature realism. In the verse from 1837 to 1841 there is very little of the Byronic self-dramatization of the earlier period. Lermontov had learned from Pushkin to see the world as it is, not either in the roseate colors of some remote ideal, or in the utter blackness of melodramatic despair. To this same period (probably January 1837) belongs the wonderful revised version, "Borodino"[66] of an earlier piece of 1830-31, "The Field of Borodino."[67] A comparison of the two versions is instructive of the new direction of Lermontov's poetry. "The Field of Borodino," in six eleven-line strophes, is put in the mouth of a survivor of the battle, a commoner who relates the experience in realistic terms, but using a language which is conventionally poetical and more appropriate to the writer than to his persona. Thus, in the first strophe, the narrator pictures the eve of the battle:

> All night long we lay by the guns without tents, without fires, sharpened our bayonets and whispered the prayer of our native land. A storm roared until morning-light. Raising my head from the gun-carriage, I said to my comrade: "Brother, listen to the song of the tempest: it's as wild as the song of freedom." But my comrade, recalling past years, was not listening.

The peasant gunner whom Lermontov makes his mouthpiece cannot with any plausibility be imagined as making the observation about the "wild song of freedom" which is attributed to him. Similar inconsitency marks the reference in the third and sixth strophes to three famous Russian victories of the past—Chesme, Rymnik and Poltava—as overshadowed by the glory of Borodino. The whole tone of the sixth and final strophe is altogether out of character with the supposed speaker:

And soundly, soundly slept our boys [*nashi*] on the fatherland's fateful night. My comrades, you fell! We could not help them. However in the traditions of glory, even louder than Rymnik, Poltava, thunders *Borodino*. Sooner shall the voice [Slavonic *glas*] of the prophet deceive, sooner shall the eye of the heavens go out, than it be blotted from the memory of the sons of the North.

"Borodino" (January 1837) is also composed in strophes constructed similarly to those of its predecessor, but with a significant difference. The strophes are four lines shorter—seven instead of eleven—and accordingly much tighter. The six lines of iambic tetrameter, rhyming aBaBcc, which open the longer strophe, convey a leisurely, meditative effect, while the shorter strophe (rhyme scheme aaBcccB), with its two sharp trimeters in lines 3 and 7, sounds breathless and impetuous.

More importantly, however, "Borodino" is formally a dialogue, and both speakers are Russian peasants. The first speaker, to whom is given the opening strophe, is an unidentified but obviously young man, who questions the veteran of Borodino: Why was Moscow given up to the Frenchmen? Surely there was some stiff fighting. All Russia remembers the day of Borodino! The old man's recollections of the battle occupy the remaining thirteen strophes. The second, repeated with minor variations as the last, contrasts, in a psychologically plausible fashion, the heroic past with the degenerate present: "Yes, there were men in our time, not like the tribe of the present day: bogatyrs you are not! An evil fate overtook them; not many came back from the field . . . If it hadn't been the Lord's will, they wouldn't have given up Moscow!" The account of the battle begins with no such historically unjustified night-long storm as in the early poem, but with the long retreat of the Russian forces before the advancing enemy, while the soldiers grumble: "What are we up to? Are we going into winter quarters? Don't the commanders dare tear the foreigners' uniforms upon the Russian bayonets?" The old gunner recalls how he loaded his cannon when the army finally made its stand at Borodino, and thought: "I'll entertain our friend! Stop there, brother M'sieu! Here's no place for sly tricks—to battle, please! We're going to break like a wall, we're going to lay down our heads for our native land!" the brief exhortation of the commanding officer in the third and final day of the battle is taken almost verbatim from the older version, but the description of the unnamed officer is new: "Our colonel was born a fighter, servant to the Tsar, a father to his men . . . Yes, too bad about him: struck with the steel, he sleeps in the damp earth." Some of the battle description is carried over from the earlier version into strophe eleven. Then in the thirteenth strophe the end of the battle is a new and far superior version: "Here darkness fell; we are all ready to start a new battle in the morning, and stand to the end. . . . and the drums began to roll, and the heathen retreated. Then we began to count our wounds, and count our comrades."

The diction of "Borodino" is colloquial and idiomatic, without being extreme. Note the young man's address to the respected old soldier as "uncle" *(diadia);* his reference to the military engagements of the war as *eshchë kakie*—"and *what* engagements, too!" The veteran tells of finding the enemy's location: *frantsuzy tut-kak-tut*—"The Frenchies were there, all right!"—and exclaims, as he recounts the course of the battle:*Vam ne vidat' takikh srazhenii*—"You'll never see such fighting." The whole feeling of the poem is authentic; there is none of the artificiality, the bookishness of the earlier poem.

The other 1837 poems are less impressive, but excellent of their kind. "The Prisoner" is a poignant song of longing for freedom, with a wistful dream of a wild, untrammeled ride on the prisoner's "good horse over the green field"; "He'll bound, gay and playful, his tail waving in the breeze." "My Neighbor" recounts the military prisoner's emotions as he listens to the sad song of another prisoner down the hall. "Supplication," addressed to the Virgin, is a fervent prayer, "not for my own forlorn [*pustynnuiu*] soul," but for "an innocent maiden" afflicted by the suppliant's fate. The poem is in a quite unusual meter, very effective in its agitated movement: a four-foot dactylic measure, with uniform dactylic rhyme.

The best of the group, however, is the four-strophe lyric that begins: "When the yellow cornland billows—" (*Kogda volnuetsia zhelteiushchaia niva).* The poem's theme, most uncommon with Lermontov and particularly surprising under the circumstances when it was written, is the calming and reassuring influence on the poet of the natural environment. After three strophes that picture the yellowing harvest, the dew-laden woodland flowers, and the murmuring rivulet, the poem ends: "Then the agitation of my soul is quieted; then the furrows on my brow are smoothed,—and I can attain happiness on earth, and I see a God in heaven." Observant critics have pointed out that the natural scene in the first two strophes is inconsistent: the "yellowing harvest" and the "crimson plum" of the first strophe belong to mid-summer, while the "silvery lily-of-the-valley"[*landysh*] of the second strophe is a flower of spring. The effect is probably deliberate: whether the season is spring or summer, the time of day morning or evening [*rumianym vecherom il' utra v chas zlatoï*], the healing and heartening effect of the natural world is the same. The three different vignettes seem to generalize the scene.

One of the noteworthy changes in Lermontov's world outlook manifest in his later verse is the relatively objective tone of the best pieces. The poet who had been in his youthful work almost narcissistically self-obsessed is suddenly able to see the world through the eyes of others, and to depict the joys and sorrows of others in a psychologically convincing fashion. "Borodino" is the description of a crucial battle as lived and remembered by a simple old soldier. "Valerik" (1840)[68] is a starkly realistic picture of a battle in the Caucasus which Lermontov himself took part in with marked heroism. There is no posing in it, no attempt to romanticize the glamor of war; it is a picture of war as it is, and the heroes of it are the common soldiers with whom the poet at this time was serving after his demotion. The poem is addressed to an unnamed lady, probably Varvara Lopukhina, in the conventional form of an epistle. The restraint and reticence of the few references to the writer's own feelings and relations with the addressee are noteworthy. In content "Valerik" is reminiscent of Polezhaev's narratives *Erpeli* and *Chir-Yurt,* especially in its tone of revulsion and horror at the spectacle of war and the needless deaths on both sides; but there is in Lermontov's poem none of the shrill, almost flippant mockery of Polezhaev. From the same year as "Valerik," and of the same inspiration—that is, direct experience of the brutality of war,—is the masterly "A Soldier's Testament"[69]—the instructions of a dying soldier to his comrade who will be going home. These poems, stylistically as in theme, are almost anti-romantic in their simple, precise vocabulary, remote from all straining for effect, all poetic diction or ornamentation.

In his earliest verse Lermontov's commonest theme, pervading everything, was love, generally in its tragic aspect as a shattering and disillusioning experience, and the resulting trauma which it leaves in the poet's life. There are far fewer verses after 1837 that can be classified as love poetry, and even in these it is not the burning passion of the youthful years that emerges, but rather a restrained tenderness. Note, for example, "We Parted" (1837);[70] "To A.O. Smirnova" (1840);[71] "To a Portrait" (1840);[72] "Vindication" (1841);[73] "No, not for you my love" (1841),[74] and especially the startlingly prophetic "A Dream" (1841).[75] "To a Baby" (1840),[76] addressed presumably to the daughter of Varvara A. Bakhmeteva (née Lopukhina) is particularly revealing of the poet's new reticence and muting of the element of passion:

> Oh, if you knew how I love you! How dear to me are your young smiles, and quick eyes, and golden curls, and your little voice! Isn't it true, they say, you resemble her?—Alas, the years fly; her sufferings changed her prematurely, but faithful dreams have preserved that image in my breast; that look, filled with fire, is ever with me. But you, do you love me? Aren't my unasked caresses tiresome to you? Do I not all too often kiss your little eyes? Do not my tears burn your cheeks? Look, do not speak either of my grief, or about me at all. To what purpose? She, perhaps, will be angered or perturbed at the childish tale.

Three poems, all probably addressed to the same unknown lady and composed 1837-38 "in Tbilisi," are good examples of Lermontov's later love lyric: "She sings—and the sounds melt on the lips"; "Like the sky, your glance shines with an azure enamel" and "When I hear your voice." The last named is remarkable for its affirmative mood:[77]

> When I hear your voice, resonant and affectionate, my heart begins to leap like a bird in its cage;

> When I meet your eyes, azure-deep, my soul wants to leave my breast to meet them.
> And I'm somehow gay, and I want to cry, and I would like to throw myself on
> your neck.

The poem is notable for its folklore intonation (e.g., "like a bird in its cage" "my soul wants to leave my breast") and for its meter, which is *tonic*—that is, without clear identification as dactylic, trochaic or the like, but with two accents in each line; e.g., the first three lines:[78]

> slýshu li gólos tvoi (two dactyls)
> zvónky i láskovy: (two dactyls)
> kak ptíchka v klétke (two trochees with anacrusis), etc.

Friendship as well as love was a theme of Lermontov's early verse, and continues to inspire some of his best mature poetry. The 1837 poem that begins: "Hastening toward the north from afar"[79] starts as a prayer to the formidable Caucasian mountain Kazbek—a prayer for a safe and comfortable journey back "to the north," i.e., St. Petersburg. But in the sixth strophe the poet turns to another concern:

> But I have still another desire! I dread to tell it! My soul trembles! What if I have
> been since the day of my banishment altogether forgotten in my native land? Shall I
> find there the embraces of former times? Shall I meet with the old-time greeting? Will
> friends and brothers recognize the sufferer, after many years?

If death has claimed some old friends, and others have grown cold, then, he declares in the last strophe, let the great mountain overwhelm him pitilessly with an avalanche.

Most affecting of Lermontov's later poems of friendship is "In Memory of Alexander Odoevsky."[80] He met the exiled Decembrist poet while in the Caucasus in 1837 and a warm friendship sprang up between the two. Odoevsky died in August, 1839, in the disease-ridden post of Lazarevsk. Lermontov's poem, written immediately after receiving the news, was published in *Notes of the Fatherland* in 1840—with the censor-dictated heading: "In Memory of A. I. ." The poem has a coolly formal appearance: six strophes, each of ten five-foot iambic lines, followed by a six-foot eleventh, and rhyming AbAbCddCCee; the final strophe differs slightly, having only ten lines, the tenth a hexameter, and rhyming AbAbCCddCee. Some of the lines in the poem, as happens quite frequently with Lermontov, were lifted in part or wholly from earlier pieces. Since almost none of the early poems had ever been published, it was not unreasonable that the poet should have used them as a quarry where it suited him. In spite of the evident calculation which the elaborate strophic form and the refurbished lines reveal, the poem has a striking inner unity and gives the impression of complete sincerity and deep personal feeling:

> But he has perished far from his dear home... Peace to your heart, my dear Sasha! Buried in the earth of foreign fields, let it sleep quietly, as [sleeps] our friendship in the mute graveyard of my memory! You died, as many have, without noise, but with firmness. A secret thought still wandered on your brow when your eyes closed in eternal sleep; and what you said before the end not one who heard you understood.

The "secret thought" which Lermontov imagined on the brow of the dying Decembrist should probably be understood as a necessarily cryptic reference to the conspirator's dream of a Russia freed from both autocracy and serfdom. Lermontov was never strongly or consistently political, and the verses which reflect a "political consciousness" are animated by a purely individualistic indignation and sense of outraged justice, not by any logical philosophy of revolution such as many of the Decembrists professed. The passionate denunciations of a hated society which thunder from "Death of a Poet" are those of an individualist and a poet, not a reformer—and such Lermontov evidently, and probably rightly, pictured Alexander Odoevsky.

Contempt and hatred of "high society" (*svet*—French "le monde") is a theme that pervades Lermontov's verse from the beginning. A memorable expression of it is in the poem that begins: "How often, surrounded by a motley throng,"[81] with the significant date: 1 January, 1840. The poem pictures the festivities of a court New Year's party: amid the cold and thoughtless merrymakers he is far away in memories of his childhood. He pictures vividly the decrepit old manor-house, the gardens, the pond, the smoke from the village huts. With the memories of physical things come poignant thoughts of a lost love, of beautiful ideals once cherished. Then, like a whip-lash, comes the final strophe, brutally breaking off the pensive melancholy of the first six strophes: "But when, coming to my senses, I realize the deception, and the noise of the populous crowd drives away my dream, a guest uninvited to the holiday—oh, how I long to confound their gaiety, and brazenly hurl in their faces an iron verse, suffused with gall and malice."

Such an "iron verse" is the short but unforgettable 1841 piece that begins "Farewell, unwashed Russia!"[82] written when the poet was once more on his way to the Caucasus. As so often, Kayden's verse translation mutes the effect; a plain prose version of this extremely direct and unpoetical poem at least preserves its vigor:

> Farewell, unwashed Russia, land of slaves, land of masters, and you, blue uniforms [the garb of bureaucratic officialdom], and you, submissive people.
> Maybe, beyond the wall of the Caucasus, I shall hide myself from your pashas, from their all-seeing eyes, from their all-hearing ears!

In eight packed lines are the poet's loathing and contempt for serfdom ("slaves"), autocracy ("masters"), bureaucracy ("blue uniforms"), subservience ("submissive people") and the omnipresent spy-system ("all-seeing eyes and all-hearing ears"), to say nothing of a general lack of civilized decency ("unwashed Russia").

The fullest expression of Lermontov's feeling toward his Russia will be found in the 1838 poem "Meditation."[83] Here in 44 lines of what has been well called a "social elegy" is the whole social criticism of *A Hero of Our Time*. Significantly, the poet puts himself in the unflattering picture he draws of a "lost generation." It is a generation that has suffered disillusion and become cynical: "Meanwhile, under the burden of knowledge and doubt, it grows old in inaction." "We are rich, hardly out of our cradle, with our fathers' mistakes and their belated wit, and life already tires us, like a level road with no goal." "Shamefully indifferent to good and evil," we are poltroons in the face of danger, "contemptible slaves before authority." We are ashamed of our best hopes and hide them under a cloak of cynicism. We are unable to enjoy fully the good things of life, for fear of satiety. "The dreams of poetry, the creations of art" leave us unmoved. We neither love nor hate wholeheartedly, but "there reigns in our soul some kind of secret cold." "We hurry to the grave without happiness and without glory, with a mocking backward glance." Leaving behind us nothing memorable, either of thought or creation, we shall be despised by our descendants as a father who has squandered all his property is despised by his deceived sons.

Yet, in spite of his full awareness of Russia's faults, Lermontov still loves her. The poem "My Native Land" (1841)[84] is a remarkable document that begins: "I love my fatherland, but with a strange love!" Passing in review a list of the usual justifications for love of one's native land—military glory, peace and tranquillity, ancient traditions—he rejects them all, and then declares: "But I do love—for what reason, I do not myself know—the cold silence of her steppes," etc. He then launches into a magnificently vivid and panoramic picture of Russia's natural features and her "people"—that is, the rural masses. The urban upper classes quite obviously have no part in the poet's love. Rather—

> With a satisfaction unknown to many I see the full threshing-floor, the log-hut covered with thatch, the window with its carved shutters, and on a holiday, in the dewy evening, I am ready to watch until midnight the dancing, with stamping and whistling, to the accompaniment of the chatter of drunken muzhiks.

In connection with this vivid and picturesque concreteness Belinsky's apt expression "poetry of actuality" comes to mind. Lermontov, it seems, has learned in his mature period to use his eyes, and at the same time to employ his observations of the real world around him for a completely different purpose than in his youthful efforts. There natural descriptions occur, but they are generally ornamental and accessory, given by way of metaphor or simile. Now they take their place as independent landscape-painting, and function as organic parts of the poem.

A development in Lermontov's later verse may be mentioned which at first glance might seem to run counter to this new appreciation of the beauty of the real world. Allegory is almost inevitably anti-realistic; yet many very effective pieces among Lermontov's later verses are allegorical. Such, for example, is "Clouds" (1840), where the poet imagines the "eternal wanderers" to be perhaps driven, like himself, by "secret envy" or "open malice," but ends with the conclusion that, altogether unlike their human questioner, to them "alien are passions, and alien are sufferings; eternally cold, eternally free, you have no homeland, you have no exile."[85] In "Three Palms" (1839)[86] the trees of the title complain to the Creator that they stand uselessly in the desert, giving no comfort to travellers, as should be their function. In answer Allah sends a caravan to the oasis, which ends by cutting down the three complaining trees for firewood. The "meaning" of the parable is nowhere explicitly set forth, but remains enigmatic. The poem, as V. N. Turbin[87] and Michael Katz[88] point out, was evidently inspired by Pushkin's ninth poem of the series "Imitations of the Koran," and both pieces go back to Zhukovsky's "An Arab's Song over the Grave of his Horse" (1810). The conventional Oriental color of Lermontov's poem perhaps also reflects Victor Hugo's *Les Orientales,* published in 1829. Lermontov's "Orientale" is pessimistic in programmatic opposition to Pushkin's optimistic tone. In Katz's words: "The palms are punished for their sin of pride—and man is depicted as both the ungrateful despoiler of natural beauty and the involuntary instrument of God's revenge." "The Gifts of Terek" (1839)[89] introduces another element into the allegory: personification. The destructive and impetuous river as well as the sea into which it flows both take human form and human passions. Here one may speak even of a kind of mythology, in which natural forces are anthropomorphized. The poem is less a ballad than a stylized version of popular song (note the threefold repetition of the Terek's plea to the Caspian), and is said in fact to be similar in a general way to some folk-tales of the Greben Cossacks. It has, however, the balladic quality of leaving many central elements unexplained, e.g., the reason for the "crimson stream" that "runs from a little wound in the breast" of the Cossack beauty, and for the death of the Cossack warrior in nocturnal battle with the Chechens. L. M. Arinshtein notes[90] that the poem is remarkable for its internal rhymes and musical repetitions, e.g., of the syllable *"-al."* Two of Lermontov's other ballads may also be cited here: "An Oak Leaf" (1841)[91] and "The Princess of the Sea" (1841).[92] In "The Dagger" (1837)[93] the weapon which "a meditative Georgian forged for vengeance" becomes the poet's "bright, cold comrade," and his model and exemplar of hardness, his "iron friend." "Contention" (1841)[94] represents two mountains in dispute: Kazbek in the Caucasus is warned by "Shat-Mountain" (Elbruz) that his proud independence will soon come to an end; to confirm his words he points to the dauntless Russian army advancing into the mountain fastness. Michael Katz's contention[95] seems justified, that the theme of civilization's benevolent advance into a semi-barbarous region is only minor and peripheral: "As in *Tri Pal'my* ["Three Palms"] Lermontov's theme in *Spor* ["Contention"] is man's destruction of natural beauty; the poet's method is the creation of vivid imagery."

The romantic poet in any language is highly conscious of the God-given nature of his inspiration and his mission to enlighten his fellows—to "burn with the Word the hearts of men," as God commands Pushkin's "prophet." Lermontov's "The Poet" (1838)[96] uses the symbol of his own Georgian dagger (the same symbol as in his 1837 poem of that name, but with a different meaning), to represent the poet's unfulfilled mission to his stagnant fellowmen. Like the gold-ornamented dagger-blade, which was created for war but has now become a mere "golden toy" as it hangs on a wall, the poet's gift, which once like "the *veche* bell" used to summon citizens to battle, has degenerated into an egoistic adornment: "But your simple and proud language has become tiresome to us; we take comfort in glitter and deceits; like a decrepit beauty our decrepit world has grown accustomed to hide its wrinkles under rouge." The naive assumption of the older romantics that the poet-prophet would necessarily find listeners to his message from above Lermontov knows from bitter experience to be an illusion. "Once was, the measured sound of your mighty words...was as necessary for the crowd as the wine-cup for the banquet...your verse, like God's spirit, hovered above the crowd." The poem ends on a doubtful note: "Shall you awake once more, O prophet scorned?" One of Lermontov's last poems is entitled simply "The Prophet" (1841).[97] The title is a demonstrative challenge to Pushkin's celebrated poem of the same name. Significantly, in Pushkin's allegory, the prophet's audience appears only in the final word of God's injunction: "Burn with the Word the hearts of *men.*" Lermontov's begins where Pushkin's ends: the first line reads: "Ever since the Eternal Judge gave me the prophet's all-seeing power." The substance of the poem is the crowd's rejection of the prophet. The spokesman for the "Eternal Judge" declares: "I began to proclaim the pure teachings of love and truth; and all those close to me hurled rocks at me in a fury." Since then the prophet has retired into the wilderness; but when by chance he wanders into the populous town, the old men point him out to their children with the mocking words: "Look! Here is an example for you! He was proud, he did not get along with us. The fool, he wanted to convince us that God spoke through his lips! Look at him, children: how sullen and thin and pale he is: See how naked and poor he is, how all despise him!" In contrast again with Pushkin's poem, which abounds with Slavonic words and archaisms, Lermontov's mingles an everyday, even commonplace, vocabulary with Biblical reminiscences.

Bitterly ironic is the poet's self-adjuration: "Do not trust, do not trust yourself, young dreamer" (1839).[98] The mood is that of Tyutchev's "Silentium": "If it should chance with you at a sacred, wondrous moment to discover in [your] soul long silent a spring still unknown and virgin, full of sweet and simple sounds,—do not listen to them, do not surrender yourself to them, throw over them the mantle of forgetfulness: with measured verses and words of ice you will not transfer their meaning." The frustration is not merely that of the incomprehension of the audience; it is the realized impossibility of putting the wonderful inner vision into adequate words. The poem ends:

> And yet among them [i.e., the poet's audience] there is scarcely one not crumpled with grievous torment, not brought to untimely wrinkles without crime or loss! ... Believe this: for them your weeping and reproach are ridiculous, with refrain learned by heart—like a made-up tragic actor, brandishing a cardboard sword!

The poem is headed by an epigraph from the prologue to Henri-Auguste Barbier's *Iambes:*

> Que nous font après tout les vulgaires abois
> De tous ces charlatans qui donnent de la voix,
> Les marchands de pathos et les faiseurs d'emphase
> Et tous les baladins qui dansent sur la phrase?

As E. E. Naidich points out in the article on the poem in the *Lermontov Encyclopedia,*[99] Lermontov made a significant change in the French original, from "que *me* font" to "que *nous* font." The epigraph in the revised form is clearly intended to reflect the feelings of the "crowd" toward the utterances of the self-centered breed of poets, those "mountebanks that dance upon a phrase." The poem is thus in a high degree ambiguous, expressing as it does both points of view—the poet's certainty of incomprehension on the part of his audience, coupled with an understanding, at least, of the "crowd's" reasons for this failure to accept the poet's self-evaluation as the proclaimer of higher truths. V. N. Shikin notes in the same *Lermontov Encyclopedia* article the sympathetic words: "Whereas there is hardly a one of them who is not crumpled with grievous torment," etc. and perhaps rather over-emphatically writes: "The idea of the significance of another personality—and precisely of a person of the crowd—appears for the first time here in Russian literature in the poem 'Do not trust yourself.'" Too much, however, should not be made of this element. The real theme of the poem is that of mutual lack of understanding and of the impossibility of overcoming this: the poet may sense that the "crowd's" concerns are just as tragic as his own, but he can no more understand them than can they his.

The theme of the poet's heaven-sent gift and the incomprehension of his fellow-men so strikingly developed in "The Prophet" merges in Lermontov's verse with the prophetic vision of his own fate, the vision of a hostile and uncomprehending world. In the 1837 poem "Do not mock at my prophetic anguish,"[100] he addresses his love with words that echo, almost verbatim, earlier verses in which he voices his dream of attempting a great exploit, presumably revolutionary, which will bring upon him opprobrium, exile, and probably death:

> Do not mock at my prophetic anguish: I knew the blow of fate would not pass me by; I knew that the head you love would pass from your breast to the block. I said to you: I should find neither happiness nor glory in the world—the bloody hour would come, and I would fall; and perfidious enmity would smilingly blacken my genius, not yet fully flowered; and I would perish, [leaving] no trace of my hopes, my torments. But I await without terror my untimely end. It has long been time for me to see a new world. Let the crowd trample upon my crown; the singer's crown is a crown of thorns!... Let it be! I have not held it dear.

Written apparently at the same time as "Do not mock . . . " is the poem "I should not like the world to know,"[101] in which he reiterates his firmness in the face of the world's hostility and his feeling that he is accountable to none but God, the author of his suffering. A similar mood characterizes the unfinished piece of uncertain date, "My future is in darkness,"[102] in which the poet asks bitterly in the first strophe: "Why did not Nature create me either later or earlier? For what purpose did the Creator prepare me, wherefore did He so terribly contradict the hopes of my youth?" Lermontov was always conscious of the high quality of his poetic gift. He continues: "He gave me the cup of good and evil, saying: I shall make beautiful your life, you shall be glorious among men!" The poem breaks off abruptly in the third strophe: "Then, readied for the arena, I boldly penetrated into the hearts of men through the uncomprehended covers of worldly proprieties and passions." The continuation, if the poet had completed the piece, would inevitably have followed the lines of "The Prophet" and "I should not like the world to know": instead of the glory of the Creator's promise—hatred and incomprehension.

But the conflict is not always between the poet and "the crowd." In the 1840 poem "I am bored and sad"[103] Lermontov looks into his own soul and finds contradiction that makes life "such an empty and stupid joke." Particularly the gulf between the romantic ideal of love and the experienced reality is a source of grief: "To love . . . But *whom?* For a time [only] isn't worth the trouble, while [to love] eternally is impossible."

The highest point reached in Lermontov's mature lyric verse is the five-strophe poem, written in the last year of his life, and first published in 1843 in *Fatherland Notes:* "Alone I walk out on to the road."[104] He asks himself the reason why, in the solemn star-spangled night, he feels unhappy and heart-sick: "Do I expect anything? Am I regretful for anything?" He answers resolutely: "I do not expect anything from life, and I have not the least regret for the past. I seek freedom and repose! I should like to forget myself and fall asleep." But the slumber he dreams of is not the total unconsciousness of the grave. He would that all night and all day "a sweet voice might sing" to him "of love," and above his head "a dark oak, ever green, might bend and rustle."

It has often been remarked that Lermontov probably found the suggestion for this poem in Heinrich Heine's little song "Der Tod, das ist die kühle Nacht," the final strophe of which contains the same images of tree and nightingale as Lermontov's:

> Über mein Bett erhebt sich ein Baum.
> Drin singt die junge Nachtigal;
> Sie singt von lauter Liebe,
> Ich hör sie sogar im Traum.

The same images, however, recur elsewhere in Lermontov, and the link with Heine is an illuminating instance of Eikhenbaum's assertion "that for the most part in Lermontov the poetic material is someone else's, and that his main concern lies in combining and fusing it."[105]

"Alone I walk out on to the road" is outstanding even among Lermontov's verse for its melodious effect; the historian V. O. Klyuchevsky, in his memorial essay on "M. Iu. L." remarks[106] that the poem "by its verse almost frees the composer from the labor of picking themes and sounds in setting it to music." The meter has been defined[107] as "five-foot iambic, with anapaestic passages"; e.g., line 1 of strophe 3: *uzh ne zhdú ot zhízni nichegó ia,* with what Nabokov calls a "scud" in the fourth foot. It can, however, be read equally well as five-foot trochees with numerous "scuds," especially in the first foot; e.g., the first strophe:

> Vykhozhú odín ia na dorógu;
> Skvóz' tumán kremnístyi pút' blestít;
> Nóch' tikhá. Pustýnia vnémlet Bógu,
> I zvezdá s zvezdóiu govorít.

Heine's German, it may be noted, has a similarly ambivalent effect (e.g., are the first two lines three-foot or four-foot? Is the basic meter iambic or trochaic?)

The tormented poet knew that he would never find freedom and repose in life. He certainly expected death in battle in the Caucasus, as the uncannily prescient 1841 poem "A Dream"[108] gives evidence. This extraordinary piece, which is constructed as a dream within a dream, or as Eikhenbaum[109] pictures it, as "two mirrors mutually reflecting the actual fates of [the lyric hero and heroine] and returning the reflections to each other," is both for its theme and its technical perfection one of Lermontov's most remarkable works. Eikhenbaum, in the notes of the four-volume *Collected Works*[110] remarks that "in [Lermontov] literature a connection has been shown between this poem and one of the songs of the Terek Cossacks.... where the story is told of a Cossack who in a dream sees himself killed." In Lermontov's "Dream" the lyric hero, in the most clear, vivid and undreamlike language, describes himself as lying in a valley of Daghestan, with a wound still smoking in his breast. Then the vision shifts to a brilliant ballroom scene in the capital, where one woman, sitting meditatively apart from her gay companions, sees a dream—of a familiar body, lying dead on a plain of Daghestan," with a black wound steaming in his breast and blood, flowing in a chilling stream." The "ring-form" of the poem, in which the last strophe repeats with slight verbal changes but with a wholly different context the substance of the first; the repetitions ("the sun burned.... and burned me"; "their gay conversation was about me.... but not entering into their gay conversation"), the subtle "instrumentation" of consonantal sounds (e.g., the first line: v po*ld*nev*n*yi zhar v *doli*n*e *D*agesta*n*a, in which l, d, and n predominate), and above all the effectiveness of the delayed subject "I" in the second line: ("In noonday heat in a valley of Daghestan with lead in breast motionless lay I")—these make "A Dream" one of Lermontov's most perfect lyrics.

Very possibly Lermontov's deliberately provoked quarrel with Major Martynov, which led to the fatal duel, was the objective expression of a death-wish so wonderfully expressed in these last poems. One might wish that over his grave an evergreen oak might rustle and a nightingale sing softly of love.

Mikhail Lermontov: The Narrative Poems

The *poèma*—a term for which no single-word equivalent exists in English—is a genre which takes the place with romantic poets that the epic had held with their predecessors of the classical era. The epic can hardly be said to have survived the eighteenth century—such a production as Küchelbecker's *David* is a literary curiosity and nothing more—and critics have generally opined that the nineteenth-century novel is its surviving heir. Somewhere between the epic and the novel is the realm of what is sometimes referred to as "the Byronic poem," although poems of the sort are by no means always marked by the special characteristics of Byron's examples.

The epic, from the *Iliad* on, is a public production: its subject is some great national event, and its heroes are always in some fashion exemplars of what are conceived to be national virtues. If they succumb at some point to the private weakness of love, as after Odysseus most of them do, this is a momentary failing, and by overcoming it they exhibit the true quality of their heroism.

Certain obligatory features are associated with the epic: supernatural powers, whether Christian or pagan, or even allegorical abstractions, intervene in the action, sometimes decisively, sometimes only as a means of postponing the ultimate decision. Figures of speech, particularly the simile, the apostrophe, metonymy and synecdoche abound. The structure exemplified first in the *Odyssey,* where the poem plunges its hearer *in medias res* at the outset, and then in a flashback explains the situation, is a favorite device. There is generally a good deal of rhetoric, as heroes explain their motives and intentions in set speeches—the only means, in fact, that the poet has of indicating psychological conditions. Linguistically, the epic is couched in a language remote from the spoken tongue, archaic, solemn and elevated.

The romantic narrative poem is essentially a private work; it deals not with a national, but with an individual fate. Its heroes are individuals; they may exhibit traits that mark them as belonging to a certain nation or class or time, but these are accessory, not essential features. When they love, as they almost inevitably do (*The Prisoner of Chillon* is a notable exception) they give themselves wholeheartedly to the passion, and no overriding sense of duty recalls them to a higher mission.

While the supernatural may play a part in the romantic narrative poem, it is not as a grandiose intervention of heaven or hell, but in the form of an apparition from the world beyond the grave, or a warning dream, or the like. The majestic deliberateness of the epic, with its burden of tropes and its sonorous verse-form (dactylic hexameter, octave stanza, or Alexandrine) is replaced by a very rapidly moving narrative, in a meter appropriately quick and voluble, most often the four-foot iambic. The figures of speech which the romantic poets favor are such conveyors of excitement as the rhetorical question and the apostrophe; the metaphor plays a greater part than the simile. The *in medias res* technique is a favorite of Byron's, but both he and many others after him love to leave situations and characters unexplained in order to hold the reader's interest. Genuine dialogue—quick interchanges of speech—is more common than the oratorical efforts of the epic. A very common device is the first-person "confession"—an account by the narrative hero to a passive listener of his past as an explanation for the present situation. Passages of description for its own sake—that is, not as one term of a simile or the like, but used independently—are ubiquitous in the romantic narrative poem; they are often used for conveying mood or for painting an ironic contrast between external nature and the actions of men. Finally, while the narrative poem is not likely to employ a vulgar idiom, neither does it resort to the high poetic diction of the epic. In its Russian form it adheres to Lomonosov's middle style rather than to the high style obligatory for the epic.

Pushkin in Russia naturalized the romantic *poèma.* His "southern poems" have been considered in this survey, as have the narratives of e.g., Kozlov, Alexander Bestuzhev, Ryleev, Küchelbecker et al. Some of the themes which appear prominently among them are: the hero's incompatibility with the society in which he finds himself (e.g., Aleko in *The Gypsies*); a conflict of duties (e.g., Ryleev's *Voinarovsky*); love thwarted by social differences (e.g., Kozlov's *The Monk*), jealousy and vengeance (e.g., Pushkin's *The Fountain of Bakhchisarai*), etc. Many of these themes we shall see recurring among the unpublished narrative poems of Lermontov.

Lermontov began writing "Byronic poems" at the age of fourteen, under the evident influence of Pushkin, whose *Prisoner of the Caucasus* was published in 1822. The fantasy and humor of *Ruslan and Lyudmila* apparently had no appeal for Lermontov at this date; his early narratives are intensely serious and exaggeratedly "romantic." The earliest seems to be "The Circassians,"[1] written in the summer of 1828. The ten-page poem is full of lines from the works of other poets, either incorporated without change, or with slight alteration—Pushkin's *Prisoner of the Caucasus,* Byron's *Bride of Abydos* in Kozlov's translation, a poem and a play by Dmitriev, etc.—evidences of Lermontov's favorite reading of the time.[2] The background of the poem is indicated by the title. Lermontov had three times in childhood been taken by his grandmother to the Caucasus, and the magnificent mountain scenery, the picturesque and exotic mountaineers, with their Muslim faith and proudly independent ways made a very vivid impression on the boy. A number of the early lyrics reflect this fascination with the Caucasus, but it is particularly in the narrative poems that it shows itself. Byron's exoticism found expression in the Near East of Greece and Turkey; Thomas Moore went to India; the Russian romantics turned to their own eastern frontier, the meeting-ground of Muslim and Christian, mountaineers and plainsmen, anarchic freedom and civilized despotism. Pushkin's *Prisoner of the Caucasus* and *The Fountain of Bakhchisarai* led the way, and other poets were not slow to follow. But Lermontov at least had real experience of the region—even his juvenile verse has a certain amount of genuine local color, not mere convention parroted from others. The poem has no plot, properly speaking: a Circassian "prince," unnamed, gathers his followers for an attack on a Russian (Cossack) "town," also unnamed, in order to rescue his captive brother. The ensuing battle is briefly described, with the habitual clichés, and the Circassians are driven back. The final section balances with the first in an atmospheric natural description. Among the numerous derivative elements in the piece one may note the lines:[3] "Coolness is wafted from the river, the young leafage merges its delightful fragrance with the spring freshness"—the same kind of deliberate confusion of sense impressions—odor and temperature— that is so notable in Zhukovsky's "Evening."

Written somewhat later in the same year 1828 and conceived as a rebuke to Pushkin for what Lermontov felt as a dearth of the romantic in the denouement of *A Prisoner of the Caucasus,* is the fourteen-year-old's own poem of the same name and basic plot.[4] Lermontov's story follows the same course as Pushkin's—the Prisoner is befriended by a compassionate Circassian maiden who falls in love with him, and eventually frees him. Pushkin's disillusioned Russian hero of course refuses the love of the girl who has saved him, and she quietly slips into a mountain torrent to drown. Lermontov's hero is felled at the moment of liberation by a Circassian bullet, sped by the girl's vengeful father. In despair she commits suicide, and her father is left to suffer a bootless remorse, over which the young poet gloats.[5]

A third narrative, also dating from 1828, and also with some Pushkin echoes (this time from *The Robber Brothers*), but still more Byronic, is *The Corsair.*[6] The poem takes the form, which becomes a favored device of Lermontov, of a confession. The speaker begins: "Friends, look at me! I am pale, emaciated, joy has gone out in my eyes like the radiance of fire." Pushkin's "bandit brother" also, it will be recalled, tells the story of his dramatic swim across a river, one arm manacled to an arm of his beloved brother, who does not survive the escape attempt. Lermontov's hero loses his brother to disease, then in despair takes to a life of piracy—in the Aegean, apparently. He has obvious Byronic traits of character: "I shall tell you only that everywhere I wander with disillusioned soul like an orphan, not daring to trust, as before, a hope that always played me false." He falls in love with a Greek girl whom he and his men rescue from a sinking boat, along with other refugees from the Turks—but alas, her misfortunes have turned her mad! "From that time, O friends, I too moan, my lot was decided by that; from that time I know no rest, but from that time I have become dead and turned to stone for tender feelings." Although the obligatory love theme appears in *The Corsair,* the principal element is the psychological. The young poet is making an attempt to explain an embittered and disillusioned character by a narration of events. The events themselves are secondary.[7] The Greek locale of the poem should be noted, however, as a reflection of the Russo-Turkish War of 1828-29, on the side of the Greek rebels.

The device of the confession recurs in *The Criminal* (1829).[8] The narrator, addressed as "ataman" in an introductory speech of his followers who ask him to tell his story, is apparently the leader of a band of brigands. His story occupies the rest of the short poem. His father married a young second wife, who fell in love with the son; their incestuous affair was discovered, the son was driven from home and became a highwayman in the company of two disreputable Jews. One of their victims, killed on a dark night on the highroad, proved to be the narrator's father. Later the band attacked and burned his paternal home and he murdered his step-mother-mistress. Since these bloody crimes he has lived, "a criminal old man, devoid of reason, afar from all, alien to all." The fifteen-year-old's attempt to picture the psychology of his criminal hero is not entirely unconvincing, although neither the father nor the stepmother is given any reality. It is a first attempt to depict a "demonic" character in Lermontov's narrative verse (the poem "The Demon" also belongs to 1829).

In 1829 Lermontov also planned a lengthy narrative poem on the career of the semi-legendary Oleg the Wise,[9] and composed a few fragments on the subject, most interesting of which is an imaginative picture of the hero's consultation of Stribog, the pagan god of war, on the banks of Lake Ilmen. The influence of Pushkin's "Lay of Oleg the Wise" and of Ryleev's *duma* on the same character may be noted. This was Lermontov's first experiment with Russian legendary history. It was to be followed the same year by another fragment, *Two Brothers,*[10] evidently intended to be the introduction to a tale of the fratricidal struggle over a girl whom both brothers love. The theme of the enmity of two brothers is a very common one in *Sturm und Drang* drama, and may have been suggested to Lermontov by Schiller's drama *Die Räuber.* It appears later in the young poet's completed tale *Izmail-Bey. Two Captive Maidens* (1830),[11] with a theme clearly derived from Pushkin's *Fountain of Bakhchisarai,* is another two-and-a-half-page fragment, in which Zaira rejects the love of Sultan Akhmet, and her rival Gülnara listens with satisfaction to a cry as someone is thrown into the sea to drown.

The first of Lermontov's narrative poems to deal quite impressively with characterization is *Giulio* (1830).[12] The piece begins with a brief description of the first-person narrator's visit to a mine in an unspecified northern land. Here the visitor is greeted by a man whom he finally recognizes as a former acquaintance, and who entrusts to him a "scroll" containing the record of his unhappy loves. The mine-motif, here entirely accessory and undeveloped, is of course a favorite of the German romantics, e.g., Tieck, Novalis and E. T. A. Hoffmann. The "scroll" contains Giulio's confession. Born on an estate near Naples, he had as a young man won the love of a young neighbor, the sweet and saintly Laura. But he was determined to "see the world," and in spite of Laura's despair, left his home and wandered about, coming finally to Venice, where he was caught up in the carnival spirit (the influence here of Hoffmann's *Prinzessin Brambilla* [1821] is very likely). Led to a sumptuous palace by a masked merrymaker, he found himself in the presence of a beautiful lady, Melina, whose lover he soon became. But one night when he entered his mistress's house unexpectedly, he detected "the sound of a kiss" (!), and, filled with jealous fury, prepared to deal with a successful rival. At that moment, as he was making his way through the dark corridor with murderous intent, an apparition stopped him—it was Laura! He fell in a faint. After a long illness, he returned to his native land, and discovered, near the summer-house which had been the scene of their youthful love-making a fresh grave—Laura's, of course. Overwhelmed with remorse, Giulio left his native Italy for the north, and sought refuge in the mine: "So I live. The subterranean dark and chill, the monotonous tapping, the flames of the torches are to my liking. I always reckon the crowd of my comrades as more contemptible than myself. Self-love gladdens my mood: so the cripple is glad when he sees the blind man."[13] The self-centered, youthful cruelty of Giulio is well pictured in his parting scene with Laura: "No, Laura, no," I exclaimed, "Leave me, forget; my former devotion is not to be inspired in a breast that is now cold to you; my heart is as free and love as light as those wanderers in the sky, the clouds."[14] In the midst of his poem, with no introduction, Lermontov inserts a free paraphrase of a famous ode of Horace (II, xvi), with some significant alterations of his own: "Cares circle in the dark of night about the soft bed, the golden tassels; scorpion-conscience at the pillow chases sweet slumber from dry eyelids. As the wind pursues in the sky afar the torn cloudlets, so sorrow in the self-same boat with us leaves us neither at meals nor in battle."[15]

One technical aspect of *Giulio* deserves mention—the meter. Lermontov's earlier narratives were written, like Pushkin's and most of Byron's, in a four-foot iambic measure—a form particularly adapted to a rapid narrative style, full of exciting turns. *Giulio* is composed in a five-foot iambic meter, with paired and always *masculine* rhymes. Lermontov often experimented in his early lyric verse with all-masculine rhymes—

probably under the influence of English prosody, in which the practice is normal. The use of the device in a long narrative had been anticipated in Russian by Zhukovsky's translation of Byron's *Prisoner of Chillon,* although both the translation and Byron's original use the four-foot, not five-foot line. The longer line harmonizes with the introspective, meditative character of the poem.

The incomplete "Oleg" was evidently to be based on Russian legendary history, and *Two Brothers,* although with an invented subject, would have been laid in pre-Christian Rus. The first major attempt, however, to utilize this material is to be found in *The Last Son of Freedom* (1830-31),[16] the hero of which is the wholly legendary Vadim, whom the chronicle pictures as an unsuccessful rebel against the Varangian Ryurik. The subject was often used by Russian writers, most notably by Knyazhnin in his tragedy *Vadim of Novgorod.* Pushkin began both a narrative poem and a tragedy on the subject, but abandoned both, and Ryleev made the Novgorodian freedom-fighter the hero of one of his *Dumy.* In Lermontov's treatment the inevitable love-element is paired with patriotic zeal in a way perhaps learned from Schiller (cf. *Don Carlos*) to bring about the tragic denouement. Vadim leaves his native city with other dissidents when Ryurik takes the throne, and plots with them to overthrow the despot. The battle is lost, however; and then Vadim discovers that his sweetheart Leda has been raped by the usurper, and mocked and abandoned by her friends, has succumbed to her woes. He makes his way alone into the city, finds Ryurik at a festival to the war-god, and challenges him to a duel. The Varangian is triumphant, Vadim is dealt a mortal blow: "Vadim fell silently to earth; he did not look around, he did not groan. He fell in blood, and fell alone—*the last free Slovenian!*" The meter here is again the swift-moving four-foot iamb, with all masculine rhymes. The poem is introduced by a dedication to Lermontov's friend N. S. Shenshin in two octave stanzas, and a "song" is introduced in the first episode, sung by Vadim's elderly friend Ingelat, and consisting of nine five-line strophes, in an irregular three-beat meter with generally dactylic clausulae, unrhymed—an attempt to utilize one form of the so-called "Russian verse" of popular song.

Lermontov returns again and again throughout his life to subjects from the Caucasus for his poems. A short and particularly successful example is *Kallý,* written in 1830-31.[17] The subject is drawn from the Caucasian tradition of the blood-feud, according to which the next of kin of a murdered man is obligated as his paramount duty in life to kill as many as possible of the murderer's family. The word *kalli* seems to be a dialect variant of the Turkish *kanli,* meaning "bloodstained"; it is given to a person who has carried out such a vengeance. Lermontov begins his poem without explanation, *in medias res,* with the words of a mullah exhorting a Circassian boy that his father was murdered and that he exists for no end but to avenge him. The boy takes the dagger that the mullah gives him, goes to the hut of one of the murderer's kin, kills him in his sleep and then, unmoved by her beauty and terror, he kills Akbulat's daughter. But filled with revulsion at his dreadful act, he then goes to the mullah's hut and kills him too. "He kept eternal silence, but not to excite the crowd's prattling attention; and he alone knew why the terrible title *'kally'* has remained with him in the mountains." The theme of this powerful little experiment seems to be the tragic consequence of the youth's obedience to the dictates of the evil tradition, in spite of an inner rebellion against it.

As a boy Lermontov during his visits to the Caucasus may have heard from the natives some of their picturesque beliefs, such as that in "the angel of death," Azrail. Two of his 1831 poems, with complex but evident ties with some of the early versions of *The Demon,* bear the titles *Azrail*[18] and *The Angel of Death.*[19] Apparently the first had been conceived as a romantic "mystery"—a pseudo-dramatic genre exemplified by Byron's *Cain* and *Heaven and Earth,* and in Russian by Küchelbecker's *Izhorsky.* It is in dramatic form, a dialogue between Azrail (in Lermontov's version a "fallen angel") and a "maiden" with whom he has fallen in love. Part of the dialogue is in prose, presumably to be subsequently versified. The theme of the "demon" whom the love of an earthly maiden might redeem haunted Lermontov, as the eight versions of *The Demon,* from 1829 to 1841, give evidence. *Azrail* uses the same theme, but instead of becoming the demon's victim, like Tamara, "the maiden" at the end of the piece abandons Azrail for another. The center of the poem is "Azrail's Confession," written, like *The Last Son of Freedom,* in four-foot iambs with exclusively masculine rhymes. In it the fallen angel tells "the maiden" of his longing for "a creature like myself, though but in torment alone," and his reproach of God for endowing him with this longing. He is punished for this blasphemy, but "the maiden's" love comforts him. The piece trails off into prose, with an ending so anticlimactic and flat as to be grotesque: "the maiden" informs her demon-lover that she is another's bride. "My bridegroom is a glorious warrior, his helmet gleams like fire and his sword is more dangerous than lightning." To this Azrail rejoins: "There's a woman for you! She embraces me and gives her heart to another!" (The Maiden) "What did you say? Oh, don't be angry!"(Azrail)"I'm not angry. (bitterly) "What is there to be angry for?"

The Angel of Death, dedicated in a separate three-stanza poem to Alexandra Mikhailovna Vereshchagina, is a more ambitious, or at least more finished, piece of work, in the most extreme tradition of romanticism. The "angel of death," according to Lermontov's plot, was once a kindly, benevolent spirit, whose coming was not terrible: "but formerly these encounters seemed a sweet destiny." But one time the angel came to take the beautiful Ada, the beloved and sole friend of the hermit Zorain, who lived in a cave in Mount Lebanon. Zorain's despair so touched the angel that he reversed fate and restored Ada to life. Later, however, young Zorain grew restive in his solitary existence, and left Ada to win military glory in a battle about to be fought in the valley below their cave. He was mortally wounded, Ada found him on the battlefield, and he died in her arms. The angel of death conveyed both souls to Paradise, but from that time forth he held only "a cold contempt for earth," and his former comforting approach has been replaced by terror: "Colder than ice are his embraces, and his kiss is a curse!" Podolinsky's *Death of a Peri* (1837) is founded on a similarly romantic dream of a supernatural intervention postponing death, but it is entirely unlikely that Lermontov's treatment could have been known to his contemporary, for it was not published until 1857. Both poems probably have their models in the German romantics, especially Jean-Paul, whose *Der Tod eines Engels* (1788) is based on a similar fantasy. The "Angel of the Last Hour" so pities the suffering beings whose souls he collects on the battlefield that he himself arranges to experience death by briefly occupying the body of a badly wounded youth. Lermontov in characterizing his hero Zorain is obviously picturing himself as he liked to be seen: "He loved the night, freedom, the mountains, and everything in nature—even men—but he shunned them."

Lermontov evinces in many of his youthful works a particular interest in Spain. His first drama is *The Spaniards;* the second version (early in 1830) of *The Demon* has its locale in Spain; and the narrative poem *Confession,* which is the germ from which the mature *Mtsyri (The Novice)* grows, is laid in Spain. The probably unfounded legend in the Lermontov family that traced the family origin back to a Spanish Duke of Lerma in the sixteenth century is doubtless largely responsible for the poet's interest in Spain.

A Confession[20] belongs to the second half of 1831. The device of letting the person most central to a tale be the narrator of it was one which Lermontov learned from Byron, and which became a favorite with him. It has the obvious advantage of providing a plausible occasion for reviewing the whole course of a life, as well as of describing feelings subjectively in the person of the one who experienced them. *A Confession* is put in the mouth of a young Spaniard incarcerated in a monastery prison and awaiting execution for some crime never revealed. Between the brief third-person exposition at the beginning and summary at the end, the poem is a monologue addressed to the priest who has come to hear the criminal's confession. In it he refers without explaining anything to his ecstatic love for an unnamed woman:

> For the last time I swear to you before the Creator that I am guilty of nothing. Say: that I did as I could without pangs [of conscience] or disquiet, that I was not parted from my fatal secret for the sake of men . . . forget that I lived—that I loved, far more than I lived! Whom did I love? Holy father, this shall die in me, with me; for life, for the world, for eternity, I shall not betray to you this secret!

The poem ends with a short third-person narrative relating how the sound of the funeral bell rung in the monastery penetrates the walls of a nearby convent and a beautiful nun, on hearing it, utters a shriek and falls senseless: "But he who heard this [shriek] thought probably, or said, that such a sound would not issue twice from one breast! . . . It carried with it life and love." The technique of lending interest and suspense to a tale by leaving the background circumstances mysterious is a common procedure with Byron; Lermontov never employed it elsewhere in quite so extreme a form as in *A Confession.*

"The Sailor" (1832),[21] a fragment, is a plotless first-person monologue by the title character, the chief interest of which is the fact that the bulk of it consists of six "Onegin stanzas"—that is, 14-line strophes rhyming aBaBccDDeFFeGG—the difficult and beautiful form that Pushkin invented for his great poem, and that other poets very seldom attempted. For a youngster who never went to sea, Lermontov shows in this poem a quite remarkable insight into the feelings of the narrator as he climbs the mast: "How mighty I felt, as I clung with elastic hand to the sail or the damp rigging; I was between the sky and the waves; I looked at the clouds, and down below, and was not confused, did not feel fright."

Of Lermontov's numerous experiments with the narrative poem there are basically two varieties—those with a conventional, literary background, spun entirely out of his imagination—*The Last Son of Freedom, The Angel of Death, Giulio, A Confession,* etc.—and those with a setting in the Caucasus and based on the poet's own observation, often on actual incidents which he remembered from his boyhood—*The Circassians, Kallý, Izmail-Bey, Aul Bastunji, Hadji Abrek,* etc. Of the two groups the second is of course far superior to the first. The mature poems *Mtsyri (The Novice)* and *The Demon* belong to the second group as far as background is concerned, to the first for incident—a quite surprisingly harmonious combination.

The best of the second group before *Mtsyri* is the "Eastern tale" *Izmail-Bey* (1832).[22] The basic plot for this was furnished by a historical incident involving Izmail-Bey Atazhukov (or Atazhukin), a prince of the Kabardá, who was educated in Russia and served in Catherine II's second war with Turkey, and who met his death after his return to his native land at the hands of his cousin Prince Roslambek Misostov. Lermontov embroiders this insufficiently romantic historical datum with the addition of a love affair between Izmail and a Russian girl, and a vengeful Russian lover of the girl who pursues Izmail and is killed by him in battle. There is also a Circassian beauty, Zara, who runs away from her family to become Izmail's mistress, and meets a mysterious fate which the poet prefers only to hint at. The hero's death by an unseen assassin's bullet conforms with the historical facts.[23] Byron's influence is obvious in a romantic embellishment of history, the theme of the ardently devoted mistress (Zara) who puts on male clothing and follows her lover in the guise of a young page (cf. *Lara:* it may be noted also that the wife of Mulla-Nur in Bestuzhev's novel of that name is another transvestite). *Izmail-Bey* begins with some personal references of Lermontov to his love of the Caucasus; the narrative is put in the mouth of an old Chechen, who relates it to the poet as a true tale of bygone days. The framing introduction and some other passages which interrupt the narrative with the author's personal comments are composed in five-foot iambic verse with irregular rhyme, the narrative proper in the four-foot iambic meter most commonly used by Byron and his Russian followers for the romantic poem, and a few lyrical interpolations (e.g., "Selim's Song" in Part III) in various short strophes.

Lermontov's love for the magnificent scenery of the Caucasus (which incidentally he often sketched very effectively in water-color) appears in the first stanza of Part I of his poem:

> I greet you, hoary Caucasus! I am a traveller not foreign to your mountains: they carried me in my infancy and accustomed me to the skies of the wilderness. And since those times I have long dreamt always of the sky of the south and the cliffs of mountains. Beautiful you are, stern realm of freedom, and you, Nature's eternal thrones, when, blue as smoke, the clouds toward evening fly toward you from afar, hover above you, whisper like shadows, like feathers undulating above the head of enormous apparitions—and the moon wanders alone over the dark blue vaults.[24]

Characterization in *Izmail-Bey* is conventionally Byronic, especially of the hero and of Zara, the mountain maiden who falls in love with him at first sight and runs away from her father's house to become his mistress. The portrait of Izmail as a mountaineer half-Europeanized through years with the Russians lends him more actuality, but he behaves quite like any Byronic hero. The background figures of the tale, on the other hand, are shown much more realistically. Here, for example, is the description of the solitary family with which Izmail obtains a night's lodging during his search for his native village (fear of the Russian advance has forced it to move from its original location):

> He himself [i.e., Izmail's host, father of Zara] was a Lesghian; it has been long since (such was heaven's decree) he has beheld his native land. Three sons and a young daughter live with him. In their company sorrow still keeps silent, and the poor refuge is dear to him. When the stars of the night are kindled, then his bold sons set out on rides hither and thither: the whole family lives by plunder! They bring fear everywhere; to steal or take by force is all one to them; they ask for wine [*chikhir*] and mead with the dagger, and pay for millet with a bullet; they lead away any horse they please whether from a native camp or a Cossack village. Their only fear is of the day, and to their possessions there is no limit! Today only one is at home, his favorite, the eldest son.[25]

Most of Lermontov's early Byronic tales have a quite simple theme: *Izmail-Bey* is in this respect quite exceptional. In the words of E. M.

Pulkhritudova: "In *Izmail-Bey* two stories are developed: the story of the gradual, inexorable ruin of the patriarchal mode of life of the Caucasian tribes; and the story of the tragic loneliness and spiritual shipwreck of a man who has thought to escape from the present with its wounds and contradictions into a past which seems to him simple, natural and harmonious." In Lermontov's picture of the patriarchal society of the mountaineers the treachery of Roslambek is just as much a part as the impulsive, open-hearted love and devotion of Zara.[26] There is no Eden in the past.

However derivative and romanticized the story of *Izmail-Bey* may be, it is a great advance over any of Lermontov's previous attempts at narrative poems, or indeed over several of the attempts that follow, such as *The Lithuanian Girl* (1832)[27] —an improbable tale laid in the period of Russian-Lithuanian wars in the fifteenth and sixteenth centuries. The old boyar Arseny (a name that recurs in *The Boyar Orsha,* and in the slightly altered form Arbenin is given to the semi-autobiographical heroes of the plays *A Strange One* and *Masquerade*), defender in his castle of a region bordering Lithuania, has taken a beautiful Lithuanian girl captive and become infatuated with her. His aggrieved wife takes refuge in a nunnery, and "Arseny was ready to sacrifice wife, children, fatherland, soul— everything for [his captive's] pleasure." Klara pretends to be loving and submissive, but one night two belated travellers seek lodging in Arseny's castle, and in the morning Klara and the travellers are gone. They were presumably her father and lover. Old Arseny is inconsolable; he seeks his revenge in war, but in a climactic battle with the Lithuanians a fierce young warrior encounters him. It is Klara! She taunts him and urges on her Lithuanians, and Arseny is overwhelmed. The poem ends with a picture of the lone convent where mass is said for the soul of the slain Arseny; there is one mourner: "God knows what came into her mind to have pity for him who had no pity for her!"

Aul Bastundzhi (1833-34),[28] like *Izmail-Bey,* is based on Lermontov's boyish recollections of the Caucasus. In the neighborhood where the Russian frontier town of Pyatigorsk was later to rise there was in the eighteenth century a Kabardian *aul* (native village) named Bastundzhi. When Georgia was annexed (1804) the Russian frontier was drawn south of Bastundzhi, and its inhabitants, along with those of several other villages, abandoned it. Originally unconnected with the village was a Circassian legend about two brothers, Kanbulat and Atvonak, who became bitter enemies because of the younger brother's passion for Kanbulat's wife. Lermontov combined the two stories, making the dreadful crime of the younger brother (Selim in his version) the reason for the abandonment of the village. In Lermontov's tale the original love and harmony of the two brothers is rudely shattered when the older (Akbulat) takes a wife (Zara). Selim falls madly in love with her, tries vainly to persuade Akbulat to give her up to him, and runs away. He returns secretly, meets Zara and is enraged when she refuses to betray her husband, even though she loves Selim. The latter wreaks vengeance by abducting Zara and his brother's favorite horse. After the abduction has been discovered, the horse gallops home, collapses and dies at his master's feet—and bound to his back is the corpse of Zara! The *aul* mysteriously catches fire, and from the mountains is heard a satanic laugh; the mullah tries vainly to overcome the evil spirit—the village is burned to the ground and its very existence is soon forgotten.

Aside from Lermontov's usual vivid and sympathetic description of Caucasian scenery and mores, the poem is remarkable chiefly for its metrical form, which is the Italian octave stanza. Pushkin's *Little House in Kolomna* (1830) had brought this difficult meter to Russian attention, and Shevyryov's essay: "On the Possibility of Introducing the Italian Octave into Russian Versification" (1831) had discussed the advantages and beauties of the meter. Shevyryov's own experiments with it in his Tasso translations were, as we have seen, less than successful. Lermontov makes no attempt, as Shevyryov did, to introduce the Italian license of eliding contiguous vowels; his lines follow purely Russian prosodic rules, and are smooth and graceful.

The first of Lermontov's narrative poems to be published was *Hadji-Abrek* (written in 1832),[29] which a friend of the poet's, acting without Lermontov's knowledge or consent, purloined and got published in Senkovsky's *Reading Library* (1835). According to Lermontov's cousin A. P. Shan-Girei, "Michel. . . . was furious." The poem, however, was quite well received.

Hadji-Abrek (Russian *Khadzhi-Abrek*) is a grim tale of blood vengeance in the Caucasus, told with great economy and restraint. The element of personal intervention in narration—the author's own comments of pity and horror at the action—is almost completely eliminated here, and the stark tragedy is so much the more effective. Beginning and ending, too, are unconventional. An old Lesghian tells the harrowing tale of the abduction of his only surviving child, a beloved daughter, to a company of sympathetic fellow villagers. He ends his story with the words: "Hither, horsemen of Dzhemet! Show me your valor! Who knows Prince Bei-Bulat? Who will bring back my daughter to me?" The challenge is met by an as yet unnamed champion, who pushes forward through the crowd and undertakes within two days to perform the mission. The identity and real purpose of the avenger are not divulged until the middle of the poem, which is in dramatic form—a dialogue between Leila, the abducted girl, now Bei-Bulat's adoring mistress, and Hadji—now designated with the ominous addition of "Abrek." "Abrek" is a Circassion term for a blood-guilty outlaw, exiled from home and kindred for a killing. Hadji becomes an "abrek" only by his dealing with Leila. She is alone when he rides up to

Bei-Bulat's house toward evening; although invited in and offered food, he strangely refuses—unwilling, of course, to accept hospitality from one whom he is about to kill. Bei-Bulat is absent on a foray, and Leila is alone. She attempts to cheer the morose stranger with song and dance, when he suddenly stops her with the words: "Enough! Cease, Leila; forget [your] gaiety for an instant. Say, has not sometimes the thought of death ever come to disturb you? Answer." (Leila) "No! What is the cold tomb to me? I have found my Paradise on earth." To her horror the visitor then reveals that Bei-Bulat is the murderer of his brother; the duty of blood-vengeance has thus fallen to him. But merely killing his enemy is not punishment enough. He has determined to wait until he can destroy what Bei-Bulat most cherishes—and now the opportunity has come! Leila reacts understandably, with abject terror and pleading, but to no avail. With a swift stroke he beheads her, puts the bloody head in a sack and spurs his restive and frightened horse down the mountain toward the village where Leila's father is waiting for his return. Wordlessly he opens the sack, and the terrible trophy rolls out. The poor father kisses his daughter's dead lips and dies that instant; Hadji-Abrek rides away. The final episode is only obliquely indicated: wandering wayfarers find two rotting bodies, covered with blood and locked in each other's embrace: "Their attire was rich, their caps were concealed with hoods. In the one they recognized Bei-Bulat. No one knew the other."

Lermontov's narrative poems, as has been noted before, fall into roughly three categories: the heroic variety, localized in some time and place furnished by the poet's own imagination; romantic tales, set in a real but somewhat overcolored Caucasian landscape; and, after 1836, a third type, which may perhaps be best described as "anti-romantic"—mocking, satirical accounts of incidents purportedly occurring in a perfectly ordinary contemporary society. One tale falls entirely outside these classifications: *The Song of Tsar Ivan Vasilyevich, the Young Oprichnik and the Doughty Merchant Kalashnikov* is a fully realistic, historically authentic reconstruction of an incident from the sixteenth century—a remarkable combination of the heroic tale of the first variety and the realistic tale of the third. It will be instructive of Lermontov's rapid artistic maturing to compare the poem *The Boyar Orsha* (1835-36) with *The Song of. . . . the Merchant Kalashnikov.*

The Boyar Orsha[30] is the best of the first group of Lermontov's narrative poems, which includes *Oleg, A Confession,* and *The Lithuanian Girl.* It is skilfully constructed and rapidly moving. The expository material is quickly given at the beginning—Orsha's long and loyal service to Tsar Ivan the Terrible, his stern and morose character, and his love for his only daughter. The catastrophe is motivated in an unique and clever fashion, as the boyar's henchman Sokol, under pretence of narrating a tale of a folklore king, discloses that Orsha's daughter has a love affair with the boyar's foundling protege Arseny. The first and most serious awkwardness in the tale comes at the end of Part I, when Orsha surprises the lovers in the girl's chamber, and proceeds to their punishment. It is perhaps not too inconceivable that a nobleman of the court of Ivan IV should consign his beloved daughter to a lingering and horrible death by locking her in her chamber and throwing the key into the Dniepr; but it is hard to believe that a man who is capable of this should merely have the girl's lover carried off to a nearby monastery to be given a formal, if hardly impartial, trial! Surely a more natural and appropriate action under the circumstances would have been a quick sword and a body hurled into the river along with the key. But no—Lermontov wants opportunity for his hero to justify himself and discourse eloquently on the power of love to level the artificial social barriers between a noblewoman and a low-born waif. To make the situation still more confusing, the poet utilizes in Arseny's speeches to the Abbot and the assembled monks portions of the earlier poem *A Confession,* where the situation is considerably different, with the result that Arseny's position is blurred and inconsistent. He has been, on the one hand, a foundling brought up by the boyar, and hence presumably in a position to have some intimacy with Orsha's daughter—a situation identical with that of Fernando in Lermontov's first attempt at a tragedy, *The Spaniards* (1829). At the same time he seems to have been, like the speaker of *A Confession,* brought up in a monastery! "People say that I was taken by you as a baby and put from my early years under the stern supervision of monks, and grew up within confining walls, a child in soul— a monk by destiny!" And somehow, in a manner left unexplained, this monk has succeeded not only in seducing Orsha's daughter, but in making himself chief of a band of brigands, who succeed at the end of Part II in rescuing him from his monastery prison! In the Third Part Arseny is leader of a Polish force which meets and annihilates a Russian army not far from Orsha's castle on the Dniepr. The ex-monk finds Orsha, mortally wounded, on the battlefield, extorts from the dying man the information that he can find his daughter in her chamber at the castle, waiting for him, and rides off in haste to recover his beloved. In a scene that surely belongs in a Gothic novel, he discovers her skeleton in the locked tower! But this scene is spoiled by the restrained and philosophical reaction of Arseny: the sight of the mortal remains of the unfortunate girl elicits this speech:

> So here is everything that I loved! Cold and lifeless dust, which[once] burned on my lips, now without feeling, without love, clasped in the embraces of the earth. Her beautiful soul, having assumed another being, now soars in a holy land, and like a reproach before me is the trace of her momentary life! She perished in the flower of her years, amid secret torments, or without perturbations, when and how, God knows![31]

The meditation is eloquent and moving, but scarcely what an ardent lover would utter in the first moment of horror at making such a discovery. And instead of killing himself on her body, as any romantic hero would naturally do, Arseny ends the poem thus: "Now one thing is left for me. I go! Whither? Is it not all the same, whether to this or another land? Here is her dust, but not she! I go from here forever, without thoughts, without goal and labor, alone with my anguish in the dark of night, and the snowstorm will cover over my tracks."[32]

The Boyar Orsha has a fascination, as Belinsky perceived, because it is, after all, the work of a great poet. The verse is magnificent—the common four-foot iambic line, with exclusively masculine rhymes, as also in *A Confession* and *Mtsyri (The Novice)*. Many of the lines in Arseny's defence (Part II) are epigrammatically eloquent: "Granting that your monastery was instituted by the hand of God, yet in this heart is another law, no less sacred to Him!" "Nay, do not threaten, holy father; what have you and I to fear? The tomb awaits us both...Is it not all the same, whether a day or a year?" "What though I die...my death will not prolong their existence, and they may not appropriate my future days..." etc. What is less satisfactory is immediately apparent: defects of motivation and characterization, as indicated, and in particular the typical romantic fallacy of an imaginative reconstruction of the past. The time and place of the poem's action are ostensibly the sixteenth century and the border between Muscovy and Lithuania. But there is nothing to distinguish this time and place from any time and place in medieval Europe, beyond the mere mention of Ivan the Terrible, Poland, and the Dniepr. Most glaring, perhaps, is Orsha's "castle" on the banks of the Dniepr, envisioned with no specific traits to distinguish it from a castle on the Rhine, or even on the Loire! And the monastery—is it Orthodox? Who can say: there are bells, the walls are painted with the figures of saints, the monks wear black habits, the Abbot holds a cross studded with diamonds and pearls, etc. These are all picturesque details, but they are drawn not from a historical reality, but from Lermontov's imagination—or from books! The same may be said of the battle briefly described in Part III:[33]

> The noisy battle had whirled far away, leaving its bloody trace... Among overthrown horses, fragments of spears and swords, a horseman was riding hither and thither at that time... A heap of bodies, disfigured by the sword, made a motley array on that hillock, and the snow, dyed with blood, had melted here and there to the ground...

The imaginative reconstruction is masterly, and often convincing, in *The Boyar Orsha,* until one compares it with a genuine historical recreation, such as is afforded by *The Song About Tsar Ivan Vasilyevich, the Young Oprichnik and the Doughty Merchant Kalashnikov.*[34]

We have seen in examining Lermontov's lyric verse how he passed in a few years from the abstract and bookish "Field of Borodino" (1830-1831) to the concrete realism of "Borodino" (1837). The same evolution can be seen here. The plot of the "Song" is an invented one, as is that of *The Boyar*

Orsha; it also is laid in the reign of Ivan the Terrible, and it also has as a principal theme that of social equality—"the doughty merchant Kalashnikov" asserts his equality with "the young oprichnik," a nobleman, who tries to make love to his wife, and kills him in a fair fight. But the differences are instructive. The "Song" is composed in the bylina meter, and put as it were in the mouth of a popular bard entertaining a gathering at a nobleman's house. *Okh ty goi esi, Tsar' Ivan Vasil'evich,* the bard begins, in the time-honored bylina manner: "Now all hail to thee, Tsar Ivan Vasilievich," in Mr. Daniels's translation. The bard addresses his audience in the first, introductory, paragraph, again briefly at the end of Part I, at the end of Part II, and at the end of the poem. Orsha, in his poem, is a "boyar," a "nobleman" without further qualification. Kalashnikov's young rival is an *oprichnik*—usually translated as "guardsman," but with a very specific connotation. Ivan IV's *oprichniki* were young men from noble families whom he recruited to be his unfailing aides in a ruthless struggle against the hereditary and semi-independent aristocracy. Among the bloodiest and most hated of Ivan's henchmen was Malyuta Skuratov. It is not without significance that in his address to young Kiribeevich the Terrible Tsar says to the youth: "For you are of the race of the Skuratovs, and you were reared by the family of Malyuta!"

It would be easy to point to other instances where the "Song" presents a concrete and specific picture of a past reality, and *The Boyar Orsha* only a conventional one. Early in the latter poem the old warrior, "aggrieved by an *oprichnik,*" addressed a plea to the Tsar that begins: "O Tsar of Hope! Let me go to my homeland. Day after day I grow older—I cannot even avenge an injury on my foe. There are many servants in your court. Let me go!" and ends with: "Let me make my bow to the Dniepr—there I shall die."[35] And what does Tsar Ivan reply to this outrageous request? Does he, as might be expected, answer: "Oh no, my friend, you'll die here," and forthwith order the boyar's execution? It is no part of Lermontov's purpose in *The Boyar Orsha* to depict Ivan IV as he really was; Orsha's request for leave is followed by no outburst; the Tsar's reply is not even reported; there is only the anticlimactic statement: "And he [i.e., Orsha] beheld his ancient house." Quite otherwise does the Tsar appear in the "Song." At a royal banquet the Tsar orders "the sweet wine from beyond the sea" to be given to his *oprichniki,* and "all drank, giving the Tsar glory." Only one of them, the love-smitten young Kiribeevich, in a gloomy revery, ignores the Tsar's wine: "Now the Tsar knitted his black brows and fixed on him his piercing eyes, just as a hawk from the height of the sky glares at a young grey-winged dove."[36] Still the young *oprichnik* is oblivious, until—"Now the Tsar brought his staff down on the ground, and with its iron end he pierced two inches into the oaken floor; but even then the young warrior did not start. Now spoke the Tsar a terrible word, and then the goodly youth came to." This iron staff of Tsar Ivan's was, it may be noted in passing, a formidable weapon: with it he had been known to pin a man's foot to the floor! Young Kiribeevich, however, is so lost in the despair of hopeless love that he bids his sovereign: "Order me executed, my head chopped off—it weighs heavy on my bogatyr shoulders, and of itself it bows down to the damp earth." When he learns the cause of the *oprichnik's* gloom, the terrible Tsar is mollified, and promises his help.

Lermontov's *Song About Tsar Ivan Vasilyevich*... faithfully reflects the mores of sixteenth-century Moscow. Here is how the Merchant Kalashnikov shuts up shop on a winter evening: "The bells rang for vespers in the holy churches; behind the Kremlin burns the misty sunset, the clouds race across the sky—a humming snowstorm is driving them. The broad merchants' mart [*gostinyi dvor*] has emptied. Stepan Paramonovich shuts up his booth with an oaken door and with a German lock with a spring; he fastens a fierce mastiff-dog with long fangs to an iron chain, and goes home, lost in thought, to his young wife across the Moskva River." He finds his wife dishevelled and in tears; the young oprichnik has accosted her in the street, kissed her in spite of her struggles, and in getting away from him she has abandoned some of her finery: "My patterned kerchief, a gift of yours, and my Bukhara veil. He has disgraced me, put me to shame, me, an honorable woman, without guilt—and what will the malicious neighbor women say? In whose sight shall I now show myself?" The boxing contest on the ice of the Moskva River, in the presence of the Tsar himself, is an historically authentic item, not a figment of the romantic imagination. Kiribeevich strikes the first blow, which bends the copper crucifix on his opponent's chest and drives it into the flesh so that he bleeds—a picturesque and credible detail. When the victorious Kalashnikov refuses to reveal why he has deliberately struck his opponent a mortal blow, the Terrible Tsar in a typical combination of vengefulness and magnanimity orders the young merchant beheaded, but his wife and brothers pensioned!

The theme of social equality is tacitly present in the poem's title, in the juxtaposition of "the young *oprichnik*," a nobleman, and "the doughty merchant," a commoner; but the theme is not stressed or developed—nor should it have been, for it would have been a glaring anachronism in the sixteenth century. The basic conflict is between two different kinds of temperament, two different ways of life. Kiribeevich is a ruthless egoist, determined to have what he wants regardless of the consequences to others or himself. When he confesses to the Tsar his infatuation with Alyona Dmitrievna, he never mentions that she is already married, and the Tsar assumes that his intervention may persuade an unmarried girl in his guardsman's favor. He boasts and struts on the boxing-ground, and tauntingly demands to know the name of the upstart who comes against him so that a proper Requiem may be sung for him. But when the unknown announces his name, and adds: "I was born of an honorable father, and I have lived in accord with the Lord's law. I have not disgraced another's wife, nor played the highwayman in the dark of night," the braggart Kiribeevich is suddenly smitten with terror: "He grew pale in the face as the autumn snow, his insolent eyes grew clouded, a cold chill ran between his powerful shoulders, upon his lips the word died away."[37] Stepan Paramonovich is the quiet, law-abiding citizen whom only an intolerable outrage drives to an exploit seemingly inconsistent with his class. The element of "rebelliousness," which some Marxist critics see in his character is simply a doctrinal mirage: it does not exist. He is touchy about his good name, and when his wife returns home in the dark, dishevelled and distraught, he warns her sternly that if she had been out carousing he will lock her up "so that she may not see God's world, may not soil my honorable name." The actions of the two fighters as they enter the ring are pointedly contrasted: "And doughty Kiribeevich comes in, in silence bows to the waist before the Tsar." When Kalashnikov appears, "he bowed first to the Terrible Tsar, afterward to the white Kremlin and the gold churches, and then to all the Russian people." The *oprichnik* is "the Tsar's man," contemptuous of "the people" and indifferent to the Orthodox faith; the young merchant bows first to the Tsar, but pays his respects then to church and people.

Kalashnikov with one blow of his mighty fist fells the guilty *oprichnik;* but his real exploit is his defiance of the Tsar. When Ivan angrily demands: "Answer me according to truth, according to conscience: of your willed intent or unwillingly did you strike dead my faithful servant?" he replies: "I shall tell you, Orthodox Tsar: I killed him with willed intent, but for what reason I shall not tell you, I shall tell it to God alone."[38] At the cost of his life he protects the good name of his beloved wife.

The Song About Tsar Ivan... is Lermontov's only experiment in historical reconstruction, but it is a most notable one, comparable in many ways with Pushkin's *Boris Godunov.* A realistic experiment of a different kind, laid not in a long past age of his native land, but in the recent past of the romantic Caucasus is *The Fugitive* [*Beglets*], subtitled "A Mountain Legend,"[39] written some time toward the end of the 1830s. The poem begins *in medias res,* most startlingly: "Harun ran faster than a fallow-deer, faster than the hare from the eagle; he ran in terror from the field of battle, where flowed Circassian blood. His father and two brothers fell there for honor and for freedom, and under the foeman's heel their heads lie in the dust." In wonderfully rapid strokes the stark tale is told. The fugitive stumbles into his native village at nightfall, and goes first to the house of his friend Selim, who lies on his death-bed. When Harun tells the story of his shameful flight, Selim says coldly: "Go—you are worthy of contempt. Neither shelter nor benediction is here with me for a coward!" Harun slinks off and tries next the house of a girl who has loved him; but as he approaches, he hears her singing a song:

The moon sails
tranquil and quiet,
but the youthful warrior
goes to battle.

The *dzhigit* loads his rifle,
and the maiden says to him:
"My dear one, more boldly
trust in destiny;

pray to the east,
be faithful to the Prophet,
be more faithful to glory.

He who has betrayed his own
with bloody treason,
who has not fought the foe,
perishes inglorious.

Rains will not wash his wounds,
wild beast will not bury his bones.
The moon sails
tranquil and quiet,
but the youthful warrior
goes to battle."[40]

Harun knows better than to knock, but goes on to his mother's house. He knocks at the window and announces himself: "I am your Harun, your youngest son; through the Russian bullets I have come to you unharmed." "Alone?" "Alone." "And where are father and brothers?"—"Fallen! The Prophet blessed their death, and angels received their souls." "You took vengeance?"—"I did not take vengeance. I made for the mountains like an arrow. I left my sword in the foreign land, in order to be a comfort to your eyes and to wipe away your tears." The old woman's answer is: "With your shame, fugitive of freedom, I shall not darken my old age. You are a slave and a coward and no son of mine!" In the morning Harun's body lies at his mother's door; a dog licks his bloody wounds and the children curse him. But his spirit still haunts the village, knocking at night at the windows. "But hearing a thunderous verse of the Koran, he runs again, under the shadow of darkness, as once he ran from the sword."

Beginning with 1836 Lermontov turned to a quite different sort of *poèma*—a semi-satirical realistic picture of his own times. There are four such experiments, only two of which were certainly finished: *Mongó* (1836), *Sashka* (1835-36?); *The Tambov Treasurer's Wife* (1837-1838) and *A Fairy Tale for Children* (1839-40). But there are also some shorter pieces which form in a way a prologue to Lermontov's realistic period. In a 1941 article entitled "On the Way to Realism"[41] the Soviet critic S.N. Durylin considers, among the landmarks leading to the realism of *A Hero of Our*

Time, "The Field of Borodino," "Valerik," etc., a group of pieces known collectively as *iunkerskie poemy,* or "Junker narratives." These have never been published in Russia, and are seldom even mentioned in Lermontov literature, their contents being, for the puritanical Russian, "unprintable." They are accorded brief consideration in the *Lermontov Encyclopedia,*[42] where they are identified as "The Hospital," "The Peterhof Holiday," and "The Uhlan's Woman." They are "erotic poems in the spirit of P. Scarron and I.S. Barkov, written by Lermontov, possibly with the participation of his comrades in the *School for Sub-Lieutenants of the Guard and Cavalry Junkers* [a "Junker" in the usage of the Russian Empire was a junior officer of noble rank]. They reflect the manners and way of life of the milieu.... Alongside a coarse naturalism, in the Junker poems are encountered exact sketches of the military life and satirical portraits of Junkers..., as also in the so-called 'Junker lyrics'[*stikhtvoreniia*] written at the same time." These latter are presumably the epistle "To Tusenhausen," "An Ode to the Privy," and a third, unidentifiable, piece.

The *Russian Literature Triquarterly* has printed the Russian text of these suppressed works[43] on the basis of two collections issued in Geneva and Leipzig. In the same issue of the periodical an article by William H. Hopkins, "Lermontov's Hussar Poems," discusses them at some length, and their importance in Lermontov's development of a realistic style. Very pertinently Hopkins cites[44] Academician P. N. Sakulin's remark on the subject: "If one forgets about an ethical evaluation of these works, then it is necessary to give them an important significance in the evolution of Lermontov's creation. Like the comical and erotic *povesti* of other poets (e.g., Pushkin) Lermontov's frivolous *poemy* brought into his poetry a stream of simplicity and liveliness, features which were so lacking in the 'Romantic' *poemy* of Lermontov and his contemporaries."[45] The writer of the *Lermontov Encyclopedia* entry (E. E. Naidich) disagrees with Durylin and Sakulin: "Nonetheless the views expressed in the literature about the significance of the Junker poems as Lermontov's first experiments in reproducing actuality in the form of a realistic narrative are an evident exaggeration. A stage on the way from the Junker poems to *The Tambov Treasurer's Wife* may be considered the poem *Mongó.* "

To an unprejudiced American observer, the "Junker poems," for all their very frank and explicit sexual language, have an engaging liveliness. The description of the town festivities at Peterhof, which forms the background for the "rape" by Junker Bibikov of a not very resistant whore, is a splendid Brueghel-like picture, and the five lines that end "The Peterhof Holiday"—Bibikov's annoyed reflection on his experience—

> Happy is he who is not acquainted with whores!
> Happy is he who, at eventide, in the garden
> Finds a kindly beauty,
> Runs after her, arranges a little intrigue,

And pays with a box on the ears for his piece of tail,
[*I pliukhoi platit za pizdu*—note the alliteration!]

exhibit all of Lermontov's remarkable skill in creating sharp, epigrammatical *pointes.*

Mongó[46] is a lighthearted versification of an actual adventure of the poet (called Mayoshka in the piece) and his cousin A. A. Stolypin, known as Mongó. The two hussars ride out of St. Petersburg one night for a surprise visit to a ballerina with whom Mongó is infatuated, and whom a Kazan squire ("N. N.") is keeping in an establishment on the Peterhof road. The lady invites the two in for tea, but unfortunately "N. N." arrives suddenly with a gang of servants and Mongó and Mayoshka have to jump out of the window and leave hurriedly. The poem is written in the four-foot iambic meter most commonly used for the "Byronic poem," but its content is designedly unheroic. Note, for example, the commonplace reflections of the ballerina:

> Leaning with her elbows at the window, meanwhile, the young danseuse was sitting at home and alone. She was bored, and yawning, was thinking silently to herself: "A marvelous thing is fate, without a doubt. My mama wears a cap of the very worst style, and my father is a simple smith! And I—upon a silken divan eat marmelade and drink chocolate!... My Pierre isn't very interesting—jealous, stubborn, no matter how much you talk to him; he doesn't like laughing or singing, but on the other hand he's rich and stupid... Now it's not what it used to be in school[i.e., the ballet school]: I eat enough for three, sometimes even more, and at dinner I drink *lunelle.* But at school!... God, what a torment! Days—dancing, posture, lessons, and nights a hard bed. It used to be you'd get up early in the morning, the piano was already tinkling in the hall, everyone singing out of tune—it made your ears ache; and then you'd be standing, one leg raised, like a stork on guard..."[47]

Mayoshka, Lermontov's humorous portrait of himself, sounds quite convincing. While Mongó is making time with the surprised and quite receptive lady, he "sits on the divan some distance away, sullen and silent as a sultan. Another's happiness is as tiresome to us as a moral novel." "Meanwhile Mongó burns and melts... Suddenly the most ardent passage is interrupted by the ill-omened clatter of an equipage flying into the court: a nine-passenger *koliaska* and fifteen riders on it... Alack! A sad denouement, the irresistible wrath of the gods!"

The Tambov Treasurer's Wife[48] is a brilliant satirical picture of "upper class" social life in a provincial town, focussed on a probably apocryphal hussars' story of the dragoon who flirted with the pretty wife of the treasurer of the town where he was quartered, was invited to dinner, and proceeded to a bout of gambling with the card-sharper husband, and literally "cleaned him out," until he was reduced at last to staking his wife—and lost her too! The tale, significantly, is composed in the 14-line strophe which Pushkin invented for *Eugene Onegin;* the fifty-three strophes are preceded by a "dedication" that begins: "What though I be reputed an Old Believer, it's all the same to me—I'm even glad. I'm writing in the Onegin measure; I sing, friends, in the old fashion." The poem was probably written in the latter part of 1837, or even in 1838—in any case, after Pushkin's death, who had himself turned in his last years to prose as a narrative medium—hence the ironic apology, "I sing in the old fashion." The piece was published in *The Contemporary* in 1838, the second of Lermontov's narratives to see the light, but outrageously mutilated by the censor. Unfortunately Lermontov's own manuscript is lost, so there is no way of filling the numerous gaps that these excisions leave.

As V. A. Manuilov remarks:[49] ... "the brilliant lightness of the exposition, the artful alternations between the narrative proper of the episode and the author's remarks, now jesting, now serious, still do not exhaust the merits of this verse tale; Lermontov has succeeded in showing the dramatism of philistine life that erodes the moral basis of existence and devalues personality, converting a person into a thing." In the latter regard one of the most notable features of the tale is the poet's sympathetic attitude toward the wife, whom he treats at first with the army-man's rough levity ("And right enough, Avdotia Nikolaevna was a very tasty bit"), but later shows as a dignified and suffering human being. Her final gesture, when the dragoon triumphantly claims his prize, is to take off her wedding ring and hurl it in the face of the husband who has so callously humiliated his wife.

In 1882 P. A. Viskovaty published a Lermontov narrative poem in two parts called *Sashka*.[50] A few fragments of Part I of this had earlier appeared in 1861, from a lost autograph of the poet. The Viskovaty publication was based on a manuscript copy made by I. A. Panafutin. The Soviet critic Boris Eikhenbaum has suggested very convincingly that "Part I" of *Sashka* is in fact a complete poem, unconnected with "Part II."[51] There is no discernible connection between the subjects of the two alleged parts, which have in common only the same ll-line strophe, rhyming AbAbAccDDcc; but this similarity has no evidential value, since *A Fairy Tale for Children* (1840) also uses the same strophe. It is quite probable that Panafutin copied two quite independent pieces from Lermontov's now lost autograph. What is still published as "Chapter I" of *Sashka* consists of 149 strophes; the fragment that figures as "Chapter II" has eight complete strophes and a fractional part of a ninth.[52]

The generating idea of *Sashka* (ironically subtitled "A Moral Poem") would appear to be a social prank which his low-class mistress Tirza suggests to the poem's hero: that he take her to the theater and flaunt her before the scandalized eyes of his upper-class world. This idea has not been carried through by the end of "Chapter I," but Sashka's black servant, Zafir, has been sent out on some secret mission, probably to procure a suitable outfit for Tirza. At this point the poem comes to an abrupt end, and it remains uncertain whether Lermontov intended to pursue the subject or not. The last strophe rather suggests that he did not:

> Whoever may be dissatisfied with my conduct, may go into a newspaper office, with a sheet in hand, with a gang of friends, and confident in their experienced eyes, may print an anathema—the rascal! I've finished ... Yes! The page is fully written. The lamp is going out ... There's a limit to everything—to Napoleons, storms and wars, and so much more, to patience—and verses, which long since have not been sounding [right], and suddenly have been falling from the pen God knows how! ... [53]

The influence of *Eugene Onegin* is very evident in *Sashka,* which follows very much the construction of Pushkin's poem: a narrative, allegedly about a friend of the poet, interrupted frequently by loosely related lyrical passages, meditations, recollections of the author, and the like, and proceeding from an episode involving the hero as a young man, to a flashback depicting his parentage and early years. There is, however, some connection also with another poem of the same genre. Strophe 32 of *Sashka* pretends to introduce the hero to the reader:

> But who is this guest? *Pardon,* at once! How absent-minded! ... *Monsieur,* let me introduce my hero, my friend Sashka! ... It's a pity that chance has brought you together at such a time, and in this place [i.e., a brothel] ... "Sashka" is an old appellation! But that "Sashka" didn't see print, and he perished immature, in exile. [54]

The reference of course concerns the 1825 poem of the ill-fated Polezhaev, who indeed "perished immature, in exile," in 1838, as a direct result of the wrath of Emperor Nikolai I over the blasphemies and obscenities of his *Sashka.* Aside from the hero's name, however, and the somewhat indecent locale of its beginning. Lermontov's poem has nothing in common with Polezhaev's.

Sashka (both poems have the title *Sashka;* Lermontov in the text calls his hero "Sasha") begins with a bewildering display of caprice. First, the hero is introduced as the poet's one-time friend, now dead in some military action in a foreign land. Then the poet expostulates with his reader when the latter appears to show some impatience for the story to begin:

> Be patient, dear reader! Whoever you may be, Eve's descendant or Adam's, intellectual or young playboy! There will be a picture—this is just the frame! I am not deviating from the rules established by antiquity. I have a strict respect for all old men—and there are so many of them now ... Isn't it true that he who is not old at eighteen is one who evidently hasn't seen people and the world, knows about pleasures only by hearsay, and has been delivered up to teachers and torments! [55]

Then he announces that Sasha was a Muscovite; this leads to two strophes of patriotic rhapsody over Moscow, and then a bit of fantasy in which he imagines himself and his Muse driving out of the Kremlin past an

astonished sentry, headed for the disreputable Presnya suburb, the
location of the brothel where Sasha is about to visit his Jewish mistress:

> I'm not a philosopher—God forbid—and not a dreamer. I don't chase after the
> flight of a bird, although in former days I wasn't altogether a stranger to this behavior
> Come, Muse, hurry up now, unfold your grubby travelling pass [*listok podorozhnyi*—
> the official pass that allowed the bearer to use the government post]: no more talk,
> now—there's a godless critic! . . . Where are we to go now from the Kremlin? There are
> many gates, the earth is large! Where? "To Presnya, and hurry up, driver!" "Off with
> you, old girl!" [addressed to the horse!]—"Out of the way, pedlar!"
> The moon is gliding in the winter clouds, like a Varangian's shield or a Holland
> cheese. A bold simile, but I'm terribly fond of all boldness, as befits gentry freedom.
> The guardian of the peace on sentry duty in his box wakes up, calling out: "Who goes
> there?"—"The Muse!"—"Who the devil! Which one?" No answer. But here are the
> ponds already—The pavement is white, the gardens to each side are sleeping
> dejectedly under the fluffy hoar-frost, the moon silvers the iron railings.[56]

Presumably invisible, the Muse and her charge make their way through the
snowdrifts to their destination, enter the door, and find a homely scene—
two girls sitting at a table, telling their fortune with cards. One, a real
beauty, is a Polish Jewess, whose history is briefly related. The other, not
so beautiful, "was cool and white and round as a snowball." Her name, the
poet remarks, was really Varvara, but since this name awakens painful
memories in him (of Varvara Lopukhina, no doubt) he will use the name
Parasha for her. The fortune-telling is abruptly halted when a visitor
dashes in—a handsome young man, hardly twenty, who has just come
from a fashionable ball. This is what gives Tirza her bright idea. She asks
naively: "A ball! What's that like?"

> "Ignoramus! It's talk, noise and rumpus, a crowd of fools, urban jollity, outward
> brilliance, deceptive disease. The young ladies circle, brag of their costumes, dissemble
> with both voice and look. One angles for a soul, another for five thousand souls [i.e.,
> 5000 serfs—a fortune]—They're all so innocent—but I'm not the man for them, and
> however much I may respect virtue, I like it better here, the moon's my witness."[57]

After an amorous interlude, which the poet modestly leaves to the reader's
imagination, Tirza springs her bright idea, and the sleepy lover says
"Maybe."

At this point begins what constitutes the bulk and the most interesting
part of the poem. A brief comparison with Polezhaev's procedure may
illuminate Lermontov's originality. Polezhaev's Sashka is very evidently
himself, and the action of the poem, the hero's words and meditations, are
faithful reflections of his own. What the reader sees, accordingly is a
picture of a particular individual, with a somewhat unusual background,
engaged in actions which are doubtless quite accurately and concretely
presented, but which nevertheless belong essentially still to one person in
one time and place. Lermontov's Sasha is *not* the poet himself, at least in

his external circumstances: there is no similarity between Ivan Ilyich N. N. and Maria Nikolavna, Sasha's parents, and Lermontov's; there is no similarity between Sashka's situation in Moscow after the Mavrusha episode and Lermontov's residence at the Moscow University Lycee. Psychologically, of course, there are many points of contact between the poet and his hero, but the picture of Sasha's parents, of the child's rearing, his first sexual experience, his student life, etc., are a *generalized* picture that might fit a large number of "heroes of the time," not in detail, but in essence. This is genuine realism; Polezhaev's method is what Russian critics call "naturalism"—a usage of the term that has nothing to do with the pseudo-scientific "naturalism" of Zola, who first introduced the term.

Sasha's father, Ivan Ilyich N.—ov, is a Simbirsk landowner, with an estate on the banks of the Volga. His personality is vividly sketched:

> He was an enemy of writers and of books; he had drawn his knowledge in legal affairs. He slept very late, ate enough for four; he paid no attention to anyone, and did not wear the chains of propriety. However, before haughty nobility he knew how to bow humbly and politely. But in that age the law of politeness demanded the bow for its fulfilment; and to bow to the law or to a big-wig at that time was considered one and the same.[58]

Ivan Ilyich married late, and it is hinted that Maria Nikolavna, who "was a very appetizing dish" (like the Tambov Treasurer's wife!) had had some previous experience. She had some typically romantic ways:

> Ivan Ilyich guarded his wife in the old-fashioned way. To put it without flattery, he conducted himself, as I like, in accordance with the rules of the old-fashioned honor of that time. His wife was notional (I make no secret of it); she loved to read trashy novels or gaze at the bright sphere of Diana, sitting in the dark gazebo until morning. But the moon and novels lead to no good—dreams are born of them....and only temptations can result![59]

"For two years Ivan Ilyich lived with his wife, and all the while her corsets grew no tighter"; but eventually a child was born—an attractive auburn-haired baby. "Already he had exchanged a little shirt for his baby clothes, and beginning his first pranks, he was already teasing the dogs and the parrot...The years passed, and Sasha grew, and at five he began to understand good and evil; but evidently by an inborn bent, he had a great inclination to destructiveness."

> He grew—his father cursed and beat him—because he himself in childhood had been frequently beaten, but, thank God, had still turned out a man: no shame to his family, neither dull nor maimed. Conceptions were low in the old days...But Sasha was born with a proud soul and a bilious disposition: before fate, before the rod he did not bow his caustic speech, nor afterwards his head. He knew how to remember who had injured him, and so he came to hate his father.[60]

The description of young Sasha's romantic early dreams is certainly autobiographical:

> He had neither brother nor sister, and no one knew his secret torments. He outgrew play prematurely, he surrendered his heart to avid doubt, and despising the dear gifts of childhood, he began to meditate, to build an airy world, and in this he lost himself in obedient thought....
>
> Oh, if he only might, like a disembodied spirit, merge with the clouds at the evening hour, incline his greedy ear to the seething waves, and long grow drunken on their talk, and embrace their breasts like a husband! To breathe in one breath with Nature in the wilderness of the steppes, to live with[Nature's] freedom! Oh, if he only might, clad in the lightning, shatter the whole world with a single stroke!...(but fortunately for you, dear reader, he was not endowed with such a power).[61]

Sasha's mother died when he was very young, and his education was put in the hands of an émigré Frenchman, the Marquis de Tesse, who used to regale the lad with gory tales about the guillotine. This leads the poet into an excursus on France, the Revolution, and Napoleon:

> And blood from that time flowed in a river, and the greedy axe thundered ... You, too, poet [i.e., André Chénier] did not preserve your lofty brow! Your living lyre had vainly carried through the universe all, all that you counted with your soul—words, dreams, with hope and longing—in vain! You trod the bloody path, unavenged, and neither caustic verse nor cold mockery visited your creative breast—even you perished fruitlessly....
>
> But after you France fell to the feet of soulless and worthless murderers. No one dared to raise his voice; out of the murk of false and fatal thoughts no one emerged with staunch soul. Meanwhile in secret the eyes of Napoleon had already seen the steps of a future throne ... And I might proceed in this tone, but truth isn't in fashion, and it's ridiculous to write about what has been two hundred times in the newspapers—so much the more on subjects such as these.[62]

When Sasha was fourteen, he fell head over heals in love—with Mavrusha, "the butler's daughter." The poet cites his own case as a parallel—probably quite honestly:

> And is it any wonder? At fourteen I myself suffered from every female face, and simple-mindedly assured the whole world that they are alike, one to the other. The tender flower of heaving bosoms and the burning breath of crimson lips awakened wondrous desires in me: I would tremble when my hand lightly touched satin shoulders; but only in dreams did I see everything unclothed that for you, of course, is no longer a novelty.[63]

Opportunity for a Russian landowner's son with a houseful of serfs was of course abundant. One summer day the boy, daydreaming in a secluded part of the garden, heard some peculiar noises, and discreet investigation disclosed Mavrusha in an amorous encounter with—his father! The encounter was unsuccessful, however, because of Ivan Ilyich's advanced years, and when the old man left the scene, his son took his place with all the ardor of frustrated virginity. Thereafter Mavrusha used to tiptoe nightly to the boy's room, until one sad evening she appeared in tears and announced that it was their last meeting. The girl's obvious love for her young master, and the helplessness of a serf's situation are movingly portrayed:

> "Listen. I'm here for the last time. I have disregarded the danger, punishment, shame, conscience—everything, just to see you, to kiss your hands in farewell and to coax a tear from your eyes. Don't turn a poor girl away—I endure enough as it is—but what's to do? The heart is free. Ivan Ilyich found out from envious people ... It's all your Vanka, the villain—it's through him that I'm ruined ... Everything is prepared! I beseech you—oh, throw me at least a look, at least a word!
>
> For your father in the first place I forgot shame—where is there any defence for a slave? He threatened me with evils. God be his judge! A week went by—the poor girl was forgotten ... but all the same it was impossible for her to love another. Yesterday he began to abuse me with infamous words ... But what's a slave before you[people]? A plaything! just so: a day, or two, or three, she's loved, and then? Please, you may as well die!" Here the tears began, and exclamations, but Sashka stopped them without attention.
>
> "Oh, master, master! I see you don't want to understand my heartfelt anguish ... Good-bye!—I can see you no longer, but I shall remember you forever, forever ... We are both to blame, and I must suffer. But so be it. Kiss me on the breast, on the eyes—kiss me where you please, for the last night! ... At daylight they'll drive me away in a kibitka to a distant farm, where sufferings and a shaggy-bearded peasant wait for Mavrusha ... And you? You'll sigh and make love to another:"[64]

The serf-girl's knowledge of the ways of masters is painfully accurate. Peeping out of his window in the morning, Sasha sees a troika at the door; Mavrusha gets in, gives a last bow in his direction, and is carried off, never to reappear in the poem, nor presumably in Sasha's thoughts.

The hero's relations with his hated and despised father worsen, however, and the boy is sent off to Moscow, first to boarding-school, then to the University. He lives with an elderly maiden aunt who keeps him well supplied with spending money. His relations with his schoolmates and the University are doubtless reflections of Lermontov's own:

> He came to see that friendship, like the bow, is an ambiguous thing; that a "fine fellow" is a boring comrade, irksome and sluggish; that the one who is hardly intelligent is both amusing and more tolerable than a thousand obliging friends. And so in a month he earned—counting only the open ones—a hundred amusing enemies.[65]

Coming to his hero's university career, Lermontov rhapsodizes:

> He entered proudly into learning's bright temple. O sacred place! I remember, like a dream, your rostra, lecture-halls, corridors, your sons' insolent disputes: about God, about the universe, and about how to drink: rum with tea, or rum neat; their proud aspect before the proud authorities, their frock-coats hanging in tatters.[66]

The "first chapter," and in all probability Lermontov's entire projected poem, comes to an end with some elegiac personal utterances; he bids farewell to his Sasha: "And you whose life, like a fugitive star, darted suddenly among us, you will never express your torments in words; you refused to drink the poison of mockery, with an unaffected smile, like Socrates; and your riddle unguessed by the stupid crowd, you died, alien to life.... Peace be with you!"

He then turns to his other friends:

> And you, all of you, to whom so many times I offered the cup of friendship—what tempest has carried you afar? What goal has killed your youth? I am here alone. The sacred fire has gone out upon my altar. The desire for fame has flitted away like a phantom. You are right: I was not born for friendship and banquets.... I am in thoughts an eternal wanderer, a son of the wild woods, the glens and freedom, and I live, knowing no nest, like a nomad bird.
> Of old I was ready to die for good, but for good I was requited with contempt; I ran through a long series of vices, and was sated with bitter pleasure.... Then I cast a cold glance backward: as from a fresh sketch, I wiped the color from the picture of past days, sighed, and put on a mask, and with a boisterous laugh drowned out the words of fools.

The words of bitter disillusion reach their climax in the next strophes:

> O eternity, eternity! What shall we find there, beyond the world's unearthly bourne?—a chaotic, shoreless ocean, where the ages have neither name nor number; where shelterless stars wander in the wake of other stars. Cast out into their mute round-dance, what shall Nature's proud king do there, who was surely created most intelligent of all, so as to devour the plants and wild beasts, though for all that (I think I'll vow), he is himself terribly like an ape.
> O vanity! And here's your demigod, your man: who by art has made himself master of earth and sea, of everything that ever he could—and yet is unable to live three days without eating! But enough—a malicious demon has lured me into such talk...[67]

The insignificant fragment that constitutes the so-called "second chapter" of *Sashka* is a vivid and atmospheric description of a decayed and run-down house in Moscow, once the scene of brilliant festivities. Since any connection between this and the "First Chapter" exists purely in a critic's imagination, it is surely better not to attempt one.

Sashka is on the borderline between the romanticism of Lermontov's early verse and the realistic traits of his late prose. It is a romantic poem in its pervasive lyricism, and in its subjectivism; at the same time the picture which it gives of an *enfant du siècle* is generalized and true to life, just as is Pushkin's of Eugene Onegin. The probably deliberate fragmentariness of it—a distinctly romantic trait—and the frank sensuality which marks it have contributed to deprive the poem of its rightful place as one of

Lermontov's most effective pieces, and a landmark in the history of emergent realism.

Of all Lermontov's attempts to write a definitive narrative poem, one preoccupied him throughout most of his creative life. The first version of *The Demon*[68] belongs to 1829, when he was fifteen; the final redaction—which was rendered final only by his death—dates to 1841. There are altogether eight different versions, partial or complete, of the poem. He was evidently anxious, as he had never been with any of his other narratives, to have it in print, and the version which became final was one which was prepared specifically to be read at court by Empress Alexandra Fyodorovna[69] and subsequently passed for publication. The reasons why, in spite of its approval by a relatively liberal censor, *The Demon* never appeared in Lermontov's lifetime are not altogether certain, but probably may be explained by a shake-up in the censor's office. Fragments of the poem were published in 1842 at the specific order of S. S. Uvarov, Minister of Education; the whole first appeared in 1856 and 1857 in Karlsruhe, Germany.

What first suggested to Lermontov the idea of a work based on the love of a supernatural being for a human girl is not known, but it was a theme that haunted the romantics (e.g., Thomas Moore, Alfred de Vigny et al.). The treatment closest to Lermontov's is De Vigny's in his poem *Eloa*. The attraction of the theme lay in the possibilities offered of raising the figure of the rebellious, self-centered, world-scorning "Byronic hero" to as it were the highest power—to a cosmic force engaged in the ultimate rebellion—against God Himself.

Through its various versions Lermontov's poem retains unchanged the basic situation: "the Demon," lonely and proud, sees a beautiful human maiden (she is a nun) and feels an awakening love which appears capable of transforming him and returning him to his former angelic state. In invisible form he seduces her—but alas, the evil of his nature destroys her physically, and he is left more alone than ever. The girl's fate varies in the versions: in a prose explanation between episodes of Version I we read:

> The Demon falls in love with a mortal maiden (a nun), and she finally loves him, but the Demon sees her guardian angel and out of envy and hate determines to destroy her. She dies, her soul flies away to hell, and the Demon, meeting the angel, who is weeping from the heights of heaven, reproaches him with a venomous smile[70]

In the final version, however, the girl's soul is saved and the Angel triumphs.

One of the most significant changes which *The Demon* underwent through the years was that of locale. In the first (1829) version this is vague and abstract. The second (1830) rather casually puts it in Spain. It is only with the 1838 version (the sixth), which subsequently had very few and not always improving alterations, that the scene is made the Caucasus, the heroine becomes Tamara, daughter of a Georgian chieftain, and she becomes a nun only after her betrothed husband has met his death through the malice of the Demon. This change makes it possible for Lermontov, who it must be remembered was in 1838 writing some of his best poetry, to embellish the rather bare outline of of his narrative with some magnificent scenic descriptions. Correspondingly the emphasis is changed, and it may; almost be said that the visible antagonist of the Demon, the representative in the poem of the Creator God, ceases to be the girl's guardian angel, and becomes beautiful, entrancing Nature itself—"God's world"[*Bozhii mir*], as the poet significantly calls it. The angel does not disappear—he tries vainly to protect his charge from the Demon's solicitations, and in the final (1841) revision, which *may* have been devised as a concession to the imperial reader and a censor's scruples, Tamara's soul is borne triumphantly heavenward as the Angel annihilates his foe with God's sentence of eternal loneliness. The figure of the Angel is a disturbing one in this piece, as it is in the famous poem "The Angel"; it partakes too much of the saccharine vulgar conception. In D. E. Maximov's marvelous phrase,[71] "the representation of heaven's messenger in the poem about the Demon.... is not devoid of an oleographic character." One is involuntarily reminded of insipid Sunday-school pictures—certainly not of the magnificent denizens of Dante's Paradise. The sixth (1838) version, which Belinsky preferred, and in my opinion with good poetical taste, to the "court version" of 1841, which is the canonical printed version, omits the episode of the final encounter of Demon and Angel, and the fate of Tamara's soul remains uncertain: "The deadly poison of his kiss penetrated her blood in a moment, a tortured but feeble cry broke the silence of the night. In it was everything: love, suffering, reproach with a last prayer, and a hopeless farewell—farewell to young life!"[72]

For the essential meaning of *The Demon* the destiny of Tamara's soul is irrelevant. What is important is that the Demon's desperate hope of redemption through love, of escape from the awful solitariness that is God's punishment for his rebellion, is destroyed with Tamara's life. It is never so formulated in the poem, but is implicit throughout that the Demon's love is purely egoistic and selfish. This is an unalterable part of his character—of the character, that is, of the demonic romantic hero, such as Pechorin in *A Hero of Our Time*—and it is inevitably destructive, whether the tragedy is played out in a Russian border fort with a simple Chechen girl ("Bela") or in a legendary Georgian convent with a young nun and a supernatural lover. It is significant that every version of the poem except the fourth, which is in a different meter from all the others, begins with the same line: *Pechal'nyi Demon, dukh izgnan'ia*—"Sorrowful Demon, spirit of exile." The last word of the line means literally "expulsion." The Demon has been *driven out* of communion with all other beings. What has driven him out? In the legend, it is God who has expelled him from Paradise for the primal sin of pride and rebellion; but in more earthy terms, it is his own monolithic egoism, which dooms any attempt at the communion of love, and destroys the being toward whom the attempt is directed. In this connection note should be made incidentally of a difficulty which non-Russian readers of the poem have sometimes expressed: since the Russian language has no article, either definite or indefinite, does *Demon* mean "*the* Demon" or "*a* Demon"—in other words, is the poem's hero to be equated with the Biblical "Lucifer, star of the morning," or is he merely one of a number of fallen angels? It would seem that the ambiguity should have been solved long ago by the insistence everywhere in the poem on the Demon's solitariness. Even in evil he has no companionship—his abode is no noisy but perhaps companionable Miltonic Pandemonium, where the whole host of rebellious ex-angels are involved in a common enterprise. His existence is much more reminiscent of Dante's solitary, monstrous Satan, lying alone in the eternal cold at the bottom of all creation. There can be only one "Demon," in Lermontov's conception.

The human characters of the poem are presented on an appropriately reduced scale. Tamara has little individuality: she is ravishingly beautiful, she is young, full of gaiety and animal spirits until the death of her betrothed at the hands of Ossetian brigands. Then she becomes despondent and gloomy. That she is good is evidenced by the Angel's attachment to her. Her part in the dialogue with her unseen demon-lover is brief and conventional and she offers no question or rebuttal to his casual disposal of her questions. She is evidently designed by Lermontov to show only one side of a woman's character—the instinctual, affectionate side. Of her betrothed we learn nothing except that he is a bold young mountaineer whose preoccupation with thoughts of his coming bliss lead him to neglect the proper prayer at a martyr's tomb on his way. Tamara's father is again a shadowy and conventional figure. From his daughter's words after the death of her betrothed we infer that he at first insists on finding her another husband, but she wins her point of taking the veil with such ease that this purpose cannot have been very seriously held. The only other human character in the poem is a decrepit night-watchman at the convent who is almost, and disturbingly, comic in his agitation at hearing the sound of the fatal kiss and Tamara's dying shriek. Lermontov would have improved his poem by eliminating him.

The gigantic figure of the Demon is balanced only by the gigantic and magnificent setting of the Caucasus:

> And above the summits of Caucasus
> the exile from Paradise was flying:
> beneath him Kazbek, like the facet of a diamond,
> glittered with its eternal snows,
> and black in the depths below,

like a crack, a snake's habitation,
coiled winding Daryal,
and the Terek, leaping like a lioness
with shaggy mane against the ridge,
roared,—and the mountain beast, and the bird
circling in the azure height,
understood the word of his waters...[73]

The Demon at first has only contempt for his surroundings, the creation of the God he hates: "And wild and wondrous was all God's world around him; but the proud spirit cast a contemptuous eye on the creation of his God, and on his lofty brow nothing was reflected." After his sudden infatuation with the beautiful Tamara the Demon's nature seems to change. Even at the beginning his relation to evil is ambiguous: "He sowed evil without enjoyment. Nowhere did he meet with opposition to his arts—and evil bored him." Men were such an easy prey that to seduce them was hardly even sporting! But when he applies his art seriously to insinuate himself into the mind of Tamara, it is with a wonderful song about the beauty and tranquillity of the natural world that he begins "Upon the aerial ocean without rudder and without sail—"[74]); after this incidental lyric, in trochaic meter, the iambics resume and there is another splendid picture of "God's world"—night in the mountains. It seems that progressively as his love grows, the Demon becomes more reconciled to creation. In his impassioned plea to Tamara, he thinks of her love as a redemption from his own sterile immortality:

To regret forever and not desire [*vsegda zhalet' i ne zhelat'*], to know everything, feel everything, see everything, to strive to hate everything and despise everything in the world!...As soon as ever God's curse was fulfilled, from that very day the warm embraces of Nature grew chilled for me forever; space shone blue before me; I saw the wedding finery of the stars I had known long since—they course in crowns of gold; but what of that?...Like Eden the world for me had become deaf and dumb.[75]

The Demon's fatal kiss, which does not bring redemption for him, infects Tamara, even in death, with some of his cold despair:

A strange smile was frozen
as it had flashed over her lips.
It spoke of many things
to the understanding eye:
in it was the cold contempt
of a soul prepared to wither,
the expression of a last thought,
a wordless farewell to earth,
the vain reflection of former life,
it was still more dead,
still for the heart more hopeless
than the eyes, forever gone out.[76]

Then, in a wonderful simile, the poet gives a last glimpse of the mountain world—the final ray of the setting sun on the snows of the Caucasus.

In the final version of the poem the Angel that bears Tamara's soul to heaven ends his speech to the Demon with the words: "She suffered and loved—and heaven opened for love!" The Demon too has suffered and loved, and his has not been the unforgiveable sin of despairing of redemption—he has sworn a solemn oath of magnificent rhetoric that he has abjured evil and hatred for heaven. Yet heaven has not opened for him, and—"once more he was left, haughty, alone as before, in the universe, without hope and without love!" The reader may well be baffled at the meaning of Lermontov's denouement. Faust, it will be remembered, despite the evil and egoism of his life, was redeemed—not by love, indeed! But Goethe had an essentially optimistic sense of life, and as he himself owned, real tragedy was impossible for him. Moreover, he was a philosopher. Lermontov was not. In his conception of his Demon there is a basic ambiguity: the figure that is conceived of in abstract terms as the embodiment of evil, the polar opposite of God, is, for the purposes of the poem, endowed with a quasi-human personality and a capacity to love and repent. The two conceptions are mutually exclusive, and philosophically the second is incompatible with the first. A "happy ending" for the poem, with the repentant Demon readmitted to the heavenly host would have been absurd and unthinkable; yet the tragic outcome as it stands seems to argue a flagrant injustice in God's handling of the situation! The difficulty is that Lermontov's Demon is two things—an allegorical personification of the principle of evil, and a human lover. The fate that is inevitable and right for the one is unjust for the other.

The ambivalence of *The Demon* is disturbing and can be explained only as unintentional. Lermontov worked too long on his poem. It displays, as one Russian critic graphically puts it, too many "geological strata." The philosophical and psychological implications of the tale were never thought out and fixed in advance, and as work on the writing progressed, Lermontov's attitude toward it inevitably changed, and yet he insisted on retaining passages of what was undeniably impressive verse even when they had become incompatible with a new understanding of his hero's character. Goethe's Mephistopheles, despite the almost sixty years of his poem's gestation, remains the same to the end—that is, from the beginning he is a cosmic force without human characteristics. There is a contradiction in his being which he himself states: ["Ein Teil von jener Kraft, die stets das Böse will und stets das Gute schafft"] "A part of that power that always wishes evil and always does good," but this contradiction is not psychological—it inheres in the nature of the universe as Goethe sees it. Lermontov's Demon is at least three mutually incompatible things: a figure from Old Testament mythology, created by a primitive imagination to account for the existence of evil; a figure embodying the romantic's dream of escape from the immutable decrees of destiny through the redeeming power of love; and a projection to a cosmic scale of the poet's own rebellious, anti-social personality. Thus, in the mythological aspect the Demon should be the Manichaean principle of evil—yet "evil bores him" (in his aspect as an aggrandized Lermontov). It is unthinkable that Ahriman should abjure evil in a mad hope of being reconciled with Ormuzd, yet the Demon does just this, and at the same time (at least in the Sixth version) he engages in a disputation with Tamara intended to undermine her faith in God!

Whether the poet fully realized the degree to which his hero was divided against himself and both philosophically and psychologically inconsistent, we shall never know. Perhaps it was uneasiness on this score that motivated him to the constant reworking which *The Demon* underwent, and which only his premature death terminated. For the reader, perhaps it is precisely this enigmatic, always tentative quality that exerts the fascination which *The Demon* has always held. For convenience, one may ignore the supernatural element altogether, and see the Demon only as the quintessentially romantic hero; one may revel in the gorgeous scenic descriptions, for whatever the Demon's attitude toward "God's world" may be, the poet sees its beauty. One may listen spellbound to the taut, resounding verse in which the Demon announces his determination to "abandon evil and do good"—some of the most magnificent rhetoric in the Russian language. *The Demon* has many and serious philosophical defects, but as a poem it is a masterpiece, and remains probably the most popular of Lermontov's narrative poems.

That Lermontov himself realized some of the inherent absurdities of the scenario which he had dreamed up in his boyhood is evidenced by a memorandum to himself written in 1831: "Note: write a lengthy *satirical* poem—the *adventures of a demon.*"[77] This immediately precedes the revision of *The Demon* in the poet's copy-book. The project was never completely carried out, but the unfinished piece entitled *A Fairy Tale for Children*[78] (1839-41) represents a move in that direction—almost, as it were, a self-parody of *The Demon*. Unfortunately, too little of the "fairy tale" was completed (27 stanzas) to permit judgment of the course it would have taken. It is composed in the 11-line stanza used also in *Sashka* and the similarity of the subject matter of the so-called "second chapter" of *Sashka* to the description in the *Fairy Tale* of the solitary and run-down house of Nina's father makes it seem likely that the "second chapter" is in fact an earlier sketch for the *Fairy Tale*.

The *Fairy Tale* begins with some interesting literary observations:

> The age of epic poems has sped by, and[Byronic] tales in verse have fallen into decline; the poets are not altogether to blame for this (although the verse of many of them is not at all smooth); the public, for the rest, is also not right. Who's to blame, who's right I don't know, but it's long since I myself have been reading verses—not because I don't

love verses, but it's like this: it's ridiculous for the sake of resounding verses to lose golden time—in our mature age, as you well know, we're all occupied with business.

The third stanza introduces the poem's "hero":

> The hero is well-known, and the subject is not new: so much the better—everything that's new is old-hat! Seething with fire and in the strength of youthful years I sang formerly of another demon; that was a mad, passionate, childish raving. God knows where the treasured copy-book is; is a perfumed glove touching its pages, and [the words] *"c'est joli!"* audible? Or is a mouse at work on it in the dust? . . . But this is a devil of a quite different sort—an aristocrat, and not resembling a devil.

This "aristocratic devil" is in a bedroom, gazing down at the sleeping occupant—a beautiful girl. The poet professes ignorance of the intruder's proper identity, and adverts again to his own poem *The Demon:*

> Was he the great Satan himself, or a petty demon [*melkii bes*—the title of Sologub's famous novel perhaps comes from here] of the most undistinguished sort, whose friendship people find so necessary for secret affairs involving family, or love? [it may be noted that one of the Russian expressions meaning "to pay court" is *melkim besom pered kem-libo rassypat'sia,* literally "to scatter oneself before someone like a petty devil!"] If he had been given an earthly form, I could have distinguished by his horns or clothing the riff-raff from the nobility; but a spirit—everyone knows what a spirit is like! Life, power, feeling, sight, voice, hearing—and thought—without body—often in various appearances: (demons in general are portrayed as ugly).
>
> But I always imagined differently the foe of pure and lovely delusions. It used to be, my youthful mind was tormented by a mighty image; amid other visions, he shone like a king, mute and proud, with such a magically sweet beauty that it was terrible— and the soul was wrung with anguish—and this strange delirium pursued my reason many years. But I, having parted with [my] other dreams, parted from him too—in verse!
>
> An outstanding weapon: throw an epigram in your enemies' faces . . . would you like to spite your friends? Have at them with a poem or a drama! But enough—[back] to business. I've told you already that in that bedroom was concealed a perfidious demon. He was not in the least touched by innocent sleep. No wonder: blood did not seethe in him, and he had a different conception of love; and his speech was full of sly temptations: not for nothing was he a genius![79]

Like Tamara's demonic visitor, this devil insinuates his thoughts into the mind of the sleeping girl—but as far as the "fairy tale" goes in its 27 stanzas, no "sly temptations" are apparent. The demon merely begins to tell the story of his acquaintance with a beautiful and innocent girl, Nina, who lives with an eccentric and aged father in a decrepit and lonely house near the Neva. The solitary child, with some prodding from the demon, daydreams in the dusty ballroom about glamorous young men with whom she dances. Comes at last the great day of Nina's seventeenth birthday, and she actually goes to a ball. Her embarrassment and trepidation are described as she enters the room, and then the poem breaks off suddenly with this stanza:

The dancing was already seething, and glittering in full radiance. There was everything that is called "the world"[*svetom:* "le monde"] . . . I didn't give it this name, though there is profound sense in this name. I wouldn't have recognized my own friends there; the smiles and faces lied so artfully that even I felt slightly sorry. I wanted to listen in—but my ears scarcely caught the flying words, the fragments of nameless feelings and opinions—the epigrams of creatures unknown! . . . [80]

How the tale would have been developed, what connection Nina's debut into society would have had with the opening scene (is she the unknown beauty by whose bedside the demon watches?), and what the promised "moral, so that children even may read" the story would have had are mysteries that are unlikely ever to be solved. One can only most heartily regret that this extremely promising beginning was fated to have no continuation.

In 1840 there was published in the first collection of *Poems of M. Lermontov* the narrative work called *Mtsyri,*[81] which had been written in 1839. Since only a few small additions to the basic text of *The Demon* are later than this (1841), *Mtsyri* is properly speaking the last of Lermontov's narrative poems and represents his most mature thought and verse technique. It is often forgotten that *The Demon,* even in its final version, is essentially a reworking of a conception that goes back to the poet's fifteenth year.[82]

The title of the poem in its printed form is explained by Lermontov's own note: "Mtsyri in the Georgian language means 'an unofficial monk,' something of the nature of 'a novice.'" In the autograph the title is *Beri,* explained as "'The Monk,' in Georgian." Mtsyri is a Russian spelling of a word that is probably related to, if not identical with, the Georgian adjective *mtsire,* "little." In Kayden's English translation the poem is entitled "The Novice."

As so often in his work, Lermontov lifted whole lines and clusters of lines from his unpublished earlier pieces for inclusion in *Mtsyri,* in this case from the unfinished narrative *A Confession* (1831) and from *The Boyar Orsha* (1835-36). Both these poems, it may be noted, are composed in the same four-foot iambic meter with exclusively masculine rhymes as is *Mtsyri*—a meter that Lermontov often used in lyric verse, and for which he had a model in Zhukovsky's translation of *The Prisoner of Chillon.* Masculine rhyme is of course normal to English verse.

The genesis of the poem is described by P.A. Viskovaty[83] on the basis of an account by Lermontov's cousins Akim Pavlovich Shan-Girei and Akim Akimovich Khastatov; the poet, wandering in 1837 along the old Georgian Military Road:

Encountered in Mtskhet. . . . a solitary monk, or rather, an old monastic servant, "Beri" in Georgian. The guardian was the last of the brotherhood of a disbanded monastery in the neighborhood. Lermontov conversed with him and learned from him that he was a mountaineer by birth, taken captive as a child by General Yermolov at the time of the expedition. The General carried him with him and left the sick boy with the monastery brotherhood. There he grew up; for a long time he was unable to accustom himself to the monastery, was homesick and made attempts to run away into the mountains. The consequence of one such attempt was a long sickness that brought him to the edge of the grave. Having recovered, the wild fellow quieted down and stayed in the monastery, where he became particularly attached to an old monk. The curious and lively account of the *Beri* produced an impression on Lermontov—and he decided to utilize what was similar in *A Confession* and *The Boyar Orsha* and he transferred the whole action from Spain and then the Lithuanian border to Georgia. Now in the hero of the poem he was able to express the daring of the indomitable free sons of the Caucasus, with which he was sympathetic, and to picture the beauties of the Caucasian natural scene.

The printed version of *Mtsyri* bears as an epigraph a line in Church Slavonic from First Samuel (Russian "First Kings"), chap. 14, verse 43: "Eating, I ate a little honey, and behold I die." The "little honey" is of course the tantalizing taste of freedom; but Lermontov may have had a little more than this in mind. In the Biblical context the words are spoken by Jonathan, son of King Saul; Saul had proclaimed a curse on the man who should eat food before the final victory over the Philistines. Jonathan unwittingly disobeyed the prohibition, but with a little honey gathered from the end of his staff, gained strength to perform a great feat, as a result of which the people intervened to save his life from his father's curse. Lermontov's use of the line may not be so entirely pessimistic as it appears out of context. The Mtsyri does indeed perform a great feat, even though he fails to win his freedom.

From the incident reported by Lermontov's cousins, the circumstances of time and place are specified; but the poem itself leaves them intentionally vague. The first lines say simply: "Not many years ago, at the spot where the streams of Arágva and Kurá foam as they join, embracing like two sisters, there was a monastery." The Arágva and the Kurá rivers join at Mtskhet, a few miles northeast of Tbilisi. An old man, guardian of the ruins of the monastery, brushes the dust from a tombstone, "whose inscription tells of past glory—and of how, weighed down by his crown, such and such a king, in such and such a year, committed his people to Russia." The year was 1801, and the king was George XIII, whose tomb is in the cathedral of Mtskhet. The second section of the poem recounts how "a Russian general" (Yermolov) brought a captive six-year-old boy, frail and sick, and left him with the monks. "He was as shy and wild as the mountain chamois, and weak and pliant as a reed. But in him the tormenting sickness had developed the mighty spirit of his fathers." With these few words Lermontov indicates two essential and contradictory features of his hero: he is physically weak and frail, and shy and timid—but in him is an indomitable spirit. He gradually becomes accustomed to the monastery, and seems ready to take his monastic vows—"in the flower of his years"—when suddenly he disappears. He is found after three days, pale and weak, and carried back to the monastery to die. Beginning with the third section of the poem, down to the twenty-sixth and last, the narrative is the Mtsyri's own story of his three days of freedom. It takes the form of the dying boy's confession to an old monk, whose only function in the poem is to listen.

It is here that the connection with *The Confession* and *The Boyar Orsha* comes in. In the first an apprehended runaway monk somewhere in Spain makes his confession before his execution; in the second, Arseny, taken at a secret rendezvous with Orsha's daughter in her chamber, tells his story at the monastic tribunal that condemns him. In neither case has the context of the confession the slightest similarity with that of *Mtsyri.*

The young Georgian novice has vague childish memories of his native mountain village, of his warrior father, of the wild, free life of his people. He is devoured by longing for his native land, and chafes inwardly at the monastery life, which he regularly refers to as his "prison." Finally one night of violent storm he runs away and heads for the mountains. His adventures are simple and symbolic. Tormented by thirst in the sultry noonday heat he clambers perilously down to the river bank and watches from hiding as a slim mountain girl appears on the opposite side to draw water. He makes no effort to communicate with her—she remains a bewitching, scarcely real vision. In the cool moonlit night that follows he encounters a snow-leopard *(bars)* frolicking alone in a glade, and impelled by some atavistic instinct, challenges the beast to single combat. He kills the leopard, but is terribly mauled. Then, half-delirious with pain and hunger, he wanders blindly, until to his utter despair he suddenly recognizes where he is—back nearly to the monastery from which he had fled! Here, doubtless from a censor's pressure, Lermontov dropped from the text that was printed a wonderful passage that voices the boy's despair and sense of defeat:

> "O God," I thought, "wherefore did you give me what you gave to all, both firmness of strength, and power of thought, desires, youth and passion? Wherefore did you fill my mind with unquenchable longing for wild freedom? Why did you give me, alone on earth, a prison instead of my native land? You refused to save me! You did not show me the longed-for way in the darkness of night, and now I am like a tame wolf." Thus I reproached. It was, old man, a mad shriek of despair, a moan forced out by suffering. Say! Surely I shall be forgiven? I was deceived for the first time! Until that moment, every hour I suppressed my obscure hope; I prayed, and waited, and lived. And of a sudden in a gloomy series the days of childhood stood before me, and I remembered your dark church and along the cracked walls the pictures of the saints of your land. How their eyes followed me slowly with dark, mute menace! And at the barred window the sunshine played on the heights . . . Oh, how I longed to be there, away from the cell and the prayers, in that wondrous world of passions and battles. . . . I swallowed my bitter tears, and my childish voice trembled when I sang praise to Him who on earth had given me alone instead of native land, a prison . . . Oh! I recognized that prescient clang [of the monastery bells]; from childhood my ears had been accustomed to it. And then I understood that I would never make my way to my

native land. And swiftly my spirit fell... I despised myself. I was without the strength for tears and fury. With a dark terror at that moment I realized my own nothingness, and smothered in my breast the traces of hopes and passions... Say, has not my feeble soul merited its fate?[84]

In the last section of the poem the runaway begs the old monk to have him carried, when he is near death, into the monastery garden under the flowering acacias:

I shall drink in the radiance of the blue sky for the last time. From there one can see the Caucasus! Perhaps he from his heights will send me a farewell greeting, will send it with a cool little breeze... And close by me before the end will resound once more the noise of home! And I shall think that a friend or a brother, bending over me, has wiped away with thoughtful hand the cold sweat of death from my face, and that in a half-whisper he is singing to me of my beloved land.... And with that thought I shall fall asleep, and curse no one![85]

The Mtsyri has characteristics that ally him with all Lermontov's protesting, freedom-loving heroes—characteristics that he shares, of course, with the poet. But in this maturest of Lermontov's narratives, the central hero has acquired a significant degree of individuality; he is far more objectively portrayed than, for example, the Arseny of *The Boyar Orsha*. Most notably, the devouring passion for which the Mtsyri sacrifices his life is love—not of a woman, but of his native land. This difference of motivation is a measure also of the near-historicism of the poem: the hero is no longer a universal human being set in an arbitrarily chosen tragic situation. He is a Caucasian mountaineer, with a childish memory of a particular historically conditioned environment, who has been subjected from near infancy to a stern, ascetic discipline altogether foreign to his earliest experience. He is the product of his environment and the society in which he was born, and his rebellion against the monastic life is natural and predictable. At the same time, he exhibits traits of the romantic hero—the exultation with which he plunges into the storm that keeps the monks cowering at the altar; the sensitive delight in the beauties of nature; the inchoate stirrings of desire at sight of the Georgian maiden drawing water; the frenzied savagery of his hand-to-hand conflict with the leopard. He is a fascinating product of mature romanticism combined with some realistic elements.

The Mtsyri is the poem's only human character, for the featureless old monk who hears the confession is only seen through the hero's words to him. The balancing element which makes the poem such a harmonious whole is the richly varied and magnificent world of nature. It has often been noted that all the realms of non-human nature play parts here: the rocky cliffs, the tumbling streams, the forests, bushes, wild flowers; the snake, the whirling eagles, the little golden fish that the delirious runaway hears singing to him—and of course the splendid great cat with which he engages in a mortal struggle. This natural world is itself an actor in the drama of the Mtsyri, not just a conventional background, as Eikhenbaum absurdly called it. It is also vividly and precisely seen, with an artist's eye for the significant detail. Note, for example the description of the scene as the thunderstorm dies away:

> The storm grew quiet. A pale light
> stretched in a long band
> between the dark sky and the earth,
> and I distinguished, like a pattern,
> upon it the jags of the distant mountains.[86]

As the boy clambers down the perilous slope to quench his thirst at the water course:

> From slab to slab I began as well as I could to descend.
> From beneath my feet sometimes a stone, breaking loose,
> would roll downward—behind it a furrow
> smoked, and the dust rose in a column;
> ringing and jumping then
> it was swallowed up by the wave.[87]

Exhausted, the Mtsyri falls asleep, and awakes in the moonlight:

> The moon already
> was shining aloft, and a single
> little cloud was stealing after it,
> as though after its prey,
> spreading out greedy arms.
> The world was dark and still;
> only like a silver fringe
> the summits of the snowy chains
> glittered before me far away,
> and the stream splashed against its banks.[88]

The relationship of this Nature to the human participant is ambivalent. At first the boy feels himself merging in it, in the mood of romantic quasi-pantheism. But in the end, for all his ardent delight in it, it proves a formidable antagonist. The sultry noonday heat wears him down; he is exhausted by the struggle with the leopard; and the trackless forest confuses him, and he can find no way to his goal. He is defeated at last by the very power that he greeted so rapturously when he first escaped from the monastery.

If Mikhail Lermontov had not lost his life to a duelist's bullet at the age of twenty-six he would doubtless have written a great deal that would have enriched Russian, and world, literature. I think it is doubtful, however, that he would have continued the line of narrative poems. *The*

Demon had reached a definitive form after years of gestation; probably the *Fairy Tale for Children* would have been completed; more doubtfully, perhaps *Sashka*. The *Mtsyri* is so definitely a culmination in its kind that it seems unlikely that the poet would have attempted anything further in that genre. By 1839 he was already turning toward prose as a medium and toward the social world of his own time and position as subject. For all the powerful attraction of the Caucasian scenery and the feudal society of the mountaineers, he was beginning to see that the typical young gentleman of St. Petersburg society afforded equal potential for tragedy. *A Hero of Our Time* was already in the making.

VI

Mikhail Lermontov: Dramas and Narrative Prose

Lermontov's Dramaturgy

Of the four categories of Lermontov's literary production, the five dramas are the least significant. Only one of these has independent literary merit and has been actually staged with some success. It will therefore be unnecessary to devote any considerable amount of space to this genre.

Aside from an insignificant script of 1829, which was to have been an opera libretto based on Pushkin's *The Gypsies,* Lermontov's first dramatic attempt is the unfinished *Spaniards* of 1830.[1] The poet's interest in the drama began in early youth, and there are accounts of home productions of which Lermontov wrote the scripts; fortunately these have not survived. By 1830 he was caught up in the fascination with Schiller's dramas which affected so many of his generation. Marks of this may be seen in his first two essays in the tragic genre: *The Spaniards,* like *Don Carlos,* is set in sixteenth-century Spain and is composed in the unrhymed iambic pentameter of Schiller's masterpiece; in the same year, 1830, Lermontov wrote a tragedy on a Russian and partly autobiographical subject, which he titled *Menschen und Leidenschaften,*[2] a name patently modelled on *Kabale und Liebe.* Like Schiller's drama, this is in prose. Lermontov's personal interest in Spain may be traced to the probably unbased fancy that his father's family descended from the Dukes of Lerma. It may be noted that the second version of *The Demon* (1830), as well as the poem *A Confession* (1831), are localized in a land Lermontov never visited.

The theme of *The Spaniards* is the Schillerian one of the rebellion of a noble and idealistic youth against the stupidity and hypocrisy of the world that surrounds him. Fernando is a foundling who has been brought up in the family of the haughty nobleman Alvarez and has fallen in love with Alvarez's daughter Emilia. Naturally the arrogant hidalgo refuses consent to their marriage and turns him out of the house. Fernando resues an old

Jew, Moses, from seizure by the inquisition, and in the Jew's house becomes acquainted with Moses' daughter Noemi, who falls in love with him. It is presently discovered, however, that Fernando is actually Moses' long-lost son. Meanwhile the odious inquisitor Pater Sorrini, who has cast lecherous eyes on Emilia, has tempted the girl's empty-headed stepmother Dona Maria to let him lure Emilia into his house on the pretext of protecting her from kidnappers. At this critical moment Fernando, warned by Moses of Sorrini's plot, breaks into the house and, unable to effect Emilia's rescue, kills her before Sorrini's eyes. He is seized and imprisoned, brought to trial before the Inquisition, and condemned to death. The drama breaks off before the end of the fifth act, but it is evident that Fernando and probably also Moses would have been the victims of an *auto da fé*. What would have been the fate of the arch-villain Sorrini must remain uncertain, but it can be conjectured that Alvarez finished him off.[3]

In spite of the obviously melodramatic implausibility of the plot, the treatment shows some dramatic merits. Neither Alvarez nor Dona Maria is a one-sided stereotype; the old hidalgo loves his daughter, and despite his contempt for low birth, seems to have some affection even for his foster-son. His wife, who is silly enough to be flattered by the Jesuit's hypocritical attentions, is stricken with remorse after her betrayal of her stepdaughter, even before the tragic denouement. Fernando, of course, is given some rousing rhetorical tirades on the subjects of genuine nobility, the equality of races, religious bigotry, and the like; neither he nor Emilia, however, emerges as a convincing human being. Still less can this be said of Sorrini, who is one of the deepest-dyed villains in Russian drama. Not content with letting his villainy speak for itself in action, Lermontov even gives him some soliloquies in which he cynically expresses his contempt for decency and his disbelief in the religion with which he cloaks his lechery.

Lermontov's second attempt at tragedy must have been written very shortly after the first, and perhaps this fact explains the apparent abandonment of *The Spaniards* with the death of Noemi. All the poet's subsequent attempts are, like *Menschen und Leidenschaften,* laid in contemporary Russia, and except for *Masquerade,* are written, like Schiller's early dramas, in prose.

The "people" of the play's German title are transparent disguises for the author himself and the most important members of his family—his father and grandmother. Although the plot is based on his own unhappy dilemma as the object of contention between his imperious and wealthy maternal grandmother (in the play, Marfa Ivanovna Gromova) and his impecunious widowed father (in the play, Nikolai Mikhailych Volin), it is complicated by the presence of a brother of Nikolai Volin's, Vasily, and his two daughters, Lyubov and Eliza, who have no real-life counterparts.

There is also Zaretsky, a friend of the hero, who is in love with the frivolous Eliza; Yury Volin's (Lermontov's) heart is inalterably given to the gentle, introspective Lyubov. Not only is his uncle's consent withheld from marriage of the two cousins, but Yury's suspicions are wrongly raised against Lyubov's constancy—he believes that she is enamored of Zaretsky, whom he accordingly challenges to a duel. Before this can take place, however, he is overwhelmed by his father's curse—the crafty Gromova has engineered a deception that leads Nikolai Mikhailych to suppose that his son has chosen his grandmother instead of him—and in utter despair drinks poison. He lives long enough to be reconciled with Lyubov but not to see the futile repentance of his father.

Such merit as the play has is in the depiction of Gromova, her servile and perfidious housekeeper Darya, and Ivan, Yury's servant. Undoubtedly drawn from life, these people are portrayed in vigorously realistic fashion. The rest of the cast, especially Yury himself and Lyubov, are highly unconvincing. The obstinacy and egocentricity of Yury in the misunderstanding with Lyubov are particularly exasperating: fortunately no genuine human being could possibly be as stupid as he is pictured. When, in his death scene, Lyubov tries to comfort him with a reunion in another world, Yury cries: "My love! There is no other world—there is [only] chaos.... It engulfs tribes... and we disappear in it... We shall never see one another... different roads... all lead to nothingness... Farewell! We shall never see one another... There is no heaven—there is no hell... people are abandoned and shelterless creatures." He sums up the apparent meaning of the tragedy in his words to Lyubov: "You and I are not created for people. My heart is too fiery, yours too tender, too weak."[4] Thus the *Menschen* and the *Leidenschaften* are almost too neatly brought together in Yury's dying words.

A realistic, but distinctly secondary, theme in the drama is the relationship between masters and serfs. Almost as odious as the tyrannical and heartless Gromova is the cringing, mealy-mouthed Darya, who is ready to abet her mistress's dirty schemes in order to save herself from a beating. Lermontov undoubtedly saw in his grandmother's home the kind of inhumanity on the part of both mistress and slave that the serf system inevitably fostered, and was revolted by it. It appears incidentally here and elsewhere, but is never a major concern of the poet at any period of his life.

Dramatically *Menschen und Leidenschaften* has good points. The situation involving Yury, his father and grandmother is plausible and well handled, although the scene of Nikolai Volin's curse and its effect on Yury is melodramatic and unconvincing. The whole sub-plot of the love between Yury and Lyubov, however, and especially the absurd misunderstanding which leads the hero to suicide is childish and patterned not on life, but on some Kotzebue-type of trashy melodrama. Worst of all are the long, stilted, tedious tirades put in the hero's mouth and intended to reveal his character as a fiery and preternaturally sensitive individual, lacerated by a callous and unfeeling world. They make the play utterly impossible to stage, and reveal all too plainly the essential failure of the poet to understand the requirements of genuine drama.

The third of Lermontov's dramatic essays has the title *Strannyi chelovek*, which Guy Daniels translates as *A Strange One*.[5] The play was written in 1831. Again it is constructed on a combination of auto-biographical situations, in this case a reconstructed and hypothetical drama between the poet's father and the mother who had actually died when he was three years old; and a dramatization of his own experience with Natalya Fyodorovna Ivanova, his first love, who had found it expedient to marry a wealthy and perhaps less "strange" man. The play's hero, Vladimir Arbenin, is an ardent, freedom-loving young poet, contemptuous of "society" and revolted by the serf system upon which upperclass existence is founded. His father, Pavel Arbenin, is estranged from his mother, Maria Dmitrievna, who has apparently left him many years before and is now living apart in poverty and dying of tuberculosis. Pavel Arbenin is a cold, calculating man, who fails entirely to understand his poet son Vladimir, and has no pity for his wife, who is desperately anxious to be reconciled with him before she dies. The story line comes to a climax when Vladimir, despite Pavel's refusal even to hear his wife mentioned, comes from his dying mother with her frantic plea that Pavel visit her and be reconciled. Pavel vacillates, first agrees to go, then reflects on what society would say, and refuses. Vladimir rails against his heartlessness, and Pavel disowns him—a theme already used in *Menschen und Leidenschaften*.

The second story-line depicts Vladimir-Lermontov's relations with his beloved Natalya Fyodorovna Zagorskina, a well-brought-up young lady who finds her ardent lover rather "strange" and is put off by his contempt for the society world which she inhabits. Vladimir makes the mistake of introducing his friend Belinsky to the Zagorskins, and this cool and suave young man, who is both wealthy and socially acceptable, is soon accepted by Natasha and her parents as her future husband. The combination of blows—his mother's death, his father's curse, and his sweetheart's and friend's faithlessness unsettle Vladimir's mind. The epilogue (scene 13) depicts the talk at a social gathering where Vladimir's madness and its causes are casually discussed. In the course of the discussion comes the announcement from Pavel Arbenin of his son's death. The "Third Guest" sums up the feelings of the group: "I'll be bound, your Arbenin wasn't a 'great' man.... He was 'a strange man!' That's all! "

A secondary theme is injected into the drama when, in the fifth scene, during a conversation at Belinsky's house between him and Vladimir, a peasant begs to see Belinsky. The peasant has heard that Belinsky is thinking of buying the village where he lives, and he has come to beg him to do so, to save its people from the tyrannical cruelty of its present mistress. The peasant's recital of the inhuman treatment that he and his fellows suffer at their mistress's hands so outrages Vladimir that he hands over a 1000-ruble note, the last money he has on earth, to Belinsky, so that he may buy the estate, which he agrees to do. Lermontov's detestation of the serf system and its attendant evils is of course apparent here; but the scene is principally designed to display Vladimir's humanitarian idealism, his impulsiveness and impracticality, in contrast to the shrewd and calculating nature of Belinsky.

Unlike Lermontov's other plays, *A Strange One* is divided not into acts, but into scenes, each provided with a very precise indication of time, from scene 1: "Morning. August 26" to scene 13: "May 12th." These indications are apparently given with the intent of lending the play a certain concreteness and immediacy. In his foreword Lermontov notes: "The persons whom I have represented are all taken from life; and I would like for them to be recognized—then repentance will surely visit the souls of these people." Although several of the dramatis personae have real-life models, it is evidently primarily Natalya Ivanova whose repentance he desires to bring about by the pathetic spectacle of the catastrophic effect which her faithlessness might have had on him. The epigraph from Byron's "The Dream" begins: "The lady of his love was wed with one / who did not love better..."

There is some question about the relation of the play's Pavel Arbenin to Lermontov's own father Yury, and it has been said that the unflattering picture which the play gives of Pavel is the result of some revelations about his father which Lermontov came to know only in 1831; this supposition, however, seems based on no evidence. Yury Lermontov died on October 1, 1831; the play had been begun earlier in that year, provisionally finished by July, and then revised and extended during the months of August and September. It is obvious that if the figure of Pavel is meant to represent Yury Lermontov—and given the unquestioned identification of Vladimir with Lermontov himself this interpretation is hard to avoid—then the poet's attitude toward his father must have suffered a radical change. Yet a poem written shortly after Yury's death seems to give a different picture— at least in this piece ("A Terrible Fate of Father and Son").[6] occurs the line: "It is not for me to judge whether you are guilty or not—you have been judged by society." The poem ends with lines that seem to hint at a possible estrangement:

> Is it possible that now you do not love me at all? Oh, if that is so, then I do not rate heaven equal with this earth, where I am dragging out my life; what though on it I do not know blessedness—at least I love!

Whatever the poet's attitude toward his father, there is no question at all about his attitude toward society. The foreword to *A Strange One* ends with this paragraph:

> Have I described society in my play justly? I do not know! At least it will always remain for me an assemblage of unfeeling people, self-loving in the highest degree, and full of envy toward those in whose soul is preserved however small a spark of the heavenly fire!
>
> To this society I surrender myself for judgment.

What he says in the poem just cited is almost identical. After the words: "You have been judged by society," he adds: "But what is society? A crowd of people, now malicious, now favorable, an assemblage of undeserved eulogies and so many ridiculous calumnies." If the avowed purpose of *A Strange One* was to present a real-life situation in exaggerated and dramatic form in order to strike some real people with penitence, at least an unavowed purpose was to portray the society that he loathed as heartless, money-mad, conformist, envious and cruel toward the "strange ones" whom it does not understand. In this satirical purpose the play is successful. As a drama, it is not. The characterizations are convincing enough, although that of Vladimir is certainly overdrawn; but as with all his plays, Lermontov fails in the most elementary requisite of a drama— that it be playable, not merely readable. The inflated, rhetorical language of the hero's speeches is ridiculous and the best actor in the world could not make his part convincing. And since the entire play is constructed around him, it is of little consequence that the other parts are somewhat more lifelike.

The last two of Lermontov's dramatic efforts abandon overt auto-biography, although the situation in *Two Brothers*[7] (1834-36), which recurs in the "Princess Mary" section of *A Hero of Our Time* and in the unfinished novel *Princess Ligovskaya,* is based on Lermontov's relations with Varvara Lopukhina, who in 1835 married N. F. Bakhmetev, probably for reasons unconnected with love. Lopukhina was sixteen years younger than her husband. The theme of a meeting between two former lovers after the girl has made a calculating and socially advantageous marriage is the background of *Two Brothers;* but as the title indicates, the development of the drama is based on the theme of the rivalry of two temperamentally opposed brothers for the love of the same woman,—a theme which has its classical example in Schiller's *Die Räuber,* and may be seen in numerous other *Sturm und Drang* dramas, e.g., *Die Zwillinge* (1776) of Friedrich Maximilian von Klinger. In Lermontov's play the two brothers, Alexander and Yury Radin, both love Vera, who is now the wife of the elderly and rather silly Prince Ligovskoi. The father of the two brothers characterizes

Alexander in an aside in the first act: "He is so cold, so calculating, that really I'd often like it better if he were impulsive and flighty...One can bet that he'll never fall in love—or commit any follies."[8] Yury is his opposite number: he is "impulsive and flighty," fiery, but entirely frank and open, and never understands his brother's duplicity until the fifth act, when Alexander himself reveals it. The enmity of the two sons brings the father to his death in the last scene: *(Yury falls senseless on the floor: Alexander stands over him and shakes his head. Alexander):* A weak soul....even this he could not endure"[i.e., his father's stroke and sudden death].[9] The pictures of Vera and her husband in the drama closely resemble those of the same-named persons in the unfinished novel *Princess Ligovskaya,* and of course Yury Radin is in some characteristics similar to Grigory Alexandrovich Pechorin in the novel. There is a distinct difference, however: "Georges" Pechorin is haughty, sharp-tongued, cynical, while Yury is open-hearted, hypersensitive and defenceless against the evil world. Pechorin seems to unite qualities of both brothers.

Two Brothers is an advance on the autobiographical plays in dramatic quality: the speeches are shorter and more natural, and it is not impossible to conceive of the work actually on the stage (it had at least one performance on the occasion of a Lermontov festival in 1915, when the famous impressario Meyerhold produced it, but this was not followed up). Lermontov himself was obviously dissatisfied with his work, and transferred to the novel certain parts of it. With it he said good-bye to the drama as a medium.

Lermontov's *Masquerade* is in several respects exceptional among the poet's dramas. For one thing, it has been a regular part of the repertoire of Russian theaters since the Soviet period. It is also, excepting the youthful *Spaniards,* the only one of Lermontov's dramas with no autobiographical content. And finally, its form is unique: it is written in the iambic free verse of Griboedov's *Woe from Wit,* to which it also owes a great deal in other respects. Lermontov correctly assessed the dramatic possibilities of his work, and pressed earnestly for its acceptance by the theater censors for actual performance; none of his other plays he apparently even envisaged on the stage. It was several times rejected, and the author made revisions of the text in a vain hope of meeting the censors' objections. The result is a bewildering situation in which no fewer than five whole or partial versions of the play exist, not one of which actually bears Lermontov's own imprimatur. The chief rivals are the four-act version of late 1835, which the censor refused in January 1836, and which is the version regularly printed in modern editions;[10] and the earlier three-act version of 1835.[11] There is also the five-act version, re-named *Arbenin,*[12] of 1836, in which the caustic social criticism of the original has been much softened. *Arbenin* is universally agreed to be the weakest of the versions, a desperate final attempt to placate the censors even at the cost of emasculating the drama.[13]

Two principal themes coexist in the several versions of *Masquerade:* a tragedy of marital jealousy, a kind of *Othello* without an Iago, which centers on the character of Evgeny Arbenin, (the title of the 1836 version is an attempt to accentuate this theme at the expense of the other); and a sweeping general criticism of the mores of capital society as these are exemplified in such typical representatives as Prince Zvezdich, Baroness Strahl and Adam Petrovich Sprich. Arbenin, a young nobleman of great intelligence and demonic power, self-centered and contemptuous of the social environment in which his lot is cast, has married a young and unsophisticated girl, Nina, whom he loves and who is devoted to him. Nina loses one of a pair of bracelets which her husband has given her while attending a masquerade; this proves to be the *Othello* handkerchief. It is picked up by Baroness Strahl, a young widow of a passionate nature but decorous public behavior. The Baroness encounters at the masquerade young Prince Zvezdich, whom Arbenin has just rescued from bankruptcy and possible suicide at a gambling place, and after an amorous conversation with him, still in domino, she gives him the bracelet as a memento. This thoughtless act leads to the catastrophe: Arbenin finds out about the lost bracelet and suspects his wife; he discovers that Zvezdich has it, and plans at first to kill him, but decides on a still more diabolical revenge—he accuses him of cheating at cards and slaps his face, and then refuses to fight with him, thus, according to the curious code of the time, irreparably smirching his honor. Finally Arbenin convinced despite her pleas of his wife's infidelity, poisons her, watches coldly as she dies, and in the 1835 version, escapes suspicion of the murder. In the canonical four-act version Arbenin is visited the day after Nina's death by Zvezdich to whom the Baroness has confessed everything in a frenzy of penitence, and by an "unknown," who proves to be a vengeful enemy of Arbenin, whom he has ruined at cards seven years before. The two assure Arbenin that they know he has caused Nina's death, and that she was innocent. Convinced at last of the truth, Arbenin goes mad; Zvezdich is balked of the opportunity to regain his honor by a duel, and the unknown retires, happy in his accomplished vengeance.

The unsettled question of which version Lermontov himself considered, or would have considered, definitive, leaves a critic rather at a loss in evaluating the play. In the earlier three-act version Arbenin most cruelly forces the innocent Nina to confess her non-existent guilt with the false promise that in that case he will call a doctor to save her life; and of course in this version the murderer suffers no punishment. This was one of the censor's chief objections; and there is no doubt that the addition of the fourth act and the unknown was Lermontov's answer to this objection, although he still retained the murder itself, which the censor wanted changed. In the version named *Arbenin* Nina is guilty, but Arbenin does not really murder her—he only pretends that a glass of lemonade she has drunk contained poison, and in this way obtains the confession of her guilt. Which ending should be considered definitive? The *Arbenin* version is out of the question—both themes are stultified in it, and all that remains is a psychological portrait of the title character. In spite of the undisputed fact that the fourth act was added after the censor's refusal to accept the play, there is some evidence that the addition of the unknown and the punishment of the murderer were voluntary changes on the author's part; moreover dramatically the spectacle of the murderer's retributive madness makes a stronger ending than that of the three-act 1835 redaction, which closes with the exit of the doctor, who has assigned Nina's death to natural causes, and Arbenin's soliloquy:

> Oho! I'm unscathed.... to whatever earthly sufferings my breast has been consigned in sacrifice... But I'm still alive! I sought for happiness and God sent it to me in an angel's form. My criminal breath sullied the godhead in it... And here it is, beautiful creature—look! cold, dead! Once in my life, risking honor, I rescued from ruin a man strange to me [i e., Zvezdich], and he, laughing, joking, saying not a word, took from me everything, everything—and in an hour.

On the whole it is probably better to accept the four-act version, in spite of the rather cheap sensationalism of the *deus ex machina* ending.

The tragedy, whichever version we accept, plunges a modern reader into a world as foreign and incomprehensible as that of *A secreto agravio secreta venganza* or *El medico de su honra*. The conventions of Calderón's Spain, where a gentleman's honor has to be vindicated by his wife's death, even if she were innocent, once her fidelity has even been put in question, seem suddenly to have been transferred to St. Petersburg. Arbenin is a powerful artistic creation, one of Lermontov's most impressive heroes.[14] He has been very properly compared with the Demon, but in his cold and monstrous egotism he is far less sympathetic than that mythological figure. The whole burden of Arbenin's complaint is: I looked for happiness, and thought I had found it; but she deceived me—*me!* So she must die. The thought obviously could never occur to such a man that perhaps his wife might also have been looking for happiness, and not finding it, had with justification looked elsewhere. Arbenin is doubtless in part a "hero of his time," the product of the odious society around him—but only in part. Lermontov does not show him, as he does Pechorin, as a strong nature warped by the false values of his caste. His psychology, like that of the Demon, is a romantic stereotype, unrelated to human reality. Nina is, by contrast, an attractive figure, very reminiscent of Desdemona, in her conflict with the husband whose Satanic nature she cannot fathom: whatever may have been Lermontov's intentions, the reader's sympathy is inevitably with her.

Of the other characters of the play, Baroness Strahl is the most complex and best portrayed. It is her thoughtless prank that begins the action, and her selfish manoeuvre in order to protect herself by casting suspicion upon Nina that makes the tragedy inevitable. Yet she is horrified and conscience-stricken when she realizes the probable consequences of her action, and endeavors to undo the damage she has done, but without effect. Prince Zvezdich might well be one of the characters of a society novel by Bestuzhev-Marlinsky. Open-hearted, insouciant, frivolous, but honorable and meaning no evil, he is utterly shattered by Arbenin's diabolical scheme to ruin his good name by the implication that he declined a duel in spite of a slap in the face. Arbenin's old comrade and fellow-gambler Kazarin is a minor character, but well delineated. The gossip and busybody Sprich, despised and yet indispensable, is the most "negative" of the cast, but even he is no villain. It must be said, to the credit of Lermontov's good sense, that after the juvenile *Spaniards* none of his dramas contains a genuine villain. Of course his people do not have the fully three-dimensional reality of Pushkin's, but they approach it.

It is doubtful that even a very good translation of *Masquerade* could ever make it acceptable on a non-Russian stage. Not only does the subject alienate the modern reader (who can tolerate *Othello* because it is so remote in time and place, but would balk at a modern version of it), but perhaps even more because of the medium in which the drama is cast. The wonderful, light, infinitely flexible and brilliantly unpredictable "free iambics" of Griboedov's masterpiece have never been naturalized in any language but Russian. In English Sir Bernard Pares' laborious attempt to render *Woe from Wit* in the original meter is an awful warning to any ambitious translator. Lermontov's handling of the same meter lacks the magnificent dexterity of his model's, but is brilliant enough to cover up and neutralize the *longueur* of many of the speeches, especially Arbenin's. A rendering in prose or even in another verse form would never do this. It is this lithe, versatile meter, capable one moment of grandiloquent solemnity, the next of epigrammatic *pointe,* now casually colloquial, now rhetorical, now caressing, now devastating, that makes *Masquerade* a stage possibility in its own language.

Perhaps a final word needs to be said about the drama's title. "Masquerade" of course refers specifically to the crucial second scene of the first act, where the bracelet is lost and Baroness Strahl finds and uses it. The censor, incidentally, in reprimanding the poet for the inadmissible aspects of his drama, wonders how he could have allowed himself such an overt calumny against the Engelhardt masquerades—social events which even members of the royal family sometimes frequented. It hardly needs to be said, however, that the actual dancing in domino, which probably did, and certainly could have, covered up a great deal of illicit philandering, is only a symbol in the drama for the whole hypocritical world of upper-class society, where everyone wears a mask and is something other than he—or she—seems. "A Diana in society, a Venus in a mask," as Arbenin remarks of the Baroness. The title thus fits the tragic and the satirical aspects of the drama equally well.

If Mikhail Lermontov were not one of the most outstanding poets in the whole course of Russian literature, and even, by virtue of his one completed novel, one of the most outstanding prose writers as well, no one would give a second thought to his dramatic production. With the dubious exception of *Masquerade,* not one of them can hold the stage, and a drama is not a drama if it exists only on paper. There are numerous extremely interesting aspects to the Lermontov plays—some, even *The Spaniards*—have fine passages of rhetoric; there are striking lines, profound observations on human life and love; there are many revealing insights into the author's own complex psychology. In this connection a remark of N. M. Vladimirskaya[15] is significant: "The attention of Soviet scholars has been concentrated on a study of the social content of Lermontov's dramaturgy, its connection with the period and the writer's view of the world, its specific artistic quality and place in the history of Russian culture." Worthy objects of attention, doubtless, and insofar as they contribute to a better understanding of a great poet, deserving the time and energy they have received. But the artistic quality of Lermontov's plays is precisely that of his lyrics or his narratives, and their place in the history of Russian culture is that of any work that must be read, a dead thing on paper, not a living presence on the stage. As dramas Lermontov's plays are null and void.

Lermontov's Narrative Prose

As has been noted, Lermontov, after the blank verse of *The Spaniards* (1830), composed the rest of his dramas except *Masquerade* in prose, using a heterogeneous mixture of stilted romantic diction and the vulgate, depending on the social caste of the speaker. It is not surprising that from the prose drama he should have turned to the prose novel. His first experiment in this line dates from 1833-34, when he was twenty, and is given in editions of Lermontov's works the conventional title *Vadim;*[16] Lermontov's own intended title is unknown, since the first page of the manuscript has been torn off. The novel is unfinished: the author was evidently dissatisfied with it for one reason or another and abandoned it with the end of Chapter 24, leaving his characters in predicaments for which no solution is in sight. Perhaps he himself could see no satisfactory resolution of his plot; but perhaps also he realized that in the course of his twenty-four chapters he had shifted his entire point of view, and the person who seemed in the early chapters to be the novel's hero had turned by the middle into its villain.

The action of the novel takes place in 1775 at the beginning of the Pugachev uprising, and its locale is the region of Tarkhany (Penza Government), the estate of Lermontov's grandmother, where he spent most of his boyhood. It is supposed that local legends of the Pugachev-shchina furnished some aspects of the plot (perhaps the striking incident of the killing of an unnamed nobleman and his beautiful daughter in Chapter 23): certainly the detailed descriptions of the region, including that of the Devil's Den, where the Palitsyns and Olga find refuge, are drawn from the author's own experience.

The novel begins with the introduction of the ambiguous villain-hero, the grotesque and ugly hunchback Vadim, who separates himself from the gang of beggars at an unnamed monastery (actually the Nizhnelomovsky Monastery about fifty versts from Tarkhany) and becomes the groom of the wealthy landowner Boris Petrovich Palitsyn. At Palitsyn's estate Vadim makes himself known to the owner's ward, the beautiful Olga, and reveals to her that she is his sister, and that their father has been betrayed, ruined and driven to his death by his one-time friend Palitsyn. The unsophisticated Olga, despite her revulsion from her hideous and ter-rifying brother, agrees at last to cooperate with him in his plans to take dreadful vengeance on Palitsyn, after the latter, in a fit of drunken lust, has nearly raped her. But everything takes a different turn when Palitsyn's son, the hussar Yury Borisovich, returns home on leave. He is stunningly handsome and as noble and open as his father is devious and craven. Olga falls in love with him and he with her, and Vadim realizes he has lost forever the only woman from whom he might ever hope to have love. He threatens Olga that he will surely kill her handsome lover when the great day of vengeance comes. This is at hand, for a mighty champion of the oppressed common people has arisen not far away, and all the gentry will be destroyed. Rumors of disquiet among the peasants reach the Palitsyns, but they discount them. The local revolt breaks out during a service at the monastery: Palitsyn's wife is lynched, but Yury and Olga escape. The proprietor himself is on a hunting expedition, and has put up for the night at the house of a buxom "soldier's wife," who is his mistress. Yury warns his father of the danger and the soldier's wife gets her half-witted son Petrusha to guide them to a refuge in a cave of sinister repute in the region, the Devil's Den. Yury returns to rescue Olga, whom he has left in a decrepit bathhouse near the Palitsyn village. On the way he is overtaken by Feodosy, one of his father's huntsmen, who has remained faithful. He lets Feodosy go to the bathhouse to find Olga, but as the huntsman steps out of the door, he is suddenly felled by an ax blow, and Vadim appears before the horrified Olga and delivers an exultant tirade over the body of the man whom he has taken for Yury. When he discovers at last his error, he is so crushed that Olga slips away unnoticed, joins Yury, and the pair eventually find their way to the Devil's Den. Vadim, meanwhile, has incited a group of Pugachev's Cossacks who have come to the village in vain search of the Palitsyns, to accompany him to the outlying farm where he knows Boris Petrovich has gone on his hunting expedition. Vadim and the Cossacks arrive just as the *soldatka* has administered a terrible beating to her seventeen-year-old son for having failed to take food to the refugees in the Devil's Den, as a result of which Yury himself has ventured out to try to find supplies. She quickly conceals Yury with some provisions in a hole under a plank in the floor, and when she is interrogated by the Cossacks, she persists, even under torture, in denying that she knows the where-abouts of the Palitsyns. Petrusha is next tortured, but the terrible effect of his mother's beating has so impressed him that he too holds out, and as the last chapter ends, Vadim and the Cossacks are deliberating on what to do next. Lermontov left no clue as to the planned outcome, although a personal confrontation between Vadim and Yury would seem to be inevitable at some point. There are hints in the course of the novel that it will end happily for Yury and Olga.

Until the appearance in the story of Yury in Chapter 9 Vadim has occupied the center of the stage and the author has obviously been sympathetic with his diabolical thirst for vengeance, and even with the more than fraternal love which he shows for Olga. With the arrival at Palitsyno of the glamorous young soldier the entire point of view changes, Yury becomes the focus and the love of the two young people takes precedence over the hunchback's scheme of vengeance. It is as though the young author has against his will been drawn into seeing his subject in an entirely different light, so that his—and the reader's—sympathies are now with the romantic lovers, and even with the vile Boris Palitsyn, little as he deserves it. This is probably the reason for the abandonment of the novel. The original plan may well have encompassed a tragedy in which Vadim's vengeance was successfully carried out but with his sister's death as the price—an outcome which the shift of sympathy would have made too monstrous to be tolerable.

Vadim is not, properly speaking, a historical novel. Although there is a certain attempt to picture the Pugachevshchina in a realistic way, this is accomplished more by the use of a lurid imagination than, as with Pushkin's *The Captain's Daughter,* by the careful use of documentary sources. *Vadim* contains neither an historical person nor an historical event. In this regard, as well as in the style, this first Lermontov experiment in prose is closely allied to such pseudo-historical verse tales as *The Lithuanian Woman* and *The Boyar Orsha.* The same stylistic means as mark the verse tales recur in *Vadim,* transposed into prose.[17]

The literary quality of the novel is not high. Lermontov's immediate model would have been Bestuzhev-Marlinsky. The juxtaposition of high-flown oratorical tirades from Vadim, Yury and Olga with the common-place, even vulgar language of the Cossacks, the *soldatka* and Boris Petrovich is quite comparable to the style of, e.g., *Menschen und Leidenschaften.* The narrative portions of the story alternate with fairly extended and realistic descriptions of the natural scene, of which that in

Chapter 28 of the Devil's den is the most notable. The influence of Sir Walter Scott may probably be seen here, although perhaps through the mediacy of Marlinsky. Certainly the abundance of far-fetched, bookish comparisons in the work is a Marlinsky trait.

Another literary presence may be felt in *Vadim*—that of Victor Hugo. It would probably be too literal an interpretation of this presence to point to the hunchback of *Notre-Dame de Paris,* hopelessly in love with the beautiful heroine, as a parallel to Vadim. Poor Quasimodo is disfigured by nature, but not by such hideous passions as Lermontov's villian-hero.[18] Bug-Jargal is another Hugo character whose romantically rebellious nature may have lent traits to Vadim. More than any specific figure, however, Hugo's theory of the effectiveness of juxtaposing the grotesque and horrible with the beautiful and the pure is likely to be the operative matter here. This theory, so antithetical to the aesthetics of classicism, he embodies in *Notre-Dame de Paris* and in various other of his earlier works, and expounds in the programmatic preface to his drama *Cromwell.*[19] Lermontov, one might say, superimposed on a Byronic hero rather similar to Lara the physical repulsiveness of Hugo's Quasimodo, with numerous hints from other literary models. In any case, the figure of Vadim is an altogether bookish construct, with few points of contact with any conceivable human being.

Princess Ligovskaya,[20] Lermontov's second attempt to write a novel, is, like *Vadim,* unfinished. This is almost the only similarity between the two fragments. From the mysterious and terrible hero with dark, volcanic passions, and the concomitant *style frénétique* (Charles Nodier's phrase) he turns in *Princess Ligovskaya* to a representation of his own age and social milieu and a style that, although uneven and occasionally showing relapses into the melodramatic manner of *Vadim,* is for the most part quite sober and matter-of-fact.

The novel was begun in 1836, and Lermontov's friend Svyatoslav A. Raevsky, as we know from the former's own testimony, had some hand in it.[21] Boris Eikhenbaum[22] conjectures that Raevsky, who is known to have been a *chinovnik* himself and a follower of the French socialist Fourier, may have been responsible for the figure of the young Polish *chinovnik* Krasiński. This seems quite probable, in view of the fact that Lermontov had no experience with bureaucratic life, and as far as we can tell was quite indifferent to such egalitarian notions as Krasiński voices in the novel.

Unlike *Vadim, Princess Ligovskaya* is patently autobiographical. The basic situation developed in the finished portion is closely parallel to that of the drama *Two Brothers;* even the name of the heroine is the same: Vera Ligovskaya. Her husband in the play is Prince Ligovsky, whose name in the novel is changed only by accent to Ligovskoi. In both cases the situation reflects Lermontov's own chagrin at the marriage of Varvara

Lopukhina to Nikolai F. Bakhmetev, a marriage which he interpreted as mercenary and refused to believe could be based on love. Moreover a secondary sub-plot in the novel, that involving Pechorin's relations with Lizaveta Nikolavna Negurova, is based on the flirtation which the poet carried on with Elizaveta Alexandrovna Sushkova, even to the anonymous letter sent by Pechorin-Lermontov in order to break off relations.[23] Elizaveta Sushkova was a lady a few years older than Lermontov, whom he met through relatives of his grandmother and courted for a while with no serious intentions. Sushkova at the time was regarded as a spinster, and according to her memoirs, was constantly plagued by her aunt, with whom she lived, to find a husband! This trait, too, is faithfully kept in the novel, transferred to Negurova's parents.

The novel breaks off at the end of Chapter 9, providing no clue as to the direction intended for its continuation. It may be presumed that the incident so graphically described in the first chapter—the accident which leads Krasiński to swear undying enmity to the arrogant Pechorin, would have led to some sort of vengeance, probably involving Pechorin's beloved Vera. Perhaps Krasiński might have taken the place of Alexander Radin in *Two Brothers*. In any case the very first words of the novel give the reader notice of the significance of the incident: "Note the day and hour, because on that day and that hour occurred an event from which stretches a chain of varied adventures which befell all my heroes and heroines"...Stender-Petersen, incidentally, cites the abrupt and compelling opening of *Princess Ligovskaya* as an apt prefiguration of the narrative technique employed by Dostoevsky in beginning e.g., *The Idiot* or *Crime and Punishment*.[24]

In this novel Lermontov is consciously attempting to overcome the schematic, one-dimensional characterization which marks his earlier narrative attempts, both in verse tales and in *Vadim*. In this regard his choice of a name for his hero is significant. Pechorin is deliberately fashioned on the model of Onegin, and according to Eikhenbaum[25] the river Pechora is picked because it runs parallel with the Onega, and is turbulent and swift while the Onega is quiet and slow-moving. Pushkin's "metonymic" technique in hinting at his hero's character by a detailed description of his dressing-room is copied by a similar description of Pechorin's study. The significance of the various items is not left to be guessed at, but explicitly pointed out. "The draperies over the windows were in the Chinese taste, and in the evening, or when the sun struck the window-panes, crimson blinds were lowered—a sharp contrast with the color of the room, but indicating a certain love for the strange, the original." The hero's dilettante interest in music and art is shown by "three alabaster caricatures of Paganini, Ivanov and Rossini" on the mantlepiece, and a powerful "primitive" painting of a man, whom Pechorin, "as an admirer of Byron, called a portrait of Lara." Pechorin has numerous characteristics of Lermontov himself: thus, he is short and stocky and plain-looking, but with lively and expressive eyes; and he is dreaded in society for his sarcastic wit. In his relations with others he exhibits in the novel a number of sides. He is naively romantic in the flashback depicting his youthful liaison with Vera; he is superior and condescending to his much younger sister; at his mother's dinner-party he deliberately shocks and needles the guests, especially Vera; yet at his first meeting with Vera after her marriage he is embarrassed and taciturn, and an acquaintance of Vera's husband has to fill in the gaps in the conversation with stupid stories.

Of the other characters none is shown with the lifelikeness of Pechorin. Vera does not appear often enough to give much impression, her husband is a mere caricature, and Pechorin's sister, although vividly portrayed, disappears after the first chapter. The most fully presented person after Pechorin is the old maid Negurova, sentimentally dreaming of an ideal love match and painfully aware that in her situation she must be satisfied with any suitor at all. She is shown sympathetically, not cynically, and one wonders what her place might have been in the novel had it been completed. The model for Negurova, Elizaveta Sushkova, was married in November 1838 to A.V. Khvostov,[26] but according to Lermontov's letter of 8 June of that year to Raevsky, "The novel which you and I began has got in a jam and is unlikely to be finished."[27]

Of the characters of *Princess Ligovskaya* Krasiński is the most bookish. He is depicted as almost a romantic cliché—exceedingly handsome, rebellious and chafing at the unfair lot which has decreed that he should be poor and despised while his hated rival is rich and a society dandy. The bookishness of Krasiński is apparent in the tirades of inflated rhetoric put in his mouth at the scenes in the opera-house lobby and outside his own shabby quarters when he encounters the man who has almost run him down, and then boasted of it. He says to his mother after Pechorin's visit (Chapter 7):

> When he was sitting opposite me, glittering with his gold epaulettes, stroking his white plume, didn't you feel, didn't you guess from the first glance that I must inevitably hate him? Oh, believe me, he and I will meet more than once on the path of life, and meet not as coolly as now. Yes, I shall go to this prince[i.e., Ligovskoi], some secret premonition whispers to me, so that I may obey the decrees of fate.[28]

It is at Prince Ligovskoi's house, where Krasiński goes in compliance with Pechorin's request, that he first meets Vera, and presumably this meeting is to "obey the decrees of fate."

The behavior of Krasiński, who is little more than a romantic stereotype, and the environment in which Pechorin finds him, are in startling contrast. The filthy, repulsive slum where the young *chinovnik* lives with his widowed mother, with its disgusting sights, sounds and smells, is descibed with the unflinching realism affected by the so-called "natural school" of the next decade in their "physiological sketches":

> You make your way first through a narrow, angular court, over deep snow or liquid mud; high pyramids of firewood threaten every minute to crush you with their fall; a heavy smell, repulsive, pungent, poisons your breathing; dogs growl at your appearance, pallid faces bearing on them the dreadful marks of poverty or vice peer out through the narrow windows of the lower floor. Finally, after many inquiries, you find the door you want, low and black as the door of Purgatory; slipping on the threshold, you fly two steps down and your feet land in a puddle that has formed on the stone pavement; then you feel with uncertain hand for the stairway and begin to mount up. Reaching the first floor and stopping on a square landing, you will see several doors around you, but alas, not one of them with a number... After suffering for about an hour, you finally find the number 49 that you want, or another one just as mysterious, and this [only] if the porter wasn't drunk and understood your question, or if there aren't two officials with identical names in the same building, and if you haven't hit upon the wrong stairway...[29]

The influence of Pushkin's "novel in verse" has been noted. A tell-tale oversight in Lermontov's manuscript makes this unmistakable: in the first chapter the hero is called not "Georges," as usually, but "Eugene!" But Pushkin's is not the only contemporary influence on the novel: the description in the first chapter of the scene on Voznesensky Prospect on the winter afternoon when Pechorin's carriage knocks down poor Krasiński owes an obvious debt to Gogol's "Nevsky Prospect":

> So, along Voznesensky Prospect was walking a certain young official, and he was walking from his department, fatigued with his monotonous work, and dreaming about a reward and a tasty dinner—for all officials dream!... It seemed he was not hurrying home, but was enjoying the clean air of the frosty evening, which was pouring its rosy rays through the winter mist over the roofs of buildings, the alluring glitter of shops and confectionaries; raising his eyes from time to time aloft with a truly poetical yearning, he would collide with some pink hat or other and excuse himself in confusion; the sly pink hat would be angry—and then look back at him under his cap and, going ahead a few steps, would turn around as though waiting for a second apology: in vain! The young official was perfectly slow-witted!... but even more often he would stop to gaze through the windows of a store or confectionary, glittering with wondrous fires and grand gilding....[30]

One should note the typically Gogolian trick of identifying a presumably human being with a part of his or her dress or other external marks—here the "pink hat" as a metonymy for the girl wearing it. A similar effect is seen in the satirical description of the ball at Baroness R**'s (Chapter 9):

> But on the other hand the ladies... Oh! The ladies were the real ornament of the ball, as of all possible balls!... How many glittering eyes and diamonds, how many rosy lips and ribbons... miracles of nature and miracles of a fashion-shop... magically little feet and wondrously narrow shoes, shoulders of white marble and the best French powder, resounding phrases borrowed from a fashionable novel, and diamonds rented from a shop....[31]

The procedure of arranging the natural and the artificial in ironic parallel—e.g., eyes and diamonds, lips and ribbons—is very like Gogol's ironic enumeration of the "rather important domestic duties" of the people who stroll along Nevsky Prospect, "such as talking to the doctor about the weather and the pimple that has come out on their nose, inquiring after the health of their horses and their promising and gifted children, reading in the newspaper a leading article and the announcements of the arrivals and departures."[32] As Eikhenbaum[33] remarks: "If one didn't know that 'The Overcoat' appeared only in 1842, one could suppose that the beginning of *Princess Ligovskaya* was written under the influence of the Gogol story."

However interesting the unfinished novel is to a student of Lermontov's development, it has to be discounted as a landmark in Russian literature. It was first published in 1882, over thirty years after the author's death, and by that time the Russian realistic novel had not only reached maturity, but was well beyond its golden age. Whatever advances in character depiction and new narrative techniques Lermontov experimented with in *Princess Ligovskaya* he had fully assimilated by the date when *A Hero of Our Time* was published (1840) and through that single complete novel these had had their effect on his country's literature.

Before we turn to *A Hero of Our Time,* however, we may take a very brief look at a few minor pieces, fragmentary and complete, which form part of the author's heritage. The six-page fragment that begins "I want to tell you the story of a woman—,"[34] dated approximately 1836, the same year as *Princess Ligovskaya,* would have been another tale of the society life of his own time. In the small portion of this project which was completed the author has not got around even to begin the story of the "woman" mentioned in the first line but has sketched the early history of the man who was presumably to have had a scandalous liaison with her. His name, it is worth noting, is Alexander Sergeevich Arbenin. Lermontov had a curious penchant for using the same name in different plays or stories. The hero of *A Strange One,* as we have seen, was Vladimir Pavlovich Arbenin, and of *Masquerade* Evgeny Alexandrovich Arbenin. Grigory Alexandrovich Pechorin is the hero of *Princess Ligovskaya* (he is familiarly called Georges, "in the French fashion") and the same name *in toto* is that of *A Hero of Our Time.* The surname Arbenin was probably suggested by his grandmother's married name, Arsenyev. Arseny, it may be remembered, is the name of the young lover of *The Boyar Orsha.* Lermontov himself was often known by his grandmother's name: thus Elizaveta Sushkova notes in her memoirs that she once disclaimed any knowledge of a person named Lermontov, having always associated "Michel" with Mme Elizaveta Alexeevna Arsenyeva![35]

The finished tale "Ashik-Kerib"[36] is Lermontov's version of a popular Turkish folk-story of the "Arabian Nights" type, which he evidently took down more or less verbatim from the lips of an Azerbaijani story-teller. The sketch *Kavkazets,*[37] written for a collection of sketches called "Our People"[*Nashi*], which appeared in 1841, was apparently withdrawn from the collection, probably as a result of Lermontov's disgrace, and not published until 1929. It is a composite picture of the Russian officer who has spent his whole life in the service in the Caucasus and become himself so identified with the people he has lived among that he is, as the first line defines him, "a half-Russian, half-Asiatic being." Aspects of this old campaigner may be seen in the character of Maxim Maximych of *A Hero of Our Time. Kavkazets* is one of the earliest Russian examples of the so-called "physiological sketch" which was to become the principal literary vehicle of the "natural school." It differs, however, from such sketches as e.g., those of Vladimir Dal, D. V. Grigorovich or N. A. Nekrasov, which are statically descriptive. In the words of B. T. Udodov:[38] "The sketch's descriptiveness is given in a definitely dynamic manner, in the aspect of the socio-psychological evolution of the 'hero.'" It had, of course, no effect on the "natural school," nor indeed any impact on Russian literature because of its belated discovery.

In the collection of articles relating to Lermontov published by the Academy of Sciences in 1979[39] V. E. Vatsuro discusses at length "Lermontov's Last Story." This story, conventionally titled "Shtoss,"[40] although the author's intended title is unknown, is available in English translation in the Ardis collection of Russian romantic prose.[41] It is unfinished, probably intentionally, and was written for a particular occasion and a particular group of auditors in 1841, when the author read it at a gathering of friends (probably at the home of Sofia Karamzina, daughter of Nikolai Karamzin). In her memoirs Countess E. P. Rostopchina recalls the occasion:[42] Lermontov had announced that he would read parts of a new novel, for which he would need about four hours, and requested only a selected few intimate friends for an audience. All preparations were made, the author arrived with "a huge copybook under his arm," and read to his select listeners for about a quarter of an hour—and stopped. It was one of his typical hoaxes.

"Shtoss," however, is, as Vatsuro points out, a more serious work than this account would indicate. The group of listeners was one that was very much interested in occult happenings, Mesmerism, "animal magnetism" (hypnosis), etc. It included Vladimir Odoevsky, the writer of Hoffmannesque tales, the poetess Rostopchina, who also wrote some similar stories, and others such as Vladimir Alexandrovich Sollogub, author of "Tarantass," "A Snowstorm," etc. Lermontov's story is deliberately constructed around an everyday, prosaic world, in contrast to some of Odoevsky's fantastic tales, such as "The Improviser," "The Salamander," etc., and is carefully devised so that a double interpretation of the related events is always possible—the entire supernatural element may be seen as a distortion of reality occasioned by the nervous disease of the painter Lugin. The tale employs several motifs which are stock elements of supernatural or horror stories of the time, e.g., a mysterious abandoned dwelling with an uncanny atmosphere, a portrait with terrible haunting eyes (cf. Washington Irving's "The Adventure of the Mysterious Picture," and Gogol's "The Portrait"; Lermontov himself had hinted at such a theme in the description of the portrait of "Lara" in *Princess Ligovskaya*), etc. The theme of a woman as a stake in a card game Lermontov had used humorously in *The Tambov Treasurer's Wife*. The story also enshrines a reference to an actual occurrence of 1839, when a "poor spinster" named Shtoss won 40,000 rubles in a lottery; according to Vatsuro,[43] "the whole town talked about this, and Vyazemsky at that time wrote to his relatives (his wife), with a punning play on the (winner's) name: 'And what about *me? [a ia-to chto-s?]*—I ask fate, did I fall to your lot, perhaps, at a game of 'fools'?" The pun is threefold in Lermontov's story, and the rationalistic interpretation of Lugin's hallucinations hinges on the suggestion conveyed by the familiar interrogation *"chto-s?"* literally "what, sir?" which is homonymous with the German surname Schtoss, and the name of a card game. Lugin's hallucinations begin with a voice which constantly repeats in his ears an address: "In Stolyarnyi Alley, at Kokushkin Bridge, the house of Titular Councillor Schtoss, apartment number 27." When he actually looks up this address and questions the unaccommodating porter about the ownership of the building, the dialogue goes as follows:

> "Whose house was it?"
> "Whose? Kifeikin's, a merchant."
> "It can't be, it was surely Shtoss's!" Lugin exclaimed involuntarily.
> "No it was Kifeikin's—but now, yes, it's Shtoss's!" answered the porter, not raising his head.[44]

When Lugin's uncanny nocturnal visitor appears, after Lugin's move into apartment 27, his first words are: "Wouldn't you like me to deal you a hand of shtoss?" On the apparition's second visit, Lugin demands of him:

> "What is your surname?" The old man smiled. "I won't play otherwise," muttered Lugin, and meanwhile his trembling hand was drawing from the pack the next card. "What, sir?" *[chto-s?]* muttered the unknown, with a mocking smile. "Shtoss? Who?" Lugin's hands sank; he was frightened.[45]

While the uncanny elements, including the ethereal figure of the old man's daughter, who in the painter's fevered imagination is the embodiment of the imagined ideal woman whom he has attempted to portray by his art, can all be explained as figments of Lugin's disordered mind, Lermontov has also provided them with what may paradoxically be called a rational supernatural explanation. As Vatsuro interprets the hints for this, it runs as follows: the old man was an inveterate professional gambler. Once, years before, when he was in the prime of life, as pictured in the portrait, he had staked his daughter at a game of shtoss, and lost. He is now condemned to return to the scene of his wicked gamble every Wednesday (the day on which it had occurred) and continue playing until he loses again. When the story breaks off suddenly, the old man has won every game, to the daughter's despair, and Lugin has lost nearly everything he owned. What the outcome would be Lermontov mockingly left to the reader's or listener's imagination.

The serious side of "Shtoss," as Vatsuro interprets it, is as an exemplification of a critical observation of Pushkin's directed at Odoevsky's kind of supernatural tale. As we have seen in a discussion of these, Odoevsky built many of his pieces on pseudo-scientific theories of abnormal mental states, and as allegorical object lessons. He remarked that writing such tales was hard. Pushkin's rejoinder was: "Then why do it? No one compels you to. A supernatural tale is good only when it is easy." "The Queen of Spades" was Pushkin's own solution of the problem of writing a good supernatural tale, and Lermontov's "Shtoss" follows the same formula: a perfectly ordinary, everyday background upon which the extraordinary fits easily and without strain, and a "double motivation," which always permits an ordinary, rational explanation of the apparently supernatural. Vatsuro might have mentioned also: no overt didacticism. The tragedy of Hermann in Pushkin's tale is no doubt the tragedy of a person who is willing to sacrifice everything for money—but this is only an inference that a moralist may draw: Pushkin never even suggests it. Probably Lugin's tragedy—assuming the "Shtoss" if completed would have ended tragically—could be interpreted as that of the ultra-romantic who turns his back on the real world to live in a world of illusions (cf. Gogol's Piskaryov in "Nevsky Prospect"), but Lermontov successfully and mercifully spares us the moral. His tale is a light trifle, with aesthetic, but no moral overtones.[46]

A Hero of Our Time [Geroi nashego vremeni]

It is unknown when Lermontov conceived the idea of writing his only completed novel.[47] There are no indications in his letters or the reminiscences of friends on the subject. He must, however, have begun writing it by at least 1838, for three of the stories which form parts of the novel were published separately in 1839. The work as a whole appeared in 1840, and the second edition, accompanied for the first time by the author's foreword, in 1841.

The novel's title was different originally from the one under which it was published, but what this original title was is still a matter of dispute.

The careless scrawl on the first page of the rough draft preserved in the Leningrad Public Library was read until 1911 as *Odin iz geroev nashego veka,* "One of the heroes of our age." The editor of the 1911 complete edition of Lermontov's works, D. I. Abramovich, first read the fourth word of the title as *nachala* instead of *nashego,* and this reading has been followed in all subsequent editions. The change makes the title read: "One of the heroes of the beginning of the century" (it should be noted that the final word *veka* means either "age" or more specifically "century.") Lermontov's editors presumably induced him to change his original version, whatever it was, to the present one.

At first glance it would seem to be a matter of only academic interest which of the readings of the original title is the correct one, but this is far from the case. To a Russian "one of the heroes of the beginning of the century" can mean only one thing: Pechorin must have been a Decembrist! Or if not involved in the actual conspiracy, at least suspected of sympathy with the cause, and hence exiled to the Caucasus, like, e.g., Bestuzhev-Marlinsky or Lermontov's friend Alexander Odoevsky. Such in fact is the interpretation which prevails in the Soviet Union; it is elaborately argued by Boris Eikhenbaum in his essay "A Hero of Our Time" in the volume *O Proze.*[48] The interpretation, and the reading of the title on which it is chiefly founded have, however, been put in question by Emma Gershtein.[49] Gershtein rightly regards the personality of Pechorin as more appropriate to the late 1830s than to the middle 1820s, and accuses Eikhenbaum of inconsistency in "wanting it both ways"; "In what way one and the same hero can belong both to the 'beginning of the century' and to 'our time,' that is, the end of the '30s of the nineteenth century, presents an insoluble puzzle." She has reexamined the manuscript and declares that the title, "carelessly written and with a bad pen... permits the disputed phrase to be read as 'One of the heroes of *our* age,' and not as the unreasonable 'One of the heroes of the *beginning* of the century.'" This reading is grudgingly admitted to be "possible" by the *Lermontovskaia Entsiklopediia.*

Eikhenbaum and others have noted that in a passage in Lermontov's foreword to the second (1841) edition of the novel, he vehemently denies any thought that his work might have a salutary effect on society: "Don't, however, suppose after this that the author of this book has any presumptuous dream of making himself the corrector of human vices. God preserve him from such a folly! It was simply amusing for him to make a sketch of a contemporary man as he understands him, and as, to his and your misfortune, he has often encountered him. It will be enough that the illness has been shown, but how to cure it, God knows!"[50] This sounds like a direct and polemical reference to de Musset's words in the final paragraph of his *Confession d'un enfant du siècle:* "Si j'étais seule malade, je n'en disais rien; mais, comme il y en a beaucoup d'autres que moi qui souffrent du même mal, j'écris pour ceux-là, sans trop savoir s'ils y feront attention." But if Lermontov had such a polemical purpose in mind, then the original title of his novel might well have reflected it, in the form that Gershtein reads, "One of the heroes of our century" as against "[Confession] d'un enfant du siècle." Since Russian has neither an indefinite nor a definite article, the French *un,* if rendered at all, must come out as *odin iz,* "one from among"; and where the French can say "*le* siècle" with the unambiguous meaning of "the *present* century," Russian, lacking the article, must make the phrase clear by such a word as "current" or "this" or "our." But "one of the heroes of the *beginning* of the century" would be too far from de Musset's title to have any relevance. This of course does not prove that Lermontov intended to do battle with de Musset over the remedial aspects of exposing the *mal du siècle,* nor that he did in fact write *nashego* instead of *nachala.* But major difficulties arise if the alternative reading is accepted. First of all, if Pechorin was a Decembrist or even only a sympathizer, one would expect at least some of his words or actions to have a bearing on social or political issues—but none do. His principal activity is directed toward the conquest, in one way or another, of feminine hearts. And is he a "hero"? For if the title is to be read as "one of the heroes of the beginning of the century," then "heroes" must be meant seriously: it would be unthinkable to treat ironically the heroism of the martyrs of 1825! Certainly Pechorin faces Grushnitsky's bullet unflinchingly, and his exploit in overcoming and disarming the drink-crazed Cossack in "The Fatalist" is heroic—but between this kind of personal valor and the idealistic, self-sacrificing heroism of the Decembrists there is a vast and umbridgeable gulf.

But if the title is either "A Hero of Our Time," or as the Gershtein alternative of the original wording can be most properly rendered, "One of the 'Heroes' of Our Century," the word "hero" is inevitably bitterly ironical. As to whether Pechorin qualifies for this designation, the best answer is that which the "primary narrator" (Lermontov himself?) gives at the end of his "Foreword" to "Pechorin's Journal":[51] "Perhaps some readers will want to learn my opinion of Pechorin's character? My answer is—the title of this book. 'But that's malicious irony!' they'll say. I don't know."

Finally, one may very reasonably wonder what could induce Lermontov to give to his novel a title ("One of the Heroes of the Beginning of the Century") which he must most certainly have known stood not the slightest chance of being permitted by the censors. He was not naive, and he knew the ways of censors by his experiences trying to get *Masquerade* printed. "One of the 'Heroes' of Our Century" would have occasioned far less difficulty, but was perhaps felt to be too cumbersome. Why "century" *(veka)* was changed to "time" *(vremeni)* remains mysterious.

At the date when Lermontov began writing his work, the Russian prose novel was still in a rather inchoate condition. The novel of adventure and the society novel were exemplified by Bestuzhev-Marlinsky; Pushkin had successfully launched the historical novel à la Walter Scott with *The Captain's Daughter;* the *picaresca* in a quite old-fashioned form had reappeared with Narezhny's *A Russian Gil Blas,* and the novel of education (German *Erziehungsroman*) with *Aristion, or Re-Education.* What was still conspicuously lacking was the type of novel which was ultimately to dominate the field so exclusively that to a modern reader it is almost synonymous with the genre itself, namely, the psychological novel, the novel devoted to the portrayal of the inner workings of a person's mind and heart. Exactly such a novel was Pushkin's masterpiece *Eugene Onegin*—but that was a "novel in verse," and it is not easy to adapt verse techniques to the kind of analytical treatment which the genre requires.

French writers had first attempted the psychological analysis of character in prose; this was manifestly an outgrowth of the classical French tragedy, so masterfully represented by Racine, which is almost wholly dependent upon such analysis; even the comedy, e.g., of Marivaux, in one of its varieties follows the same lines. Probably Rousseau's *Julie* can be considered the first attempt to introduce such a technique into narrative prose; Sénancourt's *Obermann* is another early essay along the psychological line, but so eventless and totally static as to be impossible as a model; it is certainly, however, Benjamin Constant's *Adolphe,* written in 1807 but published only in 1816, that introduced the genre to the nineteenth century. *Adolphe* has marked and obvious features of the eighteenth-century novel and the "age" which its hero exemplifies is the very beginning of the nineteenth; but it leads the way in the direction of explaining the qualities of a person's character by the social milieu in which he lives. Adolphe (the novel is written in the first person) recounts his relations with his father and with a strong-minded older woman which together, in his opinion, did most to form his character before the age of eighteen. Particularly the conventionalities of society irk him (it may be noted that he is a *German,* not a Frenchman):

Il en résulta en même temps un désir ardent d'indépendence, une grande impatience des liens dont j'étais environné, une terreur invincible d'en former de nouveaux. ...J'avais contracté dans mes conversations avec la femme qui la première avait dévelopé mes idées, une insurmontable aversion pour toutes les maximes communes et pour toutes les formules dogmatiques. Lors donc que j'entendais la médiocrité disserter avec complaisance sur des principes bien établis, bien incontestables en fait de morale, de convenances ou de religion, choses qu'elle met assez volontiers sur la même ligne, je me sentais poussé à la contredire, non que j'eusse adopté des opinions opposées, mais parce que j'étais impatienté d'une conviction si ferme et si lourde.[52]

The personality which Adolphe develops and which is responsible in the novel for the ruin of three lives—his own, that of his mistress Ellénore and of her former lover—is dominated by two conflicting characteristics: an "ardent desire for independence," and a timidity which he traces to his childish reaction to the apparent coldness and emotional distance of his father. He is impatient of the constraint on his freedom of action which his success with Ellénore entails; and he is afraid of the trauma of breaking with her.

Adolphe was translated twice into Russian in 1831: by Prince Peter Vyazemsky and by Nikolai Polevoi. In the preface to his translation Vyazemsky stressed that Adolphe's conduct was not something merely personal, but "a mark of the time":

> In this regard this work is not only a novel of today *(roman du jour),* such as the most modern society and drawing-room novels, but still more a novel of this age. ... Adolphe, created on the model and spirit of our age, is often criminal, but always deserving of sympathy; in judging him, one may ask, where will the righteous man be found who will cast the first stone at him? But Adolphe in the past century [i.e., the eighteenth] would have been simply a madman, with whom no one would have sympathized, a riddle which no psychologist would have taken the trouble to unriddle. The moral malady which possesses him and from which he perished could not have become rooted in the atmosphere of the preceding century. Then acute diseases of the heart could develop; now is the time for chronic ones. The very expression "malady of the heart" is a need and discovery of our time.[53]

Among the works in Eugene Onegin's library, in which Tatyana discovers a clue to their owner's psychology, she finds, besides "the singer of the Giaour and Don Juan," "two or three novels besides, in which the age was reflected, and contemporary man quite faithfully represented, with his amoral soul, self-loving and arid, immoderately surrendered to reverie, with his embittered mind that seethes in empty activity."[54] *Adolphe* would most certainly have been one of these novels.

Twenty years separate Constant's novel from Alfred de Musset's *La Confession d'un enfant du siècle* (1836), and the latter quite naturally has to be considered in connection with Lermontov's *A Hero of Our Time*. Its influence, except in a very general matter of theme, is slight, however. Musset begins his "confession" using the same figure of a "malady of the age" as Vyazemsky:

> Ayant été atteint, jeune encore, d'une maladie abominable, je raconte ce qui m'est arrivé pendant trois ans. Si j'étais seule malade, je n'en disais rien; mais, comme il y en a beaucoup d'autres que moi qui souffrent du même mal, j'écris pour ceux-là, sans trop savoir s'ils y feront attention; car, dans le cas où personne n'y prendrait garde, j'aurais encore retiré ce fruit de mes paroles, de m'être mieux guéri moi-même, et, comme le renard pris au piège, j'aurai rongé mon pied captif.[55]

As we have seen, it is almost as though with direct reference to de Musset's words that Lermontov writes in the last paragraph of his 1841 foreword:

You will say, morality is not the gainer from this? Excuse me. Plenty of people feed on sweets: their bellies are ruined by this. Bitter medicines are needed, caustic truths. But don't think, however, after this, that the author of this book had any sort of proud dream of making himself the corrector of human vices. God preserve him from such folly! It was simply amusing for him to sketch contemporary man as he understands him, as he met him—too often, to his and your misfortune. It will be enough that the illness has been shown—but how to cure it, God knows![56]

The general theme, then, of de Musset's *Confession* is the general theme of *A Hero of Our Time*—a "moral malady" peculiar to the first quarter of the nineteenth century; but the manner in which the two poet-novelists develop this theme is totally dissimilar. De Musset at once launches into a long historical account in order to show what his "century" is like, and then proceeds to illustrate the *maladie morale abominable* to which he is prey by descriptions of his several love affairs. Lermontov eschews all historical explanation (if he had written honestly, any such would of course never have passed the censor) and shows his "hero" in various relations with other people, only one of which is a true love affair. He does, however, for at least part of his novel, employ the first-person narrative ("Pechorin's Journal") used by both Constant and de Musset.

Apparently Lermontov early saw disadvantages in the confessional type of psychological novel. A character revealed solely by his own analysis of himself is bound to be one-sided. Doubtless no one else can ever know a person as well as he knows himself, yet there is a monotony in seeing any object from a single point of view, to say nothing of the ever possible suspicion that the writer of the confession may not be giving a completely unbiased account. To obviate these disadvantages and permit a reader what may be termed a "stereoscopic" view of Pechorin, Lermontov devised the bold experiment of presenting his hero not only as he reveals himself in his journal, but as he appears to a friendly and unsophisticated old soldier (Maxim Maximych) and as he appears briefly to the cool impartial eyes of an observer of his own class (the traveller-narrator, who *may* be identical with Lermontov himself). The effect which he desired is achieved by this means, but at the same time the unity of the whole is seriously jeopardized.

Eikhenbaum in his study of the novel[57] states at the beginning of his third section a rather dubious proposition: "It was impossible to sit down and write a new Russian novel in four parts with epilogue—it had to be collected together in the form of tales and sketches linked together in some fashion or other." To support this proposition he cites the characteristic story-cycles of the thirties: Pushkin's *Tales of the Late Ivan Petrovich Belkin,* Gogol's *Evenings in a Hamlet Near Dikanka,* and V. F. Odoevsky's *Motley Stories.* These, however, do not in any case constitute novels, and the unity which the fictional narrator in each cycle contributes (Belkin. "Red" Panko, Irenei Modestovich Gromzeika) is too flimsy to be even considered. He is on somewhat firmer ground in noting the case of Marlinsky's *Latnik* (*The Cuirassier,* 1832), in which several narrators take part, and at the end the reader is able to reconstruct for himself from fragments the whole story (but certainly not the personality) of "the cuirassier." The framework narrative, about the partisan pursuit of Napoleon's retreating army, is given by the "partisan officer"; this is interrupted after the first appearance of the cuirassier to assist in the capture of the Trepol castle by the narrative about the castle and its owners, put in the mouth of the old butler *(dvoretskii);* there is then an apparently unconnected narrative by Lieutenant Zarnitsky, interrupted by the cuirassier's own story, which completes that of the butler; and at the end the partisan officer resumes with his account of finding the body of the mysterious cuirassier.[58] This is a clever and artful means of lending variety to a story by presenting it in pieces as these become known to the principal narrator. Its relevance to Lermontov's novel, however, is slight because the substance of *A Hero of Our Time* is not a story, but the depiction of a personality. The novel has no unifying plot. It is hard to see why, had he wanted to, Lermontov could not have portrayed Pechorin in a straightforward fashion as Stendhal does Julien Sorel in *Le Rouge et le noir* (1831). That he did not choose to do so, but resorted to the extraordinary means that he did is in my opinion the result of a peculiar circumstance: he wrote the several *povesti* ("Bela," "Taman," "Princess Mary," "The Fatalist") which constitute the main substance of the novel *before* he had any idea of putting them together; in fact, in one case ("Taman") without even connecting the tale with Pechorin at all. The final structure of *A Hero of Our Time* is an afterthought, along with the personality of Maxim Maximych. That in spite of this haphazard genesis the novel is a work of art is simply because its author was a genius, if a rather eccentric one.

The technical means by which Lermontov accomplishes his purpose of welding a series of tales into what has to be granted the status of a genuine psychological novel are very interesting. Prose fiction in Russia in the 1830s took the form, above all, of such cycles of short tales as have been mentioned. In such collections the narrator contributes what unity there is: no single hero moves through all the component tales. The style of the narration may be diversified by the fictional device of introducing the individual tales as contributed by different persons, e.g., a maiden lady, a church sexton or the like. *A Hero of Our Time* is the first such collection to give a single central character (Pechorin) the burden of furnishing the unity of the whole work. When a different point of view is introduced, e.g., in "Bela," through the presentation of the tale by Maxim Maximych, this is done not arbitrarily, but with careful motivation which makes it seem perfectly natural. As Eikhenbaum points out,[59] writers such as Veltman and Marlinsky love to play with the form of their narrative by constantly intruding themselves into it in facetious dialogue with their readers. As we have noted elsewhere, practically the whole of Veltman's *Strannik* is constructed upon completely capricious alternations between a real journey and an imaginary one in which the narrator is accompanied by an admiring throng of (largely female) readers. This kind of play Lermontov completely discards. The capricious postponement of the preface to a work is another aspect of this "playing with form," of which an example may be found in the otherwise quite serious "Princess Mimi" of V. F. Odoevsky. Lermontov's postponed preface to *A Hero of Our Time* is made natural and reasonable (is "motivated," in Eikhenbaum's formalist terms) by the circumstance that the narrator comes into unexpected possession of Pechorin's journal and finds himself at liberty to publish it. Thus, in spite of the apparently fragmentary structure of the novel, Lermontov achieves a naturalness that is lacking in any of the other "cyclic" works of the period.

In one respect, however, the work is rather more akin to a *novella* than to a novel. Pechorin's character is illuminated by several points of view— Maxim Maximych's, the travelling author's, and his own—but it is a character presented statically, without development. The reader never gets any hint of the hero's past other than what comes out in the resumption of his liaison with Vera. His family background, his education, indeed even the reason for his being in the Caucasus, are all left mysterious—and yet such elements form essential features of a genuine novel—note for instance the care that Stendhal lavishes on the early life of his Julien Sorel or his Fabrice del Dongo, or that Pushkin gives to Eugene Onegin, or Lermontov himself to Sashka's "education." Nor is there in the portrayal of Pechorin any such analysis by an "omniscient author" of the workings of the hero's mind as we find, for example, in Tolstoi's treatment of Pierre Bezukhov or of Count Vronsky. Pechorin himself does what analyzing there is, but how much can one trust a person's account of his own motives?

As they are presented in the novel, the several stories are out of chronological order, like the stories in Bestuzhev's *Latnik*. There is a first-person framing narrative by a person who reveals himself as a traveller in the Caucasus, and who is also a writer. This narrator meets on his journey from Tiflis to Stavropol over the Georgian Military Road an old Caucasian soldier *(Kavkazets)* going the same way; at an unexpected overnight stop this Maxim Maximych relates to the traveller the story "Bela." The two travellers separate, but are brought together again at a stop in Vladikavkaz, where unexpectedly the hero of the story "Bela," Grigory Alexandrovich Pechorin, turns up, on his way to Tiflis and ultimately to Persia. Although Maxim Maximych greets his friend with naive effusiveness, Pechorin is very cool and distant, and when he has gone his way, Maxim in a pique hands over to the traveller several notebooks containing Pechorin's journal, which he has kept since their first acquaintance, intending to return them to their owner. From this journal the literary traveller extracts the last three stories, "Taman," "Princess Mary" and "The Fatalist," to which he prefixes a special introduction, including the information that he is led to publish these by the recent news that Pechorin has died on the way back from Persia. The chronology of Pechorin's adventures, however, has to be established as follows: "Taman," which apparently takes place on the hero's first journey to the Caucasus; "Princess Mary," which takes place at Pyatigorsk and Kislovodsk, and ends with the duel in which Grushnitsky is killed; "Bela," when Pechorin in punishment for the duel has been transferred to an isolated fort in the Chechen territory; and "The Fatalist," which takes place during a two-week stay of Pechorin in a Cossack settlement on the Terek line. Framing these events is the encounter of the author-traveller with Maxim Maximych, and forming the terminus of the whole, the statement in the Foreword to Pechorin's journal that news has lately come of the hero's death.

As Eikhenbaum points out, however, there are numerous inconsistencies which make it quite certain that the stories were originally not thought of in the context in which they finally appear. Thus in "Bela" there is no hint whatever of the events of "Princess Mary," which should have preceded it chronologically. In the separate periodical publication[60] of "The Fatalist," the following paragraph was printed by way of introduction, in Lermontov's own name:

> The story here presented is found in the notes of Pechorin, which Maxim Maximych turned over to me. I don't dare to hope that all the readers of *Fatherland Notes* will remember both these names, which I shall never forget, and accordingly I consider it necessary to remind them that Maxim Maximych is that good staff-captain who related the story of "Bela" to me, which was printed in the third volume of *Fatherland Notes,* while Pechorin is the same young man who abducted Bela. I am presenting this fragment from Pechorin's notes in the form in which it came to me.

From this it is evident that at first the travelling author who is the primary narrator of the material up to "Taman" is identified with Lermontov himself. This identification is later dropped. Finally, in the periodical publication.of "Taman"[61] the narrator remarks, apropos of his narrow escape from being drowned by the "undine" whose smuggler-lover his curiosity has endangered: "And in truth I was by no means without fault: curiosity is a thing peculiar to all travellers and writing people." It is quite evident that "Taman" was the first of the stories to be written; and in my opinion the story was not originally connected in any way with Pechorin, but was an adventure of the author-traveller.[62] The personality of the narrator of "Taman" is quite different from what is otherwise revealed of Pechorin:[63] he is naively romantic, as his identification of the smuggler's mistress as his "undine" evidences; he is principally motivated in the story by an idle curiosity, which almost leads him to a watery grave; and perhaps most telling of all, he is ridiculous. Pechorin's actions in "Bela" and "Princess Mary" are reprehensible, and perhaps not rationally explicable, but they are not the results of childish impulse, and they render Pechorin odious, but never ridiculous. But the "hero" of "Taman" is not very bright: he incautiously threatens his "undine" and the blind boy with his knowledge of their smuggling activities, and then lets the girl lure him into a midnight boat-ride in the full knowledge that he cannot swim! If she had succeeded in her efforts to drown him, one could only say that his stupidity fully justified such a fate. "Taman" is the weakest of the four stories, and the least relevant to the evolved novel; it might have been better if Lermontov had not tried to incorporate it, for it detracts from, rather than adds to, our understanding of Pechorin's character. Vladimir Nabokov[64] properly calls it "the least successful section of *A Hero of Our Time.*"

In the novel as finally put together, Lermontov has contrived with great artistry to illuminate Pechorin's character from several points of view, beginning with the most remote and "zooming in" to the most intimate. First the travelling author learns of his existence and hears one story about him at second hand, as it is related by Pechorin's friend Maxim Maximych. The "good staff-captain" is ideally designed to provide a sympathetic, but uncomprehending view of the hero's nature. He faithfully repeats, from what must have been a rather extraordinary memory, Pechorin's self-analysis and explanation of why he has tired of Bela:

> "Listen, Maxim Maximych," he replied. "I have an unfortunate character; whether my upbringing made me such, or God created me such, I don't know; I only know that if I am the cause of the suffering of others, I myself am no less unhappy.... Whether I'm a fool or a villain, I don't know, but this is certain, I too am very much deserving of pity, more perhaps even than she. The soul in me was spoiled by society. I have a restless imagination, an insatiable heart. Everything is too little for me: to sorrow I get accustomed just as easily as to pleasure, and my life becomes emptier day by day...."[65]

Maxim then asks his interlocutor if all young people of the capital are like that, and is assured that some really are, but most affect to be so because it is fashionable. The next interchange is interesting: "I guess it was the French who introduced the fashion of being bored?" asks Maxim. "No," says the traveller, "the English." Obviously such an attitude as Pechorin's words reveal is un-Russian! Were the French responsible, one might think of Chateaubriand's René or de Musset's "child of the century," though Maxim would not have. When the traveller lays the responsibility on the English, he is of course speaking ironically, but with a covert hint at Byron's Childe Harold and English "spleen."

From this second-hand picture of the "hero of our time" the novel proceeds to a first-hand, but purely external one. Pechorin himself turns up, the traveller has a chance to size him up by indications of dress, facial expression, etc., and then by witnessing his cold and distant reaction to Maxim Maximych's exuberant greetings. Finally the "journals" which are turned over to the narrator reveal Pechorin as he saw himself—first in the frank account of his actions with Princess Mary and Lieutenant Grushnitsky, then in the analysis of his motives as he sets them down, evidently honestly, since the journals, at least according to Lermontov's final draft, are intended for no eyes but his own; and then in his conversations with Dr. Werner. His relations with Vera, a former mistress, now remarried, who is a visitor at the spa, introduces another witness, and one who, he admits, is the only person to really know him: "Why she loves me, in truth I don't know. What is more, this is the one woman who has completely understood me, with all my petty weaknesses and ugly passions. Can evil be so attractive?"[66] The story "Princess Mary," which is the longest and best of the four, contributes the most to the reader's understanding of the hero. Finally, "The Fatalist" takes the whole matter into the realm of metaphysics and shows Pechorin witness of and participant in an experiment intended to demonstrate the thesis that human destiny is determined not by human will, but by "Fate."

From the self-analysis and conversations of Pechorin in "Princess Mary" it is clear that his primary moving force is an urge to impose his domination on other people. It is this which impels him to interfere deliberately in the lives of Princess Mary and Grushnitsky, and induce the Princess to love him instead of the posturing nonentity Grushnitsky. His effort of course succeeds, but as he himself recognizes, neither in this relationship nor in that with Vera, which develops simultaneously, does he give anything of himself. His desire to be loved is a form of vanity: he refuses to reciprocate. While acknowledging his emotional impotence, he refuses to accept any responsibility for it: whether, as he says to Maxim, it is his upbringing which has made him as he is, or God who has created him so, it is clear that he is himself not responsible. As he puts it in one of his meditations, he is Fate's executioner: he feels no compunction at destroying the happiness of Vera with her husband, at cruelly deceiving Princess Mary, whom he has successfully duped into believing that he loves her, or at killing Grushnitsky in a rigged duel. He regards all these actions as determined by fate. Yet, most illogically, the steps required to accomplish his mischievous purposes he regards as entirely within the power of his own will to take or not.

This ambivalence is pointed up in the climactic last story, "The Fatalist." The action of the story is precipitated by a brief discussion among some officers stationed at a Cossack fort among the Muslim Chechens: Is the Muslim belief in fate or predestination valid or not? Pechorin is present at the discussion, but takes no part in it. One of the officers, a fanatic gambler, puts the question concretely: if I put a pistol to my head and press the trigger, one of two things will happen: either I will blow out my brains, or the pistol may misfire. In the latter case, it may be concluded that I was not destined to die at that moment. Metaphysically the experiment is nonsense and proves nothing. As it turns out, the pistol does misfire, but even if the opposite had been the case, the fatalist could still legitimately conclude that fate had intended Vulich's death at that instant. But Lermontov diverts attention from the meaninglessness of the experiment by a bit of romantic folklore. Pechorin, who has watched the experiment and been as impressed as anyone must have been at the apparently miraculous outcome of it, assures Vulich that nevertheless he *is* fated to die this very day, because he has seen on the man's face the tell-tale sign of imminent death. And die he does, chopped to pieces by a drink-crazed Cossack whom he encounters late that night. This, of course, is simply a writer's trick, the importation into the story of an irrelevant bit of popular superstition. It serves the author's purpose by enabling him to have his Pechorin declare that he is convinced of the truth of predestination. In the second part of the tale Pechorin himself tries a variation of the same experiment—he succeeds in crawling into the hut where the desperate Cossack murderer is defending himself, and is able to disarm him without any injury to himself.

> After this, it seems, can one not be a fatalist? But who knows certainly whether he is convinced of something or not?... and how often we take for conviction a deceit of the feelings or a blunder of the reason! I like to doubt everything. This disposition of the mind does not hinder decisiveness of character—on the contrary. As far as I'm concerned, I always go ahead more boldly when I know what awaits me.[67]

The reasoning in this strange meditation of Pechorin is hardly lucid. Apparently the last sentence means in context that he prefers to doubt the validity of predestination, despite the apparent proofs he has witnessed, because a fatalistic belief makes it impossible to "know what awaits one." Only if the thinker is altogether "master of his fate" can he be sure of any outcome. Since for Pechorin seemingly the supreme value that he recognizes is his ability to impose his will on others, a belief in predestination would be a most discomforting doctrine to accept.

John Mersereau, Jr. in his discussion of *A Hero of Our Time*[68] considers "The Fatalist" the key to the whole of Lermontov's novel. His reasoning is philosophically most convincing: Pechorin, in spite of apparently conclusive demonstrations of the validity of the determinist position, which denies free will and asserts that an inhuman "fate" controls everything, prefers to believe—or at least to act—as if he were fully in control of his own destiny. This satisfies his egotism. But ethically, free will necessarily implies that man is responsible for his every act. This responsibility Pechorin refuses to accept; whenever the idea threatens to come up in his meditations, he resorts to the phraseology of fatalism, e.g., "Ever since I have been living and acting, somehow fate has always led me to the denouement of others' dramas, as if no one could die or come to despair without me. I was the indispensable character of the fifth act."[69] This refusal to accept personal responsibility for actions freely undertaken, such as the kidnapping which results in Bela's death, the murder of Grushnitsky or the malicious trick on Princess Mary, is in Mersereau's view the paramount sin of Pechorin, which Lermontov never expressly calls attention to in words, but by the content and positioning of "The Fatalist" leaves to the perceptive reader to deduce for himself.

Attractive as this thesis is, there are serious reasons for doubting it, which C. J. G. Turner marshals in his essay on Pechorin.[70] Thus, the present position of "The Fatalist" as the last of the five component tales of the novel is evidently an afterthought; it was originally published separately, and in the only surviving manuscript of the novel as a whole it appears between "Maxim Maximych" and "Princess Mary." With this history, it is hard to see the tale as affording in Lermontov's view a key to the whole novel. As to the content of "The Fatalist," it concerns, as Turner very well demonstrates, not the abstract problem of determinism versus voluntarism, but merely the concrete question of *terminus vitae*—the destined day of death. And finally, although in the preliminary discussion before Vulich's experiment there is a brief mention of the ethical corollary of the doctrine of free will ("And precisely if there is such a thing as predestination, why have we been given free will, judgment? Why must we give account for our actions?") this is nowhere stressed in the story and the two "experiments" do not clearly involve it. To draw the moral judgment on Pechorin's actions which Mersereau considers inherent in the tale it is necessary to pass mentally in review all the hero's acts in the preceding four parts of the novel. As to Pechorin's own conclusions in the tale itself, they are, as we have seen, ambivalent: he is provisionally convinced of the validity of the fatalist position, but on further consideration "prefers to doubt everything." In any case, he dislikes, as does Maxim Maximych, "metaphysical discussions." Pechorin prefers, as most human beings do instinctively, to act as though he controls his own destiny, and leave metaphysics to the metaphysicians. I think it is thus safer to say that Pechorin does not so much refuse to accept responsibility for his actions as refuse to concern himself with the question at all. No doubt this is an attitude both lazy and irresponsible, and as such Lermontov is perhaps tacitly presenting it to his readers as a fault in his "hero," but hardly, I think, as the key to understanding the novel as a whole. Here, I would suggest, he is doing precisely what he has done all along in depicting Pechorin: leaving him indeterminate and elusive, a puzzle both to himself and to others.[71]

Pechorin's character is the novelist's first concern. He has often been compared with Eugene Onegin, and there is no doubt that Pushkin's example played a great part in Lermontov's success with Pechorin. But

Pechorin is not another Onegin. Eugene is passive, and bored; Pechorin is demonically, aggressively active—but also bored. In Onegin's place Pechorin would have gleefully accepted Tatyana's naive declaration of love, not to reciprocate it, but to dominate her. The tragedy of Onegin's duel with his friend and Lensky's death is the result of the passivity of the hero's character and his tame submission to a public opinion that he inwardly despises. Grushnitsky's death is the result of Pechorin's egoistic interference in the affair between him and Princess Mary, which has driven Grushnitsky to an unworthy but natural desire for revenge. Finally, in Pechorin's relations with women there is nothing analogous to Onegin's belated but very genuine passion for Tatyana after she is married. Pechorin is morally incapable of such a passion, because it would mean sacrificing some of himself to the loved one.

The "stereoscopic" portrayal of Pechorin's character as viewed by two observers and himself, and as manifested in interrelations with four women and three men, should, one would suppose, illuminate him quite completely; yet he remains a puzzling enigma. How is one to understand him? First of all, it is misleading and irrelevant to look for any explanation outside of the text itself. Soviet criticism is prone to seek reasons for Pechorin's character in the social and political conditions of the Russia of Nikolai I. Not a shred of evidence for this exists in Lermontov's text, and unless we accept unequivocally the notion that Pechorin is Lermontov himself, this approach is invalid. Pechorin is a literary character, and has only the background that his creator gives him. But Lermontov gives his hero *no* background at all, which is one of the principal reasons why he remains such an enigma. The question of background is momentarily raised in Pechorin's words to Maxim Maximych in "Bela": "whether my upbringing made me such, or God created me such, I don't know." But what this upbringing was is never revealed. Pechorin's character is not shown as developing in the novel, nor is any hint given of the reasons for it.

But can it be equated with Lermontov's own, as hostile critics assumed it could when the novel first appeared, and if so, is it presented self-approvingly or deprecatingly? There can be no doubt that many traits of Pechorin's portrait, even to the semi-autobiographical elements of the liaison with Vera (i.e., Varvara Lopukhina-Bakhmeteva), coincide with what we know of Lermontov's own personality and history.[72] In the text itself there is no evidence of disapproval or moral censure—but equally there is none of adulation. The attitude is studiously impartial and objective. And taking the question one step farther back, what do we surely know about Lermontov's character anyway except what can be inferred from this and other works? Any conclusions on this question are dangerously circular. The only relatively safe basis for a conclusion lies in the forewords, first, to Pechorin's journal, and second, to the 1841 edition of the novel, in which Lermontov decisively denies that Pechorin is a self-portrait. "*A Hero of Our Time,* my dear sirs, is a portrait indeed, but not of a single person: this is a portrait compounded of the vices of our whole generation in their full development." This is explicit enough, but can the Foreword itself be altogether trusted? Nabokov calls it "a stylized bit of make-believe in its own right."[73] That it is stylized there is no question, but I think we have to accept as genuine the two major points that it makes, first, that Pechorin is not being presented as an admirable figure, and second, that he is not a self-portrait, but a composite.

As to the question of the author's opinion of the character he has created, the Foreword to Pechorin's journal, which must be attributed, if not to Lermontov himself, then at least to a persona who resembles him very closely, puts it explicitly: "Perhaps some readers will want to know my opinion of Pechorin's character? My answer is the title of this book.—'But that's malicious irony!' they'll say. I don't know." Is "hero" in the title ironical? If the original title can be read, as Gershtein believes, "One of the 'heroes' of our century," and if the Foreword to the 1841 edition can be taken at face value, then the definitive title must be ironical. The Foreword starts out straightforwardly: "In every book the foreword is the first and therewith the last thing: it serves either as an explanation of the purpose of the work, or as a justification and an answer to critics." Then, however, it comments on the disinclination of readers to read a preface, and remarks that this is a pity because "Our public is still too young and simple to understand a fable unless they find a moral at its end. It doesn't unriddle jests, it doesn't sense irony: it is simply badly educated." Having thus gratuitously insulted his readers, the author then turns to the question with which we are at the moment concerned: "It [i.e., the public] still doesn't know that in proper society and in a proper book open abuse can have no place; that contemporary propriety has discovered a much sharper weapon, almost invisible, and none the less deadly, which under the cloak of flattery inflicts a sure and irresistible blow."[74] This weapon is of course irony. From the author's words one must infer that the public's first conclusion on reading *A Hero of Our Time* was that "hero" was meant seriously, and that the author was presenting a revoltingly immoral character for the public's admiration, whereas he had all along intended "hero" to be taken ironically and Pechorin's character to be recognized as vicious, but as a well-bred "modern" author he had refrained from overtly saying as much, but left it to the public's sagacity to guess his intention. Of course, the Foreword itself may be ironical, and this is probably Nabokov's reason for commenting: "We should not take, as seriously as most Russian commentators, Lermontov's statement in his Introduction. . . . that Pechorin's portrait is 'composed of all the vices of our generation.'"[75] Probably we should not; but there is no reason to doubt that the portrait is, at least, a composite, into which of course some of Lermontov's own traits enter. After all, Lermontov created it, and "our time" was his time; but such traits belong to the whole age, not to the novelist individually. That he means what he says in the "Foreword" is borne out by the impressive poem "Meditation" *(Duma)* of 1838, which indicts "our generation" for almost exactly the same faults as the novel shows in Pechorin. "And we hate and love accidentally, sacrificing nothing either to malice or to love, and in our soul there reigns some sort of mysterious cold, even while fire seethes in our blood"; these words apply precisely to Pechorin in his every relation with other human beings.

But how did Pechorin come to be what he is? To this question the author leaves no clue, and this omission I see as deliberate. It is a significant fact that in earlier drafts of the tales, and even in the separate periodical publication of "Bela," "Taman" and "The Fatalist" there are a few—not indeed very significant—hints that refer to Pechorin's past. Thus, in the draft of "Princess Mary" Pechorin writes, apropos of Princess Mary's curiosity about himself: "But now I am convinced that at the first opportunity she will inquire who I am and why I am here in the Caucasus. They will probably tell her the terrible story of the duel, and particularly the reason for it, which here is known to a few, and then—why, I'll have a marvelous means for infuriating Grushnitsky!"[76] This, and all other references to Pechorin's past that might conceivably serve to explain his present Lermontov carefully cancelled. All we are left with is the novel's title and the disclaimer "I don't know" when a reader is envisaged as saying that that is "malicious irony."

Russian Marxist commentators regularly attempt to prove that there is a covert political message in *Hero of Our Time.* Thus, in his otherwise admirable essay on the novel,[77] Boris Eikhenbaum devotes considerable space to discussing the political message in Scott's novel *Old Mortality,* which Pechorin reads the night before the duel (under the title of the French translation "The Scottish Puritans"). If in the novel Scott does in fact denounce, or have his characters denounce, royal tyranny, this does *not* mean that Lermontov was portraying his hero as a Decembrist sympathizer. Categorically, the novel has *no* political overtones or implications, and any attempt to read such into it is sheer perversity. The problem of Pechorin's character is a moral one, and is so presented by the author. Whatever he may have thought about Russian autocracy—and we know what he thought from "The Death of the Poet"—in his novel at least he is totally apolitical.

Of other characters in the novel, Princess Mary is the best developed. She is certainly inspired by Tatyana, but is no copy. She is naive, open-hearted, and impulsive; she has spirit and fire, and also intelligence. She is romantic, and like Tatyana has formed some impressions of the world and its people from books, such as Byron's poems, rather than from experience, of which she has had little. When Pechorin makes fun of Grushnitsky, she angrily comes to his defence; yet she is intelligent enough, when he is not directly attacked, to see his inferiority to Pechorin. She falls genuinely in love with Pechorin at last, and frankly tells him so; but when she realizes that his feelings for her have been pretense all along, she says: "I hate you!" and means it. She has a nervous breakdown after the incident, but she will recover; she will not succumb, like Bela, to the knowledge that she is not loved. She is a real woman, and after Tatyana the first such in the Russian novel, and the worthy predecessor of Turgenev's strong-minded heroines.

Vera is the only person, according to Pechorin's own confession, who really knows him through and through—and she still loves him. We see her, of course, only through Pechorin's eyes, and since he has known her before the novel opens, he does not sketch her as fully as he does Princess Mary. She appears rather a passive figure, contrasting with the more vivid Mary. Yet if there exists in Pechorin's solipsistic make-up any place at all for real love, it is she who inspires it. When, after the duel, he receives her letter of farewell, his reaction is unexpectedly vehement—a wild, frantic pursuit, and when the futility of this becomes apparent, a childish, hysterical fit of weeping. Has he been really in love with her? So it would seem; and yet he has used his liaison with her quite cynically as one adjunct in his campaign against Grushnitsky and Princess Mary. Perhaps one is to infer that he realizes when it is already too late that he has really always been in love with Vera; but perhaps also, as Turner suggests, his frenetic reaction to her farewell is no more than discomfiture at seeing a victim escape his domination.

The fifth chapter of C. J. G. Turner's monograph on Pechorin[78] is entitled: "The Hero dons a mask." It is the author's contention that Pechorin throughout "Princess Mary" is playing a consciously chosen part, in a scenario in which he is both actor and director. An impressive number of verbal references to his actions in the story picture them as episodes in a drama, specifically a comedy. The final one, of course, is his sarcastic announcement when his bullet has tumbled Grushnitsky into the ravine: "Finita la commedia." All of Pechorin's ostensibly self-revealing monologue in his final interview with Princess Mary is calculated and mere play-acting, as, according to Turner's theory, are most of the utterances which his journal records as made to Grushnitsky, Mary or Vera. If any of his "self-revelation" is to be taken as entirely frank, it is those journal passages in which he records his thoughts and feelings as they present themselves to himself alone, not as he presents them to others.

But Grushnitsky too is playing a part, as Pechorin notes from the first. A symbol of this is his "soldier's great-coat," that is, the coarse, heavy garment of the common soldier, which he ostentatiously wears, hoping it will make Princess Mary suppose that he has been demoted to the ranks for duelling, while actually he is only a cadet waiting for his officer's commission. Despite his total artificiality, Grushnitsky emerges from the novel as a credible person. He is a sham from beginning to end. In his propensity to see himself in the role of a hero of a society novel à la Marlinsky, he is a kind of parody of Pechorin, who sees himself as a Byronic hero, mysterious and fascinating, dominating all around him. In other respects too Grushnitsky is as it were a vulgarized copy of Pechorin. He is a poseur, a would-be wit, in his offhand moments likable and amusing, and charming enough to attract the sympathy of the rather unsophisticated Mary. In contrast to Pechorin, however, he is a person of weak will, readily inveigled into a dishonorable scheme for avenging himself on his rival. It is perhaps precisely because Pechorin senses in Grushnitsky much of himself that he pursues him with such unmotivated relentlessness.

The other male character in Pechorin's "comedy" is Dr. Werner, whose portrait is drawn largely from life. His model was a certain Dr. Maier, whom Lermontov met in 1837. He is in some aspects another Pechorin—at least they understand one another well enough to exchange ironical smiles as, according to Cicero, Roman augurs did when they met. But in the construction of the story Dr. Werner plays a very minor part, mainly, as Turner puts it in terms of classical Greek drama, that of "messenger." He gathers news and reports it to Pechorin, who plots his actions accordingly. Although he and Pechorin converse on serious subjects, Pechorin does not confide to him any significant revelation of his own character. It is significant, however, that Dr. Werner, who has been Pechorin's second in the duel, turns away in horror when Grushnitsky is killed; his note to Pechorin contains the only moral censure on the hero from another person: "There is no evidence against you, and you may sleep peacefully, *if you can.* Farewell."[79]

Perhaps the most sympathetic portrait of all in the novel is that of Maxim Maximych. He is a simple old soldier, rather sentimental (it hurts him when Bela on her death-bed has nothing to say to him, though he has loved her like a father), open-hearted, wise in the ways of the world, but altogether at sea in the alien milieu of the modish products of capital society. It is significant that amid all the hostile criticisms that greeted the first appearance of *A Hero of Our Time,* Maxim Maximych was accorded universal praise.

The device which Lermontov employed in the construction of the novel—that is, the use of several individually complete short stories unified only by the presence in each in some fashion of a central character—was one which he was able to carry through with brilliant success, but which no other Russian novelist after him attempted. As we have noted, it has several advantages, particularly that of exhibiting the central character from different points of view, of heightening the interest by allowing material to be presented out of chronological sequence, of permitting only a limited period of the hero's life to be shown, as in a *novella,* without a full description of education, early life, and the like. But the method also involved Lermontov in some awkwardnesses. A first-person narrative, such as he adopts for all of the component tales, is always difficult to manage when certain actions or situations involving other people have to become known to the narrator. How does he find out about them? How does Maxim Maximych, for example, find out about Azamat's attempted deal with Kazbich? He has to overhear a conversation between the two from behind a fence. How does Pechorin learn that Grushnitsky and the Captain of Dragoons are planning to make a fool of him by challenging him to a duel which they will render harmless by using unloaded pistols? He has to eavesdrop outside a lighted window with "an improperly closed shutter!" Nabokov counts no fewer than eight occasions in "Princess Mary" alone where Pechorin acquires needed information by fortuitously listening in on other peoples' conversations. In itself the overheard conversation is a harmless convention, very much like the soliloquy in classical drama: it is absurd and unrealistic, but convenient, and a reader can accept it for its utility and ignore its improbability; but there is no doubt that in *A Hero of Our Time* Lermontov runs the convention into the ground.

Although *A Hero of Our Time,* when it was published, could be seen as a unique work, quite isolated from anything else by Lermontov's pen, the publication after his death of *Princess Ligovskaya* and the drama *Two Brothers* makes that impossible today. The reader of these two incomplete pieces will realize at once that the same basic situation on which they are built is used also in the story "Princess Mary." Confusingly, the name "Princess Ligovskaya" in the latter tale is transferred from Vera to Princess Mary, a character who has no analogue in the unfinished novel or play. But the triangle consisting of Pechorin (or Yury Radin in *Two Brothers*), Vera and Vera's husband remains the same in all three pieces, and, as we have seen, reflects Lermontov's real-life affair with Varvara Lopukhina. Vera and Pechorin, in *Princess Ligovskaya,* have been childhood lovers, but Vera has "married for money." The situation is the same in *Two Brothers.* It is apparent from "Princess Mary" that Vera has yielded to Pechorin and deceived her first husband; she has a son, by whom is not mentioned. Her first husband has died, and in "Princess Mary" Pechorin seduces her again and ruins her life with her second husband. One may perhaps surmise that this situation might have been utilized in *Princess Ligovskaya* had that fragment been carried to completion. In any case, in "Princess Mary" Vera, as we have noted, is the only person who has ever wholly understood the hero. Is this element autobiographical? We shall never know, for Varvara Lopukhina's husband had all her correspondence with Lermontov destroyed after the poet's death. For purposes of his novel, Lermontov has Vera in her farewell letter to Pechorin summarize his character as she sees it. This is doubtless the way Lermontov intended his hero to appear to the reader as he says good-bye to him:

She who has loved you once cannot look without a certain contempt on other men, not because you are better than they—oh, no! But in your nature there is something especial, something peculiar to you alone, something proud and mysterious: in your voice, whatever you may be saying, there is an unconquerable power; no one can so constantly wish to be loved; in no one is evil so habitually attractive, no one's glance promises so much bliss, no one is better able to exploit his superiorities—and no one can be so genuinely unhappy as you, because no one strives so much to convince himself of the contrary.[80]

The last part of the final sentence of this encomium, however, is arrant nonsense, and an example of Lermontov's inveterate love of striking off aphorisms. Where in the whole novel is there any evidence that Pechorin is striving to convince himself that he is happy? Quite the contrary, he everywhere evades like the plague any implication that he is or could conceivably be happy. He seems almost to pride himself on his inability to experience such a vulgar and commonplace condition. But on the whole Vera's summary catches the essence of the hero as Lermontov wanted him to appear; and although Pechorin is certainly not a replica of Lermontov, the qualities that she ascribes to him are those with which he has endowed most of the heroes of his poems, plays and prose pieces, and which he would very evidently like to have seen in himself.

A great deal remains and will probably always remain enigmatic about *A Hero of Our Time*. Some of the puzzles, I think, are part of the author's intention. But still there is a good deal that can be said about it without too great risk of dissent. It is composed of several short stories, in a fashion otherwise unexampled, but yet remains a genuine novel. The several points of view create a picture in depth of the novel's hero which is almost unique. This picture is presented *sine ira et odio,* but equally *sine amore et studio,* as of a character given, not developing. It is a composite picture, of the upper-class Russian of Lermontov's own time, and inevitably contains numerous elements of its author without ever being a mere self-portrait. Pechorin's character is given, I think deliberately, no hint of the reasons for its being what it is and the author with vehemence disclaims having any notion of how it could be made otherwise: "It will be enough that the malady has been shown, but how to cure it, God knows!" The "Hero of Our Time" must be accepted as he is, whether as a product of bad upbringing, or as the work of an inscrutable God. Beyond this all that we can say of the novel is that it is a masterpiece of vigorous, swift-moving, picturesque narration, unlike anything else in Russian, including other prose by Lermontov himself.

Regardless of genre—lyric, narrative verse, drama or prose—Lermontov's work remains very much all one. It is characteristic that lines from lyrics reappear in narrative poems and vice versa, while one of the speeches from the play *Two Brothers* appears in part in the novel *Princess*

Ligovskaya. The characteristics that mark one genre are equally present in them all, and the influences that he imbibed from his youth can be traced throughout his life. One of the outstanding characteristics of all Lermontov writing is an intensely rhetorical quality. Whether he is denouncing a perfidious sweetheart in a lyric, or through the mouth of his Demon criticizing God's handiwork in the universe, or through the mouth of Arbenin in *Masquerade* or of Krasinski in *Princess Ligovskaya* denouncing the falsity and hypocrisy of society, his voice is that of an orator, and the sharp, epigrammatic style is one that suits declamation more than meditation. The low-keyed, harmonious, restrained style of Pushkin was altogether alien to him, however much he admired Pushkin.

Like any young writer—and one must remember that Lermontov died at 26—he absorbed many literary and philosophical influences, and after a short period of assimilation, they became his own. Only in his very earliest, apprentice work is he imitative in the usual sense. He lifts whole lines and parts of lines, as we have seen, in his first narrative poem, *The Circassians,* and in other pieces, though less frequently, for a few more years. But we must not forget that these are all "practice pieces." Almost nothing that he wrote in the first nine years of his literary life (1828-37) was written for publication, or probably, had he lived, would ever have been published. When we detect in this immature work the influence of Pushkin, of Byron, of Schiller and others, we are seeing these influences often before they have had time to be thoroughly assimilated. To us Lermontov looks far less original that he did to his contemporaries, who had not the privilege of ransacking his notebooks and sometimes tracing through several different versions in quite different contexts the same or nearly the same line or image.

Pushkin was Lermontov's earliest literary idol, and the older poet's influence was probably the longest lasting. But Lermontov's attitude was by no means one of uncritical acceptance. We have noted the curious instance of the early narrative poem *A Prisoner of the Caucasus,* constructed on the same plot as Pushkin's poem, with the same title, and full of Pushkinian lines and tags, and yet demonstratively given a wholly different dénouement—one more satisfyingly "romantic" in the young poet's eyes. Pushkin's famous lyric "The Demon" is evidently the inspiration for Lermontov's "My Demon," but the two demons are markedly different. Pushkin's "Prophet" hears God's voice bidding him "burn with the Word the hearts of men"; Lermontov's "Prophet" goes before men with his burning words, and is reviled and ridiculed and pointed out as an anti-social monster. Perhaps only from *Eugene Onegin,* which he revered most of all Pushkin's work, did Lermontov accept without essential change Pushkin's lessons: the new, proto-realistic style, the idea of a hero who should be a composite picture, a type of his age,— even, as we have seen, some of the technical devices which Pushkin used in portraying his hero, e.g., the "metonymic method." Pechorin is not another Onegin, but it is safe to say that he would never have existed without Onegin's example.

Pushkin's literary background was one that differed radically from Lermontov's. It can be considered to some degree symbolic that Pushkin was born in the last year of the eighteenth century. His earliest verse belongs in the line of eighteenth-century light verse—madrigals, anacreontics, epigrams, anthology verses and the like, and until he began *Eugene Onegin* his lyric falls chiefly in the categories of elegy, epistle and the like which typify the Karamzinian sentimentalist fashion. The chief model for his prose was Voltaire. All this is past history for Lermontov, fifteen years younger. Of Russian influences Pushkin himself, but also Zhukovsky and Batyushkov and Kozlov, even such minor figures as Polezhaev and Podolinsky, contribute to Lermontov's formation as a poet. The tremendous importance of French models for Pushkin is evident in all his work; even Shakespeare and Byron were accessible to him principally through French translations. He paid lip service to Goethe's greatness, but did not know him in the original, and he despised the German romantics. The French romantics, especially the *école frénétique* of Victor Hugo, Jules Janin et al. left him entirely cold. For Lermontov, on the other hand, it was German rather than French influence that was representative of the West. Before he learned English, he read *Macbeth* in Schiller's translation. He read Goethe and Schiller and Heine in their original language, and if, as Eikhenbaum contends,[81] his ignorance of Novalis, Tieck, Von Arnim and Brentano, as also of Shelley, Keats and Coleridge, may echo the French neglect of these poets, it is also certainly true that temperamentally they must have been altogether uncongenial to him. Of French writers those who most attracted him were his contemporaries Alfred de Vigny, whose *Eloa* is significant for *The Demon,* Alphonse de Lamartine, Chateaubriand, and especially Victor Hugo. Pushkin's poem "André Chénier" inspired Lermontov to read that last great French poet of the eighteenth century, but it was probably Chénier's tragic story rather than his verse that formed the attraction.

Lermontov's relations with Byron are complicated. While the English poet was unquestionably the most important and long-lasting foreign influence on Lermontov, this influence was not always direct. Before 1829, when Lermontov learned English, such works as Zhukovsky's translation of *The Prisoner of Chillon* and Kozlov's of *The Bride of Abydos* established the first contacts. Even after he began to read Byron in the original and pore over Thomas Moore's edition of Byron's letters and journals, much of the Byronic influence came not directly but through the "Byronic poems" of Pushkin, Kozlov, Podolinsky and other Russian poets, and even by way of French imitations, e.g., by Victor Hugo and Alphonse de Lamartine.

It was Byron's tales that first attracted Lermontov, and such early attempts as *Giulio, The Lithuanian Woman* and *The Confession* are examples of youthful imitation. In late narratives such as *Hadji Abrek* and *The Boyar Orsha* the imitation is less direct, only certain structural and psychological characteristics being retained; *Mtsyri* shows almost complete independence of Byronic influence beyond the confessional form. The features of Byron's verse which are chiefly apparent in Lermontov's lyric are well summarized by N. Ya. Dyakonova:[82]

> The qualities inherent in Byron of hatred for political and national oppression, the celebration of revolutionary struggle, the contraposition of nature and natural feelings to society, disillusionment with people and concentration within oneself answered the needs of Lermontov's inner development and stimulated him; in Lermontov's lyric verse Byronic motifs acquired an independent sonority. In portraying passion that reveals the personality of the lyric hero, Lermontov follows the oratorical, declamatory style of Byron, with his penchant for hyperbole, absolutes, antitheses, for the use of aphorisms and a sharpening of thought. Lermontov's metric is close to the metric of Byron's verse line, freer than the Russian. In conformity with the practice of English versification, Lermontov uses, for example, five-foot iambics with only masculine rhymes and variants of ternary measures which are not normal to Russian poetry. In the four-foot iambic he admits certain deviations from "correctness," e.g., two unaccented syllables between accents.

Besides the narrative and lyric verse of Byron's earlier period Lermontov was attracted to the quasi-dramatic "mysteries," particularly *Cain* and *Heaven and Earth*. Of the later masterpieces of Byron the influence may be seen in such Lermontov works as *The Tambov Treasurer's Wife, Sashka* and *A Fairy Tale for Children*. To quote Dyakonova again,[83]

> The introductory strophes to *Sashka*, the account of the hero's education, the digressions, the ironical remarks in parenthesis, the parodies of romantic cliches, the lowering of images and vocabulary, their approximation to conversational speech, and of the line and the rhythm to the syntax of prose, the comic utilization of quotations, have parallels in *Don Juan* and *Beppo*. Like Byron and Pushkin, Lermontov combines civic and lyric, pathetic and comic elements.

While there are undoubted elements of Byronism in *A Hero of Our Time*,[84] Lermontov's hero is no such self-portrait as Byron's Don Juan, and the novel is a generalized picture of a concrete time and place, which Byron's poem decidedly is not. By the date when he wrote his novel, indeed even by the date of *Princess Ligovskaya*, the Byronic influence on Lermontov was largely a thing of the past. Eikhenbaum[85] queries: why did Lermontov fall under the spell of Byron while Pushkin was casting it off, and answers convincingly: "The fact amounts to this, that Pushkin only met with Byron, and after paying his talent its due, went his own way, while for Lermontov Byron was the school which he failed to find in Russian literature."

Eikhenbaum[86] adduces another West European model for young Lermontov—Friedrich Schelling, particularly in the ethical sphere. Apparently it is not fashionable at present among Soviet scholars to find any connection between Lermontov and Schellingism: the *Lermontov Encyclopedia,* for example, contains no entry on either Schelling himself or on the *Lyubomudrye* who were his Russian followers, although the writer (R. B. Zaborova) of the article on Lermontov's close friend V. F. Odoevsky notes:[87] "Odoevsky and Lermontov belonged to different trends in the literature of Russian romanticism, but they were united by a common interest in F. Schelling, E. T. A. Hoffmann, and the fantastic genre in literature." Schelling's philosophy left a considerable mark on Lermontov's youthful work, particularly, as Eikhenbaum notes, in his treatment of the problem of good and evil. Rejecting the Augustinian and Leibnizian explanation of evil as purely negative, the absence of good, as darkness is the absence of light, Schelling gave it a dialectic turn: "Good and evil are one and the same, only viewed from different sides." This doctrine is clearly apparent in, for example, such poems as Lermontov's "June 11, 1831." Man, in Schelling's view, alone of the created world contains both the two principles of good and evil; Lermontov, in the 25th strophe of his poem writes: "I am wonted to this condition, but to express it clearly tongue neither of angel nor of demon would be able: they have no such perturbations; in one all is pure, in the other all evil. Only in man might the holy and the vicious be both encountered. All his torments have their origin from this." The same notion occurs also in the youthful novel *Vadim,* e.g., "Moreover did not angel and demon have their origin from a single principle?"[88] From this Schellingian doctrine of good and evil as the same thing from different sides derives Lermontov's so-called "demonism." His Demon can be wholly evil, and yet long for good and abjure the principle of his own nature; and in *Masquerade* Arbenin can commit monstrous evil, and yet remain a tragic figure because he has vainly longed for good and himself destroyed it.

Of the other German romantics Schiller undoubtedly exercised the strongest influence on Lermontov. We have seen evidence of this in, for example, his early dramas. Naturally it is in the drama that this connection is most obvious, although it must be remembered that some of Schiller's poems were among the earliest of Lermontov's translations. Of the dramas it was those of Schiller's *Sturm und Drang* period—*Die Raüber* (cf. *Two Brothers), Don Carlos* (cf. *The Spaniards*) and *Kabale und Liebe* (cf. *Menschen und Leidenschaften)*—that chiefly attracted Lermontov. There are no traces of Schiller's mature tragedies, such as *Wilhelm Tell* or the *Wallenstein* trilogy. There are traces, however,[89] of Schiller's theoretical writings (e.g., *Über die tragische Kunst* and *Über das Erhabene*) in Lermontov's *Masquerade.* In these treatises Schiller opposes, for example, the "tragic flaw" theory on the grounds that audience sympathy is alienated when a character is responsible for his own misfortunes, and advocates a kind of tragedy in which both doer and sufferer evoke sympathy and the doer suffers no external punishment. This Lermontov attempts with Arbenin and Nina, but unfortunately the confused state of the text of the tragedy robs it of full effectiveness.

When Lermontov died in 1841 the Russian literary scene was very different from that of a decade before. The age of poetry was temporarily over. Tyutchev still wrote, and magnificently, but for himself, not for the public. Benediktov's flashy and vulgar verse enjoyed a short-lived popularity; but the age of great prose was already under way. Pushkin in his last years had initiated it with masterpieces like *The Queen of Spades* and *The Captain's Daughter;* Gogol had enriched it with masterful tales and his strange prose "poem" *Dead Souls;* and Lermontov had made his contribution of *A Hero of Our Time.* We need not trouble ourselves with the idle question of literary fashion—which, if any, of these works are "romantic," which "realistic." The significant thing is what they led to. Russian literature for the next fifty years is primarily a literature of prose,—of the novel and short story (e.g., Turgenev, Dostoevsky, Goncharov, Tolstoi, Leskov et al.) and of the drama (e.g., Ostrovsky and Chekhov). Even verse (for example, that of Nekrasov and Kozma Prutkov) tends to be prosy. In this great literary revolution Lermontov's novel plays a leading part. And when verse once again moves into the foreground with the beginning of the Silver Age, such poets as Blok and Bely find in Lermontov almost a contemporary, a spiritual brother and satisfying master.

Lermontov, 1837.

Lermontov's drawings on an autograph of "Vadim."

A View of the Caucasus from Sakli, painting by Lermontov, 1837.

Lermontov, 1840.

Gogol, 1838.

Gogol, 1830s.

Gogol, 1842.

VII

Nikolai Gogol:
Juvenile Poem and Ukrainian Tales

The present study is deliberately titled "Russian Literature in the Romantic Period"—a period which is rather arbitrarily defined as from about 1800 to 1840. By no means all of the writers who flourished in these forty years, and who have been passed in review in our survey, can be properly regarded as romantics, at least unambiguously and all the time. On the other hand, almost none of them escaped some infection from the dominant literary tendency of the time.

Assignment of a writer to one or another literary fashion—classicism, romanticism, realism et al.—is always a difficult and controversial matter. The difficulty is inherent in the changeableness which is normal to the human being—not many writers or artists of any kind remain true to the same artistic principles from the beginning of their creative life to its end. But the difficulty becomes exacerbated when an irrelevant value judgment is imposed on an artistic style. Western scholars accept the artistic and literary styles which go under the names of classicism, romanticism, realism et al. as neutral descriptive labels, useful for all their vagueness, but implying nothing either meliorative or pejorative. An individual critic may be more sympathetic to one trend than another, but his attitude is dictated by no ideology. Not so the Marxist: for him certain styles are "progressive," others "reactionary." Marx declared that romanticism was a world outlook fostered by the possessing classes in reaction to the Enlightenment and the French bourgeois revolution; it is therefore inherently "wrong" and stands in the way of the "right" artistic mode of realism. Romanticism as such being a phenomenon of the past, the twentieth-century Marxist cannot combat it, but he deprecates it and tries to restrict it to a few and less important representatives. A consequence of this doctrinal bias against romanticism and its modern kin is Marxist insistence in placing Russia's greatest writers of the first half of the nineteenth century, Pushkin and Gogol, in the realist camp. Few western critics will deny that Pushkin's *Eugene Onegin* and *Boris Godunov*, Gogol's *Inspector General* and *Dead Souls* show strong realistic tendencies and must be accounted as at least in the ancestry of the developed movement of the second half of the century; and even Marxist critics have to admit grudgingly that Pushkin's "Byronic poems" and Gogol's Ukrainian tales belong in the romantic tradition; this admission, however, is usually qualified by the claim that in their artistic maturity these great writers "overcame their illusions" and became convinced realists. The claim is false: neither Pushkin nor Lermontov nor Gogol was ever unequivocally a realist. The ambiguity of Gogol's position is best explained not by psychological factors, which are in general too uncertain to explain much of anything, but by the transitional age in which he lived—a time when the romantic fashion had nearly run its course and the trend toward realism was just beginning. The simultaneous presence in all of Gogol's writing of elements of both romanticism and realism is the key to its fascination.

Thousands of studies have been made from Gogol's time to our own, by both Russians and non-Russians, of Gogol's literary heritage. It seems as though all possible approaches to this heritage have been explored, yet none can be accepted as definitive. I take it as self-evident that an artist must be judged as an artist, and not as a political reformer, religious prophet or philosopher. Unfortunately Gogol built up delusions in his later years that he was all of these, and these delusions have been reflected in numerous studies of his own time and later. The critic Belinsky, as is well known, hailed Gogol ecstatically as one who really understood Russia and depicted her as she was, in all her sordidness, especially in all the horror of her "peculiar institutions," serfdom and autocracy. The Gogol Belinsky saw, a stout opponent of these manifest evils, never existed: he was a mirage of Belinsky's own devising, perpetuated by Chernyshevsky and ultimately by many Marxist critics up to the present. But in any case, Gogol's political views do not and cannot explain his writing, and are strictly speaking irrelevant to it. The same must be said for his religious convictions, except in so far as their contagion destroyed the artist in him.

Gogol as a person was, to put it mildly, peculiar—many would say, morbid. He left a vast collection of private letters, in which he may be supposed to lay bare his soul; and throughout his literary creations are scattered passages which psychologists, Freudian and other, have gleefully seized upon as "explaining" the real meaning of his work. Such studies explain nothing consequential. The work may explain much about the man—how much is debatable—but to infer the writer's psychology from the work, and then explain the work from his psychology is an exercise in futility that only a psychologist would be capable of.

The only critics who have come close to dealing in a meaningful way with Gogol's literary creation are the formalists, but even their interpretations are often stultified by doctrinal rigidity. Formalism at least has the advantage of making the work itself the sole object of study, and not the psychology of the man who wrote it, or his beliefs, political, religious or whatever. It focusses on his purposes as an artist, and the means he employs to effect these purposes. When these purposes, and of course the means with them, change, as they do with Gogol in the course of his creative life, there is no need for invoking biographical motivation for this:

a conscious artist may very well change his technique without undergoing any inner cataclysm.

To return to our earlier question: to what extent does a study of Gogol's writing show him to be a realist? Unquestionably such tales as "Ivan Fyodorovich Shponka and His Auntie," the story of the two Ivans, "Old-World Landowners," and "The Overcoat," as well as *The Inspector General* and *Dead Souls* picture aspects of contemporary Russian reality, although by no means photographically or comprehensively. But is this picture the kind that we see in writers who are universally recognized as realists, let us say, Flaubert or Thackeray or Goncharov? Flaubert, for example, draws an unforgettable portrait of Monsieur Homais, or of those archetypical bourgeois Bouvard and Pecuchet, and the reader is left with no doubt of the author's disgust and contempt. But the portrait is itself low-key, objective, dispassionate. Goncharov's Alexander Aduev is ridiculous, pathetic and shallow, but one can believe in his existence. He is a living figure, and so are Bouvard and Pecuchet. But is Akaky Akakievich a credible human being, or are Ivan Ivanovich and Ivan Nikiforovich, or Khlestakov, or Plyushkin? Probably the only Gogolian characters one can think of who are portrayed in the Flaubert or Goncharov manner are the two pathetic "old-world landowners"—and they were an experiment that Gogol never repeated. Gogol saw all the pettiness, ugliness and vulgarity around him, but he depicted it as a caricaturist, like a George Grosz, emphasizing to enormity certain prominent features, but ignoring others. We shall see later some of the devices he uses for this. One of them is humor: he makes the ugliness he sees laughable that it may not be terrifying. But this is not a realist's technique: one may almost say that Gogol is an antirealist, in the sense that his picture of external reality is really a picture not of the world existing around him, but of the assumed opposite of an ideal world of beauty and harmony; the degree to which he exaggerates is a measure of the degree to which he sees it fall short of the ideal. But such an approach marks the romantic. Gogol is indeed, as Donald Fanger calls him, a "romantic realist"—a category in which he places three other great transitional writers of the nineteenth century, Dostoevsky, Balzac and Dickens. For an English reader Gogol shows closer kinship with Dickens than with either of the others, largely because both use humor as a prime device, and often obtain their effects by a piquant contrast between humor and pathos. This we shall see in Gogol as this study proceeds. The realist unqualified makes an effort to render a cool, objective report, *sine ira et odio;* but of these "romantic realists," and preeminently of Gogol, one must emphatically reverse Matthew Arnold's famous dictum about Sophocles: he saw life neither steadily nor saw it whole.

At this point in our survey we have come at last into an area of full illumination. All of Gogol's important work, and some of the unimportant, has been translated into English, often more than once. We may accordingly dispense with tedious plot summaries as we consider it. Of course not all the translations available are equally accurate, nor can any of them convey the very peculiar flavor of the original; this, however, can be said of all translations. A reader would be well advised to seek out modern, rather than Victorian translations: the latter are likely to be prissy and to omit "indelicate" passages. Leonard J. Kent's edition of the *Collected Tales and Plays of Nikolai Gogol* is a careful revision of the Constance Garnett translation, and despite some inaccuracies, is a handy and readable volume, which together with Guerney's *Chichikov's Journeys or Dead Souls* will provide nearly all of Gogol that is worth reading. Jesse Zeldin's translation of *Selected Passages from a Correspondence with Friends* is the only English version of that late and controversial work. Gogol's voluminous letters have been judiciously selected and translated by Carl R. Proffer.[1]

Hanz Küchelgarten[2]

Gogol began his literary career under a pseudonym with the publication in 1829 of the poem: *Hanz Küchelgarten: an Idyll in Pictures.* In the brief editorial comment that precedes the poem of "V. Alov" the composition of the poem is referred to 1827, "when the author was eighteen." Modern critics have often questioned the truth of this dating, on the grounds that in 1827 Gogol was still a student in the Nezhin Lycée and could scarcely have had the time to write such an ambitious piece, and if he had done so, would not have been likely to conceal the fact from all his fellow students. On the other hand he would have had ample leisure for writing the poem during 1828-29, when he was jobless in St. Petersburg. But it is hard to see why he should have falsified the date of a work which he was publishing anyhow under an assumed name! The poem had three reviews, one (by Orest Somov) mildly favorable, the others devastating. The author promptly called in all the unsold copies (which was most of the edition) and burned them. The work was never acknowledged as his during his lifetime, and direct proof of Gogol's authorship was not discovered until 1909.

Hanz Küchelgarten has never been put into English, and so a brief account of it is in order. It consists of eighteen "pictures" and an epilogue, composed in various meters. The locale is a small German town near Wismar in Mecklenburg; the hero, a moody, introspective romantic, breaks away from his placid, idyllic existence as the betrothed of the charming Luisa, granddaughter of an old Lutheran pastor, and after some wanderings abroad—the only one specifically shown is his visit to Athens—returns home sad and disillusioned and receives a warm and forgiving welcome from Luisa and her parents; the old pastor has died in the meantime.

The rather odd choice of a German background for the poem by an author who had at the time of its composition never been outside of Russia is explained by the fact that *Hanz Küchelgarten* (the "z" in the prenomen is Gogol's own eccentric spelling) is obviously modelled on the idyll *Louise* of the Mecklenburg poet Johann Heinrich Voss[3] (1783-84), which had appeared in 1820 in a Russian translation by P. Teryaev. The entire picture of the pleasant bourgeois existence of a sleepy little north German village is lifted from Voss, along with the description of appetizing meals, the pastor's afternoon nap, and similar details. Voss used the accentual dactylic hexameter in his poem, as he had done in his translation of the Odyssey (1781), and imitated the Homeric manner in the use of constant epithets, epic repetitions, and the like. Gogol did not try the hexameter, but imitated Voss in his other Homeric devices. The verse of the poem is somewhat labored and lifeless, but not bad, in view of the author's immaturity. It was almost his only venture of the kind.

The theme of the poem—the disillusion of a fugitive from domestic tranquillity—may have been suggested by Zhukovsky's ballad "Theon and Aeschines." The nature of the disillusionment, however, seems original with Gogol. Hans meditates (Picture III) on the glories of Athens as he envisions the city from the classical writers; then in Picture XIII sees the sad reality:

> Vainly the avid wanderer craves to resurrect the past in spirit; vainly he strives to unroll the decayed scroll of deeds gone by—worthless is the labor of his powerless efforts; everywhere the troubled glance reads destruction and shame.[4]

When he finally returns to his Lunensdorf, Hans has apparently been further disillusioned by some vaguely hinted experience presumably in a big city where he has tried his hand at poetry: "They treat shamefully the wondrous gift, and trample upon inspiration, and despise revelation."

Among the influences detectable in *Hanz Küchelgarten* is that of Pushkin's *Eugene Onegin:* the meditations of young Lensky contribute to those of Hans; and Louisa's dream (picture XI) owes some features to that of Tatyana.

There is no point in lingering over this ill-starred work of Gogol's youth. It is totally derivative, has nothing Russian in it whatever, and gives little evidence of the Gogol to be. Only the moody, introspective meditations of the poem's hero and his evident craving for literary fame have autobiographical significance—and Gogol's letters attest to these traits more directly.

Evenings on a Farm Near Dikanka, Parts I and II[5]

When he arrived in St. Petersburg Gogol discovered a number of other Ukrainians in the literary life of the capital, notably Professor Maximovich, who had published in 1827 a collection of Ukrainian folk songs, and Orest Somov, whom he met soon after his arrival, and whose Ukrainian stories (e.g., "Rusalka," 1829; "Stories about Treasures," 1830; "Haidamak," etc.) often were based on popular legends of supernatural doings. Somov also utilized Great Russian folklore in some of his stories, e.g., "The Werewolf" (1829) and "Kikimora" (1830). There is little question that it was these and similar tales (e.g., by Olin and Pogorelsky) that first turned Gogol's literary efforts in this direction. He wrote to his mother that "people here are all interested in everything Little Russian." He determined to begin exploiting the same material, but found himself handicapped by an inadequate knowledge. He accordingly wrote to his mother and other relatives with urgent requests for material of all kinds bearing on the life of the Ukrainian people—legends of ghosts, demons, witches and the like, popular songs, customs, festivals—even details about the typical dress of Ukrainian women. All this information he carefully copied into his notebooks, and used it in the composition of *Evenings on a Farm near Dikanka.*.

The first collection of *Evenings* appeared in the autumn of 1831, the second in the spring of 1833. One story of the first collection ("St. John's Eve") had been published anonymously under another title in *Fatherland Notes* in 1830,[6] as had a couple of chapters from what was apparently to have been a long story, *"The Terrible Boar."*[7] There are four tales in each of the two parts of *Evenings on a Farm near Dikanka,* and it is possible to arrange the eight pieces in pairs of roughly analogous content, atmosphere and style. The two love-stories "A May Night" (Part I) and "The Night before Christmas" (Part II) form one pair; two tales attributed to Foma Grigoryevich, the Dikanka sexton, are anecdotes involving devils and witchcraft—"The Lost Letter" (Part I) and "An Enchanted Spot" (Part II). The horror tales "St. John's Eve" (Part I) and "A Terrible Vengeance" (Part II) constitute a third pair. The remaining two, "The Fair at Sorochintsy" (Part I) and "Ivan Fyodorovich Shponka and His Auntie" (Part II) are much more loosely related, but are both based on a somewhat stylized "real life," and are both nearly or entirely free from the supernatural which plays such a large part in all the others.

Taking a cue from Sir Walter Scott's *Tales of My Landlord* or Washington Irving's *Tales of a Traveller,* Gogol invents as the "editor" of his collections a simple Ukrainian bee-keeper, "Red" Panko, at whose house the gatherings are supposed to take place at which various story-tellers narrate their tales. The editor introduces each of the collections in a naive and garrulous foreword and explains the apparently fragmentary state of the Shponka story by the loss of the second part of his manuscript, which his wife had used to line her pie-pans! The character of this editor and the Ukrainian atmosphere of the whole collection are admirably conveyed in these forewords.

With the exception of "Ivan Fyodorovich Shponka and His Auntie," which is best considered as a forerunner of Gogol's quasi-realistic later style, all the Dikanka stories develop the general theme that human life is precarious, always beset by the powers of evil that may at any moment break in to turn the happiest existence into tragedy. This essentially pessimistic world outlook is mitigated by a belief in the possibility of human goodness and pluck as saving agents. In the midst of a crowded and carefree fair the rumor suddenly goes round that the devil is abroad, trying to collect the pieces of his red blouse, which a peasant has chopped up ("The Fair at Sorochintsy"); a cap with an important letter sewed in it is purloined by the devils, but recovered by the cap's intrepid owner, who goes to Hell for the purpose and beats the powers of evil at a game of cards ("The Lost Letter"); a pair of young lovers have their lives and happiness destroyed by the lure of gold with which a sinister demon tempts them ("St. John's Eve"); an innocent girl is persecuted and driven to suicide by her malevolent witch-stepmother, but her ghost, as a *rusalka,* enables a bold young Cossack to win his beloved ("A May Night"); another bold and God-fearing young Cossack outwits a rather stupid devil whom he forces to whisk him to St. Petersburg and back on Christmas Eve in order to win his girl ("The Night before Christmas"); in "A Terrible Vengeance" the theme of evil encroaching upon life becomes so overpowering that neither human innocence nor bravery are of any avail, and only another supernatural power is able at long last to destroy the portentous sorcerer in whom this evil is embodied. Whether Ukrainian folk belief actually justifies this pessimistic outlook on life is immaterial: this is the fashion in which Gogol interprets it—and the same outlook extends to much later tales, e.g., "The Portrait," where no folklore background is involved.

Evil in most of the Dikanka tales is an external, quasi-human bearer of supernatural power—a witch, a sorcerer, a demon; but evidently Gogol began quite early to identify the evil principle in human lives with the loathsome vulgarity and vacuity which constitute the opposite of ideal beauty and worth. For this principle Gogol uses the word *poshlost',* a term that embraces far more than any single English synonym.[8] The first Gogolian work to employ *poshlost'* as a central concept is the third tale of the second part of the Dikanka series, "Ivan Fyodorovich Shponka and His Auntie." Significantly, this is the only one of the tales that is entirely free of the supernatural element (in "The Fair at Sorochintsy" the supernatural is a hoax, to be sure, but the atmosphere assumes its reality). The narrow, timid, futile, life-denying existence of Ivan Fyodorovich is by implication as potent a form of evil (or ugliness) as the demons and witches

of the other tales. Of Shponka and his later compeers Akaky Akakievich,
the two Ivans, Khlestakov, et al.,Dante's terrible words might be spoken,
with which he condemns the trimmers:

> Questi non hanno speranza di morte,
> E la lor cieca vita e tanto bassa
> Che invidiosi son d'ogni altra sorte....
> Non ragionam di lor, ma sguarda e passa.

But Gogol does not, like Dante, cast a mere contemptuous glance at these
"low lives"—he expends his incomparable artistic skill in showing them in
all their ugliness, so that passersby may be moved, like the Dikanka
churchgoers at the sight of Vakula's painting of the devil, to spit as they look.

Evenings on a Farm near Dikanka, when analyzed, proves to be a
strange amalgam of several quite incongruous elements. Constructionally,
as we shall see, one of the author's most characteristic devices is contrast.
Here this takes the form of a juxtaposition of boisterous humor side by side
with romantic beauty and horror. Valerian Pereverzev, in his volume
Tvorchestvo Gogolia (1914), Chapter 2, remarks on the arrangement of
the tales in Evenings: "The author seems deliberately to have placed each
story in such a way that a picture of ordinary life in all its pettiness and
comic absurdity is followed by a picture of heroic exploits and the clash of
powerful passions in all their tragedy and pathos."[9] He sums up in the next
paragraph: "Nearly every one of the stories, then, is structured according
to the principle of antithesis—petty versus profound passions, trivial
versus heroic deeds—as is the book as a whole." Exception must be taken
to Pereverzev's assumption that the tales anywhere deal with "ordinary
life," but the fact of the antithetical arrangement, both of individual tales
and of the two collections as wholes, is indubitable The very device of
contrast, of course, is itself romantic—cf. Victor Hugo's Notre-Dame de
Paris or Ruy Blas, for example. But in the Evenings the two elements come
from widely different sources. A good deal, perhaps most, of the romantic
component is borrowed from the Germans Tieck and Hoffmann. The
borrowing is concealed by a heavy coating of Ukrainian local color. A case
in point is "A Terrible Vengeance." The basic plot of the wicked sorcerer
who suddenly appears to his daughter's family, tries to lead his son-in-law
into a life of brigandage, and kills his daughter's infant son, is taken from
E. T. A. Hoffmann's tale "Ignaz Denner," with some amplifications from
Tieck's "Pietro von Abano." The motif of the sorcerer's incestuous plots
against his daughter and her successful resistance is added by Gogol, who
provides also the whole Ukrainian setting. The son-in-law becomes a
valiant Cossack, who perishes in battle with the foes of his native land, the
Poles; the sorcerer is made an even more heinous sinner by becoming a
collaborator with his country's enemies. Another addition to the tale for

which Gogol is apparently responsible is the bizarre, almost grotesque pseudo-legend in Chapter XVI (the bandura-player's recital) which purports to motivate the career of the wicked sorcerer, and which is by far the least successful portion of the tale. Along with the elements of German romantic horror and Ukrainian patriotic history goes an occasional and very effective use of the phraseology and atmosphere of Ukrainian popular song—e.g., the conversation of Katerina and her husband during the boat ride across the Dniepr, Katerina's lamentation at her husband's death, et al.

"A Terrible Vengeance" exceptionally contains no humor. Usually the uncanny and supernatural are balanced in the tales by scenes of almost slapstick comedy. Thus, in "The Fair at Sorochintsy" a gathering of peasants, already apprehensive at the rumors of the appearance at the fair of a devil in the form of a pig, is suddenly startled by a pig's snout breaking through the window. One man jumps so high in the air that he hits the planks of a roosting-place under the ceiling where the lover of the woman of the house is hiding, and brings it down; another of the peasants bolts through the door, runs until exhausted, and falls down in the street in a faint of terror; one climbs into the stove and shuts the door on himself, etc.—a hilarious scene that can be traced back to similar scenes in the popular Ukrainian Christmas farce *(vertep)*. Gogol's father, Vasily Gogol-Yanovsky, composed such comedies, which his son asked to have sent to him in St. Petersburg when he was writing the *Evenings,* and which unquestionably were the inspiration for some of the horseplay of the comic scenes. Unfortunately, only one of the elder Gogol's comedies is extant, but in this ("The Simpleton, or the Tricks of a Woman Outwitted by a Soldier") a church sexton *(dyachok),* as in "The Fair at Sorochintsy," plays the part of a lover. The same motif reappears in "The Night before Christmas," where it is part of the age-old theme of the woman with several lovers, whom she conceals one after another as the next appears. The ignominious fate of the devil in "The Night before Christmas" probably also belongs to the Christmas farce tradition: Vakula seizes him by the tail and compels him, under threat of making the sign of the cross over him, to carry him to St. Petersburg and back. In the midst of the horrors of "The Lost Letter" comes the scene in which the narrator's grandfather plays "Fools" (a woman's card game) with a band of devils and witches in Hell; when he realizes that they are cheating him, he makes the sign of the cross over his cards under the table, and wins the game.

The content of most of the tales is based on actual Ukrainian peasant beliefs—e.g., in witches which can take other forms at will (witch into cat in "May Night"), treasures which for some reason the devil covets but cannot himself touch, so must seduce a human being into getting for him ("St. John's Eve"), the transformation of a drowned maiden into a water-nixie or *rusalka* ("May Night"), the manifestation of the devil in the form of a human being with a dog's or a pig's head ("The Fair at Sorochintsy," "The Lost Letter"), etc. Gogol is of course not alone in utilizing such material (note Pogorelsky's *Lafertovskaia Makovnitsa* or Somov's *Rusalka*), but in one respect his tales differ notably from those of his contemporaries using similar material. Other writers are prone to treat their material condescendingly, as the naive superstitions of ignorant peasants: Gogol conveys in his tales a sense of real terror in the face of the supernatural— perhaps because he himself did believe in it, at least half-heartedly.[10]

When analysis indicates that the material from which the *Evenings on a Farm near Dikanka* was drawn is of very diverse origin—Ukrainian popular farce, historical legends, popular superstitions, German romantic *diablerie,* etc.—this must not be taken as in any sense derogatory to the artistic quality of the *Evenings.* Quite the contrary: out of this disparate material Gogol is able to weave a fabric of the most fascinating pattern and color. The phenomenal success with which he accomplishes this task is due in very large measure to his fascinating language. The nuances of this are of course impossible to appreciate in translation, although some devices— e.g., the illogical use of certain adverbial particles, such as "even"—can be felt in another language. We shall postpone consideration of the language, however, until after a review of some later aspects of Gogol's work, where it will be more appropriate: there is no marked difference in Gogol's use of language until after *Dead Souls: Part I.* One peculiar aspect of the language in the Dikanka and Mirgorod cycles, however, may be noted— the presence in the narration, especially in dialogue passages, of a good deal of Ukrainian linguistic material. Some passages, e.g., snatches of song (Levko's serenade in "May Night") or short exchanges of dialogue are given entirely in Ukrainian; otherwise there are numerous local words from the southern language (e.g., *liulka,* "pipe," or *pechko,* "ball"), used frequently enough in the tales to make the author feel it necessary to provide a glossary in the introduction to each of the two parts. Moreover, in "The Fair at Sorochintsy" each section is headed by an epigraph, always in Ukrainian. Several of these are from the comedies of Gogol's father; some are from the *Aeneid Travestied* of Kotlyarevsky; and some are from popular songs, legends, or proverbial sayings. All this conveys for the Great Russian reader a peculiar, exotic flavor.

Whatever the material he is using, Gogol transforms into Ukrainian semblance; but to this must be immediately added a caveat. What he creates is *not* the Ukraine of reality, but a stylized Ukraine, as the legends, songs, comedies, etc. present it. In no sense is it a realistic picture, either of the everyday life of the country or of the people who live there. He is at great pains to give the details, for example, of the women's costumes, e.g., the skirt made up of separate front and back panels (the *plakhta* and *zapaska*), the ship-like head-dress *(korablik),* etc.—but these costumes are worn by a set of pretty puppets. Gogol's young women and young men are conventionalized abstractions, totally without reality. It is impossible to imagine any lad, Ukrainian or of any other nationality, addressing his girl in the flowery terms that Levko uses to Ganna, for example, or for any wife to address her husband as Katerina does Buralbash as they ride across the Dniepr. They are persons from popular song and heroic epic, not real people. Gogol is much more convincing with his old men and old women—e.g., the mayor *(golová)* in "May Night," with his eternal reminiscences about the time when he escorted Empress Catherine on her Ukrainian tour; his crony the eternally smoke-enveloped distiller; the old drunk Kalenik, who can't find his own hut in his befuddled condition, and placidly goes to sleep on a bench in the mayor's house, etc. But even with these much more vividly pictured persons, their reality is that of the stage, not the genuine Ukrainian village.

An exception must be made in this regard, as in most others, for "Ivan Fyodorovich Shponka and His Auntie." As V. V. Vinogradov has very cogently remarked:[11] "A writer's artistic heritage almost never presents a straight line of objects that move in a single direction." There are several directions present, as we have seen, in the two cycles of *Evenings*—light-hearted farce, sentimental love-stories, somber Gothic horror tales, quasi-folk epic, etc. "Shponka" stands alone in the Dikanka group as a representative of the "realistic" direction—of the direction, that is, which has as its later monuments *The Inspector General*, "The Tale of How Ivan Ivanovich Came to Quarrel with Ivan Nikiforovich," and the first part of *Dead Souls*. In "Ivan Fyodorovich Shponka and his Auntie" the psychological characterization is brilliantly in advance of anything else in the *Evenings:* not only is the title "hero" given full treatment, as a kind of Russian Mr. Milquetoast, but his strapping, Amazonian "auntie" (the diminutive is of course deliberately ironical) Vasilissa Kashporovna, is a marvelous creation, not only credible as a human being but in the highest degree sympathetic. There is no doubt that the placid, narrow, timid, unimaginative existence of Ivan Fyodorovich is felt by Gogol as a form of evil as life-destroying as that of the demon Basavryuk ("St. John's Eve"), but it is portrayed with a tolerant good humor that is disarming. Who can help forming a certain amused affection for a young man whom the mere presence of a young woman beside him so intimidates that all the "conversation" he can muster is the remark: "There are a great many flies in summer." When elsewhere Gogol remarks that Shponka was never very lavish with words, whether "from timidity, or a desire to express himself elegantly," the reader is left to add his own alternative, "or from invincible stupidity." But stupidity is at least a quality not deliberately chosen: Nature, not man, must be held responsible, and so Ivan Fyodorovich Shponka, for all his hesitations, is a pleasanter acquaintance than, let us say, either Khlestakov the "Revizor" or Chichikov the collector of "dead souls."

The literary quality of *Evenings on a Farm near Dikanka* has been very differently appraised by different critics in different ages. Pushkin in a letter to the editor of the supplement to the periodical *Russkii Invalid* apropos of the first collection of tales, wrote: "I have just read *Evenings near Dikanka*. They have astonished me. Here is genuine gaiety, sincere and unforced, without affectation, without primness. And in places what poetry! What sensitivity! All this is so unusual in our current literature that I haven't yet come to my senses."[12] Vladimir Nabokov[13] excuses Pushkin's somewhat exaggerated praise by the reminder that in 1831 very little Russian prose of quality was being published, and appends his own, as usual, iconoclastic view:

> Their charm and their fun have completely faded since then. Curiously enough, it is on the strength of *Evenings* (both first and second volumes) that Gogol's fame as a humorist has been based. When a person tells me that Gogol is a "humorist," I know at once that person does not understand much in literature.... I have never been able to see eye to eye with people who enjoyed books merely because they were in dialect, or moved in the exotic atmosphere of remote places.... There is nothing more dull and sickening to my taste than romantic folklore or rollicking yarns about lumberjacks or Yorkshiremen or French villagers or Ukrainian good companions. It is for this reason that the two volumes of the *Evenings* as well as the two volumes of stories entitled *Mirgorod* (containing *Viy, Taras Bulba, Old World Landowners*, etc.) which followed in 1835, leave me completely indifferent.

Nabokov adds a little later: "When I want a good nightmare I imagine Gogol penning in Little Russian dialect volume after volume of *Dikanka* and *Mirgorod* stuff about ghosts haunting the banks of the Dniepr, burlesque Jews and daring Cossacks."

One may not see eye to eye with either of these critics in their contradictory appraisals. Significantly, neither Pushkin nor Nabokov has a word to say about the feature which constitutes what is genuinely fascinating and permanently valuable about *Evenings on a Farm near Dikanka,* as also in the *Mirgorod* tales—the marvelous language, with its extraordinary combination of poetical cadences and colloquialism, of grotesquerie and breath-taking beauty. What if the charm of "local color" has faded (it is not "a fast color," quips Nabokov) and the horrors of such a tale as "A Terrible Vengeance" provide yawns instead of goose-flesh—Gogol's rich, rhythmical, gorgeous prose is an enduring delight As Fanger remarks:[14] "Though from our vantage point the chief interest of *Evenings* lies in technique and style (and in the quasi-autonomous thematic value they always carry in his writing), Gogol's contemporary success rested to a large extent on his subject matter."

Mirgorod[15]

At the beginning of 1835 Gogol's third collection of tales was issued, consisting of two parts, each comprising two tales. The whole bore the title *Mirgorod,* a name that seems to have been chosen from two considerations. First, most obviously, it is the name of a Ukrainian town, the metropolis of the area where Gogol grew up (he was born, it may be noted, in Sorochintsy, the site of the "fair"). But the name Mirgorod (spelled in Ukrainian with a "dotted i") means "world-town," or something akin to "cosmopolis,"—i.e., a town which is in some fashion a microcosm of the world.

The title signals the Ukrainian atmosphere of the collection, just as does that of the first two groups (Dikanka is a village of the Mirgorod district, once owned by the Yusupov family). In *Mirgorod* Gogol continues his exploitation of Ukrainian themes: "Taras Bulba" follows in the developmental line of "A Terrible Vengeance," "The Viy" in that of e.g., "St. John's Eve" or "The Lost Letter," and "The Tale of How Ivan Ivanovich Came to Quarrel with Ivan Nikiforovich" belongs with "Ivan Fyodorovich Shponka and His Auntie." Only "Old-World Landowners" marks an entirely new direction.

In *Mirgorod* Gogol dispenses, barring one exception, with the device of a fictional story-teller, and relates his stories in his own person, in various tones of voice. In the Dikanka cycles he had distanced himself from his readers at two removes, first by the creation of an "editor," Rudy Panko the Beekeeper, who presumably collected the tales from the lips of the tellers; and then, in some instances at least, by the intervention of the actual narrators, whose style of speaking he imitated. This is most apparent in the three tales ("St. John's Eve," "The Lost Letter," and "An Enchanted Spot") which are specifically said to be related by "the sexton of N—church," Foma Grigoryevich. Donald Fanger[16] points out the great gain in vividness in the second version of the tale "St. John's Eve" over the anonymous first version, written before the invention of "Red" Panko. In Foma Grigoryevich's three tales there is even the trace of a third narrator— the second two relate adventures of Foma's "grandfather," who has told them at some previous occasion; and some of the circumstances of the tragic tale of Petro and Pidorka in "St. John's Eve" are given as reminiscences of "grandfather's aunt," who used to run a tavern. By the use of these devices Gogol was able, like Scott and Irving, to mimic a colloquial and individual style of oral narrative—a technique called *skaz* in Russian. Thus, for example, the sexton frequently interjects into his narratives asseverations of veracity in the form of "may I never again sing Alleluias in N—church, if—" such and such is not true. It was a useful device, but by the time he wrote the Mirgorod stories, Gogol had come to rely more upon interpolations of his own auctorial person to provide the contrast which was needed between the content of the narrative and the narrator.[17] The effect is somewhat like that of a stereoscopic picture: a narrative given by an "omniscient author," who objectively records all aspects of an action in a cool, dispassionate voice, is flat, lacks depth; but when the narrator obtrudes his own comments and interpretations regarding the action, a certain depth is achieved by the contrast between two levels. There are, of course, obvious dangers in the overuse of the device of auctorial intervention, which may at worst completely over-balance the narrative so that it becomes as it were only a series of running exemplifications of the author's feelings, as is so often the case with Sterne's *Tristram Shandy* and *A Sentimental Journey*. Gogol, however, generally uses the device discreetly, and by varying his tone in the several tales achieves a diversity as great as would have been possible by the use of *skaz*. In the case of the tale of the two Ivans, indeed, the *skaz* element and the personal intervention are both employed, as we shall see.

The first of the Mirgorod stories is told directly in the first person, as though the two "old-world landowners," Afanasy Ivanovich and Pul-kheriya Ivanovna, had been personal friends of the author. As has been pointed out by Russian critics, this device is very similar to Karamzin's in *Poor Liza,* where too the author represents himself as a friend of one of the lovers, and as moved by their sad tale to some sentimental meditations. But despite similarities of construction, Gogol tells his sentimental idyll in an entirely different style. The background of "Old-World Landowners" is depicted in loving and realistic detail, from the squeaky doors, each with its own peculiar voice, to the chronically overheated rooms and the storeroom, bulging with Gargantuan supplies of fresh fruit and vegetables in season, and with pickles and preserves beyond all reasonable expec-tations of use. Against this background stand out the two old people, wonderfully and sympathetically portrayed. Their lives flow as placidly as some sluggish stream, with few interests beyond those of eating and preparations for eating. Belinsky was appalled by their almost vegetable existence, and thought the tale was a satire, an expose of the mindless, parasitic life of the Russian country gentry. A more perverse misinter-pretation could hardly be conceivecd: Gogol is tenderly amused by the gormandizing, not revolted; and the whole picture is dominated by the touching love of the old couple for each other, which marks their every action. Early in the tale he calls Afanasy and Pulkheriya his "Philemon and Baucis": it may be recalled that Ovid's hero and heroine ask from the grateful gods they have unwittingly entertained that when their time comes to die, they may die together, neither surviving the other. Their Russian counterparts are less fortunate, and the story ends tragically, when poor old Afanasy Ivanovich is left to live some five years after the death of his Pulkheriya. The description of the old man's rapid degene-ration, and his uncontrollable childish tears when he endeavors to utter his wife's name with the terrible word *pokoinitsa,* "the late," before it, is harrowing, but *not* sentimentalized. Throughout the whole marvelous tale the author pictures a kind of existence which, as it seemed to Belinsky and might well seem to most readers, almost sub-human, with a tender humor and humanity that transform it into what is indeed an "idyll," as Gippius terms it. Of this kindly human sympathy there are not many traces in Gogol. Afanasy Ivanovich and Pulkheriya Ivanovna are ridiculous, but lovable; but even Akakii Akakievich, for all the famous pathos that some critics find in him ("The Overcoat") is not lovable—and indeed Gogol's attitude toward him is cool and tolerant, but almost contemptuous. Most of Gogol's characters are grotesques, humanity caricatured. The "old-world landowners" are real and touching and even dignified in their artless simplicity. The story is the highest point artistically in *Mirgorod,* but it represents a direction that Gogol's writing never took again. In its plotlessness, it constitutes what is really the beginning of a new genre, the sketch, the characteristics of which Fanger[18] defines by observing that in creating "Old-World Landowners" Gogol "alters the code of Russian fiction, producing something midway between a story and a performance—a verbal artifact whose charm lies entirely in the modulations of its unfolding..."

The contrast between "Old-World Landowners" and the second story of the cycle is startling. "Taras Bulba," which Russians are likely to know almost by heart, and which many non-Russians for some reason know better than any other of Gogol's stories, is thoroughly uncharacteristic of the author, and is on the whole an artistic failure. It must be said at once, however, that there are two versions of the tale, the one that was published in *Mirgorod* in 1834,[19] and the completely revised and expanded form in which the tale entered into the complete works of 1842.[20] The latter is the one that is always read, as is the second version of "The Portrait." In both cases the original form is artistically superior, although at least the 1842 "Taras Bulba" is not, as is the later "Portrait," a completely different story.

As early as the second Dikanka cycle, in which appeared "A Terrible Vengeance," Gogol can be seen striving to create in prose a kind of Ukrainian national epic. His efforts take the form of appropriating the themes and style of popular song, and it should be noted that his essay printed in the second part of *Arabesques* in 1835, "On Little Russian Songs," was written at the same time that he was working on "Taras Bulba." As was noted in connection with "A Terrible Vengeance," the prose of that piece is so highly poeticized that it flows with a rhythm almost like that of free verse, and is marked by numerous devices characteristic of verse, such as inversions of normal word order, alliterations and assonances. The same may be said of "Taras Bulba," especially in the second version, and more particularly in the exalted battle passages. As we shall see in considering this second version, Gogol had by 1842 encountered

Homer (in Gnedich's translation of *The Iliad)* and incorporated many Homeric devices in his Ukrainian epic.

Anonymous Ukrainian popular verse is the first ingredient of "Taras Bulba." Gogol was not interested in attempting to recreate the real life of the Dniepr Cossacks; indeed, it is impossible to discover even the date he envisions as that of his tale (Fanger speaks of it as "set in an aoristic past"[21]). In the first chapter he describes his hero as "one of those characters who could exist only in the harsh fifteenth century," and adds: "when Batory organized regiments in Little Russia ... he [i.e., Bulba] was among the first colonels." Stefan Batory was King of Poland from 1576 to 1586, so Bulba could hardly have belonged to the *fifteenth* century! Moreover the Kiev Academy to which Bulba's sons are sent was founded only in 1631! There are even some incidental hints that point to other dates; but the two-century gap between the fifteenth and the seventeenth, contained within a page, is enough to show Gogol's complete disregard for the reality of his picture. This picture is the most successful part of the tale, and although constructed largely out of the author's imagination, is a striking work of art.

The characterization is crude and conventional, with the exception of that of Bulba himself. Both sons, and Andrii's Polish innamorata, are mere puppets—the idealized youthful romantic hero, the idealized romantic youthful lover, and the idealized—and totally unlifelike—capricious maiden respectively.[22] Taras is given more solidity, but even he fails to be altogether convincing as an epic hero. He does, however, embody the qualities which Cossack legend and popular song impute to the champions of the Ukraine against Polish tyrants and Turkish marauders.

The construction of the story is its weakest point. Gogol was notoriously inept at putting together a plot, which no doubt explains his abandonment of his aborted novel *The Hetman,* to which we shall return. Since in "Taras Bulba" he deliberately avoids any genuinely historical framework, which usually in such tales provides a readymade skeleton, he is constrained to invent one, and this invention is hackneyed and feeble. Gippius, in his *Gogol,*[23] quotes a passage from an anonymous review in *The Moscow Herald* of the *Neva Almanac* of 1828, in which a historical tale by Faddei Bulgarin is the principal butt. From this review one may readily see the degree to which Gogol in "Taras Bulba" was utilizing conventional plot clichés:

> We are gradually beginning to discover the secret of how to compose historical tales [the reviewer begins ironically]. Let us set down certain basics of this new theory. Take a few historical persons, dress them in national costumes and concoct some sort of intrigue among them. By preference our writers choose the fall and destruction of cities and towns as subjects, and here Bulgarin, following his predecessors' example, has destroyed Wenden. The choice is most advantageous: first, in the description of the siege there can be a great deal of military crash and thunder; in the second place,

the choice permits the introduction of two lovers, one of whom must belong to the besiegers, the other to the besieged, for greater interest[cf. Andrii Bulba and his Polish girl]. Among the historical persons must infallibly be placed an invented person of supernatural powers—either a wizard, as Mr. Bulgarin has it, or a gypsy, as in *The Haidamak* [of Orest Somov], and best of all, a Jew, as Mr. Aladyin had [in his *Kochubeí*]. These Jews are very much in fashion; they descend from Shakespeare's Shylock and Walter Scott's Isaac. He must be an omniscient person, must appear everywhere, like a *deus ex machina,* tie and untie all the knots of the transaction.... As regards the form of narration, best of all is to divide it arbitrarily into chapters, and begin each chapter with a description, either of morning, or of night, or of a storm, after the example of Mr. Aladyin. In style, the more florid the expressions, the better.

This ironic review was published some five years before the first "Taras Bulba," but many of the points that it makes would apply as well to Gogol's story as to Bulgarin's. To be sure, there are no historical characters in "Taras Bulba," but the siege of Dubno is a major episode in the tale, and the infatuation of Andrii Bulba for the daughter of the Polish commander of the town forms the principal complication. There is no warlock or other supernatural person, but the Jew Yankel plays an important part, with several other Jews in minor roles. And as for the final point, one has only to read Chapters 2 and 5 to see that Gogol has done his part—magnificently, it must be said—with the description.

The original element in the plot is the relation of the father toward his two sons. When Andrii discovers (by the preposterously improbable device of a secret underground passage) his enchanting Polish princess starving inside the beseiged city and forthwith turns traitor to his Cossack heritage and joins the Poles, old Taras Bulba consigns his son to death and eternal damnation, and himself executes him. Ostap is captured by the Poles, taken to Warsaw for execution; the old man with the help of the Jew Yankel goes to Warsaw in disguise, witnesses Ostap's public tortures, and even risks his life to call an encouraging word to the dying boy. Afterward he and his Cossacks perpetrate a terrible vengeance on an innocent Polish population in retaliation for Ostap's death. By this device Gogol is able to raise the picturesque figure of his Cossack hero to a genuinely tragic stature. One may not believe in the reality of the figure, but there is no question of his dramatic effectiveness.

In this connection some attention must be paid to a literary influence on Gogol which is most apparent in "Taras Bulba," and which fortunately disappears shortly after 1834. This is the effect of the widely read and imitated French "horror school" of the 1830s, typified by such works as Victor Hugo's *Han d'Islande, Bug-Jargal* and *Le dernier jour d'un condamné à mort;* Eugène Sue (*Les Mystères de Paris,* etc.), Frédéric Soulié (*Les Mémoires du diable, Robert Macaire,* etc.) and even early Balzac are usually bracketed with the so-called *École frénétique.* A novelist now thoroughly, and properly, forgotten, but who was very much in the public eye in both France and Russia in the 1830s is Jules Janin. Janin's novel *L'Âne mort et la femme guillotinée* (1832) was a sensation in its time. Professor V. V. Vinogradov surveys exhaustively the specific influence of Janin's novel on Gogol, and in so doing gives a précis of the novel itself.[24] It is a programmatic work, in essence sentimentalism turned inside out, so that instead of an "embellished nature" we have "naked nature," in all its hideous ugliness and horror. The "dead ass" of the title is a farm donkey associated in the narrator's mind with the figure of his mistress Henrietta, whose career as a prostitute ends at the guillotine after she has murdered the man who first seduced her. The donkey is torn to pieces at a "baiting" by savage dogs; Henrietta's headless body is piously buried by the narrator, but dug up by ghouls for dissection at a medical school. Janin provocatively contrasts his method with the conventional picture of rustic "nature embellished":

> But what is a shepherd in actuality? A tattered unfortunate, dying of hunger, who for five sous follows a few mangy sheep alongside the high road . . . And a shepherdess? A fat chunk of meat, with a red face, red arms, greasy hair that stinks of butter and garlic. Theocritus and Virgil lied about them . . . So, boldly on! And we shall come to terms with nature, which we have had the honor of being the first to discover![25]

But it is not merely the "seamy side" of human existence which the novelist takes credit for discovering. He also, ostentatiously, as the title of his novel gives evidence, flaunts before his readers' horrified gaze the most revolting pictures of violence and cruelty:

> Upon the Olympus which I have constructed, I have heaped up crimes upon villainies, physical vileness upon moral baseness; I have flayed nature, and having deprived her of her plump, white envelope, adorned with a tender ruddiness and peach-bloom, have disclosed all her so numerous vessels, have shown how the blood circulates, how all the veins intersect in *all* directions . . . so that one may hear the drily beating heart in the breast. . . . A genuine living slaughter-house! Picture the operation: a young, healthy human being lies on a broad black slab, and two experienced executioners are flaying the skin from him, steaming and bloody, as from a rabbit, not separating a single shred from the whole. This is the nature I have chosen.[26]

Janin's horrible picture is of course metaphorical—it is "nature" who is skinned alive—and introduced only to symbolize his naturalistic method. Gogol, however, on one occasion tried to present the same picture literally, unquestionably under Janin's influence. Among the unpublished papers, or pieces published as fragments, in Gogol's complete works, are several that are headed either "from an unfinished novel" or from "a novel to be called *The Hetman*."[27] One of these is a fragment, which Gogol tried to publish in the *Reading Library:* it was banned by the censors as being too revolting to permit in print. It is called "The Bloody Bandura-Player," and depicts literally the horrifying spectacle of a man who has been skinned alive. The man appears to be the intended hero of *The Hetman,* a historical figure named Stepan Ostranitsa. The torturers are Poles who have captured both him and his mistress. Whether Ostranitsa actually did meet this gruesome fate is not recorded.

Fortunately, after 1832, when "The Bloody Bandura-Player" was written, Gogol moderated his "naturalistic" trend; but even so, "Taras Bulba" abounds in scenes of violence over and above the descriptions of battle, which must be considered apart. When they leave the Sich, for no particular reason the Cossacks decide to kill all the Jews who have been furnishing them with vodka and other necessities in their military town. The unfortunates are dumped into the Dniepr, to the accompaniment of Cossack guffaws. Ostap's tortures are not described in detail, "lest a reader's hair stand on end," but enough is given to make one grateful for the restraint. The bloody vengeance which Bulba exacts for his son's death includes the butchery of innocent women, babies thrown in the flames, etc., which Gogol notes apologetically as traits "of a cruel and barbarous time." Taras himself ends his tumultuous career burning at the stake.

Nothing of this sort mars the stories of the Dikanka cycle. There the horror is metaphysical, an encroachment of the evil principle into human lives in an uncanny and supernatural fashion: and it is to this type of horror that Gogol returns in the third story of the Mirgorod cycle, "The Viy," and in "The Portrait" in *Arabesques*. Naturalism of the Janin sort was obviously a wrong turn for Gogol, and he had the good sense to abandon it after "Taras Bulba."

Cossack life, as Gogol envisioned it, inevitably involved a good deal of fighting, as well as carousing, pillaging and casual murder. Gogol was not a soldier, and for battle descriptions in "Taras Bulba" he had to rely on a combination of literary borrowing and imagination. Note the following description from Chapter 9 of the rewritten 1842 version:

> But Bovdyug [never previously mentioned] had already fallen from the wagon. A bullet had hit him directly under the very heart, but the old man gathered all his spirit and said: "There's no regret in parting from this world. May God grant everyone such an end! May the Russian land be glorious to the end of time!" And Bovdyug's soul was borne to the heights to tell the elders long since departed how men know how to fight in the Russian land, and still better, how they know how to die there for the holy faith.
>
> Balaban [never previously mentioned], a village commander [*kurennyi ataman*], also crashed to the ground soon after him. Three mortal wounds were his lot: from a spear, from a bullet and from a heavy broadsword. He was one of the doughtiest Cossacks; many expeditions had he accomplished by sea during his commandership, but the most glorious of all was his expedition to the shores of Anatolia,...[28]

Here is a technique of very obvious derivation—from the oldest and greatest of all epics. Pages of battle description in the *Iliad* proceed in this fashion: the death of a warrior on one side or the other, previously unmentioned, or if at all, only casually, together with a detailed anatomical description of the wound that kills him, and a brief précis of his former career or a note about his attitude toward death. From Homer comes also Gogol's frequent use in the more epic portions of "Taras Bulba" of formal speeches from his hero or others, followed by the phrase (e.g., Chapter 9, paragraph 3): "thus spake the chieftain"—the familiar Homeric *hôs ephat'*, followed by the speaker's name and rank. Gogol's source was of course the Gnedich translation of the *Iliad* (1829); the formula *ták govoríl atamán*, it may be noted, even forms the first hemistich of a hexameter line. These Homeric borrowings, furthermore, belong only to the expanded 1842 version: the corresponding passage in the 1835 version is very brief, generalized and entirely devoid of Homeric coloration. There is a telltale folk-song cliché ("To the whistle of bullets they advanced, as to the sound of wedding music") and Bulba's voice is compared to "the distant neighing of a stallion," but otherwise the passage is remarkably restrained and free of ornamentation.

Carl Proffer, in his excellent study *The Simile and Gogol's "Dead Souls,"* argues[29] that the author's motive for rewriting "Taras Bulba" was to make it a complete polar opposite of *Dead Souls,* a heroic, patriotic and essentially optimistic picture of the side of Russian character most antithetical to the meanness and triviality of his "poem." In this connection Proffer notes[30] the substitution everywhere in the 1842 version of the terms "Russia" and "Russian" for the earlier "Ukraine" and "Ukrainian." Part of the process of heightening and ennoblement involved the use of Homeric elements. Proffer notes, for example,[31] in an entire chapter which he devotes to "The Simile and Other Homeric Elements: *Taras Bulba* and the *Iliad*" (Chapter 12) that "there are no Homeric [i.e., developed] similes in the 1835 edition of *Taras Bulba,* but in the 1842 edition there are thirteen." Other Homeric features which he notes are: compound epithets of a particularly poetic type, often coinages of Gogol's own, catalogues of the names of warriors; the use of mutual mockery by warriors in battle; and particularly the almost clinical, detailed descriptions of the carnage of battle. By the use of such features borrowed from Europe's oldest and greatest epic Gogol evidently hoped to create a short prose epic of his own and with it counteract in part the depressing and vulgar effect which he feared critics would find in *Dead Souls.*[32]

Each of the four tales which make up *Mirgorod* stands by itself, with nothing thematically to connect it with the others; and each represents a different direction of Gogol's art. "Old-World Landowners" is Karam-zinian sentimentalism in realistic dress; "Taras Bulba" is an attempt at national epic in a naturalistic mode; "The Viy"[33] is folklore super-naturalism, also in a naturalistic mode. Two seemingly quite incongruous elements make up the tale: the realistic, and comic, description of the life of bursary students, largely derived from Narezhny's novels *The Two Ivans* and *The Bursary Student,* and a much embellished horror tale of folklore origin involving the theme of the witch who rides on a man's back. A third, subsidiary, element is that which gives the tale its title. Gogol's note on the name "Viy" declares: "The 'Viy' is a colossal creation of the imagination of the simple folk. The chief of the gnomes is called by such a name among the people of Little Russia: the eyelids over his eyes reach to the very ground. All this tale is popular tradition. I was unwilling to change it in anything, and I relate it with almost the same simplicity as I heard it."[34] This is evidently a bit of mystification, for neither the name "Viy" nor any traditions about gnomes exist in Ukrainian folklore. The "colossal creation" is of Gogol's own imagination, probably stimulated by vague memories of Scandinavian and Celtic mythology.[35]

In the horror tales of the Dikanka cycles, e.g., "St. John's Eve" or The Lost Letter," the supernatural is juxtaposed with a conventionally faithful background of Ukrainian peasant life. This background, however, is a mere sketch, lacking in concrete detail, and entirely overshadowed by the supernatural element. Thus, for example, the description in "The Lost Letter" of the Konotop fair is a vivid episode, but much too slight to balance the story of "Granddad's" card game with the denizens of Hell. The case is different with "The Viy." Here some eight pages of perfectly realistic description of the bursary student's life, its quasi-republican Roman organization, and the vacation journey of three students, including the "hero," Khoma Brut, lead up to the first encounter of Khoma with the witch, her transformation from old hag to a beautiful girl, and Khoma's ride on her back, her death, and his flight back to Kiev. Then follow about eighteen pages of again detailed realistic, and often humorous, description of Khoma's summons to read the funeral service for the daughter of a Cossack captain, his journey in a huge antique carriage with six elderly and bibulous Cossacks, of the picturesque old-fashioned *khutor* of the Cossack captain, and of the servants' talk at supper before the beginning of Khoma's duties. All of this description is entirely realistic, with no intrusion of the supernatural element except Khoma's recognition of the dead daughter of the Captain as the witch whose death he had unintentionally caused. The final portion of the tale, about ten pages, depicts the horrendous happenings on the three nights of Khoma's vigil with the dead witch, culminating in the appearance of the monstrous Viy, the triumph of the forces of evil, and the death of the "philosopher" Khoma. Even interspersed with this, however, are the commonplace daytime events at the Captain's estate, which accentuate the nightmarish atmosphere of the vigils. This technique, of sharp and glaring contrast of both content and tone, between everyday life and an extraordinary world of folklore horror, is extremely effective. Gogol was to use it again, but much less strikingly, in "The Portrait."

The element of contrast extends to the characters of "The Viy." Nothing could be further from the idea of a champion of the Church against the forces of evil than Khoma Brut as Gogol depicts him—a lazy, gluttonous, hard-drinking fellow, ignorant and sensual. It is not by the sanctity of his character that he succeeds during the first two nights in holding at bay the demonic rout, but by the magic of exorcism and a charmed circle. It is implied that his final defeat and death result from no moral deficiencies, but from his uncontrollable impulse to look at the Viy at the moment when his eyelids are propped up so that he can see where his antagonist is. Presumably if Khoma had not looked at the Viy, the Viy could not have seen him and pointed him out to the demons.

Among the characters who populate the tale are several of Gogol's delightful grotesques—persons designated and individualized by single, striking traits: such are the old Cossack Yavtukh, who when in his cups weeps bitter tears because he is an orphan; Dorozh, who under the same circumstances becomes extremely inquisitive about the teachings in the seminary; and the "theologian" Khalyava, who when drunk always retires to lie down in a patch of weeds and never fails, drunk or sober, to purloin some small object, whether he has any use for it or not. The witch, of course, like all of Gogol's young beauties, is totally without individuality—or perhaps it might be said that she is too schizoid to have personality, since she is first seen as a penurious old hag, and then without warning or explanation assumes what is apparently her true form as a dazzling, but uncanny, beauty. Gogol had trouble with her: in his manuscript she remains an old woman, whom Khoma in a hallucination sees otherwise; in the original *Mirgorod* edition she has youthful traits in an old woman's face; only in the 1842 version does she become an entirely different person. The change is instructive: there is something inherently reasonable and hence less horrifying in a combination of ugliness and horror; the horror engendered in the scenes of Khoma's nightly vigils in the church is precisely the result of the combination of superhuman beauty with evil. The climax of horror, whatever may have been Gogol's intent, is not in the grotesque figure of the Viy, but in the spectacle of the supremely beautiful witch as she gropes vainly after Khoma, protected within his magic circle, her sightless eyes glaring with green fire. It may be noted here that at the period when "The Viy" was written, Gogol was preoccupied with the theme of beauty as evil; it appears, with no supernatural traits, in a sordid urban setting in "Nevsky Prospect."

The story of Khoma Brut's heroic exploit in the old church ends with an abruptness that leaves some essential questions unanswered. The Viy and the rest of the hellish rout are so intent on getting their prey that they ignore the first cock-crow, and are caught by the second, and hence must remain eternally stuck in the windows and doors of the church—a grotesque fancy that seems to be original with Gogol. The priest who should have performed the requiem mass for the dead girl refuses to do so in the desecrated church, which is thenceforth abandoned. But what happens to the "living dead" witch? Is she too trapped, like the monsters, in the church for all time? It may be noted that the whole final scene is ambivalent. The church is stormed by a host of monsters—one thinks of a Hieronymus Bosch painting—but their object is not to take possession of the witch's soul, as in Zhukovsky's translation of the Southey ballad "The Old Woman of Berkeley," but to help the witch take vengeance on the man who has caused her death. And the monsters, including the Viy, are described not as traditional devil figures, but as "gnomes"—earth spirits of a pre-Christian mythology. Moreover, when Khoma reads his "book," there is pointedly no mention of its Christian content, and it is curses and exorcisms that hold his foes at bay. There is something pre-Christian about the whole supernatural element in "The Viy."

The effectiveness of "The Viy" depends in large measure on Gogol's superb use of several quite ordinary narrative devices—contrast, atmosphere and tempo. The contrast between the gay, boisterous, earthy life of the seminary students, including Khoma, in the first part of the story, with his eerie encounter with the witch, the wild, nightmarish (and mutedly erotic) ride on her back and her transformation, and the contrast in the second part of the tale between Khoma's days at the Cossack captain's *khutor,* filled with with most prosaic and ordinary activities, and his terrifying nights, locked in the solitary church with the witch's corpse, is exceedingly telling. That Gogol was particularly conscious as an artist of the uses of contrast is plain from a remark in his essay: "On the Architecture of the Present Time":[36]

> Genuine effectiveness consists in sharp contrast; beauty is never so clear and evident as in contrast. Contrast is bad only when it is put to use by a crude taste, or to put it better, by a complete absence of taste; but when it is in the hands of a lofty and subtle taste, it is the prime condition of everything, and acts equally upon all. Its several parts harmonize in accordance with the same laws whereby a light yellow color harmonizes with blue, white with light blue, pink with green and so on,—It is all dependent on taste and on the ability to arrange.

In "The Viy" Gogol's "ability to arrange" his effects is superlative. Gukovsky somewhat schematically, but with genuine insight, sees the whole tale founded on the antinomy of "night" and "day." He even notes the evidently intentional contrast in the "hero's" name: Khomá (the vulgar Ukrainian deformation of Fomá, i.e., "Thomas"), and the heroic Roman cognomen Brut, i.e., "Brutus."[37]

Atmosphere is a somewhat intangible quality, conveyed most effectively by a few telling words. Note how the terror of Khoma's nights is conveyed by the understated eeriness in the paragraph which begins the account of his final vigil:

> "It's time," said Yavtukh.—"Let's go."
> "A splinter in your tongue, you damned swine [*knur*]," thought the philosopher, and getting to his feet, he said: "Let's go." Going along the road, the philosopher kept

constantly glancing to the side, and started feebly to converse with his guides. But Yavtukh was silent, Dorozh himself was uncommunicative. The night was hellish. Wolves were howling in the distance, a whole pack of them. And the very barking of the dogs was somehow terrible. "It seems as though something different were howling; that's not a wolf," said Dorozh.

Yavtukh was silent. The philosopher could not find a thing to say.[38]

Again, the scene with the servants after the second vigil, when the flirtatious and vain cook's helper greets Khoma:

"Greetings, Khoma!" she said, on seeing the philosopher. "Ai, ai, ai! What's happened to you? she screamed, throwing up her hands.
"What do you mean, you foolish woman?"
"Oh, my God! Why, your hair has turned all white!"
"Aha! Why, she's speaking the truth," declared Spirid, giving him an intent look.
"You've turned quite as white as our old Yavtukh!"[39]

A terror story that drags on can become tedious and boring. "A Terrible Vengeance" is a case in point. Gogol avoids the danger in "The Viy" by a remarkable feat of acceleration in his treatment of the three nights in the church. The climactic effect of the threefold repetition of almost the same situation is of course a familiar folklore device, which Zhukovsky also uses in the "Ballad in which is described how a certain old woman rode double on a black horse, and who rode before her."[40] In Zhukovsky's poem the first night's happenings are described in four four-line strophes; those of the second night are given in five strophes, of the third and final night in twelve. Gogol's treatment almost reverses the emphasis: the description of Khoma's first night occupies a total of 117 lines, of the second 51 lines, and of the third 70 lines. The pace of the narrative is leisurely in the first night, hectic in the second, and in the third just enough more expansive to allow for the epilogue that tells of the death of Khoma and the final fate of the church. The seemingly abrupt ending, which, as we have noted, never returns to the witch's father or to the Cossack servants with whom Khoma has been associated during his days at the Captain's *khutor,* conveys a sense of almost breathless haste, against which is contrasted the quiet, humorous, normally-paced final scene, of Khoma's seminary friends Khalyava and Tiberius Gorobets drinking to the memory of their lost companion. It is a marvelously effective device.

"The Tale of how Ivan Ivanovich Came to Quarrel with Ivan Nikiforovich"[41] had been published separately in the almanac *Novosel'e* in 1834, a year before its inclusion in the collection *Mirgorod.* In the original publication it is accompanied by the note: "One of the unpublished true stories [*bylei*] of the Beekeeper 'Red' Panko," and is dated 1831.[42] It therefore belongs to the period and inspiration of the Dikanka cycles, although scholars are inclined to doubt the authenticity of the 1831 date, and actually place it in 1833. It is in any case the earliest of the *Mirgorod* tales, and the only one of the four to be composed in the *skaz* style, which its attribution to "Red" Panko explains. It may be observed that the "I" who tells the story "Old-World Landowners" may be identified with Gogol himself, and is thus a different person from the "I" who tells the story of the two Ivans. Imperceptibly, however, the narrator's personality changes, and the *skaz* style disappears. By the end of the story the remark: "It's dreary in this world, gentlemen!'" seems to belong more to the author's own persona than to "Red" Panko.

"The Viy" returned for a final time to the world of Ukrainian folklore first exploited in *Evenings on a Farm near Dikanka:* "The Tale of how Ivan Ivanovich Came to Quarrel with Ivan Nikiforovich" returns to "Ivan Fyodorovich Shponka and his Auntie," of the same cycle. Like the earlier story, it depicts in humorous and satirical manner the stupid, mindless existence of a provincial gentry which certainly is not far from the animal level, and yet in some strange fashion remains likable. Critics since Belinsky have almost unanimously settled upon the quality of *poshlost'* as the prime object of Gogol's detestation. It is a concept for which it is difficult to find an appropriate English equivalent (Nabokov devotes ten pages to the subject, but leaves the reader no closer to an equivalent).[43] It is usually translated as "commonplaceness," "banality," or "vulgarity," sometimes even "Philistinism." Ivan Ivanovich and Ivan Nikiforovich are classical examples of the quality—two "noblemen" whose entire existence before their quarrel consisted of lounging on their porches, eating melons and saving the seeds, visiting each other and exchanging snuff, and commenting with incredible fatuousness on "world affairs." Ivan Ivanovich has "a book which he looks at occasionally," but "he did not remember its title, because the servant girl had long ago torn off the upper part of the title page to amuse a child." He also whittles bowls and other useful things out of wood. Ivan Nikiforovich is so grossly corpulent that he practically never moves from his house, or even goes to church. Yet in spite of the utter worthlessness of these absurd creatures, one comes to like them and feel regret when they quarrel over a ridiculous trifle, and spend the rest of their lives in a futile lawsuit.

It may be noted in this connection that Gogol may have been indebted to Narezhny for the generating idea and the title of his story, but for nothing else. *The Two Ivans, or A Passion for Litigation* describes a neighbors' quarrel which arises from an incident as trivial as that which sets Ivan Ivanovich and Ivan Nikiforovich at odds; and Narezhny's quarrel results in some retaliatory depredations comparable to that of Ivan Ivanovich in bringing down Ivan Nikiforovich's goose-pen; but here the similarity between the tales ends. Narezhny, as we have seen, is resolutely and overtly didactic, and *The Two Ivans* ends with an improbably wealthy and philanthropic uncle who brings the litigants to see the error of their ways and rescues them from the certain ruin which rapacious courts threaten them with. Gogol's story has of course serious moral implications, but the author leaves them wisely for the reader to work out for himself, and his only comment *in propria persona* is the pessimistic one that ends the tale.

Certain aspects of Gogol's comic technique may be very clearly observed in the story. Description by comparison, in which the second element is as absurdly remote as possible from the first, is a favorite device. Thus, the physical features of the tall, scrawny Ivan Ivanovich and of the obese Ivan Nikiforovich are memorably caught in the simile: "Ivan Ivanovich's head resembles a radish, root downward; Ivan Nikiforovich's, a radish root upward." One of the carriages brought by guests to the mayor's party "was like a huge haystack or a fat merchant's wife"; another "was in profile a perfect pipe without a mouthpiece." The roofs of Mirgorod, seen from a distance, are "very much like a plateful of pancakes." Ivan Ivanovich has a mouth that looks like the letter *izhitsa* (more or less equivalent in shape to an English "V"); Ivan Nikiforovich has a nose that looks like a ripe plum. The mayor's uniform coat has eight buttons, sewn on "as a peasant woman sows beans, one to the right and the next to the left," etc.

It is part of the *skaz* technique, seen already in the Dikanka stories, for the fictional narrator to interpolate occasional references to people and events presumably familiar to fellow townsmen, but mysterious to the uninitiated. Thus, early in the story of the two Ivans, in the rhapsodic description of Ivan Ivanovich's astrakhan coat, comes the abrupt note: "He had had it made at a time before Agafya Fyodorovna went to Kiev. You know Agafya Fyodorovna? The same who bit the assessor's ear." Agafya is of course introduced later, but no further reference explains the incident assumed to be common knowledge. Similarly, in verifying the eulogy of Ivan Ivanovich's fine qualities, the narrator remarks: "Dorosh Tarasovich Pukhivochka, when he is travelling from Khorol, always stops in to see him." Dorosh Tarasovich, of course, has never been mentioned before nor is ever heard of again.[44]

Gogol is prone, in referring to sexual matters in any way, to employ a tone of wide-eyed innocence. Thus, when Agafya Fyodorovna ("the same who bit the assessor's ear") comes into the story a second time (Chapter 3), the following dead-pan paragraph describes her advent:

> On the evening of the same day [as the quarrel] Agafya Fyodorovna came to Ivan Nikiforovich's, Agafya Fyodorovna was neither a relative nor a connection by marriage, nor even a spiritual relative[*kuma*—a woman who had been associated with him as godmother to a child when he had been a godfather] to Ivan Nikiforovich. It would seem, she had absolutely no reason to come visit him...[45]

In the same way, in Chapter I, the narrator remarks:

> God, how time flies! At that time ten years had already passed since he [i.e., Ivan Ivanovich] became a widower. He had no children. Gapka [Ivan's buxom housekeeper] has children and they are constantly running around the yard. Ivan Ivanovich always gives each of them a pretzel or a piece of melon or a pear.[46]

Later (Chapter 6) the passage of the time between the quarrel and the mayor's party is indicated by the following:

> A large number of marriageable girls have succeeded in getting married; one of the judge's molars has fallen out, and two bicuspids; around Ivan Ivanovich's yard more little urchins are running than before—God alone knows where they come from![47]

A very typical Gogolian trick, which is to be seen in abundance in "The Overcoat" and others of the Petersburg tales, has a single brilliant example in the tale of the two Ivans. This consists in presenting two totally unrelated ideas in a grammatically logical connection: "Ivan Ivanovich is of a somewhat timorous character. Ivan Nikiforovich, *on the other hand* [my italics], has trousers of such broad dimensions that if you were to blow them up, the whole courtyard with its barns and outbuildings could be accommodated in them."[48] This passage of course also illustrates what Valery Bryusov regards as the key trait of Gogol the writer—hyperbolism, outrageous exaggeration.[49] Trivial particles such as *zhe,* which emphasizes a preceding word, or *dazhe,* "even," or *i,* a weaker "even," often appear in Gogol's prose, where they emphasize, in defiance of logic or common sense, some particularly unimportant word. In "The Tale of How Ivan Ivanovich Came to Quarrel with Ivan Nikiforovich," however, the campaign against logic is mostly waged more overtly. Thus, for example, in the first chapter the narrator expostulates indignantly at the baseless rumor that Ivan Nikiforovich has been married. The rumor, he declares, is as ill-founded as the absurd and unseemly allegation, also current, that Ivan Nikiforovich "was born with a tail in the rear." In refuting the latter calumny the narrator remarks that to his "enlightened readers it is well known, without any doubt, that only witches, and an extremely small number even of them, have a tail in the rear,—and what is more, these belong more to the female sex than the male." Here, it may be noted, the assault on logic is multiple. The tautology "tail in the rear" is of a piece with the alogical use of "even"; then it is casually admitted that certain members of the human race *do have* tails; and then comes the absurd remark that witches "belong *more* [my italics] to the female sex than the male!" The Russian *ved'ma* is of course uncompromisingly feminine.

A literary narrative, under most circumstances, or a conversation forming part of a narrative, proceeds logically, that is, from presumed relationships of cause and effect. Laurence Sterne in *Tristram Shandy* was one of the first writers who systematically flouted this narrative expectation, and proceeded according to what in modern terms would be called "free association of ideas," which is, of course, very often the way in which actual conversations, or the monologues of talkative people, are carried on. Gogol, especially in his *skaz* narratives, often uses this procedure for humorous effect. A beautiful example is this, in Chapter 5 of our tale; the mayor of Mirgorod calls on Ivan Ivanovich to complain that that gentleman's grey pig has wandered into the police courtroom, picked up Ivan Nikiforovich's formal petition against his neighbor, and run off with it. Ivan Ivanovich indignantly protests that the streets are free, and "a pig is God's creature," to which the mayor retorts:

> "Agreed! This is well known to everybody, that you're a learned person [an inference presumably based on the profound truism that 'a pig is God's creature!'], you know the sciences and various other subjects. Of course, I never learned any sciences: I began to learn handwriting only in the thirtieth year of my life. I am, of course, as you all know, of the rank and file."
>
> "Ha!" said Ivan Ivanovich.
>
> "Yes," continued the mayor. "In the year 1801 I was in the 42nd regiment of chasseurs, a lieutenant in the fourth company. Our company commander was, if you will allow me to say so, Captain Yeremeev...."[50]

The mayor manages, after this digression—the mention of Captain Yeremeev leads to nothing—"to get back to his sheep," or in this case, pig, and Gogol now creates just as humorous an effect by the use of rigorous logic as he has been able to do before by the flouting of it. The mayor solemnly proposes that the law declares that "the one guilty" must be punished; he is therefore obliged to arrest and castigate the grey pig! Ivan Ivanovich eventually disposes of this threat by agreeing to keep the pig in custody until slaughtering time, when he will deliver some sausages to the mayor.

A rich source of humorous effect is always available in parody, and it is naturally legalese, which is just as impenetrable in Russian as in English, that in this tale Gogol employs for the purpose. Both Ivans submit formal charges to the court, each against the other. That of Ivan Ivanovich begins with the deadly insult which was the primal cause of the quarrel: in a heated argument Ivan Nikiforovich had called him "a gander" *(gusak)*. It may occasion some surprise that the name of a male goose should be regarded as so indecent that it cannot even be pronounced by the squeamish Ivan Ivanovich in polite society; but I can recall that in my childhood the specific name of the male of the bovine kind was never uttered by well-brought-up ladies, a bull being always referred to delicately as "animal" or "creature." Presumably "gander" similarly had too great a connotation of male sexuality. In any case, Ivan Ivanovich, in denouncing the slander, feels it necessary (rigorous logic again) to assure the court that he really isn't a gander, but has been duly and properly christened, whereas "a *gander,* as is well known to all who are in any way conversant with the sciences, cannot be registered in a church record, because a gander is not a human being, but a bird, as is quite well known to everyone, even one who has not been in a seminary."[51] Ivan Nikiforovich's first petition—the one the pig stole—is couched in the same legal jargon as his rival's, with the addition of a larger number of insulting personal references. After the loss of this document, a second petition had to be made, which was drawn up by a hired scribe versed in the art. The result is a hilarious spoof of legalese, in which most of the ostensible sentences hang precariously in the air, e.g.: "In consequence of the said my petition the which did be from me, the gentleman Ivan Nikifor's son, Dovgochkun to that effect, jointly with the gentleman Ivan Ivan's son, Pererepenko, to which also the Mirgorod district court itself has displayed its partiality."[52] The substance of the petition, which can hardly be made out from the jumble, lies in the accusation that the laxity of the district court in allowing free access to Ivan Ivanovich's pig demonstrates the court's criminal connivance with the pig's owner to obstruct the course of justice.

There are, of course, numerous other devices in the tale which Gogol employs for comic effect, but those mentioned are the most notable. The tone of the tale until the final chapter is uniformly comic, more so than in any earlier tale of Gogol except "Ivan Fyodorovich Shponka and his Auntie." Fanger declares: "The story of the two Ivans is an exercise in generating and sustaining comic narrative—by a sheer creative energy that exceeds the needs of objective observation or objective statement so far as to make them irrelevant."[53] Gogol himself, or at least the persona which he had used in "Old-World Landowners," intervenes abruptly toward the end of the tale, with a radical change of tone: the narrator now seems to be no longer "Red" Panko, but the author himself, and the atmosphere shifts from the sultry Ukrainian summer of the rest of the story, to a sodden autumn day when the narrator revisits Mirgorod after a long absence and finds both litigants terribly aged, but each still convinced that his case will very shortly be decided, and in his favor—the only thing, it seems, that he now lives for. The ending is gloomy in the extreme:

> I sighed even more profoundly and was even more in a hurry to say goodbye, because I was travelling on extremely important business, and took my seat in the *kibitka*. The scrawny horses, known in Mirgorod as "post horses," dragged themselves off, making an unpleasant sound with their hooves as they sank into the grey mass of mud. The rain was pouring down in torrents on the Jew sitting in the box, covered with a piece of bast sacking. The dampness penetrated me through and through. The gloomy gate with its sentry-box, in which a discharged soldier was cleaning his grey gear, passed slowly by. Again the same open country, in places dug up and black, in places green; drenched jackdaws and crows; the monotonous rain, the tearful sky without a gleam of light—it's dreary in this world, gentlemen![54]

Summing up the *Mirgorod* collection, Fanger states:[55] "The four stories, taken together, represent a lost world [i.e., of antique patriarchal life, of heroic valor and patriotism, of an alluring but fateful beauty, of tranquillity and friendship].... *Mirgorod* then is elegiac overall. Each of the stories represents a new experiment in using some earlier literary source as starting point for a markedly original narrative embodying some intimate Gogolian concerns." It may be added that this elegiac tone, so almost startlingly stressed at the end of the tale of the two Ivans, takes on an emphasis applicable to the whole by coming as it does at the end of the entire collection.

VIII

Nikolai Gogol:
St. Petersburg Stories and Comedies

Arabesques

Mirgorod and *Arabesques* were both issued early in 1835, and the stories and articles that make up the two collections were all written during the same years 1833-34. The two collections, however, are very different in content: the *Mirgorod* stories continue Gogol's earlier Ukrainian subjects, while the pieces in *Arabesques* belong to the environment of St. Petersburg. Moreover *Arabesques* is a very motley miscellany, mainly consisting of pieces of a critical content, of essays emanating from Gogol's short period as a lecturer on history in St. Petersburg University. The two parts of the collection are listed below. The three stories, which are starred, have been frequently translated into English ("The Portrait," however, in its revised 1842 version). The entire collection, with the exception of the two fragmentary portions from the unfinished historical novel *The Hetman,* has been translated by Alexander Tulloch, with an introduction by Carl R. Proffer.[1]

Part I	*Part II*
Preface	Schlözer, Miller and Herder
Sculpture, Painting and Music	*Nevsky Prospect (a tale)
On the Middle Ages	On Little Russian Songs
Chapter from a Historical Novel	Thoughts on Geography (for children)
[i.e., *The Hetman*]	The Last Day of Pompeii (Bryullov's
On the Teaching of General History	Painting)
*The Portrait (a tale)	The Captive (fragment of a historical
A Glance at the Make-up of Little	novel [*The Hetman*])
Russia	On the Movement of Peoples at the End
A Few Words About Pushkin	of the Fifth Century
On the Architecture of the Present	*The Diary of a Madman
Era	
Al-Mamun	

Most of the historical essays are valueless as literature, although they show more competence than is customarily credited to Gogol as a historian. The essay on Little Russian songs is very interesting, and the detailed critique of Karl Bryullov's famous painting, "The Last Day of Pompeii," the essay on modern architecture, and that on "Sculpture,

Painting and Music" reveal a good deal about Gogol's aesthetic ideas of the period before his religious crisis. Only the three tales, however, are of much literary interest. Of these "Nevsky Prospect,"[2] which was written between 1833 and August 1834, may be considered first, as its history is less complicated than that of "The Portrait," written during the same year.

"Nevsky Prospect," which Pushkin greatly admired, is quintessential Gogol. Side by side, in unforced juxtaposition, tragedy and farce, against an impressionistic big-city background; and pervading the whole the same pessimistic theme as of "The Viy": evil is most dangerous and horrible when conjoined with beauty. The "plot" of the tale is simple in the extreme: two young men, an artist and a soldier, strolling along St. Petersburg's most fashionable street, encounter two attractive women. To the painter the gorgeous brunette whom he follows is the very reincarnation of Perugino's Bianca; but it is to a brothel that she leads him, and she turns out to be a common prostitute. The discovery shatters his life; he takes to opium, and loses his sanity; at the end of the story his body is found, his throat cut with a razor. The soldier follows a buxom blonde, who turns out to be a German ironmonger's wife. He tries his wiles on her, but is discovered by her husband, who with the help of friends undresses the hapless Lothario and throws him into the street. He soon recovers from his humiliation and forgets the whole incident.

The names of the two friends are significant: Piskaryov and Pirogov. The first is a derivative of the word *piskar'*, a variant of the commoner *peskar'*, which is the name of a fish, the gudgeon; the variant form is evidently used because the syllable *pis-* suggests the verb *pisat'*, which means either "to write" or "to paint." Gogol had originally thought of giving the young artist the more obvious "speaking name" Palitrin, from *palitra*, "palette." Pirogov's name is a derivative of *pirog*, "a pie"—a commonplace and pedestrian comestible, quite in keeping with the lieutenant's earthy and self-assured character. It should be noted that Gogol's proper names are seldom of the banal and obvious kind represented by the eighteenth-century Zmeyad ("snake-poison") or Cheston ("honest")—cf. Sir Benjamin Backbite or Lady Sneerwell. He provided many of the characters in his Ukrainian stories with absurd *cognomina*, such as Golopupenko ("bare belly-button") or Tiberii Vorobets ("Tiberius Sparrow"), but his later practice seems to have been to use actual names, chosen often for merely acoustic effect, e.g., "the inn-keeper Zuzulya" or "Shponka" (the name means "a cross-partition," but the meaning here is irrelevant to the use of the name, which is based simply on its silly sound). There are anecdotes about Gogol's perusing the registers of post-stations while on a journey, in search of particularly outlandish names (telephone directories, unhappily, had not yet been invented!). Sometimes he deliberately chose an absurd name in order to provide himself with an opportunity for a pun, e.g., Yaichnitsa ("omelette") in the play *Marriage,* or Bashmachkin (the owner of "The Overcoat") whose name is derived from *bashmak,* "shoe."

The two episodes which make up the narrative portion of "Nevsky Prospect" are carefully arranged in parallel so as to give maximum effect to the contrast: Piskaryov suffers a psychological trauma that shatters his entire life and drives him to suicide; Pirogov suffers a painful physical humiliation which some pleasant company and a very successful exhibition of his dancing prowess enable him to forget in a moment. The published version of the tale softened both incidents considerably—in the case of Pirogov's beating, as a result of censorship. A restoration of the two original passages makes the effect in each case more obvious. Piskaryov, after his experiments with opium dreams, conceives the mad plan of searching out his beautiful prostitute and persuading her to marry him and lead a poor but moral life. He retraces his steps to the brothel and makes his proposal to the bewildered girl:

> "O God! Help me to prevail!" pronounced Piskaryov in a voice of desperation, and was already prepared to gather all the thunder of a powerful eloquence, poured forth from the very soul, in order to shake the beauty's unfeeling, deadened soul, when suddenly the door opened and a certain officer came noisily in. "Hello, Lipushka," he said, unceremoniously slapping the beauty on the shoulder. "Don't disturb us," said the beauty, assuming a stupidly serious air. "I'm getting married and have to give my acceptance at once of the match proposed to me." Oh, this he had no more strength to bear! He dashed out, losing both feelings and thoughts.[3]

As for Pirogov's case, the received text merely indicates that the three German artisans overpowered him, stripped him, and threw him out into the street. Gogol's manuscript gives a more logical version:

> If Pirogov had been in full uniform, then evidently respect for his rank and calling would have stayed the rowdy Teutons. But he had come quite as an ordinary private person, in a frock-coat and without epaulettes. With the greatest fury the Germans tore all his clothes off him, Hoffmann with all his weight sat on his legs, Kunz held him by the head, and Schiller seized in his hand a bundle of twigs that served as a besom. I have to acknowledge with grief that Lieutenant Pirogov was very painfully flogged.[4]

Censorship, of course, prohibited even fictional references to any such insult to a Russian officer, so, to Pushkin's sorrow, "the scene of the beating" had to be toned down to the merest hint.

Professor Vinogradov argues convincingly that De Quincey's *Confession of an English Opium-Eater,* translated into Russian in 1834, influenced Gogol in his description of the dreams which Piskaryov induces by his use of the drug.[5] Another influence is unquestionably that of E. T. A. Hoffmann, whose student Anselmus, hero of the *novella* "The Golden Pot" [*Der Goldene Topf*], lives just such a dream-life as Piskaryov's, although without benefit of opium and with an oneiric happiness instead of suicide as his ultimate fate.

In "Nevsky Prospect" as in so many of Gogol's tales of the middle period there is enough description of the actual world to give color to the mistaken notion that the author was a realist unqualified. Most of this, naturally, comes in Pirogov's story. The description of the honest ironmonger Schiller and his methodical habits is a good example:

> I think it is not superfluous to acquaint the reader somewhat briefly with Schiller. Schiller was a perfect German, in the full sense of this entire term. Even from his twentieth year, from that happy period in which a Russian lives heedlessly, Schiller had marked out his whole life and made no exception in any circumstance. He had resolved to get up at seven o'clock, have dinner at two, to be exact in everything, and get drunk every Sunday. He resolved in the course of ten years to accumulate a capital of 50,000 and this resolution had already been as dependable and inexorable as fate, since sooner will an official forget to glance into his chief's vestibule, than a German think of changing his mind. Never under any circumstances did he increase his expenditures, and if the price of potatoes rose too greatly above the normal, he added not a penny but only lessened the quantity, and although he sometimes remained quite hungry, he got used to this. His punctuality even went so far that he had resolved to kiss his wife no oftener than twice in twenty-four hours, and in order not by any chance to kiss her an extra time, he never put more than one teaspoon of pepper into his soup [pepper was regarded as an aphrodisiac]; on Sunday, however, this rule was not so strictly carried out, since Schiller then used to drink two bottles of beer and one bottle of caraway-flavored vodka, which, however, he always cursed.[6]

The opening of "Nevsky Prospect" is an extremely good example of Gogol's quasi-realistic style. It belongs in the line of the so-called "physiological sketch," which Russian writers of the group dubbed by Belinsky "the natural school" had borrowed from such French writers as Jules Janin, Eugène Sue, Dumas père and Frédéric Soulié. The "physiological sketch" in its usual form is a detailed and realistic enumeration of the external characteristics of a particular urban environment, the manners of a particular class of city dwellers (e.g., "St. Petersburg Hurdy-Gurdy Players") or the like. As employed by e.g., Butkov, Nekrasov and other realists, the sketch is painstakingly detailed and accurate, as though a zoologist were giving a scientific account of a certain type of fauna. Gogol's method, however, is quite different. In "Nevsky Prospect" he follows the succession of different types of St. Petersburg humanity who may be found on the great avenue at different times of day and night, e.g., workmen, nursemaids, officials of various classes, off-duty military men, street-walkers, etc. In this regard he is precisely within the tradition; but his descriptions are impressionistic in the extreme. Note, for example:

> Here you will meet with extraordinary whiskers, tucked with unusual and astonishing artistry under cravats; whiskers of velvet, of satin, black as sable or as coal, but alas, belonging solely to the Ministry of Foreign Affairs alone. For those who serve in other departments Providence has banned black whiskers; they are obliged, to their supreme dissatisfaction, to wear red ones.[7]

Or the equally impressionistic picture of the ladies who promenade the avenue:

> Here you will meet with such waists as you have never so much as dreamed of: slender little, narrow little waists, not a bit thicker than the neck of a bottle; when you meet them, you will politely step to one side, in order not by any means to jostle them incautiously with a boorish elbow; timidity and terror possess your heart, lest somehow or other even by your unguarded breathing that most charming product of nature and art might be shattered. And what ladies' sleeves you will meet on Nevsky Prospect! Oh, what a delight! They are rather like two aerial balloons, so that the lady might suddenly rise into the air, if her husband were not holding her down; for it is as easy to lift a lady into the air is it is a champagne-filled goblet carried to the mouth.[8]

Gogol's procedure, it may be remarked, is here, as often, what may be called "synecdochical," that is, a portion of the human figure (whiskers, moustaches, waists, sleeves) is taken for the whole. It is not far, we may observe, from this procedure to such a tour de force as the tale "The Nose," in which that anatomical fraction of a man's figure assumes an independent, and high-ranking, existence! The discussion of the ladies on Nevsky Prospect constitutes also a perfect example of Bryusov's thesis that hyperbole is Gogol's *faculté maîtresse*.

But the "synecdochical method" is not Gogol's only means for picturing the human denizens of Nevsky Prospect.

> There is a multitude of such people who, when you meet them, infallibly look at your shoes, and if you continue on your way, they turn around in order to gaze at your coat-tails. I am to this day unable to understand why this happens. At first I thought they were cobblers, but nothing of the sort: they serve for the most part in various departments, and many of them are able in superlative fashion to refer a case from one official location to another.... [9]

Or consider this sketch of the genus "St. Petersburg artist," to which Piskaryov belongs: "In general they are very timid: a star and a thick epaulette put them in such confusion that they involuntarily lower the price of their works. They sometimes love to dress smartly, but this smartness on them seems too garish and has somewhat the look of a patch."[10] The descriptive means vary, but never take the form of simple exhaustive enumeration of presumably typical traits.

One of Gogol's themes, as has been noted, is the pessimistic one, that evil, which a more naive romantic would unhesitatingly equate with ugliness, can infect even the most perfect beauty (one may remember in this connection Baudelaire's *Fleurs du mal*). The artist, whom nature has endowed with the greatest sensitivity and appreciation of beauty in its spiritual aspect, is through his very superiority to ordinary humanity more peculiarly vulnerable to the horror of beauty perverted. The gross natural man (Pirogov) is not even attracted by perfect beauty; the object of his pursuit is a commonplace creature whom the artist ignores. And the natural man, having no ideal vision to be shattered by sordid reality, suffers no spiritual disillusion, only momentary frustration. But the overriding theme of "Nevsky Prospect" is that which the story's ending so beautifully states: "Oh, do not trust that Nevsky Prospect.... All is deception, all is dream, all is not what it seems!"[11] Perugino's Bianca is a stupid prostitute, a seemingly easy conquest (Pirogov's German *Hausfrau*) has a strong and vindictive husband. Schiller is an ironmonger, Hoffmann a cobbler! And the last line of the tale—"the demon himself lights the lamps only to show everything in an unreal guise"—hints that the city's deceptive character is just as much a diabolic doing as any of the illusion (e.g., "An Enchanted Spot") in the Dikanka tales.

"The Portrait"[12] is the only tale in the first part of the *Arabesques* miscellany. Gogol responded to the adverse criticism of this piece by Belinsky and others by rewriting it completely for his *Collected Works* in 1842. In most respects the rewritten tale is inferior to the original version, but for some unexplained reason is the form selected in all available translations. Belinsky, whose preference for the "natural school" of incipient realism made him intolerant of fantasy and the supernatural, was harshly critical of the *Arabesques* version, so Gogol's revision endeavored to eliminate as much of this as possible, with a result that is neither one thing nor the other. As we shall see later, however, it has considerable interest as an aesthetic tract.

Like "Nevsky Prospect," "The Portrait" is constructed of two tales, connected only by the physical object which gives its name to the whole. The portrait is the literal embodiment of evil, which works upon the artist Chertkov, who buys it in the first tale, to pervert his artistic integrity and drive him to eventual madness and death; in the second tale, the artist who has innocently created the portrait succeeds by repentance and religious devotion in redeeming himself and destroying the evil. The theme of the tale, which haunted Gogol obsessively, especially after the phenomenal success of his play *The Inspector General,* is that of the artist's responsibility for the moral effect of his creation. The powerful satiric picture of an amoral world which the "comedy" *Revizor* presents frightened its creator into the belief that by creating an "evil" work of art he had imperilled his soul. Unfortunately the resulting religious crisis which he underwent, while it may, we hope, have relieved his soul, certainly ruined his art. Father Grigory, the painter of the demonic portrait of the old usurer Petromikhali, atones for his artistic sin by picturing the Holy Virgin in unearthly beauty. Gogol, to his despair, proved incapable of creating any "good" character to match his all too successful Khlestakovs, Chichikovs and Skvoznik-Dmukhanovskys.

The motif of a painting with such lifelike and terrifying eyes that those who look at it are disquieted and imagine that the figure comes out of its frame to haunt them comes to Gogol most immediately from Charles Robert Maturin's Gothic novel *Melmoth the Wanderer*. One of Washington Irving's *Tales of a Traveller* ("The Italian") uses the same motif, but only incidentally, not as a constructional feature. In Maturin's novel the title character, Melmoth, has achieved a kind of unnatural prolongation of life by being artistically incarnated in a portrait, from which he can at will emerge for various activities. The old usurer, according to Father Grigory's revelation at the end of Gogol's tale, is none other than the Antichrist in a partial or conditional incarnation (since the Antichrist's final incarnation must be contrary to the laws of nature, he must wait for this until the laws of nature weaken and can be breached, as the old monk believes is soon to happen). Even the incomplete, unfinished portrait, in which the eyes are the only portion artistically perfected, receives at the usurer's death enough of his spirit to be able to accomplish his diabolic purpose at least with Chertkov. It is never hinted what has been the portrait's career between the time when it disappeared from Father Grigory's possessions and the time it turns up at the auction where Chertkov buys it; but the fact that the artist first spies it at the art shop so covered with dust that he has to wipe it clean before he recognizes its extraordinary artistry would indicate that it has lain unnoticed among other rubbish during the interval (in the revised version the portrait has caused several other disasters in the interval between the two tales). Chertkov bids with another man for the portrait, finally gets it at the price of his entire stock of ready money, and then, appalled by the terrible eyes, he runs abruptly from the shop, leaving his costly purchase behind. It appears mysteriously in his studio, however, and even though its new owner covers it so that the eyes may not haunt his dreams, it is in vain. The old man steps from his frame in the night and whispers to Chertkov that he should abandon his poor but honorable pursuit of beauty and instead cater to the crass tastes of his clients and thus amass a fortune. This suggestion is the beginning of Chertkov's tragedy.

There is no doubt of Gogol's intention of emphasizing the diabolical and corrupting power of money. It is this which turns Chertkov from a young, idealistic painter of genuine talent into a fashionable dauber interested only in the rich fees he collects. It should also be noted that the evil subject of "the portrait" is a hard-fisted usurer, who grinds down the faces of the poor. But I think that Gukovsky goes much too far in insisting that at this date in his life (1834-35) Gogol of course did not believe literally in the Antichrist or in religious supernaturalism, and was using both only symbolically, with the equation: money is the Antichrist.[13] The symbolism is of course obvious, and doubtless the author intends to leave the lesson that the artist who follows Mammon loses his artistic soul; but to Gogol, here as elsewhere, the Devil is real and his machinations are not mere poetic symbol.[14]

By following the diabolical suggestion of old Petromikhali,Chertkov makes himself incapable of creating beauty; his timid attempts to put some reality into the portraits which he does for the fashionable élite come to an abrupt end when his first patroness takes his idealized picture of Psyche for a portrait of her pallid and pouting daughter! After this he takes a kind of malicious satisfaction in giving what his patrons want, and pocketing their fees. But the crisis comes when he sees at the Academy some really great work by a former acquaintance of his who has persisted in following the ideals of his youth: Chertkov is overwhelmed, frantically tries to regain what he has lost, and realizes with horror that he cannot relearn his art. From this point he falls into the ultimate and unforgivable sin: he uses his ill-gotten wealth to buy up all the genuinely beautiful creations he can get his hands on, and savagely destroys them. This is the last perversion of the artist's soul—to become a destroyer instead of a creator of beauty.

Chertkov's story is given first: by itself it is complete, but the mysterious power of the portrait remains unexplained at the end. The second tale puts this in context. The parallelism of the two tales is deliberately brought out by the device of repeating in the second the scene at the art auction which began the first: and again the strange and terrible portrait appears among the pictures to be sold. A military man, just chancing to pass, sees the portrait and recognizes it as his father's work; he recounts to the throng gathered at the shop the story of its creation and his father's sufferings and penance for painting it. His account begins with an irrelevant excrescence—a two-page "physiological sketch" of the Kolomna quarter of St. Petersburg where his father and old Petromikhali lived. Then follows the tale of how the old usurer on his death-bed sent for the artist to make his portrait; how the latter at first saw his task only in purely artistic terms, and rose to the challenge of putting on canvas the repellent and terrifying features of the dying man, to the point of capturing in the eyes all the hypnotic power of the original; and how, frightened by his own success, he broke off and refused to finish the portrait; how in desperation the old man revealed that his sinful soul could have a reprieve from Hell if it could lodge at death in a finished portrait; and how the artist in horror abandons his work and flees, for which he receives the old man's curse and a prophecy of woes and unhappiness to come. As with Chertkov, the unfinished portrait mysteriously appears in the artist's house after the usurer's death. Twice the artist attempts to confess to a priest the sin he has committed in giving the demonic soul a material earthly dwelling-place in the portrait, and twice at the moment of confession an appalling tragedy occurs in his family—his wife swallows a packet of needles she has put in her mouth, and dies in agony; and a younger son, the narrator's brother, falls out of the second-story window and dashes out his brains. After these dreadful experiences, the artist abandons the world, becomes a monk, and atones his sin by painting icons for the church. His son visits him before the old man's death, and hears the whole story, together with the prophecy, revealed to the artist in a vision, that fifty years from the painting of the picture, at the new moon, the story of the portrait will be recounted to a crowd of people, and as a result the portrait itself will disappear. The crowd looks at the easel where the painting had stood—and in its place sees only an insignificant landscape. The prophecy has been fulfilled.

The tone of "The Portrait" is solemn and semi-poetical for the most part, but with occasional bits of satire, as for instance in the description of Chertkov's fashionable patroness and her daughter. The most glaring breach in the general tone is that at the beginning of the narrative in the second part, when apropos of the usurer Petromikhali the unnamed son of the artist Father Grigory describes the peculiar character of the Kolomna district. Gogol must have had an unreasoning affection for this inappropriate *tour de force,* for it was kept almost unchanged in the second version of "The Portrait," in which so much else was completely made over.

In its original version "The Portrait" is free from the offensively "preachy" tone of the revision. The moral lesson implicit in the sad fate of Chertkov is left to be apprehended by the reader with little comment from the author. Thus, the apparition of the old usurer addresses Chertkov in his uneasy dreams in these words:

> You think that it is possible by long exertions to attain art, that you will win and receive something? Yes, you will receive [something] . . . you will receive the enviable right to throw yourself off the Isakievsky Bridge into the Neva, or tie your neck in a shawl and hang yourself on the first nail you come across. . . . Everything in this world is done for profit. Take up your brush with all speed and sketch portraits of the whole town. Take every commision offered; but don't fall in love with your work, don't sit over it day and night! Time flows rapidly, and life doesn't stand still.[15]

Chertkov starts to follow these cynical injunctions, and soon "he grew great in general fame, jingling with his gold pieces, and beginning to believe that everything in the world is simple and ordinary, that revelation from above does not exist in the world, and that everything must infallibly be put under a strict regimen of punctuality and monotony."

Chertkov in the degradation of his art evidently in Gogol's meaning sins particularly against realism, since he paints his subjects not as he sees them, but as they would like themselves to be seen. But realism, evidently, can go too far. At the beginning of Part II of the tale the onlookers at the art auction are appalled by the mysterious portrait: "They felt that this was the acme of truth, that only a genius can represent truth in such a degree, but that this genius has already overstepped with too great audacity the limits of man's freedom."[16] Here must be seen the sense of Gogol's pessimistic aesthetics: Father Grigory at the end of the story says to the narrator: "Marvel, my son, at the terrible power of the Devil. He strives to insinuate himself into everything: into our actions, into our thoughts, and even into the very inspiration of the artist."[17] It is the "overstepping of the limits of man's freedom" in art that gives the opportunity for the penetration into the artist's inspiration of the principle of evil.[18] But Father Grigory does not preach a sermon on this text; he only goes on to elaborate on the might of the Devil and the helplessness of man without the aid of the heavenly powers. All of this is changed, as we shall see, in the 1842 version of "The Portrait."

The third and last completed narrative in *Arabesques* is the short "Diary of a Madman."[19] This has always enjoyed an irrelevant popularity, analogous to that of Pushkin's "Stationmaster," as a humanitarian treatment of the theme of the "little man"—the downtrodden civil servant at the bottom of the official hierarchy. It is questionable how much importance Gogol attached to this theme, here or in "The Overcoat"; but in any case the author's social attitude is of no literary concern. The tale is an attempt to show the progressive stages of a psychopathic delusion as revealed in the jottings of a certain Poprishchin. Apparently the trauma which is the immediate cause of the diarist's madness is the realization that the daughter of the director of the department, with whom he is hopelessly in love, is to be married to a glamorous young court chamberlain. But it is clear that even before this blow descends, Poprishchin's mind is somewhat unbalanced, for the first entry in his journal, otherwise perfectly factual and normal in appearance, records an unusual occurrence: he overhears a conversation on the street between two dogs—Madgie, the pet of the girl whom he worships from afar, and another poodle named Fido. Poprishchin occupies a bureaucratic position by no means at the bottom of the hierarchy: he is a titular councillor (ninth in the table of ranks, in which fourteenth is the lowest), corresponding to the rank of staff captain in the military. He is evidently not very bright, however, since he is normally employed for the not very demanding task of trimming the director's quill pens! In his spare time he lies on his bed and daydreams. On one occasion he manages to find Madgie alone and tries to engage her in conversation, but the stubborn beast pretends she cannot talk. Finally he discovers and confiscates a correspondence from Madgie in Fido's dog-box. The letters are quite well written, he has to admit, but in rather a doggy style. They reveal the infatuation of Madgie's mistress for the young court chamberlain Teplov, and this revelation completes the derangement of the diarist's mind. He breaks off his reading of Madgie's letter with the entry: "Everything that's best in the world, everything goes to either court chamberlains or generals. You find yourself some poor treasure, you think to put out your hand to take it—and some court chamberlain or general grabs it from you. The devil take it! I wish I might be made a general ... "[20] This seems to lay the ground for the next stage in his delusion. In the following entry he reverts to the subject:

What of it, if he's a court chamberlain? That's nothing more than a rank; it's not some visible object that one might take into his hands.... Several times I've tried to make out where all these distinctions originate. Why am I a titular councillor and on what basis am I a titular councillor? Maybe I'm a count or general, and I only appear to be a titular councillor? Maybe I don't know what I am.[21]

The next thing we know the diarist has read in the day's news that Ferdinand VII, King of Spain, has died and there is no male heir. This is the final jolt needed. Up to now the entries have been dated normally, from October 3 through December 8 (presumably in 1833, the year of the death of Ferdinand VII). After December 8 the next entry is dated: "April 43rd, year 2000." It records the happy news that Spain has a new king: it is the diarist himself. All he waits for is the arrival of a delegation from Spain to make the official proclamation. The dating becomes even more erratic, e.g., "Martober 86th. Between day and night"; "No date. The day was dateless"; or "Madrid, February 30th." The last entry of all is mere gibberish, part of it written upside down.

In his last entries Poprishchin has become totally absorbed in the consciousness of his new dignity, and we read nothing more about the lovely Sophia and her court chamberlain. "King Ferdinand VIII" cuts up his new uniform and sews it together again as a royal cape, to the consternation of his housekeeper; and he stops going to the office. Eventually the delegation from Spain arrives and conducts him to his kingdom, which is of course the madhouse. Unexpectedly the final entry is a despairing *cri de coeur* as the poor lunatic complains of the cruel and inhuman treatment to which the madhouse attendants are subjecting him. It is to his doubtless long dead mother that the cry is directed, and it is harrowing: "Mummy, save your poor son! Drop a little tear on his poor sick head! See how they're torturing him! Clasp the poor orphan to your breast. There is no place for him on earth! They're persecuting him! Have pity on your poor sick child!"[22] But at once comes the final reminder that the "sick child" is mad: "And do you [plural, not addressed to "Mummy"] know that the Bey of Algiers has a lump [*shishka*] under his very nose?"

The pathos of the final entry of the madman's diary, which is reminiscent of the passage in "The Overcoat" in which the tormented Akaky Akakievich turns on a young fellow who has been teasing him, with the famous words: "Leave me alone: why do you hurt me?" has led commentators to ascribe to Gogol a good deal more humanitarian sympathy than the circumstances warrant. It must be remembered that Gogol loved the stage and was, according to contemporaries, a consummate actor. He undoubtedly had the actor's instinct for knowing what precisely will move an audience, and made full use of the instinct. As Diderot remarks in his *Paradoxe sur le comédien,* it is not at all necessary for the actor himself to feel the emotions he conveys on the stage—in fact, the "paradox" is that he is more effective precisely when he does *not* feel moved himself, but can coldly calculate his effect. It of course cannot be proved that Gogol's effects do not derive from a warm human sympathy for a miserable fellow-man; no more can the converse be proved. But I think that all we know otherwise of the artist indicates that the pathos is purely literary and calculated.

Contemporaries seemed to feel that Gogol by artistic intuition had grasped the very essence of madness in his tale: but it is difficult to see exactly where this can be made out. There are many awkwardnesses that cannot be or at least are not, explained. For example, the dogs' correspondence is treated throughout as factually existing: the diarist discovers a packet of letters in Fido's box and confiscates them; and from them he learns for the first time the unwelcome news that his adored Sophia is in love with Teplov—and what is more, that she makes fun of him, Poprishchin, whom she considers ridiculous. It would be possible to assume that Poprishchin has been subconsciously aware of these unpleasant truths all along, but there is nothing in the piece itself to warrant such an assumption. The whole tale had best be considered an excursion into fantasy, into deliberate irreality masquerading as sober fact, of exactly the same sort as "The Nose." Madgie's epistolary exploit is no different in kind from Major Kovalyov's runaway nose, and the author's final comment in that tale can serve the former case just as well as the latter: "Well then, and where don't absurdities occur?—Still, however, when you think about it, in all this there really is something. Whatever you may say, such happenings do occur in the world—not often, but they do occur." It is the principle of indeterminacy at work in this mad world. One dog can write to another, and a nose can leave its customary place and become a bureaucrat—seldom, but it can happen!

Incidentally, it should probably be pointed out that the motif of the dog's conversational and epistolary ability was gleaned by Gogol from E. T. A. Hoffmann, who had followed up Cervantes' *Coloquio de los perros* with his tale *Nachricht von den neuesten Schicksalen des Hundes Berganza.* Berganza, as with Cervantes, can speak only on occasion, by the special intervention of heaven; and he is quite incapable of writing. But Hoffmann's tomcat Murr can not only write, but becomes something of an author—at any rate, he contributes his part to a rather complex work by writing his "Views on Life" on the reverse of some page-proofs of his master Kreisler's autobiography! The reactions of Poprishchin and of Hoffmann's narrator to hearing a dog speak are remarkably similar: when Hoffmann's persona hears groans and bitter words as he crosses a city park in the night, and sees a large bulldog, he reflects: "Without a doubt it was he who had sighed and spoken those words; and this of course struck me as a little strange, since I had never heard a dog speak so intelligibly."[23] Poprishchin, having first overheard the two poodles exchanging greetings on the street, reflects: "I admit, I was quite astonished at hearing him talking in human fashion. But afterward, when I considered all this properly, I ceased to be astonished. Actually, a great number of such occurrences have already happened in the world."[24] He then gives as instances the report that in England a fish was heard to utter "two words in an unknown language," while two cows reportedly walked into a shop and asked for a pound of tea! After such incidents, who could be surprised at hearing two dogs discuss their interrupted correspondence!

Later Tales

In the period between the publication of *Mirgorod* and *Arabesques* (1834) and Pushkin's death (1837) Gogol wrote two stories "The Nose" and "The Carriage," which Pushkin published in 1836 in his periodical *The Contemporary*. During 1839-40 Gogol wrote his last great tale, "The Overcoat," which was first published in the author's *Complete Works* in 1842. Gogol had spent considerable time abroad during 1836 and 1837; under the influence of his experiences in Paris and Rome he started what was intended to be a serious novel, named for its heroine *Annunziata*. Only a fragment was ever completed of this work, which was revised in 1841 and also published in *Complete Works,* 1842. The fragment is titled "Rome." It is very inferior Gogol, and gives no indication that the world has lost much by the author's failure to complete the work. "The Portrait" was entirely rewritten, and the new version also published in 1842 in *Complete Works.*

"The Carriage"[25] is a trifle, no more than an amusing anecdote. Unlike the other tales written after *Mirgorod,* it is laid not in St. Petersburg, but in an unnamed southern town.[26] The entire story seems to have been constructed as background for the "punch line," when the General on opening the carriage door discovers Chertokutsky, hung over and in his dressing-gown, cowering inside, and simply remarks: "Ah, so you're here!" and departs with his officers. Leading up to this climax are some entertaining sketches of the sleepy little country town, suddenly brought to life by the arrival of a cavalry regiment to be stationed in the locality, and of the local gentry, and especially of Chertokutsky, who is described as a very typical officer, who never lets anyone forget that his service was with the cavalry:

> Pythagoras Pythagoravich Chertokutsky, one of the provincial aristocrats of B— district, was the most noteworthy of the landowners. He made more noise than anyone else at the elections, and had arrived there in a small equipage. He had served previously in one of the cavalry regiments and was one of its notable and conspicuous officers. He was conspicuous at least at numerous balls and assemblies, wherever the regiment had wandered: for the rest, inquiry could be made about this of the young ladies of Tambov and Simbirsk provinces. It is very possible that he might have developed in other provinces this profitable reputation, if he had not gone into retirement through a certain circumstance which is usually designated as an "unpleasant-

ness"; whether in years gone by he had given someone a box on the ear, or someone had given him one, I have no certain recollection: the fact is only that he had been asked to retire. For the rest, he had by no means been put off balance by this; he wore a frock-coat with a high waist after the pattern of a military uniform, [he wore] spurs on his boots, and moustaches under his nose, because without these the gentry might have supposed that he had served in the infantry, which he contemptuously referred to sometimes as "the infantrance" and sometimes as "the infantillery." [...] He seemed to smell out where a cavalry regiment was stationed, and always used to turn up to visit the officers....[27]

"The Carriage" has never been seen as a particularly significant piece, even by those who believe that Gogol always wrote his humorous sketches with serious intent. The satire in it is harmless and whimsical, rather than devastating; and the tale is of interest chiefly as a splendid example of Gogol's ability to make something of the merest shadow of a plot.

"The Nose,"[28] on the contrary, is one of the most complex, and certainly one of the most controversial things that Gogol ever wrote. The most diverse interpretations have been put upon it, from the solemn Marxist orthodoxy, that it was written as an expose of the vulgar, trivial capital society of the reign of Nikolai I, to the predictable Freudian analysis in which Major Kovalyov's nose becomes a sexual symbol.[29] As a matter of fact, a certain amount of truth can be found in most of these interpretations. Their chief failing is the claim to exclusiveness. Even the Freudian interpretation cannot be rejected *in toto:* Gogol's principal literary model for "The Nose" was Laurence Sterne's *Tristram Shandy,* in which also a nose plays a very large part—not, to be sure, as an independent entity—and Sterne's needlessly emphatic assertions that when he says "nose," it is precisely a nose that he means, and not some other part of the anatomy, as dirty-minded people may suspect, are evidence enough that the ambiguity was intended. Gogol's Kovalyov, moreover, is portrayed as a confirmed woman-chaser, beginning with the incidental note that "if he met with some pretty little [seller of false shirt-fronts], he used to give her in addition to this, a secret commission, adding: 'Just ask, darling, for Major Kovalyov's apartment.'" But a reader approaching "The Nose" without interpretive preconceptions must certainly find the chief clue to its meaning to be precisely that which Gogol's admired friend Pushkin mischievously appended to his verse tale *The Little House in Kolomna:* "Here's a moral for you: in my opinion it's dangerous to engage a cook gratis; and for him who has been born male it's odd and useless to deck himself out in a petticoat; it will sometimes be necessary for him to shave his beard, which is inconsistent with a lady's nature ... More than this you'll squeeze nothing out of my tale."[30] In other words, the tale exists for itself, and any attempt to read instructive meaning into it is time wasted. The most satisfactory interpretations of "The Nose" to be found, in either Russian or English are, in my opinion, those of Vsevolod Setchkarev and of Donald Fanger.[31]

"The Nose" underwent a number of partial revisions. It was first submitted (in 1835) to the periodical *Moscow Observer,* which rejected it as "vulgar" and "dirty." In this original version the whole incident of Major Kovalyov's disappearing nose was explained as a dream[32]—exactly as Pushkin's coffin-maker's encounter with a group of his late clients is explained. Gogol dropped this motivation for the version published in *The Contemporary* (1836), to the great benefit of the story. It is his purpose precisely to leave the extraordinary incident unexplained. Both published versions (1836 and that of the 1842 *Collected Works*) were subjected to some vexatious and ridiculous changes imposed by censorship. Particularly, the episode in which the Nose, as a state councillor, visits the Kazan Cathedral to pray and is approached there by a deferential Kovalyov, had to be omitted, and a visit to the Merchants' Mart substituted. There was also some alteration required in the description of the district superindent of police, who is characterized in the original manuscript as "a great patron of all arts and manufactures; but he preferred the government banknote to everything else. 'That's a material thing,' he habitually said, 'there's nothing better than that: it doesn't ask for food, it doesn't take up much room, there's always place for it in the pocket, and it doesn't break if you drop it.'"[33]

According to Viktor Vinogradov, who has made an exhaustive study of the subject and composition of "The Nose,"[34] the subject of the tale is less novel than it would appear: a great deal of what Vinogradov calls "nosology," both literary and quasi-medical, was appearing in the press during the 1830s. Much of this had to do with so-called "rhinoplastic surgery," or the restoration of noses accidentally or purposely cut off. Gogol's fantasy, accordingly, fitted the current "nosological" fashion; but it can by no means be explained as inspired by the fashion. It has its own raison d'être.

The story is constructed as two parallel episodes, tantalizingly juxtaposed as though supplementing each other, and yet never actually coming in contact. In the first the drunken barber Ivan Yakovlevich discovers a nose baked in a loaf of his wife's bread, and recognizes it as belonging to Collegiate Assessor Kovalyov, whom he shaves twice a week. He is appalled at the thought that the police may find stolen goods on him (!), and succeeds in dropping the nose, wrapped in a rag, into the Neva, but is picked up by the police as a suspicious character. The second, which purposely begins with the same sentence as the first, but with a different subject: "The barber Ivan Yakovlevich woke up quite early—"; "Collegiate Assessor Kovalyov woke up quite early,"—continues with Kovalyov's discovery that his nose is unaccountably missing, leaving in its place only a blank space "as smooth as a pancake." The rest of the second section recounts the efforts of the Major (Kovalyov prefers to sport the military title equivalent to that of his civil rank) to recover his nose and put it back in place. At the beginning of the third section the nose is back in place as unaccountably as it had disappeared. The barber comes in to shave his client; both men are painfully self-conscious about the nose, but neither has a word to say on the subject, and no explanation is ever hinted at that would connect the one incident with the other. In fact, Gogol deliberately negates any such connection. When the Major meditates on the strange occurrence, he notes that the barber shaved him on Wednesday, and the nose was in place all day Wednesday and Thursday. It was apparently on Friday that it disappeared. Ivan Yakovlevich is picked up by the police, but although the officer who returns the nose to Kovalyov speaks darkly of the barber's complicity in the affair, it is for the theft of a strip of buttons that he is held. Ivan Yakovlevich's wife accuses him vociferously as a careless drunkard and assumes that he has cut off the nose unwittingly, but her suspicion is clearly unfounded—and in any case, its presence in a loaf of her freshly baked bread would seem to implicate her in carelessness equal to her husband's! In short, the author has made every possible effort to cancel every explanation, rational or irrational, for the mystifying occurrence.

The second section is the longest of the three. Kovalyov, on discovering the absence of his nose, goes out of the house and looks for a cab. To his surprise, he sees his nose get out of a carriage at a house door, where he is evidently leaving a calling-card. Kovalyov trails the nose, who is wearing the uniform of a State Councillor (three ranks above Kovalyov's own!), and follows it into the Kazan Cathedral, where he timidly accosts it, and is snubbed. Kovalyov then goes to the Police Chief, who is not at home. He next tries to put a notice in the newspaper, but is told that this is impossible—someone might be offended! The clerk gives him an instance of such an unpleasantness:

> "Last week there was such a case. An official came in, in just the same way you did just now, and brought a notice—the price came to two rubles seventy-three kopecks—and the whole content consisted of the fact that a black-haired poodle had run away. What could there be in this, it would seem? But it turned out to be a libel: the poodle was a cashier—in what department I don't remember."[35]

Kovalyov goes next to the local police inspector (the amateur of government banknotes), who offends him by the curt pronouncement that a respectable man doesn't have his nose pulled off. On reaching home Kovalyov meditates on the matter, and concludes that the staff-officer's widow Podtochina, whose daughter Kovalyov has been playing around with without serious matrimonial intentions, has employed some witches to steal his nose. But at this moment a police officer appears, with the nose wrapped in a piece of paper. The double character of the nose appears here most clearly: the appendage is a mere inanimate thing at this moment, stuffed into the officer's pocket. But in explaining the circumstance, the officer notes:

"It was apprehended almost on the road. He had already taken a seat in the diligence and was intending to ride off to Riga. And a passport had even been made out in the name of a certain official. And the strange thing is that I myself took him at first for a gentleman. But luckily I had my glasses with me, and I saw at once that it was a nose. I'm nearsighted , you know, and if you were to stand right in front of me, I would see only that you had a face, but I couldn't distinguish a nose or a beard or anything. My mother-in-law, that is, my wife's mother, also can see nothing."[36]

Incidentally, the officer's speech affords two splendid instances of Gogol's comic devices: the complete illogicality of citing a mother-in-law's nearsightedness as an explanation of one's own; and the solemn elaboration of the obvious—"my mother-in-law, *that is, my wife's mother,*" as though the word *teshcha* could mean anything else!

Kovalyov's joy in recovering his nose is soon dashed, when he discovers that it won't stick to the blank spot on his face, and even the doctor who is summoned can do nothing to help matters beyond suggesting that the nose be pickled in spirits and kept in a bottle! Kovalyov then returns to his suspicions about Mme Podtochina, to whom he writes a letter of accusation. To this he receives a ludicrously ungrammatical reply that convinces him that his charges are unfounded. The section ends with a description of how Major Kovalyov's predicament becomes the subject of the wildest rumors throughout the city (cf. the rumors that fly about town in *Dead Souls* after the Governor's ball).

Section 3 begins again with Kovalyov's waking—happily, this time, with his nose quite mysteriously back in place. The barber shaves him, and Kovalyov gaily resumes his interrupted social life.

The final paragraph of the story is in the form of a scolding review, pointing out the various incongruities and absurdities in the tale, and ending with the significant passage:

But what is stranger, what is the most incomprehensible of all, is this: how can authors pick such subjects? I acknowledge, this is *quite* incomprehensible, it is perfectly—no, no, I don't understand it at all. In the first place, there is decidedly no profit to the country in it; in the second place—but in the second place too there is no profit. I simply don't know what this.... [37]

Of course the incoherence and the unfinished sentence are intended as a spoof of the style of reviews in such a periodical as *The Northern Bee;* but I think Gogol is using the word *pol'za* in this context in two senses: there is "no profit to the country"—that is, "The Nose" has no didactic purpose, overt or hidden; and there is "also no *profit*"—financial, that is, for the author. Gogol was not writing for gain; his story "The Portrait," especially in its second version, is indication enough of his aversion to art perverted for financial profit.

The form in which Gogol chose to cast his tale is that of a sober, factual newspaper account, complete with dates and names, where possible. It begins: "On March 25th there occurred in St. Petersburg an unusually strange event. The barber Ivan Yakovlevich, who resides on Voznesensky Prospect (his surname is lost, and even on his sign—on which there is the representation of a gentleman with a lathered cheek and the inscription 'Also lets blood'—nothing further is set forth)." At the end of the first section, apologetically, as it were, the reporter breaks off at the moment when the district police officer accosts Ivan Yakovlevich in the tavern: "But here the incident is completely shrouded in fog, and of what happened next absolutely nothing is known." In just the same way the second section ends with the words: "Following this—but here again the whole incident is shrouded in fog, and of what happened next absolutely nothing is known." The third section records the return of Kovalyov's nose, and adds merely: "This happened on April 7th."

A modern reader must inevitably be reminded in reading "The Nose" of the opening of Franz Kafka's story "The Metamorphosis": "After an unquiet night, Gregor Samsa awoke one morning to find himself transformed into some kind of enormous cockroach."[38] The phlegmatic report of an utter absurdity is the same in both tales, but the entire tone of Kafka's nightmarish masterpiece is entirely different. The absurdity of "The Metamorphosis" is the image of the depressing absurdity of life itself, and Samsa's plight reflects in a mostrous physical form the metaphysical *Angst* of Everyman faced with a realization of this absurdity. Not so with "The Nose": Major Kovalyov's life is momentarily deranged (from March 25 to April 7), his social career and his amorous conquests curtailed; but the moment his nose resumes its wonted place, everything is as though nothing had happened, and it can be assumed that he forgot the whole incident and hoped everyone else would do the same. *Angst* has no place in the wholly superficial world of a Major Kovalyov.

A word should be said about Gogol's use in "The Nose" of his favorite comic devices. The illogicality of the police officer's references to his mother-in-law's near-sightedness has been noted. Other instances are numerous. Thus, the reporter's first mention of Ivan Yakovlevich's wife takes this form: "Ivan Yakovlevich woke quite early and smelled hot bread. Raising himself up a little on the bed, he saw that his wife, a quite respectable lady, *who loved to drink coffee* [my italics], was taking out of the oven some freshly baked loaves." Praskovya Osipovna's fondness for coffee is totally irrelevant to the case, and merely contributes a specious air of factual accuracy to the reporting. Again, having trailed his errant nose into the Cathedral, Kovalyov tries to "put it in its place" in a blundering speech that ends with:"Why, you are my own nose!" The nose replies: "You are mistaken, my dear sir. I am myself independently [*sam po sebe*]. Furthermore, there can be no close relationship between us. Judging by the buttons of your uniform, you must be serving in a different department." The final sentence is a prime example of the pseudo-logical deduction: you are employed in a different department; *therefore* there can be no close relation between us.

Sometimes Gogol's absurd effects derive, like these examples, from the apparatus of logical thought applied to nonsense; but sometimes it is syntax rather than logic that suffers. Mme Podtochina, the staff-officer's widow, displays this kind of absurdity with particular brilliance. She begins her letter to Major Kovalyov as follows: "Your letter astonished me extraordinarily. I acknowledge to you frankly, I didn't at all expect, and still more with regard to the unjust reproaches on your part." This is almost a match for the tangled *non sequiturs* of Ivan Nikiforovich's legal petition.

During his short literary career Gogol wrote a number of critical articles, beginning with the 1829 essay "*Boris Godunov, a* Poem by Pushkin" and ending with the several "letters" in *Selected Passages from a Correspondence with Friends* which deal with literary subjects. The latter will be considered in their appropriate place; but two other works of the intervening period deserve at least brief mention. "A Few Words about Pushkin" (published in *Arabesques* in 1835, but written in 1832) and "On the Development of Periodical Literature in 1834 and 1835" (published in 1836 in Pushkin's journal *The Contemporary*). Both these pieces belong to Gogol's apogee as a writer and are still uncontaminated by the morbid religiosity of his last decade, when he misread both his own and his friends' work so consistently as to vitiate his criticism.

"A Few Words about Pushkin,"[39] although like most contemporary criticism lacking in concrete analysis and inclined to dwell on the exotic— the Caucasus mountains and "Crimean nights"—in its subject's verse, does at least correctly distinguish the salient features of Pushkin's style. It begins with the definition of Pushkin as a "national poet," noting however that "genuinely national character consists not in description of the *sarafan,* but in the very soul of the people." "A poet can be national even when he is describing a quite alien world, but yet looks at it with the eyes of his national element, the eyes of the whole people, when he feels and speaks so that it seems to his countrymen that it is they themselves feeling and speaking." Gogol then goes on to a very perceptive definition of the peculiar qualities of Pushkin's style. "If one must speak of those qualities which constitute Pushkin's proper character, that distinguish him from other poets, these consist in an extraordinary rapidity in description and in an uncommon art of signifying a whole object in a few traits."

The exotic in Pushkin's poems—Gogol obviously has the *Prisoner of the Caucasus* and *The Fountain of Bakhchisaray* particularly in mind, though he does not name them—attracts the crowd, particularly the younger element, but they find depictions of everyday life (probably *Eugene Onegin, Count Nulin, The Little House in Kolomna,* etc.), flat and disappointing. Here Gogol drops in a personal reminiscence. As an amateur painter he had done a landscape with a dead tree in the foreground. A country neighbor criticized it with the words: "A good artist chooses a sturdy, beautiful tree, on which the leaves would be fresh and well grown, not dry." The young artist remarks that in his childhood he was vexed by such a judgment, but later extracted from it a certain wisdom: "to wit, what pleases and does not please the crowd." Applying this anecdote to Pushkin he declares: "The more ordinary an object is, the higher must the poet be to extract the uncommon from it, and for this uncommon to be, *inter alia*, the perfect truth."

Pushkin's lyric verse ("his small compositions, that delightful anthology") is marked by the utmost simplicity. "Here is not that cascade of eloquence that attracts only by verbosity.... Here there is no eloquence, here there is only poetry: no kind of external brilliance, everything is simple, everything decorous, everything filled with an inner brilliance which is not at once descried; everything is laconism, such as pure poetry always is." The essay ends with the lamentation that the number of readers capable of appreciating the great poet's true merits can be counted on one's fingers.

"On the Movement of Journalistic Literature in 1834 and 1835"[40] is a polemical document, containing in essence a program for the future development of criticism in Russia. It takes the form of, first, a review of the leading periodicals of the two years in question—the *Reading Library*, the *Northern Bee*, the *Son of the Fatherland* with its adjunct the *Northern Archive*, *Literary Supplements to the Invalid*, the *Moscow Telegraph* with its supplement *Molva*, which Donald Fanger neatly englishes as "Talk of the Town." The *Reading Library* with its enormous circulation of 5000 dominates the scene journalistically, and its editor Senkovsky has things his own way in matters of criticism, although he has avowedly no principles of criticism to serve as a guide; according to Gogol:[41] "in his reviews there is neither positive taste, nor negative—there is none of any kind at all." Serious writers, irked by this situation, banded together to issue the new periodical *Moscow Observer*, in an attempt to break the *Reading Library's* virtual monopoly. The new periodical began with a programmatic and polemical article by Shevyryov in its first issue, directed against literary commercialism. Gogol judges this blast to be unfortunate, in that the rise of commercialism was inevitable, given the increasing market for periodicals. But in inveighing against commercialism Shevyryov was writing in the interests of his own class of literary men, and in a manner scarcely comprehensible to the ordinary reader. He should rather have "directed his attention to the poor subscribers," who had "purchased inferior goods and still congratulated themselves on their purchase." In any case, the *Moscow Observer* had got off to a bad start by having as its editor an unknown (Androsov), by lack of advance advertising (its adversaries, the *Reading Library* and the *Northern Bee* controlled the advertising media) and by carelessness in punctuality of issuance. After a blast at "Baron Brambeus" (i.e., Senkovsky), who had impudently characterized himself in an article in the *Reading Library* as the legislator of a new literary school, the *Moscow Observer* had lapsed into silence and thereby won the contempt of its entrenched foes.

Gogol goes on to declare that a periodical must have a set of principles, a direction of its own, but he fails to find such in any of the leaders of the field. For example, the *Moscow Herald,* which he regards as one of the best, promised its readers to keep them abreast of Russian and West European literary events of importance: yet in the two years reviewed (1834-35) one would gather the impression that *nothing* of importance had taken place in the literary world. In these two years, however, as Gogol indignantly points out, (1) Walter Scott died, "the great chronicler of the heart, of nature and life, the fullest, vastest genius of the XIXth century"; (2) A disquieting literary phenomenon had arisen and swept like a comet over Europe from the country of its birth—by which cryptic description he means the so-called *école frénétique* of Jules Janin and his ilk. This phenomenon had its repercussions even in Russia; he does not mention that he himself was strongly affected by it! (3) "The reading of novels, of cold, boring tales, was popularized to a great degree, and a general indifference to poetry became very evident"; and (4) new editions of Derzhavin and Karamzin had come out, which should have been the occasion for a reappraisal of the significance of these great figures for their country's literature. None of the questions raised by these capital developments in European literature found treatment in the Russian periodicals of 1834-35.

What did the journalists then write about? They wrote about their present concerns, to wit, themselves. He breaks down this accusation into four heads: (1) "Disregard for their own opinions": the critics never analyze a work they approve and state in what regards it is good. Rather they write: "This book is marvelous, unusual, unheard of, a work of genius, the first in Rus; it is sold for fifteen rubles; its author is above Walter Scott, Humboldt, Goethe, Byron. Get[the book], have it bound and put it in your library; buy the second edition too and put it in your library; there's no harm in having two copies of a good thing." Yet after all this extravagant praise the same reviewers presently have exactly contrary words about the same books, to the readers' utter bewilderment. (2) "Literary unbelief and literary ignorance." One never sees the names of the great and established (Russian) writers of the past, with whom a new writer under review might be compared, so that it appears as though Russian literature is simply without roots. Yet the reviewers will always compare some miserable hack work with Shakespeare, whom they have never read! (3) "Want of a pure aesthetic enjoyment and taste." Glimmers of such qualities may be seen in the Muscovite journals, but never in those of St. Petersburg. The writings of Shevyryov form an honorable exception. (4) "Triviality in ideas and a trivial dandyism." Important questions and ideas are shunned, and the reviewers strive above all to be amusing. An instance is Senkovsky's ridiculous nit-picking over the somewhat archaic but perfectly intelligible demonstratives *sei* ("this") and *onyi* ("that"). This is the level of Russian criticism!

Why have no contemporary writers of real merit spoken out against this debasement of criticism? He names Zhukovsky, Krylov and Vyazemsky. Are they loath to soil their hands in the dirty business of journalism? "We must only observe, that criticism founded on profound taste and intelligence, the criticism of a lofty talent has an equal value with every kind of original production: in it is visible the writer being reviewed; in it is visible even more the one reviewing. Criticism marked by talent outlives the ephemeral character of a journal's existence. For the history of literature it is priceless."

As Donald Fanger rightly notes,[42] this article should forever dispel the mistaken picture of the young Gogol as an esthete lost in rapturous abstractions. "Here he calls in the most practical terms for what amounts to the deliberate fostering of a literary culture—the marshaling of a usable past, the illuminating of present tendencies at home and abroad—by writers turned critics."

Gogol underwent a spiritual and emotional crisis in 1841, the results of which were catastrophic for his art. Nothing written after that date is comparable to the early pieces, and most of it is embarrassingly bad. To the beginnings of the post-crisis period belongs the revised version of "The Portrait,"[43] which is in every way inferior to the original. Gogol was always very sensitive to criticism, and the unfavorable reaction of critics, especially Belinsky, to the supernatural elements in "The Portrait" induced him to attempt a version in which the sinister influence of the old usurer's likeness is given a presumably naturalistic interpretation: the painter (significantly his name, originally Chertkov, obviously derived from *chert,* "devil," is now changed to Chartkov) has a nightmare in which the old man in the portrait visits him; the accidental discovery in the frame of the portrait of a secret niche with a roll of gold coins is the push needed to turn him away from "pure" art to a crass commercialism. The denouement of the story is the same as in the original version. The second part of the tale suffered more serious alteration than the first. A group of buyers at an art auction is puzzled and repelled by the extraordinarily lifelike eyes of a dusty old portrait. The lively bidding for the painting is interrupted by a young artist (a soldier in the original), who tells the company what he knows of its story. It had been painted by his father, the portrait of a mysterious old usurer; but the painter had been so repelled by his subject and so disquieted by the emotional effect of his work on himself that he had refused to finish the painting. The old man died, and the unfinished painting passed through several hands, each time accompanied by a strange psychological change in its possessor and in some cases by tragedy. The artist's father, who in the second version is a very unimpressive and banal figure, explains to his son that he has always regretted having painted the picture, and asks the younger artist to destroy it, if he ever comes across it. The entire theme of the old man as Antichrist and the painting as a physical habitation for his soul after death is dropped in the revision. The older artist, as in the original, becomes a monk, and wins spiritual peace through asceticism and religious painting. A hint of the original motivation is retained, as the artist's confession to his son evidences:

> "There is one occurrence in my life," he said,—"To this day I cannot understand what that strange figure was, of which I painted a representation. It was precisely some kind of diabolic phenomenon. I know, the world rejects the existence of the Devil, and for that reason I shall not speak of him. But I shall say that I painted him with revulsion, and I did not feel at that time any love for my work. I tried to subdue myself by force, and callously, suppressing everything, to be faithful to nature. That was not a creation of art, and therefore the feelings which take possession of everyone when they look at it are rebellious feelings, disturbing feelings—not the feelings of an artist, because an artist, even in agitation, breathes repose."[44]

At the end of the young artist's narrative the company at the auction turn toward the easel where the painting has stood—and it is gone! "Stolen!" echoes through the crowd. In the original, of course, the painting is supernaturally replaced by a banal landscape.

In this version of the story may be seen Gogol's increasing revulsion against what might be termed "realism at all costs," and his feelings of horror at his own "sin" in picturing evil in such works as *The Inspector General* and *Dead Souls*. There is also, even more pronounced than in the first version, the feeling that the artist who creates with material gain as his goal sells his soul and creates nothing of worth. We have seen a hint of this latter conviction in "The Nose," but the anti-didactic bias of the latter story, which perhaps derived from Pushkin and was never strongly felt by Gogol, has been wholly given up in "The Portrait." In the second version the tone is extremely preachy; Gogol has become obsessed by this period with the unfortunate notion that he has a mission and must instruct his readers both morally and aesthetically. The whole of the older artist's instruction to his son is a sermon of a content patently intended for the reader:

> You have talent; talent is the most precious gift of God—do not ruin it. Pursue, study everything that you see, submit everything to your brush, but in everything know how to find the inner thought, and above all strive to understand the lofty secret of creation. Blessed is the chosen one who possesses it. For him there is no lowly object in nature. In the trivial the artist-creator is just as great as in the great; in the despicable there is for him no longer the despicable, because it is permeated by the beautiful soul of its creator, and the despicable has already taken on lofty expression because it has passed through the Purgatory of his soul.[45]

Although the second version of "The Portrait" suppresses all the overtly supernatural elements of the first, and substitutes obscure psychological effects for them, the change was too slight to placate Belinsky, who continued to dislike the tale—and with good reason: the second version is neither a good horror story nor a convincing psychological thriller.

It is, however, something else, which the first version was to a much lesser degree—an aesthetic tract. Carl Proffer, in the final chapter of his work *The Simile and Gogol's "Dead Souls,"* presents the thesis that Gogol, anticipating the hostile criticisms which he knew his "poem" *Dead Souls* was certain to evoke, rewrote three of his earlier pieces for publication in his *Collected Works,* issued immediately after *Dead Souls,* Part I. These three pieces—the only ones so completely rewritten—are "Taras Bulba," "The Portrait," and the pseudo-dramatic sketch "Leaving the Theater after the Presentation of a New Comedy." Proffer believes, and offers cogent evidence for his theory, that the rewriting enabled Gogol, as he thought, to meet the criticisms of *Dead Souls,* either positively, by presenting in "Taras Bulba" a picture of a heroic Russian past, or didactically in the two other pieces. The second version of "The Portrait," in Proffer's words:[46] "develops the theory that the great artist must be a model of moral and spiritual perfection. Firmly and, as it turned out, tragically he believed that, like the artist-monk in 'The Portrait,' he had to devote years to conscientious self-purification before he could create the heroes of virtue he envisaged as the antitheses of the characters in the first part of *Dead Souls.*" Proffer does not touch on the point that Gogol may have thought of his intended positive heroes in the second part of the *poema* as a species of atonement, parallel with Father Grigory's ecclesiastical painting, created to compensate for the monstrous depiction of evil (the portrait), but this seems to be implied in the parallelism. It is certain that Gogol's "realism" tends to the psychological and eschews the crassly material and external portraiture of his earlier work in both the second "Portrait" and the second part of *Dead Souls.*

"The Overcoat"[47] is generally conceded to be Gogol's finest story; it is also the last complete one, and marks the end of the genuinely literary period in Gogol's life. It was begun in 1839, and not put into final form until 1841. It appeared in print for the first time in the 1842 edition of Gogol's *Complete Works.*

The first impetus toward the story, according to a reminiscence told by P. V. Annenkov,[48] was an anecdote told in Gogol's hearing by some of his acquaintances in the civil service about a poor official who was a passionate hunter. Having by untold privations accumulated 200 rubles to buy a new rifle, on his very first hunting expedition into the Finnish marshes he had lost the new acquisition into a tangle of rushes from which it was impossible to recover it. He returned home, took to his bed, and probably would have died of grief had not his friends, learning of the disaster, taken up a collection to buy him a new rifle. Gogol, perhaps remembering his own experience of having had to weather the St. Petersburg winter in a light summer overcoat, translated the rifle into a new overcoat, and let his hero actually die of the shock of losing it. But the "plot" of "The Overcoat" is the least significant thing about the tale. After stating it in four extremely short sentences, Vladimir Nabokov continues:[49] "This is all in the way of plot, but of course the *real* plot (as always with Gogol), lies in the style, in the inner structure of this transcendental anecdote." Elsewhere Nabokov states in his habitual provocative fashion: "His [i.e., Gogol's] work, as all great literary achievements, is a phenomenon of language and not one of ideas." However extreme this dictum may seem, it is most certainly valid for "The Overcoat."

    "The Overcoat" has been the object of many and diverse interpretations. The orthodox Marxist reading attributes to Gogol a profound feeling of sympathy for the ill-paid, down-trodden "little man" at the bottom of the official hierarchy, and a concomitant feeling of indignation against the callous officials of the upper ranks. On the other extreme, the "formalist school" of Russian criticism, represented here by Boris Eikhenbaum, sees in the tale only Gogol's consummate mastery of technical devices for effective composition. Eikhenbaum's essay "How Gogol's 'Overcoat' was Made" (first published in 1919)[50] deals in detail with these devices, among which the author lists the "humanitarian" passages which so impress the orthodox Marxist, and which the formalist sees as no more than rhetoric coolly devised to contrast with the humorous elements in the tale. Without a doubt Eikhenbaum goes too far in his rejection of any personal emotional involvement in Gogol's tale, but the formalist interpretation is a much needed antidote to the deplorable "social" misreadings of the radical critics of the 1850s and 1860s. Chernyshevsky, for example, writes: "Does Gogol mention any kind of defects in Akaky Akakievich? No, Akaky Akakievich is unconditionally right and good; his whole misfortune is attributed to the callousness, vulgarity, crassness of the people on whom his fate depends."[51] This is the most arrant nonsense, possible only in a critic wearing blinders. Gogol makes pitiless fun of Akaky Akakievich as so intellectually impoverished as to be incapable of even framing an intelligible sentence, a copying-machine whose mental capacities are not even equal to the arduous task of changing the first to the third person in extracting from a document! No defects indeed![52]

    There is no doubt that Gogol was a very conscious artist, and at the period in his life when "The Overcoat" was written, averse to overt didacticism. The tone of his tale is, as Eikhenbaum notes, not so much that of a narrator as of an actor performing a monologue.[53] The effects which the tale produces are certainly not haphazard or unconscious. Some of these, perfectly comparable with those in "The Nose" or "Nevsky Prospect," are humorous, e.g., the description of the tailor Petrovich who makes the overcoat; some are sharply satirical, e.g., the description of the "certain important person" whose cruel rebuff of Akaky Akakievich leads directly to the latter's death; and some are sentimental, e.g., the humanitarian passage referred to above, when the little man, teased by his fellow clerks, says so movingly: "Why do you torment me?" None of these passages has any greater emphasis than any other, and none can be taken accordingly as determining the tonality of the whole.[54] Gogol's attitude toward his story is that of an artist—coolly detached, fully aware of what he wants to do and how to do it. His attitude toward his subject is perhaps best seen in the passage that immediately follows the account of Akaky's death:

> There disappeared and went out of sight a being whom no one had defended, who was dear to no one, who was neither interesting to anyone nor had even drawn to himself the attention of so much as the naturalist who does not fail to fix on a pin a common fly and look at it under the microscope; a being who had borne submissively office mockeries and had gone to his grave without any kind of extraordinary fuss, but before whom, all the same, though just at the end of his life, there had flashed a bright stranger in the shape of an overcoat, which had for a moment animated the poor life, and upon whom also unendurable misfortune had thereafter descended, as it has descended upon the kings and the chiefs of this world.[55]

The very careful finish of this sentence, its rhythmical cadence, the deliberate build-up of the period to its climax, are typical of Gogol's rhetorical style at its best; and the image of the little man as so much less consequential to any fellow-man than even a common fly to a naturalist, places him in the writer's estimation. Looking back from this passage to the account of the feelings of the impressionable young clerk who seems to hear in Akaky's pleading "Let me alone! Why do you torment me?" the further words: "I'm your brother, you know," the earlier passage takes on a slightly different implication. The young clerk's distress may be interpreted as a reaction to the unwelcome notion: "Yes, this insignificant little insect is indeed my brother!" In any event, whatever Gogol's attitude toward Akaky Akakievich, and whatever the attitude he wishes his reader to take toward him, it is evident that the passage about the young clerk's reaction to Akaky's plea does *not* hold the key to the interpretation of the tale as a whole: the passage is not found in the original draft of the story, but was added later.

The author's skill in portraying the little man is evidenced in many details. His ridiculous name is one: Gogol goes to considerable pains to describe the scene at the baby's christening, when all the names suggested for him are real, but outlandish and very uncommon saints' names, so that at last it seems inevitable to give the child his father's name. And that name, together with the patronymic, creates an absurd impression with its fourfold repetition of the syllable "ak." Moreover, for the reader with a little knowledge of Greek, the name itself is significant: *akakos* means literally "guileless, innocent," and then "simple," with the connotation of "silly" or "simple-minded."

Another of Gogol's devices for portraying his "hero" is to be seen in reproduction of his speech. One of the first quotations of Akaky's own words is his halting explanation to Petrovich when he brings his old "dressing-gown" to be mended: *"A ia vot k tebe, Petrovich, togo—,"* an untranslatable series of vocables that if more or less literally put into English come out as: "But I [have] here for you, Petrovich, you know . . . " Gogol then remarks:

> It must be realized that Akaky Akakievich used to explain himself for the most part with prepositions, adverbs, and finally with such particles as have absolutely no meaning. If indeed the matter was very difficult, he even had the habit of not ending his phrase at all, so that very often, after beginning a speech with the words: "This really is perfectly, you know . . . ," nothing more was forthcoming, and he himself forgot, imagining that he had already said everything.[56]

This verbal impotence is a perfect clue to the nature of the man himself.

Doubtless the office teasing which he endured clouded to a certain extent Akaky's serene and routine-bound existence, but no unprejudiced reader of the story can interpret it as Gogol's intention to make an oppressive social system responsible for Akaky's lowly position. It must be remembered that one well-intentioned director had even tried to reward the faithful copyist by giving him a slightly more demanding kind of work to do, with the result that Akaky was so thrown off balance by having to change an original first person to the third in the documents that he begged to be allowed to go back to his safe routine. For such a clerk promotion could hardly be thought of in any system. Recognition of this fact, of course, does not imply that Gogol saw no faults in the system. His savagely sarcastic portrayal of "a certain important person" of general's rank (actual privy councillor, grade 2), who made it a custom to address all petitioners of lower rank than his with "How dare you?" and "Do you know to whom you are talking?" is sufficient to absolve him from the charge of seeing only good in the Russian bureaucracy. But it must be noted, even so, that the rank-conscious "important person" has pangs of conscience for his all too successful crushing of Akaky Akakievich, even before the latter's vengeful ghost makes his dramatic appearance to recover or replace his stolen overcoat. And Akaky's office companions take up a collection for him after that misfortune—inadequate, to be sure, to replace the precious garment, but evidencing at least a certain humanitarian impulse.

For those critics who believe that Gogol in "The Overcoat" or *The*

Inspector General or *Dead Souls* was a consistent realist, who had safely overcome "the illusions of romanticism," the ending of "The Overcoat" constitutes a serious stumbling-block. Why, after the "realism" of the pitiful story of Akaky and the sunset glamor of his new overcoat, does Gogol suddenly abandon the real world and introduce the little man's corpse haunting St. Petersburg's streets by night and robbing frightened officials of their overcoats? The answer is that there is just as much, and just as little "realism" in "The Overcoat" as in "The Nose," and it is just as reasonable in the one story for a poor man in death to turn highwayman as in the other for an official's nose to leave its normal place and assume an independent existence. Gogol is a pseudo-realist, who, when it suits him, can convey the illusion that he is portraying the real world, while actually his world is one of fantasy.

Thus, for example, the new overcoat which Petrovich fabricates is described in full and realistic detail—or so it seems. It is made of the best cloth, has a calico lining; the collar is of cat-fur, because marten is too expensive; it is sewn with silk thread, with double seams, etc. But what color is it? That important detail is somehow missing. And what of the overcoat's creator? We learn that Petrovich had been a serf, but was liberated; that he had a wife; and that he made a habit of getting drunk on holidays; and that when he was sober, as Akaky unfortunately found him, he charged more for his work than when drunk. As for his appearance:

> ... he was sitting at a broad, unpainted wooden table, and had crossed his feet under him, like a Turkish pasha. His feet, after the fashion of tailors who sit at their work, were bare. And the first thing that struck the eye was his big toe, which was very familiar to Akaky Akakievich, with a sort of huge nail, thick and strong, like a turtle's shell. On Petrovich's neck hung a skein of silk and one of thread, and on his knees was some sort of rag. He had already been trying for about three minutes to put a thread through the eye of a needle, had not succeeded, and so was very angry with the darkness and with the thread itself, muttering under his breath: "She won't go in, the bitch; you try my patience, you bastard!"[57]

But about Petrovich's face, for instance? Does he wear spectacles? What is his nose like? (Gogol is very fond of grotesque noses—perhaps because his own "resembled a duck's bill!") Do his ears protrude? The description, in which the big toe with its nail like a turtle's shell looms largest, is impressionistic. Only certain details are given, vivid in themselves, and covering up the absence of a complete picture.

Observing his insignificant subject at the moment of crisis brought on by the realization that his old "dressing-gown" is no longer reparable, and he must absolutely have a new overcoat, Gogol notes that once the initial shock had passed, and Akaky had resigned himself to the inevitable scrimping necessary to scrape together the money, a great change takes place in him:

From that time on his very existence became as it were somehow fuller, as though he were getting married, as though some other person were sharing his existence, as though he were not alone, but some sort of pleasant life companion had consented to walk the path of life with him—and this companion was no other than that same overcoat.... He became somehow livelier, even firmer in character, as a man who has at last defined and set a goal for himself.[58]

The tragedy and the comedy as well of "The Overcoat" are precisely in this spectacle of a drab, meaningless existence taking on a momentary, almost sexual excitement—when the exciting object is only an artifact of cloth, fur, etc. Moralists have sometimes seen Akaky's downfall as a justified retribution for so passionately attaching himself with all his being to such a trivial and mundane thing. Gogol makes this attachment both ridiculous and touching—and given the nature of Akaky Akakievich, inevitable.

As for the story's fantastic ending, it is a bravura piece, with the chief emphasis precisely on the realistic description of the supernatural. Thus, the first appearance of the apparition is carefully localized: "Throughout St. Petersburg rumors were suddenly circulated that at Kalinkin Bridge and far more distantly a corpse had begun to appear of nights in the form of an official." It should incidentally be noted that Gogol uses the word *mertvets,* "a dead man," "a corpse," for the apparition, *not,* as in the final paragraph, *prividenie,* "an apparition." The word conveys a far more concrete, "realistic" impression than would the word "ghost." The "realism" continues with the matter-of-fact treatment accorded the rumors: "Measures were taken by the police to apprehend the corpse at all costs, alive or dead [!], and punish him in the cruelest fashion, as an example to others [i.e., other corpses!]"[59] The corpse is, as a matter of fact, apprehended in the very act of snatching a frieze overcoat from someone's shoulders, but when the policeman making the arrest tries to revive his frost-bitten nose with a pinch of snuff, the "dead man" gives such a violent sneeze that everyone is spattered, and in the ensuing confusion the corpse disappears, after which the police have such a horror of the dead that they are afraid to arrest even the living!

The climax of the supernatural comes in the most realistic fashion. The "certain important person," on his way back from a party, decides to visit his mistress instead of going directly home. While he day-dreams in a luxurious glow in his sleigh, running over in his mind the delights of the evening, past and anticipated, he feels himself seized by the collar, and turning around, sees "a short man in a shabby uniform," in whom he recognizes with terror the dead Akaky Akakievich. The identification is made complete when the corpse addresses him with his habitual meaningless "you know" [*togo*], but more vigorously and decisively than in life: "Aha! So you're here at last! At last I've got you, you know, by the collar! It's *your* overcoat I want! You wouldn't exert yourself over mine, and bawled me out besides. Now give me yours!" In a terrible fright the "important person" throws off his overcoat and orders his driver to head for home—and with this episode the "haunting" ceases—on Akaky's part, that is. The final, soberly reported, incident evidently has nothing to do with him, but doubtless the "apparition" here is none other than the thug who had stolen Akaky's overcoat:

> And as a matter of fact, a certain Kolomna policeman saw with his own eyes an apparition [*prividenie*] appearing from behind a certain house; but being by nature somewhat weak.... he did not dare stop it, but just followed after it in the darkness until at last the apparition suddenly turned around and stopping, asked: "What do you want?"—and showed such a fist as you won't see even among the living. The policeman said: "Nothing," and immediately turned back. The apparition, however, was a good deal taller, was wearing an enormous moustache, and directing his steps, so it seemed, toward Obukhov Bridge, disappeared totally in the darkness of night.[60]

In all this account Gogol expends, mockingly, it seems, every effort to render the "corpse" as realistic as possible; the "apparition," on the other hand, whose supernatural fist so intimidates the policeman, is of course a living robber.

As in all his best mature work Gogol exploits in "The Overcoat" all the possibilities of the illogical. Note for example the solemn discussion of the origin of Akaky's surname, Bashmachkin. It is obvious, says the author, that this name derives from *bashmak,* "shoe." But how this could have come about is obscure, because "both his father, and his uncle, and even his brother-in-law, and absolutely all the Bashmachkins used to go in boots, having them resoled only about three times a year." There is a triple absurdity in this passage. Conceivably, though with little likelihood, the fact that the Bashmachkins wore boots instead of shoes could have some connection with the surname; but where does the brother-in-law fit in? (There is incidentally a slip here on Gogol's part, not apparent from an English translation, since "brother-in-law" in English can mean either a sister's husband or a wife's brother; but the Russian *shurin* can mean *only* the latter—and Akaky was never married!) As a final bit of illogic, the sentence trails off into mention of the Bashmachkins' habit of having their boots resoled *only* three times a year, as though this information were relevant to anything! Something of the same sort results from Gogol's frequent use of the adverbs meaning "even," which put an apparently important emphasis on certain words which on closer inspection prove to deserve no emphasis at all.[61] Thus for example summing up his preliminary expositional account of Akaky's service, Gogol writes:

> Thus flowed on the peaceful life of a person who knew how to be content with his lot on a salary of 400[rubles a year], and would perhaps have so flowed on up to advanced old age, had it not been for the various misfortunes that are piled up on life's road not only for titular, but *even* [my italics] for privy, court and every kind of councillors, and *even* [my italics] for those who give no counsel, and do not *even* [my italics] accept it from anyone themselves.[62]

Here the first "even," if interpreted logically, would imply that while titular councillors (grade 9) might be expected to meet with misfortune "on life's road," privy councillors (grade 3), actual (grade 4) and court councillors (grade 7) ought to be exempt, but are not! The second "even" suddenly takes the word *sovetnik* out of its bureaucratic sense ("councillor") and gives it its etymological sense ("counsellor") and solemnly assures the reader that misfortunes may befall *even* people who have nothing to do with "counselling" at all—who do not *even* accept it, much less give it— surely a rather gratuitous bit of information! In the description of Petrovich's lair it is noted that the tailor's wife, while frying some fish, had produced so much smoke in the kitchen "that it was impossible to see *even* the cockroaches"—with the absurd implication that these insects should have been the most conspicuous objects in the kitchen.

The significance of "The Overcoat" is too subtle and elusive to be formulated in any definitive fashion. Chizhevsky[63] interprets the matter from a religious point of view, and sees in Akaky's fixation of his whole human capacity for love on such an unworthy object as an overcoat Gogol's condemnation of such a perversion, and perhaps even the workings of the Devil himself through the tailor Petrovich as "Tempter." It is of course impossible to prove that this reading of the tale ("Gogol's story of the poor clerk is not humorous, but terrible") is wrong, but I think very few readers would accept it. Fanger puts the evaluation in my opinion more convincingly:[64]

> The metaphor [i.e., of a "pattern" in the story] is only approximate, but to the extent that it is valid it may suggest why those who claim "The Overcoat" is *not* about Christian charity and arbitrary authority, meekness and pride, poverty and comfort, justice, bureaucracy, city life, even literature itself—why such readers are as mistaken as those who assert that it *is* about these things. Respecting the peculiar mode of its being, it would be more accurate to say that the story is ultimately about significance and insignificance as such, in literature no less than in life.

Gogol left Russia in June 1836, for what turned out to be a very lengthy stay in western Europe. Except for eight months in 1839-40 and another eight months in 1841-42, he remained abroad for twelve years. He visited Switzerland, where he found the mountains appallingly ugly; he visited Germany briefly, where he derided the inhabitants as backwoods boors; he lived for a time in Paris, which he found at first intellectually stimulating, but ended by rejecting as empty and frivolous; and he spent most of his time in Italy, which he hailed ecstatically as his second homeland. He particularly loved Rome, and familiarized himself with the city in all its phases, ancient, medieval and modern. In 1839 he began what was to have been a serious novel, to be titled *Annunziata* after its heroine, a beautiful Roman girl of the lower classes, with whom the hero, an unnamed prince of old Roman family, falls in love. The novel never progressed beyond some forty pages, which were published under the title "Rome" after some revision in 1841, in *Complete Works* (1842).[65] The completed portion of the work consists of, first, an extravagant and rather ridiculous panegyric of the surpassing beauty of the girl Annunziata;[66] then a long explanation of the early life and education of the Prince, and of his impressions of the two cities Paris and Rome—material which despite an unconvincing disclaimer on Gogol's part patently reflects his own experiences; and finally a relatively short section describing the carnival at which the Prince first sees Annunziata, and his first attempt to discover who she is, for which purpose he enlists the help of a lower-class Roman named Peppe, who is amusingly described in a way faintly reminiscent of some of Gogol's Russian characters. The fragment breaks off, perhaps significantly, with the Prince's absorbed reverie as he views the panorama of his native city from the Janiculum:

> The sun was shining lower toward the earth; redder and more fiery became his radiance on the whole architectural mass; still more lively and still closer did the city become; still darker were the outlines of the pines; still bluer and more phosphorescent became the mountains; still more solemn and better prepared to go out, the air of the sky.... God, what a night! The Prince, absorbed by it, forgot both himself, and the beauty of Annunziata, and the mysterious destiny of his people, and everything on earth.[67]

The passage, incidentally, is a fair sample of Gogol's style in "Rome," which Belinsky, not altogether unjustly, described as Marlinskian. Gogol seems in the piece to be determinedly striving to be not himself, with unfortunately a great deal of success. There are unbroken pages of involved, turgid, semi-poetical rhapsody, ungraced by a spark of Gogol's habitual humor. The only exception is a passage relating the Prince's visit to one of Rome's back streets to find Peppe and his encounter with a group of typically gossipy and officious Roman women. About half of the fragment is devoted to the description of the Prince's gradual disillusionment with Paris, which comes to seem to him shallow and trivial, and his deepening love for the Rome he returns to after his father's death and which now satisfies all his instincts, aesthetic and spiritual.

"Rome" is one of Gogol's works which has apparently never had an English translator, and it is not hard to see why. As the impressions of a sensitive northerner, overwhelmed by the sensuous beauty of southern nature and southern people, "Rome" has some interest. It is closely akin in spirit to the paintings of the same period by Russian artists domiciled in Italy—e.g., Silvester Shchedrin, M. I. Lebedev, Karl Bryullov, etc. But Gogol, divorced from his native land, loses, like these artists, his originality and attractiveness and becomes only another nineteenth-century traveller, eager to record his impressions of a fascinating, exotic land. He contributes nothing to the literature either of Italy or of Russia.

Gogol's Dramatic Works: *The Inspector General* [*Revizor*]

In his "Author's Confession," written in 1847 as a kind of apologia for *Selections from a Correspondence with Friends,* Gogol looks back on his literary career and divides it sharply into two parts: before and after *The Inspector General.* Of the earlier period he writes:

> The reason for that gaiety which was remarked in my first writings to appear in print consisted of a certain spiritual need. I was afflicted by attacks of melancholy, inexplicable to me myself, which originated perhaps in my unhealthy condition. In order to distract myself, I used to think up for myself everything amusing that could possibly be imagined. I would think up perfectly ridiculous persons and characters, put them mentally into the most amusing positions, altogether without concern for the reason for this, the purpose of it, or what profit anyone would derive from it. Youth, a time when no kind of questions occur to the mind, instigated this. Here is the origin of those first works of mine, which made some people laugh as light-heartedly and uncontrollably as they did myself, and brought others into perplexity as to how such absurdities could enter into the head of an intelligent man. Perhaps with years this gaiety along with the need for self-distraction would have disappeared, and with it my writing. But Pushkin made me look at the matter seriously.[68]

Gogol goes on to explain how Pushkin chided him for not using his extraordinary ability to intuit character and "present it suddenly entire, as though alive," in a work of large compass. Pushkin gave Gogol the subject of *Dead Souls,* as he did also, says Gogol, of *The Inspector General.*[69]

> At this time I had myself already begun to think seriously,—the more so as those years had begun to approach when of itself the question arises for every action: why and for what purpose are you doing this? I saw that in my works I was laughing to no purpose, idly, myself not knowing why. If one is to laugh, then it is better to laugh powerfully, and at what actually merits general ridicule. In *The Inspector General* I decided to gather into one heap everything bad in Russia, such as I knew it then, all the injustices such as are done in those places and in those conditions where justice is most of all demanded of man, and laugh at it all at one stroke.[70]

As Gippius rightly remarks apropos of this passage:[71] "The words that in youth 'no kind of questions occur to the mind,' cannot be taken literally; not a few questions are posed and decided throughout Gogol's youthful work, beginning with *Hanz,* but they are all questions of the aesthetic consciousness, of the same origin as Gogol's early laughter." Beginning with *The Inspector General* Gogol is conscious of a mission, that of the comic artist "who can 'produce a good influence on society.'"

Of Gogol's sincerity in seeking by his later works "to produce a good influence on society" there can be no question. But precisely what kind of influence has he in mind? Belinsky and the liberals of his camp, and older Marxist writers such as Gukovsky, view his efforts as revolutionary and entirely political in nature: according to them, Gogol was campaigning against the social institution of serfdom and the political institutions of autocracy and bureaucracy. I believe this is an absolutely false interpretation: Gogol saw the tyranny and cruelty of landlords, the corruption of justice, the flagrancy of bribe-taking, the sloth and servility of officialdom, the ruthless chase after wealth and rank, and all the other vices which he pillories in *The Inspector General* and *Dead Souls,* but he saw them as private, individual vices, which the individual can correct by his own efforts once his eyes are opened to them. He had no thought whatever of altering the basis of his society, but was naively optimistic that if the individual sinners could be brought to mend their ways, Utopia would automatically result. When he appends to *The Inspector General* the epigraph: "Don't blame the mirror if your mug is crooked," the words are addressed not to society, or to the landowning class or to officialdom, but to the individual member of the comedy's audience.

Although his friend Sergei T. Aksakov reports that as early as 1832 Gogol was already seriously interested in the drama, it was only in the following year that he began writing a comedy called *Order of Vladimir, Third Class.* The comedy was never completed because the author realized, as he himself said, that the censors would never pass it. He later published four separate scenes—"The Morning of a Man of Affairs" (originally entitled "An Official's Morning"), "The Lawsuit," "Servants' Quarters," and "Fragment"—in his *Complete Works* (1842).[72] Two other fragments are preserved in manuscript: the first of these is a duplicate of much of "The Law-Suit," the second of the last part of "Servants' Quarters." The plot of the comedy was evidently fairly complicated, and perhaps occasioned too much difficulty in handling. A minor official (the "man of affairs") covets a decoration as a reward for his evidently rather commonplace services, and mentions his ambition to a "friend" who secretly envies and detests him. This "friend" finds the ideal opportunity of damaging the official (Ivan Petrovich Barsakov) when he discovers that Christopher Petrovich, Ivan's brother, is bringing a lawsuit against the former for falsification of their aunt's will. Perhaps this intrigue was to have resulted in keeping Ivan Petrovich from receiving "the order of Vladimir, Third Class," a blow which was to have unhinged his mind in the last act so that he imagines himself to be "the order of Vladimir, Third Class." A second plot line, with no discernable connection with the first, concerns a young official named Mikhail Andreevich, whose tyrannical mother plots to break up a love affair between him and a girl of "poor but honest" family. "Servants' Quarters" introduces several typical lackeys, household maids, a portly major-domo, etc., who discuss among other things a coming servants' ball and their contributions to it. Again there is no apparent link with the other plot lines.

It is clear, however, from the somewhat enigmatic fragments that

Gogol was already a master of pithy, character-revealing dialogue. The characteristics of mother and son in "Fragment" are particularly vivid, as is that of the major-domo Lavrenty Pavlovich in "Servants' Quarters." A disturbing awkwardness, however, is the extensive use of asides in these fragments, revealing the contrast between a speaker's real feelings and his words. Such asides are of course an old comic convention, but Gogol had learned by the time of *The Inspector General* to make more sparing use of them.

In 1834 Gogol was working on another comedy, to be called *Suitors,* which with considerable change was eventually published (in *Complete Works*) as *Marriage.* Work on this play had been suspended during the composition of *The Inspector General.* The comedy was staged (unsuccessfully) in 1843.

In a letter dated October 7, 1835, from St. Petersburg, to Alexander Pushkin, Gogol begs for the speedy return of his comedy *Marriage,* which he had submitted to the older writer for comments, mentions that he has begun *Dead Souls* and become bogged down in the third chapter, and then adds the following:

> Do me a favor, give me some subject,—it can be amusing or not, but at least a purely Russian anecdote. My hand is a-quiver to write a comedy in this [spare] time. If this doesn't come to pass, then my time will have been wasted, and I don't know what to do with my circumstances.... Do me a favor, give me a subject; in a trice there will be a five-act comedy, and I swear it will be funnier than the devil. My mind and belly are both starved...[73]

Pushkin's reply to this letter is lost, but since Gogol began writing *The Inspector General* almost at once, and in his "Author's Confession" states that Pushkin gave him the subjects of both *Dead Souls* and *The Inspector General,* it is generally assumed that the suggestion for the comedy was given in the lost letter. It is said that during his travels in the Volga region gathering material for his *History of Pugachev,* Pushkin had himself at one time been taken for a Petersburg official travelling incognito. But the "anecdote" was a familiar one, and many versions of it exist. Senkovsky[74] called the subject of *The Inspector General* "an old anecdote, known to everyone, a thousand times printed, told, and elaborated in various forms and in various languages." Of Russian parallels the closest seems to be Veltman's story "Roland Mad," considered earlier in this study.

In most respects *The Inspector General* is a most unconventional comedy. There is no conflict which must be brought to a satisfacary conclusion in the denouement. The complication consists of the age-old device of mistaken identity, which here becomes almost the whole plot substance, instead of a mere device of plot construction, as customarily. Moreover, most unusually, the mistaken identity is accidental, not planned: when Khlestakov is taken for the expected St. Petersburg official, he does nothing himself to further the deception, but simply takes advantage of the situation passively. Then the age-old convention that a comedy must turn on the plight of two lovers frustrated by some obstacle which will be triumphantly overcome in the denouement is not merely disregarded, but ridiculed: Khlestakov's "engagement" to Maria Anto-novna is a blatant parody. Finally, and perhaps most serious of all, the convention of *bonnes moeurs,* which demands that virtue be triumphant in a comedy, and vice properly punished, is defiantly flouted. There *is* no virtue in the play: all the characters are rascals in one degree or another, or at least vulgar and stupid; and Khlestakov goes successfully away with a considerable amount of money which the obliging mayor and his official associates have "lent" him as covert bribes. To be sure, the play ends with the announcement of the arrival of the real Inspector General, and the mayor and all his officials are flabbergasted: but there is no indication in the play itself that this Inspector will be any different from the one whom their fear has created in the person of Khlestakov. He *may,* of course, be averse to taking discreet bribes to close his eyes to geese in the courtroom, filth in the infirmary, a soldier's widow flogged, and the town merchants despoiled—but Gogol's play gives no indication of such a likelihood. Mayor Skvoznik-Dmukhanovsky has, according to his own word, hood-winked three governors; he will probably be able to take care of the real Inspector. Gogol's allegorical interpretation of the comedy—Khlestakov is the flighty, superficial, easily lulled conscience, the real Inspector is the genuine human conscience, which sternly arraigns the sinner on his death-bed—is a later fabrication, in no way pertinent to the original comedy.[75]

Other comedies have existed before *The Inspector General* which have flouted the conventions in one way or another: Molière's *Le Misanthrope* rejects the happy ending with the lovers united; Lesage's *Turcaret* lets rascality escape unpunished, etc.—but before Gogol no comic writer flouted all the established conventions so pointedly. The whole tenor of the comedy is satirical, and no one of the characters escapes ridicule. It is also, as Gogol promised Pushkin it would be, "funny as the devil."

In this respect it is instructive to compare *The Inspector General* with two of its Russian predecessors, Fonvizin's *The Minor* and Kapnist's *Chicane (Iabedá).* Both the latter have very funny individual scenes, but viewed on the whole, they are not so much funny as frightening. The tyrannical Prostakova of *The Minor* is too sinister to be amusing, and the comedy's "happy ending" is too flimsy and contrived to carry conviction. The cynical villainy of the corrupters of justice in Kapnist's play bids fair to prevail and rob an honest young man of his paternal inheritance. Only a most improbable *deus ex machina* ending saves the proprieties. In *The Inspector General* there may be no honest character, but equally there are no villains. The Mayor is guilty of accepting a bribe to let off an unmarried potential recruit from military service and of sending instead a married man; he has a woman flogged for insubordination, through a mistake; and he has squeezed numerous merchants into supplying him gratis with samples of their goods. The merchants themselves, however, are cheats and rogues, and deserve little sympathy. Everybody accepts and, when necessary, gives bribes (the Judge limits his takings to hunting dogs!); the Superintendent of Charitable Institutions is not only slovenly in the maintenance of the hospital, but also proves to be a malicious back-biter, denouncing his colleagues to Khlestakov; the School Superintendent is an incompetent ignoramus; and the town doctor is a German who can't even understand Russian. The landed proprietors, represented by Dobchinsky and Bobchinsky, are fools and busybodies. As for Khlestakov, he is no villain, only an empty-headed nobody. The good things of life—food, fine clothes, comfort, sex—are his passion, and his mind does not rise above them. He has lost all his money at cards on his way from the capital to his father's estate in Saratov, has run up a bill at the local inn which he has no means of paying, but would still rather go hungry than miss out on impressing the Saratov yokels with his modish St, Petersburg clothes. He is purely passive in his relations with the Mayor and the officials. Assuming that he does not want his incognito violated, the latter never reveal to him that he is being taken for an Inspector General; when the Mayor invites him to his own house and arranges it so that his hotel bill is evaded, and then one after another the various town officials offer him three-hundred ruble notes in "loan," he accepts it all as simple courtesy, obviously due to a person of his elegance and refinement. He "shoots a line" of the most outrageous nonsense at the Mayor's house, but this is clearly with no intent to foster the deception—he will doubtless treat the gullible backwoods society of Saratov to the same line when he returns home. He professes love to the Mayor's daughter in absurd clichés from romantic novels, and then with complete unconcern repeats the same nonsense to the girl's mother. He finally catches on that he is being taken for some sort of bigwig, and is so amused that he writes an account of his experiences for a St. Petersburg writer friend. Even in the matter of the "engagement" he takes no active part. When he is discovered on his knees in front of Anna Andreevna, the latter explains the embarrassing situation to her husband as Khlestakov's ardent suit for their daughter's hand, and Khlestakov acquiesces and plays his part. The "hero" of *The Inspector General* is one of the most passive characters in comedy. He is not even responsible for his timely getaway, which his servant Osip suggests as an act of elementary prudence, and his master accepts quite casually.

As Donald Fanger remarks,[76] "There is genius already in Gogol's making the false inspector a naif." A standard comic plot is that of the trickster tricked—Gogol himself was to use it later in his unsuccessful play *The Gamblers*—but by making Khlestakov merely passive he allows the creation within his comedy of what Gippius[77] calls an "internal" plot running parallel with the external. This internal plot hinges on the Mayor's self-deluded vision of himself as the father-in-law of a Petersburg bigwig and thus destined to rise to general's rank. The Mayor himself is totally responsible for this delusion—Khlestakov has no hand in creating it. At the same time the gullibility of the provincial officials and their evident awe of him encourage Khlestakov to create his own dream-world situation, that of a social lion, rich, powerful, a literary and musical genius (he has, so he admits, written not only *The Frigate Hope* [Marlinsky], and *Yury Miloslavsky* [Zagoskin], but *The Marriage of Figaro* [Mozart], *Robert le Diable* [Meyerbeer] and *Norma* [Bellini]!) and an intimate of the great. It must be noted that this double-sided "internal" plot has no structural connection with the external one. There have been many comedies about liars—Alarcón's *La Verdád sospechosa* is one of the best—but the liar's activity ordinarily brings about the denouement and is duly punished (cf. Shakhovskoi's "If You Don't Like It, Don't Listen"). Khlestakov "shoots his line" unpunished and gets away; the Mayor dreams his roseate dream until the Postmaster's fateful revelation, but neither Khlestakov nor the Mayor is responsible for the denouement: the internal and external plots come to a simultaneous but unconnected end with the announcement of the real Inspector's arrival.

The picture of the society of the small town into which Khlestakov has blundered as a sink of vice and corruption, inhabited by an "assemblage of monsters," and thus wholly unrepresentative of the real Russia, which the critics of the play conjured up, is entirely unfounded. It is a society of blatant vulgarity and wrongdoing, of gossip and backbiting and frivolity, of provincial ignorance and of arrogance paired with servility. This is not a pretty picture, but the vices portrayed are not serious enough to arouse indignation and loathing, as they are in *Chicane,* only a contemptuous amusement.

Is the picture realistic? In a literal sense, of course not. As Gogol has his critic complain, in "The Denouement of *The Inspector General,*" "everyone without exception is agreed that there exists no such city in all of Russia." The picture is a caricature, not a portrait, and like all caricatures, owes its effectiveness to exaggeration. The Judge's conclusion that an incognito visit from a *revizor* to an obscure provincial town must mean that Russia is about to go to war is a logical absurdity in itself, but typical of the kind of "thinking" that one might really have found in a backwoods town. The ridiculous Dobchinsky (Peter Ivanovich) and Bobchinsky (Peter Ivanovich), a pair who inevitably recall Tweedledum and Tweedledee, are not likely to have really existed anywhere—but their characteristics individually existed, and Gogol's art has simply combined these characteristics and exaggerated them. In a higher sense, realism is achieved in the play, even though no single figure is a copy of actuality. Exactly the same may be said of Gogol's masterpiece, *Dead Souls*.

What motivates the action of the play? In a classical comedy the action is set in motion when a pair of young lovers meets an obstacle to their happiness and steps are taken to overcome it. Thus, in Molière's *L'École des femmes,* Arnolphe is "educating" his ward Agnès to make her a good wife for himself, and the play consists of the successful ruses by which Agnès and her lover Horace outwit him and marry in his despite. In *The Inspector General,* however, there is no such mechanism, since there is no pair of young lovers. The whole action stems from a single primal emotion, to be sure,—but this is fear, not love. Every official in the unnamed town of the comedy has an uneasy conscience, especially the Mayor, and in the face of a visitation from a St. Petersburg inspector general, is frightened into taking action. This action consists in attempts, mostly monetary, to propitiate the visitor. The visitor himself, as we have seen, takes no action.

Fear creates a curious, unreal situation. Gippius has pertinently noted the prevalence in Gogol's mature writing of such unreal, chimerical situations. In *Marriage,* Kochkaryov busies himself with almost frantic zeal to get his friend Podkolyosin married, and his gratuitous efforts are matched by an equally gratuitous resistance on Podkolyosin's part. The "marriage" of the title is a pure chimera; no one in the play talks or thinks about anything else—and nothing whatever comes of all this fuss. In *Dead Souls Part I* the whole denouement—Chichikov's discomfiture and flight—results from the totally unmotivated rumor that his purchase of "dead souls" is somehow linked in sinister fashion with a plot to kidnap the governor's daughter! Here the fear of the town officials conjures up the chimera of Khlestakov as Inspector General; when the bubble bursts (the reading of Khlestakov's letter), the play is of course at an end.

The manner in which Gogol individualizes his characters is masterly. Except perhaps for Bobchinsky and Dobchinsky, who are intentionally an identical character duplicated, all the dramatis personae are given traits that mark them out as individuals. Thus Amos Fyodorovich, the Judge, has not only a penchant for hunting dogs, but a supposedly Voltairean, "free-thinking" cast of mind, which makes the Mayor's hair stand on end. The superintendent of schools, Luka Lukich Khlopov (his surname, not without significance, is derived from *khlop,* "bedbug"), is not only easy-going and lazy, but excessively timid. He has to be literally pushed by his fellow-officials into the room where the awe-inspiring "inspector" is receiving them one by one, and when in the presence, his wits fail him to such a degree that he can't find the right honorific for addressing Khlestakov, and professes himself incapable of having an opinion even on such a matter as whether blondes are preferable to brunettes! One of the most vividly characterized of the minor persons of the comedy is the locksmith's wife *(slesarsha),* whose husband the Mayor has put on the list of recruits. Her tirade against His Honor is hilarious:

He did it, the bastard, he did it! God strike him down in the other world and in this! If he has an aunt, may his aunt too have every kind of rotten luck, and if his father's alive, may he, the bastard, croak or cough his head off all his life, damn him! The tailor's son ought to have been taken—he was a drunkard, too—but his parents gave a rich present, and he lit on the son of the merchant's wife Panteleeva, but Panteleeva too sent his wife three pieces of cloth on the sly. So then he came to me. "What good's your husband to you?" says he. "He's no use to you at all." I'm the one to know about that, whether he's any use or not. That's my business, the bastard! "He's a thief," says he, "If he hasn't done any stealing now," says he, "that's all the same," says he. "He will steal, and anyway they'll take him next year for a soldier." And what's it like for me without a husband, the bastard! I'm a weak person, you low-life! May your whole family never see God's world! And if you have a mother-in-law, may your mother-in-law too—[78]

Gogol is always least successful in creating attractive women; but his satirical portraits of women are quite as vigorous and lifelike as those of the male sex. An example in *The Inspector General* is Anna Andreevna, the Mayor's wife, whose chief traits are an overpowering curiosity, an arrogant disdain for the other ladies of town, and a petulant impatience with her daughter, who cannot utter the simplest word without being contradicted by her mother. The girl receives the sharpest rebuke when she inadvertently enters the room where Khlestakov is on his knees in front of her mother, making this high-sounding declaration: "My life hangs on a hair. If you do not crown my constant love, then I am unworthy of earthly existence. With a flame in my breast, I entreat your hand." Bewildered, but obviously delighted with this homage from a great Petersburg official, Anna Andreevna stammers: "But permit me to point out: I am in a certain fashion.... married." As Khlestakov brushes aside this irrelevant circumstance with a quotation from Karamzin, Maria Antonovna rushes in with a message from her father. Anna scolds her for flightiness and lack of decorum, and ends her tirade rather surprisingly, considering the circumstances: "Some sort of cross-breeze is always blowing through your head. You model yourself on Lyapkin-Tyapkin's daughters. Why should you look to them? You oughtn't to look to them. You have other models—you have your mother before you. That's the kind of model you ought to follow."[79]

The ending of Gogol's comedy is quite as unconventional as the rest of its construction. The catastrophe is convincingly motivated: the Postmaster has been introduced in the first act as an avid reader of other people's letters, which if their elegant style particularly catches his fancy, he sometimes fails to send on. And Khlestakov, it has been hinted, has some amateurish literary pretensions, which lead him to put his experiences into a letter to a writer friend. It can therefore be no great surprise that the Postmaster is the first to discover the mistake in identity. The reactions are predictable: the Mayor flies into a towering rage, chiefly at his own stupidity; his enemies gloat malevolently; Bobchinsky and Dobchinsky accuse each other of having been the first to recognize in the insignificant Khlestakov a great Petersburg official; and in the midst of the hubbub a gendarme enters with the announcement: "The official who has arrived from Petersburg with personal instructions summons you to his presence at once. He has put up at the inn." Then follows the famous, and up to that time unprecedented, "tableau scene," during which the entire cast of the play stands frozen in typical attitudes for a minute or two, wordless, until the curtain comes down. Gogol was much concerned with the effectiveness of this novel ending, and deeply distressed by the failure of the Petersburg cast to follow his intentions with it, in spite of the elaborate half-page of instructions that ends the printed text of *Revizor.* The actors complained that they needed a ballet-master to compose such a tableau; the scene, however, when Gogol's intentions are precisely followed, is extremely effective.

Gogol's Dramatic Works: *Marriage* [*The Suitors*]

The comedy which eventually (in 1840) was completed under the title *Marriage (Zhenit'ba)* had been begun seven years earlier, and had undergone several partial or complete revisions. In one of these earlier versions it is called *The Suitors: a Comedy in Three Acts.*[80] In this there is no trace of either the "utterly improbable event" which ends *Marriage,* nor of the two protagonists of the completed comedy, Kochkaryov and Podkolyosin. The action takes place in a provincial town; the heroine, Avdotya Gavrilovna, is desperately looking for a husband, and through the good offices of the matchmaker Marfa Fominishna (who later turns into Fyokla Savishna), is visited by four suitors—Yaichnitsa, Onuchkin, Zhevakin and Panteleev. The fragment breaks off inconclusively with the appearance of Panteleev (scene 11). The several suitors have characteristics that are retained for the most part in *Marriage:* Yaichnitsa is crude and domineering; Onuchkin is looking for a well-bred wife who can speak French, Zhevakin is a retired naval officer who has been in Sicily and retains a nostalgic memory of the "black-eyed beauties" of that exotic land. Panteleev is characterized only by a stammer—he is dropped in the final version in favor of the merchant Starikov, who may be presumed to be the finally successful suitor. *The Suitors* has no plot, and dialogue constitutes its only interest. The final scene presents each of the four suitors proposing marriage, and the heroine still undecided as to her choice.

The completed comedy *Marriage* was first published in the 1842 *Complete Works,* first played in St. Petersburg December 9, 1842, and in Moscow February 5, 1843, in both places badly and with little popular success. As with *The Inspector General,* the comedy requires a style of acting quite different from that habitual in Russian theaters of the time, and the author's careful explanation of his intentions fell on deaf ears.

Belinsky, who saw the first Petersburg performance, wrote:[81] "If the actor who plays the part of Kochkaryov, on hearing of Podkolyosin's intention of getting married, assumes a meaningful air, as of a person with some sort of purpose, he spoils the whole part from the very beginning." Here Belinsky certainly caught the clue to the whole intent of the little comedy. Kochkaryov's officious efforts to get his friend married are deliberately left unmotivated. A motive, to be sure, could be plausibly devised: when Kochkaryov first encounters the matchmaker Fyokla in Podkolyosin's apartment, he greets her with the words: "Oh, it's you!... to what a devil you got me married!" Fyokla replies: "What's wrong? You carried out the law." "Carried out the law! What a wonder of a wife! I suppose I couldn't have got along without her?" The implication is that Fyokla hasn't done so well in providing Kochkaryov with a wife, and hence he is perhaps eager to spite the old woman by taking her business away from her. But this possible motive is so merely hinted, and then quickly dropped, that Gogol evidently intended it to be understood only as a perhaps subliminal suggestion, not even consciously recognized by Kochkaryov. How then explain Kochkaryov's unflagging efforts, which will certainly continue even outside the framework of the play (he goes in pursuit of the runaway Podkolyosin after the latter's self-defenestration at the end of the play) to get his friend into the toils of matrimony? Quite simply, Kochkaryov is what the Germans call a "Tuer"; he revels in purposeless, gratuitous action for its own sake. He has no conscious purpose, either of spiting old Fyokla or of doing Podkolyosin a favor, although he charges his friend with base ingratitude when he balks at such a precipitate change of life. He sees a beautiful situation in which he can display his virtuosity, and rushes headlong into it without any premeditation. In this he is precisely in the position of Khlestakov on his first appearance in the Mayor's house. Khlestakov opens his mouth and the most ridiculous flow of verbiage pours forth, mounting in extravagance as he sees his audience impressed. He is not consciously falsifying, he has no purpose in his display—as we say, "he likes the sound of his own voice." Kochkaryov likes the feel of his own activity: he is not acting *for* anything—the action itself is its own end.

Podkolyosin's attitude toward matrimony is equally unmotivated. He apparently enjoys the thought of getting married, as long as this thought remains comfortably abstract, and far enough in the future not to be frightening. He quizzes his servant as to whether the tailor who is making him a new frock-coat didn't perhaps suggest that maybe the master is getting married, and is disappointed when Stepan answers "No." But when Fyokla, and later Kochkaryov try to push him into taking positive action, he is horrified. Marriage, after all, is "somehow strange. To be unmarried all your life, and then suddenly—married!" He is rather like Ivan Fyodorovich Shponka, but far less passive. Shponka, perhaps, had Panko's "old woman" not used the second part of the manuscript of his story to line her pie pans, would have obeyed his auntie's injunctions and submitted to the strange estate of matrimony. In any case, one cannot envisage his jumping out of a window to avoid it—and without his hat besides! Podkolyosin, in his very resistance, is an active character.

Against the active and mutually neutralizing efforts of the two friends—the unmotivated insistence of Kochkaryov and the unmotivated resistance of Podkolyosin—are projected the fully motivated efforts of the other suitors to win Agafya Tikhonovna. Most positive is the civil servant Yaichnitsa, who is crassly and avowedly interested not in Agafya herself, but in annexing a very comfortable piece of property, and who regards the whole affair as a mere business deal. Onuchkin is evidently less interested in Agafya's property than in her social graces, which he hopes may enhance his position in society. Kochkaryov puts him out of the race entirely by assuring him that the lady knows no French! As for Zhevakin, his everlasting reminiscences about the charms of the black-eyed girls of Sicily identify him as something of a sensualist. He would like to marry Agafya Tikhonovna because she is attractive, and because he is getting on in years and has been frustrated often before—seventeen times, in fact! The merchant Starikov, who plays a very small part in the comedy, is likely to be the lucky man in the end: he is Aunt Arina's choice, and probably it may be expected that the disgraceful evasion of the "gentleman" Podkolyosin may bring Agafya to revise her romantic views and consent after all to become a merchant's wife.

Marriage was not a success when it was first performed chiefly no doubt because of its completely unorthodox construction. The play's explanatory description, "A quite incredible incident," characterizes it very well. It has no plot, in the meaning usually understood by that word. The generating idea—Kochkaryov's ingenious and energetic efforts to get Podkolyosin married—produces all the action, and it all comes to nothing. The situation at the end of the play is the same as it was at the beginning. The title of the play is mockingly ironical: no one gets married, and there is no immediate prospect that any one will. The conventional expectations are ruthlessly flouted, even more perhaps than in *The Inspector General*— in that there was at least the parody of a "happy ending" with love rewarded. In *Marriage* at the very moment when the hero paints for himself a roseate picture of the bliss of a married life, and the audience is preparing itself for the appearance of the priest and the ceremony that will bring all this into being, he suddenly destroys the whole illusion and the audience which has been expecting Agafya and Podkolyosin to live happily ever after in marital bliss discovers that there will be no marriage at all: instead of rejoicing, the comedy ends with frustration and recrimination. In this drastic rejection of a dramatically satisfying ending, *Marriage* is rather like the tale "The Carriage." The whole effect lies precisely in the absence of the expected conclusion.

Gogol's Dramatic Works: *The Gamblers*

Gogol's only other completed drama is the comedy *The Gamblers*,[82] published in *Complete Works* in 1842, and performed in both Moscow and St. Petersburg in the following year. Regarding the latter performance Belinsky wrote:[83] "This work, in its profound truth, its creative conception, the artistic elaboration of character, its consistency in the whole and in details could not have any meaning or interest for the greater part of the audience of the Alexandrinsky Theater." Belinsky's praise in this instance is wholly undeserved, and the audience is likely to have been right in its unfavorable verdict. In the comedy's twenty-five scenes the whole action consists in the successful swindling of the cardsharp Ikharev by a group of other gamblers. When Ikharev proves to be a match for the gang at conventional card cheating, and they respectfully acknowledge his mastery, they turn to another form of deception and introduce two accomplices as an elderly landowner Glov and his supposedly unsophisticated son: the latter pretends to gamble with the gang and lose a Treasury note which his father has left him, the proceeds of a mortgage on his estate. Ikharev is apparently sharp only in card-playing, and falls easily for the deception when the gang offers him the Treasury note in return for a solid bit of cash which he has previously acquired by cheating at cards. The whole trick goes off all too smoothly, and Ikharev is successfully despoiled. There are no sympathetic characters in the play: and indeed, no interesting characters. One can hardly care much at the spoliation of the comedy's "hero"; and the spoilers appear only in their assumed, and false, identities, so that the audience has no way of knowing what they are really like. Moreover, the plot succeeds too easily to be interesting, and Ikharev is impossibly gullible. The whole comedy is a bore. It may be noted that here the conventional comedy situation has been not so much flouted as ignored. In *The Inspector General* young love is parodied in Khlestakov's "engagement" to the Mayor's daughter; in *Marriage* the "happy ending" is rejected and the title of the play becomes a mockery; in *The Gamblers* there are no female parts at all, and not even a ghost of a "love interest" enlivens the comedy.

In the final volume of Gogol's *Collected Works* appear his dramatic pieces: the completed comedies *The Inspector General, Marriage* and *The Gamblers,* and the fragments of *Order of Vladimir, Third Class*. His abortive attempt at a serious play on a historical subject, *Alfred* (the Great), begun in 1835 and soon abandoned, was not published until after his death. Along with the genuinely dramatic material Gogol included a curious piece in dramatic form, but obviously not intended for actual presentation, entitled "Leaving the Theater After the Presentation of a New Comedy" (*Teatral'nyi raz"ezd posle predstavleniia novoi komedii),* a cumbersome title which Fanger simplifies to "After the Play."[84]

Structurally this is evidently inspired by Molière's similar response to criticisms of one of his comedies, *Critique de "l'École des femmes,"* but it lacks the wit of its model, and is literarily valueless. Gogol began it in 1836, after his disillusionment by the hostile reception of *The Inspector General,* but most of it was written in 1842, after his change of heart regarding the direction of his own work.

The "author of the comedy" begins the scene as he waits in the lobby of the theater, unobtrusively placed so as to listen unobserved to the comments of the audience as it files out. As a comic artist he needs, so he says, to find out at first hand what impression his work has made on people, and is eager to learn from this criticism where he has gone wrong. What he learns from an assortment of play-goers constitutes the bulk of the piece; at the end the author emerges from his concealment and sums up his feelings about what has been said.

Most of the comments are irrelevant and superficial; the negative predominate, but a few presumably perceptive critiques are voiced, e.g., by a "very simply dressed man," by the "second young lady," and by a gentleman identified only as "first spectator." Only a few have to do with the artistic side of the comedy: for example, the "second young lady" vehemently disputes the criticism that the comedy (*The Inspector General,* of course) should have had a love affair as its complicating factor *(zaviazka);* another spectator opines that passions other than love dominate modern life and so should have their place in comedy: "Is there not more electricity nowadays in rank, financial capital, an advantageous marriage, than in love?" The objection that all the characters of the comedy were negative; the author should have included at least one good character—is countered by the undoubtedly valid point that had such a character been presented, he would have attracted all the spectators' sympathy, and they would have all too easily forgotten the evil which it was the author's purpose to expose. The trivial criticism that the language of the comedy is "low" is easily disposed of.

The chief issues discussed, however, are ethical and religious; do such rascals as the comedy depicts really exist? Is it possible for "an actual state councillor to be a goose" (Mr. P's indignant question—he *is* an actual state councillor). Doesn't the exposure of such rascality discredit the government? (No, Gogol hastens to say, for it is evident from the announced appearance of the real Inspector General that rascality is going to be punished.) Granting that abuses of the kind shown in the comedy do exist, should such "public wounds" be exhibited? Wouldn't it be better to conceal them? Implicit in all the discussion is the ancient assumption that comedy's function is didactic: indeed a "second officer" even adduces a not inappropriate example. To the "first officer's" objection: "But this amounts to giving comedy some sort of general significance," the "second officer" rejoins: "And isn't this its direct and genuine significance? At its very beginning comedy was a public, popular creation. At any rate that was how its very father, Aristophanes, showed it. Only afterward did it get into the narrow canyon of a private plot, introduce a love theme as the one and indispensable plot complication."[85] Gogol's principal mouthpiece in "Leaving the Theater," after the "Author" himself, is a petty official from a provincial town, "a very simply dressed man," who responds to the question: "Surely such people [as the stage rascals] don't exist?" with this rejoinder:

> "A person first of all puts this question: 'Surely such people don't exist?' But when has it been known for a person to put this kind of question: 'Surely I myself am not altogether free from such vices?' Never, never! But here's what—I'll speak frankly with you—I have a good heart, real love in my breast, but if you but knew what spiritual exertions and perturbations have been necessary for me so as not to fall into many vicious propensities into which one falls without realizing it, when he lives among people! And how can I say now that there aren't in me this very minute those very propensities at which all were laughing ten minutes ago, and at which I too was laughing?"[86]

The "very simply dressed man" acknowledges that in his provincial service he has seen such abuses as the comedy has shown, and put out of patience, has sometimes thought of quitting the service: "In our little town not all the officials are of the honest sort; one often has to climb up the wall to do any kind of good action. Several times before now I've been minded to chuck the service; but now, precisely after this performance, that is, I feel refreshed and therewith a new strength to continue my career. I am comforted by the thought that baseness among us will not remain hidden or countenanced, that there, in the sight of all honorable men, it has been smitten with ridicule, that there is a pen which will not hesitate to lay bare our base movements, even though this does not flatter our national pride, and that there is a noble government which permits this to be shown to the eyes of all who should see it; and this alone gives me zeal to continue my useful service." This is exactly the sort of stuff that fills *Selected Passages from a Correspondence with Friends,* and has nothing in common either with Aristophanes or with *The Inspector General* as Gogol originally conceived it. It may very possibly, however, as Proffer astutely conjectures,[87] embody a preliminary defence of the "new comedy" *Dead Souls,* published in 1842.

At the end of "Leaving the Theater," after all the audience has left, the Author comes forward and in a final monologue deplores the general assumption that there has been no positive character in the play. There *has* been one positive character—laughter. Laughter sets free; it can come only from a bright soul, who sees evil but is moved thereby not to anger but to a cleansing ridicule. What seems to trouble the Author most is the tirade pronounced by one spectator, who contemptuously dismisses this "comedy" and all others as mere "stories" *(pobasënki)*. Such "stories," the Author declares, are the precious possessions of mankind; "the wondrous finger of Providence has been constantly upon the heads of their creators." Sometime, in the ever-recurring vicissitudes of the world, "he who often sheds spiritual, profound tears, he will laugh more than all the others in the world!" With this cloudy prophecy the piece ends.

IX

Gogol's *Dead Souls* and *Selected Passages*

Dead Souls: A Poem. Part I[1]

Gogol's last years were very much occupied with labor on a project which, although never brought to completion, resulted in his greatest work—the "poem," as he called it, *Dead Souls*. He began the first part in 1835, on an idea which he received, as he records, from Pushkin. The first reference to it is in a letter to Pushkin dated October 7, 1835: "I have begun to write *Dead Souls*. The plot has stretched out into a very long novel, and it will, I think, be extremely amusing. But now I've stopped it on the third chapter. I'm hunting for a good slanderer with whom one can become intimate. I want to show all Russia—at least from one side—in this novel."[2] The word which Carl Proffer translates here as "slanderer" [*iabednik*] is, of course, a derivative of *iabedá,* usually translated, for want of an equivalent English term, with the French *chicane.* A *iabednik* is a person always on the lookout for a shady deal and a specialist in legal inconsistencies and complexities that will enable him to bring a case into such confusion that no decision is possible: such is Samosvistov in *Dead Souls: Part II.* Gogol evidently felt the need for some technical expertise to be able to handle Chichikov's project convincingly!

Dead Souls in a first draft was carried through the sixth chapter, and portions at least were read to Pushkin, whose comments will be considered hereafter. It is apparent from a manuscript copy of a second version that Gogol's original characterization of the landowners whom Chichikov visits was far more exaggerated and ridiculous than the toned-down version which was finally published.

The bulk of Part I of the "poem" was written after Pushkin's death and during Gogol's residence abroad (note the reference in Chapter 11 to Rome: "Rus! Rus! I behold you, from my wondrous, beautiful distant place I behold you!").[3] When the work was completed, Gogol returned to Russia, and during a period in Moscow made numerous revisions and additions to the manuscript. After some difficulties with the censors, the work was finally passed by the St. Petersburg office, with only minor excisions, and published in June, 1842.

The standard text of *Dead Souls: Part I,* based on the first two printed editions of the work supplemented by dated and certain corrections in

Gogol's own hand, consists of eleven chapters. Bernard Guerney in his translation of the work[4] adds with no explanation an extra chapter, which he numbers 10, thus changing the numeration of the last two chapters to 11 and 12 instead of 10 and 11. The material which Guerney inserts as Chapter 10 is an undated fragment headed simply "Chapter," without number, and printed in the Academy edition of Gogol's works (1940-52), Volume 6.[5] The material is genuine Gogol and interesting in itself (an official and fruitless investigation of Sobakevich and Korobochka by the Public Prosecutor and the Chairman of the Administrative Offices respectively), and contributes to the portraits of the two landowners already presented. There is, however, no warrant for assuming that Gogol intended such a change. The editors of the 1889-96 tenth edition, Nikolai Tikhonravov and V. T. Shenrok, rejected the supplement as probably an early section which Gogol threw out before any of the existing versions, and this is the verdict followed also by the editors of the Academy edition. It should be noted, however, that Gogol himself felt that he had left his story with various loose ends, one of which the material in question would have tied up;[6] and a hint in Gippius's *Gogol*[7] would indicate that that astute critic believed the material to represent a later revision by Gogol: "subsequently Gogol tried to rectify the defects, by developing, for example, the interrogation of Sobakevich and Korobochka." Thus there is considerable likelihood that the "chapter" in question should take its place, as Guerney has made it, in the body of the text. Nevertheless, in view of the uncertainty of the matter, it seems better to follow the accepted version of the "poem," as Magarshack in his translation[8] does. There are, after all, innumerable excluded passages of a wide range of dates connected with *Dead Souls*.

In earlier references to *Dead Souls,* e.g., the letter to Pushkin quoted above, Gogol calls the work simply a "novel." The designation *poèma* occurs first in 1836. In normal Russian usage, as we have noted elsewhere, a lengthy piece of narrative verse is so called, such as for instance Baratynsky's *Eda,* Lermontov's *Mtsyri* or Gogol's own *Hanz Küchelgarten.* The application of the term to a piece of narrative prose is unique in Russian, and requires some explanation.

Perhaps the suggestion, certainly the best precedent, for such a usage may be found with one of the western writers whom Gogol most admired: Henry Fielding. In his Preface to *Joseph Andrews* Fielding refers to his work as a comic romance, and continues (paragraph 5): "Now, a comic romance is a comic epic poem in prose; differing from comedy, as the serious epic from tragedy; its action being more extended and comprehensive; maintaining a much larger circle of incidents and introducing a greater variety of characters." In earlier paragraphs Fielding refers to Fénelon's *Les Aventures de Télémaque* as a serious epic, although it is in prose, and denies it to the category of what he elsewhere calls "serious romance," exemplified by such French works as *Clélie, Astrée, Le Grand*

Cyrus, etc. He continues with a further description of the "comic romance":

> It differs from the serious romance in the fable and action, in this; that in the one these are grave and solemn, as in the other they are light and ridiculous; it differs in the characters by introducing persons of inferior rank, and consequently of inferior manners, whereas the grave romance sets the highest before us; lastly in its sentiments and diction; by preserving the ludicrous instead of the sublime. In the diction, I think, burlesque itself may be sometimes admitted.[9]

In this connection Gippius remarks:

> In the versions of *Dead Souls* written abroad there was a very important acknowledgement of Gogol, which has come down to us in three variants. Apropos of the ladies who demand a hero "without spot," Gogol replies to this assumed "fool's court": "He (the author) hasn't the habit of looking aside when he is writing. If he raises his eyes, it is only to the portraits hanging before him of Shakespeare, Ariosto, Fielding, Cervantes, and Pushkin, who reflected nature as she is, not as certain people would be pleased to have her be."[10]

Of course in its context this passage which Gippius quotes, and which Gogol deleted from the printed version of *Dead Souls,* refers to the author's attitude toward realistic characterization as opposed to romantic idealization; but it is significant that of the authors named in the passage, all but Shakespeare have left visible traces even in the construction of *Dead Souls:* and Fielding and Cervantes belong precisely in Fielding's category of writers of "comic romance."

Fielding and Cervantes are again mentioned together in Gogol's unpublished *Literary Primer for Russian Youth*[11] as writers of "the lesser sorts of epic," which "although written in prose, can none the less be reckoned with works in verse." In his primer Gogol refers both the classical verse epic and the novel to the genre "epic," and also the "lesser sorts of epic," verse and prose, of which he has adduced Fielding as an exemplar. The epic, he says—that is, the national verse epic, such as the *Aeneid* or *The Lusiads,* takes as its subject the whole life of a people or nation. "The novel is not an epic. It can rather be called drama. Like the drama, it is a too restricted [*uslovlennoe*] work.... The novel does not take a whole life, but a significant event in a life, such as has made the life reveal itself in a brilliant form, despite its restricted scope."[12] The "lesser epic," intermediate between the true epic and the novel, creates "a true-to-life picture of everything significant in the traits and manners of the time picked [by the author], that earthy, almost statistically captured picture of the defects, abuses, vices and everything that he has discerned in the chosen period and time worthy of attracting the attention of every observant contemporary."[13] The hero of the epic must be an important figure; of a novel, the hero can be anyone; of a lesser "epic" the hero should be "though a private person and of no distinction, yet significant in many regards for an observer of the human soul." The lesser epic will have no universality, but "a full epic volume of significant private phenomena."

Gogol's *Primer* evidently means by novel the nineteenth-century historical type created by Scott and carried on by e.g., Victor Hugo and Alfred de Vigny. The novel of the sixteenth, seventeenth and eighteenth centuries, from Cervantes to Fielding, and exemplified in Russian by e.g., Chulkov's *The Comely Cook* or Narezhny's *A Russian Gil Blas,* which is predominantly the "novel of manners," falls into his category of "lesser epic." And since such a work as Pushkin's *Eugene Onegin,* which although its author called it a "novel," falls otherwise within what in Russian is ordinarily called a *poèma,* and which Gogol terms a "lesser epic," it follows that the term "poem" which both he and Fielding extend to narrative in prose as well as verse, is perfectly applicable to *Dead Souls,* the more so as the work abounds, as we shall see, in stylistic devices, such as apostrophe, sentence periodicity, alliteration, inversions of normal word order, etc., as well as in narrative devices, e.g., lyrical digressions, similes, interpolated stories, etc., which are particularly characteristic of serious verse.[14]

The title of the novel or "poem," cited above, was a compromise between Gogol and the censorship office. Gogol's original title, and the one by which the work is now universally known, aroused the indignation of the ecclesiastical authorities, who protested, according to Gogol: "...the soul is immortal, there cannot be any dead soul; the author is taking up arms against immortality."[15] This was of course a willful misunderstanding of the title: the word *dusha* has two distinct meanings in nineteenth-century Russian. Its original, and ecclesiastical, meaning applies to the immaterial, and presumably immortal, portion of the human being; but after Peter the Great the word had a political and material meaning: a male serf. The "souls" that Chichikov collects are the physically defunct but fiscally existing male serfs upon whom their owner must pay the government a head-tax in the intervals between the five-year revisions of the census. Gogol's title, however, although applying specifically to Chichikov's ingenious and shady enterprise, certainly has an accessory metaphorical meaning, implying that perhaps the owners of these deceased serfs are the real "dead souls." After some difficulties, and some legerdemain with the manuscript, so that it might reach the hands of a more tolerant censor, Gogol had to agree to turn his original title around, so that the less objectionable portion of it was the first to strike the eye: *Chichikov's Adventures, or Dead Souls.*

Gogol's indebtedness to his predecessors, western and Russian, is almost entirely a matter of external form. "Chichikov's Adventures" immediately suggests Narezhny's picaresque novel *A Russian Gil Blas, or The Adventures of Prince Gavrila S. Chistyakov.* It should be noted that the suggestion of "purity" or "honesty" inherent in the name of Narezhny's hero is deliberately dropped from that of Gogol's: Chichikov has no very obvious Russian etymology, although there is a suggestion of sneezing *(chikhnut')*. It is possible that Gogol had in mind the Italian word *ciccia,* a childish term for meat, and its derivative *ciccione,* "a fat man." Chichikov is portly![16] *Dead Souls,* like Narezhny's novel and Lesage's *Gil Blas,* takes the form of a series of episodes, externally united only by the continuous presence in each of the principal character, and in Gogol's case, by the enterprise which is Chichikov's reason for visiting the several landowners of the district of N—. Both Gogol's and Narezhny's novels, of course, have plots in addition to the episodes which form the body of the works (Chichikov through malicious gossip is obliged to take abrupt leave of the town of N—), but these plots are subordinate and more or less ornamental. The depiction of manners in the episodes is the main thing. Narezhny's novel, like all his work, is heavily didactic: the ultimate repentance and redemption of Prince Chistyakov through the uplifting influence and example of his benefactor is the denouement of the work. Such a denouement is typical of the *picaresca* in general, and must quite certainly have been in Gogol's mind from the beginning; but the notion that the work was begun with any such grandiose scheme in mind as that of a "Russian *Divine Comedy,*" ending with a hero purified and transformed and burning with zeal to lead his compatriots upon the path of salvation, is ridiculous nonsense. Though Gogol's knowledge of Dante was doubtless superficial and derived from inferior translations, it was certainly adequate to save him from the heresy of imagining the denizens of hell (*Dead Souls* was supposed to be his *Inferno*) as ultimately saved, as we know he did at least in the case of Plyushkin.[17] *Dead Souls: Part I* is in form a picaresque novel of quite normal type, except that the "rogue" is not the narrator, and even the fragments preserved from the projected second part do not depart essentially from the characteristics of the genre. There is no hint in Part I of the repentance which Chichikov does exhibit in the final fragment of Part II.

Narezhny's didactic developmental novel *Aristion, or Re-Education* also certainly contributed to *Dead Souls.* It may be recalled that young Aristion in the process of his "re-education" visits in his mentor's company a number of presumably "negative" landowners—the boorish and tyrannical Sylvester (cf. Nozdryov), the miser Tarakh (cf. Plyushkin) and the bon vivant Paramon (cf. Petukh in *Dead Souls, Part II*). After this he is conducted to the model establishment of German (cf. Skudron-zhoglo/Kostanzhoglo in Part II). It may be noted, however, that Gogol's use of his model here is entirely original. Chichikov is not accompanied on his visits by a raisonneur like Kassian to point the moral, and he does not evince any great spiritual improvement as a result of his visits. Only in Skudronzhoglo's model establishment does he give evidence of being affected by his experiences—and then only in the direction of an improved economic arrangement. His contacts with negative examples of the landowning class leave him morally unaffected.

The subject of *Dead Souls*—Chichikov's quest—dictates the principal element of structure. Since the hero, in order to obtain his peculiar commodity, is obliged to travel from one to another of the local gentry, these peregrinations serve as the framework for the first part of *Dead Souls,* and for most of the fragmentary second part. From the point of view of subject, there is no reason why one such visit should precede or follow another; insofar, however, as the five landowners visited are symbols of various perversions of the "Russian soul," as James Woodward maintains,[18] the progression from the saccharine Manilov (Woodward's "effeminized male") through Korobochka (the "masculinized female"), Nozdryov (the violent, animalistic "hunting" male), Sobakevich (the dominating, acquisitive, misanthropic male) to Plyushkin (the sexless, unreasoning accumulator of useless rubbish) is right and inevitable The first six chapters of the work form a static, essentially descriptive unit, the first chapter forming as it were a kind of prologue, in which Chichikov becomes acquainted with the officialdom of the town of N—and with three of the landowners whom he subsequently visits—Manilov, Sobakevich and Nozdryov. The following five chapters (7-11) form a corresponding dynamic unit, mostly dramatic, recounting Chichikov's resounding success with his official acquaintances when he registers his purchases, then the beginnings of the catastrophe when at the governor's ball he makes the mistake of paying too much attention to the governor's schoolgirl daughter; and finally the ensuing scandal when the drunken Nozdryov appears with the indiscreet revelation of Chichikov's dealings in "dead souls," and Korobochka arrives in town to inquire the going price of the same commodity, in the suspicion that she has been cheated. As a result of the public stir which his activities have caused, the purchaser of "dead souls" takes the prudent course of getting out of town—not, however, it must be emphasized, thwarted and defeated: he takes with him the duly registered list of his purchased "souls," which can be utilized elsewhere according to plan. Here may be noted, as Gogol's contemporaries pointed out, a good deal of similarity with *The Inspector General:* the rascally principal character in both cases succeeds in making his getaway, leaving confusion behind; there is a parody of a love-affair: Khlestakov's "engagement" to the Mayor's daughter in the one case, the cock-and-bull story dreamed up by the two "agreeable ladies" that Chichikov is planning to abduct the governor's daughter in the other; and finally, and particularly close, the rumor that strikes terror into the bewildered officials of N—that a new governor-general has been appointed, who is likely to make inconvenient scrutiny of some of their unorthodox doings. The structural kinship of the second half of the "poem" with a comedy is notable in the episode of Chichikov's getaway, with its several frustrating obstructions: the horses have to be shod; his carriage has to be repaired; and finally, when he is already safely launched, he is halted by the funeral procession of the Public Prosecutor.

The final chapter (11) of *Dead Souls: Part I* serves as an epilogue to the whole work, as Chapter 1 served as a prologue. While Chichikov is dozing as his troika whirls him along the road farther and farther from the scene of his discomfiture, the author in a flashback at last explains who he is and what his background has been. From his days as a schoolboy he has been guided by his father's precepts, always to keep on the good side of his superiors, and above all to respect the power of money. In following these precepts he has already been involved in several questionable enterprises and once been dismissed in disgrace from the service; and in an effort to regain wealth and a respectable position he has concocted the scheme of which the whole work is the record.

A certain amount of suspense is created by the device of leaving the reader in the dark as to Chichikov's motives until the final chapter: why does he want the "dead souls?" This question is naturally the first raised by each of the squires from whom he tries to acquire them. He either gives no answer, or gives one that is quite patently a lie (he tells Nozdryov that he is about to be married, and his bride's father insists on his son-in-law's possessing at least three hundred serfs!—a fabrication that he uses again, more successfully, with General Betrishchev in Part II). Unless the reader of the work is gifted with considerably more perspicacity than the officials of the town of N—, he will accordingly not understand the full purport of Chichikov's project until the author explains it in Chapter 11. The intended swindle consists in this: Chichikov will register his purchase of "dead souls" in the regular way; since he cannot own them except as adjuncts to a landed estate, he will declare them as bought for "resettlement," and in the remote province of Kherson, where in fact he may obtain land very cheaply from the government if need be. Then he will obtain a government loan on the security of his "souls"—and presumably disappear with the money. With the revelation in the final chapter of Part I the suspense inevitably disappears. Part II loses the advantage of this mystery: the reader knows all about Chichikov's enterprise, and the only uncertainty left to intrigue him is that of when and how he will be caught.

What was Gogol's purpose in writing *Dead Souls?* Belinsky, who hailed Gogol as the founder of the "natural school" (his designation for what a later age would call nascent realism) saw in the "poem" both a denunciation of the iniquity of serfdom and a pitilessly accurate portrayal of contemporary Russia. It is neither. Gogol himself gives the lie to the notion that the picture of Russia in *Dead Souls* is a true one. It is a caricature, not a portrait: "Everything I have written is remarkable only in a psychological regard....[it should not be regarded as a model for young writers, for] it will force them to produce caricatures... I have never had the intention of being an echo of the entirety [of Russian life] and of reflecting in myself the actuality as it exists around us—an intention that worries the poet all his life long, and dies in him only with his own death."[19] Elsewhere[20] he recounts Pushkin's reaction on hearing the author read the first versions of some chapters of *Dead Souls:* "Finally he became absolutely gloomy and pronounced in a voice of melancholy: 'God, how sad is our Russia!'—This amazed me. Pushkin, who had such a knowledge of Russia, had not noticed that all this was caricature and my own proper invention." Apropos of Belinsky's comparison of Gogol with Columbus, Gippius[21] notes: "Belinsky hardly suspected how apt was his comparison: Gogol is the Columbus of naturalism. Gogol really, like Columbus, discovered a country which he did not intend.... his greatest work, constructed of realistic material, he consciously and assiduously romanticized before its very issuance, subjecting realism to emotionalism, converting the novel into a poem." It is of course irrelevant to the present significance of the Americas that Columbus thought he had discovered a new route to China; so it is irrelevant to the subsequent rise and triumph of realism that Gogol never meant to be a realist.

Much the same may be said about Belinsky's other delusion. Gogol's attitude throughout his work, and quite notably in *Dead Souls,* toward individual serfs is one of detached and amused contempt. Note the description of Petrushka, who carries about with him his own inseparable "atmosphere," so potent that he need only lay down his pallet and hang up his jacket in a room for it to smell as though it had been occupied for years; and of Selifan, with his edifying discourses to his horses and his philosophical resignation—when drunk!—to receiving a beating. For Gogol the serf is a creature of another world, whom he regards with ironic amusement, in exactly the same way he regards for instance the antics of Chichikov's dappled trace-horse. In this connection it is pointless to adduce Chichikov's meditations on the possible biographies of the "dead souls" he has acquired: thoughts which an author puts into the head of a character have no necessary pertinence to the author's own thoughts. Certainly Gogol at no time in his life envisioned the abolition of serfdom as a desirable possibility, and *Dead Souls* was most decidedly never intended as an abolitionist document; yet this does not in any way alter the fact that the work inspired many earnest young men, such as Alexander Herzen, to thoughts of abolition. "*Dead Souls* shook all Russia," writes Herzen;[22] "To present contemporary Russia with such a denunciation was essential. It is the story of a disease, written by the hand of a master. Gogol's poetry is the cry of horror and shame uttered by a man who has sunk beneath the influence of a base life, when he suddenly sees in a mirror his own bestialized face." Inaccurately though Herzen may have interpreted the work and Gogol's intentions, he certainly recorded its effect correctly.

But if Gogol did not write his masterpiece as a manifesto against serfdom, what was his purpose? In his letter to Pushkin, quoted above, he notes of the work's beginning that it will be "extremely amusing." Perhaps it was begun with no more serious purpose, but it is hard to believe. Although in his earlier work didacticism is not overt and obtrusive, as it is in *Selected Passages from a Correspondence with Friends,* there is usually a hint of it. In *Dead Souls* there is rather more than a hint. Certainly he had not conceived the work at the beginning as a "Divine Comedy" or a "Pilgrim's Progress," with his shabby and mediocre hero ultimately and edifyingly redeemed; but he certainly did intend in the work to expose the crassness of Chichikov's mercenary motives, the timidity, conformism and banality of Russian officialdom and the vulgarity, ignorance and callousness of the landowning class. All of these things, as we have emphasized before, Gogol viewed as personal, not institutional vices, and remediable by personal reformation, not by alteration of the country's public institutions. He expects by his "poem" to open the eyes of his countrymen to their own faults, and leave it to them to take steps for self-improvement.

But certainly a didactic intent does not exhaust the author's purpose with *Dead Souls.* The work is after all a magnificent literary creation and represents Gogol at the very height of his powers. What is didactic in it is muted and oblique. As Fanger says:[23] "The Gogolian masterpieces without exception can be read either as hilarious or horrifying, and whichever way they are read, an awareness of the alternative is always present." The ambivalence, however, is not merely between the "hilarious" and the "horrifying." Almost everything in Gogol is capable of the same alternative readings. *Dead Souls* has an extra-literary, didactic purpose; but it is also "art for art's sake," a work that is justified by its own being. To quote Fanger again in his excellent summation:[24]

> The bedrock allegory of Gogol's art thus concerns the miracle and meaning of its own existence. Authentic art, he insisted in "The Portrait" and elsewhere, must serve a great idea; the great idea that informs all his mature writing is the transforming and liberating power of literary creation, its ability to transcend limitations in the present. This is not a matter of assertion, but of demonstration. As his fictions transform the least promising matter into occasions of delight, they open the possibility of a like transformation in the area of life.

The chief matter of the first six chapters of *Dead Souls* is character description. The landowners from whom Chichikov tries to purchase their "dead souls" are not numerous—only five are described in Part I—and it is ridiculous to claim, as many Russian critics do, that this "assemblage of monsters" is typical of the landowning class of all Russia. Part II, with Tentetnikov, Betrishchev, Petukh and Platonov, does something to extend the coverage, as it were, and rectify the balance, but even with this addition, *Dead Souls* is by no means a true and comprehensive picture of the whole gentry class of the Russia of Nikolai I. Gogol has picked certain perhaps common but certainly not universal types, and as usual exaggerated their characteristics to caricatural proportions. The relations of these with their estates constitutes one of the chief features of their characterization. Manilov leaves everything in the hands of a dishonest bailiff, and knows or cares nothing himself about the management of his lands, and as a result his peasants are shiftless and idle. Korobochka, for all her invincible stupidity, which puts Chichikov in such a sweat, is an admirable manager of a small estate, and is described with amused sympathy; Sobakevich is methodical and a hard task-master, but surprisingly is the only one of the estate-owners who shows some appreciation of his peasants—at least of the dead ones; as for Plyushkin, his miserliness has reduced both himself and his whole estate to abject misery. Nozdryov can hardly be characterized in this regard: he is personally a bully, a boaster, a liar and a cheat, but nothing consequential is said about his relations with his estate. Although Gogol's focus is primarily on the relations of these landowners with their lands, he shows little interest in their treatment of their serfs as human beings, only as economic objects.

As for the humanity of the landowners themselves, more is implied than explicitly stated. In James B. Woodward's volume Gogol's "Dead Souls" the five landowners of Part I are convincingly shown as representatives of psychological types of what he terms perversions of the "Russian soul." From obscure hints in the portrayal of Manilov, for instance, the deduction is made that this originally "most modest, tactful, and educated [army] officer" was "superficially feminized" by marriage and has become the vacuous, uxorious sentimentalist that he is through the influence of the gentle but dominating Mme Manilova, the personification of "the superficial feminine." Korobochka, on the other hand, is for Woodward the "masculinized" female. A bedraggled and literally "hen-pecked" rooster in Manilov's yard symbolizes him, while it is significant for Korobochka's position that almost every human figure whom Chichikov encounters on her estate is a stalwart female. Korobochka's name, which means "little box," is significant of her thrifty, frugal nature. Nozdryov's name, as Woodward points out, derives from the Russian word for nostril (nozdria), and coupled with his inordinate love of hunting dogs, identifies him as the aggressive, instinctual "hunter," whose being is summed up, as Woodward puts it, in "a single, unchanging impulse—the impulse to challenge and destroy."[25] In the Sobakevich household Woodward sees the contrary of the Manilov situation—Mme Sobakevich, under the influence of her husband's overwhelming masculinity, has become a "superficially masculinized" parody of a woman. Sobakevich himself, with all his solidity and xenophobia, certainly represents one unmistakable type of "Russian soul." As for Plyushkin, he is dehumanized, sexless. When Chichikov first sees him, he takes him for a housekeeper because of a vaguely feminine costume and a bunch of keys, and even addresses him as "matushka."[26] His name again is significant—pliushch means "ivy," and the famous description of the neglected garden on Plyushkin's estate is dominated by the figure of the hop-vine—a surrogate for ivy—which embraces and throttles everything. As Woodward very properly says:[27] "It has been customary to regard him simply as a miser, but here the acquisitive instinct is only a manifestation of the rapacious spirit of nature that has supplanted his human soul. Avarice is not the cause of his inhumanity, but rather the dominant symptom, just as Nozdryov's passion for hounds is a symptom of his ebullient 'masculinity.'"

In Chapter 5 Chichikov's carriage, en route from Nozdryov's to Sobakevich's estate, has a minor collision with another carriage, through the carelessness of Selifan, Chichikov's driver. The occupant of the barouche turns out to be a beautiful sixteen-year-old girl—the governor's daughter, returning home from school, as Chichikov learns later. She is more interestingly and convincingly pictured than most of Gogol's young women, and her sudden appearance and equally sudden departure once the horses have been untangled has a profound effect on the susceptible Chichikov. Whether, as Woodward suggests, she was intended as the counterpart of Dante's Beatrice, destined in the unwritten third part of the work to effect Chichikov's redemption, is rather doubtful. She represents, for Woodward, the spiritual purity of true, not superficial, femininity. She of course plays an unwitting part in the denouement: it is Chichikov's attentions to her at the Governor's ball that bring down upon him the ire of the rest of the ladies. She plays no further part in the "poem," but amid the vulgarity and ugliness of the rest she is a strikingly bright and attractive spot.

A word should be said here on the matter of Gogol's arrangement of his five portraits. I think that Woodward successfully refutes the notion that their ordering is random and governed by no logic. Certainly contrast is a very important factor in the arrangement. Korobochka and Sobakevich share certain characteristics—thrift and careful attention to their estates—and they alternate with two other portraits which exemplify, in Woodward's words:[28] "sharply contrasting attitudes to earthly possessions—attitudes of total disregard (Manilov) and total disrespect (Nozdryov)." But contrast is probably not the only factor that dictates the arrangement. There is an obvious heightening of seriousness between the first and the last, Manilov and Plyushkin, but does the whole sequence show a crescendo? Gogol himself says in the third of the "Four Letters to Various Persons Apropos of *Dead Souls*":[29] "My heroes are not villains at all; were I to add just one good trait to any one of them, the reader would be reconciled to them all. But the vulgarity [*poshlost'*] of the whole together frightened readers. They were frightened by the fact that my heroes followed one after another, one more vulgar than another, that there was not one comforting phenomenon, that there was not even anywhere for the poor reader to catch his breath and recover his spirit, and that after reading the whole book it seems as though one had come out of some stifling cellar into God's light." The phrase *odin poshlee drugogo,* "one more vulgar than another," could be no more than a stereotyped expression, not to be taken literally; but it may, and probably does, convey Gogol's true intention. Woodward's arguments[30] here are subtle and for me less than convincing—I fail to see, for instance, why the "masculinized female" (Korobochka) should be on a lower level than the "superficially feminized male" (Manilov) or why of the two exemplars of masculinity, Nozdryov and Sobakevich, the latter should occupy the place nearest to the totally "vegetablized" Plyushkin. But perhaps Gogol meant it so; perhaps, again, the real key to his meaning has yet to be found.[31]

The first six chapters of *Dead Souls: Part I* are devoted to Chichikov's encounters with the landed gentry of N—district. In the following four the attention is shifted to town society. The characterizations in the first portion of the work are individual, those in the second part collective—the local officials as a class, and their wives as an undifferentiated group. As with the portraits of the gentry in the first half of the work, the treatment is impressionistic and satirical, but by no means denunciatory. Chichikov's remarkable success in town begins with his appearance at the Administrative Offices to register his purchases, which amount to such a number that it is immediately concluded that he is a millionaire—and a millionaire, Gogol notes, is always looked upon favorably, even by people who expect no personal gain from him. The equally rapid decline in Chichikov's popularity begins with his unfortunate appearance at the Governor's ball, and is traceable to the pique of the ladies present when he snubs them to devote all his attention to the alluring blonde daughter of the Governor. The appearance of the drunken Nozdryov at the ball and his indiscreet revelation of Chichikov's quest for "dead souls" completes the hero's discomfiture and leads directly to the denouement—his abrupt departure from town. The final chapter, as mentioned above, is a flashback in which Chichikov's background and previous career are detailed, and an explanation finally given of his peculiar interest in acquiring title to a collection of "dead souls."

The portrait of the "hero" of *Dead Souls* is in the nature of things developed in a way totally different from those of the minor characters. While these are presented either overtly or tacitly as seen through Chichikov's eyes, Chichikov himself has to be shown as seen by the author's eyes. In the very first paragraph of the work the hero's external characteristics are tellingly reported: "In the brichka sat a gentleman, not a good-looker, but also not of a bad exterior, neither too thick nor too thin; it couldn't be said that he was old, however it also couldn't be said that he was too young."[32] Thus at the very outset we see Chichikov as the epitome of the "average man." There is nothing really distinctive about him—he is "middle-of-the-road" in everything. As the work proceeds, we see that he is finical about his dress and his personal cleanliness; he likes good food and drink, but is by no means either a gourmet or a gourmand; he has an eye for a pretty girl, and daydreams a bit about the Governor's attractive daughter whom a minor carriage accident throws literally in his path—but he is too realistic to let the day-dreams interfere with his real business. He is polite and affable to everyone, with varying degrees of familiarity according to the rank of his acquaintances. His conversation is entrancing to the officialdom of N—, but the samples of it which Gogol mischievously gives are made up mostly of platitudes. He makes mistakes in the course of the work, and reproaches himself for them, e.g., in broaching the subject of "dead souls" to Nozdryov, and more seriously, in paying too much attention at the Governor's ball to his host's pretty daughter. He never divulges anything about his past or his business beyond the vague hint that he has been in the service and has been persecuted, presumably for his own uprightness, by envious rascals.

It is not until the final chapter that the author gives a full account of Chichikov's birth, upbringing and previous career. This account is presumably meant to confirm Chichikov's mediocrity. There is nothing in the story to mark him as either very good or very bad.[33] He is not exceptionally intelligent, but very shrewd and hard-working. His aim from the beginning has been to acquire wealth with which to make himself a comfortable life and a respected place in society. In his efforts to attain this end he has engaged in somewhat shady practices which Gogol implies are neither exceptional nor heinous—they are simply the usual thing, such as a thoroughly average person might be expected to engage in. The enterprise which Chichikov is embarked on throughout the work is more ingenious, but differs little in seriousness from those which he has previously tried. It is notable above all that in this life history there has been no question of penitence. Chichikov has been caught pocketing huge sums through a profitable collaboration with large-scale smuggling operations. In such an operation it is the faceless "government" that loses, just as it would be if he mortgaged his "dead souls" and disappeared with the money. It never occurs to him or to any other "average man" that there is anything reprehensible about such conduct, and he can quite honestly picture himself as an innocent man persecuted unjustly when his doings have led him to dismissal from the service.

Whatever Gogol's original intention may have been regarding the finale of his "poem," certainly by the time the final revision of Chapter 11 was written he had planned a "conversion" of sorts for Chichikov. As has been noted before, such an ending is quite in the tradition of the picaresque novel—for example *Gil Blas de Santillane* or *Guzman de Alfarache*—and may have been intended from the start. It would represent an ostensible moral lesson for the reader, as such endings regularly do elsewhere in the *picaresca,* and justify the prior inclusion of all manner of wickedness. Let the readers gloat over the hero's sins through most of the work, as long as in the last chapter he repents of his past and begins a new life!

Such is Chichikov's character in Part I of *Dead Souls*—that of a man so thoroughly average as to have little distinction at all. Most of the other characters in the work are exaggerated to grotesqueness. Not so Chichikov. He is no monster to be viewed with horrified disbelief. He is Everyman in a nineteenth-century Russian garb.

The author's obvious declarative remarks about his hero, however, do not by any means exhaust the devices by which Chichikov's character is portrayed. In Chapter 3 Chichikov goes to his travelling-case *(shkatulka)* to get some official paper, and Gogol takes the opportunity of describing this interesting article in detail. It is palpably a symbol of its owner, with contents ranging from miscellaneous useless junk ("visiting cards, funeral announcements, old theater tickets, and the like") to a secret money-drawer at the bottom. Nabokov[34] writes: "Andrey Bely, following up one of those strange subconscious clues which are discoverable only in the works of authentic genius, noted that this box was the *wife* of Chichikov..." At least, he guards it as the apple of his eye. Nabokov also notes that the case is a sort of *"korobochka"* or "little box" and thus symbolizes a degree of kinship between Chichikov and his hostess. Perhaps also the useless odds and ends in the case may similarly indicate his affinity with Plyushkin, that inveterate collector of lost buttons and bits of string. Bely noted[35] that Chichikov's servants Petrushka and Selifan are bearers of certain aspects of their master's personality. The malodorous Petrushka is, according to Bely, "the bearer of Chichikov's stench," which frequent bathing and the use of imported soaps and eau de cologne physically eliminate in Chichikov himself. Woodward disagrees with Bely's contention that the coachman Selifan represents the "poetry" in his master's nature, and equates him instead with the "element of irrationality in Chichikov's character... the irrationality which constantly frustrates the realization of his plans and which is most blatantly revealed in his attempts to acquire dead serfs from the two landowners, who plainly regard him as a quarry to be hunted."[36] Another quite obvious symbol of Chichikov is the lazy and cunning dapple-grey trace-horse with which Selifan wages unremitting war with words and whip.[37] An ironic turn is given this symbol when Selifan addresses the horse with admonitions to live respectably, like the master.[38] Bely sees Chichikov's slippery and elusive nature symbolized by the "sideways movements" which Gogol constantly gives him, e.g., when he is trying to escape being stepped on by the clumsy Sobakevich. Doubtless many other less obvious symbols serve to emphasize various traits in Gogol's hero which he chooses to leave inexplicit, but these are the most striking.

Gogol's entire approach toward his character portraits—of landowners and officials, men and women, who populate his "poem"—is by way of humorous and ironical exaggeration. In this regard it is instructive to consider the difference in tone between Gogol's work and another depiction of presumably typical specimens of nineteenth-century landed gentry—Saltykov-Shchedrin's *The Golovlyov Family*. Saltykov's Golovlyovs are modelled largely on members of his own family, which perhaps accounts for the downright savagery with which they are pictured. Not a glimmer of humor or human kindliness illuminates that black picture. "Little Judas" is of course a monster unparalleled in Russian literature, but even the rest of the family, although slightly less repulsive, are none of them viewed with the amused good humor with which Gogol sees his characters. Gogol's words in his *Author's Confession* come to mind: "If one is to laugh at something, it is better to laugh powerfully, and at what really deserves general ridicule."[39] Korobochka and Plyushkin, the Governor who does such beautiful needlework, and the registrar of purchase deeds who finds a twenty-ruble note insufficient reward for the proper performance of his assigned duties—these and many others are figures deserving of general ridicule—but not of horror. "Yudushka" Golovlyov, his sinister mother Arina Petrovna, feckless father and drunken brother Pavel are not ridiculed—they are mercilessly bludgeoned, and it is horror and revulsion not laughter, that they evoke.

In connection with Gogol's character portrayal, mention must be made of two very effective and typical devices which he employs with particular mastery in *Dead Souls*—contrast and the "metonymical method." Consider the chapter (6) devoted to the miser Plyushkin, which is developed very largely by the use of contrast, both explicitly in the picture of the neighboring landowner who "burns the candle at both ends," and implicitly in several striking symbols. As Chichikov approaches the manor house, he notes the extravagantly luxuriant vegetation surrounding it. Gogol's description of this is a veritable tour de force, the total impression from which is of some tropical jungle, growing in fantastic profusion. Immediately comes the contrasting picture of the owner and his surroundings: Plyushkin is as niggardly and grudging as nature is lush and redundant.[40] Then, after some description of the spidery Plyushkin and his ways, his past is described, and the picture of the affable, generous, well-liked, sociable gentleman that he was before his wife's death forms another effective contrast with the ridiculous and unseemly creature whom Chichikov finds.[41]

The pictures of Manilov and Korobochka make a good deal of use of the device so beautifully exploited by Pushkin in *Eugene Onegin*—description through association with material objects. As the traveller nears Manilov's house he notes a pastel-painted arbor inscribed "A Temple for Solitary Meditation," and a garden pool covered with green slime. These natural accessories foreshadow Chichikov's impressions of the owner's character: he is vapidly sentimental, and he is negligent, not to

say shiftless. Korobochka's plump feather-beds and extremely tasty
pancakes characterize her. But the apogee of the method comes in the
chapter devoted to Chichikov's visit to Sobakevich. At his first introduction to that gentleman, Chichikov has his feet stepped on—Sobakevich
is solid, clumsy, and lumbering.   So are his house, his furniture, and all
his accessories.

> When Chichikov gave a sidelong glance at Sobakevich, he seemed to him this time
> extremely like a medium-sized bear. To clinch the similarity, the coat he was wearing
> was perfectly bear-colored, his sleeves were long and his trousers long, he stepped
> every which way and was perpetually treading on other peoples' feet. . . . Chichikov
> gave him another sidelong glance when they were moving into the dining room: a bear!
> a perfect bear! Only such a strange affinity as this was needed—his name was Mikhail
> Semyonovich

[Mikhail or "Misha" is the generic Russian pet-name for a bear]. The
pictures on the wall of his drawing-room are mostly of burly heroes (and
heroines) of the Greek revolution: "Next followed the Greek heroine
Bobelina, whose one leg was bigger than the whole trunk of those fops who
fill present-day drawing-rooms." Bobelina, incidentally, is a prime exhibit
in Woodward's case to prove that the overpoweringly masculine Sobakevich "masculinizes" everything around him.

> Chichikov again glanced over the room, and everything that was in it—everything was
> solid, awkward in the highest degree and had a certain strange resemblance to the
> master of the house himself; in the corner of the drawing-room stood a paunchy
> walnut bureau on perfectly absurd legs, a perfect bear. The table, the armchairs, the
> regular chairs—everything was of the heaviest and most uneasy character—in a word,
> every object, every chair, it seemed, was saying: "I too am Sobakevich," or "I too am
> very like Sobakevich."[42]

Gogol had demonstrated in his comedies, particularly *The Inspector
General,* his mastery of the art of characterization through dialogue. The
same skill is apparent also in *Dead Souls: Part I.* The first portion of the
"poem" is narrative and descriptive, with occasional subjective digressions; the second portion (chapters 7-11) is dramatic, consisting largely of
dialogue, reported in direct or indirect form. The dialogue concerns the
two sexually differentiated waves of gossip—the ladies' story of Chichikov's designs on the Governor's daughter, and their husbands' conjectures
on the meaning of his dealings in "dead souls." A superb example of
character depiction through dialogue is afforded by the conversation on
the morning after the Governor's ball and Korobochka's arrival in town
between the two ladies whom Gogol designates, with deadly irony, as "The
Lady Agreeable in All Respects" and "The Agreeable Lady." These two
"friends" in an amiable conversation that runs from the latest fashions to
the latest gossip, and includes some barbed innuendoes at each other's

expense, ends by concocting out of nothing the absurd story that Chichikov's object in the town of N—— is to abduct the Governor's daughter—the "dead souls" are just a screen! Again, the conversation of the two town officials with Korobochka and Sobakevich in the fragment that Guerney calls "Chapter 10" is also beautifully handled, but of course merely confirms the characterizations of the participants already made in the first six chapters. Again, the free-for-all, all-male discussion of the town officials of the possible identity of the mysterious Chichikov is most revealing of their individual characters. Incidentally, it is noteworthy that among all the far-fetched possibilities suggested, no one hits on the right one. The officials are all utterly nonplussed by the strange action, but never suspect a swindle, even though the Vice-Governor suggests that Chichikov may be an ex-bandit who is wanted, and whose latest exploit has been passing counterfeit banknotes. Oddly enough, the town officials, who are certainly familiar with a good many artful dodges for appropriating government funds in an inconspicuous way, seem to see nothing in the purchase of "dead souls" but an inexplicable eccentricity on Chichikov's part.

The writer of a "lesser epic" such as Gogol envisions his work must always be on guard against a too rapid pace. We have seen, for instance, in the novels of Bestuzhev-Marlinsky various techniques for retarding the action. Many of the same techniques are employed also by Gogol—and they are essentially the same as those employed by his admired models Fielding and Cervantes, and can be traced back to a hoary—and Homeric—antiquity. When, for instance, in the second book of the *Iliad* the poet has marshalled the Trojan and Achaean hosts for their first encounter (in the epic, at least), he pauses for a tremendous five-fold simile before the clash of battle actually begins. The expanded comparison or "Homeric simile" became the most commonly employed epic mannerism with Homer's successors, and Gogol in his "poem" makes frequent use of it.[43] Thus, for example, the stunned condition of the masculine officials of the town of N—— at the bewildering news about the amiable Chichikov that is now current is likened to the state of a suddenly awakened school-boy up whose nose his mates have thrust a paper full of snuff (Chapter 9); and in Chapter 8 the general pleasure of N—society at Chichikov's arrival at the Governor's ball evokes an ironical, tongue-in-cheek comparison that runs to fifteen lines:

> Thus upon the faces of the officials is [an expression of general satisfaction] on the occasion of an inspection by a travelling chief of the posts entrusted to their governance; after their first fright has already passed, they have observed that a great deal is to his liking, and he himself has deigned at last to joke a little—that is, to pronounce a few words with a pleasant smile. The officials nearest him in rank and location laugh loudly in reply to his sally; those laugh with all their hearts who, however, have not heard very well the words pronounced by him; and finally some

policeman standing far off at the very entrance doors, who has not from birth laughed in his whole life, and who has only just a moment before been displaying his fist to the people,—even he in accordance with the immutable laws of reflection expresses on his face a sort of smile, although this smile is more like someone preparing to sneeze after some strong snuff.[44]

This simile, incidentally, is a good example in its involved, formal structure, unnatural word order and absurd climax, of Gogol's style when he chooses to be elaborate.

Another very common device of retardation is the interpolated story. Even in Homer a whole novella may be inserted into the narrative, e.g., the story of Ares and Aphrodite in *Odyssey* VIII, and with later epic writers examples are legion. Readers of Ariosto may even sometimes find one small story dexterously tucked into a larger tale which is itself interpolated into the main narrative. In *Don Quixote* the most notable example of the interpolated tale is the episode called *El curioso impertinente*—the story of the man whose unseasonable curiosity about his wife's fidelity brings about the very result he dreads. The story of "The Man of the Mill" occupies several chapters of *Tom Jones*. In Gogol's "lesser epic" there is only one example of this device—the story which the Postmaster tells the other officials about Captain Kopeikin, whom his active imagination identifies with the mysterious Chichikov.[45] Strictly speaking, this tale thus has more relevance to the immediate situation than is usually the case. The story is couched in the peculiar "embellished" style supposed to be habitual with the Postmaster—that is, it is a kind of *skaz*. Gogol is said to have been particularly satisfied with the story, and to have been indignant when the censors imposed a much softened version of it on him.[46] In itself the story is a strong protest at bureaucratic red tape and callousness when a man's very life is at stake, and as such is predictably given great prominence in Soviet textbooks. It is likely that Gogol valued it chiefly as the stylistic *tour de force* which it is. It clashes in tone, however, with the rest of *Dead Souls,* and is not artistically an unqualified success.

To the ordinary reader the clearest claim that Gogol's *Dead Souls* can have to designation as a "poem" is the omnipresent interposition of the writer. This element too can be listed among the devices for retarding the action, but such is very evidently not its principal function. It is a usage very familiar from the novels of Bestuzhev-Marlinsky, who may have been Gogol's model for it. But the lyrical element in *Dead Souls* is far more than a stylistic device—it is almost the principal component of the work. It alternates with passages of quasi-realistic description, usually taking the form of a meditation on what has just preceded. Its tone varies widely from the satirical to the sentimental, with all manner of shadings and nuances. Note, for example, the passage at the beginning of Chapter 7, contrasting the quite different fates of the idealizing writer, who deals only with model specimens of humanity, and the realist, such as Gogol himself, who portrays characters who are repugnant to himself and outrage his readers: "And for a long while yet it is destined for me by a wondrous power to go hand in hand with my strange heroes, to contemplate the whole of enormously-rushing life, to contemplate it through laughter visible to the world and tears invisible and unknown to it."[47] Chapter 10 provides several examples of the subjective excursus; it begins with an account of the official gathering at the house of the Police Chief to discuss what measures to take following the revelations about Chichikov. The second paragraph is an ironical meditation on Russian inability to get anything done in a deliberative assembly. After the "Tale of Captain Kopeikin" and the wild conjecture that Chichikov may be Napoleon, escaped from St. Helena, comes another ironical paragraph in which the author discusses the prevalence of belief in improbabilities, and then another apropos of the officials' decision to question Nozdryov about Chichikov, even though everyone knows that Nozdryov is a notorious liar; this leads to an excursus on the human propensity to believe the most preposterous things: "Man does not believe in God but he does believe that if the bridge of his nose itches, he is inevitably destined to die soon." After the interrogation of Nozdryov and the sudden death of the Public Prosecutor the reader is envisioned, protesting that it is absurd that officials should be so frightened by a lot of nonsense. This leads to a serious meditation on human perversity in passing by the truth and espousing falsehood:

> What crooked, narrow, out-of-the-way impossible detours, which lead one far aside, has humanity chosen in striving to reach the eternal truth, when all the while before it the straight path was wholly open, like the path that leads to a magnificent edifice destined for a king's palace. It is wider and more luxurious than all other paths, shone upon by the sun and illuminated by fires all night, but men have streamed past in blind darkness.[48]

The most famous of these subjective digressions, and the most elaborate, is that which ends Part I—the apostrophe to the speeding troika, with its comparison with Russia, racing to an unknown but heaven-determined goal and astounding mankind as she whirls ahead.[49]

Such lyrical digressions are nothing new in Gogol's prose—we have seen them from the beginning; they are one of the most recognizable characteristics of his style. They alternate and contrast with his often humorously developed, ludicrously exaggerated pictures of the everyday world. But in *Dead Souls* they reach their highest point. They are built up with all the devices of ancient rhetoric—long periodic sentences, anaphora, apostrophe, oxymoron, and all the rest.[50] The contrast between them and the humdrum narrative portions of the poem is extreme, and scarcely reproducible in another language. Gogol, in the second of the "Four Letters to Various Persons Apropos of *Dead Souls,*" writes apologetically of these lyrical digressions, which evidently were particularly singled out by critics for attack; but they are in fact almost the highest points of his wonderful verbal art.[51]

The reception of *Dead Souls: Part I* in the Russian critical world was quite generally unfavorable.[52] The chief exceptions to the chorus of disapproval were Gogol's friends Vissarion Belinsky and Stepan Petrovich Shevyryov, who wrote perceptive and laudatory reviews. Shevyryov in particular perceived and appreciated the extraordinary mingling in *Dead Souls* of two quite contradictory elements, which he generalizes to claim as a quality of all works of art:

> Every production of an artist has two sides: its one side is turned toward life, from which it draws its material, its content, but with its other side it belongs to the creator, it is all the fruit of his creative spirit, a secret of his internal life. Judges are for the most part divided into two sides: one group looks only at the content and at the connection that subsists between the production and life, particularly contemporary life; the other group is delighted with the artist's artistry, whether or not they explain this, and are undisturbed by the question about life. It is long since we have encountered works in which external life and content presented such a sharp and extreme contrast with the wondrous world of art, in which the positive side of life and the creative power of the beautiful were in such a decisive conflict together, from which only Gogol's talent could have constantly issued with the victor's crown.[53]

Gogol's peculiar artistry then, in Shevyryov's view, is the mingling of "real" and "ideal" in apparently irreconcilable opposition which only the author's genius succeeds in bringing off. Most of the critics, evidently, belonged to Shevyryov's first group, and were appalled by the apparently exclusive allegiance of Gogol's art to the "low" and seamy side of life. As was to be expected, Osip Senkovsky in his *Reading Library* (1842, No. 8) was hostile; he spent a good deal of his review in an extremely heavy-handed ironical ridicule of the use of the word "poem" in Gogol's title. But the most serious attack came from Nikolai Polevoi, in the *Russian Herald* (1842, Vol. VI). Polevoi, the admirer of Hugo and western romanticism, was outraged by what he saw as Gogol's "defection" from romantic idealism to the "natural school." He begins with the accusation that the content of *Dead Souls* is a mere repetition of that of *The Inspector General* (the similarities are indeed striking), and—"need it be said, a joke, repeated a second time, becomes a bore, and so much the more if it is dragged out to 475 pages?" Then he settles down to serious business:

> But if we add to this that *Dead Souls,* consisting of gross caricatures as it does, is founded on fantastic and imaginary details, that the persons in it are all to the last man fantastic exaggerations, repulsive scoundrels or banal fools—all to the last man, we repeat; that the details of the narrative are filled with such descriptions that you sometimes involuntarily throw the book down; and finally, that the language of the narrative, like Gogol's language in "Rome" and *The Inspector General,* can be called an assemblage of errors against logic and grammar—we ask, what is one to say of such a creation?[54]

What irks Polevoi mostly, it would seem, is that a writer of what he somewhat grudgingly admits is real genius, such as Gogol, should stoop to seek his material where he does:

> Not a word as to whether the loathsome articles in taverns, prisons, gambling-dens, the pictures of shame, poverty, humanity's ruin, are deserving of the attention of a genuine talent, whether they themselves, without an aesthetic purpose in representing them, are to the artist's purpose. Who will maintain the contrary, we will retort to him, that after this a waxen representation of a rotting corpse, a picture of a drunkard vomiting and taken with delirium tremens can be objects of art?

It will be seen that Polevoi's indignation has led him far afield from *Dead Souls* in pursuit of some of the more extreme exemplars of the "natural school." His final point is more cogent: granting, as one must, that there *exist* Sobakeviches, Plyushkins and Nozdryovs, must a writer depict them exclusively, and not occasionally put in a decent person, who also exists in nature? Gogol's answer was hinted at even in the First Part of his poem: wait a bit and if I live long enough, I shall present you with a gallery of positive types. Of course he did not live long enough, or else his powers proved insufficient for the task; but in any case, in the fragments of Part II of his poem, he did create some credible, uncaricatured types of ordinary human beings.

Selected Passages from a Correspondence with Friends

Vasily Gippius begins the tenth chapter of his masterly *Gogol* with the statement: "The first part of *Dead Souls* and the *Collected Works* of 1842 were the last appearance in print of Gogol the artist."[55] *Selections from a Correspondence with Friends,* published in 1847, belongs wholly to Gogol the moralist and preacher, who had already made some inroads even upon earlier writings, e.g., the second version of "The Portrait." The extant portions of *Dead Souls: Part II,* which were composed between 1845 and Gogol's death in 1852, and are rough drafts and not finished work, were published posthumously in 1855. Even in their unsatisfactory condition, some of these are, as Gippius would agree, the work of "Gogol the artist."

The change from one Gogol to the other seems to us at first sight, and seemed to his contemporaries, abrupt and inexplicable. Yet the two had coexisted from the beginning, and one may find numerous traces of the moralist even in the best works of the earlier period, and of course in the seldom read minor works, such as the essays which constitute the bulk of *Arabesques*. It is not that Gogol underwent a complete and revolutionary reversal of outlook about 1840-41, as it seemed to Belinsky. Most emphatically he did not turn from a liberal to a reactionary, from a free-thinker to a religious conservative from a "Westernizer" to a "Slavophile."

In his political and philosophical views he had always been what he overtly and provocatively proclaimed himself in the *Selections from a Correspondence with Friends,* and it was only the misunderstanding of Belinsky and the liberals that allowed them to interpret *The Inspector General* as an attack on bureaucracy, and implicitly, on autocracy; and *Dead Souls* as a pitiless exposé of the evils of serfdom.

Belinsky and his friends misinterpreted Gogol and made him out to be what he had never been. But Gogol equally misinterpreted himself. "Leaving the Theater after a Performance of a New Comedy," as revised in 1842,[56] is a complete misinterpretation of the meaning of *The Inspector General.*[57] The allegorization explained in "The Denouement of *The Inspector General,*"[58] which equates the final tableau of the comedy, when the real Inspector General is announced, with a sinner's arraignment by his own conscience, is a blatantly absurd afterthought. And the concept of creating out of *Dead Souls* a Dantesque "earthly comedy" with Chichikov as a pilgrim passing through Hell and Purgatory into Paradise, if Gogol ever had it, which is dubious, is surely not one that he held when he first began his poem. What Gogol himself says, in tendentious explanations written after the fact, is of no evidential value; he was very prone to falsify, and quite capable of deceiving even himself. The letters which he wrote *at the time* of composing his comedies and his poem give no hint of allegorical interpretations of these works, which in their original intentions were no more and no less than works of art, created to stand or fall as such.

Gogol's political and philosophical outlook after 1842 is the same as it had always been. What then had changed?—for it is idle to say that nothing had. What had changed was quite simply Gogol's attitude, not toward the world around him, but toward his own work. From the moment he had entered the literary world he had been motivated, like any artist, by the thought of winning fame in that world. He had succeeded in a quite spectacular way, and for a decade or so expended all his efforts at perfecting his craft. By 1839 he had made himself one of the greatest artists of the word in the history of his native land. What he had written during these years was written for its own sake sometimes (e.g., "The Nose") quite ostentatiously in defiance of the demands for extra-textual "meaning." But Gogol was a complicated and contradictory person, and there had always been in his make-up a religious bent and a latent sense of mission. He was dismayed and depressed by the storms of controversy which *The Inspector General* and later the first part of *Dead Souls* aroused. His detractors found fault with his naturalistic method, and decried his work as vulgar, dirty, mere caricature. His defenders applauded it on grounds completely irrelevant to his intentions. Shaken by these misunderstandings the artist in Gogol retreated, and the moralist and prophet took his place. It is said that a serious illness he suffered in the summer of 1840, and what seemed to him like an almost miraculous recovery, were the turning point: he felt that

God had spared his life in order that he might perform a mission. The change, however, was not quite as abrupt and dramatic as this would make it: there had been evidences before 1840 of the eclipse of the artist in Gogol (e.g., "Rome"), and some superlative artistic work after the allegedly crucial date (e.g., "The Overcoat"). But, as Gippius remarked, 1842 marks the end of the published works of Gogol the artist.

Gogol the moralist made his first public appearance with "The Denouement of *The Inspector General*" (1846) and "Addition to the Denouement of *The Inspector General*" (1847), followed shortly by *Selections from a Correspondence with Friends* (1847). Up to the date of *The Inspector General* (1836) Gogol wrote as an artist, consciously seeking effects by the use of literary devices, particularly, as we have noted, by the device of contrast between comedy and pathetic rhetoric. But even in the work of this period it is evident that he was disquieted by his perhaps too great success in recreating artistically the characteristics of evil and ugliness. "The Portrait" in its original form gives clear indications of this: the painter of the sinister portrait of the wicked old usurer catches all too vividly the evil in the old man's eyes, and thus quite innocently creates a means whereby that evil is perpetuated as long as the portrait exists. When *The Inspector General* was produced and published, it was met by almost universal reprobation, chiefly on the grounds that all the characters in the play are base and despicable, and the "comedy" contains no moral uplift. Gogol's futile attempt to counter these criticisms by protesting that the audience had overlooked the one positive character in the play, "Laughter," is ingenious, but unconvincing, evidently even to himself. He became even more uneasy at his appalling ability to create ugliness and his sheer impotence where beauty was concerned. Probably the fragment "Rome," with its extravagant rhapsody over the beauty first of Annunziata, and then of the eternal city itself, is an attempt, which he had to recognize as unsuccessful, to accomplish the creation of the positive. When the first part of *Dead Souls* appeared (1842) its reception repeated that of the comedy: again all the characters are rascals or fools—it is an "assemblage of monsters," and even the rhapsodic final paragraphs, with their somewhat ambiguous vision of Russia dashing forward toward an unknown future, were insufficient to offset the depressing effect of the whole. Perhaps most disturbing of all was the misinterpretation of Belinsky and his school, which seized upon both the comedy and the poem as social and not artistic documents and hailed their author as a bold apostle of democracy and emancipation. It must be most emphatically reiterated that Gogol's concern in both works, indeed in all his work hitherto, had been primarily that of an artist. There is no evidence that he had ever at any time looked on serfdom as the intolerable evil it appeared to the liberals; as for the common peasants, Gogol was always contemptuous of them, and depicted them uniformly as savages and fools. While he was acutely aware of the bureaucratic abuses which he so tellingly pictures in his comedy, he never dreamed of attacking the autocracy, or even the bureaucracy itself, which in his view needed not abolition, but the reform, personal and individual, of its erring members.

The short and specifically directed pieces which were aimed at interpreting *The Inspector General* made little stir in the critical world: they were too late to change the impact of the play, and probably most people regarded them as a disingenuous attempt to rid the author of the odium of calumniating his native land. The effect was very different, however, when in 1847 he published, despite pessimistic warnings from many friends, his last major work, *Selections from a Correspondence with Friends.*[59]

The work consists of 32 "selections" on a wide range of topics, from "Woman in the World" to "Easter Sunday." The title is a literary pretense: the pieces are essays, sometimes composed in an ostensibly epistolary form, but all written for the occasion and not taken from a genuine correspondence. Several of them are addressed, however, to specific friends, e.g., Zhukovsky, Count Alexei Tolstoi, Mme A. O. Smirnova, and the poet Nikolai Yazykov. Tolstoi and Yazykov, it may be noted, were both in the Slavophile camp; Gogol fancied himself above party affiliations, but most of the ideas which he voices in *Selected Passages* are those of the Slavophiles, but considerably farther to the right!

On the surface, *Selected Passages* is a literary production. It is written in the heavily rhetorical style that marks such earlier pieces as "A Terrible Vengeance," "Taras Bulba," and "Rome," as well as the lyrical digressions of *Dead Souls: Part I.* In narrative context this style contrasts with passages of realistic description, e.g., in "The Overcoat"; but already in "Rome" the tone of the fragment is so preponderantly didactic that the unrelieved rhetorical style becomes tedious; in *Selected Passages* it becomes intolerable. From an artistic point of view the work is a catastrophic failure.

But Gogol's motives in writing it were no longer those of an artist.[60] In the years 1842 to 1846 he had come more and more to show another side of his complex nature, a side that had always been there, but which had been obscured by his strong aesthetic conscience. Now a moral conscience replaced that of the artist. Gogol, after periods of physical and spiritual illness, had come to see himself as a teacher and prophet, with a message which he devoutly believed was "needful to Russia." With incredible naiveté he set himself up in *Selected Passages* to instruct everyone in his proper duties, from a housewife to a Governor-General. It was this presumption to omniscience which more even than the substance of the precepts given roused indignation among Gogol's friends—some of them even among the ostensible addressees of the "Letters."

The central idea running through *Selected Passages* is that erring humanity must not be rejected, but shown its errors and through Christian love led to self-reformation. With this abstract program little fault can be found. It is Gogol's concrete applications of it that raise opposition. First of all, the world that he envisages in his lectures on rural economy, provincial administration, wifely duties, etc., is no real world of any time or place, but a never-never land of Golden Age simplicity and harmony. Again and again he emphasizes the word "patriarchal": the Governor-General must be a patriarch, a father to all the junior officials of his staff; the landowner must be a stern but loving father to his peasants, to whom he must explain that their servile condition is a part of God's plan; the bureau chief must reprimand a peccant subordinate with fatherly admonitions so that he will be ashamed and thenceforth behave irreproachably; the parish priest must stir his peasant flock with fatherly exhortations to abandon drunkenness and sloth, which will infallibly be followed by their reformation; the governor's wife must ostentatiously wear the same gown three or four times at social functions and thus check the vicious chase after needless luxury in her female associates. This patriarchalism reaches even into literature. In the seventh "Letter"—"The *Odyssey* in Zhukovsky's Translation"—the magnificent Russian version of the Homeric epic is lauded less as a work of art than as a picture of a patriarchal society where a king made his own bedstead and a princess did the family laundry—a picture that should have a salutary effect in turning luxury-loving ladies and gentlemen of Moscow and St. Petersburg back to the primeval simplicity of early Russian life.

All this could probably have been dismissed as no more than an eccentric and belated Rousseauism, but for its social and political implications. If human error is to be eradicated by individual reformation effected by Christian example and precept, one may theoretically envisage two avenues by which this may be accomplished: by brotherly love and by fatherly direction. The first implies equality among men, the second implies subordination; the first was Jesus' way; the second is that of the Church. Gogol unequivocally chooses the second alternative, however much he may protest that he regards men as his brothers. He sees the hierarchical structure of Russian society as a God-ordained order, in which the peasant is in a child's relation to the landowner, the soldier to his officers, the petty clerk to the bureau chief, the rural nobleman to the Marshal of the Nobility, and everyone to the Tsar. This means, as Belinsky angrily declared, that Gogol had come forward as the defender of the knout and of ignorance. It must be reiterated that Gogol's ideas had not changed; he had never deplored serfdom, only abusive landlords—and for their iniquity individual reformation was the cure; and he had always been a loyal defender of autocracy and an admirer of Nikolai I. What had changed was not his political philosophy, but his attitude toward his craft as a writer. The purpose of art, as he now sees it, is instruction. In *Selected Passages* all is blatant didacticism: art, literature, the theater exist solely to preach the truth and are justified only as they do so. It is Tolstoi's perverse aesthetic long before "What is Art?" Gogol's defection was from art, not ideology.

A number of the *Selected Passages* have an ostensibly literary subject: the one already cited on "The *Odyssey* in Zhukovsky's Translation" (VIII); "On Public Readings of Russian Poets" (V); "On the Lyricism of Our Poets" (X); "Karamzin" (XIII); "On the Theater, on the One-Sided View towards the Theater, and on One-Sidedness in General" (XIV); "Subjects for the Lyric Poets of the Present Time" (XV); and "What, in the Last Analysis, is the Essence of Russian Poetry and in what Does its Originality Consist?" (XXXI). In many of these there are extremely perceptive critical insights, particularly in the long one on the essence and originality of Russian poetry; but like leitmotifs running through the whole are two entirely unliterary themes: an emphasis primarily on the *moral* effect of poetry; and a constant reiteration of the peculiar virtues of Russianness, of Russians' spiritual superiority to people of other nations—a point of view which gives evidence of Gogol's ideological affinity with the Slavophiles. But even in dealing with purely literary matters, Gogol's critical sense can no longer be trusted, particularly where Pushkin is concerned. Everywhere in *Selected Passages* Gogol misinterprets and misrepresents Pushkin, and presents to his readers a false image of Russia's greatest poet. Thus, in Letter X, "On the Lyricism of Our Poets," ostensibly addressed to Zhukovsky, who must surely have been aware of the falsification, Gogol cites a poem by Pushkin,[61] which is actually addressed to Gnedich, the translator of the *Iliad,* beginning "For long you conversed alone with Homer." Gogol[62] says "I am repeating this entire—it is all in one strophe"—and then proceeds to quote only the first sixteen lines, omitting the last eight, which would have given him away. With the most brazen effrontery he refers the poem's genesis to a probably apocryphal anecdote in which Emperor Nikolai I was supposed to have arrived late at some function because he had been so absorbed in reading the *Iliad* that he forgot the time! In the same Letter X he cites lines from Pushkin's *Exegi Monumentum,* and continues:

> Although you, of course, are responsible for the "column of Napoleon"[instead of the self-censured "column of Alexander," which Pushkin had originally written], yet even if the verse had remained in its original form, it would nevertheless have served as a proof, and an even greater one, that Pushkin, while feeling his own personal preeminence as a man over many wearers of crowns, was aware at the same time of all the pettiness of his calling in comparison with the calling of the wearer of the crown, and knew how to bow reverently before those of them who have shown the world the greatness of their calling."[63]

This is the most perverse nonsense: Pushkin meant precisely, as did Horace in the original *Exegi Monumentum,* that the poet's achievement stands higher and will be more enduring than any achievement of any *"ventseno-sets* (crown-wearer)." Gogol may have had a laudable motive in thus misrepresenting Pushkin as a loyal and admiring subject of Nikolai I, but the fact remains that the interpretations he gives were false, and Gogol knew it.

The publication of *Selected Passages from a Correspondence with Friends* has significance primarily from a biographical point of view. The work itself hardly deserves consideration as a piece of literature.[64] But since Gogol himself, at least at first, regarded it as his best work, indeed almost his only really valuable production, it is necessary to consider to some degree its public impact. One of the best witnesses in this regard is Sergei Timofeevich Aksakov, about whom a few preliminary words are necessary.

Aksakov's friendship with Gogol began in 1832, when Pogodin introduced the young writer to the older man. Sergei Aksakov (1791-1859) was a Moscow gentleman, civil servant and one of the leaders of the Slavophile movement. His sons Ivan (1823-86) and Konstantin (1817-60) became the movement's chief spokesmen. Sergei Aksakov had not, at the period of his acquaintance with Gogol, distinguished himself as a writer: he was known only as a lover of the theater, a translator, and the author of numerous theatrical criticisms. In 1847, the same year as saw the publication of *Selected Passages,* Aksakov's charming *Notes on Angling,* a sort of Russian *Compleat Angler,* saw the light. His classical *Family Chronicle* (1856) and *Childhood Years of Bagrov-Grandson* (1859) and his *Memoirs* (1856), which reveal him as a very great stylist and one of the founders of Russian realism, all belong to a period after Gogol's death. To this period also belongs his very important and fully documented *History of My Acquaintance with Gogol, Including All Correspondence from 1832 to 1852,* published shortly after Gogol's death in 1852. We shall give a few extracts from Aksakov's letters to Gogol of the year 1846-47, just before and just after the fateful publication of *Selected Passages.*

Under date of December 9, 1846, Aksakov writes:

> Long ago I began to dislike your religious bent. Not that I, as a bad Christian, understood it badly and hence was fearful; but because [your] display of Christian humility seemed to me a display of your spiritual pride.... Meanwhile your new trend developed and grew. My fears were renewed with great force; every letter of yours confirmed them. Instead of the former warm, friendly effusions, there began to appear the exhortations of a preacher, mysterious, sometimes prophetic, always cold, and, worst of all, full of pride in the garb of humility.... Shortly after this dark rumors began to circulate that in Petersburg a whole book was being printed of your works, in which was included your correspondence with friends, consisting of sermons and prophecies, your avowal that everything you had previously written was worthless and undeserving of attention, your announcement that you had burned the continuation of *Dead Souls,* and that you were setting out for Jerusalem...[65]

Gogol had planned a new edition of *The Inspector General,* to be printed with his allegorical fantasy "The Denouement of *The Inspector General*" in revised form, the proceeds of the sale of which were to be turned over to a group of the author's friends to be given to the poor. Why such ostentation in your charity? Aksakov queries. Christ directed us to give, so that "the left hand shall not know what the right hand doeth."

> Finally, I turn to your last action—to the new "Denouement of *The Inspector General*"—... Tell me, for God's sake, laying your hand on your heart: surely your explanations of *The Inspector General* are not sincere? Surely it cannot be that you, frightened of the absurd interpretations of ignoramuses and fools, are yourself blasphemously conspiring to spoil your own living creation by calling them allegorical persons? Can it be that you don't see that your allegory of an inward city no more sticks to it than peas to a wall; that calling Khlestakov a "worldly conscience" makes no sense, since Khlestakov's being taken for the Inspector is an accident?[66]

In his reply to Aksakov's letter,[67] Gogol assumes a patient and conciliatory tone, and assures his friend that there is no new trend in his views: what Aksakov calls his mysticism has been a part of him since early youth. As for *Selected Passages,* they "will be necessary to many (in spite of all the incomprehensible passages) in many essential respects." He expects to be attacked from all quarters, and these attacks will show him what he is! He admits that some actions should be done so that "the left hand shall not know what the right hand doeth," but there are others that should have full publicity, and this is one of them. He says nothing whatever to the charge that the allegorical interpretation of *The Inspector General* is a disingenuous afterthought.

In the meanwhile Aksakov had read *Selected Passages,* and sent off an indignant letter to his son Ivan, who had evinced sympathy with the work, doubtless because of its markedly Slavophile outlook. Aksakov *père* picks out various individual passages in the *Selections* for acid comment, as for instance this one, which also more than any other raised the ire of Belinsky:[68]

> I could not without a bitter laugh listen to his exhortation to landowners, that they should plow, reap and mow in front of their peasants; how they must force them to kiss certain words of Holy Scripture, *poking them with a finger,*[69] how they must perform judgment and punishment, and how they must convince the intelligent Russian folk that the landowner imposes corvée only in order that they may eat their bread in the sweat of their brows....
>
> I could not without regret listen to this language, banal, dry, flabby and lifeless, that you revelled in, and only the article about Russian literature and literatures [in general] and the letter about Ivanov reminded me of the former Gogol.... The whole book is full of fawning and terrible pride under the mask of humility. He fawns on woman, her beauty, her charms; he fawns on Zhukovsky, he fawns on authority. He wasn't even ashamed to say in print that nowhere is it possible to tell the truth so freely as with us [Russians].... "[70]

To the author himself of *Selected Passages* Aksakov wrote in even sharper terms on January 27. He begins with an ironical comment that if Gogol meant to raise a stir with his book, he had certainly succeeded. But the writer finds himself unfortunately unable to believe that Gogol had meant his book other than seriously.

> You sincerely thought that your calling consisted of proclaiming high moral truths to people in the form of dissertations and precepts, a sample of which is contained in your book.... You made a gross and pitiable mistake. You have gone completely astray, got muddled, you contradict yourself constantly, and thinking that you are serving heaven and humanity, you insult both God and man.
>
> If an ordinary writer had written this book—God be with him! But the book was written by you; in it shines in places your former powerful talent, and for that reason your book is harmful: it disseminates the falsehood of your intellectualizations and delusions.

Probably quite wrongly Aksakov blames Gogol's delusions on his prolonged residence abroad and on false—Catholic—friends. "These friends of yours will render their account to God, blind fanatics and illustrious Manilovs, who not only allowed, but even themselves aided you to get entangled in the net of your own intellect, of devilish pride, which you take for Christian humility."[71]

A few days before this (January 23) Aksakov had written again to his son Ivan with further comments inspired by a second reading of *Selected Passages.*

> Thank God, I am by now perfectly convinced of the writer's sincerity, and his spiritual condition has an explanation for me: he is in a state of transition, which is always full of excess, delusions, blindnesses. I have a glimmer of hope that Gogol will emerge triumphantly from this condition; but his book is extremely harmful; everything in it is false, in consequence even the impressions, being false... You yourself are the closest and living proof of this... In speaking of the reconciliation of art with religion he shows with all his words and acts that the artist in him is dead; God grant that this be only for a time.[72]

Sergei Aksakov's comments about *Selected Passages,* both to others and to Gogol himself, are typical of the reactions of the author's friends and well-wishers. Gogol's shock and disillusionment can be imagined. He had been floating in a state of euphoria, expecting admiring plaudits for the work which he considered so necessary for the whole Russian people; instead, as he ruefully remarks in a letter to Zhukovsky:[73] "The publication of my book burst forth exactly like a slap in the face—a slap in the face of the public, a slap in the face of my friends; and, finally, a stouter slap in my own face." Deflated and downcast, he repents of having published it, and most of all, of having mistakenly thought himself fit to be the teacher of the Russian people. He now realizes, so he protests in his letters, his own immaturity and the presumption of his trying to instruct others in

Christian principles before having himself mastered them. Nowhere, however, do his letters admit that the precepts themselves which *Selected Passages* preach can be wrong; the mistake, as he sees it, was chiefly in timing—he should have waited for his own perfecting. As for future conduct, he will renounce the role of teacher, for which he is evidently not yet ready, and return to his literary task, which at this time is principally to complete his "poem," *Dead Souls*.

Dead Souls: Part II[74]

There is no doubt that Gogol had intended from the first to continue *Dead Souls* beyond the first part. As has been suggested earlier, the picaresque genre, to which the work belongs in a formal way, generally brings the *picaro* to an edifying reformation after the major part of the work has been devoted to his rascalities. Such a conclusion was certainly planned for Chichikov, and it is likely that Gogol had also in mind to draw a brighter picture of life in a continuation than he had given in the first part, with the inclusion of characters who, if not models, would at least be no "assemblage of monsters." But Gogol's genius lay precisely in bringing to uncanny life such repulsive grotesques as the two Ivans, Plyushkin, or Khlestakov. He had seldom tried his hand with what might be termed "ordinary people," and almost never with a character's psychological development. The portrait of the prince in "Rome" is an attempt in this direction, but can hardly be considered a brilliant success. It is perhaps this inability that may explain what happened to his first attempt to complete his poem. After five long years of labor on the project, he suddenly, in the summer of 1845, burned it all. In the fourth of the "Four Letters to Various Persons apropos of *Dead Souls*," which is the XVIIIth of *Selected Passages*,[75] he explains, rather enigmatically, his motives for the act:

> The reason why the second volume of *Dead Souls* was burned was because it was necessary. "[That which thou sowest] is not quickened, except it die," says the Apostle [Paul: 1 Corinthians xv, 36]. It is necessary to die first, in order to be resurrected. It was not easy to burn the work of five years, produced with such painful exertions, where every line shook me up in the getting, where there was much that constituted my best thinking and had occupied my soul. . . . Just as soon as the flame had carried away the last pages of my book, its content suddenly was resurrected in a purified and radiant form, like the phoenix from its pyre, and I suddenly saw in what disorder still had been what I had counted as already ordered and harmonious. The appearance of the second volume in such form as it was would have sooner caused damage than profit.

In the first of these "Four Letters" he apologizes for what he sees as the deficiencies of the first part of his poem, and which undoubtedly are also those which caused him to burn the second part: they are the result, he says, of his own insufficient knowledge of Russian, especially provincial life. In the third letter he claims to have portrayed all his own "abominations" in the pictures he has drawn of the characters in Part I, and again complains that his work would have been far better if his friends and readers had provided him with samples of real life:

> Now if you...had collected....pertinent observations on my book, both your own and those of other intelligent people, occupied like you with an experienced and practical life, had joined to this a multitude of events and anecdotes such as have happened in your neighborhood and in the whole province, in confirmation or confutation of every doing in my book...you would have done a good deed, and I would have said a hearty thank-you to you.

What all these rather vague and cryptic indications come to is that the first part of *Dead Souls* had been written too subjectively and needed the corrective of exact, and, as he says elsewhere, "statistical" knowledge of Russian life, which the author feels he did not have. In the first of the "Four Letters," moreover, Gogol writes rather apologetically of the "lyrical digressions" of his work, which are of course one of the best justifications for calling it a "poem," and belong also to the prevailing subjectivism of its style.

Subjectivism of style and caricatural exaggeration are the two characteristics of Gogol's writing which most clearly set him apart from the literary trend of which nevertheless he was generally acknowledged to be the leader—what Belinsky had called the "natural style." The years just following the publication of *Dead Souls: Part I* saw the beginnings of this trend, of which, besides Gogol, Dal and Sollogub were early adherents, to be followed very shortly by the greatest writers of the next decade. The collection *Physiology of Petersburg,* to which Nekrasov, Belinsky, Grigorovich, Dal, Panaev and Grebenka were contributors, came out in 1845; Dostoevsky's *Poor People* in 1846; Grigorovich's *Village* also in 1946; Goncharov's *A Common Story,* Grigorovich's *Anton the Luckless* and the first of Turgenev's *Huntsman's Sketches* in 1847. All these works Gogol read assiduously, as his letters testify. He was very evidently making a serious effort to refashion his own style in what he now recognized as a better mold: "Our literature of late years," he said in 1849 to Arnoldi, "has taken a sharp turn and hit upon the right road." It is highly probable that the first burning of the second volume of *Dead Souls* resulted from his feeling that in it he had failed himself to "hit upon the right road" of realism; but since he destroyed the evidence, we shall never know certainly.

The last years of Gogol's life were occupied in rewriting *Dead Souls: Part II,* a task which had probably been again completed by 1852. He read large portions of it to friends, whose reminiscences allow us to reconstruct the main lines of the plot. On February 11, 1852 OS, a few days before his death, he again burned his probably complete final draft of Part II. The burning was certainly deliberate, not an accident suggested by the Devil, as he afterward claimed, and he was evidently in his right mind, however insane the act may seem. No satisfactory reason has ever been advanced to account for the act.

Fortunately, however, in this case the destruction was not total: rough drafts of four successive chapters were found among his papers, and one of an unnumbered chapter that evidently came toward the end of the work, or perhaps constituted the actual finale. These, together with the recollections of persons such as Sergei Aksakov, Lev Arnoldi and Shevyryov, who had heard the author read it, make possible a tentative reconstruction, and a consideration of the first four chapters allows some conclusions about the completely different style of Part II. A convenient, although incomplete, summary of the content of some of the missing chapters, as recalled by Lev Arnoldi and his sister, Gogol's devoted friend A. O. Smirnova, may be found in David Magarshack's translation of *Dead Souls*.[76] Arnoldi's account in full may be found in the original language in the fifth volume of Gogol's *Collected Works*.[77]

The preserved chapters of Part II consist of two layers of corrections and alterations imposed on a basic text. Printed Russian texts, going back to the original printed edition of 1855, give the same material twice: first the basic text with alterations that can be dated as prior to 1848; and then the same basic text with alterations that belong to 1848 and 1849. Nothing is preserved of the definitive version which Gogol burned in 1852. Translators of Part II take their own choice of material from either the first or second recension, including the names of some characters, which Gogol altered; thus the Tentetnikov of the second recension is called Derpennikov in the earlier version, and Kostanzhoglo is named Skudronzhoglo.

In spite of the very unsatisfactory nature of the extant chapters of Part II, certain features of it are obvious, and may be inferred as probably belonging also to the lost final text. First, the basic plot line—Chichikov's quest for "dead souls"—continues to be the chief axis of the work, although with some changes. In the first place, while plot in the first part is a decidedly secondary element, Part II is a great deal more conventional in this regard, and if the reconstruction of the lost portions is reliable, the plot must have been quite complicated. Chichikov in the first chapter becomes involved with Tentetnikov, a wealthy young landowner with whom he takes up residence and whose affairs take most of his attention in the extant chapters. He endeavors to reconcile his young friend with General Betrishchev, with whom he has quarreled, and whose daughter Ulinka he still loves. Chichikov more or less incidentally acquires some "dead souls" from the General on a fictitious pretext that amuses the latter highly; and he tries to purchase some others from Colonel Koshkaryov, but is thwarted by the ridiculous red-tape of the latter's bureaucratic menage. In the lost chapters summarized by Arnoldi, Chichikov tries on Tentetnikov the same ruse he had employed on the General, and his host, overwhelmed with gratitude for Chichikov's having successfully brought him together again with his beloved Ulinka, instead of ceding him "dead souls," makes out a purchase deed for 300 "living souls," which he is to show to his fictitious uncle as proof of his solidity, and then destroy. Whether Chichikov's better nature restrained him from taking unscrupulous advantage of the opportunity thus afforded is uncertain. This story line ends, as it was doubtless intended from the beginning to end, with Chichikov's arrest (for falsifying a will—an episode which was given in the lost portion of the work), his imprisonment and despair, and the introduction of an improbably wealthy and philanthropic gentleman who effects the release of the more or less repentant sinner. There are indications, however, that Chichikov's reformation was not definitive in Part II, that phase being reserved for the unwritten Part III. Apparently not only Chichikov was intended to be transformed, but also Plyushkin, as a note from Gogol makes evident, and doubtless other characters from Part I.

But from the very first chapter of Part II another storyline, evidently destined to be at least as important as that of Chichikov's doings, emerges: that of Tentetnikov and Ulinka Betrishcheva. In the extant chapters Chichikov intervenes with General Betrishchev in favor of his young friend Tentetnikov; in the lost chapters, the reconciliation took place, the lovers were betrothed, but Tentetnikov was suddenly arrested as a member of an illegal secret society, and sent to Siberia (it can hardly be coincidental that on April 23, 1849 the Petrashevsky circle, including Fyodor Dostoevsky, suffered exactly this fate!). Ulinka accompanied him and married him in Siberia; in the final chapter the two would have been recalled through the agency of the good Governor-General. From even this unsatisfactory and conjectural sketch it can be seen that Gogol was attempting to leave the framework of the quasi-picaresque adventure novel, and essaying a realistic love story together with a psychological study of Tentetnikov's character, of which a sketch is given in the first extant chapter. This sketch includes, in proper realistic fashion (cf. Pushkin's *Eugene Onegin* or Lermontov's *Sashka*) a revealing account of a marvelous teacher whom the young boy idolizes, but who dies before their relations have led very far, leaving Tentetnikov the prey of a routine and stultifying educational system. It is implied that the young man's indolent and apathetic character is not inborn, but the direct result of his unfortunate education. In the first chapter Tentetnikov is portrayed as a listless daydreamer, totally unable to accomplish anything; he lies abed half the day and never even starts the monumental work on "all Russia" which he dreams about. He is an early prototype of Goncharov's Oblomov, but unlike Oblomov, apparently capable through the transforming power of love of shaking off his lethargy. The lost account, sketched by Arnoldi, of Tentetnikov's reveries in General Betrishchev's garden after winning Ulinka's hand, was evidently a high point of the story: Arnoldi describes it as a lyrical and descriptive masterpiece:

> Here Gogol had two wonderful lyrical pages. On a hot summer day, just at noon, Tentetnikov is in a thick, shady garden, and around him is deep, dead silence. This whole garden was described with marvelous brush, every branch on the trees, the burning heat in the air, the crickets and all the insects in the grass, and finally everything that Tentetnikov was feeling, happy, loving and being loved in return! I have a vivid memory that this description was so good, there was so much power, color, poetry in it, that it took my breath away. Gogol read superbly![78]

It may be noted that what Arnoldi refers to as the lyricism of this lost passage is not at all the kind of subjective effusion typical of Part I of *Dead Souls,* but is rather the sort of atmospheric natural description of which for instance Turgenev's *Huntsman's Sketches* provide so many instances.

Besides the psychological studies of the radical dreamer Tentetnikov and his beloved, the "superfluous man" Platonov is pictured in the extant chapters; he has everything, and is always bored—a Eugene Onegin carried to extremes. To match him, there appeared in the lost chapters an emancipated young woman; the two fall in love, according to the account left by Arnoldi's sister, but after a period of initial bliss, discover that it is too late; they are no longer capable of real love:

> But this animation, this happiness, was only for a moment, and a month after their first avowal, they realize that it was only a flash in the pan, a caprice, that real love was not there, that they are not even capable of it, and later ensues a coolness on both sides, and then again boredom and boredom, and of course this time they begin to be bored even more than before.[79]

Among the psychological, or perhaps rather, sociological, portraits in Part II is that of Khlobuev; along with Platonov he represents Gogol's unflattering notion of the evils of a modish modern education. The two characters are complementary: Platonov is rich, and, relieved of the necessity of any kind of work by his wealth and an energetic brother, Platon Mikhailovich is oppressed by invincible boredom and a melancholy which is the result of a realization of his uselessness and the needlessness of exerting himself toward any end. Khlobuev, an intelligent, good-hearted, religious person, is poor, mired in debt, and perfectly helpless to take any effective measures to better his situation. His estate is hopelessly run down, he is often without the necessities of life for himself and his five children, yet he cannot bring himself even to take a post in the civil service. He complains that he is too old, it is too late to make anything of himself. Yet he serves champagne and gives expensive parties, and keeps a foreign tutor for his children. He is, according to Gogol, a victim of an education which not only fitted him for no useful place in society, but taught him to crave all manner of luxuries and superfluities.

Khlobuev would not be believable, perhaps, as a person, were it not for such confirmatory creations of other novelists as Goncharov's Oblomov or Turgenev's Rudin. The pathologically useless nobleman was a genuine

Russian phenomenon of the nineteenth century. But Khlobuev is awkwardly pictured in Gogol's work, mainly by the author's declarative description rather than by words or acts of his own; and he is evidently devised to be a negative example, as Kostanzhoglo is a positive one, of the sermons of *Selected Passages from a Correspondence with Friends.*

It will be seen that several of the major characters in *Dead Souls: Part II* were depicted naturalistically, without Gogol's habitual exaggeration, and instead of the merely static snap-shots which we have of such people as Plyushkin or Manilov, these were portrayed in action, in interrelation with others, and their inner selves, not merely their exteriors, analyzed. This is the technique of realism, such as Gogol learned it from writers of the "natural school." Even more significant is his choice of characters: Tentetnikov is a real person, not a caricature; so is Khlobuev, and so is Platon Mikhailovich. They are also typical—composite creations, embodying traits from many individuals. Korobochka, on the other hand, or Sobakevich, or Manilov, are powerful grotesques, not real people; their features are indeed generalized from individual originals, but there is no possibility of believing in them as living beings. They are romantic abstractions, idealizations in reverse. It should also be noted that nowhere in the extant portions of *Dead Souls: Part II* do we find any such lyrical digressions as are so marked a feature of Part I. The author has evidently made a strenuous, and not altogether unsuccessful, effort to remake his entire style. Vasily Gippius puts the matter most cogently:[80]

> In entering upon this new creative path Gogol was obliged to refashion completely the structure of his *poèma.* It was a matter not merely of introducing "positive" heroes. . . . everything now had to be altered—the plan and the material and the artistic devices. . . . It is precisely in this—in the effort to create a real (in contemporary terminology) and psychological novel on a broad and diversely worked out plan—that the reasons must be sought for the failure of the second volume of *Dead Souls,* and not at all in the introduction of "positive" types. . . . Gogol's task was not one of representing "ideal" characters—on the contrary: it was because of its ideality that everything written up to 1845 was burned; only Gogol slipped inescapably into schematization and idealization, having had no experience in the past in the representation of psychological complexity.

In a letter to Konstantin I. Markov[81] dated December 3, 1849, Gogol denies any thought of creating "positive" characters:

> As for volume II of *Dead Souls,* I did not have in mind precisely a *hero of virtues.* On the contrary, almost all the characters can be called heroes of shortcomings. The point is simply that the characters are *more significant* than the earlier ones and that the intention of the author here was to enter more deeply into the meaning of the life we have vulgarized, to do this by revealing more clearly the Russian man not from *one* side.

Gogol's inexperience with the new style which he felt obliged to adopt explains, in Gippius's view, the inadequacy of most of Part II, and the relative success of the parts where the author is closest to his old style.

For there are still traces in Part II of the old Gogol. Chapter 2, with its delightful description of Chichikov's unexpected and unplanned visit to the estate of the genial epicure Peter Petrovich Petukh, is a gem that can rank beside any of the descriptions of Part I. Petukh is described in the hyperbolic terms familiar from Part I: he is so corpulent that he could never possibly drown—he would float like a cork. His meals are gargantuan feasts on which Petukh lavishes all his money and attention. Just as Sobakevich is pictured in terms of a bear, Petukh figures as a watermelon. Yet in spite of the exaggeration and grotesqueness of the picture, Petukh is a credible human being, and likeable. The same cannot be said of Colonel Koshkaryov: he is a schematic comic-strip character and nothing more, and it is impossible to believe in the existence either of the Colonel himself or of his absurd bureaucratic estate, where his peasant officials have had a university education and "German" enlightenment, including foreign dress, has been spread over his whole domain. He is an exaggerated figure, but not one like Petukh, drawn from real life. He is a figment of Gogol's own imagination.

It is possible, although not provable, that the final version of Part II, which is irretrievably lost, would have eliminated some of the schematism of such characters as Koshkaryov, Kostanzhoglo, Murazov and the Governor-General. But it is also quite possible that such figures represent a tendency which would have pervaded the whole, and which might indeed have been the reason for its destruction. Certain it is that Murazov and the Governor-General, to whom are given such very important roles in the drama of Chichikov's arrest and subsequent release, are totally without distinctive traits of character—they are the shadowiest figures in the whole work. Murazov is simply the idealized millionaire, the Governor-General the idealized functionary such as the one whose duties Gogol the preacher lays down so tediously in *Selected Passages*. Not quite the same can be said about Kostanzhoglo/Skudronzhoglo: he has some individual traits, although in the main he is nothing more than the phenomenally hard-working and successful landowner of the old school whom Gogol depicts in *Selected Passages*. Almost his sole human characteristics are his splenetic disposition and his contemptuous disregard of his wife's expostulations. Otherwise the whole episode in which he figures is little but a feebly dramatized lecture from *Selected Passages*. It is interesting, incidentally, that Gogol, who had absolutely no experience of farming or estate management, should have imagined himself capable of giving advice on these subjects—on the basis, it must be assumed, of a certain amount of research of a purely theoretical kind. It is also interesting that he should have felt it necessary to give his ideal landowner a non-Russian name.

Whether this is Skudronzhoglo or Kostanzhoglo, the name is Greco-Turkish (the final element of the name is a Turkish suffix equivalent to the Russian "-vich"), and although Gogol insists that Konstantin Fyodorovich was entirely Russian, he refers frequently to his "southern blood." It seems that, like Goncharov, who made *his* successful man (Stolz) the son of a German schoolmaster, Gogol could not quite visualize a genuine Russian in such a role!

Gogol began his literary career with a poem (his only attempt at verse), entirely derivative and entirely lacking in the features that mark his mature style—hyperbolism and humor. He ended it, curiously, with another work—*Dead Souls: Part II*—that is almost as alien to the style that is generally recognized as Gogolian. Once again the typical grotesque exaggeration is missing, as is most of the humor. Just as the picture of Hanz Küchelgarten is a clumsy attempt at psychological portraiture, so are the pictures in his last work of Tentetnikov, Platonov and Khlobuev. The first work is universally regarded as a failure, in which verdict Gogol himself must have concurred, since he never acknowledged it as his; it represented a false direction to which he never returned. *Dead Souls: Part II* is hard to evaluate, since it exists only in fragments, and even these are only early drafts. Unquestionably the writing in Part II is greatly inferior to that in the first part. It tends toward clumsy, over-long sentences, unrelieved by the verbal gymnastics of Part I, and as Andrei Bely remarks,[82] "it horrifies one by the quantity of empty tautologies." Proffer notes[83] the prevalence in Part II of similes which almost repeat others successfully used in Part I, and of other banal comparisons that in his opinion give evidence of Gogol's failing powers of invention. It should be remembered, however, that what we have is only a rough draft; had Gogol's final version survived, we might have seen these and other stylistic defects eliminated. It seems unjust, therefore, to call Part II a failure only because it lacks the typical Gogolian features of Part I and of the author's other mature work. It was not intended to have these features, but represents an entirely new direction. It should be judged against such achievements of the "natural school" as Grigorovich's *Village* or Goncharov's *A Common Story* or Turgenev's "Khor and Kalinich." Seen from such a vantage point, the work does not look so bad. We might be very much surprised if some miracle could restore to us the lost definitive version of *Dead Souls: Part II.*

With the advent of the "natural school" and Gogol's attempts to remake his style to conform with the new direction, it seems reasonable to terminate this survey of Russian literature of the Romantic period. Most of the great writers of the period were dead: Pushkin and Lermontov, Bestuzhev and Yazykov, Küchelbecker and Baratynsky. Of the pioneers of romanticism Batyushkov was insane and long silent; only Zhukovsky survived (until 1852).

The first fifty years of the nineteenth century had been a dazzlingly brilliant period in Russian letters. To it belong the greatest names in Russian poetry: it had indeed been a "Golden Age." Prose had taken a distinctly minor, but still respectable place. During the century's last fifty years the contrary would be true: poetry would languish until nearly the end of the century, while prose in the hands of the great novelists would reach the highest point.

The "Romantic period" had been dominated by the literary fashion to which it owes its name; but by no means all the literary heritage of the period can be claimed as romantic. At the beginning of the century sentimentalism still flourished, and such a figure as Narezhny belongs to that transitional fashion. The greatest poets of the age, Pushkin and Lermontov, and the greatest prose writer, Gogol, all approached by the end of their careers the new realistic trend, Pushkin most closely of all, and many of the minor writers of the era show some traits of the new fashion, e.g., Polezhaev and Koltsov. Of the poets of the age the most uncompromising romantics are the Decembrist group and the so-called "Pushkin Pleiad."

Romanticism did not die a sudden death in 1850, however. A respectable group of minor poets continued to follow the trend, such as Karolina Pavlova, Apollon Grigoryev, Yakov Polonsky, Apollon Maikov, the Slavophiles Ivan and Konstantin Aksakov, and the Stankevich circle. Turgenev in his first literary efforts (e.g., *Parasha*) continued the tradition and one very great poet, Fyodor Tyutchev, who survived from the Pushkin generation, carried a modified romanticism even into the 1870s, forming a bridge into symbolism. Indeed, even Soviet critics acknowledge that the "socialist realist" Maxim Gorky is a romantic in his earliest tales. But as a period style romanticism does not survive the early 1840s; after that it is a relic, a minority trend, an old-fashioned mode, no longer dominant.

Notes

CHAPTER 1

1. F. I. Tiutchev, *Lirika* (M. Nauka, 1966), I, 315.
2. N. A. Nekrasov, *Sobranie sochinenii v vos'mi tomakh* (M. Gosudarstvennoe izdatel'stvo khudozhestvennoi literatury, 1965-1967), VII, 192-210.
3. I. S. Turgenev, *Sobranie sochinenii v desiati tomakh* (M. Gosudarstvennoe izdatel'stvo khudozhestvennoi literatury, 1961-1962), X, 239-242.
4. K. V. Pigarev, *Zhizn' i tvorchestvo Tiutcheva* (M. Nauka, 1926).
5. Pushkin, *Sobranie sochinenii v desiati tomakh* (M. Gosudarstvennoe izdatel'stvo khudozhestvennoi literatury, 1958-1962), VI, 138-139.
6. Tiutchev, II, 31-33.
7. Tiutchev, II, 43-46.
8. Tiutchev, II, 49-50.
9. Tiutchev, II, 53.
10. Tiutchev, II, 80.
11. *Heines Werke in Fünfzehn Teile* (Berlin, etc.: Bong & Co., n.d.): Part VII, pp. 61-64.
12. Heine, p. 65.
13. Heine, pp. 67-68; Tiutchev, II, 85-87.
14. Tiutchev, II, 78-79.
15. Tiutchev, I, 165.
16. Tiutchev, I, 19.
17. Tiutchev, I, 20.
18. Tiutchev, I, 81-82.
19. Tiutchev, I, 12.
20. Tiutchev, I, 16.
21. Tiutchev, I, 31.
22. Tiutchev, I, 39.
23. Tiutchev, I, 30.
24. Tiutchev, I, 81-82.
25. Tiutchev, I, 29.
26. Tiutchev, I, 74.
27. Tiutchev, I, 9.
28. Tiutchev, I, 75.
29. Tiutchev, I, 57.
30. Tiutchev, I, 98.
31. Tiutchev, I, 44.
32. Tiutchev, I, 22.
33. Tiutchev, I, 13.
34. Tiutchev, I, 34.
35. Tiutchev, I, 50.
36. Tiutchev, I, 61.
37. Tiutchev, I, 78.

38. Tiutchev, 1, 32.
39. Tiutchev, 1, 73.
40. Tiutchev, 1, 83.
41. Tiutchev, 1, 96.
42. Tiutchev, 1, 46.
43. B. Bukhshtab, *Russkie poety* (L. Gosudarstvennoe izdatel'stvo khudozhestvennoi literatury, 1970), p. 34.
44. Tiutchev, 1, 84.
45. Tiutchev, 1, 53.
46. Tiutchev, 1, 63.
47. Tiutchev, 1, 42.
48. Tiutchev, 1, 56.
49. Tiutchev, 1, 59.
50. Tiutchev, 1, 64.
51. Tiutchev, 1, 85.
52. Tiutchev, 1, 36.
53. Tiutchev, 1, 43.
54. Valerii Briusov, *Sobranie sochinenii v semi tomakh* (M. Nauka, 1975), VI, 205.

CHAPTER 2

1. A. I. Polezhaev, *Stikhotvoreniia i poemy* (L. Sovetskii Pisatel', Biblioteka poeta, bol'shaia seriia, 1957).
2. V. G. Belinskii, *Sobranie sochinenii v trekh tomakh* (M. OGIZ, 1948), II, 247.
3. Polezhaev, pp. 248-249.
4. Polezhaev, pp. 189-214.
5. Polezhaev, p. 189.
6. Polezhaev, p. 190.
7. Polezhaev, pp. 192-193.
8. Polezhaev, pp. 194-195.
9. Polezhaev, pp. 196-197.
10. Polezhaev, p. 209.
11. Polezhaev, p. 214.
12. Polezhaev, pp. 215-226.
13. Polezhaev, pp. 64-75.
14. Polezhaev, pp. 56-57.
15. Polezhaev, pp. 51-53.
16. Polezhaev, pp. 53-54.
17. Polezhaev, pp. 60-61.
18. Polezhaev, pp. 61-63.
19. Polezhaev, pp. 80-83.
20. Polezhaev, pp. 87-90.
21. Polezhaev, pp. 97-101.
22. Polezhaev, pp. 116-117.
23. Polezhaev, pp. 123-125.
24. Polezhaev, pp. 125-127.
25. Polezhaev, p. 130.
26. Polezhaev, pp. 132-136.
27. Belinskii, II, p. 249.
28. Polezhaev, pp. 172-178.
29. Polezhaev, pp. 227-260.
30. Polezhaev, pp. 230-231.

31. Polezhaev, p. 234.
32. Polezhaev, pp. 239.
33. Polezhaev, pp. 245-247.
34. Polezhaev, pp. 248-249.
35. Polezhaev, pp. 259-260.
36. Polezhaev, pp. 281-309.
37. Polezhaev, p. 283.
38. Polezhaev, pp. 295-296.
39. Polezhaev, p. 298.
40. Polezhaev, pp. 307-309.
41. Polezhaev, pp. 318-321.
42. Belinskii, II, 276.
43. Polezhaev, pp. 322-341.
44. Belinskii, II, 276.
45. Polezhaev, pp. 406-412.
46. Belinskii, II, 264.
47. Belinskii, II, 265.
48. Belinskii, II, 257.
49. *Poety 1820-1830-kh godov* (L. Sovetskii pisatel', Biblioteka poeta, bol'shaia seriia, 1972), I, 598-602.
50. A. S. Pushkin, *Sobranie sochinenii v desiati tomakh* (M.-L. Gosudarstvennoe izdatel'stvo khudozhestvennoi literatury, 1958-1962), VI, 159.
51. *Poety 1820-1830-kh godov*, I, 668-674.
52. *Poety 1820-1830-kh godov*, I, 776-777.
53. Pushkin, II, 13.
54. *Poety 1820-1830-kh godov*, I, 598.
55. *Poety 1820-1830-kh godov*, I, 676-677.
56. *Poety 1820-1830-kh godov*, I, 679-682.
57. *Poety 1820-1830-kh godov*, I, 677-679.
58. *Poety 1820-1830-kh godov*, I, 608-660.
59. *Poety 1820-1830-kh godov*, I, 608-609.
60. *Poety 1820-1830-kh godov*, I, 610-611.
61. For Bobrov's utilization of the theme, see W. E. Brown, *A History of Eighteenth-Century Russian Literature* (Ann Arbor: Ardis, 1980), p. 499.
62. *Poety 1820-1830-kh godov*, I, 648.
63. *Poety 1820-1830-kh godov*, I, 613-615.
64. *Poety 1820-1830-kh godov*, I, 617-621.
65. *Poety 1820-1830-kh godov*, I, 622-627. Gebedzhin (or Gebedzhe) is at present called Beloslav; it is not far from the Varna airport.
66. *Poety 1820-1830-kh godov*, I, 654-655.
67. *Poety 1820-1830-kh godov*, I, 628-633.
68. *Poety 1820-1830-kh godov*, I, 634-640.
69. *Poety 1820-1830-kh godov*, I, 658.
70. *Poety 1820-1830-kh godov*, I, 640-647.
71. Pushkin, VI, 150-161.
72. A. B. Kol'tsov, *Polnoe sobranie stikhotvorenii* (L. Sovetskii Pisatel', Biblioteka poeta, bol'shaia seriia, 1958).
73. Kol'tsov, p. 76.
74. Kol'tsov, pp. 56-57.
75. Kol'tsov, p. 55.
76. Kol'tsov, pp. 52-53.
77. Kol'tsov, p. 271.
78. Kol'tsov, pp. 88-89.

79. Kol'tsov, pp. 89-90.
80. Kol'tsov, pp. 90-91.
81. Kol'tsov, p. 92.
82. Kol'tsov, pp. 121-122.
83. Kol'tsov, pp. 182-183.
84. Kol'tsov, pp. 196-197.
85. Kol'tsov, pp. 198-199.
86. Dmitrij Tschižewskij, *Russische Literaturgeschichte des 19. Jahrhunderts. 1. Die Romantik* (München: Eidos Verlag, 1964), p. 138.
87. Adolf Stender-Petersen, *Geschichte der Russischen Literatur* (München: C. H. Beck, 1957), II, 94.
88. Kol'tsov, p. 40.
89. Kol'tsov, p. 183.
90. Kol'tsov, pp. 114-117.
91. Kol'tsov, pp. 148-149.
92. Kol'tsov, p. 106.
93. Kol'tsov, pp. 126-127.
94. Kol'tsov, pp. 145-147.
95. Kol'tsov, pp. 141-142.
96. Kol'tsov, pp. 143-144.
97. Kol'tsov, p. 169.
98. Kol'tsov, pp. 149-150.
99. Kol'tsov, p. 150.
100. Kol'tsov, pp. 156-157.
101. Kol'tsov, pp. 95-96.
102. Kol'tsov, pp. 114-117.
103. Kol'tsov, pp. 107-110.
104. Kol'tsov, pp. 168-169.

CHAPTER 3

1. *Poety 1820-1830-kh godov* (L. Sovetskii pisatel', biblioteka poeta, bol'shaia seriia, 1972), I, 318-347.
2. *Poety 1820-1830-kh godov*, I, 342-343.
3. *Poety 1820-1830-kh godov*, I, 345.
4. A. S. Pushkin, *Sobranie sochinenii v desiati tomakh* (M. Gosudarstvennoe izdatel'stvo khudozhestvennoi literatury, 1958-1962), IX, 48.
5. *Poety 1820-1830-kh godov*, I, 335-337.
6. Pushkin, IX, 54.
7. *Poety 1820-1830-kh godov*, I, 348-367.
8. *Poety 1820-1830-kh godov*, I, 352.
9. *Poety 1820-1830-kh godov*, I, 352-355.
10. *Poety 1820-1830-kh godov*, I, 358.
11. *Poety 1820-1830-kh godov*, I, 351-362.
12. *Poety 1820-1830-kh godov*, I, 360-361.
13. *Poety 1820-1830-kh godov*, I, 263-264.
14. *Poety 1820-1830-kh godov*, I, 487-497.
15. *Poety 1820-1830-kh godov*, I, 488.
16. *Poety 1820-1830-kh godov*, I, 491.
17. *Poety 1820-1830-kh godov*, I, 490.
18. *Poety 1820-1830-kh godov*, I, 491-492.
19. *Poety 1820-1830-kh godov*, I, 494.

20. *Poety 1820-1830-kh godov*, 1, 496; for the Mickiewicz original, see Adam Mitskevich, *Sonety* (L. Nauka, 1976), p. 20.

21. *Poety 1820-1830-kh godov*, 1, 398-428.

22. *Poety 1820-1830-kh godov*, 1, 401-402.

23. *Poety 1820-1830-kh godov*, 1, 407.

24. *Poety 1820-1830-kh godov*, 1, 403-404.

25. *Poety 1820-1830-kh godov*, 1, 424-426.

26. *Poety 1820-1830-kh godov*, 1, 411-416.

27. *Poety 1820-1830-kh godov*, 1, 419-423.

28. *Poety 1820-1830-kh godov*, 1, 252-311.

29. *Poety 1820-1830-kh godov*, 1, 23-24.

30. *Poety 1820-1830-kh godov*, 1, 259.

31. *Poety 1820-1830-kh godov*, 1, 262-264.

32. *Poety 1820-1830-kh godov*, 1, 283-284.

33. *Poety 1820-1830-kh godov*, 1, 280-282.

34. *Poety 1820-1830-kh godov*, 1, 291.

35. *Poety 1820-1830-kh godov*, 1, 26.

36. *Poety 1820-1830-kh godov*, 1, 299-302.

37. *Poety 1820-1830-kh godov*, 1, 306-307.

38. *Poety 1820-1830-kh godov*, 1, 294; 297-298.

39. *Poety 1820-1830-kh godov*, 1, 551-579.

40. *Poety 1820-1830-kh godov*, 1, 567.

41. *Poety 1820-1830-kh godov*, 1, 568.

42. *Poety 1820-1830-kh godov*, 1, 368-397.

43. *Poety 1820-1830-kh godov*, 1, 372-373.

44. *Poety 1820-1830-kh godov*, 1, 388.

45. *Poety 1820-1830-kh godov*, 1, 389-394.

46. *Poety 1820-1830-kh godov*, 1, 386-387.

47. *Poety 1820-1830-kh godov*, 11, 258-277.

48. *Poety 1820-1830-kh godov*, 11, 268.

49. *Poety 1820-1830-kh godov*, 11, 276.

50. *Poety 1820-1830-kh godov*, 11, 226-257.

51. *Poety 1820-1830-kh godov*, 11, 231.

52. *Poety 1820-1830-kh godov*, 11, 251-252.

53. *Poety 1820-1830-kh godov*, 11, 252-253.

54. *Poety 1820-1830-kh godov*, 11, 256-257.

55. *Poety 1820-1830-kh godov*, 1, 429-439.

56. *Poety 1820-1830-kh godov*, 1, 432-436.

57. V. G. Benediktov, *Stikhotvoreniia* (L. Sovetskii pisatel', 1939); *Sochineniia V. G. Benediktova*, ed. Ia. P. Polonskii (M. M. O. Vol'f, 1902), Vol. I.

58. Polonskii introduction, Vol'f edition, I, xiv.

59. Polonskii introduction, Vol'f edition, I, xii.

60. V. Belinskii, *Polnoe sobranie sochinenii* (M. 1955), VII, 500.

61. Benediktov, Vol'f ed., I, 14-15.

62. Benediktov, *Stikhotvoreniia*, p. 174; Benediktov, Vol'f ed., I, 166-168.

63. *Brannaia krasavitsa*, Vol'f ed., I, 24.

64. Benediktov, *Stikhotvoreniia*, p. 1; Benediktov, *Sochineniia*, Vol'f ed., p. 8-9.

65. Benediktov, *Sochineniia*, Vol'f ed., Vol. I, pp. 48-49.

66. Benediktov, *Sochineniia*, Vol'f ed., Vol. I, pp. 48-49.

67. Benediktov, *Stikhotvoreniia*, p. 81; Benediktov, *Sochineniia*, I, 27-28.

68. *Poety 1820-1830-kh godov*, 11, 167.

69. Benediktov, *Sochineniia*, Vol'f ed., I, 87.

70. Benediktov, *Sochineniia*, Vol'f ed., I, 52-53.

71. Benediktov, *Sochineniia*, Vol'f ed., I, 78-79.

72. *Poety 1820-1830-kh godov*, II, 526-588.

73. *Poety 1820-1830-kh godov*, II, 548-549.

74. *Poety 1820-1830-kh godov*, II, 574.

75. *Poety 1820-1830-kh godov*, II, 566.

76. *Poety 1820-1830-kh godov*, II, 415-452.

77. A selection of Sokolovsky's verse is printed in *Poety 1820-1830-kh godov*, II, 362-414.

78. *Poety 1820-1830-kh godov*, II, 368.

79. *Poety 1820-1830-kh godov*, II, 421-425.

80. *Poety 1820-1830-kh godov*, II, 426-429.

81. *Poety 1820-1830-kh godov*, II, 430-445.

82. Friedrich Schiller, *Gedichte* (Leipzig: Reclam, n.d.), p. 197.

83. *Poety 1820-1830-kh godov*, II, 449-451.

84. P. P. Ershov, *Konek-Gorbunok. Stikhotvoreniia* (L. Sovetskii pisatel', Biblioteka poeta, bol'shaia seriia, 1976).

85. A. N. Afanas'ev, *Russkaia narodnyia skazki A. N. Afanas'eva* (M. I. D. Sytin, 1914), 5 vols.; II, 246-254.

CHAPTER 4

1. Boris Eikhenbaum, *Stat'i o Lermontove* (M.-L. Nauka, 1961), p. 42.

2. *A Lermontov Reader*, edited and translated by Guy Daniels (New York: Macmillan, 1965), pp. 214-303.

3. *Russian Literature Triquarterly* (Spring 1972), pp. 69-80; reprinted in *Russian Romantic Prose: An Anthology*, ed. Carl R. Proffer (Ann Arbor: Translation Press, 1979), pp. 196-209.

4. Mikhail Lermontov, *Vadim*, translation and introduction by Helena Goscilo (Ann Arbor: Ardis, 1984).

5. M. Iu. Lermontov, *Sobranie sochinenii v chetyrekh tomakh* (M.-L. Nauka, 1961-1962), I, 603.

6. Lermontov, I, 11.

7. Lermontov, I, 10.

8. Lermontov, I, 15.

9. Lermontov, I, 57.

10. Lermontov, I, 390. Blagoi in his volume *Lermontov i Pushkin* (M. 1941), pp. 365-366 notes another difference between the two poets' demons: "For Pushkin his demon is an objectively opposing figure; Lermontov's demon is almost directly identified with the subjective consciousness of the poet himself." It should be remembered that there is some evidence to support the notion that Pushkin's "Demon" had indeed an objective existence—in the person of Alexander Nikolaevich Raevsky!

11. See Boris Eikhenbaum, *Lermontov*, translated by Ray Parrot and Harry Weber (Ann Arbor: Ardis, 1981), pp. 30-31.

12. Lermontov, I, 65; Lermontov, *The Demon and Other Poems*, translated from the Russian by Eugene M. Kayden (Yellow Springs, Ohio: The Antioch Press, 1965), p. 3.

13. Lermontov, I, 74.

14. D. P. Murav'ev in *Lermontovskaia entsiklopediia* (M. Sovetskaia entsiklopediia, 1982), pp. 283-284 points to the mutually conflicting elements of this "Prayer," which he considers "one of the high points of [Lermontov's] early lyric." The petitioner on the one hand prays the Almighty for forgiveness for a course of life that seems unlikely to lead to salvation, while at the same time pointing out to the Creator in no uncertain terms that the passions, including that for verse-writing, are inborn and an integral part of his personality, to which he will be doing violence by suppressing them. The only solution is to beg the Almighty to abolish them!

15. Lermontov, I, 83.

16. Lermontov, IV, 512.

17. Lermontov, I, 87.

18. Lermontov, I, 121.

19. Lermontov, I, 114-117.

20. Kayden, p.6.

21. Lermontov, I, 231.

22. L. M. Shchemeleva in *Lermontovskaia entsiklopediia*, p. 227.

23. Lermontov, I, 214; Kayden, p. 13.

24. Lermontov, I, 228.

25. Lermontov, I, 300; Kayden, p. 10.

26. Lermontov, I, 59.

27. Lermontov, I, 323.

28. Lermontov, I, 239; Kayden, p. 14; Daniels, p. 74; *Penguin Book of Russian Verse,* introduced and edited by Dmitri Obolensky (Harmondsworth, Middlesex: Penguin Books, 1962), p. 154.

29. Lermontov, I, 390; Kayden, p. 17; Daniels, p. 74.

30. Lermontov, I, 372.

31. Lermontov, I, 316.

32. Lermontov, I, 183-193.

33. See V. I. Korovin in *Lermontovskaia entsiklopediia*, p. 586. Eikhenbaum (*Lermontov,* Parrott and Weber translation, p. 40) notes: "In 1831 it[i.e., the iambic pentameter] acquires an especially sharp, prosaic character as in the poem 'June 11, 1831,' which goes wholly beyond the bounds of the customary lyric genres and represents a free form of the meditation (like Byron's 'Epistle to Augusta,' which probably served as a model)...After 1831 Lermontov completely abandons the iambic in lyric poetry as well as in narrative poems."

34. Lermontov, I, 292.

35. Lermontov, I, 361; Kayden, p. 17; Daniels, p. 74.

36. Lermontov, I, 49.

37. Lermontov, I, 140; Kayden, p. 7; Daniels, p. 73.

38. Lermontov, I, 149.

39. Lermontov, I, 256-257.

40. Lermontov, IV, 517-518; 668.

41. Lermontov, I, 248.

42. Lermontov, I, 258-259.

43. Lermontov, I, 288.

44. A. S. Pushkin, *Sobranie sochinenii v desiati tomakh* (M.-L. Gosudarstvennoe izdatel'stvo khudozhestvennoi literatury, 1958-1962), II, 289-292.

45. Pushkin, X, 11; Shaw, *The Letters of Alexander Pushkin:* three volumes in one, trans. J. Thomas Shaw (Madison, Milwaukee, and London: The University of Wisconsin Press, 1967), pp. 452-453.

46. Lermontov, I, 234-235.

47. Lermontov, I, 251-252. Lermontov seems to have found some of the motifs for this poem in Thomas Moore's piece beginning: "When he who adores thee has left but the name of his fault and his sorrows behind."

48. Lermontov, I, 366.

49. Lermontov, I, 243-244.

50. Lermontov, I, 217-218.

51. Lermontov, I, 197-198.

52. Lermontov, I, 384.

53. Lermontov, I, 232.

54. Lermontov, I, 271-272.

55. Lermontov, I, 318.
56. Lermontov, I, 348-349.
57. Lermontov, I, 249.
58. Lermontov, I, 403-404; Kayden, p. 25.
59. Lermontov, I, 405.
60. Lermontov, I, 406.
61. Lermontov, I, 412-414; Kayden, p. 31. I. S. Chistova gives an exhaustive analysis of the poem in the *Lermontovskaia entsiklopediia*, pp. 511-513, noting the intensely rhetorical quality of it, and the combination in it of the elegiac (the second part, lines 34-56) with the oratorical and denunciatory (last 16 lines). This extraordinary combination has given rise, as she notes, to widely divergent attempts to define its genre ("political satire": I. Borichevsky; "political ode": B. Eikhenbaum; "Ode-satire": K. Barkhin)—all of them unsatisfactory.
62. Lermontov, I, 417-418; Kayden, p. 56; Daniels, p. 103.
63. Lermontov, I, 419-420; Kayden, p. 37.
64. Lermontov, I, 421; Kayden, p. 38; *Penguin Book of Russian Verse*, p. 155.
65. Lermontov, I, 422; Kayden, p. 39.
66. Lermontov, I, 408-411. "Borodino," published in the sixth issue of *The Contemporary* (1837) in connection with the 25th anniversary of the battle, was Lermontov's first poem to be published with the author's knowledge and consent. See D. E. Maksimov in *Lermontovskaia entsiklopediia*, p. 67.
67. Lermontov, I, 297-299.
68. Lermontov, I, 497-505; Kayden, pp. 77-83. After "Borodino," "Valerik" is one of the earliest attempts in Russian verse to represent the reality of war in a common, uninflated language. See D. E. Maksimov (p. 67) and E. M. Pul'khritudova (p. 79) in *Lermontovskaia entsiklopediia*.
69. Lermontov, I, 506-507; Kayden, p. 84; Daniels, p. 105.
70. Lermontov, I, 423; Kayden, p. 40.
71. Lermontov, I, 494; Kayden, p. 73.
72. Lermontov, I, 495; Kayden, p. 74.
73. Lermontov, I, 508; Kayden, p. 86.
74. Lermontov, I, 549; Kayden, p. 106.
75. Lermontov, I, 530; Kayden, p. 96.
76. Lermontov, I, 492-493; Kayden, p. 71. The identification of the "baby" to whom the poem is addressed is a matter of debate (see T. G. Dinesman in *Lermontovskaia entsiklopediia*, p. 464). The usual belief, first voiced by P. A. Viskovaty in 1891, is somewhat weakened by the masculine gender of the verbs and adjectives of the poem; but since the addressee is a "baby" (*rebënok*, masc.), this difficulty seems slight. Moreover Lermontov was extremely careful in all his allusions to Varvara Lopukhina, especially after her marriage, to disguise her figure, so it is not impossible that he here deliberately employs the wrong gender to make identification less easy.
77. Lermontov, I, 436. It has been very plausibly suggested by V. S. Shaduri ("Lermontov v Gruzii," in *Za khrebtom kavkaza* [Tbilisi: "Merani," 1977] that the addressee of these three poems was Ekaterina Alexandrovna Chavchavadze, daughter of the Georgian poet Alexander Garsevanovich Chavchavadze (1786-1846). She had blue eyes and a fine voice, and was a friend of several poets.
78. See V. S. Shaduri in *Lermontovskaia entsiklopediia*, p. 510.
79. Lermontov, I, 432-433; Kayden, pp. 44-45.
80. Lermontov, I, 461-463; Kayden, p. 59.
81. Lermontov, I, 466-467; Kayden, pp. 62-63. Although earlier writers on Lermontov even identified the New Year's masquerade of the poem, and speak of an unpleasant incident involving the poet's rudeness to two masked daughters of the Tsar, this is all, according to modern research, a legend (see L. N. Nazarova and E. E. Naidich in *Lermontovskaia entsiklopediia*, p. 215). The poem is an example of Lermontov's trend in his later verse toward

a declamatory style, noted by Eikhenbaum (see his *Lermontov,* Parrott and Weber translation, p. 128). The theme of the masquerade and of the reversal of levels of reality in the piece—i.e., the poet's bright recollections of a happy childhood are more "real" than the shadowy, masked figures around him—are notable. The first part of the poem approaches the romantic elegy in character, while the last, as in "Death of a Poet," belongs to the satire—a combination which, as Eikhenbaum notes, may be found in such French poets as André Chénier, Henri-Auguste Barbier (1805-1882) e.g., in his *Les Iambiques* and Gilbert, as well as Victor Hugo.

82. Lermontov, I, 524; Kayden, p. 76.

83. Lermontov, I, 442-443; Kayden, pp. 46-47.

84. Lermontov, I, 509-510; Kayden, p. 87. V. A. Manuilov (*Lermontovskaia entsiklopediia,* pp. 469-470) suggests that Khomyakov's Slavophile poem "Native Land" (*Otchizna,* 1839) may have been the stimulus for Lermontov's piece. Khomyakov emphasizes the meekness of the Russian people, their devout Orthodoxy, etc. Lermontov's poem differs markedly from all earlier Russian patriotic verse, in the absence of the usual civic theme: his emphasis is entirely on the land itself and the common people who almost form a part of it, rather than on the rights and duties of the abstract citizen.

85. This piece is composed of three four-line strophes, each consisting of four dactyls acatalectic—an extremely musical meter, conveying strong emotion. Lermontov had used it earlier in his "Prayer" *(Molitva)* of 1837.

86. Lermontov, I, 454-456; Kayden, p. 52.

87. In *Lermontovskaia entsiklopediia,* p. 580.

88. Michael R. Katz, *The Literary Ballad in Early Nineteenth-Century Russian Literature* (Oxford: Oxford University Press, 1976), pp. 176-177.

89. Lermontov, I, 458-460; Kayden, pp. 56-58.

90. *Lermontovskaia entsiklopediia,* p. 127.

91. Lermontov, I, 541-542; Kayden, pp. 102.

92. Lermontov, I, 545-546; Kayden, pp. 104.

93. Lermontov, I, 434; Kayden, pp. 43.

94. Lermontov, I, 526-529.

95. Katz, *The Literary Ballad...,* p. 179.

96. Lermontov, I, 448-449; Kayden, pp. 48-49.

97. Lermontov, I, 547-548; Kayden, pp. 107.

98. Lermontov, I, 452-453; Kayden, pp. 50-51.

99. *Lermontovskaia entsiklopediia,* p. 336.

100. Lermontov, I, 425. This piece has traditionally been interpreted as a somewhat hysterical reaction to the poet's arrest after the circulation of his "Death of a Poet." It can, of course, hardly be imagined that Lermontov feared a death on the scaffold for writing a poem, no matter how outspoken! There is an evident connection between "Do not mock ... " and Pushkin's poem "André Chénier" (1825), and there have been attempts to show that Lermontov thought at one time of writing a cycle of poems on the fate of the French poet (see E. Gershtein in *Lermontovskaia entsiklopediia,* p. 337); to such a project this unfinished piece might readily be attributed. Gershtein, however, has still another interpretation: she would date the poem *before* the composition of "Death of a Poet": "It may be supposed that 'Do not mock ...' immediately precedes 'Death of a Poet,' preparing its poetical phraseology, and in part its problematics, and is connected with numerous moments of spiritual crisis in the youthful Lermontov occasioned by biographical or creative causes...." Might it not even be possible to interpret the poem as the utterance not of Lermontov himself, but of Pushkin in the quality of André Chénier?

101. Lermontov, I, 424; Kayden, p. 41.

102. Lermontov, I, 567.

103. Lermontov, I, 468; Kayden, p. 64.

104. Lermontov, I, 543-544; Kayden, p. 103; Daniels, p. 115.

105. *Lermontov*, Parrott and Weber translation, p. 46.

106. *Sochineniia v vos'mi tomakh* (M. Izdatel'stvo sotsial'no-ekonomicheskoi literatury. 1959), p. 123.

107. I. B. Rodnianskaia in *Lermontovskaia entsiklopediia*, p. 96.

108. Lermontov, I, 530; Kayden, p. 86.

109. *Literaturnoe nasledstvo*, Vol. 43-44 (M. Nauka, 1941), p. 252.

110. Lermontov, I, 706.

CHAPTER 5

1. M. Iu. Lermontov, *Sobranie sochinenii v chetyrekh tomakh* (M.-L. Akademiia Nauk, 1961-1962), II, 7-16.

2. Boris Eikhenbaum, *Lermontov*, trans. Parrott and Weber (Ann Arbor: Ardis, 1981), pp. 23-26, exhibits side by side some of Lermontov's borrowings and their sources in "The Circassians." As noted by L. N. Nazarova in *Lermontovskaia entsiklopediia*, p. 613, this early essay in the genre lacks the love interest which is otherwise almost an obligatory feature of the Byronic poem.

3. Lermontov, II, 11.

4. Lermontov, II, 17-39.

5. Boris Eikhenbaum, *Lermontov*, p. 26, notes the young poet's indebtedness, not only to Pushkin, but to Kozlov and Bestuzhev-Marlinsky. L. N. Nazarova (*Lermontovskaia entsiklopediia*, p. 213) notes that the traits of disillusionment and weariness with life which characterize Pushkin's Prisoner are not present with his fourteen-year-old imitator—"they were not understood by the young poet."

6. Lermontov, II, 40-53.

7. Eikhenbaum (*Lermontov*, p. 26-27) shows in detail the borrowings in *The Corsair*, most surprising of which is one from a Lomonosov ode: "He does not simply imitate his chosen 'favorite' poet, as usually happens in one's school years; rather he takes ready-made excerpts from various sources and forms a new work from them. We will see that later he does the same thing with his own verses, constructing new poems from old bits and pieces."

8. Lermontov, II, 54-60.

9. Lermontov, II, 61-65.

10. Lermontov, II, 66-68.

11. Lermontov, II, 69-71.

12. Lermontov, II, 72-88.

13. Lermontov, II, 88.

14. Lermontov, II, 77.

15. Lermontov, II, 79.

16. Lermontov, II, 89-117. In the style of Ryleev's *Dumy* and other Decembrist documents, Lermontov ignores the historical differences between the era of Vadim's legendary revolt and the present, and injects into his piece various "allusions" applicable to the contemporary scene. Thus, Vadim is one of only a handful of surviving fighters for freedom—an obvious allusion to the fate of the Decembrists; and the reproach of Vadim's contemporaries for inactivity is of course pointedly aimed at Russians of 1831 (see T. A. Nedosekina in *Lermontovskaia entsiklopediia*, p. 437).

17. Lermontov, II, 118-123.

18. Lermontov, II, 124-132.

19. Lermontov, II, 132-150.

20. Lermontov, II, 151-158.

21. Lermontov, II, 159-163.

22. Lermontov, II, 164-242.

23. There seems, however, to be recent evidence that Atazhukin, instead of being the

victim of Roslambek's treachery, actually himself contrived the death of his cousin (see K. N. Grigor'ian in *Lermontovskaia entsiklopediia,* p. 189).

24. Lermontov, II, 164-165.

25. Lermontov, II, 180-181 (st. 24).

26. See also E. M. Pul'khritudova in *Istoriia romantizma v russkoi literature, 1825-1840* (M. Nauka, 1979), pp. 285-287; E. M. Pul'khritudova in *Lermontovskaia entsiklopediia,* p. 188.

27. Lermontov, II, 243-260.

28. Lermontov, II, 261-287.

29. Lermontov, II, 288-303.

30. Lermontov, II, 304-339.

31. Lermontov, II, 338.

32. Lermontov, II, 339.

33. Lermontov, II, 329-330.

34. Lermontov, II, 415-432; *A Lermontov Reader,* edited and translated by Guy Daniels (New York: Macmillan, 1965), pp. 78-98; Lermontov, *The Demon and Other Poems,* translated from the Russian by Eugene M. Kayden (Yellow Springs, OH: Antioch Press, 1965), pp. 111-128. In her article on "Song of Tsar Ivan Vasilievich...." I. S. Chistova (*Lermontovskaia entsiklopediia,* p. 410) notes Lermontov's indebtedness to Slavophile friends, especially Svyatoslav Afanasievich Raevsky (1808-1876) for collections of actual folklore material. He seems also to have utilized the song about Mastryuka Temryukovich in Kirsha Danilov's collection of popular songs (see *Drevnie rossiiskie stikhotvoreniia sobrannye Kirsheiu Danilovym;* 2nd revised edition (M. Nauka, 1977), pp. 27-32.

35. Lermontov, II, 305.

36. Lermontov, II, 416.

37. Lermontov, II, 427-428.

38. Lermontov, II, 429-430.

39. Lermontov, II, 461-466.

40. Lermontov, II, 463-464. As so frequently, Lermontov in *The Fugitive* re-uses material originally composed for another work. In this case the maiden's song is almost a repetition of Selim's song from *Izmail-Bei.* In that dreary political tract which N. G. Chernyshevsky aggrandized with the title of "novel," *What is to be Done? [Chto delat'?],* the songs of Selim and "the maiden" are misinterpreted in typical fashion as covertly revolutionary utterances, and this circumstance has led otherwise rational critics to misread accordingly Lermontov's splendidly stylized bit of mountain folklore (see I. Ia. Zaslavskii, *Lermontovskaia entsiklopediia,* p. 52).

41. "Na putiakh k realizmu," in the collection *Zhizn'i tvorchestvo M. Iu. Lermontova.* Sbornik I: *Issledovaniia i materialy* (M. 1941), pp. 163-250.

42. *Lermontovskaia entsiklopediia,* pp. 639-640.

43. *RLT,* No. 14, pp. 416-429.

44. *RLT,* No. 14, p. 42.

45. Cited by Hopkins from Durylin, p. 198; see P. N. Sakulin, "Zemlia i nebo v poezii M. Iu. Lermontova," in *Venok M. Iu. Lermontovu* (M.-P. 1914), pp. 37-38.

46. Lermontov, II, 340-348. *Mongo* has never found an English translator.

47. Lermontov, II, 344-345.

48. Lermontov, II, 433-460. There is a good translation of *The Tambov Treasurer's Wife* by Guy Daniels, pp. 39-69.

49. *Lermontovskaia entsiklopediia,* p. 561.

50. Lermontov, II, 349-414. There is no English translation of *Sashka.*

51. Boris Eikhenbaum, "Literaturnaia pozitsiia Lermontova," *Literaturnoe nasledstvo,* Vol. 43-44, pp. 58-60.

52. E. E. Naidich (*Lermontovskaia entsiklopediia,* pp. 498-499) rejects categorically any connection of the so-called "Chapter II" of *Sashka* with the "first chapter," and identifies

"Chapter II" as a variant of the first part of *A Fairy-Tale for Children*, in my opinion probably correctly. He also says: "*Sashka* can be considered as a completed work." On the latter point there are still differences of opinion. Maksimov (*Poeziia Lermontova* [M.-L. 1964], p. 89) remarks: "The poem *Sashka*, despite its brilliant verse and a series of noteworthy descriptions and lyrical passages, as a whole did not completely satisfy Lermontov. Apparently for this reason it remained unfinished, or was artificially brought to a close, halted abruptly in mid-course." In a lengthy note, however, he presents the opposing view, that *Sashka*, on the analogy of such intentionally "incomplete" works as de Musset's *Namouna* and Gogol's "Ivan Fyodorovich Shponka and His Auntie," was deliberately left a "fragment" by its author.

53. Lermontov, II, 410-411.
54. Lermontov, II, 362, stanzas 32-33.
55. Lermontov, II, 351, stanza 5.
56. Lermontov, II, 352-353, stanzas 9-10.
57. Lermontov, II, 365, stanza 40.
58. Lermontov, II, 370, stanza 51.
59. Lermontov, II, 371, stanza 54.
60. Lermontov, II, 376-377, stanzas 67, 68.
61. Lermontov, II, 378-379, stanzas 71, 73.
62. Lermontov, II, 381-382, stanzas 79-80.
63. Lermontov, II, 386, stanza 90.
64. Lermontov, II, 592-593, stanzas 105-107.
65. Lermontov, II, 397, stanza 116.
66. Lermontov, II, 398, stanza 118.
67. Lermontov, II, 406-407, stanzas 139-141.
68. Lermontov, II, *The Demon*, final version, pp. 504-541; earlier version, pp. 545-641.
69. *M. Iu. Lermontov: Issledovaniia i materialy* (M. 1974), p. 411.
70. Lermontov, II, 547
71. D. E. Maksimov, *Poeziia Lermontova* (M.-L. Nauka, 1964), p. 80.
72. Lermontov, II, 635.
73. Lermontov, II, 505, sect. 3.
74. Lermontov, II, 515-516.
75. Lermontov, II, 527.
76. Lermontov, II, 535-536.
77. Lermontov, IV, 517 (note 14).
78. Lermontov, II, 492-503; Guy Daniels translates the "Prefatory Note" to the poem (first six stanzas) in his *A Lermontov Reader*.
79. Lermontov, II, 493-495.
80. Lermontov, II, 503.
81. Lermontov, II, 467-491; full translation in Kayden, pp. 134-158, "The Novice."
82. See Maksimov, *Poeziia Lermontova*, p. 179.
83. Lermontov, II, 690, quoting *Russkaia starina*, vol. 10 (1887), pp. 124-125.
84. Lermontov, II, 689-690.
85. Lermontov, II, 491.
86. Lermontov, II, 475.
87. Lermontov, II, 477-478.
88. Lermontov, II, 480.

CHAPTER 6

1. M. Iu. Lermontov, *Sobranie sochinenii v chetyrekh tomakh* (M.-L. Akademiia Nauk, 1961-1962), III, 10-168. For a study of all of Lermontov's dramatic attempts, see K. N. Grigor'ian, "Dramaturgiia M. Iu. Lermontova," in *Istoriia russkoi dramaturgii: XVIII-pervaia polovina XIX veka* (M. Nauka, 1982), pp. 368-401.

2. Lermontov, III, 169-253.

3. N. M. Vladimirskaia in *Lermontovskaia entsiklopediia* (M. Sovetskaia entsiklopediia, 1981), p. 200 calls *The Spaniards* "Lermontov's first completed dramatic production." It is possible that the drama is complete, for by the point when the manuscript breaks off the three principal characters—Fernando, Emilia and Noemi—have all been disposed of. It seems difficult to believe, however, that the poet would have left the fate of Moses undecided, and particularly that Sorrini's villainy would have been tamely left for heaven to punish.

4. Lermontov, III, 251-252.

5. Lermontov, III, 254-346; Guy Daniels, *A Lermontov Reader* (New York: Macmillan, 1965), pp. 214-303.

6. Lermontov, I, 243.

7. Lermontov, III, 489-538.

8. Lermontov, III, 491.

9. Lermontov, III, 538.

10. Lermontov, III, 347-488.

11. Lermontov, III, 541-638.

12. Lermontov, III, 639-716.

13. For a complete discussion of the textual variants of *Masquerade*, see Boris Eikhenbaum's article "Piat' redaktsii 'Maskerada'" in his volume *O Poezii* (L. 1969), pp. 215-233.

14. The dualistic character of Arbenin is explained by A. M. Dokusov in *Lermontovskaia entsiklopediia* (P. 274) as a reflection of the Schelling doctrine, familiar to Lermontov through contacts with the "Wisdom-Lovers" of the oneness of good and evil. It must be noted, however, that the character of the Demon, even in the earliest versions of the poem, before Schelling's philosophy became known to the poet, is very similar to that of Arbenin.

15. *Lermontovskaia entsiklopediia*, s.v. *dramaturgiia*, p. 146.

16. Lermontov, IV, 7-136. On the development of Lermontov's prose style and the place of *Vadim* in his work in general see the excellent discussion in John Mersereau Jr., *Mikhail Lermontov* (Carbondale, IL: Southern Illinois University Press, 1962), pp. 26-46.

17. See Eikhenbaum, *Lermontov* (Ann Arbor: Ardis, 1981), pp. 148-150.

18. On the connection between Vadim and Quasimodo, see the article of A. M. Dokusov, "M. Iu. Lermontov i V. Giugo," in *Puti russkoi prozy XIX veka* (L. 1970), pp. 3-15. On the echoes of Bestuzhev-Marlinsky in *Vadim*, see A. V. Fedorov, *Lermontov i literatura ego vremeni* (L. 1967).

19. The influence of the *école frénétique* in French prose of the 1830s, of which Hugo is only the most conspicuous example, is evident throughout *Vadim*, e.g., in the detailed and intentionally shocking descriptions of violence and horror, such as the death of Mme Palitsyna, of the murder of the unnamed landlord's daughter, of the horrible old beggar-woman who revolts even Vadim, etc. See Eikhenbaum, *Lermontov*, pp. 150-153.

20. Lermontov, IV, 164-257; complete translation in Daniels, pp. 117-213. See also Mersereau, pp. 47-62.

21. Raevsky's part in the composition of the novel is very uncertain. According to a note in the *Lermontovskaia entsiklopediia* (signed by I. A. Kryazhinskaya and L. M. Arinshtein), "V. Kh. Khokhryakov in the '50s asked Raevsky about the degree of his participation in the creation of the novel, and recorded: 'S[vyatoslav] Af[anasievich] said that he wrote only at Lermontov's dictation.'" Eikhenbaum, however, in the notes to *Lermontov* (IV, 642) remarks, after quoting the words of Lermontov's letter to Raevsky: "The question, evidently,

is of *Princess Ligovskaya,* work on which was interrupted in January 1837. Raevsky's part in work on the novel is confirmed by the MS: a considerable part of it is written in his hand—'at Lermontov's dictation' (according to Raevsky's own words spoken in the '50s to V. Kh. Khokhryakov), but obviously not without his verbal advice, stories, descriptions, etc. It must be supposed that his assistance was particularly called for in those chapters where *chinovniki* are concerned, and in particular about Krasiński. Lermontov, who had just finished Junker school. could not have known the *chinovnik* way of life in detail."

22. *Istoriia russkogo romana v dvukh tomakh* (M.-L. Akademiia Nauk, 1962), I, 286.

23. See article "Lermontov i E. A. Sushkova" by Antonia Glasse in *M. Iu. Lermontov: Issledovaniia i materialy* (L. Nauka, 1979, pp. 80-121.

24. Adolf Stender-Petersen, *Geschichte der Russischen Literatur in Zwei Bänden* (München, C. M. Beck, 1957), II, 151-152.

25. *Istoriia russkogo romana v dvukh tomakh,* I, 287.

26. *M. Iu. Lermontov: Issledovaniia i materialy,* p. 119.

27. Lermontov, IV, 606.

28. Lermontov, IV, 236-237.

29. Lermontov, IV, 231-232.

30. Lermontov, IV, 164-165.

31. Lermontov, IV, 251.

32. N. V. Gogol', *Polnoe sobranie sochinenii v desiati tomakh* (Berlin: Slovo, 1921), VIII, 216-217.

33. *Istoriia russkogo romana,* I, 286; Benediktov's verse often exploits the same effect, e.g., "The Waltz."

34. Lermontov, IV, 258-263.

35. *Issledovaniia i materialy,* p. 88.

36. Lermontov, IV, 264-274.

37. Lermontov, IV, 475-479.

38. *Lermontovskaia entsiklopediia,* p. 213.

39. *Issledovaniia i materialy,* pp. 223-252; see also I. S. Chistova, "Prozaicheskii otryvok...'Shtoss' i 'Natural'naia shkola' " in *Russkaia literatura,* XXI, 1, 116-122.

40. Lermontov, IV, 480-500.

41. *Russian Romantic Prose: An Anthology,* ed. Carl R. Proffer (Ann Arbor: Ardis, Translation Press, 1979), pp. 198-209 (translation by David Lowe).

42. Lermontov, IV, 658.

43. Vatsuro, in *Issledovaniia i materialy,* p. 237. For the game of shtoss, see *Eugene Onegin: A Novel in Verse by Aleksandr Pushkin,* translated from the Russian with a Commentary by Vladimir Nabokov, 4 volumes (New York: Bollingen Foundation, Pantheon Books, 1964), II, 258-261.

44. Lermontov, IV, 487.

45. Lermontov, IV, 497-498.

46. For the aesthetic implications of Lermontov's tale, see John Mersereau Jr., "Lermontov's 'Shtoss,' Hoax or Literary Credo?", *Slavic Review,* XXI (1962), pp. 280-295.

47. Lermontov, IV, 275-474.

48. Boris Eikhenbaum, *O proze* (L. Khudozhestvennaia literatura, 1969), sect. 5, pp. 265-274.

49. Emma Gershtein, *"Geroi nashego vremeni" Lermontova* (M. 1976), pp. 25-31.

50. Lermontov, IV, 277.

51. Lermontov, IV, 340.

52. Benjamin Constant, *Adolphe* (Paris: Garnier, n.d.), pp. 7-8.

53. *Istoriia russkogo romana,* I, 280-281.

54. A. S. Pushkin, *Sobranie sochinenii v desiati tomakh* (M.-L. Gosudarstvennoe izdatel'stvo khudozhestvennoi literatury, 1959-1962), IV: *Eugene Onegin,* ch. vii, strophe 22. The poet Anna Akhmatova has examined the whole question of the place of Constant's

Adolphe in Pushkin's works, especially *Eugene Onegin:* see the translation of her essay by Sharon Leiter in *Russian Literature Triquarterly,* No. 10 (Fall, 1974), pp. 157-179.

55. Alfred de Musset, *Confession d'un enfant du siècle* (Paris: Charpentier, 1899), pp. 1-2.

56. Lermontov, IV, 276-277.

57. Eikhenbaum, *O proze,* p. 249.

58. A. A. Bestuzhev-Marlinskii, *Sochineniia v dvukh tomakh* (M. 1958), I, 548-594.

59. Eikhenbaum, *Lermontov* (Ardis, 1980), pp. 157-161.

60. *Otechestvennye zapiski,* Vol. VI (1839), No. 11, sec. iii, p. 146.

61. *Otechestvennye zapiski,* Vol. VIII (1841), No. 2, sect. iii, p. 153.

62. The whole matter of the chronology of the constituent stories that make up *A Hero of Our Time* is disputed. The most recent opinion is briefly summarized in the section "History of Composition" under the entry *Geroi nashego vremeni* in the magnificent *Lermontovskaia entsiklopediia,* editor V. A. Manuilov (M. 1981). The writer (B. T. Udodov) states:

> The compositional history of "A Hero . . . " is almost undocumented and is established on the basis of text analysis and in part from indications in memoir literature (frequently inexact or controversial). Possibly "Taman" was written earlier than the other stories; according to the recollections of P. S. Zhigmont it was sketched "in rough draft" in the apartment of S. O. Zhigmont (Autumn 1837). There is foundation for the assumption that "The Fatalist" was written subsequently to "Taman," and perhaps before the idea of the whole novel was formed. According to other suppositions, "The Fatalist" was written before "Maxim Maximych" (B. Eikhenbaum) and "Taman." the last of the tales that go into the novel (E. Gershtein). The idea of the novel as "a lengthy series of tales" was definitively established with Lermontov, probably in 1838.

Emma Gershtein in her book *"Geroi nashego vremeni" Lermontova* argues, in my opinion unconvincingly (pp. 7-20), that, contrary to Zhigmont's evidence, "Taman" was the last tale to be written. Her argument relies principally upon the fact that Lermontov's first outline of the sequence in which the separate tales were to be printed in the novel does not include "Taman." But this does not exclude the possibility that that tale had been written earlier but not originally considered appropriate for the novel. Gershtein's opinion of the literary excellence of "Taman," which she rates as more mature than "Bela," and therefore presumably written later, is entirely subjective and one with which few critics concur. She admits that "Taman" gives a picture of Pechorin that is inconsistent with what emerges from other tales, but regards this as evidence of Lermontov's skill in creating a three-dimensional personality. But the inclusion of contradictory traits in a character sketch which is consistent in the other tales certainly renders this argument unconvincing. There is every reason to believe that the narrator in "Taman" was conceived of originally as the "travelling writer," and the tale was put in its present position, regardless of inconsistency, at the last minute, probably merely to give the "novel" greater bulk. Lermontov was never the patient and careful writer that Pushkin was. Such is very nearly the conclusion also of B. T. Udodov (*M. Iu. Lermontov. Khudozhestvennaia individual'nost' i tvorchestskie protsessy* [Voronezh, 1973], pp. 482-497). Eikhenbaum (*O proze,* article "Geroi nashego vremeni," p. 260) tends to the same conclusion, but with some reservations. "It is possible, accordingly, that the words about 'writing people' at the end of 'Taman' are a relic of the original intention; while [my] first conclusion remains: 'Taman' was written before 'Bela,' and most likely earlier than all the other tales that make up the novel."

63. It is of some interest to note that Lermontov's teacher of Russian language and literature in the Junker school, Vasily Timofeevich Plaksin, who had earlier greeted the young author of *Hadji Abrek* as "Russia's future poet," was rather critical of *A Hero of Our Time,* and in particular "expressed the thought that there was a certain inconsistency in the figure of the principal hero in 'Bela' and 'Taman.' " (*Lermontovskaia entsiklopediia,* p. 109).

64. Nabokov, *Onegin* Commentary, III, 287.

65. Lermontov, IV, 315-316.

66. Lermontov, IV, 398.

67. Lermontov, IV, 493-494.

68. Mersereau, *Mikhail Lermontov,* pp. 132-143.

69. Lermontov, IV, 411.

70. C. J. G. Turner, *Pechorin: An Essay on Lermontov's "A Hero of Our Time"* (Birmingham: Birmingham Slavonic Monographs, No. 5, 1978), pp. 55-62.

71. O. V. Miller in a review of Turner's book (*Russkaia Literatura,* 21, iv, pp. 203-208) criticizes the author for failing to take into account the socio-political background of "our time" in his discussion of Pechorin's character. Commenting on Turner's rejection of the usual Soviet interpretation of "fatalism" as a reflection of the mood of hopelessness and apathy that characterized the Russian intelligentsia after the failure of the Decembrist coup, Miller writes (p. 206): "Such an attitude on the author's part leads to a superficial interpretation of the figure of the principal hero. Lermontov was writing the novel for his contemporaries, and to take into account the philosophical, literary and historical background against which *A Hero of Our Time* was apprehended by its first readers is absolutely essential for an understanding of the novel." Some validity must of course be conceded to this approach, but Lermontov's deliberate suppression of all overt reference to background elements in the formation of Pechorin's character makes it clear that he wished to emphasize rather the volitional aspects. Moreover, even if one accepts the Marxist interpretation of "fatalism," it still remains true that Pechorin rejects fatalism as an explanation of his own behavior. Even after two striking "experiments" that apparently demonstrate the truth of fatalism, Pechorin remains a voluntarist. The socio-political background of *A Hero of Our Time* is therefore largely irrelevant.

72. See Turner, chapter "The Hero and His Author," pp. 63-72.

73. Vladimir Nabokov, trans., *A Hero of Our Time* (New York: Anchor Doubleday, 1958), p. xvi.

74. Lermontov, IV, 275.

75. Nabokov, *A Hero of Our Time,* p. xvi.

76. Lermontov, IV, 650.

77. Eikhenbaum, *O proze,* pp. 271-274.

78. Turner, pp. 45-54.

79. Lermontov, IV, 452.

80. Lermontov, IV, 453.

81. Eikhenbaum, *O poezii,* p. 186.

82. *Lermontovskaia entsiklopediia,* p. 43.

83. *Lermontovskaia entsiklopediia,* p. 44.

84. See W. J. Entwhistle, "The Byronism of Lermontov's 'A Hero of Our Time,'" in *Comparative Literature,* 1 (1949), 140-146.

85. *O poezii,* p. 185.

86. *O poezii,* pp. 186-191.

87. *Lermontovskaia entsiklopediia,* p. 352.

88. Lermontov, IV, 27.

89. Eikhenbaum, *O poezii,* pp. 192-199.

CHAPTER 7

1. Vladimir Nabokov, *Nikolai Gogol* (New York, New Directions, 1944), p. 61, writes: "The old translations of 'Dead Souls' into English are absolutely worthless and should be expelled from all public and university libraries." Isabel Hapgood's hapless version receives the master's particular contempt (see pp. 79, 89). On the other hand, he says of B. G.

Guerney's translation of *Dead Souls,* "it is an extraordinarily fine piece of work," marred in his opinion chiefly by the use of the alternate censor-imposed title "Chichikov's Journeys." As to Guerney's subtitle, "Home Life in Old Russia," one may gather Nabokov's opinion of the degree to which *Dead Souls* reflects genuine Russia from the remark (pp. 70-71): "Moreover their [i.e., Gogol's heroes] surroundings and conditions, whatever they might have been in 'real life,' underwent such a thorough permutation and reconstruction in the laboratory of Gogol's peculiar genius that (as has been observed already in connection with *The Government Inspector*) it is useless to look in *Dead Souls* for an authentic Russian background as it would be to try and form a conception of Denmark on the basis of that little affair in cloudy Elsinore." Carl Proffer's article *"Dead Souls* in Translation," *Slavic and East European Journal,* VIII, 4 (1964), pp. 420-433, gives a somewhat soberer and more factual account of the accuracy of translators in reproducing Gogol's peculiar stylistic effects.

2. Gogol', *Polnoe sobranie sochinenii* (M.-L. Akademiia Nauk, 1937-1952), I, 59-100.

3. *Poetische Werke von Johann Heinrich Voss:* Erster Teil, *Louise, ein ländliches Gedicht* (Berlin: Gustav Hempel, n.d.).

4. Gogol', *Polnoe sobranie,* I, 89.

5. Gogol', *Polnoe sobranie,* I, 103-316; *The Collected Tales and Plays of Nikolai Gogol,* ed. Leonard J. Kent (New York: Modern Library Giant, 1969), pp. 3-206.

6. This earlier version, "Bisaryuk, or St. John's Eve," is given in Gogol, *Polnoe sobranie,* I, 349-366.

7. Gogol', *Sobranie sochinenii v shesti tomakh* (M. Gosudarstvennoe izdatel'stvo khudozhestvennoi literatury, 1959), I, 268-281.

8. *Poshlost'* is the subject of a rambling but entertaining dissertation by Nabokov (*Nikolai Gogol,* pp. 63-74). The reader may come away from this discourse with a clearer idea of the word's connotations, but no better off with a translation.

9. Robert A. Maguire (ed.), *Gogol from the Twentieth Century: Eleven Essays* (Princeton: Princeton University Press, 1974), p. 136.

10. Gogol's relations with the infernal are discussed at considerable length and occasional plausibility by Dmitry Merezhkovsky in the essay "Gogol and the Devil," in Maguire, pp. 55-102.

11. V. V. Vinogradov, *Izbrannye trudy: poetika russkoi literatury* (M. 1976), p. 76.

12. A. S. Pushkin, *Sobranie sochinenii v desiati tomakh* (M.-L. Gosudarstvennoe izdatel'stvo khudozhestvennoi literatury, 1958-1962), VI, 88-89.

13. Nabokov, *Nikolai Gogol,* pp. 30-31.

14. Donald Fanger, *The Creation of Nikolai Gogol* (Cambridge, Mass.: Harvard University Press, 1979), p. 87.

15. Gogol', *Sobranie sochinenii,* II, 7-245; *The Collected Tales and Plays of Nikolai Gogol,* pp. 207-420.

16. Fanger, pp. 86-87.

17. The ostensibly personal intervention of Gogol in the Mirgorod stories has led modern critics to a good deal of psychological interpreting of them, some of it rather convincing (e.g., Fanger's remarks on the erotic subtext of Khoma Brut's encounter with the witch, pp. 100-101, and on the possible phallic significance of Ivan Ivanovich's desire for his neighbor's rifle, p. 105) and much of it grotesquely ridiculous, e.g., Yermakov's nonsensical misreading of the passage in the story of the two Ivans regarding the rumor that Ivan Nikiforovich possessed "a tail behind" (see Maguire, p. 170). Cf. F. C. Driessen, *Gogol as a Short-Story Writer* (The Hague: Mouton, 1965) and Hugh McLean, "Gogol's Retreat from Love. Toward an Interpretation of *Mirgorod,*" in *American Contributions to the Fourth International Congress of Slavists* (The Hague: Mouton, 1958), pp. 225-245.

18. Fanger, p. 97.

19. Gogol', *Sobranie sochinenii,* II, 32-153.

20. Gogol', *Sobranie sochinenii,* II, 249-320.

21. Fanger, p. 98.

22. Bryusov, in his excellent essay on Gogol ("Ispepelennyi: K kharakteristike Gogolia," in Valerii Briusov, *Sobranie sochinenii v semi tomakh*, VI, 134-159), quotes part of one of the "Taras Bulba" battle scenes and then queries: "In what period are these heroic deeds taking place? In the Little Russia of the sixteenth century or in the mythological times of the expedition of Troy? Who are these who chop their foes in two, overcome five singlehanded, put everyone in a fright with an *inhuman* shout? Zaporozhie Cossacks, or the heroes of Homer, the godlike Diomede, the goddess's son Achilles, Agamemnon, shepherd of the people?" It is of course the 1842 version to which Bryusov is referring.

23. Vasilii Gippius, *Gogol'* (L. 1924; Brown University Slavic Reprint Series no. 1, Providence, R.I., 1966), pp. 69-70. Translated by Robert Maguire (Ann Arbor: Ardis, 1981).

24. V. V. Vinogradov, "Romanticheskii naturalizm: Zhiul' Zhanin i Gogol'," *op. cit.*, pp. 76-100.

25. Vinogradov, pp. 81-82.

26. Vinogradov, p. 81.

27. Gogol', *Sobranie sochinenii*, I, 282-327.

28. Gogol', *Sobranie sochinenii*, II, 122-123.

29. Carl R. Proffer, "Gogol's Defense of *Dead Souls.*" *The Simile and Gogol's "Dead Souls"* (The Hague: Mouton, 1967),Chap. 13.

30. Proffer, p. 193.

31. Proffer, p. 169.

32. Even the 1835 version of "Taras Bulba" struck Belinsky as epic. He wrote of it in his essay "On Russian Stories and the Stories of Gogol"[*Sobranie sochinenii v trekh tomakh* (M. OGIZ, 1948), I, 144]: " 'Taras Bulba' is a fragment, an episode from the great epic of the life of a whole people. If the Homeric epic is possible in our times, here you have its loftiest example, ideal, and prototype!"

33. Gogol', *Sobranie sochinenii*, II, 154-194.

34. Gogol', *Sobranie sochinenii*, II, 154, note.

35. Andrei Siniavskii ("Abram Terts"), *V teni Gogolia* (London: Collins, 1976), p. 546, resorts to the Jungian "archetype" to explain Gogol's Viy: the figure arises from the author's subconscious and corresponds thus to no specific Ukrainian myth but to other widespread primitive beliefs, not consciously known to Gogol.

36. Gogol', *Sobranie sochinenii*, IV, 48-49.

37. G. A. Gukovskii, *Realizm Gogolia* (M.-L. 1959), p. 191.

38. Gogol', *Sobranie sochinenii*, II, 191.

39. Gogol', *Sobranie sochinenii*, II, 187.

40. V. A. Zhukovskii, *Sobranie sochinenii v chetyrekh tomakh* (M.-L. Gosudarstvennoe izdatel'stvo khudozhestvennoi literatury, 1959), II, 48-53.

41. Gogol', *Sobranie sochinenii*, II, 195-245.

42. Gogol', *Sobranie sochinenii*, II, 346.

43. Nabokov, *Nikolai Gogol*, pp. 63-74.

44. In his book on Gogol, Nabokov alludes several times to the intriguing secondary characters who appear only momentarily, never to be heard of again (e.g., in *The Inspector General*—see Nabokov's Chapter 2, section 3).

45. Gogol', *Sobranie sochinenii*, II, 212.

46. Gogol', *Sobranie sochinenii*, II, 296.

47. Gogol', *Sobranie sochinenii*, II, 233.

48. Gogol', *Sobranie sochinenii*, II, 199.

49. See Valerii Briusov, "Ispepelennyi: k kharakteristike Gogolia," *Sobranie sochinenii v semi tomakh*, VI, 134-159; translated by Robert Maguire, *Gogol from the Twentieth Century*, pp. 103-131.

50. Gogol', *Sobranie sochinenii*, II, 229.

51. Gogol', *Sobranie sochinenii*, II, 220.

52. Gogol', *Sobranie sochinenii*, II, 231.

53. Fanger, *The Creation of Nikolai Gogol,* p. 107.
54. Gogol', *Sobranie sochinenii,* II, 245.
55. Fanger, p. 108.

CHAPTER 8

1. Nikolai Gogol, *Arabesques,* trans. by Alexander Tulloch, introduction by Carl R. Proffer (Ann Arbor: Ardis, 1982).
2. N. V. Gogol', *Sobranie sochinenii v shesti tomakh* (M. Gosudarstvennoe izdatel'stvo khudozhestvennoi literatury, 1959), III, 7-43.
3. Gogol', *Sobranie sochinenii,* II, 309.
4. Gogol', *Sobranie sochinenii,* II, 308.
5. Vinogradov, "O literaturnoi tsiklizatsii po povodu 'Nevskogo Prospekta' Gogolia i 'Ispovedi opiofaga' De Kvinsi," *Izbrannye trudy: poetika russkoi literatury* (M. Nauka, 1976), pp. 45-62.
6. Gogol', *Sobranie sochinenii,* III, 38-39.
7. Gogol', *Sobranie sochinenii,* III, 10.
8. Gogol', *Sobranie sochinenii,* III, 10-11.
9. Gogol', *Sobranie sochinenii,* III, 11.
10. Gogol', *Sobranie sochinenii,* III, 15.
11. Gogol', *Sobranie sochinenii,* III, 42.
12. The original version of "The Portrait" may be found in Gogol, *Sobranie sochinenii,* III, 239-281; translation in Nikolai Gogol, *Arabesques,* by Alexander Tulloch.
13. G. A. Gukovskii, *Realizm Gogolia* (M.-L. Gosudarstvennoe izdatel'stvo khudozhestvennoi literatury, 1959), pp. 329-330.
14. See Dmitrii Merezhkovskii, "Gogol' i chert," *Polnoe sobranie sochinenii* (St. Petersburg-Moscow, 1911), Vol. X; translation in Robert A. Maguire, *Gogol from the Twentieth Century* (Princeton, N.J.: Princeton University Press, 1974), pp. 55-102.
15. Gogol', *Sobranie sochinenii,* III, 247.
16. Gogol', *Sobranie sochinenii,* III, 265.
17. Gogol', *Sobranie sochinenii,* III, 280.
18. Fanger notes (*The Creation of Nikolai Gogol* [Cambridge, Mass.: The Belknap Press, 1979], pp. 114-115): "Demonism and moralizing aside, Gogol's passionate estheticism produces a cloudy message about the 'horrible reality' art can reveal when it pursues nature too slavishly. The suggestion seems to be that God and the Devil are copresent in the world and that any representation of phenomena must serve one side or the other. The artist who succumbs to vanity and courts social acceptance—or even the artist who allows himself to pursue the phantom of truth unguided by a vision of beauty—does the Devil's work." But Father Grigory's artistic sin seems to be rather that of yielding to the temptation to treat his repellent task from the point of view of mere technical mastery: he is at first gratified by his success in capturing on his canvas the whole terrifying evil of the old man's eyes, and only when he suddenly realizes that his triumphant "realism" has literally created evil does he throw down his brush and flee. Would it have been possible for him as an artist to have depicted this "phenomenon" at all without hazarding his soul? Is one left with the scarcely satisfactory suggestion that had he been an inferior artist, technically incapable of showing the usurer's eyes as they were, all might have been well? Gogol's message is indeed "cloudy," and it is better not to attempt to formulate it.
19. Gogol', *Sobranie sochinenii,* III, 173-193.
20. Gogol', *Sobranie sochinenii,* III, 185.
21. Gogol', *Sobranie sochinenii,* III, 185.
22. Gogol', *Sobranie sochinenii,* III, 193.
23. E. T. A. Hoffmann, *Sämtliche Poetische Werke* (Berlin und Darmstadt: Insel Verlag, 1963), I, 83-84.

24. Gogol', *Sobranie sochinenii*, III, 175.

25. Gogol', *Sobranie sochinenii*, III, 160-172.

26. "The Carriage" was written in 1835, when Gogol was beginning *Dead Souls*, and represents the author's first excursion into provincial Russian life other than that of the Ukraine. He had no experience of the provinces of Great Russia, and Belinsky's assertion that *Dead Souls* was an authentic portrait in which one could find the whole of Russia in all its ugly reality is ridiculously wrong.

27. Gogol', *Sobranie sochinenii*, III, 162-163.

28. Gogol', *Sobranie sochinenii*, III, 44-70.

29. A typically humorless and pretentious Freudian reading of "The Nose" is that of Ivan Yermakov in *Ocherki po analizu tvorchestva N. V. Gogolia* (M.-L. 1924), pp. 167-216. Maguire includes an edited translation of this in his *Gogol from the Twentieth Century*, pp. 156-198.

30. A. S. Pushkin, *Sobranie sochinenii v desiati tomakh* (M.-L. Gosudarstvennoe izdatel'stvo khudozhestvennoi literatury, 1958-1962), III, 261.

31. Vsevolod Setchkarev, *Gogol: His Life and Works* (New York: New York University Press, 1965), pp. 155-172; Fanger, *The Creation of Nikolai Gogol*, pp. 118-122.

32. Yermakov makes much of the fact that a nose is a dream, and vice versa—that is, the Russian *nos*, read backward is *son*, "dream." If Gogol ever had this Nabokovian whimsy, he suppressed it in his final version.

33. Gogol', *Sobranie sochinenii*, III, 58.

34. Vinogradov, *op. cit.*, article "Naturalisticheskii grotesk (siuzhet i kompozitsiia povesti Gogolia 'Nos')," pp. 5-44.

35. Gogol', *Sobranie sochinenii*, III, 56.

36. Gogol', *Sobranie sochinenii*, III, 61.

37. Gogol', *Sobranie sochinenii*, III, 70.

38. Franz Kafka, *Das Urteil* (Frankfurt a/M: Fischer-Bücherei, 1935), p. 23.

39. N. V. Gogol', *Izbrannye stat'i* (Moskva: Sovremennik, 1980), pp. 37-42; the essay is translated by Alexander Tulloch in *Arabesques* (Ann Arbor, Mich.: Ardis, 1982), pp. 109-114.

40. Gogol', *Sobranie sochinenii*, VI, 87-108.

41. Gogol', *Sobranie sochinenii*, VI, 91.

42. Fanger, *The Creation of Nikolai Gogol*, pp. 78-79.

43. Gogol', *Sobranie sochinenii*, III, 71-127.

44. Gogol', *Sobranie sochinenii*, III, 126.

45. Gogol', *Sobranie sochinenii*, III, 125-126.

46. Carl R. Proffer, *The Simile and Gogol's "Dead Souls"* (The Hague: Mouton, 1967), p. 197.

47. Gogol', *Sobranie sochinenii*, III, 128-159.

48. P. V. Annenkov, *Literaturnye vospominaniia* (L. Academia, 1938), pp. 61-62. Dmitrii Chizhevsky (or Chyzhevsky or Tschiževskij!) gives the whole anecdote in his article "O 'Shineli' Gogolia" in *Sovremennye zapiski* (Paris, 1938), Vol. LXVII, pp. 172-195; see Maguire's translation, "About Gogol's *Overcoat*" in *Gogol from the Twentieth Century*, p. 312.

49. Nabokov, *Nikolai Gogol* (New York: New Directions, 1944), p. 144.

50. Reprinted in Boris Eikhenbaum, *Literatura: teoriia, kritika, polemika* (Chicago, IL: Russian Language Specialties, 1969), pp. 149-165. For an English translation see Maguire, *Gogol from the Twentieth Century*, pp. 267-291.

51. N. G. Chernyshevskii, "Ne nachalo li peremeny?", *Sovremennik* (1861); reprinted in N. G. Chernyshevskii, *Literaturnaia kritika* (M. Khudozhestvennaia literatura, 1981), II, 215.

52. As Donald Fanger very justly points out (*op. cit.*, p. 160), over the years critics have seen the meanings of "The Overcoat" as primarily falling "into four overlapping categories: the social, the ethical, the religious, and the esthetic." None of the four can be accepted as exclusively valid, but—"What these analyses have in common is a respect for the idiosyncracy

of the form that allows full appreciation of the capriciousness of the story, its legitimate transcendence of singleness of message—the way it 'triumphantly asserts literature's independence from the repressive forces of reality and gleefully demonstrates its freedom to play with the realms of matter and spirit, life and death, to which it refers but by which it is not bound.'" The quotation is from an excellent article by Charles Bernheimer, "Cloaking the Self: The Literary Space of Gogol's 'Overcoat,'" *PMLA*, Vol. 90 (January, 1975).

53. Aleksandr Slonimskii, *Tekhnika komicheskogo u Gogolia* (Petersburg, 1923: Providence, R.I.: Brown University Reprint II, Brown University Press, 1963), p. 15, pairs "The Overcoat" with "Old World Landowners": "Here the plot itself has no comic significance. In plot 'The Overcoat' is the same kind of sentimental tale—a 'pitiful story'—as 'Old-World Landowners,' only with a sharper comic coloration. In both the comic quality is created by definite comic procedures, which give a comic coloration to events and persons."

54. "The complex of narrative attitudes is more devious than in 'Old-World Landowners,' the narrator himself more elusive. Where in that story he had voiced personal attitudes and claimed involvement in the events, here he is a disembodied voice, shifting levels bewilderingly, so that as a source of perspective he resembles the Petersburg wind he describes as blowing from all four directions at once" (Fanger, *op. cit.*, p. 154).

55. Gogol', *Sobranie sochinenii*, III, 154-155.

56. Gogol', *Sobranie sochinenii*, III, 136.

57. Gogol', *Sobranie sochinenii*, III, 135.

58. Gogol', *Sobranie sochinenii*, III, 141.

59. Gogol', *Sobranie sochinenii*, III, 155-156.

60. Gogol', *Sobranie sochinenii*, III, 159.

61. Chizhevsky (in Maguire's translation of his essay "About 'The Overcoat,'" in *Gogol from the Twentieth Century*, p. 297) puts the matter statistically: "Within the thirty-two to forty pages that 'The Overcoat' takes up in the usual editions of Gogol, this little word ["even"] crops up no fewer than seventy-three times."

62. Gogol', *Sobranie sochinenii*, III, 133.

63. Essay "About 'The Overcoat,'" in Maguire, *Gogol from the Twentieth Century*, pp. 315-321.

64. Donald Fanger, *The Creation of Nikolai Gogol*, pp. 162-163.

65. Gogol', *Sobranie sochinenii*, III, 194-236.

66. Briusov, "Ispepelennyi," *Sobranie sochinenii*, VI, 145 (translated in Maguire, "Burnt to Ashes," pp. 103-131), giving typical examples of Gogol's penchant for hyperbole, remarks:

Gogol's pen was particularly unrestrained when he was sketching his Annunziata: "Try to gaze at a lightning flash, when cleaving the coal-black clouds it begins to quiver unbearably in a veritable flood of brightness: such were the eyes of the Alban girl Annunziata [not "Albanian," as Maguire translates *albanki:* the girl was native Italian, from Albano, in the hills south of Rome] ... Howsoever she turns the radiant snow of her face—her image is wholly imprinted on the heart.... Whether she turns the back of her head with its marvelous upswept hair showing a dazzling neck and a beauty of shoulders never seen by earth—even there she is a marvel. But most marvelous of all, when she looks straight at one eye to eye, inducing a chill and a sinking of the heart.... No lithe panther can compare with her in swiftness, strength and pride of movement. Everything in her is the crown of creation, from shoulders to antique, fragrant foot and the last little toe on her foot"—What is this? The description of a living person, or an uninhibited flight to the world of the fabulous and the impossible?

67. Gogol', *Sobranie sochinenii*, III, 236.

68. Gogol', *Izbrannye stat'i*, pp., 235-236.

69. There is no doubt that Gogol in his habitual fashion greatly exaggerated his intimacy with Pushkin. Pushkin's few letters to him are short, polite and cool; Gogol's to him are effusive and mannered. Bryusov in his essay on Gogol (*op. cit.*, p. 150) records what may be

Pushkin's real opinion of his admirer: "Not only does it seem to Gogol that 'all the delight of his life had disappeared' with Pushkin's death, but Gogol even believes that 'he undertook nothing, wrote nothing' without Pushkin's advice and that *Dead Souls* is not only a task inspired by him, but actually his, Pushkin's, creation, whereas we have P. Annenkov's testimony that Pushkin yielded the subject of *Dead Souls* to Gogol *not altogether willingly* and in his own household circle said: 'One has to be pretty careful with that Ukrainian; he robs me so that it's impossible even to cry out.' L. Pavlishchev confirms the same thing."

70. Gogol', *Izbrannye stat'i*, p. 236.

71. Vasilii Gippius, *Gogol'* (L. Mysl', 1924; reprint Providence, R.I.: Brown University Press, 1966), p. 87.

72. Gogol', *Polnoe sobranie sochinenii v desiati tomakh* (Berlin: Slovo, 1921), VII, 59-107. For a general discussion of all Gogol's dramatic works, see Iu. V. Mann, "Dramaturgiia N. V. Gogolia" in *Istoriia russkoi dramaturgii: VXII-pervaia polovina XIX veka* (L. Nauka, 1982), pp. 426-473.

73. Gogol', *Sobranie sochinenii*, VI, 324-325; *Letters of Nikolai Gogol*, selected and edited by Carl R. Proffer (Ann Arbor: The University of Michigan Press, 1967), p. 52.

74. *Biblioteka dlia chteniia*, Vol. 16 (May, 1836).

75. See "The Dénouement of *The Inspector General*" [*Razviazka Revizora*] in Gogol', *Sobranie sochinenii*, IV, 389.

76. Donald Fanger, *op. cit.*, p. 130.

77. See Maguire's edited translation of V. V. Gippius, "Problematika i kompozitsiia 'Revizora,'" *N. V. Gogol'. Materialy i issledovaniia* (M.-L. 1936), pp. 215-265.

78. Gogol', *Sobranie sochinenii*, IV, 71-72.

79. Gogol', *Sobranie sochinenii*, IV, 76.

80. Gogol', *Polnoe sobranie sochinenii v desiati tomakh*, VII, 305-325.

81. Belinskii, *Polnoe sobranie sochinenii* (M. 1955), VI, p. 575.

82. Gogol', *Sobranie sochinenii*, IV, 150-197.

83. Belinskii, *Polnoe sobranie sochinenii*, VII, 85-86.

84. Gogol', *Sobranie sochinenii*, IV, 235-271.

85. Aristophanes did of course employ comedy as a means of castigating through public ridicule what he regarded as the "public wounds" of Athens. He certainly did not, however, envision the kind of private reformation of the individual citizen which Gogol has in mind. For a stimulating modern discussion of this question, see Vyacheslav Ivanov's essay "*Revizor* Gogolia i komediia Aristofana": *Teatral'nyi Oktiabr'* (M. 1927), translated by Maguire in his *Gogol from the Twentieth Century*, pp. 200-214.

86. Gogol', *Sobranie sochinenii*, IV, 246.

87. Carl R. Proffer, *The Simile and Gogol's "Dead Souls"*, pp. 183-200.

CHAPTER 9

1. N. V. Gogol', *Sobranie sochinenii v shesti tomakh* (M. Gosudarstvennoe izdatel'stvo khudozhestvennoi literatury, 1959), V, 7-260. For a complete, scholarly and impartial account of all aspects of Gogol's masterpiece, see Iurii V. Mann, *V poiskakh zhivoi dushi: "Mertvye dushi": pisatel'—kritika—chitatel'* (M. Kniga, 1984).

2. Gogol', *Sobranie sochinenii*, VI, 324-325; *Letters of Nikolai Gogol*, selected and edited by Carl R. Proffer (Ann Arbor: The University of Michigan Press, 1967), p. 52.

3. Gogol', *Sobranie sochinenii*, V, 231-232.

4. Nikolai Gogol, *Dead Souls: Chichikov's Journeys, or Home Life in Old Russia*, translated by Bernard Guerney (New York: The Heritage Press, 1942).

5. Gogol', *Polnoe sobranie sochinenii* (M.-L. 1937-1952), VI, 629-639.

6. See the "Second Letter Apropos of *Dead Souls*," in Gogol', *Sobranie sochinenii*, VI, 146-147; Nikolai Gogol, *Selected Passages from Correspondence with Friends*, translated by Jesse Zeldin (Nashville, Tenn.: Vanderbilt University Press, 1969), p. 90.

7. Gippius, *Gogol'* (L. "Mysl'," 1924), p. 144.

8. Gogol, *Dead Souls,* translation by David Magarshack (Harmondsworth, Penguin Books, 1961).

9. Henry Fielding, *The Adventures of Joseph Andrews and his Friend Mr. Abraham Adams* (London: J. M. Dent & Co., 1908), I, xxxviii-xxxix.

10. Gippius, pp. 139-140.

11. Gogol', "Uchebnaia kniga slovesnosti dlia russkogo iunoshestva,"*Izbrannye stat'i* (M. 1980), p. 209.

12. Gogol', "Uchebnaia kniga...," pp. 211-212.

13. Gogol', "Uchebnaia kniga...," p. 209.

14. Konstantin Aksakov, an almost idolatrous admirer of Gogol, in his article "A Few Words about Gogol's Poem: *Chichikov's Adventures, or Dead Souls*" [K. Aksakov, "Neskol'ko slov o poème Gogolia: *Pokhozhdeniia Chichikova, ili Mertvye dushi* (M. 1842); reprinted in *Russkaia estetika i kritika 40-50-kh godov XIX veka* (M. Iskusstvo, 1982), pp. 42-53] contends that Gogol's "poem" is a modern version of the Homeric epic—an opinion that both Belinsky and, predictably, Senkovsky rejected and ridiculed. In Fanger's discussion, *The Creation of Nikolai Gogol,* pp. 165-168, of Gogol's use of the term*poèma* for *Dead Souls,* he touches on a possible connection with the universally recognized *poèma* of Dante ("quite apart from the plan of a tripartite work following that of the *Commedia*"), and hits on an original and in my opinion most significant connection between the "dead souls" who constitute the *dramatis personae* of Gogol's *poèma* and the souls of the trimmers in *Inferno,* whom Dante calls (*Inf.* III, 62-64) "la setta dei cattivi / A Dio spiacenti ed ai nemici sui, / Questi sciaurati, *che mai non fur vivi*" (my itialics). Fanger continues his Dantean parallel by emphasizing "the road" as the chief organizational feature of both "poems."

15. Letter of January 7 to Pletnyov: Gogol', *Sobranie sochinenii,* VI, 362; translated in Proffer, *Letters of Nikolai Gogol,* p. 105.

16. Boris Eikhenbaum quotes the memoirs of Olga Nikolaevna Smirnova to the effect that Gogol found the name Chichikov "on a house—in the old days there were no numbers, just the name of the owner" (see Maguire's translation of his essay "How 'The Overcoat' was Made," in *Gogol from the Twentieth Century,* p. 273).

17. Gogol', *Izbrannye stat'i,* p. 143.

18. James B. Woodward, *Gogol's "Dead Souls"* (Princeton: Princeton University Press, 1978).

19. From Gogol's open letter to Pletnyov, "About *The Contemporary,*" Gogol', *Izbrannye stat'i,* p. 225.

20. "Four Letters to Various Persons Apropos of *Dead Souls,*" in Gogol, *Sobranie sochinenii,* VI, 153. Proffer (*The Simile and Gogol's "Dead Souls,"* p. 40) notes of Gogol's technique in describing characters, "In each one, as in a caricature, certain salient features are exaggerated. One of the most persistent traits of his writing is his emphasis on the characters' physiognomy, in lengthy physical portraits of them and their surroundings." Elsewhere (p. 43) he remarks: "Sometimes a character remains nameless; he is totally identified with an external feature, by a physical characteristic or article of clothing." We have noted examples of this Gogolian procedure in, for example, the description of the promeneurs on Nevsky Prospect, identified only as whiskers of different colors (masculine) or billowing sleeves (feminine). A caricaturist by definition proceeds by exaggerating real characteristics in his subjects. Vasily Rozanov (*Legenda o velikom inkvizitore* [SPb. 1906], p. 276) declares: "Gogol looked upon all phenomena and objects not as they were in reality, but in their extreme." It should be noted, however, that Gogol seems to have been himself aware of the dangers of excess; he very considerably toned down the hyperbole of the earlier versions of *Dead Souls* in the final one (see Proffer, *op. cit.,* p. 147).

21. Gippius, *Gogol',* p. 202.

22. A. I. Gertsen, *Sobranie sochinenii* (M. 1956), III, 447.

23. Fanger, *The Creation of Nikolai Gogol,* p. 258.

24. Fanger, *The Creation of Nikolai Gogol,* p. 261.

25. Woodward, *Gogol's "Dead Souls,"* p. 37.

26. Woodward strangely misunderstands this passage (p. 82) and attributes the description actually to Pliushkin's housekeeper!

27. Woodward, *Gogol's "Dead Souls,"* p. 111.

28. Woodward, *Gogol's "Dead Souls,"* p. 106.

29. No. XVIII, *Selected Letters from a Correspondence with Friends;* Gogol', *Sobranie sochinenii,* VI, 151.

30. Woodward, *Gogol's "Dead Souls,"* pp. 107-108.

31. Fanger (*The Creation of Nikolai Gogol,* pp. 180-181) denies the claim of Andrei Bely [*Masterstvo Gogolia* (M.-L. 1934)] that "the landowners Chichikov visits.... represent a progressively greater degree of deadness; the individualizing moral principle in each is *equally* absent. What they rather represent are differing degrees (and kinds) of *aliveness*—an aliveness that reaches its apogee in Sobakevich and Nozdryov, the one impressing his selfhood on everything around him and so reifying it, the other making everything a possession (or attribute) of himself and so perpetually dispersing that selfhood." With this reading the crescendo of arrangement disappears, leaving only the drastic contrast between the more or less animal "aliveness" of the first four and the vegetable, parasitic "aliveness" of Plyushkin.

32. Gogol', *Sobranie sochinenii,* V, 7.

33. Note Gogol's remark in the third of the "Four Letters to Various Persons Apropos of *Dead Souls"* (Gogol', *Sobranie sochinenii,* VI, p. 151) that "my heroes are not villains at all; were I to add just one good trait to any one of them, the reader would be reconciled to them all." Nabokov makes "Our Mr. Chichikov" (the "our" identifies him as "Satan's home-bound, hell-bound agent," Nabokov, *Gogol,* p. 111) a very sinister character indeed: "for Chichikov is a fake and a phantom clothed in a pseudo-Pickwickian rotundity of flesh, and trying to smother the miserable reek of inferno . . . permeating him by means of maudlin perfumes pleasing to the grotesque noses of that nightmare town." With all due respect for a great writer and an often subtle critic, I think this is a gross perversion, belied by the very apparent efforts which Gogol makes to show Chichikov as an average, unexceptional person. He is *not* a Sologubian *melkii bes* nor even a *besënok.* Proffer is certainly close to the mark when he asserts (Proffer, *The Simile and Gogol's "Dead Souls,"* p. 124): "But we should not consider Chichikov as an evil agent of Satan—that would be too flattering for him. He is simply a chubby little swindler who has a particular ability to hop around in a servile manner for the pleasure of others." He is also, as Proffer notes on the next page, not bright enought to make a good devil!

34. Nabokov, *Gogol,* p. 91.

35. Andrei Belyi, *Masterstvo Gogolia,* p. 100.

36. Woodward, *Gogol's "Dead Souls,"* pp. 90-93.

37. Gogol', *Sobranie sochinenii,* V, 227.

38. Gogol', *Sobranie sochinenii,* V, 42.

39. Gogol', *Izbrannye stat'i,* pp. 235-236.

40. One of Woodward's most astute and satisfying intuitions is concerned precisely with the significance of the description of Plyushkin's garden (Woodward, *Gogol's "Dead Souls,"* pp. 108ff.). He notes the ambivalence of the description, typical of Gogol, which emphasizes the beauty of the wilderness, which however is "the beauty of savagery, destruction and death." The dominant symbol is that of the "spreading, voracious" hopvine, which represents the "rapacious spirit of nature" embodied in Plyushkin himself. Further in Chapter 6 Gogol introduces the figure of the spider, which like the hop-vine or the ivy implicit in Plyushkin's name, is nature in its destructive, asphyxiating aspect. Woodward's elaboration of the other figures in Chapter 6 is typical of his approach. Much of it is ingenious and carries conviction, e.g., the interpretation of the headless white birch standing like a column amidst the encroaching green, as a last vestige of humanity destined for suffocation; but a great deal of it is absurdly over-subtle, e.g., the following; "Nature, in Gogol's description, does not rend and

tear. Hence Plyushkin's lack of teeth." Surely an aged man's toothlessness does not have to be a symbol! Similarly, the fact that housekeeper Mavra's name means "dark" in (modern) Greek is a pretty fine point and one not certain to have been even known to Gogol.

Woodward's book is in general an exasperatingly uneven work, filled with brilliant intuitions, elaborated with gossamer subtleties such as no great writer, and certainly not Gogol, could ever have consciously spun. A great many of these take the form of images and symbols which are forced in the most Procrustean fashion to serve his purposes. Thus the mention in Chapter 3 of a variety of vegetables in Korobochka's kitchen garden initiates the "natural produce" motif, of which Woodward says (p. 27): "Just as Sobakevich himself is presented as a creation of nature, so the 'Sobakevichan' soul, in both senses of the term, is presented in the form of natural produce—as a grain of wheat, a nut, a cucumber, a pumpkin, and a radish." Thereupon, in an evident effort to dispose of a rather recalcitrant bit of evidence, Woodward (p. 27) wrenches Sobakevich's impatient protest to Chichikov: "Really, with you a human soul is all the same as a stewed turnip" *(Pravo, u vas chelovecheskaia dusha vsë ravno chto parenaia repa)* into the impossible: "Truly, your soul is just like a stewed turnip,"—a remark that makes no sense at all in the circumstances, and ignores the essential word "human." Often, however, Woodward hits upon very pertinent points that have been ignored or misunderstood, e.g., his ingenious reconstruction of Manilov's life as an army officer. He is less successful, however, in reconstructing the career of Korobochka's deceased husband, whose progressive erosion he sees symbolized in an extended simile in which the director of a government office, grand as Prometheus in his own domain, becomes progressively smaller as he encounters his superiors, becoming metaphorically an eagle, then a fly, and finally a grain of sand. Unfortunately for this ingenious fabric, Korobochka's nameless husband was a lowly collegiate secretary (grade 10, fourth from the bottom), and could under no circumstances have ever occupied any "Promethean" post.

Gogol was unquestionably a very careful and conscious artist, and no doubt the similes in *Dead Souls,* at least the more elaborately developed ones, e.g., the famous simile of the flies and sugar in Chapter 1, are designed to illuminate more than the most obvious similarities to tenor and vehicle. But that every image, every name, every allusion has some arcane significance in terms of the meaning Gogol attaches to his "poem" is altogether beyond belief, and Woodward's insistence on such subtleties detracts seriously from the credibility of his work as a whole.

Still in connection with the Plyushkin garden, Nabokov (*Gogol,* pp. 86-88) calls attention to the painterly effect of Gogol's description, so different from the stereotyped and unsubtle renditions of color and chiaroscuro in earlier Russian works: "I doubt whether any writer, and certainly not in Russia, had ever noticed before, to give the most striking instance, the moving pattern of light and shade on the ground under trees or the tricks of color played by sunlight with leaves. The following description of Plyushkin's garden in *Dead Souls* shocked Russian readers in much the same way as Manet did the bewhiskered Philistines of his day." He then gives a careful and beautiful translation of the passage.

41. Proffer (*The Simile and Gogol's "Dead Souls,"* p. 110) calls attention to an unobtrusive pun in the description of Plyushkin's habitation. As the manor-house first comes into Chichikov's sight, it is referred to as "the strange *castle" (sei strannyi zámok),* the word castle having been substituted for *dom,* "house," in an earlier version. But with a change of accent *(zamók)* the same word means "lock." "The house, the castle is also a *lock,"* says Proffer. "Plyushkin is locked off from life."

42. Gogol', *Sobranie sochinenii,* V, 98-100. Sobakevich's extreme sturdiness and solidity appeared to have left no place in his make-up for a soul: "It seemed that in this body there was no soul at all, or that with him it was not at all where it should have been, but as with Koshchei the Deathless, somewhere beyond the mountains and enclosed by such a thick shell that everything that stirred on its bottom produced absolutely no disturbance on the surface" [*Sobranie sochinenii,* V, 105]. This negative appearance, however, is belied by the kulak's care for his living serfs and by his affectionate remembrance of those that are "no longer existent,"

in Chichikov's careful phraseology. Evidently Gogol's second alternative in the above passage—Sobakevich's soul is, like that of the folklore enchanter Koshchei, hidden in an egg safely remote from his body—is the one he wants his reader to accept. As Proffer remarks (*The Simile and Gogol's "Dead Souls,"* p. 103): "Here he actually says that Sobakevich bears no evidence of having a soul—except (and this part of the simile is the key to the whole thing) that it *might* be there somewhere, but hidden very deeply." This alternative would allow the author in a subsequent never-written volume to arrange for the redemption of a character for whom it seems apparent that he feels some affection.

43. Andrei Belyi, *Masterstvo Gogolia* (M. 1934), p. 277, compares the pauses in the narrative produced by extended similes to the passages in a song where the voice is silent and the accompaniment takes over.

Gogol's use of the simile as a stylistic, even structural device in his "lesser epic" is the subject of Proffer's magisterial monograph *The Simile and Gogol's "Dead Souls."* See in the present connection especially his Chapter 6, "The Homeric Simile in *Dead Souls.*" Proffer notes incidentally (p. 81) that by his use of the simile Gogol was enabled to give a far broader picture of contemporary Russia than his narrative unadorned would have allowed. It should be added that the same is true of the simile in the *Iliad,* which is very often drawn from the peace-time life of Homer's time, deliberately chosen to extend the picture of Achaean existence, as well as to afford a striking contrast with the narrative content, which is entirely confined to the "abnormal" condition of war.

44. Gogol', *Sobranie sochinenii,* V, 169.

45. Gogol', *Sobranie sochinenii,* V, 208-214.

46. The Postmaster was, as Gogol says, "flowery in his words, and loved, as he himself said, to embellish his speech." The embellishments consisted chiefly of such locutions as "my dear sir" (even when addressing more than one auditor), "some kind or other, you know, you understand, you can imagine, relatively, so to speak, and in a kind of way." The interpolated story of Captain Kopeikin is so thoroughly "embellished" that, as Proffer says (*op. cit.,* p. 65): "We can hardly believe that any real person ever used these words and phrases so frequently. By exaggerating the mannerism, Gogol creates a device by which he can make fun of the usual poetic simile. He presents it (through the Postmaster) and then explodes it by the use of these meaningless *vvodnye slova.*"

47. Gogol', *Sobranie sochinenii,* V, 139-140. Woodward (*Gogol's "Dead Souls",* pp. 145ff.) maintains that this passage is intended to refer not to two different kinds of writers, but to the subjects (Woodward's "Masters and Slaves") with which the "poem is primarily concerned."

48. Gogol', *Sobranie sochinenii,* V, 220.

49. Gogol', *Sobranie sochinenii,* V, 259-260.

50. Proffer (*The Simile and Gogol's "Dead Souls,"* pp. 20-21) has a perceptive discussion of some of the rhetorical devices which Gogol employs in his lyrical passages.

51. Gogol', *Sobranie sochinenii,* VI, 147.

52. For a more detailed account of the critical reception of the first part of *Dead Souls* see Proffer, *The Simile and Gogol's "Dead Souls,"* p. 67.

53. *Russkaia literatura XIX veka. Khrestomatiia kriticheskikh materialov* (M. 1964), pp. 352-353.

54. *Russkaia literatura XIX veka. Khrestomatiia kriticheskikh materialov,* pp. 348-350.

55. Gippius, *Gogol',* p. 153.

56. Gogol', *Sobranie sochinenii,* IV, 235-271.

57. "Leaving the Theater after a Performance of a New Comedy" was first sketched in 1836, and as the title intimates, was conceived as a rebuttal of some of the hostile criticisms directed at *The Inspector General.* Even in its original form, however, the pamphlet misrepresents the comedy. As it was revised in 1842 it may, while still overtly referring to *Revizor,* though never by name, be actually intended to anticipate and meet the expected attacks from the same reactionary critics against *Dead Souls.* Carl Proffer (*The Simile and Gogol's "Dead Souls,"* pp. 184ff.) makes a very good case for this interpretation.

58. Gogol', *Sobranie sochinenii*, IV, 379-391.

59. Gogol', *Polnoe sobranie sochinenii* (M.-L. 1937-1952), VIII; English translation by Jesse Zeldin, (Nashville, Tenn.: Vanderbilt University Press, 1969). Five of the essays are given in Gogol', *Sobranie sochinenii*, VI, 125-203.

60. In one of his letters of this period (*Polnoe sobranie sochinenii*, XII, 366) Gogol remarks: "For a long time now I have looked at men not as an artist...I look at them as brothers, and that feeling is several times more heavenly and better."

61. A. S. Pushkin, *Sobranie sochinenii v desiati tomakh* (M. Gosudarstvennoe izdatel'stvo khudozhestvennoi literatury, 1958-1962), II, 353.

62. Gogol', *Izbrannye stat'i*, p. 121.

63. Gogol', *Izbrannye stat'i*, p. 122.

64. Merezhkovsky said that it sounded as if Chichikov had written it, after having gone insane and embraced Christianity!

65. S. T. Aksakov, *Sobranie sochinenii v chetyrekh tomakh*, III, 335-337.

66. Aksakov, III, pp. 337-338.

67. Aksakov, III, pp. 338-340. Proffer, *Letters of Nikolai Gogol*, pp. 168-169.

68. V. Belinskii, *Sobranie sochinenii v trekh tomakh*, III, 709. Belinskii's famous "Salzbrunn Letter" to Gogol is available in English in *Belinsky, Chernyshevsky and Dobrolyubov: Selected Criticism*, edited and with an introduction by Ralph E. Matlaw (New York: E. P. Dutton & Co., 1962), pp. 83-92.

69. See "The Russian Landowner" in Zeldin's translation of *Selected Passages from a Correspondence with Friends*, p. 138.

70. Aksakov, III, 341-342.

71. Aksakov, III, 343-344.

72. Aksakov, III, 345.

73. Aksakov, III, 338-340; Proffer, *Letters of Nikolai Gogol*, pp. 168-169.

74. Gogol', *Sobranie sochinenii*, V, 263-528.

75. Gogol', *Sobranie sochinenii*, VI, 156-157.

76. Gogol, *Dead Souls*, trans. David Magarshack (Harmondsworth: Penguin Books, 1961), pp. 12-15.

77. Gogol', *Sobranie sochinenii*, V, 553-558.

78. Gogol', *Sobranie sochinenii*, V, 556.

79. Gogol', *Sobranie sochinenii*, V, 357-358.

80. Gippius, *Gogol'*, pp. 208-210.

81. Carl Proffer, *Letters of Nikolai Gogol*, p. 200.

82. Andrei Belyi, *Masterstvo Gogolia*, pp. 258-259.

83. Carl Proffer, *The Simile and Gogol's "Dead Souls,"* pp. 157-160.

Selected Bibliography

Afanas'ev, A. N. *Narodnyia skazki A. N. Afanas'eva*, ed. A. N. Gruzinskii. M. I. D. Sytin, 1914.

Aksakov, S. T. *Sobranie sochinenii v chetyrekh tomakh*. M. Gosudarstvennoe izdatel'stvo khudozhestvennoi literatury, 1956.

Alekseev, M. P. "Russko-angliiskie literaturnye sviazi XVIII veka-pervaia polovina XIX veka." *Literaturnoe nasledstvo*, Vol. 91. M. Nauka, 1982.

_____. *Pushkin: Sravnitel'no-istoricheskie issledovania*. M. Nauka, 1972.

Annenkov, P. V. *Literaturnye vospominaniia*. L. Academia, 1938.

Baratynskii, E. A. *Polnoe sobranie stikhotvorenii*. Introduction, notes and ed. E. N. Kupreianova. L. Sovetskii pisatel', Biblioteka poeta, bol'shaia seriia, 1957.

Batiushkov, K. N. *Opyty v stikhakh i proze*. Ed. I. M. Semenko. M. Nauka, 1977.

_____. *Polnoe sobranie stikhotvorenii*. Introduction, notes and ed. N. V. Fridman. M.-L. Sovetskii pisatel', Biblioteka poeta, bol'shaia seriia, 1964.

Bayley, John. *Pushkin: A Comparative Commentary*. Cambridge: University Press, 1976.

Belinskii, V. G. *Polnoe sobranie sochinenii*. M. Akademiia Nauk SSSR, 1955.

_____. *Sobranie sochinenii v trekh tomakh*. M. OGIZ, 1948.

Belyi, Andrei. *Masterstvo Gogolia*. M.-L., 1934. Reprint Ardis, 1983.

Benediktov, V. G. *Sochineniia V. G. Benediktova*. Ed. Ia. P. Polonskii. M. M. O. Vol'f, 1902.

_____. *Stikhotvoreniia*. Introduction, notes and ed. L. Ia. Ginzburg. L. Sovetskii pisatel', Biblioteka poeta, bol'shaia seriia, 1939.

_____. *Stikhotvoreniia*. Introduction F. Ia. Priima. Notes and ed. B. V. Mel'gunov. L. Sovetskii pisatel', Biblioteka poeta, bol'shaia seriia, 1983.

Bestuzhev, N. A. *Izbrannaia proza*. M. Sovetskaia Rossiia, 1983.

Bestuzhev-Marlinskii, A. A. *Polnoe sobranie stikhotvorenii*. Introduction, notes and ed. G. Prokhorov. M. Sovetskii pisatel', Biblioteka poeta, bol'shaia seriia, 1948.

_____. *Sochineniia v dvukh tomakh*. M. Gosudarstvennoe izdatel'stvo khudozhestvennoi literatury, 1958.

Blagoi, D. D. *Dusha v zavetnoi lire*. M. Sovetskii pisatel', 1977.

_____. *Ot Kantemira do nashikh dnei*. M. Khudozhestvennaia literatura, 1973.

_____. *Tvorcheskii put' Pushkina*. M. Sovetskii pisatel', 1967.

Bocharov, S. G. *Poetika Pushkina: Ocherki*. M. Nauka, 1974.

Bondi, S. M. *O Pushkine*. M. Khudozhestvennaia literatura, 1978.

Boratynskii, E. A. *Razuma velikolepnyi pir. O literature i iskusstve*. M. Sovremennik, 1981.

Bowra, C. M. *A Book of Russian Verse*. London: Macmillan, 1947.

Briusov, Valerii. *Sobranie sochinenii v semi tomakh*. M. Khudozhestvennaia literatura, 1975.

Brown, W. E. *A History of Eighteenth-Century Russian Literature*. Ann Arbor: Ardis, 1980.

_____. *A History of Seventeenth-Century Russian Literature*. Ann Arbor: Ardis, 1980.

Bukhstab, B. *Russkie poety*. L. Khudozhestvennaia literatura, 1970.

Byron, George Gordon, Lord. *The Complete Poetical Works of Lord Byron*. Boston: Houghton-Mifflin, 1905.

Čiževskij, Dmitrij. *History of Nineteenth-Century Russian Literature*. Trans. Richard Noel Porter. Vol. 1: The Romantic Period. Nashville: Vanderbilt University Press, 1974.

Dal', V. I. *Izbrannye proizvedeniia*. M. Pravda, 1983.

_____. *Povesti i rasskazy*. M. Sovetskaia Rossiia, 1983.

Davydov, Denis. *Stikhotvoreniia*. Introduction, notes and ed. Vl. Orlov. L. Sovetskii pisatel', Biblioteka poeta, malaia seriia, 1959.

_____. *Stikhotvoreniia*. L. Sovetskii pisatel', Biblioteka poeta, bol'shaia seriia, 1984.

_____. *Voennye zapiski*. M. Voennoe izdatel'stvo, 1982.

Dees, Benjamin. *Evgeny Baratynsky*. New York: Twayne, 1977.

Dekabristy: Antologiia v dvukh tomakh. L. Khudozhestvennaia literatura, 1975.

Del'vig, A. A. *Polnoe sobranie stikhotvorenii*. Introduction, notes and ed. B. V. Tomashevskii. L. Sovetskii pisatel', Biblioteka poeta, bol'shaia seriia, 1959.

Derzhavin, G. R. *Stikhotvoreniia*. Introduction, notes and ed. D. D. Blagoi. L. Sovetskii pisatel', Biblioteka poeta, bol'shaia seriia, 1957.

Dmitriev, I. I. *Polnoe sobranie stikhotvorenii*. Introduction, notes and ed. G. P. Makogonenko. L. Sovetskii pisatel', Biblioteka poeta, bol'shaia seriia, 1967.

Dostoevskii, F. M. *Sobranie sochinenii v desiati tomakh*. M. Gosudarstvennoe izdatel'stvo khudozhestvennoi literatury, 1958.

Drevnie rossiiskie stikhotvoreniia sobrannye Kirsheiu Danilovym: Second ed. M. Nauka, 1977.

Druz'ia Pushkina. Perepiska. Vospominaniia. Dnevniki. M. Pravda, 1984.

Eikhenbaum, B. M. *Lermontov*, trans. Ray Parrott and Harry Weber. Ann Arbor: Ardis, 1981.

_____. *Literatura: Teoriia, kritika, polemika*. Rpt. Chicago: Russian Language Specialties, 1969.

_____. *O poezii*. L. Sovetskii pisatel', 1969.

_____. *O proze*. M. Khudozhestvennaia literatura, 1969.

_____. *Stat'i o Lermontove*. L. Nauka, 1961.

Eng, Jan van der, ed. *The Tales of Belkin of A. S. Puškin*. The Hague: Mouton, 1968.

Ershov, P. P. *Konek-Gorbunok. Stikhotvoreniia*. Introduction I. D. Lupanova, notes and ed. D. M. Klimova. L. Sovetskii pisatel', Biblioteka poeta, bol'shaia seriia, 1976.

Fanger, Donald. *The Creation of Nikolai Gogol*. Cambridge, Mass.: Harvard University Press, 1979.

Fridman, N. V. *Poeziia Batiushkova*. M. Nauka, 1971.

_____. *Proza Batiushkova*. M. Nauka, 1965.

Gershtein, E. G. *"Geroi nashego vremeni" M. Iu. Lermontova*. M. Khudozhestvennaia literatura, 1976.

Gertsen, A. I. *Pis'ma izdaleka*. M. Sovremennik, 1981.

_____. *Polnoe sobranie sochinenii*. M. Nauka, 1954-62.

Ginzburg, Lidiia Iakovlevna. *O starom i novom*. L. Sovetskii pisatel', 1982.

Gippius, Vasilii. *Gogol'*. L. Mysl', 1924; rpt. Providence, R. I.: Brown University Press, 1966.

Gippius, Vasily. *Gogol*. Trans. Robert Maguire. Ann Arbor: Ardis, 1981.

Glinka, F. N. *Izbrannye proizvedeniia*. Introduction, notes and ed. V. G. Bazanov. L. Sovetskii pisatel', Biblioteka poeta, bol'shaia seriia, 1957.

_____. *Stikhotvoreniia*. Introduction, notes and ed. V. Bazanov. L. Sovetskii pisatel', Biblioteka poeta, malaia seriia, 1951.

Gnedich, N. I. *Stikhotvoreniia*. Introduction, notes and ed. I. N. Medvedeva. M.-L. Sovetskii pisatel', Biblioteka poeta, malaia seriia, 1963.

Goethe, J. W. von. *Goethes sämtliche Werke in sechs Bänden*. Stuttgart and Tübingen: V. G. Cotta'scher Verlag, 1854.

Gogol, N. V. *Arabesques*, trans. Alexander Tulloch. Introduction Carl R. Proffer. Ann Arbor: Ardis, 1982.

_____. *The Collected Tales and Plays of Nikolai Gogol*, ed. Leonard J. Kent. New York: Modern Library, 1969.

____. *Dead Souls*, trans. David Magarshack. Harmondsworth, Middlesex: Penguin Books, 1961.

____. *Dead Souls. Chichikov's Journeys, or Home Life in Old Russia*, trans. Bernard Guerney. New York: The Heritage Press, 1942.

____. *Izbrannye stat'i*. M. Sovremennik, 1980.

____. *Letters of Nikolai Gogol*, ed. Carl R. Proffer. Ann Arbor: University of Michigan Press, 1967.

____. *Polnoe sobranie sochinenii*. M.-L. Akademiia Nauk SSSR, 1937-52.

____. *Selected Passages from Correspondence with Friends*, trans. Jesse Zeldin. Nashville, Tenn.: Vanderbilt University Press, 1969.

____. *Sobranie sochinenii v shesti tomakh*. M. Gosudarstvennoe izdatel'stvo khudozhestvennoi literatury, 1959.

Griboedov, A. S. *Sochineniia v dvukh tomakh*. M. Pravda, 1971.

____. *Sochineniia v stikhakh*. Introduction, notes and ed. I. N. Medvedeva. L. Sovetskii pisatel', Biblioteka poeta, bol'shaia seriia, 1967.

Grikhin, V. A., ed. *Russkaia romanticheskaia povest'*. M. 1983.

Gukovskii, G. A. *Pushkin i russkie romantiki*. M. Khudozhestvennaia literatura, 1965.

____. *Realizm Gogolia*. M.-L. Gosudarstvennoe izdatel'stvo khudozhestvennoi literatury, 1959.

Gulyga, A. V. *Shelling* (Zhizn' zamechatel'nykh liudei). M. Molodaia gvardiia, 1982.

Heine, Heinrich. *Heines Werke in fünfzehn Teile*. Berlin, etc.: Bong & Co., n.d.

Hoffmann, E. T. A. *Werke*. Berlin and Darmstadt: Tempel Verlag, 1963.

Iazykov, N. M. *Polnoe sobranie stikhotvorenii*. Introduction, notes and ed. K. K. Bukhmeier. M.-L. Sovetskii pisatel', Biblioteka poeta, bol'shaia seriia, 1964.

Istoriia russkoi dramaturgii XVII-pervaia polovina XIX veka. L. Nauka, 1982.

Istoriia romantizma v russkoi literature, Vols. I, II. M. Nauka, 1979.

Istoriia russkogo romana v dvukh tomakh, Vol. I. M.-L. Nauka, 1962.

Istoriia russkoi literatury, Vols. V, VI. M.-L. Nauka, 1941-53.

Istoriia russkoi poezii v dvukh tomakh. L. Nauka, 1968,

Ivan Andreevich Krylov. Problemy tvorchestva. L. Nauka, 1975.

Kantor, V. K. and A. L. Ospovat, eds. *Russkaia estetika i kritika 40-50-kh godov XIX v*. M. Iskusstvo, 1982.

Karamzin, N. M. *Polnoe sobranie stikhotvorenii*. Introduction, notes and ed. Iu. M. Lotman. M.-L. Sovetskii pisatel', Biblioteka poeta, bol'shaia seriia, 1966.

Katenin, P. A. *Izbrannye proizvedeniia*. Introduction, notes and ed. G. V. Ermolova-Bitner. M.-L. Sovetskii pisatel', Biblioteka poeta, bol'shaia seriia, 1965.

____. *Razmyshleniia i razbory*. M. Iskusstvo, 1981.

Katz, Michael R. *The Literary Ballad in Early Nineteenth Century Russian Literature*. Oxford: Oxford University Press, 1976.

K istorii russkogo romantizma. M. Nauka, 1973.

Khomiakov, A. S. *Stikhotvoreniia i dramy*. Introduction, notes and ed. E. F. Egorov. L. Sovetskii pisatel', Biblioteka poeta, bol'shaia seriia, 1969.

Kiukhel'beker, V. K. *Izbrannye stikhotvoreniia v dvukh tomakh*. Introduction, notes and ed. N. V. Koroleva. M.-L. Sovetskii pisatel', Biblioteka poeta, bol'shaia seriia, 1967.

____. *Puteshestvie. Dnevnik. Stat'i*. Eds. N. V. Koroleva, V. D. Rak. L. Nauka, 1979.

Kodjak, Andrej and Kiril Taranovsky, eds. *Alexander Puškin. A Symposium on the 175th Anniversary of His Birth*. NYU Slavic Papters 1. New York: New York University Press, 1976.

Koehler, Ludmilla. *Anton Antonovich Delvig: A Classicist in the Time of Romanticism*. The Hague: Mouton, 1970.

Kol'tsov, A. V. *Polnoe sobranie stikhotvorenii*. Introduction and notes L. L. Plotkin, eds. M. I. Maleva and L. L. Plotkin. L. Sovetskii pisatel', Biblioteka poeta, bol'shaia seriia, 1958.

Kozhinov, Vadim. *Kniga o russkoi liricheskoi poezii XIX veka*. M. Sovremennik, 1978.

Kozlov, I. I. *Polnoe sobranie stikhotvorenii.* Introduction, ed. and notes I. D. Glikman. L. Sovetskii pisatel', Biblioteka poeta, bol'shaia seriia, 1960.

Krylov, I. A. *Polnoe sobranie sochinenii v trekh tomakh.* M. OGIZ, 1946.

Lazhechnikov, I. I. *Sochineniia v dvukh tomakh.* M. Gosudarstvennoe izdatel'stvo khudozhestvennoi literatury, 1963.

Lednicki, Waclaw. *Pushkin's Bronze Horseman.* Berkeley: University of California Slavic Studies, Vol. I, 1978.

Lermontov, M. Iu. *The Demon and Other Poems,* trans. Eugene M. Kayden. Yellow Springs, Ohio: The Antioch Press, 1965.

——. *A Hero of Our Time,* trans. Vladimir Nabokov. New York: Anchor Doubleday, 1958.

——. *A Lermontov Reader,* ed. and trans. Guy Daniels. New York: Macmillan, 1965.

——. *Sobranie sochinenii v chetyrekh tomakh.* M.-L. Nauka, 1961.

——. *Vadim,* Introduction and trans. Helena Goscilo. Ann Arbor: Ardis, 1984.

Lermontovskaia Entsiklopediia. M. Izdatel'stvo "Sovetskaia entsiklopediia," 1982.

Lezhnev, A. *Proza Pushkina.* M. Khudozhestvennaia literatura, 1966.

——. *Pushkin's Prose.* Trans. Roberta Reeder. Ann Arbor: Ardis, 1983.

Lotman, Iu. M. *Roman A. S. Pushkina "Evgenii Onegin." Kommentarii.* L. Prosveshchenie, 1980.

Maguire, Robert A., ed. *Gogol from the Twentieth Century: Eleven Essays.* Princeton: Princeton University Press, 1974.

Maimin, E. A. *Russkaia filosofskaia poeziia.* M. Nauka, 1976.

Maksimov, D. E. *Poeziia Lermontova.* M.-L. Nauka, 1964.

Mann, Iurii Vladimirovich. *V poiskakh zhivoi dushi. "Mertvye dushi": pisatel'—kritika—chitatel'.* M. Kniga, 1984.

Manuilov, V. A. *Roman M. Iu. Lermontova "Geroi nashego vremeni". Kommentarii.* M.-L. Prosveshchenie, 1966.

Mastera russkogo stikhotvornogo perevoda. Introduction, notes and ed. E. G. Etkind. L. Sovetskii pisatel', Biblioteka poeta, bol'shaia seriia, 1968.

Mersereau, John, Jr. *Mikhail Lermontov.* Carbondale, Il.: Southern Illinois University Press, 1962.

——. *Russian Romantic Fiction.* Ann Arbor: Ardis, 1983.

Merzliakov, A. F. *Stikhotvoreniia.* Introduction, notes, and ed. Iu. M. Lotman. L. Sovetskii pisatel', Biblioteka poeta, bol'shaia seriia, 1958.

Meshcheriakov, V. P. *A. S. Griboedov. Literaturnoe okruzhenie i vospriiatie.* L. Nauka, 1983.

Mirsky, D. S. *Pushkin.* New York: E. P. Dutton, 1963.

Mitskevich, Adam. *Stikhotvoreniia. Poemy.* M. Khudozhestvennaia literatura, 1979.

M. Iu. Lermontov. Issledovaniia i materialy. M. Nauka, 1979.

Nabokov, Vladimir. *Nikolai Gogol.* New York: New Directions, 1944.

Narezhnyi, V. T. *Izbrannoe.* M.-L. Sovetskii pisatel', 1983.

——. *Izbrannye romany.* Introduction, notes and ed. V. F. Pereverzev. M.-L. Academiia, 1933.

——. *Rossiiskii Zhilblaz, ili pokhozhdeniia Kniaz'nia Gavrily Simonovicha Chistiakova.* Petrozavodsk, 1983.

O'Bell, Leslie. *Egyptian Nights. The Biography of a Work.* Ann Arbor: Ardis, 1984.

Odoevskii, A. I. *Polnoe sobranie stikhotvorenii.* Introduction, notes and ed. M. A. Briksman. L. Sovetskii pisatel', Biblioteka poeta, bol'shaia seriia, 1958.

Odoevskii, V. F. *Povesti i rasskazy.* M. Gosudarstvennoe izdatel'stvo khudozhestvennoi literatury, 1959.

——. *Russkie nochi.* L. Nauka, 1975.

——. *Sochineniia v dvukh tomakh.* M. Khudozhestvennaia literatura, 1981.

Orlov, P. M. *Russkii sentimentalizm.* M. Izdatel'stvo Moskovskogo Universiteta, 1977.

The Oxford Book of Russian Verse. Oxford: Clarendon Press, 1924.

Ozerov, V. A. *Tragedii. Stikhtvoreniia.* Introduction, notes and ed. I. N. Medvedeva. L. Sovetskii pisatel', Biblioteka poeta, bol'shaia seriia, 1960.

The Penguin Book of Russian Verse. Introduction and ed. Dmitri Obolensky. Harmondsworth: Penguin Books, 1962.

Poety-Radishchevtsy. Introduction and ed. P. L. Orlov, notes P. L. Orlov and G. A. Likhotkin. L. Sovetskii pisatel', Biblioteka poeta, bol'shaia seriia, 1979.

Poety-satiriki kontsa XVIII-nachala XIX veka. Introduction, notes and ed. G. V. Ermolova-Bitner. L. Sovetskii pisatel', Biblioteka poeta, bol'shaia seriia, 1959.

Poety 1790-1810-kh godov. Introduction Iu. M. Lotman. Ed. Iu. M. Lotman and M. G. Al'tshuller. L. Sovetskii pisatel', Biblioteka poeta, bol'shaia seriia, 1971.

Poety 1820-1830-kh godov. Vol. I. Introduction and general ed. L. Ia. Ginzburg, notes and ed. V. E. Vatsuro. L. Sovetskii pisatel', Biblioteka poeta, bol'shaia seriia, 1972.

Poety 1820-1830-kh godov. Vol. II. Introduction, notes and ed. V. S. Kiselev-Sergenin; general ed. L. Ia. Ginzburg. L. Sovetskii pisatel', Biblioteka poeta, bol'shaia seriia, 1972.

Poety XVIII veka v dvukh tomakh. Introduction and ed. G. Makogonenko. Biographical notes. I. Z. Serman. Notes and ed. N. D. Kochetkova. L. Sovetskii pisatel', Biblioteka poeta, bol'shaia seriia, 1972.

Pogodin, M. P. *Povesti. Drama.* M. Sovetskaia Rossiia, 1984.

Polezhaev, A. I. *Stikhotvoreniia i poemy.* Introduction N. F. Bel'chikov, ed. V. V. Baranov. L. Sovetskii pisatel', Biblioteka poeta, bol'shaia seriia, 1957.

Poliarnaia zvezda, excerpts from the almanac published by A. Bestuzhev and K. Ryleev [1823-25]. M. Sovetskaia Rossiia, 1982.

Povest' vremennykh let. M.-L. Nauka, 1950.

Proffer, Carl R. *The Simile and Gogol's "Dead Souls."* The Hague: Mouton, 1967.

Proza russkikh poetov XIX veka. Ed. with notes by A. L. Ospovat. M. Sovetskaia Rossiia, 1982.

Pushkin. Introduction and ed. by John Fennel, with plain prose translations of each poem. Baltimore, Md.: Penguin Books, 1964.

Pushkin. Issledovaniia i materialy, Vol. X. L. Nauka, 1982.

Pushkin, A. S. *Alexander Pushkin, Complete Prose Fiction.* Trans. Paul Debreczeny. Stanford: Stanford University Press, 1983.

____. *Alexander Pushkin. Collected Narrative and Lyrical Poetry.* Ed. and trans. Walter Arndt. Ann Arbor: Ardis, 1984.

____. *The Bronze Horseman. Selected Poems of Alexander Pushkin.* Trans. with an Introduction by D. M. Thomas. New York: The Viking Press, 1982.

____. *The Captain's Daughter and Other Great Stories.* New York: Random House, Modern Library Paperback, n.d.

____. *The Critical Prose of Alexander Pushkin.* Ed. and trans. Carl R. Proffer. Bloomington: Indiana University Press, 1969.

____. *Eugene Onegin.* Trans. Charles Johnston. New York: The Viking Press, 1977.

____. *Eugene Onegin: A Novel in Verse.* Trans. in the Onegin stanza with an Introduction and notes by Walter Arndt. New York: E. P. Dutton & Co., 1963. Second revised ed. New York: E. P. Dutton, 1982.

____. *Eugene Onegin: A Novel in Verse.* A new revised edition trans. Babette Deutsch. Ed. with an Introduction by Avrahm Yarmolinksy. Baltimore: Penguin Books, 1965.

____. *Eugene Onegin, A Novel in Verse by Alexander Pushkin.* Trans. with a Commentary by Vladimir Nabokov. Four volumes. New York: Bollingen Series LXXII, Pantheon Books, 1964. Second, revised edition, 1975.

____. *A Journey to Arzrum.* Trans. Birgitta Ingemanson. Ann Arbor: Ardis, 1974.

____. *The Letters of Alexander Pushkin.* Three volumes in one. Trans. J. Thomas Shaw. Madison: University of Wisconsin Press, 1967.

____. *Little Tragedies.* Trans. Eugene M. Kayden. Yellow Springs, OH: The Antioch Press, 1965.

——. *Perepiska Pushkina v dvukh tomakh.* M. Khudozhestvennaia literatura, 1982.
——. *The Poems, Prose and Plays of Alexander Pushkin,* ed. Avrahm Yarmolinsky. New York: Modern Library Giant, 1936.
——. *Pushkin's Fairy Tales.* Trans. Janet Dally. New York: Mayflower Books, 1979.
——. *Pushkin Threefold: Narrative, Polemic and Ribald Verse.* The originals with linear and metric translations by Walter Arndt. New York: E. P. Dutton, 1972.
——. *The Queen of Spades and Other Stories.* Trans. Rosemary Edmonds. Harmondsworth: Penguin Books, 1962.
——. *Ruslan and Liudmila.* Trans. Walter Arndt. Ann Arbor: Ardis, 1977.
——. *Sobranie sochinenii v desiati tomakh.* Ed. D. D. Blagoi, S. M. Bondi, V. V. Vinogradov, Iu. G. Oksman. M. Gosudarstvennoe izdatel'stvo khudozhestvennoi literatury, 1959-1962.
——. *The Tale of Tsar Saltan,* etc. Trans. Louis Zellikoff. Drawings by I. Bilibin. M. Progress Publishers, n.d.
——. *Three Comic Poems.* Ed. and trans. William G. Harkins. Ann Arbor: Ardis, 1977.
Radishchev, A. N. *Stikhotvoreniia.* Introduction, notes and ed. V. A. Zapadov. L. Sovetskii pisatel', Biblioteka poeta, bol'shaia seriia, 1975.
Raevskii, V. F. *Polnoe sobranie stikhotvorenii.* Introduction A. V. Arkhipova and V. G. Bazanov. Ed. and notes V. G. Bazanov. M.-L. Sovetskii pisatel', Biblioteka poeta, bol'shaia seriia, 1967.
Rannie romanticheskie veianiia. Iz istorii mezhdunarodnykh sviazei russkoi literatury. L. Nauka, 1972.
Rassadin, St. *Pushkin Dramaturg.* M. Iskusstvo, 1977.
Richards, D. J. and C. R. S. Cockrell, eds. *Russian Views of Pushkin.* Oxford: Meeuws, 1976.
Russian Romantic Prose: An Anthology. Ed. Carl R. Proffer. Ann Arbor: Translation Press, 1979.
Russkaia basnia XVIII-XIX vekov. Introduction N. L. Stepanov; ed. and notes by V. P. Stepanov and N. L. Stepanov. L. Sovetskii pisatel', Biblioteka poeta, bol'shaia seriia, 1977.
Russkaia epigramma vtoroi poloviny XVIII-nachala XIX v. Introduction by L. F. Ershov; ed. and notes by M. I. Gillel'son and N. G. Zakharchenko. L. Sovetskii pisatel', Biblioteka poeta, bol'shaia seriia, 1975.
Russkaia literatura XIX v. Khrestomatiia kriticheskikh materialov. M. Vysshaia shkola, 1964.
Russkaia romanticheskaia povest'. Introduction, notes and ed. V. I. Sakharov. M. Sovetskaia Rossiia, 1980.
Russkie esteticheskie traktaty pervoi poloviny XIX veka. Ed. Z. A. Kamenskii. Vol. II. M. Iskusstvo, 1974.
Russkie pisateli o literaturnom trude, v chetyrekh tomakh. Vol. I. M. Sovetskii pisatel', 1954.
Russkie poety XIX veka. Khrestomatiia. Ed. N. M. Gaidenkov. M. Gosuchpedgiz, 1960.
Russkie povesti XIX veka. Povesti 20-30-kh godov. Ed. and notes B. S. Meilakh. M.-L. Gosudarstvennoe izdatel'stvo khudozhestvennoi literatury, 1950.
Russkii romantizm. L. Nauka, 1978.
Rydel, Christine, ed. *The Ardis Anthology of Russian Romanticism.* Ann Arbor: Ardis, 1984.
Ryleev, K. F. *Polnoe sobranie sochinenii.* Introduction, commentary and ed. A. G. Tseitlin. M. Academia, 1934. "Academia" Reprints, No. 4. The Hague: Europe Printing, Mouton, 1967.
——. *Polnoe sobranie stikhotvorenii.* Introduction V. G. Bazanov and A. V. Arkhipova; ed. A. V. Arkhipova, V. G. Bazanov and A. E. Khodorov; notes by A. V. Arkhipova and A. E. Khodorov. L. Sovetskii pisatel', Biblioteka poeta, bol'shaia seriia, 1971.
Schiller, Friedrich. *Sämtliche Werke* [in acht Bänden]. Sans-Souci Ausgabe. Potsdam and Berlin: Müller & J. Kiepenhauer Verlag, n.d.
Semenko, I. M. *Poety pushkinskoi pory.* M. Khudozhestvennaia literatura, 1970.
Semenko, Irina. *Vasily Zhukovsky.* Boston: Twayne, 1976.

Serman, Ilya Z. *Konstantin Batyushkov.* New York: Twayne, 1974.

Setschkareff, Vsevolod. *Alexander Puškin, sein Leben und sein Werk.* Wiesbaden: Harrassowitz, 1963.

Setchkarev, Vsevolod. *Gogol: His Life and Works.* New York: New York University Press, 1965.

Shakhovskoi, A. A. *Komedii.* *Stikhotvoreniia.* Introduction, notes and ed. A. A. Gozenpud. L. Sovetskii pisatel', Biblioteka poeta, bol'shaia seriia, 1961.

Slonimskii, A. *Masterstvo Pushkina.* M. Gosudarstvennoe izdatel'stvo khudozhestvennoi literatury, 1959.

____. *Tekhnika komicheskogo u Gogolia.* Petersburg, 1923; rpt. Brown University Reprint II. Providence, R. I.: Brown University Press, 1963.

Somov, O. M. *Byli i nebylitsi.* M. Sovetskaia Rossiia, 1984.

Stender-Petersen, Adolf. *Geschichte der Russischen Literatur,* Vol. II. München: C. H. Beck, 1957.

Stikhotvornaia komediia kontsa XVIII-nachala XIX v. Introduction, notes and ed. M. O. Iankovskii. M.-L. Sovetskii pisatel', Biblioteka poeta, bol'shaia seriia, 1964.

Stikhotvornaia tragediia kontsa XVIII-nachala XIX v. Introduction, notes and ed. V. A. Bochkarev. M.-L. Sovetskii pisatel', Biblioteka poeta, bol'shaia seriia, 1964.

Tamarchenko, D. E. *Iz istorii russkogo klassicheskogo romana. Pushkin, Lermontov, Gogol'.* M.-L. Nauka, 1961.

Timofeev, L. V. *V krugu druzei i muz. Dom A. N. Olenina.* L. Lenizdat, 1983.

Tiutchev, F. I. *Lirika.* Ed. K. V. Pigarev. M. Nauka, 1966.

Tomashevskii, B. V. *Pushkin.* M.-L. Nauka, 1956; 1961.

____. *Pushkin i Frantsiia.* L. Nauka, 1960.

____, P. Bogatyrev & Viktor Shklovskii. *Ocherki po poetike Pushkina.* Berlin: Epokha, 1923; rpt. The Hague: Slavistic Printings and Reprintings, Mouton, 1969.

Tschižewskij, Dmitrij. *Russische Literaturgeschichte des 19. Jahrhunderts.* Vol. I. *Die Romantik.* München: Eidos Verlag, 1965.

Turner, C. J. G. *Pechorin: An Essay on Lermontov's A Hero of Our Time.* Birmingham: University of Birmingham Press, 1978.

Tynianov, Iurii. *Poetika. Istoriia literatury. Kino.* M. Nauka, 1977.

____. *Pushkin i ego sovremenniki.* M. Nauka, 1960.

Udodov, B. T. *M. Iu. Lermontov. Khudozhestvennaia individual'nost' i tvorcheskie protsessy.* Voronezh, 1973.

Vel'tman, A. F. *Strannik.* M. Nauka, 1977.

Venevitinov, D. V. *Izbrannoe.* M. Gosudarstvennoe izdatel'stvo khudozhestvennoi literatury, 1956.

____. *Stikhotvorenniia, proza.* M. Nauka, 1980.

Viazemskii, P. A. *Sochineniia v dvukh tomakh.* M. Khudozhestvennaia literatura, 1982.

____. *Stikhotvoreniia.* Introduction, notes and ed. L. Ia. Ginzburg. L. Sovetskii pisatel'. Biblioteka poeta, bol'shaia seriia, 1958.

____ *Zapisnye knizhki. (1813-1848).* Ed. V. S. Nechaeva. M. Nauka, 1963.

Vickery, Walter N. *Alexander Pushkin.* New York: Twayne, 1970.

Vinogradov, V. V. *Izbrannye trudy: Poetika russkoi literatury.* M. Nauka, 1976.

V mire Pushkina. Sbornik statei. M. Sovetskii pisatel', 1974.

Vostokov, A. Kh. *Stikhotvoreniia.* Introduction, notes and ed. Vl. Orlov. L. Sovetskii pisatel', Biblioteka poeta, bol'shaia seriia, 1935.

Woodward, James B. *Gogol's "Dead Souls."* Princeton: Princeton University Press, 1978.

Zagoskin, M. N. *Iurii Miloslavskii, ili Russkie v 1612 godu: Istoricheskii roman v trekh chastiakh.* M. Khudozhestvennaia literatura, 1967.

____. *Roslavlev, ili Russkie v 1812 godu.* M. Khudozhestvennaia literatura, 1980.

Zhirmunskii, Viktor M. *Bairon i Pushkin: Iz istorii romanticheskoi poemy.* L. Academia, 1924.

Zhukovskii, V. A. *Sobranie sochinenii v chetyrekh tomakh.* M.-L. Gosudarstvennoe izdatel'stvo khudozhestvennoi literatury, 1959.

Index

1876) **IV** 113, 114

Grimm Brothers (Jakob, 1776-1865; Wilhelm, 1787-1859) **III** 163

Kinder- und Hausmärchen **III** 163

Grosz, Georg (1893-1959) **IV** 265

Grotius, Hugo (Hugo de Groot: 1583-1645) **I** 248

Gruzintsev, Alexander Nikolaevich (1779-the 1840s) **I** 37, 48, 49, 53, 57, 58

Guereiro, I. **III** 265

Guerney, Bernard Guilbert **IV** 266, 342, 395

Guizot, François Pierre Guillaume (1787-1874) **III** 48

Gukovsky, Grigory Alexandrovich (1902-1950) **I** 193, 197, 228, 230, 271, 341; **III** 66, 413; **IV** 285, 299, 325

Gusev, Vladimir **II** 215

Hadrian (Publius Aelius Hadrianus), Roman Emperor (76-138 A. D.) **I** 188

Hanka, Vaclav (1791-1861) **I** 175

Hannibal, Carthaginian general (247-183 B.C.) **IV** 116

Hanski, Eva, wife of Honoré de Balzac **III** 427

Hapgood, Isabel **IV** 394

Harkins, William E. **III** 51, 408

Harlin, Anna (d. 1787) **III** 217

Hauptmann, Gerhart (1862-1946) **II** 36

Hebel, Johann Peter (1760-1826) **I** 193, 209, 267, 342

Hedylus (fl. 270 B.C.) **I** 248, 249; **III** 180

Hegel, Georg Wilhelm Friedrich (1770-1831) **I** 214

Hegesippus *de Bello Judaico* (a medieval Latin translation of the *Jewish War* of Josephus) **II** 45

Heine, Heinrich (1797-1856) **I** 17; **III** 241; **IV** 13, 15, 18, 19, 172, 258

Reisebilder **IV** 16-18

Helvétius, Claude-Adrien (1715-1751) **I** 138, 164; **III** 341, 414

hendecasyllabic verse: see Phalaecean verse

Henri IV King of France (1553-1610)

Henry IV, King of Germany and Holy Roman Emperor (1050-1106) **II** 47

Henry VII Tudor, King of England (1457-1509) **III** 108

Herder, Johann Gottfried (1744-1803) **I** 171, 172, 188, 208, 271, 287, 307, 308, 316; **IV** 293

Stimmen der Völker **I** 171, 200

Hérédia, José-Maria de (1842-1905) **II** 44

Les Trophées **II** 44

Herod the Great, King of Judaea (73?-4 B. C.) **I** 51, 52

Herodotus (490/480-430/425 B.C.) **I** 118, 202; **III** 168; **IV** 73

herois **I** 231

Herwegh, Georg (1817-1875) **I** 212

Herzen (Gertsen), Alexander Ivanovich (1812-1870) **I** 212; **II** 78, 141; **III** 84, 303, 348, 414; **IV** 38, 128, 129, 131, 348

The Thieving Magpie **II** 274

Hesiod (end of 8th century B. C.) **I** 137, 247, 248, 302

Hesse, Hermann (1877-1962) **II** 229

historical novel **II** 279-301; **III** 226-235; **IV** 229, 240

historicity, historicism **I** 23, 57, 112, 273; **II** 49, 92, 160, 279; **III** 228

Hoffmann, Ernst Theodor Amadeus (1776-1822) **I** 17 19, 208; **II** 139, 228, 241, 259; **III** 208, 220, 237, 346; **IV** 179, 260, 270, 295, 304

Die Lebensansichte des Katers Murr **II** 266; **IV** 304

Die Serapionsbrüder **II** 222, 223, 230

Holbach, Paul Heinrich Dietrich, Baron de (1723-1789) **III** 341, 414; **IV** 45

Hölderlin, Johann Christian Friedrich (1770-1843) **I** 228, 229; **II** 22; **III** 150; **IV** 20

Empedokles auf Etna **II** 24

Hölty, Ludwig Heinrich Christoph (1748-1776) **I** 171

Homer (?) **I** 46, 146, 163, 200, 208, 210, 225, 239, 241, 247, 248, 259, 261, 271, 273, 316, 320; **II** 21, 37, 47, 65; **III** 19, 90, 144, 280, 363; **IV** 131, 282, 357, 358, 366, 396, 401, 404

Homeric hymns **I** 179, 264

Iliad **I** 55, 200, 209, 210, 253, 262, 273; **II** 32, 36; **III** 26, 402; **IV** 175, 281, 282, 357, 366, 404

Odyssey **I** 187, 200, 210, 240, 272, 308; **II** 36; **III** 21; **IV** 175, 358

Hopkins, William H. **IV** 194

Horace (Quintus Horatius Flaccus: 65-8 B. C.) **I** 24, 117, 127, 137, 139, 145, 146, 151, 154, 157, 166, 178, 228, 233, 235, 236; **II** 14, 21, 65, 180, 245; **III** 144, 164, 185, 277, 278, 280, 339, 350, 414, 426; **IV** 88, 179, 367

vol. 4